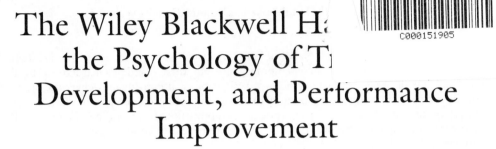

The Wiley Blackwell Handbook of the Psychology of Training, Development, and Performance Improvement

Wiley Blackwell Handbooks in Organizational Psychology

Series Editor: Jonathan Passmore

The aim of the Wiley Blackwell Handbooks in Organizational Psychology is to create a set of uniquely in-depth reviews of contemporary research, theory, and practice across critical sub-domains of organizational psychology. Series titles will individually deliver the state-of-the-art in their discipline by putting the most important contemporary work at the fingertips of academics, researchers, students, and practitioners. Over time, the series will grow into a complete reference for those seeking to develop a comprehensive understanding of the field.

Published

The Wiley Blackwell Handbook of the Psychology of Training, Development, and Performance Improvement

Edited by Kurt Kraiger, Jonathan Passmore, Sigmar Malvezzi, and Nuno Rebelo dos Santos

WILEY Blackwell

This paperback edition first published 2020
© 2015 John Wiley & Sons Ltd

Edition history: John Wiley & Sons Ltd (hardback, 2015)

Registered Offices
John Wiley & Sons, Inc., 111 River Street, Hoboken, NJ 07030, USA
John Wiley & Sons Ltd, The Atrium, Southern Gate, Chichester, West Sussex, PO19 8SQ, UK

Editorial Office
111 River Street, Hoboken, NJ 07030, USA

For details of our global editorial offices, customer services, and more information about Wiley products visit us at www.wiley.com.

Wiley also publishes its books in a variety of electronic formats and by print-on-demand. Some content that appears in standard print versions of this book may not be available in other formats.

Library of Congress Cataloging-in-Publication Data

The Wiley Blackwell handbook of the psychology of training, development, and performance improvement / edited by Kurt Kraiger, Jonathan Passmore, Nuno Rebelo dos Santos and Sigmar Malvezzi.
    pages cm
  Includes bibliographical references and index.
  ISBN 978-1-118-73701-9 (cloth) | ISBN 978-1-119-67366-8 (Paperback)
1. Employees–Training of.   2. Organizational learning.   3. Employee motivation.   4. Career development.   5. Personnel management–Psychological aspects.   6. Psychology, Industrial.
I. Kraiger, Kurt, 1957–
  HF5549.5.T7W49155 2014
  658.3′124019–dc23

Cover Design: Wiley
Cover Image: © busypix/Getty Images

Set in 9.5/11pt Galliard by SPi Global, Pondicherry, India

Printed and bound by CPI Group (UK) Ltd, Croydon, CR0 4YY

10   9   8   7   6   5   4   3   2   1

Contents

About the Editors

Jonathan Passmore (Series Editor) is the Professor of Coaching and Behavioural Change at Henley Business School, University of Reading and a professor of psychology at the University of Evora, Portugal. He is a chartered psychologist, holds five degrees, and has an international reputation for his work in coaching and leadership, including being listed by Thinkers50 as one of the top 10 coaches in the world. He has published widely books on the themes of leadership, personal development and change, and served as editor for the *Association for Coaching* book series. He speaks widely at conferences across the world and has published over 100 journal papers and book chapters.

Kurt Kraiger is a Professor and Chair of the Department of Management, Fogelman College of Business and Economics, University of Memphis. He is a Fellow and former President of the Society of Industrial/Organizational Psychology (SIOP). He has edited three books on training, published over 65 scholarly papers, given nearly 40 invited talks, and made over 110 scientific presentations. He is currently an Associate Editor of the *Journal of Business and Psychology* and is on the editorial board of the Academy of Management: Learning and Education, Journal of Management, and Journal of Applied Psychology.

Sigmar Malvezzi is Professor and Researcher of Fundação Dom Cabral, Brazil. He received his PhD at the Department of Organizational Behavior at the University of Lancaster, UK, and the degree of "Livre Docente" at the University of São Paulo, Brazil. He has lectured at the Institute of Psychology of the University of São Paulo and at the Business School of Fundação Getulio Vargas. His research has explored professional and career development with focus on the building of professional identity. His most recent book is Temas e Investigaciones en Psicología Organizacional y del Trabajo (2017)..

Nuno Rebelo dos Santos is Professor of Psychology at the University of Evora, Portugal. He is a chartered psychologist and has been invited speaker in many international scientific and professional meetings. He is a faculty member of several PhD and master courses, including the Erasmus Mundus Master Program in Work, Organizational and Personnel Psychology, as well as the PhD on Management at the University of Evora. He has worked for more than 25 years in executive training and development and his research is focused on performance development, cooperation and decent work.

About the Contributors

Gardênia da Silva Abbad, PhD Gardênia is professor in the Social, Work, and Organizational Psychology and in the Management Master's and doctoral programs at the University of Brasilia (UnB), Brazil. He is the coordinator of the Research Group on the Impact of Training on the Job and the Organization and a member of the Organizational and Work Psychology Working Group of the National Research Association. He also teaches on Master's and doctoral psychology programs. He can be contacted at: gardenia.abbad@gmail.com.

Lisa Anderson, PhD Lisa is senior lecturer in Management Education at the University of Liverpool Management School. She has a PhD in Management Learning and her research interests center on social learning, critical reflection, action learning and management, and leadership development and evaluation. She is also particularly interested in the nature and purpose of business school education.

Linda Argote, PhD Linda's research and teaching focus on organizational learning and memory, knowledge transfer, and group processes and performance. Her book, *Organizational Learning: Creating, Retaining and Transferring Knowledge*, was a finalist for the Terry Book Award of the Academy of Management. She has published numerous articles and book chapters. She is a fellow of the Academy of Management, Association for Psychological Science (APS), and the Institute for Operations Research and the Management Sciences (INFORMS). The Organization Management and Theory (OMT) Division of the Academy of Management recognized her as their Distinguished Scholar in 2012.

Patricia L. Baratta Patricia is currently pursuing an MA in Industrial/Organizational Psychology at the University of Guelph, Canada. She completed her BSc in Psychology at the University of Toronto. Her research focuses on state boredom and how it relates to discretionary workplace behavior.

Simon Beausaert, PhD Simon is an assistant professor in the field of professional development of teachers at the Université Catholique de Louvain-la-Neuve and senior researcher in workplace learning at Maastricht University. His current research focuses on assessment, formal and informal learning and their relation with (aging) employees' professional development and employability.

Jairo Eduardo Borges-Andrade, PhD Jairo has a PhD in Instructional Systems from Florida State University. He is a full professor at the University of Brasilia, Brazil. His areas of interest are informal and formal workplace learning. In addition he teaches at the undergraduate, Master's, and doctoral levels and consults on training and development evaluation systems for public and private organizations.

Thomas M. Cavanagh Thomas is a PhD student in the Industrial/Organizational Psychology program at Colorado State University. His research interests include training and development, technology in organizations, older workers, and statistics and methodology. His work has appeared in *Academy of Management: Learning and Education*, and *Human Resource Management Review*.

Charlotte Coleman Charlotte is a doctoral candidate at Leeds University Business School. Her doctoral research examines corporate responses to institutional pressures, such as community resistance and environmental activism. She is a qualitative researcher with wider interests in research methods and skills training and business and public engagement.

David G. Collings, PhD David is professor of Human Resource Management at Dublin City University Business School and visiting professor at King's College London. His research and consulting interests focus on management in multinational corporations with a particular emphasis on staffing and talent management issues. His work in these areas has been published in outlets such as the *Journal of World Business*, *Journal of Vocational Behavior*, and *Human Resource Management*. He has edited six books, sits on the editorial board for a number of journals, and is editor of the *Human Resource Management Journal*.

Valéria Vieira de Moraes, PhD Valeria has a degree in Economics, a Master's in Education and a PhD in Organizational Psychology. She currently works in public policy and management. Her research interests are related to work-based learning, particularly in the generation of learning opportunities through participatory management instruments.

Karen Evans, PhD Karen is professor and chair in Education at the Institute of Education, University of London. Her main fields of research are learning in life and work transitions, and learning in and through the workplace. She is an academician of the Academy of Social Sciences and a leading researcher in the UK Economic and Social Research Council Centre for Learning and Life Chances in Knowledge Economies and Societies (LLAKES).

Rodrigo R. Ferreira, PhD Rodrigo is professor in the Management Department at the University of Brasilia (UnB), Brazil. He has a doctorate in Social, Work, and Organizational Psychology from UnB. He is coordinator in the Study and Research Group on the Management of People in Public Administration (GEPAP – Master's in Business Administration/UnB). He can be contacted at ferreirarods@gmail.com.

Clive Fletcher, PhD Clive is professor emeritus in Occupational Psychology at Goldsmiths' College, University of London, and managing director of Personnel Assessment, Ltd. He has published extensively on psychological assessment, performance management, multisource feedback, and leadership development. Clive is a consultant to many organizations in these fields; he can be contacted at c.fletcher@personnel-assessment.com.

Thomas Garavan, PhD Thomas is research professor in Leadership at Edinburgh Napier Business School. He has authored or co-authored 14 books and over 100 refereed journal papers and book chapters. Thomas is editor-in-chief of *European Journal of Training and Development* and associate editor of *Personnel Review*. He is a member of the editorial board of *Human Resource Development Review*, *Advances in Developing Human Resources*, *Human Resource Management Journal*, *Human Resource Development International*, and *Human Resource Development Quarterly*. He can be contacted at T.Garavan@Napier.ac.uk.

Darryl Gauld Darryl is in his fourth decade in education and training roles, having taught learners from most countries at primary, secondary, and tertiary schools, RTOs/TAFEs, universities, and corporations. Now, Dr Gauld is the principal of Macquarie Grammar School, in Sydney, a Top 50 High School attributed to Effective Teachers.

Therese Grohnert Theresa is a researcher in professional development at the Department of Educational Research and Development, Maastricht University. She is interested in informal learning in the workplace, especially learning from failure and judgment and decision making.

Rebecca Grossman Rebecca is a doctoral candidate in the Industrial/Organizational Psychology program at the University of Central Florida, and a graduate research associate at the Institute for Simulation and Training. Her research focuses on team cohesion and related variables in traditional and complex settings, and on improving such variables through training interventions.

Jean-Luc Gurtner, PhD Jean-Luc is professor of educational psychology at the University of Fribourg/Switzerland. He was visiting fellow at Concordia University in Montreal, Stanford University, and visiting professor at the Institute of Education, London, and at the Pontifical University of Curitiba/Brasil. His research interests are Information and Communication Technologies in vocational education and training (VET), Language Learning, as well as Motivation and Learning.

Kyle Heyne Kyle is a PhD student in Industrial and Organizational Psychology at the University of Central Florida/Institute for Simulation and Training. His research focuses on how technology can be used to improve individual and team effectiveness, including research on virtual teams as well as simulation- and game-based approaches to training.

Nina Keith, PhD Nina is professor of Organizational and Business Psychology at Technische Universität Darmstadt, Germany. Her research focuses on formal and informal learning in organizations and has been published in various international journals, including the *Journal of Applied Psychology*, *Personnel Psychology*, and *Journal of Experimental Psychology: Applied*.

Natasha Kersh Natasha is a researcher and tutor at the Faculty of Policy and Society, Institute of Education, University of London. Her research work and publications relate to issues of workplace learning, vocational education and training (VET), and lifelong learning in the United Kingdom and international contexts.

Manuel London, PhD Manuel is dean of the College of Business at the State University of New York at Stony Brook. He is also professor and director of the Center for Human Resource Management at Stony Brook. He received his PhD from The Ohio State University in Industrial and Organizational Psychology and taught for three years at the business school at the University of Illinois in Champaign-Urbana.

Tyree Mitchell   Tyree is a PhD student in the Industrial/Organizational Psychology program at DePaul University. His research interests include training and development, transformational leadership, and the role of goal-orientation in the workplace. He has presented his research at several conferences such as the Midwestern Psychological Association and Association for Psychological Science.

Edward M. Mone   Edward has more than 25 years of experience in career, leadership, and organization change and development. He is currently president of Edward M. Mone & Associates, a firm specializing in organization and leadership development, and adjunct professor of Management at the State University of New York at Stony Brook. He was previously vice president for Organization Development for CA, Inc.

Luciana Mourão, PhD   Luciana is professor in the Master's in Psychology program at the Salgado de Oliveira University (UNIVERSO), Brazil. He has a doctorate in psychology from the University of Brasilia and is a researcher in the Organizational and Work Psychology Working Group of the National Research Association and Master's in Psychology program – ANPEPP.

Fergal O'Brien, PhD   Fergal is a lecturer in Finance at the Kemmy Business School, University of Limerick. He completed his PhD at Lancaster University and also holds an MBA, which was awarded the Guinness Irish Management Institute Sir Charles Harvey Award in 1999. He has published in the areas of finance and graduate career progression in journals such as *Derivatives Use, Trading and Regulation, Irish Accounting Review*, and *Personnel Review*. He is undertaking research primarily in the area of derivative instruments and specifically investigating the profitability of option trading strategies, the returns to horse-racing wagers, and the ability of forward-looking systematic moments to explain asset returns.

Leonor Pais, PhD   Leonor is professor at the University of Coimbra and also teaches at Porto Business School of University of Porto, Portugal. She is the Portuguese coordinator of the European **WOP-P Master Course** supported by the European Commission through the Erasmus Mundus Program. Her research interests are focused on knowledge management, human resources management, cooperation, decent work, and organizational performance. She is the author of various book chapters and scientific papers.

Robert A. Roe, PhD   Robert is emeritus professor of Organizational Theory and Organizational Behavior at Maastricht University (the Netherlands), and visiting professor in Vancouver (Canada), Valencia (Spain), Trento (Italy), and Leipzig (Germany). His publications cover a broad range of topics, including motivation, competence and performance, assessment and selection, leadership and teams, organizational culture and change, and research methodology. Currently his major research focus is on temporal facets of behavioral and organizational phenomena.

Alan M. Saks   Alan is a professor of Organizational Behavior and Human Resources Management at the Centre for Industrial Relations and Human Resources, University of Toronto. He is the author of *Research, Measurement, and Evaluation of Human Resources* and co-author of *Organizational Behaviour: Understanding and Managing Life at Work,* and *Managing Performance through Training and Development.*

Eduardo Salas, PhD   Eduardo is Pegasus and Trustee Chair Professor of Psychology at the University of Central Florida (UCF) and holds an appointment at UCF's Institute for Simulation and Training. Salas earned a PhD in Industrial/Organizational Psychology at Old Dominion University, and has co-authored over 375 articles and chapters on topics like teamwork, team training, and performance assessment.

Mien Segers, PhD Mien is professor in Corporate Learning at the Department of Educational Research and Development. Her research addresses the role of informal learning in the workplace, on the individual as well as the team level. Her work has been published in many high-ranking journals and is the chief editor of the EARLI (European Association for Research on Learning and Instruction) book series New Perspectives on Learning and Instruction.

Jeffrey R. Spence, PhD Jeffrey R. Spence is an assistant professor of Industrial/ Organizational Psychology at the University of Guelph, Canada. He received his PhD in Industrial/Organizational Psychology from the University of Waterloo, Canada. His research examines employee performance appraisals and intra-individual work performance, focusing on organizational citizenship behavior and workplace deviance.

Annette Towler, PhD Annette is an associate professor of Psychology at DePaul University. Her work has appeared in *Human Resource Development Quarterly*, *Journal of Applied Psychology*, *Personnel Psychology*, and *Organizational Research Methods*. Her research has primarily focused on improving training design features to increase transfer of employee skills to the workplace.

Piet Van den Bossche, PhD Piet is associate professor at the University of Antwerp, Belgium, and at Maastricht University, the Netherlands. His research activities are centered around issues of learning and cognition in teams and collaborative environments.

Janine van der Rijt Janine is a PhD candidate at Maastricht University's School of Business and Economics. Her research addresses proactive help seeking and feedback seeking in the workplace. She is appointed as educational consultant at Erasmus MC University Medical Center Rotterdam and is affiliated to the Institute of Medical Education Research Rotterdam.

Sara Van Waes Sara is an instructional developer and researcher at the University of Antwerp, Belgium. She works at a center for faculty development: the Center for Excellence in Higher Education. She is currently working on her PhD, which focuses on the professional development of faculty in higher education, drawing on social network theory.

Maria Joao Velez Maria Joao Velez is a teaching assistant at Nova School of Business and Economics. She has an MSc in Psychology from the University of Evora. She is currently attending the doctoral program in Management at Nova School of Business and Economics. She has published articles in the field of organizational behavior and management. Her main research interests focus on toxic workplaces and followership.

Sandra Watson, PhD Sandra is assistant dean at Edinburgh Napier University's Business School, Edinburgh, UK. She is professor in Human Resource Development and has published many articles and edited texts on human resource management and development. She has guest edited special issues in human resource development and hospitality journals and sits on the editorial board of a number of international journals.

Christian Wolff Christian received his Bachelor's (2010) and Master's (2012) degrees in Psychology at the University of Münster. Since 2013 he has been a PhD student and part of the work group of Organizational and Business Psychology at Technische Universität Darmstadt, Germany. His research interests include learning, self-regulation, leadership, and research methods.

Foreword

The editors of this book – Kurt Kraiger, Jonathan Passmore, Nuno Rebelo dos Santos, and Sigmar Malvezzi – are each internationally respected scholars in their own right. Together, they have assembled an outstanding cadre of academic and intellectual thought leaders to provide us with a stimulating, scholarly perspective on what may be the top organizational challenge of the day – building a talented workforce.

To remain competitive, organizations must crack the code on how to train, develop, and appraise talent. As a result, many books have been written purporting to offer practitioners advice on this topic. However, this book is different. It is grounded in empirical research and sound theoretical foundations rather than anecdotal examples. As such, it is an ideal starting point for the researcher, student, or intellectually curious practitioner who is interested in current research findings and future research needs.

It focuses on the *psychology* of training, development, and performance improvement. This is both important and distinctive, for it is only by truly understanding the psychological factors the underlie these topics that we can hope to make sound organizational decisions about employee development across various complex, diverse settings. Simple lists of best practices may appear helpful, but unfortunately experiences in one setting often don't transfer well to the next. Deeper understanding of psychological phenomena requires solid research and strong theory. That is a strength of this book. It reveals the state of the current research and what we can learn from it. I'm confident that it will also stimulate a tremendous amount of future research.

The editors were wise to include several interrelated topics in this single volume. In organizational settings, training, development, and performance improvement do not operate in isolation, but instead co-mingle to influence the readiness of talent. It is helpful to think of them as connected and this book addresses a range of key topics such as coaching, training, socialization, personal development, e-learning, performance appraisal, and informal learning.

Finally, a book is only as good as its authors. The quality of the chapters is top notch, as the editors have assembled a set of content experts. This is readily apparent as you read the book. The globally diverse set of authors comprehensively and intelligently summarize what is known about a topic and stretch our thinking for the future. They advance our understanding and make us smarter about a set of key organizational challenges and related psychological dynamics.

Scott I. Tannenbaum, PhD
President, The Group for Organizational
Effectiveness, Inc.

Series Preface

Welcome to this third book in the Wiley Blackwell Organizational Psychology series. This title in the series focusses on training, development, and performance improvement and builds on the previous two titles in the series that have focussed on leadership and change and on coaching and mentoring.

Over recent years we have seen a growing number of universities and organizations offer e-learning-based programs for employees and students, including the development of massive open online courses (MOOCs). At the same time our understanding of training design and delivery has developed alongside the methods for supporting employee learning and the transfer of knowledge to improve organizational practice.

We believe this series differs in three significant ways from other titles in the field.

Firstly, the book is aimed at the academic researcher and student, as opposed to the practitioner, although scholar practitioners may also find this an interesting read. The aim is to offer a comprehensive coverage of the main topics of inquiry within the domain and in each of these to offer a comprehensive critical literature review of the main topic areas. Each chapter is thus an attempt to gather together the key papers, book chapters, and ideas and to present these for the serious researcher, student, and academic as a starting point for research in the key topics of I/O (industrial and orgainzational) psychology in a focused chapter. The book thus aims to operate as a starting point for any in-depth inquiry into the field.

Secondly, while many books take a UK/European or a US/North American approach with contributors drawn predominately from one continent or the other, in this series we have made strenuous efforts to create an international feel. For each title in the series we have drawn contributors from across the globe, and encouraged them to take an international, as opposed to national or regional, focus. Such an approach creates challenges. Challenges in terms of language and spelling, but also in the way ideas and concepts are applied in each country or region. We have encouraged our contributors to highlight such differences. We encourage you as the reader to reflect on these to understand better how and why these differences have emerged and what implications these have for your research and our deeper understanding of the psychological constructs that underpin these ideas.

Thirdly, the chapters avoid offering a single perspective, based on the ideas of the contributor. Instead we have invited leading writers in the field to critically review the literature in their areas of expertise. The chapters thus offer a unique insight into the literature in each of these areas, with leading scholars sharing their interpretation of the literature in their area.

Finally, as series editor I have invited contributors and editors to contribute their royalties to a charity. Given the international feel for the title we selected an international charity – The Railway Children – a charity that supports run-away and abandoned children across the world. This means approximately 10 percent of the cover price has been donated to charity and in this way we are collectively making a small contribution to making the world a slightly better place.

With any publication of this kind there are errors; as editors we apologize in advance for these.

Jonathan Passmore
Series Editor, I/O Psychology

Railway Children

Railway Children supports children who are alone and at risk on the streets of India, East Africa, and the United Kingdom. Children migrate to the streets for many reasons, but once there they experience physical and sexual abuse, exploitation, drugs, and even death. We focus on early intervention, getting to the street kids before the street gets to them, and where possible we reunite them with their families and communities.

In addressing the issue we work through our three step change agenda to:

- Meet the immediate needs of children on the streets – we work with local organizations to provide shelter, education or vocational training, counseling, and, if possible, reintegration to family life.
- Shift perception in the local context – we work with local stakeholders to ensure that street children are not viewed as commodities to be abused and exploited – but as children in need of care and protection.
- Hold governments to account – if we are to see a long-term, sustainable change for the children with whom we work, we must influence key decision makers, ensuring that provisions for safeguarding children are made within their policies and budgets.

Last year we reached over 27,000 children; 14,690 of these were in India where we reunited 2820 with their families. In the United Kingdom we launched our research "Off the Radar," which revealed the experiences of over 100 of the most detached children in the United Kingdom. Many of these children received no intervention either before leaving home or once they were on the streets. We have made recommendations that include emergency refuge for under 16s and a wrap-round of other services, such as Misper schemes, local helplines, outreach, and family liaison, to allow children and young people to access interventions in a variety of ways.

To find out more about our work, or to help us support more vulnerable children, please go to www.railwaychildren.org.uk or call 00 44 1270 757596.

1

The Psychology of Training, Development, and Performance Improvement

Kurt Kraiger, Jonathan Passmore, Sigmar Malvezzi and Nuno Rebelo dos Santos

Introduction

It is well established that the management and development of human resources is critical to the well-being and effectiveness of organizations. In their recent monograph, Salas, Tannenbaum, Kraiger, and Smith-Jentsch (2012) concluded: "Continuous learning and skill development is now a way of life in modern organizations. To remain competitive, organizations must ensure their employees continually learn and develop. Training and development activities allow organizations to adapt, compete, excel, innovate, produce, be safe, improve service and reach goals" (p. 1). While the emphasis of the Salas et al. chapter is on training and development, training is but one of many methods by which organizations shape the knowledge, skills, and competencies of its workforce. In this volume, we focus on training and instruction, personal and professional development, and appraisal and feedback.

In concept and in practice, distinctions among training, development, and appraisal are at times artificial if not distracting. When a manager or supervisor appraises the performance of a subordinate and gives feedback, the purpose of that action is (often) to stimulate if not guide the development of the subordinate's skills and competencies. When organizations establish formal development programs for members (e.g., leader self-development activities), formal and informal training are also critical components. Finally, training at its best is a multifaceted approach to stimulating change and can incorporate both personal development and assessment and feedback of trainees.

The effective development of human resources is one of the best ways that organizations can differentiate themselves in the marketplace (Huselid & Becker, 2011). This point is made by Boudreau and Ramstad in a 2005 paper. They argued that organizations are increasingly unable to differentiate themselves by access to capital, better product design, or unique markets. All organizations now compete in relatively the same marketplaces, with similar products, and with similar access to financing. Thus, it is the extent to

The Wiley Blackwell Handbook of the Psychology of Training, Development, and Performance Improvement,
First Edition. Edited by Kurt Kraiger, Jonathan Passmore, Sigmar Malvezzi, and Nuno Rebelo dos Santos.
© 2015 John Wiley & Sons Ltd. Published 2020 by John Wiley & Sons Ltd.

which organizations can locate, procure, train, develop, and retain human capital that best enables them to compete.

Research in strategic human resource (HR) management typically finds that it is not isolated HR practices that lead to greater organizational effectiveness, but the bundling of practices. For example, Delaney and Huselid (1996) reported that the coupling of staffing and training practices by organizations related to staffing and training correlated to organizational performance. Similarly, Huselid (1995) defined high-performance work practices as integrated systems of recruitment and selection, performance management, and training, and found that use of such systems predicted employee retention, individual performance, and long-term corporate financial performance. Crook and colleagues (2011) reported a meta-analysis of 66 studies and found that aggregate human capital (knowledge, skills, and abilities) within organizations strongly predicted firm performance; human capital relates strongly to performance, especially when that human capital is not readily acquirable in the labor market. Finally, Aguinis and Kraiger (2009) reviewed multiple studies conducted in Europe that showed the impact of sound training policies and practices on measures of organizational effectiveness. Indeed, the integration of training, development, and appraisal is so well accepted, that texts on job and work analysis (Brannick, Levine, & Morgeson, 2007), industrial/organizational psychology (Cascio & Aguinis, 2011), and performance improvement (Mager & Pipe, 1997) all emphasize the importance of first identifying the skills and knowledge needed to perform jobs effectively, and *then* assigning the skill to one or more HR systems that include training, development, and performance appraisal. In other words, each system is seen as an alternative path to the same goal: a competent workforce.

Looked at another way, organizations can best accomplish their goals, continually innovate, and differentiate themselves from competition by optimizing talent within the organization. Katz and Kahn (1978) model organizational effectiveness as input–throughput–output systems, with talent – partly in the form of member knowledge and skills – as a major input. How do organizations optimize talent? In the simplest sense, they find it, manage it, or grow it. That is, the effective organization institutes systems for attracting, selecting, and assigning new employees; setting performance standards and maintaining efficient and effective work procedures; and training and developing its members. We do not argue here that training and development are more important than selection and management systems, but simply that they are necessary components of effective organizations.

Why the Psychology of Training, Development, and Performance Improvement?

Browsing the business section of the airport book store can reveal a number of practice-oriented books on training, development, and performance appraisal and feedback. Similarly, while not all business management students are required to take a course in human resource development, those that do are exposed to multiple systems for how to train and develop human capital. Why then a handbook on the *psychology* of training, development, and appraisal? The direct answer is that the consumers of all these systems are human beings who can be best be characterized as unpredictable in terms of how they respond to any intervention geared towards personal or professional improvement.

Industrial and organizational psychology (I/O) is the study of human behavior, emotion, and cognition at work. In short I/O brings science to investigating how individuals, organizations, and states can support, train, develop, and provide feedback to their human resources to optimize performance and well-being.

Consider two examples. First, in the area of workplace training: multiple meta-analyses reveal that in general training works – individuals who received training show more knowledge and better skills than they did before training, or in comparison to those who did not receive training (see Salas et al., 2012, for a summary of such meta-analyses). However, anyone who has delivered training or taught in a classroom can attest that there is a wide range of responses to even effective instruction. Some learners are attentive and appear to get it, others seem puzzled, and yet others are more interested in engaging with other distractions, from technology to doodling on the page. Similarly, in nearly all aforementioned meta-analyses, there are broad confidence intervals around the mean effect sizes for interventions – meaning that the effectiveness of training varies considerably across studies, settings, populations, and so forth. In one meta-analysis, Kraiger and Jerden (2007) examined the effectiveness of providing learner control in computer-based training. Learner control refers to the extent to which the learner can influence his or her learning experiences by determining features of the learning environment such as the topics or sequencing of learning activities. Learner control is generally perceived as not only advantageous to learning, but also desirable to learners. While Kraiger and Jerden found some support for the learner control leading to more learning for certain outcomes, in general, the mean effect sizes for most outcomes were near .00 with large confidence intervals, suggesting that as often as learner control helped learning, it hindered it. Perhaps more striking, similar results were found for reactions to (or liking) of the provision of control. Across studies, trainees were almost as likely not to like learner control as to endorse it. These findings led Kraiger and Jerden to propose a construct of "preference for control," which moderates both the extent to which trainees respond (affectively) to learner control and benefit by it. Put more simply, people are different and those differences matter in the training environment.

Second, in the area of performance management, it is well documented that feedback is essential to performance improvement. For example, Cascio and Aguinis (2011) contend: "One of the central purposes of performance management systems is to serve as a personal development tool. However, the mere presence of performance feedback does not guarantee a positive effect on future performance" (p. 104). Again, anyone who has had to provide feedback to a subordinate or graduate advisee knows that there is considerable variability in how individuals respond to feedback (e.g., information vs. motivational vs. threatening). Indeed, Alvero, Bucklin, and Austin (2001) reviewed 68 feedback studies and concluded that "feedback does not uniformly improve performance" (p. 3). More specifically, Kluger and DeNisi (1996) conducted a meta-analysis of 131 studies and showed that while performance feedback had an overall small positive effect on subsequent performance, in 38 percent of the interventions, it had a *negative* effect on performance. In a meta-analysis of the effects on multisource feedback on performance, while most effect sizes were positive, overall effects were small (Smither, London, & Reilly, 2005).

To be certain, much of the variability in the effectiveness of performance feedback depends on characteristics of the feedback itself (cf., DeNisi & Kluger, 2000). But, it is also the case that receiving, processing, and responding to feedback represents a series of psychological behaviors (Ilgen, Fisher, & Taylor, 1979). As such, different individuals are likely to respond to identical feedback in different ways. Consistent with this, London and Smither (2002) proposed the construct of feedback orientation, a characteristic of individuals that includes affect towards and perceived value of feedback, propensity to seek feedback, the propensity to process feedback mindfully, sensitivity to others' perspectives, and a sense of accountability to act on feedback. Once again, the point here is that people differ, and those differences matter in how feedback is received, processed, and acted upon.

Similar examples can be found for other training methods, as well as other interventions such as career guidance and performance appraisal. While there is value in "how to" guides, the delineation of best practices should ideally follow an empirically based understanding of the role of the person in context, or the psychology of training, development, and appraisal. That is the objective for this handbook.

The Scope of the Handbook

This handbook is a unique contribution to the field, as it joins together training and appraisal as tools for promoting individual development within organizations. The handbook is divided into four sections: training, e-learning, personal and professional development in organizations, and performance management.

Training

Training and development are often discussed together as a systematic process, initiated by the organization, resulting in relatively permanent changes in the knowledge, skills, or attitudes of its members. The distinction between training and development is that the former is typically reserved for events facilitating the acquisition of knowledge, skills, and attitudes (KSAs) relevant to an immediate or forthcoming role, whereas development refers to activities leading to the acquisition of KSAs or competencies for which there may be no immediate application. Further, training is typically sponsored by the organization as training outcomes have direct benefits to the organization. Development activities may be sponsored by the organization as well, but may also be initiated by individuals within the organization without recognition or even awareness by the organization.

Section I's focus is on training. The aim of this section is to present the state of the art of training processes examined from a psychological perspective. A set of training scholars, researchers, and professionals review and discuss different processes and concepts relevant to the design, delivery, and evaluation of training.

In **Chapter 2 Sigmar Malvezzi** explores the development of training from an intuitive to a manageable, institutionalized instrument that is now used to explicitly support explicitly wider organizational development. The chapter seeks to analyze the path training has taken to become a strategic social institution as it has evolved from medieval guilds through the era of industrialization into the technology-integrated practices used by organizations in the twenty-first century.

In **Chapter 3 Rodrigo R. Ferreira, Gardênia da Silva Abbad, and Luciana Mourão** focus on training needs analysis (TNA) as an intervention that is used to understand development needs within organizational settings better. The contributors review the wide range of literature, some 200 papers, and note there is still relatively little theoretical or empirical research on TNA. In spite of this they note that TNA does offer processes for the collection, analysis, and interpretation of data in order to define when formal instructional actions are the best option, help inform the profile of who needs to be trained, and shape the content should be taught.

In **Chapter 4 Karen Evans and Natasha Kersh** review workplace learning. They review three aspects of learning, namely those of *individual*, *environmental*, and *organizational*. The contributors then review the concept of competence development at work, and factors such as the development of the knowledge economy and rapidly changing workplace environments.

In **Chapter 5 Alan M. Saks** focuses on the transfer of socialization in learning. The chapter explores the implications of the transfer of training for organizational socialization and argues that research and practice on organizational socialization can be significantly improved by applying what we know about the transfer of training to the design and delivery of socialization programs. In the first section Saks describes how similar training and socialization programs are in that learning is the most fundamental and primary objective and outcome of training and organizational socialization. Second, Saks reviews the socialization research on employee orientation and training before finally offering a new construct to the socialization literature based on Baldwin and Ford's (1988) model of the transfer of training process.

In **Chapter 6 Nina Keith and Christian Wolff** review the literature from active learning. The chapter explores active learning approaches as well as benefits and challenges associated with their use in organizational training including a discussion of theory and findings regarding the effectiveness of active learning approaches as well as cognitive, motivational, and emotional processes that may underlie their effectiveness.

In **Chapter 7 Darryl Gaud** focuses on the competences of effective teachers and trainers. The chapter examines the literature on competencies, processes, and personal characteristics of workplace trainers through a lens of Knowles' (1980) model of training. The chapter suggests that training is the strategic linchpin of modern productivity, business innovation, and renewed employee commitment that results in higher morale and lower employee turnover when high-quality delivery is achieved by competent trainers.

In **Chapter 8 Jonathan Passmore and Maria Joao Velez** consider the question of training evaluation. The chapter sets out a brief critical review of some of the commonly used training evaluation models, including Kirkpatrick, Phillip's ROI, CIPP, CIRO, Brinkerhoff, IPO, HRD Evaluation and Research, Success Case Method, Dessinger-Moseley Full-Scope (DeSimone, Werner, & Harris, 2002), as well as the SOAP-M evaluation model. The chapter notes the difficulties of evaluation and recognizes that evaluation needs to take account of organizational practice and available resources.

In **Chapter 9 Linda Argote** reviews knowledge transfer and organizational learning. She argues that the characteristics of the organizational context explain variation in organizational learning and knowledge retention and transfer. The organizational context interacts with experience to affect organizational learning and the retention and transfer of knowledge acquired through learning. Similarly, the context can promote knowledge retention or facilitate knowledge decay.

E-Learning and virtual learning

Because of the growing popularity of various forms of technology-distribution instruction, Section II addresses issues specific to the design and delivery of e-learning. E-learning is a deliberately broad term that includes various methods of delivering training via technology (e.g., multimedia learning, computer-assisted instruction, web-based training, and virtual learning environments). Virtual learning is often used synonymously with e-learning, but also connotes immersion in a virtual world, for example, through simulations or even alternative worlds such as Second Life or massive multiplayer online games. The aim of this section is to present evidence of best practices with respect to the management and delivery of e-learning and virtual learning.

In **Chapter 10 Annette Towler and Tyree Mitchell** examine facilitation in e-learning environments, specifically the role of the trainer. While trainers typically have less direct contact with learners in e-learning (compared to face-to-face instruction), they nonetheless play critical roles in encouraging learner engagement and active processing of training content. In their chapter, Towler and Mitchell focus on both the relationship between the trainer and the trainee within the e-learning environment, and recommend specific trainer behaviors conducive to trainee learning.

In **Chapter 11 Jean-Luc Gurtner** reviews current trends and future directions in virtual learning environments (VLEs). Gurtner discusses the growing prevalence of VLEs in higher education, and contrasts them with blended or hybrid learning systems. He presents a thorough discussion of design and delivery characteristics of effective VLEs, based on research, and concludes with a discussion of psychological and social issues to consider as VLEs become more prevalent.

In **Chapter 12 Rebecca Grossman, Kyle Heyne, and Eduardo Salas** review and discuss two more increasingly popular training methods – simulations and serious games. Simulations are artificial scenarios or environments that represent some aspect of reality. Serious games do as well, but add established rules or constraints, as well as a specific goal. Both simulations and games enable trainees to develop new skills and practice new or old skills in a relatively safe environment with high potential for feedback. Grossman and colleagues review evidence for the effectiveness of both simulation-based and game-based training, as well as discussing best practices for the design and delivery of each.

Development

Section III of the book covers personal and professional development in organizations and at work. Various authors bring several ideas, concepts, and tools for promoting development within organizations and in the professional field. They review, present, and discuss the state of the art on the subject from a psychological perspective.

In **Chapter 13 Kurt Kraiger and Thomas M. Cavanagh** review the literature on training and personal development. They focus on the strategic importance of training and its effectiveness, identify established and emerging best practices, and emphasize that the promotion of active learning, among others, is still one best practice in maximizing learning outcomes.

In **Chapter 14 David G. Collings** explores the contribution of talent management to employee development. He highlights research from Cornell University, USA, that has identified that talent management is the top human resources priority on CEOs' agenda. The chapter critically reviews the evidence as to whether talent management contributes to organizational success.

In **Chapter 15 Lisa Anderson and Charlotte Coleman** review the research on the use of action learning sets as a learning methodology. They focus on the development of action learning and its role in the development of managers. The most widespread approaches to action learning are presented as well as a reflection on the reasons why it is becoming more and more used in management education and development.

In **Chapter 16 Leonor Pais and Nuno Rebelo dos Santos** discuss the contribution of knowledge sharing (where it is seen as a cooperation process) to employee development. The authors approach the literature on knowledge sharing focusing on aspects where this is oriented to people instead of technology. They consider in knowledge sharing the several competing drivers that make the situation a social dilemma. The literature on knowledge sharing as a social dilemma is reviewed and summarized. The authors discuss how this approach can promote personal and professional development.

In **Chapter 17 Robert Roe** discusses the roles of the organization and the employee in development of the employee's career. The author focuses on the design of an employee-development system based on the concept of the person's agency. He discusses this employee-development system and reviews theoretical concepts and methods suitable to ground this system. The roles of people involved and practical illustrations of the concepts are also explored in the chapter.

In **Chapter 18 Simon Beausaert, Mien Segers, and Therese Grohnert** discuss the use of personal development plans as learning and development tools. They define the concept, explore the theories on which use of the tool is based, and characterize the purposes of its use. The required conditions (person related and context related) critical to personal development plans are discussed. The authors underline the feed-forward function and present a critical perspective on the informal learning brought about by personal development plans. Suggestions for future research are given.

In **Chapter 19 Thomas Garavan, Fergal O'Brien, and Sandra Watson** consider leadership development's contribution to organizational success. They explore what leadership development is and what the different types of leadership development practices are in organizations. They review published work on the organizational outcomes of leadership development practices and present an agenda for future research on the subject.

In **Chapter 20 Nuno Rebelo dos Santos and Leonor Pais** explore reflection-on-action as a means for personal and professional development within organizations. Balint Groups, supervision, communities of practice and mentoring are presented as structured actions of intentional development based on reflection on real professional practice. The authors characterize those practices according to the literature review, showing how they have blurred boundaries and at the same time have a strong conceptual identity. They present an overview of the state of art of their research.

Finally in **Chapter 21 Valéria Vieira de Moraes and Jairo Borges de Andrade** consider informal learning as a process for development within organizations. De Moraes and de Andrade start by describing informal learning and its role for the development of individuals in workplaces.

Performance management

The fourth and final section covers the use of formal and informal feedback as tools to encourage performance improvement. The section contains five chapters focusing on appraisal and feedback.

In **Chapter 22 Jeffrey Spence and Patricia Baratta** from review the literature on performance appraisal as a tool for employee development. They note that the great conundrum of appraisals is that they are needed to fulfill a number of important personnel and organizational needs, yet increasingly they have a reputation for being a waste of manager and employee time. The contributors consider whether performance ratings are accurate and whether reviews contribute to improvements in performance.

In **Chapter 23 Manuel London and Edward Mone** explore the issue of feedback design and how the design of feedback sessions can be enhanced to optimize their contribution to organizational life. The contributors note that feedback needs to form part of a wider set of organizational interventions, if it is to be successful. Specifically feedback needs to be part of a performance management process that includes: articulation of the department's mission and alignment of the employee's job and strengths with department and company goals, ongoing discussions about expectations, developmental experiences, regular discussions about performance, clear standards of performance, training in the use feedback, and employee surveys to track satisfaction.

In **Chapter 24 Clive Fletcher** considers how individuals can use 360-degree feedback as a development tool. The chapter focuses on the practical aspects of using 360-degree feedback in development. Fletcher considers whether differing views of an individual do really emerge from such feedback processes and notes that the research concludes that differences between rater groups have often been found to be large. This raises questions about the justification for using the same rating dimensions for each group and whether use of the same rating dimensions across different groups is valid.

In **Chapter 25 Piet Van den Bossche, Sara van Waes, and Janine van der Rijt** explore social networks and their role in feedback, specifically the idea that professional development is for a large part driven by discursive interactions with others. The contributors start by reflecting on the different strands of research and theoretical perspectives before describing how a social network perspective can be used to provide a common angle to grasp the role of the relationships that provide feedback. They move on to consider the different aspects of networks and their contribution to development.

Conclusion

This volume seeks to adopt a truly international feel to the study and practice of professional development in organizations. Contributing to it are leading international scholars who collectively have provided critical literature reviews and discussions across a wide area of training, development, and appraisal topics. In doing so, we hope to encourage stronger cross-fertilization between these areas of research, integrate research and practice across different geographical areas, and encourage researchers to draw on the wider psychological (research-based) literature to inform further research and practice.

References

Aguinis, H., & Kraiger, K. (2009). Benefits of training and development for individuals and teams, organizations, and society. *Annual Review of Psychology*, 60, 451–474.

Alvero, A. M., Bucklin, B. R., & Austin, J. (2001). An objective review of the effectiveness and essential characteristics of performance feedback in organizational settings (1985–1998). *Journal of Organizational Behavior Management*, 21, 3–29.

Baldwin, T. T., & Ford, K. J. (1988). Transfer of training: A review and directions for future research. *Personnel Psychology*, 41, 63–105.

Boudreau, J., & Ramstad, P. (2005). Talentship, talent segmentation, and sustainability: A new HR decision science paradigm for a new strategy definition. *Human Resource Management*, 44, 129–136.

Brannick, M. T., Levine, E. L., & Morgeson, F. P. (2007). *Job and Work Analysis* (2nd ed.). Thousand Oaks, CA: Sage.

Cascio, W. F., & Aguinis, H. (2011). *Applied Psychology in Human Resource Management* (7th ed.). Upper Saddle River, NJ: Prentice-Hall.

Crook, T. R., Todd, S. Y., Combs, J. G., Woehr, D. J., & Ketchen, D. J., Jr. (2011). Does human capital matter? A meta-analysis of the relationship between human capital and firm performance. *Journal of Applied Psychology*, 96, 443–456.

Delaney, J. T., & Huselid, M. A. (1996). The impact of human resource management practices on perceptions of organizational performance. *Academy of Management Journal*, 39, 949–969.

DeNisi, A., & Kluger, A. (2000). Feedback effectiveness: Can 360-degree appraisals be improved? *Academy of Management Executive*, 14, 129–139.

DeSimone, R. L., Werner, J. M., & Harris, D. M. (2002). *Human Resource Development* (3rd ed.). Orlando, FL: Harcourt College Publishers.

Huselid, M. A. (1995). The impact of human resource management practices on turnover, productivity, and corporate financial performance. *Academy of Management Journal, 38*, 635–670.

Huselid, M. A., & Becker, B. E. (2011). Bridging micro and macro domains: Workforce differentiation and strategic human resource management. *Journal of Management, 37*, 421–428.

Ilgen, D. R., Fisher, C. D., & Taylor, M. S. (1979). Consequences of individual feedback on behavior in organizations. *Journal of Applied Psychology, 64*, 349–371.

Katz, D., & Kahn, R. (1966). *The Social Psychology of Organizations*. New York: John Wiley & Sons, Inc.

Kluger, A. N., & DeNisi, A. (1996). The effects of feedback interventions on performance: Historical review, a meta-analysis and a preliminary feedback intervention theory. *Psychological Bulletin, 119*, 254–284.

Knowles, M. S. (1980). *The Modern Practice of Adult Education from Pedagogy to Andragogy*. Englewood Cliffs, NJ: Cambridge Book Company.

Kraiger, K., & Jerden, E. (2007). A new look at learner control: Meta-analytic results and directions for future research. In S. M. Fiore & E. Salas (Eds.), *Where is the Learning in Distance Learning? Towards a Science of Distributed Learning and Training* (pp. 65–90). Washington, DC: American Psychological Association.

London, M., & Smither, J. W. (2002). Feedback orientation, feedback culture, and the longitudinal performance management process. *Human Resource Management Review, 12*, 81–100.

Mager, R. F., & Pipe, P. (1997). *Analyzing Performance Problems* (3rd ed.). Atlanta, GA: Center for Effective Performance, Inc.

Salas, E., Tannenbaum, S. I., Kraiger, K., & Smith-Jentsch, K. A. (2012). The science of training and development in organizations: What matters in practice. *Psychological Science in the Public Interest, 13*(2), 74–101.

Smither, J. W., London, M., & Reilly, R. R. (2005). Does performance improve following multisource feedback? A theoretical model, meta-analysis, and review of empirical findings. *Personnel Psychology, 58*, 33–66.

Section I
Training

2

The History of Training

Sigmar Malvezzi

Introduction

Training is an age-old activity broadly applied to support humankind's process of adaptation to the world. Adaptation is a condition of humans that requires the development of the skills of individuals. Individuals are not born with the internal instruments they will require for their adaptation but have to develop them out of their many potentialities (Baxter, 1982). Human potentialities are developed into skills through the various means available to them such as routines, experiences, education, and training. Among those tools of development, training became the most commonly applied to the professional need of adaptation. Correlated to the open-ended human condition and dependent on knowledge and technology, training has developed into a heterogeneous activity, carried out through a wide variety of means and deployed to an almost infinite number of human functions.

The study of an object endowed with an identity so vaguely outlined as to its contents, functions, and boundaries as is training, aligns the researcher with those of the sciences whose objects of study are hardly reproducible for observation. Its grasp requires scrutiny of its institutionalization as a historical development to expose its open-ended condition, and the evolution of its identity, functions, and boundaries.

Historical study is always a helpful path to the unveiling of the articulation of complex social, technological, and economic contexts functioning much like a stage on which the different social, cultural, technological, and economic factors at play may be observable. In the case of training, the conditions it has had available for the achievement of its aims, and the many circumstances in which it has been applied, have evolved and made its observation and the interfaces it has built with work and society complex. Thus the study of the history of training is a fertile path for the understanding of its needs, structures, systems, and tools. Grounded in that potentiality, the analysis of the history of training's institutionalization is taken as the objective of this chapter.

The Wiley Blackwell Handbook of the Psychology of Training, Development, and Performance Improvement,
First Edition. Edited by Kurt Kraiger, Jonathan Passmore, Sigmar Malvezzi, and Nuno Rebelo dos Santos.
© 2015 John Wiley & Sons Ltd. Published 2020 by John Wiley & Sons Ltd.

A historical review of training will highlight its function as a permanent service of human civilization and an instrument through which human potentialities are turned into skills. That service has never been a technically readymade solution as medicines have been for illnesses. Training is an activity materialized by different rhythms, presented through distinct visions, deployed according to several purposes, and regulated by the dynamics of economic competition. As an institutionalized service, training is a manageable structured activity of work characterized by regular elements and necessary for the effectiveness of production. As such, it is a transcendent object that has traversed societies, contingencies, political systems, and economic conditions.

The aim of this chapter is the construction of the path training has taken from an intuitive to a manageable, institutionalized instrument that supports ongoing organizational development. The strategy designed for this purpose does not consist of the exposition of the historical details and figures involved since such an aim would go way beyond the scope of a chapter and become the objective of an entire book. This chapter seeks rather to analyze the path training has taken to become a strategic social institution. The plan of this chapter is to set out the evolution of training, bringing to light the agency of its institutionalization and expounding the variety of issues related to it and the challenges it poses for its management in modern organizations.

The Ontological Roots and Evolution of Training's Requirements

Training's contribution to the development of potentialities into skills has raised it to an irreplaceable position in the tiers of human strategic actions. Its role has become one that contributes to the development of human performance by fitting it to the demands of tasks and to human emancipation by endowing individuals with the capacity to pose and to achieve targets for living and self-fulfillment. By making these two broad contributions, training enables individuals to be effective agents and subjects, by empowering them with the subjective structures and the biological conditions required by making and thinking. These are two mandatory means in the chain of events, which together support human existence and the achievement of the desired projects of which it consists. Necessarily linked to performance effectiveness, training is a crucial link in the string of routine tasks and in the thread of sophisticated strategic events. That broad deployment of training suggests that probably it was not invented by a mind, community, or culture of genius, in a particular historical time, but has been omnipresent in societies and communities since their rise. Probably training emerged out of the routine of social life and slowly evolved as a rational and complex action impelled by the necessary transmission of procedures, skills, and knowledge across successive generations on all continents and in all societies. Its evolution towards a sophisticated action is like the blossoming of a vine on a pole, always growing in step with the development of civilization. A society deprived of training was likely to fail in its own continuity and development.

The steps from a simple activity into a highly sophisticated, regulated, expensive institutionalized service reveal training's interdependence on fundamental factors of civilization such as the development of knowledge, the mastering of, and the technology necessary for, the process of "making by art" – as Aristotle conceived work. The matching of the primitive methods necessary for the qualification of the members of a community to till the land and the sophisticated methods for the qualification of commercial pilots to fly sophisticated aircraft reveals training's dependence on the grammar of society. Training is like a liquid that assumes the shape of the vessel that contains it. Its omnipresence and deployment in the arts, sports, economic production, social life, professional qualification, driving, war, and many other fields of activity disclose the broad range of faces and shapes it presents and the role it plays in human adaptation to the world. By creating the identity of a regulating and emancipating agent dependent on the evolution of civilization, training exposes the openness of the human condition.

Human beings are open-ended individuals constituted by almost countless kinds of potentialities, which to be useful require transformation into effective competences. They are always dependent on the building, broadening, and sustaining of biological and subjective structures to enable them to achieve the aims they pose for themselves both individually and collectively. Through the development of their potentialities into competences, human beings are instrumentalized to attain an almost infinite range of goals the achievement of which out of the properties of the material world is grounded in "making by art." Competences are the outcome of continuous learning to adapt, build new skills, and sustain those previously acquired. Training is the activity through which competences are produced by its potentiality to organize human development. Although endowed with that potentiality, training is not a "factotum," but has limitations, as everybody can see in its ineffectiveness on the development of elderly people. Old age is a time of life in which, by reason of a person's biological condition, potentialities are diminished and training is of limited effect in its capacity to develop many competences and thus to play its role in enabling older individuals to adapt fully to the world. Being one of the main human tools for adaptation to the world, training is a kind of power potentially available to everybody but also potentially inaccessible to many individuals. The inaccessibility to training compromises the sustainability of adaptation of many individuals and communities.

Just as happened with other services and institutions such as trading, taxes, and economic production, in early societies, training was an ever-present activity, calling for effective performance and regulated by community traditions and social and even religious systems. Before the creation of guilds and the industrial era, training was an active power the visibility of which was limited to the sports, arts, and warfare. In other fields training was integrated into the routine of life as a part of it. In general, training applied to work was understood, regulated, and conducted within and by the community's life routine as part of the process of secondary socialization. The development of individuals' skills enabling them to live and to work required little systematic knowledge and was managed in the light of the community's practical experiences. Every community member was entitled and obliged to learn the common basic techniques of routine social life and the fundamental means of survival. This learning was undertaken through the process of socialization and in most cases located in the realms of the family's duties. Accordingly, in medieval Britain every father had to start training his male offspring in the art of archery, just as girls were trained in sewing. Anthropological studies of indigenous communities reveal their training activities within social structures and life regulations (Wallman, 1979). In the primitive Inca civilization every individual had to engage in agricultural activity during the first part of the day and could engage in crafts during the rest of the day. Through that differentiated work engagement new members were able to learn most of the ordinary techniques required for that people's adaptation and survival. Those individuals who did not engage in the agricultural tasks were considered outcasts. The training received during those activities, chiefly agricultural skills, was mediated by the community's traditions and their entire social system.

That traditional community control of training has steadily declined since the introduction of industrialization. The split between work and family life in the industrial era removed training activities from the realm and control of the latter, transforming their design, costs, and regulation into a rational action requiring scientific knowledge, managerial coordination, and economic resources. The outcome of that evolution from community to rational control reached such a point at the turn of the twenty-first century that most enterprises found themselves unable to take on their workers' skilled training as required for the achievement of the goals in view. Today, to develop working skills individuals have to enroll in schools and sometimes to buy training as an outsourced resource from various specialized organizations, such as professional bodies. At the beginning of the twenty-first century, the development of workers' skills related to the prevailing technologies transformed training into a complex activity requiring multiple competencies drawn from various fields of specialized knowledge. These conditions fostered the creation of specialized training organizations capable of designing and applying training projects in partnership with industries, airlines, hotels, and any other kind of organization. Besides its evolution as a complex activity, training became big economic business. Training is a financially expensive activity but a necessary means for the sustainability and quality of businesses and therefore ended up as a mandatory item in the strategic and financial planning of most organizations. In times of fierce economic competition and highly sophisticated production technologies, training emerges as a paradox because it is a crucial requirement of competition and an expensive resource. The management of training thus requires special care on the part of enterprises.

The Origin of Training

Since World War I, the word "training" has been a popular item in everyday vocabulary to express a routine activity common to the professional experience of most adults. It bears an intuitive meaning of the development of skills often associated with education, professions, and sports. In general terms, "training" describes actions such as the intentional and organized development of skills, purposeful learning, formal preparation, professional upgrading, and the development of human potentialities. It appeared in the English language around the fifteenth century to express and communicate the idea of instructing, developing, and teaching, probably taken from an earlier sense of disciplining, or bringing something into a desired form. The main hypothesis drawn by historians presumes that the word originated from the performance of rural growers arranging branches and vines in a desired position or shape and was applied by analogy to human performance. Practical exercises, verbal instructions, and observation of the environment have always existed as an essential part of life. These were spontaneous instrumental activities integrated into the processes of primary and secondary socialization, education, and the integration of all kinds of newcomers. Children and adolescents were admitted within adult groups through the acquisition of language, behavioral patterns, and rituals of interaction with adults in a spontaneous and intuitive but complex kind of training. As society evolved, complex and rapid tasks stemming from emerging technologies were developed, and as these required not only specific skills but synergy between several performers, training evolved *pari passu* with the increasing complexity of the process of production of goods and services.

Throughout that evolution, training itself became a realm of specific technologies leading to the creation of an ample repertoire of instrumentalities. The training technologies within primitive community life consisted mainly of the elaboration and communication of narratives, the observation of others making things, and the on-the-job-training of working together or solo whether or not under the supervision of another trained individual. The objective was simply the transference of traditions and knowledge from older people to youngsters and newcomers. The traditions developed by assimilating new technologies – such as that involved in the preparation of the stained glass windows of cathedrals as a means of communicating the deeds and the values of heroes and saints with a view to developing moral, civic, and quality standards to inspire others' actions. On the basis of those technologies available to all citizens, training attained, in the twenty-first century, to the deployment of techniques such as those necessary to the production of sophisticated software and situational tests to simulate concomitant stock market operations to prepare professional brokers to operate in several countries. At the beginning of the twenty-first century, many training technologies are not exposed to everybody but are in the hands of a very few qualified people, with implications for the development of democracy.

References giving evidence of concern with training practices, procedures, and effects have been registered since the earliest historical times, revealing the recognition of integrated activities related to the learning of knowledge, skills, and procedures as part of society's sustainability. One of the most ancient registers of training is the famous and widespread phrase attributed to the Chinese philosopher Lao Tse who lived in the fifth century BCE, "If you tell me, I will listen. If you show me, I will see. But if you let me experience, I will learn." This affirmation points to the awareness of Chinese society regarding the differentiation of activities in their capacity to develop differentiated actions. The voice, the listening, and the practice are related to distinct subjective structures, which constitute human competences. Yet Lao Tse's affirmation reveals the recognition that the development of skills resulted from the organization of activities such as the making and not only from listening or observation.

Other references to training appear in historical studies on various topics, such as the understanding of military effectiveness on the sustainability of a conqueror's power. In his studies on social power, Lattimore (1962) observed that training was a necessary complement to military might to sustain the Roman conquests. Armies were the main instrument of conquest to sustain domination. They were effective in guaranteeing the control of tax gathering and the recognition of the suzerainty of the Roman leader, ensuring social obedience up to as far as 300 kilometers away. Beyond that distance military power was limited for those purposes and had to be shared with and supported by the "education of men and women." The subjection of conquered peoples required investments in their education and in their adaptation to their new political condition. In this case, training did not seek to develop skills related to "making by art" but was rather deployed for the change of subjective structures such as systems of attitudes, values, and beliefs which later were explained as part of kinetic intelligence (Gregory, 1994) in the process of adaptation. Similar deployment of training was observed in the 1980s, in the era of total quality management. The adaptation of workers to the booming economic competitiveness required cultural changes in workers – a requirement that set training as a necessary instrument of that cultural change (Legge, 1995). The implementation of new strategies of management just required the support of the kinetic intelligence exactly as the Roman army required cultural change for the consolidation of the conqueror's power.

Yet another topic to which training was related is found in the role it played in the replacement of manpower. Even in ancient societies, the supply of labor was not a spontaneous action limited to the replacement of a worker but was also dependent on the systematic reconstitution and transmission of the expertise, the technology, and the performance able to produce the desired outcome. The preparation of people for work was a fundamental question that may be observed in the attention paid to it by responsible authorities and in the dedication of professionals and artists to organizing activities capable of the effective development of skills. Plutarch offers an account of the concern of the early Roman state with the availability of good workers. Good artisans can transmit their expertise in their various crafts to apprentices and newcomers. He registered the deeds of Numa

Pompillius, the second king of Rome, to whom he attributes the creation of a new model of teaching in small groups of people. He organized the teaching of skills in the shape of lessons to groups of youngsters, just as society has institutionalized it in schools nowadays. According to Plutarch, Numa Pompillius invested in that initiative because he sought the development of the new city of Rome. To support this achievement he instituted classes, and organized their pedagogical activities and the teachers for them (see Plutarch, 1952). He hoped, as a result of that initiative, to qualify skilled workers to construct the new city. The novelty described in that record is Numa Pompillius's concern with the general organization of the students, their relation to their masters, and pedagogical activity as an effective means for the transmission of expertise. That kind of strategy later appears in more complex fields of knowledge, such as the development of navigation in Portugal in the year 1417. At the beginning of the fifteenth century, the Portuguese prince Dom Henrique founded and sponsored the School of Sagres, in the south of Portugal. That school is another evidence of a step forward in the slow institutionalization of training.

The main mission given to that school was the preparation of sailors for the purpose of boosting Portuguese overseas domination. Prince Dom Henrique enlisted expert sailors, craftsmen, cartographers, and thinkers and brought them together to develop the art of navigation by the mutual complementation of each other's knowledge and expertise aiming at the training of new sailors. That group built caravels, replotted routes, developed sailors' competences, and sent them to sea on several expeditions. To that school is to be attributed Portugal's success in its discoveries of the fifteenth century. Although many do not accept that example of entrepreneurship as a school, it was, nonetheless, recognized as a kind of laboratory for the study of the sailing business and technology as well as the qualification of new sailors. The School of Sagres reveals an awareness of the fact that sailing could not be as effective as it might be if technology and training were not integrated into a unified rational architecture. It may be seen that in that experience the concept of the sailor-apprentice and his intentional training were directly related to a strategic dimension of investments in future discoveries.

At this point of its institutionalization training discloses its potentialities to evolve *pari passu* with society. Its early stage discloses the mere deployment of potentialities; the next step reveals the awareness of the need of competences and the exploration of training to develop them. The following step shows the transformation of the awareness and needs into plans to exploit and integrate the development of potentialities according to long-term projects for the advance of society. Notwithstanding the slow pace of its development, in the period of the discoveries training already possessed both visibility as a differentiating factor in society and increasing importance as an instrument of social, political, and economic achievement. Both the visibility and importance of training emerge clearly after the fall of the Western Roman Empire. Fostered by the expansion of trade, training was a general concern materialized in the attempts to organize the development of skills and apprenticeships. From that point onwards, every new experience dedicated to the transmission of expertise contributed to the gradual institutionalization of training given its first impulse by the guild, which was the emblematic feature of the preindustrial era and was later consolidated by the conditions created in the industrial context. The greater the regulation of the production of goods in the quest for business speed and complexity, the greater became the complexity and regulations of training, a feature that materialized its institutionalization. Although guilds were a significant step forward in the institutionalization of training, industries consolidated that process by offering endless opportunities for qualitative leaps in its expansion, regulation, and capabilities. If those two steps are compared, guilds were advanced institutions but still organized within the contingencies of the medieval context in which the boundaries between social systems and rational action in the regulation of training were intertwined. Industries created particular conditions that enhanced the distance between social systems and the rational action.

The Emergence of Medieval Guilds

The origin of guilds is a matter of well-known controversy. Guilds were the advanced stage of the evolution of the *collegia* of Roman culture under the form of professional associations. They were quite popular in the European sixth century for butchers, fishermen, merchants, artists, weavers, shoemakers, and many other sorts of business (Muniz, 1975). Guilds became not only a source of wealth and labor but also an effective means for the training of new professionals. Their organization was regulated in such detail that they expose to view a primitive but already institutionalized model of training. Guilds integrated two broad objectives: the production of goods and the training of apprentices. In brief, guilds were institutions that hired youngsters to put them into a kind of on-the-job training. Within that model, apprentices were admitted between 12 and 15 years old, lived in the workshops under the guidance and control of the master, and there lived out a primitive form of professional career. The guild masters had full authority over the apprentices much like parental power such that on occasion they could even apply physical punishment. The apprentices would only start with the small, simple tasks of the particular craft, or were merely limited to the cleaning of tools and the workshop. Quite often their families had to pay for their training before they started to merit their own wages. The training could take two years as in the case of cooking or last even a decade depending on the nature of the craft concerned and on the apprentice's results. The average duration of training was about seven years, as Adam Smith (1981) registered it. Beginning with cleaning, observation, and small tasks, apprentices were given progressively more complex work according to their ability. There were no formal appraisals, nor written guidance, or books. Most of the exercise of the profession was guided and regulated by codes and social norms. Guilds were a successful model that came to be reproduced not only all over Europe but also transplanted to European colonies overseas.

In the guilds, the apprentices were classified by degrees of ability. The first step in the training was a role termed trainee from which the apprentice could be promoted to journeyman and then, finally, to master – the last stage or highest point in the professional hierarchy. The schooling of trainees consisted of the performance of tasks under the master's guidance. In general, the trainee was not entitled to wages and had no tools of his own. At a certain stage in his apprenticeship, the trainee could be promoted to journeyman. The latter was a professional who mastered most of the technology and could work without the immediate supervision of the master. He could possess tools bought with the money he earned from his work. He was entitled to the position of master and actually promoted to it when he proved by the production of an "opera prima" that he was in fact an expert in that particular craft. As a master the individual was entitled to leave the shop and attempt to organize his own workshop in accordance with the rules and codes of the association of the particular place in which he lived.

One of the main features that turned guilds into a significant step forward in the institutionalization of training was the development of a culture of the organization of training by the institution of rules, discipline, hierarchy, and procedures. That culture was an important element in the removal of training from the control of traditions and social systems by subjecting it to a need for both technical and business regulation. Guilds were a kind of specialized cell of the social texture subject to the social system but contextualized as a space in which it was possible to work under specific conditions legitimized by the technological contingencies and commercial conditions. The contribution of guilds to the training culture, in which the success of industries was rooted, consisted of the recognition of characteristics such as that professional qualification takes time, requires discipline, consists of the transfer of knowledge and expertise, and is an important step towards professional emancipation. These four features although within another context and with other values and technologies have been sustained and kept even in times of virtual and high-speed work. The guilds were the seed out of which the basic training concepts blossomed to constitute the prevailing identity of the development of skills later in the industrial context. They made the relationship between training and costs more consistent. The stability and regularity of economic production became dependent on the systematization of the development of skills and the guild satisfied that requirement.

Notwithstanding the step forward that guilds represented in the institutionalization of training, they inspired some criticisms that ever since their time have haunted training under the most varied circumstances. Guilds brought out the two potentialities of training. On the one hand they contributed to the regulation of work in the quest for high-quality performance through the development of potentialities into competences. But on the other hand training may be organized in such a way as to compromise human emancipation if the conditions under which it is exercised restrain the possibilities of the individual's deployment of his competences. The main criticism of guilds relates to their creation of a system of the development of skills that permitted the economic exploitation of apprentices as cheap labor, the unnecessarily drawn-out period of training, and the elitism of the masters. These criticisms are supported by evidences set out in many historical research findings and disclose the strong influence of the organization of medieval society on the early institutionalization of training.

From within the context of the guild, training evolved into the forms it assumed in the industrial context rooted in the experiences gained from the former. Industries were started grounded in many of the beliefs developed in the guilds. The first was the certainty that the training of apprentices, the development of senior workers, and the perfection of experts are activities that give room for the legitimate exploitation and expansion of human potentialities as a condition that enables individuals to accomplish tasks that are hardly achievable by spontaneous learning. Another belief was the certainty that training is part of the broad social and economic system and that it should be organized to provide the necessary development of workers' skills at both low and more advanced levels of expertise. Further, guilds transferred to industries the understanding that training is a complex activity because of its several interfaces with the world as represented by time, supervision, results, costs, and techniques. The belief that the rationalization of the development of skills was not only a social but also an economic phenomenon will become more evident in the next sections dedicated to the reshaping of training in industry.

The Institutionalization of Training

The industrial era began with the creation of mass production methods and machines in the eighteenth century. The fast, broad, and fertile implementation of those novelties steadily redesigned working conditions, reshaped work performance, and reshuffled workers' skills. These changes first became visible in the serialization of tasks and thence sprang up in the intermediation of machines between human performance and the transformation of materials into products. They dismantled the art of craftsmanship and gradually replaced it by an endless technological and managerial innovation disclosing the high potentiality of productivity intrinsic to the evolution of mass production. Soon, industries created the trajectory of engineered, repetitive, and fragmented tasks, which went on evolving into the mechanization, the automation, the robotic, and then the teleworking linking fragmented production stations. The initial intermediation of machines easily expanded its realms to the mediation of informational intelligent systems within networked enterprises. That evolution imposed new demands of adaptation to both work and the working life for which training became a crucial resource that ended up institutionalized as an activity as complex as the very organization of production itself.

The onset of the industrial era can be tracked from the invention of the "factory system" (Hobsbawm, 1987) in the early eighteenth century. That new way of production became the seed of potentialities and structures that were later developed into organizations out of which virtual enterprises have emerged in the twenty-first century.

> The industrial system emerged on the basis of the "factory system," a form of work organization, not a new technology. At the heart of the "factory system" were the following features: fencing of the factory and the imposition of control over the access or departure ... the allocation where possible, of fixed geographical working points ... a detailed division of labor. (Emmery, 1982)

Probably, the pioneers of the factory system had not envisaged the high potentiality and necessity of training as a crucial factor of production and productivity effectiveness. At the onset of industries, management pioneers did not recognize training as a crucial link in that new compound nor were they concerned with the need of any special managerial care of the process of adaptation. Training's contribution to the success of production and of services sprang up gradually in correlation with the demands of skills stemmed from the technological and managerial development of industries.

In the first stages of the factory system, workers were recruited and hired by the foremen or by intermediary agents who assigned tasks to them and provided the raw materials they required either to work within the plant or at home as ways of mass production. The hiring of workers was carried out under the contracts and rules imported from the guilds and the artisan shops. When hired, workers had to accomplish the tasks assigned to them under the rule of "swim or sink," without any systemic activity to prepare and adapt them to tasks. Recruiters presumed that the hired workers were skilled weavers, potters, carpenters, spinners, metalworkers, or experienced manpower in some other craft and were thus able to learn and to perform the new tasks assigned to them in the factory. There are records of foremen spending some time teaching their team, but that attention on the part of the supervisor was not organized, nor obligatory and not even regular. Impelled by factors such as the steady technological evolution and the development of administration, the demand for specialized and accurate performance came to constitute a constant difficulty. Recruitment and training were two means whereby solutions could be found. The need for the development of the skills of a larger number of workers to perform accurate and precise tasks was gradually realized and integrated into managerial concerns. Soon the mismatch between the demands of production, the limitations of workers' competences, and the difficulties encountered in preparing them became apparent and were routine problems on managers' desks.

By the end of the nineteenth century personnel selection and training were two activities recognized as crucial managerial instruments of production effectiveness. They required a rationalization analogous to that of the managerial care of the production line. The recognition of the contribution of recruitment and training to performance effectiveness turned managers' eyes towards the search for ways to skill workers. From the turn of the eighteenth to the end of the nineteenth century, there are records of managerial initiatives aimed at the skilling of workers. Gradually these initiatives have become integrated into managerial routines and have undergone improvements born from the experience of their implementation. Various scattered actions to recruit and train workers during the nineteenth century shaped the institutionalization of personnel management as part of the hierarchical structure through the gradual organization of regularities in each of its services. In the course of that process, although solutions grounded in intuition were still quite frequent, the demand for the rationalization of those services brought systematic and scientific knowledge into personnel management. That demand fostered the alliance between enterprises and the academy creating a partnership that was already visible by the close of the nineteenth century. The integration of thinkers and makers in the search to adapt workers to their tasks stimulated the development of articulated actions capable of managing the development of workers' skills. It was one of the main features of the institutionalization of training.

One of the pioneer training initiatives was the gathering of small groups of workers in classrooms distant from the shop floor where they could be taught how to operate the machines and perform the tasks. That experience proved to be a good tactic in terms of time-saving but not so effective in its main aim:

> Since workers were now learning away from the job, they had to remember not only what they had learned in classroom until they could get onto the floor of the production line, but they also had to transfer what they had learned abstractly in the classroom onto a real machine in a real work environment. (Sleight, 1993, p. 3)

Notwithstanding their limitations, the classrooms were deployed and gradually improved, becoming the so-called "vestibule schools," in the late 1800s. That step forward "consisted of a room or area set off from the plant floor where workers not only received formal instructions for several days or weeks but also were given hands-on-training in the operation of specific machines or performance of technical tasks" (Kauffman, 2008, p. 128). The "vestibule schools" proved to be an effective means and became a widespread technique for the training of apprentices in factories. The successful experience of the "vestibule schools" fostered their improvement in terms of the better elaboration and design of the content taught to workers and apprentices, thus shaping the training programs. This was specific content to bring to fruitful effect the understanding of tasks and the learning of performances, which were molded into regular activities. These training programs consisted of organized learning trajectories. Soon managers discovered that they only needed to be elaborated once and could then be deployed in other units of production to be replicated to distinct groups of workers. The training programs gave visibility to the workers' skilling as rational and regular managerial service contingencies that promoted their legitimacy within the young culture of scientific administration. As a comprehensive regular set of activities, programs rapidly proved to be much more effective than the previous intuitive foreman initiatives in preparing newcomers or in helping workers to adapt to the new technologies. The success and visibility of these programs soon led to the inclusion of training in budgets and in the list of issues discussed at meetings where managerial plans were elaborated. Training programs became a common practice and gradually were identified with the very training activity thus giving visibility to the institutionalization of the professional qualification. The institutionalized training presented after World War I had been shaped in the late nineteenth century through the consolidation of those scattered initiatives with the support of some measure of scientific knowledge.

The gradual shaping of training together with other activities dedicated to the fitting of performances to tasks such as recruitment, selection, career paths, and rewards as rational managerial actions, built the differentiation of personnel management as a specialized and necessary service within the hierarchical structure of enterprises. Training gradually appeared in a formal locus within personnel management as one of its mandatory activities consolidating its specific identity as a specialized action within personnel management. As such, training undertaken as a visible and manageable activity became daily more evident. Training was implemented everywhere and became as visible in the enterprise's structure as maintenance and finance. Notwithstanding such visible legitimacy and development, training was not an easy task as the concern with it required more than programs and visibility. That required plus was found in the deepening of the alliance between managers and the young applied human sciences.

Recognized as a technical support susceptible of rational design, leading to practical effective results, the accomplishment of training required inputs found mainly in scientific knowledge. That need attracted the attention of the academic pioneers in the fields of psychology and pedagogy, motivating them to study and investigate issues such as human abilities, their identification and differentiation, the best ways of applying them, techniques for their measurement, and methods to develop them within the contingencies of the organizations. Personnel management itself, as a set of differentiated services, became an object of science, and as such was regularly investigated and continuously enriched by the creation of practices stemming from scientific investments. Training programs started to be elaborated under the guidance of and matched with the theories, concepts, and empirical findings developed by practitioners and researchers. That integration of thinking and making fostered the development of work psychology as a specialized field of knowledge grounded in the researches and experiences carried out in the last two decades of the nineteenth century by those pioneers. The involvement of professionals and researchers in the understanding of those problems impacted managers stimulating them to learn the difference between intuitive and scientific procedures. As part of those movements and discoveries, from the development of professional schools to the organization of lectures within the shop floor to prepare skilled workers on the grounds of the certainty of science was but a short step. Those schools started in the nineteenth century and expanded quickly after World War I as another training instrument placed outside the walls of enterprises and potentially integrated into the broad educational system as its new branch. They fostered another alliance in the interface between factories and the educational systems as a result of which the concept of professional education became more visible and legitimated. That alliance was a strategic turning point in society following the awareness of the matching between the academy and the economy, which ended up in the twenty-first century in executive and professional education becoming big business and a widespread service.

Theodore Struck captured that link between the academy and the economy. He investigated the progress made in the development of workers' skills and, looking for a qualitative leap in its advance, concluded that the educational system did not fit into the demands of the "new economy." His findings led him to regard schools as places restricted basically to the teaching of writing, reading, mathematical skills, and some classes on liberal arts. According to his view, in limiting their activities to that humanistic knowledge the schools were not in tune with the declining preindustrial society since they had not integrated work apprenticeship into their goals. To fill that gap, industries should revise their teaching goals to fit them to the demands of the new economy in order to produce a competent labor force. Beliefs and proposals such as those of Struck emerged and were reinforced by the success of training programs in industries and the possibility of transferring them to schools. The practical success of those programs inspired the possibility of their transfer to schools. That inspiration fostered the creation and development of special schools that could be the partners of enterprises. In keeping with that spirit, in 1902, the

YMCA created their Industrial Department to bridge the gap between youngsters and the manpower requirements of the railroads of the United States. Its aim was to expand its welfare work into the realm of industry. YMCA's initiative was so successful that by1915 there were almost 100 YMCA facilities serving various industries, not only the railroads (Kaufman, 2008).

At that point, the need for training had become a key concept in managerial and academic concerns, the achievement of which was accomplished through the definition of learning targets. Schools and personnel management started to design trajectories aimed at the development of workers' and apprentices' skills both for implementation in schools as a propaedeutic action and in organizations as part of the managerial duty of adaptation of performances to tasks. The training programs whether undertaken in schools or on the shop floor reinforced training's identity as a necessary service, linked to personnel management, to science, to the educational system, and to organizational effectiveness. Programs became a kind of mandatory instrument for the materialization of training and had expanded their deployment not only to shop-floor workers but also to the skilling of foremen and managers. That expansion of the realms of training activities led to the perception of the complexity of skilling and the understanding of human abilities. Through the 1920s and 1930s various research projects were undertaken and several theories emerged in that field reinforcing the need for the scientific approach to training and providing more evidence for its legitimacy.

Notwithstanding their consolidation and scientific support, the elaboration of training programs created tensions within both academia and the managerial field. Organizational demands and the programs developed in schools and in factories did not always match exactly because industries were evolving from manual to "all round mechanical" work. The technology shifted skilled craftwork to broadly previously defined minimally differentiated machine-tending tasks requiring only unskilled or semiskilled manpower (Douglas, 1921). Those mismatches revealed the existence of distinct paces between training and labor demands. Training programs and chiefly schools moved at a conservative pace while the shop floor was a locus of continuous innovation. Besides that technical aspect within industries, many schools were not prepared to adopt the target of training apprentices as enterprises required them to do. That mismatch brought out the need for broader actions than just technical modifications of syllabuses and programs.

Along with programs and professional schools, the institutionalization of training took another step forward impelled by managerial endeavor to link it to negative events such as turnover and manpower shortage, which posed serious difficulties for the regularity of production. Training and personnel selection were together envisaged as preventive instruments to overcome those difficulties. At the beginning of the twentieth century training was conceived of as a good tool to prepare for the replacement of incompetent workers as this testimony of Taylor's gives evidence:

> It becomes the duty of those on the management's side to deliberately study the character, the nature and the performance of each workman with a view to finding out his limitation, on one hand but even more important, his possibilities for development, on the other hand; and as deliberately and as systematically, to train and teach this workman, giving him, wherever it is possible those opportunities for advancement which will enable him to do the highest and most interesting and most profitable calls of work for which his natural abilities fit him. (Taylor, 1947, p. 256)

This testimony shows the visibility of training's potentialities as a resource that could be considered in management's routine concern for the adaptation of workers to tasks. The achievement of those potentialities deepened the shaping of the identity of training and therefore of its institutionalization as part of management and as part of society with impacts whose effect extends beyond factory boundaries. The broad deployment of all those skilling activities already under the control of the academy and management fostered the vision of training as a technology conceived much as engineering was and as such treated as a commodity that could be bought and sold. The quest and deployment of those programs and models were not limited to the industrialized world but contaminated business management wherever the "factory system" was applied. Even then unindustrialized countries such as Brazil, where railroads were being built, required that kind of managerial technology that was imported from Europe through the hiring of foreign engineers. That conception of training as a resource that could be found readymade somewhere made its deployment an easier and legitimate action much as was the purchase of any other technology. The conception of training as technology was first proposed by William Stern, a German psychologist and philosopher who invented the word *psychotechnique* in 1903 to express the emerging experimental research on work and its deployment in schools and professional settings (Carroy, Ohayon, & Plas, 2006, p. 119). A new word is a helpful means to foster the institutionalization of a resource like training that, seen as a commodity, could be transferred from one enterprise to another.

All those developments contributed to the recognition of a new area of knowledge which, integrating distinct fields of science around the same question, was a complex issue whose handling required the cooperation of several expertises. That emergent field of research dedicated to the validation of professional practices reinforced the visibility and identity of training by establishing it as an object of scientific investigation and of managerial systemization. Education for work could not be effectively accomplished by intuitive knowledge nor controlled by social systems and traditions but should be taken as a field of science to feed the institutions in charge of society's management and economic production. That consolidation of training as a crucial element of management and a complex issue in scientific knowledge impacted broadly in the reshaping of professional boundaries and in public policies. That consolidation progressed in such a way that after World War I training was no longer an issue restricted to the four walls of factories but a general topic investigated by academics, handled by managers, taken into consideration by workers' associations, and regulated by public administration. Over the first three decades of the twentieth century, training had its identity and institutionalization recognized by academic literature, by schools, by workers' associations, and by governments, as seen in the many initiatives taken to regulate it and to foster its expansion and improvement as the analysis of the case of France gives some evidence.

In France, an industrialized county for more than a century, training's institutionalization stimulated the integration of endeavors to promote the development of work skills, a fact that deepened its enrichment and investigation. The work of several psychologists pioneered the complementarity of those institutions in the promotion and development of training. Binet, Ribot, Lahy, Buisson, and Henri were researchers whose investigations contributed significantly to the development of training in their country through their attempts to understand skills and their learning in distinct contexts such as schools and workplaces. Through distinct initiatives they realized that it was possible, in all the phases from infancy to adult life, to improve the learning process of abilities by applying the results of research to the learners (Carroy, Ohayon, & Plas, 2006, p. 99). That belief opened the eyes of managers and government to the need for investment in the investigation of performance and the development of skills. The good results of the application of the findings of new sciences in professional contexts awoke an important echo among both researchers and practitioners. Training was favored by those studies not only from the point of view of the understanding of learning skills but also from that of other aspects such as the influence of prejudices in work performance.

The view of Jean Maurice Lahy, one of the pioneers mentioned, was not limited to performance effectiveness but his interest also extended to the social deployment of skills. With the support of the printing workers' association, he investigated differences between male and female linotypers as an expected managerial concern and as a social bias. Grounded in empirical evidences statistically analyzed, Lahy demonstrated that males and females had equal potentiality to learn and perform – a very important finding at that time. The observed differences in their outcomes, particularly in their speed, were grounded in factors related to conditions strange to skilling and related to other features of management such as financial rewards and foremen's attitudes. These external factors were created by managerial policies and managers' attitudes. Those findings broadened the vision of the factors comprised in skilling by linking the deployment of skills to social contingencies as an important step in the investigation of the social nature of intelligence (Carroy, Ohayon, & Plas, 2006, p. 121). That link was expanded two decades later by the classical Hawthorne studies in which training was taken to be an activity directed not only towards the development of physical capacities but also towards the social capacity that was part of the determinants of workers' skills. Those studies impacted the understanding of training by the expansion of its object of attention from abilities to other aspects of subjective structures such as attitudes and values. That widened concept of skilling expanded the objective of training and some decades later it was taken as the outcome of the acquisition of knowledge, the development of skills, and the change of attitudes. From the 1960s, that popular model of training comprising those three disclosed that skilling was an action directed to the person and not restricted just to mental and motor skills. That expansion of training as an institution responsible for work skilling did not stop at that point but moved on into other significant realms.

Motivated by the strategic concerns of enterprises, the lack of manpower generated by the war, and the new technological developments, authorities and managers soon realized the urgent need for professional education and training as a complementary action to be promoted by the educational system. At that time, the discussion on those topics was as to whether all children and youngsters should be better instructed in order to be earlier prepared to face the new requirements of jobs (see Carroy, Ohayon, & Plas, 2006, p. 122). The answer to that question was given in France in 1922 by a government decree instituting professional guidance with a view to the technical training of future workers as a school subject. That government move arose from the recognition of the joint responsibility of enterprises and government for workers' skilling to perform in response to emerging technologies and changing working conditions. Six years after that government decree, the Institut National d'Orientation Professionnelle (INOP) was created in France and similar institutions were created in other countries, like the SENAI in Brazil. That institute was a new kind of organization dedicated entirely to professional skilling, which became a further part in the chessboard of the institutionalization of training. As a result of the influence of such initiatives training easily became related to several other factors such as work satisfaction, as seen in the 1921 testimony of another French researcher, Fontégne. According to him, training should be an activity by which if "the professional's performance produces the minimum tiredness and the maximum bliss, trainees will present the optimum level of productivity."

At that stage in its evolution, training increased its visibility as an organized service, fully recognized as an indispensable instrument of adaptation in fundamental fields of society such as education, professionalization, business management, sports, the arts, and even war. As such, it was a service with a scope of far-reaching consequences for individuals' capabilities and seen to have an identity easily differentiated from that of other services also required for and related to adaptation, such as socialization, education, selection, motivation, and appraisal. Training was another component of society heard of in primary socialization even before the beginning of professional life. Most people knew the meaning of the word training intuitively, used it in their daily discourse, and were aware of its main locus, potentialities, values, and the high probability of experiencing it in their own way. After World War II, the generalized application of training revealed its coming of age as a service clearly autonomous of and complementary to other services related to adaptation. Training was an available and regular public resource, which should be applied for the sake of the effectiveness of the various activities of society with the aim of ensuring both the individual's ordinary as well as his special capabilities. From that level of recognition and appliance, training evolved – maximizing its potentialities, sophisticating its instrumentality, enriching the values it could add to society, and achieving the status of a compulsory path for the legal exercise of many activities. The recognition of that level of maturity and of its fundamental contribution made training a valuable asset in regard to strategic issues, a step forward that put it into the big business by which specialized enterprises create and plan, implement, assess, and develop training projects.

Training at the Dawn of the Twenty-First Century

Since the theory of systems and the computer were introduced into organizations in the early 1950s, the demands for adaptation to managerial evolution have steadily increased. The answer to those demands found in training a service already available as a mature institution that could be shaped to and deployed on behalf of different programs, targets, conditions, loci, and approaches. Training was a tool already at hand for managers and available to academic research as a trustworthy activity in its potentialities for adaptation, able to contribute to the qualification of adequate work performance. The necessary mediation of training for effective performance was no longer in doubt, nor was its locus in the personnel management structure, but it had pervaded other institutions like government and schools. From that point in its evolution, training was set in an endlessly increasing differentiation of its own structure and agency in its adaptation to the pace of a broad demand for skills – as was later to be observed in the role it played in its implementation for semi-autonomous teams, quality circles, organizational development, and the like in the 1960s and 1970s. That differentiation was observed from east to west in enterprises and other kinds of organization consolidating training's identity as an open-ended and mandatory instrument related to the regulation of work performance and individual emancipation. From the experience of its broad deployment, which ranged from sophisticated strategic business plans to high performance in sports and arts, training was remolded in its contents, functions, and boundaries, as earlier mentioned, in a way that made it difficult to describe it as a serialized instrument. The potentialities found in training confirmed once again the open-ended character of the human condition and the range of tasks to which people could be adapted. As such a rich and highly mature institution, training was able to offer adequate service for the needs of both beginners and experts, for complex and routine performances and for short- and long-term adaptations, thus becoming highly differentiated along with its general deployments. The conditions to which work performance had to adapt in the tele-information era exposed training to harder challenges that gained momentum at the beginning of the twenty-first century when society and particularly business were moved by the confluence of the virtualization of "making," digital technology, and economic fragmentation. Under these conditions, training faced the challenge of having to qualify workers for constantly varying demands of skills. Within that new grammar people have to interact with invisible processes of production, to decide under and react to high-speed patterns of performance, absorb new technologies, and work in interdependent relationships with other performers. Training has met that challenge by amplifying the diversity of its actions and means as evidenced by and clearly expounded in the several chapters of this book.

Under that grammar, business management became a continuous movement of articulation, change, differentiation, integration, qualification, projection, and assessment. The adaptation of performance to that grammar turned the understanding of skills into a more complex issue by the difficulties stemmed from the integration of mental, social, and motor operations, cross-referencing judgments, entrepreneurship, self-designed tasks, and the management of synergy with others. These requirements – more to be expected of gods or supermen – fostered the differentiation of training in its targets, instruments, and boundaries, impacting the need for distinct expertise for trainers. Today, many workers in realms such as those of finance, security, and strategy face demands for skills analogous to those required by the character Pi in the beautiful Ang Lee movie *The Life of Pi* (2012). Pi had to coexist with Richard Parker, a carnivorous tiger on a boat adrift at sea. It would be hard, even for a training expert, to anticipate the set of skills that the adaptation to that situation would require. Pi had to be a resilient entrepreneur of the development of his own skills to succeed in facing the threat of his coexistence with Richard Parker. Analogously, many workers today have to be resilient builders of their own skills, just as Pi had to be. Accordingly, training is not limited to institutionalized activities but emerges as a set of tasks shared by personnel management and the autonomous individual's action – as has been well documented in the recent literature of career development.

The skills required for jobs performed within virtualized fast activities, with a high level of autonomy and interwoven with several protagonists, are the significant challenge for training today, because they cannot be easily discriminated nor differentiated one from the other. Many jobs require the adaptation of workers to a sequence of unforeseen surprises – as seen in Pi's adventure. Today, a common challenge of training programs is that of the preparation of workers to deploy distinct skills in the face of the need for the rapid understanding of the context within which they perform, the skills for which they have to craft just as Pi had to create the tasks from a restricted range of materials. Under these working conditions, training emerges as a creative instrument to consider adaptation as a kind of continuous necessity that can never be considered adequate because the needs to which it has to respond are molded and remolded in accordance with the constant changes of the context. This adaptation to oscillating needs stemming from contexts under the metamorphosis of emergent properties requires high levels of differentiation of training itself. The alliance between academia and enterprises continues to enable training to be a reliable tool to meet that demand. The leap taken by training in its evolution from the "vestibule schools" to this highly open-ended demand for programs resulted in the individualized training programs known as coaching. These differentiations suggest that although already institutionalized, training is still a service in progress.

The "vestibule schools" were created to serve groups of workers aiming at optimizing the possibility of the serialization of teaching, within a context characterized by the high regularity of the events in view. The serialization succeeded and it is still required for and applied to certain stages and sorts of training. The institutionalization of training during the first half of the twentieth century occurred on the grounds of the potentiality of the serialization of learning. More than a century later, as an already mature institution, training moved back to a model more similar to the guilds concerning the apprentice/master relationship. It moved to the singularization of workers' qualification because they perform tasks surrounded by emergent properties. Today the effectiveness of many performances depends on the capturing of the particular conditions created by spontaneous events emerging in the working context and on interdependence of others' performances, seen as a routine within the structure of networks. Under these conditions, performance is created from the quest for the best reaction to the task, just as seen in the case of Pi. To carry their jobs out safely, workers require close supervision, a kind of mirror where they can see and appraise their own performance and craft the skills it requires. That is an age-old practice in the case of musicians and singers. In those cases, adaptation required more inputs than those given in classrooms and on the job. They require frequent technical feedback to mold their skills properly. They rely on coaching. The training answer to that kind of differentiation in its service was the expansion of its boundaries to integrate coaching in its repertoire.

That long differentiation of training after its institutionalization revealed an artful capacity to exploit its own hidden potentialities to adapt itself to innovations on many sides: the academic and technological development, the fierce commercial competitiveness within globalized business, and the increasing complexity of society. That effective adaptation of training to the evolution of organizations is a good sign that it possesses the ability to continue to innovate to face the challenges that will be posed by the era of networked enterprises. Training may not have changed its main function since the time of the guilds, traversing the centuries constantly dedicated to workers' qualification with a view to their adaptation to the demands of their tasks, but the way the function of qualification was set as a need and the way skills were developed have. The steady commitment of training to that function could be compared to a kind of resilience in which challenges are met with creativity. Training has absorbed the evolution of the very concept of skills (Attewell, 1990), diversified the span of activities through which skills could be developed, recreated its instruments to explore and deploy the potentialities of new technologies, expanded the realms of the assessment of its results, and amplified its interfaces with society and with people.

The merits of that positive adaptation are grounded in the sustainability of the alliance between academy and organizations, as easily seen in the several chapters of this book. That interdependence between the shop floor and academic research has opened the eyes of both sides to the importance of both inputs. On the one side, sciences like psychology have contributed to the understanding of skills while, on the other side, administration contributed with concrete situations, problems, and projects in which skills could be observed, deployed, and investigated. What skills are and how they should be differentiated, categorized, and developed are still open questions. If the main function of training is workers' skilling, the cooperation of both sciences contributed as indispensable conditions of training, its institutionalization, and differentiation. That cooperation fostered the development of the understanding of skills. At the beginning of the twentieth century, when training already had a public face and a consistent identity as a service aimed at qualification within the personnel management structure, the prevailing concept of skill was the positivistic vision of independent structures seen as the subjective instrument of performance to be developed by activities in classrooms and on the job. That concept of skill evolved under the influence of a diversified range of paradigms, which opened up new paths (Attewell, 1990) enriching training with alternative concepts and countless instruments elaborated for its measurement. From Wechsler to Golleman and later to Sternberg and Hovart the concept of skill posed more complex tasks to training because the issues resulting from any new research had their impact in the revision of the activities through which training could exercise the accomplishment of qualification.

On the side of administration, since the 1970s, organizations have witnessed and undergone the emergence of many models of management ranging from Total Quality Management, Re-Engineering, Manufacturing Cells to Self-Managed Teams and Networked Enterprises, among many others. In the implementation of all those models training was always a mandatory means to promote the required workers' qualification to each one of those management rationales. The flexibility and repertoire of potentialities brought about by training enabled it to adjust itself to all management rationales, thus disclosing its open-ended condition to offer diverse varieties of service within a countless range of contexts to achieve ample diversity of long- and short-term development targets. That adjustment has demonstrated that training is a tool, rather like the interview which is an organized structure of face-to-face communication that can be applied to all sorts of investigation, learning, and persuasion. Analogously, training is a complex integration of learning activities organized to qualify people for their adaptation to and integration into the world, a structure developed in step with the evolution of work and society constantly differentiating its potentialities and achievements.

Along its historical path training has faced various kinds of challenge that have only served to enrich it and enabled it to take each successive step. The challenge posed to it by the guilds were the organization of learning with few instruments and under the limitations imposed by social controls and community traditions. The challenges posed by industries were in the rigidity of the tasks needed to operate machines at regular speed, which divorced the creating mind from the making hands and thus imposed meaningless and repetitive tasks. The challenges posed by the structure of networks are the creation of tasks within a context of emerging properties at a synergic pace with others that also have to be frequently negotiated. In the face of all those challenges, training has proved itself capable of understanding its function and of offering appropriate services to satisfy most of the demands placed in its hands. It is not possible to forecast what work performance will be like in the coming decades but nobody doubts that training will be able to continue to answer its forthcoming challenges. As a mature and open-ended service supported by the alliance between academics and practitioners it is prepared to face any storm. Its success will be an outcome of its care for the double contribution it will continue to make, that is, the regulation of work performance and the individual's emancipation which although in a kind of paradoxical relationship can be integrated and function complementarily.

References

Attewell, P. (1990). What is skill? *Work and Occupations*, 17(4), 422–448.

Baxter, B. (1982). *Alienation and Authenticity*. London: Tavistock.

Carroy, J., Ohayon, A., & Plas, R. (2006). *Histoire de la psychologie en France*. Paris: La Découverte.

Douglas, P. (1921). *American Apprenticeship in Industrial Education*. New York: Columbia.

Emmery, F. (1982). New perspectives in the world of work. *Human Relations*, 35(12), 1095–1122.

Gregory, R. (1994). Seeing intelligence. In J. Khalfa (Ed.), *What is Intelligence?* (pp. 13–26). Cambridge: Cambridge University Press.

Hobsbawm, E. J. (1987). *Mundos do trabalho*. Brazil: Editora Paz e Terra.

Kaufman, B. E. (2008). *Managing the Human Factor*. Ithaca, NY: ILR Press.

Lattimore, O. (1962). *Studies in Frontier History*. London: Oxford University Press.

Legge, K. (1995). *Human Resource Management: Rhetorics and Realities*. London, Macmillan.

Muniz, M. A. G. (1975). *Historia social del trabajo*. Madrid: Jucar.

Plutarch. (1952). *The Lives of Noble Greeks and Romans*. Chicago: Encyclopaedia Britannica, Inc.

Sleight, D. A. (1993). A developmental history of training in the United States and Europe. http:// www.msu.edu/~sleightd/trainhst.html (accessed May 19, 2014).

Smith, A. (1981). *The Wealth of the Nations.* Indianapolis: Liberty Fund.

Taylor, F. W. (1947). *Taylor's Testimony Before the Special House Committee: A Reprint of the Public Document, Hearings Before Special Committee of the House of Representatives to Investigate the Taylor and Other Systems of Shop Management Under Authority of House Resolution 90.* New York: Harper & Row.

Wallman, S. (1979). *The Social Anthropology of Work.* London: Academic Press.

3

Training Needs Analysis at Work

Rodrigo R. Ferreira, Gardênia da Silva Abbad, and Luciana Mourão

Introduction

Training needs analysis (TNA) is an important component of instructional systems because the success of the planning, execution, and evaluation of training in organizational environments depends on the quality of information generated in the TNA stage. However, there is still relatively little theoretical or empirical research in TNA (Kraiger, 2003; Aguinis & Kraiger, 2009). Literature reviews dedicated to the topic are rare (Gould et al., 2004; Chiu et al., 1999; Abbad & Mourão, 2012; Ferreira & Abbad, 2013). The characteristics and theoretical-methodological gaps in this field are, to some extent, still unknown.

It seems that the prescriptions of seminal authors (Mahler & Monroe, 1952; McGehee & Thayer, 1961; Moore & Dutton, 1978, among others) have not yet been completely adopted in practice or in TNA research. For over 50 years, training and development (T&D) literature has been concerned with the importance of systematic procedures for TNA and the investigation of internal and external variables that influence or originate needs for training in work contexts (McGehee & Thayer, 1961). However, the scientific production in the area has yet to provide plausible answers to important theoretical and methodological questions surrounding the topic.

For McGehee and Thayer (1961), training needs are derived from poorly developed skills, insufficient knowledge, or inappropriate attitudes. For Mager and Pipe (1979) training needs are differences identified between the current performance of employees and the performance that an organization would like to have from them. For Borges-Andrade and Lima (1983), training needs can be defined as a discrepancy between a prescribed and a real situation or between "what is" and "what should be" in terms of individuals' dominance of different competencies. Asku (2005) said that a training need is the hiatus between the hoped-for success and the real success of an organization or an individual.

The Wiley Blackwell Handbook of the Psychology of Training, Development, and Performance Improvement,
First Edition. Edited by Kurt Kraiger, Jonathan Passmore, Sigmar Malvezzi, and Nuno Rebelo dos Santos.
© 2015 John Wiley & Sons Ltd. Published 2020 by John Wiley & Sons Ltd.

On the other hand, TNAs are processes for the collection, analysis, and interpretation of data in order to define: (a) when formal instructional actions are the best option (or not) to remedy gaps in competencies; (b) the profile of who needs to be trained; and (c) what content should be taught (Clarke, 2003). For Wright and Geroy (1992) a TNA should be a systematic process of collection, analysis, and interpretation of data referring to gaps in individuals', groups', and/or organizations' competencies, and should possess seven principal characteristics: (a) be based mainly in the organizational culture and philosophy; (b) be proactive instead of reactive; (c) have a method that allows the distinction between situations that can be resolved through training from those that cannot; (d) allow the participation of various organizational actors who are interested and involved directly or indirectly in the training; (e) be based in observable competencies instead of the perceptions of directors, managers, and professionals; (f) consider the varied use of techniques to collect and analyze data; and (g) finally, have a cost/benefit analysis.

It is in this context that this chapter makes its mark since the aim is to critically review (Baumeister & Leary, 1997) the scientific literature on TNA, addressing topics such as: the areas in which these studies are applied, the nature of research, research design, participant profiles, the main instruments used to collect data, procedures for collecting data, analysis methods, training needs predictor variables, the use of multilevel approaches in TNA, among others. As such, the following text is organized in to three parts: methodological and conceptual issues, future research, and conclusions.

The initial search for articles was conducted based on literature reviews published in the *Annual Review of Psychology* (Wexley, 1984; Latham, 1988; Tannenbaum & Yukl, 1992; Salas & Cannon-Bowers, 2001; Aguinis & Kraiger, 2009). In reference to the multilevel approach in organizational and TNA research, three important texts were used as the basis for this study: Ostroff and Ford (1989), Koslowski et al. (2000), and Brandão et al. (2012).

We intend to design the global scenario in regards to the production of scientific knowledge about TNA. As such, the following databases were consulted: Web of Knowledge (ISI), Ovid, Proquest, Wiley Online Library, Emerald, PsycNet (APA), Higher Education Coordination Agency's (CAPES) online periodical portal (Brazil), Scielo (of the Americas), and the Brazilian Digital Library of Theses and Dissertations. The year of publication of the selected articles was not determined.

The articles were analyzed based on conceptual and methodological dimensions in order to choose meta-themes that emerged as being the most important. As such, our analysis of the literature is divided into the following topics: **multilevel TNA analysis** (organizational, tasks, groups, processes, individual and multilevel theoretical or empirical models); **methodological characteristics** (design, nature of the data collected, instruments/procedures used for data collection); **conceptual questions and TNA models** (theoretical issues and models prevalent in TNA research); and **predictors of needs** (predictors of training needs in the literature). One hundred and ninety-one articles were analyzed that deal specifically with TNA.

TNA: Methodological and Conceptual Issues

In regards to the **year of publication**, one can say that the TNA literature showed enormous quantitative growth in the past decade. More than 75 percent of the articles analyzed were published in the decade of 2000. Between the decades of 1980 and 2000 there was an increase in the publication of articles about TNA, showing a possible increase in researchers' and professionals' interest in the topic in those years. Authors such as Aguinis and Kraiger (2009) have already shown that the scientific field

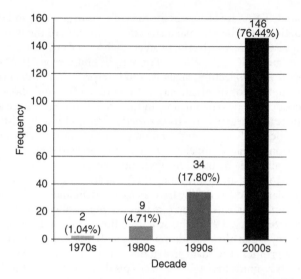

Figure 3.1 Articles analyzed distributed by decade (2000s include the period from 2000 to 2014, which can inflate the numbers presented only in this series).

of T&D in organizations as a whole grew exponentially in the past decade, which, certainly, also applies to TNA, a sub-area of the T&D field.

In relation to the **continent in which the article was produced**, taking into consideration the country in which the institution where the authors were affiliated is located, there is hegemony of Anglo-Saxon production, mainly from North America (United States) Europe and England. Together, these continents are responsible for 72 percent of the articles analyzed.

Regarding the **area of application**, based in the area of knowledge in which the results of the studies were applied, surprisingly, health (mainly nursing, medicine, and occupational health) is the area that produced the most studies about TNA. Almost 42 percent of the studies analyzed aimed to test and develop TNA technologies to instruct professionals in the area of health (e.g., Hicks & Henessy, 1997; Powell, Wallace, & Wild, 2013; Hicks & Tyler, 2002). Business administration (24 percent) and organizational psychology (13 percent) were the second and third areas, respectively, that produced the most articles about TNA. Even in military contexts, TNA is an important procedure to human resource management (Alliger et al., 2013).

Methodological issues

Regarding the **nature** of research, there was a predominance of empirical articles (78 percent). In terms of theoretical development, two important studies stand out and are considered to be seminal: that of McGehee and Thayer (1961) and that of Ostroff and Ford (1989). The former identified three critical and interdependent components of TNA (the O-T-P Model): organizational analysis (O), task or operational analysis (T), and personnel analysis (P). Organizational analysis emphasizes the study of the internal and external organizational context: the objectives, resources, and the allocation of these resources according to the strategic plan. This analysis supplies information about where training actions are needed. Subsequently, an analysis of the task will determine which activities are performed in the work environment and the conditions in which the work is done. This analysis supplies information about which knowledge, abilities, and attitudes need to be trained. Thereafter, the personnel analysis will determine who needs to be trained and what type of training is needed.

Ostroff and Ford (1989) proposed a multilevel theoretical approach. Accordingly, it is possible to conduct studies about how organizational changes and challenges are transformed into training needs. The Multilevel Model proposed by Ostroff and Ford (1989), is represented by a cube: content, level, and application. The first component (content) is composed of organizational content, tasks, and individuals, and it deals with the main types of information regarding the internal and external organizational environment that can be related to the training needs. The second component (level) expands upon the approach, dividing the content areas into three levels of training needs: organizational, sub-unit, and individual. This segmentation makes it clear that the training need should be seen according to the organizational level in which it is found (isomorphism[1]). The third component of the model (application) adds depth to the cube, incorporating the needs of conceptualization, operationalization, and interpretation of the other two components. Operationalizing means developing measures that explore the constructs at each level and the content area to which it pertains. Conceptualizing and interpreting means guaranteeing that the inferences made from the TNA are consistent with the conceptual and operational definitions previously defined.

In reference to the **design**, there is a predominance of descriptive (59 percent), followed by correlational studies (40 percent). These results reinforce the predominantly descriptive character applied to studies about TNA and indicate a need for more correlational or causal–explicative studies, which could identify the main predictors of learning needs. Ommani and Chizari's study (2009), for example, intended to identify the training needs of extension experts related to environmental security in agriculture (ESA) in Khuzestan Province, Iran. The results showed that 61 percent of the variability of the training needs for the ESA was due to level of education, social participation, and level of satisfaction at work.

In reference to the **nature of the data collected**, 61 percent of the empirical studies exclusively utilized quantitative data. Twenty-four percent reported the use of mixed data (qualitative/quantitative; e.g., Aelterman et al., 2013; Clarke, 2003; While, Ullman, & Forbes, 2007), while 15 percent analyzed exclusively qualitative data. There was a preponderance of quantitative studies in the sample. Despite the fact that there was a certain consensus in the literature that mixed methods are far more comprehensive and allow for the crossing of disciplinary boundaries (Tashakkori & Teddlie, 1998; Creswell, Goodchild, & Turner, 1996; Greene, Caraceli, & Graham, 1989; Onwuegbuzie & Teddlie, 2003), it seems that the production of knowledge about TNA is still characterized by the use of limited techniques for data collection and analysis.

The work of While, Ullman, and Forbes (2007), an example of multiple research procedures, intended to develop and validate a scale to evaluate learning needs for professionals who take care of patients with multiple sclerosis. Different methods were used to collect data from the participants (nurses, members of medical care departments, and patients with multiple sclerosis), such as document analysis, focus groups, personal interviews, telephone interviews, and surveys. The study was carried out in three phases: (1) description of competency items and the development of the questionnaire, (2) investigation of the face validity of the questionnaire, and (3) pilot test of the questionnaire. The factorial analysis demonstrated that the instrument is reliable at 0.97 (Cronbach's Alpha). Correlational analyses showed the construct validity of the scale. The authors also called attention to the importance of developing valid psychometric scales to measure learning needs.

In relation to the **research method**, the sample of articles analyzed showed a predominance of surveys (131; 69 percent), including three bibliographic studies. The use of mixed methods (survey and observation) is infrequent (see, for example, Robertson et al., 2013). Studies that make use of observation or experimental/quasi-experimental design are practically nonexistent in the area of training needs.

An example of a quasi-experimental study, which focused on the sequences of communication in work teams as a form of understanding training needs, was conducted by Bowers et al. (1998). The results indicate that the groups that had their communication sequences mapped out before the task, indicating their learning needs for communication, presented better subsequent performance than those that were not submitted to needs mapping. The sequential communication analysis and the TNA process revealed themselves as important factors to understand and improve the performance of the teams.

In relation to the **sampling techniques** used in the empirical articles, a strong, nonprobabilistic predominance of convenience samples was observed (122; 82 percent). Probabilistic (12 percent) and census techniques (6 percent) to select research participants were used infrequently to investigate training needs. There was little investment in research designs that require the application of probabilistic sampling techniques, which could make the generalization of results to the population of interest more viable. Apparently, the TNA studies are focused on positions, occupations, and exclusive professions of a determined type of organization or professional area, accessed by convenience or in isolation, without a connection with organizational macroprocesses or value chains that integrate diverse levels of analysis and their relationships with internal and external stakeholders to identify training needs.

In relation to the **participants' profiles**, there was a relative balance between those that focused on only employees who were not in managerial positions (41 percent) and those that used mixed samples (30 percent). Studies that had samples composed exclusively of managers (9 percent) or executives (1 percent) were a minority. This criterion did not apply to 17 percent of the empirical studies because they used samples with other profiles, such as clients, suppliers, students, and patients (e.g., Allen et al., 2013; Jenkins, 2010; Lazarowitz & Lieb, 2006). On the one hand, this result can be considered exciting because it shows that some of the TNA studies partially operationalized premises of diverse authors about the need to involve the most heterogeneous gamut possible of stakeholders in the TNA process (McGehee & Thayer, 1961; Moore & Dutton, 1978; Wexley, 1984; Ford & Noe, 1987; Ostroff & Ford, 1989; Taylor, O'Driscoll, & Binning, 1998; Clarke, 2003). On the other hand, one can note that the exclusive participation of employees who were not in managerial positions is predominant in the studies, showing that managerial levels need to be contemplated in future studies.

Magalhães and Borges-Andrade (2001) developed a study that aimed to investigate the relationship between self and hetero-evaluation of learning needs, involving workers (n = 325) and managers (n = 344) of a Brazilian banking institution. The self-evaluation questionnaire was composed of 34 competency items, including items on knowledge, abilities, or attitudes. The hetero-evaluation questionnaire was answered by immediate supervisors. To analyze the difference between self and hetero-evaluation, the Pearson correlation with two-tailed significance and the paired student's t-test were used. The results show that there is a significant relationship between self and hetero-evaluation of training needs, although supervisors tend to indicate greater training needs in their subordinates than the self-evaluations from the same sample.

In relation to the **instruments and procedures for data collection**, the results show a strong predominance of questionnaires (61 percent), that is in consonance with the empirical and quantitative nature and with the survey methods that were widely adopted in TNA research. Studies about TNA also show the use of mixed instruments/ methods (27 percent), interviews (5 percent), focus groups (3 percent), document analysis (3 percent), and observation protocols (1 percent). Apparently, the great gap with respect to instruments/procedures for data collection is the use of images and/or sound in the studies about TNA, typical strategies of observational studies.

Jenkins' study (2010) intended to create a multifaceted formative assessment approach that better enabled students to engage in the assessment process. A formative assessment approach, consisting of six key initiatives, was outlined. Firstly, a subject-specific reader was created to more clearly focus independent and assessment-based study. Secondly, the assessment process was refocused around the number of hours involved and not the number of words produced. Thirdly, the number of assignments was reduced. Fourthly, the assessment process was supported by detailed guidance notes on the assignment to help create a more effective self-regulated study environment. Fifthly, an assignment-based tutorial was introduced to facilitate student discussion of the assignment that served to break down the linear transfer of knowledge from teacher to student, and in doing so, enhance dialogue, which serves to improve the effectiveness of learning. Finally, an e-learning environment was also embraced to facilitate rapid submission and feedback on the assessment, which is a fundamental feature of effective formative assessment.

In regards to the **procedures for data analysis**, the use of statistical analyses is predominant. There is equilibrium between descriptive statistics (30 percent) and inferential statistics (31 percent). These results are compatible with the quantitative nature of methods used in many studies. Mixed analysis procedures are also discussed in parts of the articles (24 percent) and some qualitative strategies are used (15 percent). Clarke (2003) intended to investigate the influences of organizational policies (these were the result of a conflict of interest and of power relationships established in the organizations) in the TNA processes. Questionnaires, focus groups, and semi-structured interviews were used as strategies for data collection. Categorical thematic content analysis techniques were used to analyze the qualitative data, and nonparametric statistical inferences (Mann-Whitney U) were used to analyze the quantitative data.

Conceptual issues

In the literature, the hegemonic use of the term **"training needs"** to refer to the gaps in competencies needed for a job is noted. Nevertheless, this term does not seem to be the most precise to refer to the gaps in competencies at work since there are innumerable strategies to manage learning at work that can be applied to aid in or diminish gaps in knowledge, abilities, and attitudes, besides training per se. The expression "training needs," despite the fact that it is most frequently used, is problematic since it includes only one solution to resolve different problems and needs for new learning at work. Before the diagnosis the solution to be applied to eliminate the competency gap has already been defined, which is a strategy that restricts instead of amplifies the choice of alternatives to meet the broader educational needs or even training needs at work. With the intention of proving the empirical bases for this discussion, initially, we tried to investigate which **concepts were most adopted** in the scientific literature on TNA: training, learning, or educational needs.

The results indicate the predominant use of the term "training needs" (68 percent). The term "learning needs" (13 percent) is also found in the literature, although less frequently.

The term "educational needs" (7 percent) and others, such as "development needs," "competency needs," or "skills needs" are also used. It is important to pay attention to an analysis of these concepts and their uses in order to investigate eventual differences between them and to avoid confusion and unnecessary increases in the creation of these technical expressions. The use of resources for formal strategies for teaching-learning at work can be rationalized in function of what is understood by needs. Training sessions are costly strategies and demanding in terms of financial, structural, and human resources. Through a process called evaluation of training needs, one can identify the instructional strategy and the management of performance or of learning at work best suited to resolve the problem in function of the nature, magnitude, priority, or dominion sphere of a competencies gap. Besides this, the definition of the teaching-learning solutions should be analyzed according to its reach and complexity, from the most simple, such as instructions about services and the use of job aids, to the most elaborate personnel development (postgraduate courses or language courses, for example).

A recommendation that is registered in the seminal texts by Ostroff and Ford (1989), McGehee and Thayer (1961), and Moore and Dutton (1978) is that all of the TNA processes should take into consideration the **internal/external organizational context to investigate competency gaps**. Nevertheless, it can be noted that such a recommendation is still not frequently found in TNA practices or research. Only some of the studies (39 percent) discussed the importance of analyzing the internal and/or external context of the organization to investigate training needs. Most of the studies (61 percent) did not discuss this practice and most of the theoretical articles did not explore the importance of such a procedure.

Another theoretical-conceptual question, which has been present in the literature for many years, is the adoption of a **multilevel approach to TNA research,** (Koslowski et al., 2000; Pilati, 2006; Abbad, Freitas, & Pilati, 2006). Thanks to the introduction of multilevel investigations of training needs, it has become necessary to identify training needs for entire teams, evaluating the amount and the way tasks overlap and are interdependent in relation to diverse levels of analysis. Mossholder and Bedeian (1983) were pioneers in proposing the use of such an approach in organizational studies related to TNA. More recently, this literature received contributions from Koslowski et al. (2000) and Puente-Palácios (2003).

Among the texts analyzed, few recommended the adoption of a multilevel approach in TNA studies. Among them, the study by Ostroff and Ford (1989) stands out. Even though they did not adopt a multilevel approach, as defined by these authors, many other authors indicated the importance of investigating variables at macrolevels (of the organization), mesolevels (of groups and processes), and at the microlevel (individuals) (McGehee & Thayer, 1961; Moore & Dutton, 1978; Wexley, 1984; Ford & Noe, 1987; Abbad, Freitas, & Pilati, 2006; Ferreira et al., 2009; Coelho Junior & Borges-Andrade, 2011; Abbad & Mourão, 2012). It can be noted, however, that there is theoretical and empirical support for the conception and testing of multilevel models in TNA research. However, what happens in the field is the opposite: one can say that the multilevel approach has not yet in fact been adopted. Only 1 percent of the studies analyzed used a multilevel approach to investigate needs (Mossholder & Bedeian, 1983; Ostroff & Ford, 1989). As such, this question gives rise to a rich and long agenda for TNA research.

Authors such as Pilati (2006), Aguinis and Kraiger (2009), and Iqbal and Khan (2011) emphasized that, in the perspective of learning needs diagnosis in organizations, the current tendencies are to develop methods that attempt to **align the training actions to organizational strategic plans**. However, one notes that a considerable portion of the studies (72 percent) did not discuss this focus. The use of techniques to reveal future needs and strategies is very important for the planning of the instruction so that it is in accordance with the individual competencies that will need to be developed in order for the organization to be able to meet its goals. This finding demonstrates that both the concept of training needs and the current practices of needs analysis only cover the problem-centered skills gaps, thus tending to uncover the training needs that arise from organizational strategic planning and actions.

Iqbal and Khan (2011) affirmed that the TNA process should base itself in organizational strategies and in learning needs described in such a way as to allow the elaboration of instructional objectives that are focused on the individual. The authors propose a conceptual model of TNA that is comprised of three main components: (a) antecedents to the effectiveness of the process (importance attributed by the organization to the process of TNA, performance and managerial interest in the TNA process); (b) evaluation of needs (description of the learning needs); and (c) results (definition of the training objectives and the organizational objectives, development of personnel, motivation to learn, carrier development, effectiveness of expenditures).

Another important category in this literature review refers to the **models for investigation** (Alvarez, Salas, & Garofano, 2004; Abbad & Mourão, 2012). The theoretical elaboration necessary for the conception and testing of a model facilitates the elaboration of constitutive and operational definitions of antecedent and consequential variables of individuals' learning needs at work. The methodological rigor to test a TNA model can subsidize the development of organizational tools that support the learning and which are more efficient and effective. However, the proposition of TNA models, be they theoretical or empirical, is still in initial stages in the literature. Only 6 percent of the articles analyzed discussed the proposal of TNA models.

Jacobson, Ruben, and Selden's study (2002) aimed to develop a TNA model (Strategic Systems Training Model) for the municipal sector in 35 cities in the US. The model proposed by the authors puts individual training needs as its first component. The authors observed that the workers' needs varied according to the complexity level of the task. The simplest needs of the individual would be those considered to be the most basic to perform the job, how to use computers, or how to write. The needs considered to be the most complex are those competencies that are more strategic for the organization and that demand study or previous experience from the worker, such as leadership and strategic planning. The second component of the model contemplates the organizational training needs. The authors define organizational training needs as those that arise in function of their essential competencies, that is, in function of their reason for existing, of their business. As such, they would be organized into the most basic (means), such as finance, management of personnel, for example, and the most advanced related to the construction of citizenship for public organizations. The relationship between the organization's needs and the individual's needs arises in function of the needs individuals will have according to the structure of the organization's needs (e.g., if a manager or employee indicates that they have learning needs in the area of tax accounting, it is because the organization has learning needs in its finance area).

The results of this literature review also show that, besides being scarce, the **existing TNA models are still rarely cited or adopted**. Only 12 percent of the articles analyzed adopted or cited a TNA model, while 88 percent referred to no model at all. One of the most pervasive criticisms in the literature (that the current TNA processes in organizations, for the most part, have an ad hoc character) could have its roots in the fact that there is not a habit of adopting a guiding model to conduct competencies gaps diagnoses. The contributions of models for the investigation of social phenomena and also for the structuring of organizational practices could be relevant (Wellington & Szczerbinski, 2007). The results suggest that, besides being scarce, the TNA models currently available in the literature have not found support for their use in the managerial practices of T&D in organizations.

The use of the results of **taxonomies for learning** to describe needs could be very useful for the integration between the subsystems of TNA and planning and instructional execution, in that they supply important subsidies for one to choose the modality of the course, the means and instructional strategies, and the order for presenting the content, among others. The taxonomies of learning results can supply important subsidies to adapt the instructional strategies to the nature and complexity level of the competencies that need to be learned (defined in the TNA stage) (Abbad, Freitas, & Pilati, 2006). Nevertheless, what one notes in the literature in the field is that the use of taxonomies is almost nonexistent to describe and investigate learning needs at work. Only around 4 percent of the studies adopted taxonomies or at least cited the importance of doing so; 96 percent do not make any mention of taxonomies for learning results whatsoever.

Hauer and Quill's study (2011) described the necessary stages to determine the learning needs and propose instructional actions for doctors in a hospital in the US. The main stages proposed by the authors were: (a) evaluate the learning needs, (b) describe the educational objectives, and (c) plan and implement the instructional actions. For the authors, an instructional objective is a sentence that defines the knowledge, abilities, and/ or attitudes (as well as their nature and complexity) that the student needs to know how to execute after an instructional event. These objectives should come from the individual's competencies gaps and have as their base their description, learning results taxonomies that demonstrate the complexity, and the dimension of the dominion the individual needs to have from that competency. As such, the authors propose the adoption of taxonomies similar to those proposed by Bloom (1956) and Fink (2003).

The study of **training needs predictor variables** could help in the management of organizational instructional actions in the measure that they could reveal internal and/ or external variables related to the rise of competencies gaps in workers. However, the results show that only a small percentage of the studies investigate antecedent variables of learning needs (7 percent).

Al-Khayyat and Elgamal's study (1997) aimed to develop and empirically test a training and development model based on systems theory. The authors' proposal contemplates the whole T&D system, not only the needs evaluation stage. The predictors of the quality of instructional actions would be: objectives in the area of personnel development; long-term personnel management policies; workers' perceptions about the role of the organization's development actions; climate and managerial attitudes; and resource allocation (physical, human, and financial). Their consequences would be: worker satisfaction; application of knowledge; performance improvement; productivity; profitability; and managerial satisfaction.

A synthetic analysis of the methodological and conceptual questions shows that there is still a huge potential for growth in terms of TNA research. In the case of methodological questions, some critical points should be highlighted: (a) there is a hegemony of empirical articles, which is positive, however, it is evidence of a need to develop theories that sustain the new demands for TNA; (b) the design of TNA studies is predominantly descriptive, showing that there is a demand for more explicative-causal studies; (c) most of the studies are exclusively quantitative, with a predominance of surveys, a few studies adopt more than one method or research procedure; (d) the sampling techniques used are also inherently weak since convenience samples, not probabilistic samples, predominate; (e) in relation to the research participants, those that include samples of workers and managers still correspond to a minority of the studies reviewed; (f) the data analysis procedures also require attention since few of the studies are inferential or utilize more sophisticated multivariate statistical analysis strategies.

In the same way, in reference to the conceptual aspects, the literature review conducted indicates several gaps that should be understood as challenges to be overcome by the researchers and professionals in the area. The main conceptual weaknesses found were: (a) the internal or external organizational context is infrequently considered in the investigation of competency gaps; (b) the multilevel approach, although it is recommended, is still not used in TNA studies; (c) there are few studies that deal with the question of aligning training actions to the organizational strategies; (d) the TNA investigation models are still scarce and they are not frequently cited or adopted; (e) the area still lacks development and utilization of learning needs taxonomies; (f) there are still few known predictor variables of training needs; (g) what constitutes training needs is still little discussed, especially what would be the possibilities and implications of adopting other concepts to refer to competencies gaps, such as learning needs, for example. Having this group of gaps in mind, an agenda for future research in the area is presented below.

Future Research

With a base in the results reached and the gaps in the TNA research and practices, we propose a research agenda based in the methodological and conceptual dimensions of the area.

TNA: Methodological agenda

The results of the literature review identify a relative advance in TNA practices and research. This means that the practices and studies based exclusively on the opinion of managers, without the use of methodological procedures that intend to adapt the instructional action to the real needs of the target audience, are no longer the rule, as they were until the end of the 1990s. Nevertheless, there are still many aspects that need to be observed so that TNA methods can become more robust: (1) generate more precise and reliable results; and (2) permit the investigation of mediator, moderator, antecedent, and consequent training needs factors.

The descriptive-applicative design, which is predominant in the studies in the field supply important diagnostic bases for making decisions in the organizational environment. Nevertheless, studies with such design show only one part of the phenomenon of training needs. Little is yet known about which variables can be related to the origin of a worker's competency gap. Are they in the environment that is external to the organization, in society, or in the worker's world? Are they changes in the tasks, jobs, occupations, or professions? Are they changes in organizational strategies? Are they changes in the relationships between the organization and the stakeholders? Are they changes in the structural arrangement of the organization? Are they changes in the work flow? Are they individual factors related to the attitudinal predisposition of the subject? Or are they all of these together or none of them? The literature shows us that these questions still do not have answers based on reliable, precise empirical results. The existing theories cannot supply all of the answers either. As such, this gap can be related not only to the adoption of more robust research methods and design but also to the low interest of researchers in developing theories that are able to identify predictor (antecedent) variables and as such serve as the basis to conduct empirical studies with correlational or causal-explicative design.

From the methodological perspective, another gap is the fact that studies depend almost exclusively on surveys. At the same time that this method offers an objective basis for making decisions, if it is used as the only source of information it can lead to limited conclusions with a wide margin of error. In this sense, it is necessary that the studies and practices in the area develop in order to find multiple methods and sources, human and documental, of information and procedures for data collection and analysis. The opportunity to triangulate data (Ma & Norwich, 2007) that a multimethod study offers can contribute to making a more efficient decision from a more precise description of the competencies gap, which supplies important information for the subsystems of instructional design and training evaluation. The use of strategies such as focus groups, Delphi methods, document analysis, interviews, and observation should be in the foundation of the conception of TNA practices and research.

Despite the fact that TNA studies are mainly conducted using surveys, the statistical analyses applied could be more advanced. Even though, for diagnostic ends, the descriptive statistics are adequate, other multivariate and inferential statistical indicators, whether they are parametric or not, need to be explored by researchers, thus allowing the cross analysis of data and guaranteeing more precision and reliability for the results of the TNA process. Some examples are tests of difference of means or medians (Median Test, Mann-Whitney U, ANOVA, t Test) and correlational tests (Spearman Rho, Pearson Bivariate Correlation). These statistical techniques and tests, if adopted, would allow for the identification of predictor or correlated variables to training needs, among which, those that are relative to the respondent's profile (e.g., be of the area, means, or ends of the organization, be of job X or Y, age, time in that position, level of education, professional training, besides other variables connected to the motivational and cognitive profile of the target audience, such as: professional self-efficacy, locus of control, learning strategies), support and organizational climate, demands and external organizational changes, are among other pertinent variables at different levels of analysis. Some variables are commonly included in the studies, but are not investigated as possible explanatory variables of training needs and learning.

In future TNA studies it would also be useful to employ linear statistical techniques such as multiple linear regression, structural equation modeling (SEM) and hierarchical linear models (HLM). The use of HLM is still not a reality in TNA research. Despite the fact that there are sufficient conceptual justifications for the elaboration and testing of multilevel theoretical models available in the literature in the area (McGehee & Thayer, 1961; Mussholder & Bedeian, 1983; Ostroff & Ford, 1989; Klein & Kozlowski, 2000; Koslowski et al., 2000; Baldwin & Magjuka, 1997; Abbad & Mourão, 2012), the use of hierarchical statistical analyses (Raubendush & Bryk, 1986; Snijders & Bosker, 1994; Kreft & De Leeuw, 1998; Hox, 2002; Hox & Roberts, 2011) is still not a reality in the scientific and professional field of TNA. Multilevel regression would be an appropriate statistical technique to investigate the relationship between the training needs of the individual and groups of individuals and variables in multiple and at different levels of analysis, which is not done routinely (e.g., organizational strategy, challenges and changes for the organizations, characteristics of the organizational unit, characteristics of the position, characteristics of work groups).

The use of nonprobabilistic samples suggests that research about training needs are case studies that do not intend to generalize findings for contexts other than that of the organization itself as a field of inquiry. This reveals an inherent characteristic of the object of the study – learning and training needs: it is context dependent and, for this reason, specific for certain organizations, units, work flows, positions, and occupations. The descriptions of competency gaps of nurses in a hospital dedicated to the care of adults with cancer, for example, might not be the same for nurses who work in a hospital that is dedicated to the care of children with cancer. The gaps of competencies for union employees in the Netherlands might not be the same as those for union workers in England or Brazil. It is important to note, nevertheless, that a training need is a strong phenomenon influenced by the context in which it is found, assuming, as such, its peculiarities. One can say that TNA research generally utilizes convenience samples in part because it is that and only that study context that one desires to investigate, given its idiosyncrasies, without intending to generalize the results. However, there are competencies (and, as such, their respective gaps) that are common to different types of organizations or even groups of individuals in the same organization. In this sense, the use of probabilistic techniques or sampling census, which guarantee a representation in relation to a larger population of interest, could be useful to investigate if the training needs phenomenon really is specific to the study context or if it could be generalized to other contexts.

Related to sampling techniques is the gap of participants' profiles. The samples chosen by convenience privilege only one professional segment in the organization. Even if the focus is elaboration of courses for only one segment of professionals (e.g., nurses), it is important that the TNA process contemplate other stakeholders, such as intermediary and direct supervisors, subordinates, directors, and even clients, suppliers, and competitors for future students' services. It is also recommended that when applying training needs scales and hetero-evaluation strategies be utilized since the target professionals of the instructional action might not be conscious of their own work-based competency gaps.

TNA: Conceptual agenda

As previously highlighted, the empirical nature of the TNA field creates a gap in the development of theories about the phenomena connected to the training needs. What the literature presents as a training need, learning need, or competency gap is a concept still strongly related to the individual's occupational space. As such, these competency gaps are dealt with in isolation. It is rare in the definitions of gaps or learning needs for the authors to make reference to variables that are related to the expression of these competencies at work, such as: those that are relative to the organizational context (mission, vision, strategy, goals, economy, technology, client behavior, image, work flows, support, and situational restrictions), lacking, with these omissions, a contemplation of a broader and more precise ecological vision about the phenomenon. The studies that intend to investigate competency gaps and propose instructional actions that are aligned with the organizational strategies are relatively rare. The internal and/or external context of the organization and the articulations of these environments with the rise of learning needs were practically absent in the TNA studies analyzed. Seminal studies on the topic have already prescribed how the organizational context could be related to the concept of training needs (Mahler & Monroe, 1952; McGehee & Thayer, 1961; Moore & Dutton, 1978, among others), nevertheless, to date, the articles analyzed seem to be neglecting these theoretical prescriptions from the definition and operationalization of the concept of needs, and in the choice of research design.

This brings us to another conceptual gap in the field, which is closely related to a methodological gap that was previously noted. The multilevel approach, that is, the conception of theoretical models that organize the phenomenon of training needs in a hierarchical manner, nesting it in relation to antecedent, consequent, moderator, and mediator variables, have not yet been adopted in TNA research. Many recommendations about the need to adopt a multilevel approach to investigate competency gaps at work have not found support in the studies analyzed (99 percent of the studies analyzed did not adopt or report the importance of adopting a multilevel approach). It is also important to note that in this respect there is an apparent discrepancy in the classical literature in the area (between the years 1950 and 1980) and the contemporary literature (1990 and 2000s). Seminal authors such as Mahler and Monroe (1952), McGehee and Thayer (1961), Moore and Dutton

(1978), Wexley (1984), Ford and Noe (1987), Ostroff and Ford (1989), Mossholder and Bedeian (1983), Roberts, Hulin, and Rousseau (1978), and Rousseau (1985) had already proposed theoretical-methodological alternatives to conceive and test multilevel TNA models. However, what one sees analyzed in the literature, principally in that published between 1990 and 2000s, is an almost entire abandonment of these recommendations. As such, certainly, a rich and extensive research agenda related to the adoption of a multilevel approach opens up in TNA.

Another important conceptual gap in the area is in regards to the conception and adoption of theoretical models. At the same time in which there are few existing models, one can say that they have not been readily adopted (78 percent of the studies analyzed did not adopt or cite TNA models). The lack of valid modeling parameters to investigate the learning needs produces knowledge that is not systematic, with ad hoc characteristics and organizational practices that do not contribute to effective management of learning in work contexts. As such, we recommend the elaboration and adoption of theoretical-methodological TNA models. The models could substantially help the conception and testing of theories and methods in such a way as to confer scientific rigor to the practices and research and allow more precise decisions in the work environment.

The use of taxonomies of learning results (Bloom, 1956; Gagné, 1985; Fink, 2003) also constitutes a gap in the TNA research. The use of taxonomies to describe needs can be very useful for the integration among the TNA subsystems as well as with instructional planning and execution (Ferreira & Abbad, 2013). The taxonomies of learning results can supply important subsidies to align the instructional strategies (defined in the planning and execution stage) to the nature and level of complexity of the competencies that one wishes to learn (defined in the TNA stage) (Abbad, Freitas, & Pilati, 2006). Nevertheless, what one notes in the literature in the field is that the use of taxonomies to describe and investigate the learning needs at work is almost nonexistent since 96 percent of the articles analyzed did not cite or adopt taxonomies of learning results.

Finally, it appears to us that perhaps the main conceptual gap in the field regards the discussion of what is and what is not, in fact, a training need. Here we see not only a gap in the researchers' disposition to discuss the concept but also an important bias in respect to the adoption of the term "training needs." The results indicate a predominant use of the term "training needs" (68 percent) to refer to the gaps in competencies at work. The term "learning needs" (13 percent) is also found in the literature, however, less frequently. The term "educational needs" (7 percent) and others, such as "development needs," "competency needs," or "skills needs" are used infrequently. The concept of learning needs is still not well defined or discussed in the T&D area nor in organizational literature. The most common are terms such as training needs, development needs, qualification needs, educational needs, among others, to refer to that which the worker needs to know and do to achieve competency at work. Rigorous investigation of the nature, magnitude, amplitude, level of analysis, target audience, and priority of a competency is essential before a decision on which instructional action(s) (training, information, job aid, etc.) and which learning condition(s) (formal or informal) can best meet the needs of the worker and the organization in terms of which competencies both need to dominate and/or apply at work. As such, one asks: why would one use a term that defines, a priori, the action or solution to be applied? In this case, there is a clear misalignment between the process (evaluation of training needs) and product created (informal learning, which is not formal training). The adoption of the term "learning," as opposed to "training, "education," or "qualification," would be recommended since it would increase the possibility of actions to solve the competency gaps of workers, not only through formal instructional events, but also for all of the forms of informal learning at work, management of performance, and of knowledge in organizations (Vargas & Abbad, 2006). Define the problem (need) connect it to a unique solution (training) weakening the evaluative and decisive process which makes the search for other possible solutions to diminish or attenuate competency gaps. In this context, one can say that the learning needs refer to the competencies that the worker and organization, at their different levels – groups, teams, units, work flows – need to acquire, retain, develop, and apply so that their production is effective in the context, given the mission, vision, and organizational strategies.

To attempt to respond to some of these gaps, Abbad and Mourão (2012) proposed a TNA model based on Birdi's (2006) model of training evaluation. This model comes from a group of results from empirical studies and goes beyond the analysis of tasks and people, including the organizational and group levels. The application of this model supplies the necessary information to design the learning and training situations that can promote and develop the complex competencies that are valued by work environments, the development of which requires varied educational actions, curricula, and continuous learning programs as well as permanent education. In this sense, testing this model is part of a research agenda that can connect empirical TNA research with practical applications in organizations.

Conclusion

TNA research has advanced qualitatively as well as quantitatively in the past fifty years. The processes of needs analysis, which occupied a secondary role in the planning, execution, and evaluation of instructional events before, frequently did not take advantage of theory and methods that now find support in scientific T&D literature around the world. The great increase in TNA articles published in the past two decades shows that this is a hot topic in organizational psychology. Increasing interest in the topic, on the part of researchers as well as professionals, shows that TNA is an important step for conferring scientific rigor to the practices and studies of T&D, which as a result increases the effectiveness of investments in instructional actions in the work environment. Nevertheless, the field of TNA is still young and as such has a long way to evolve theoretically and methodologically.

In general, there are no studies comparing the effectiveness of training with and without TNA. This is a hot topic for the research agenda that can contribute significantly to the knowledge on training needs. The literature suggests that most of the investments in training do not result in positive transfer nor improve organizational outcomes. Probably, one of the reasons for this is due to the lack of TNA aligned with organizational goals and strategies. If we understand organizations as organic systems, we can say that your performance depends on how appropriately your strategies are outlined, how effective your ecological analysis is and, therefore, what your available processes and resources, including human resources are. In this context, the assessment of knowledge, skills and attitudes necessary to desirable organizational and individual performance is one of the important processes that need to be considered in organizational studies. The absence of TNA aligned to organizational strategy can lead to serious problems, including: (a) offering training to people who do not need it; (b) not developing skills critical to achieving strategic objectives; (c) developing obsolete skills; (d) wasting financial resources; and (e) discrediting T&D systems in organizations.

It is necessary to increase the scope of possible methods and research designs used to analyze needs such that the phenomenon can be investigated in a wider spectrum than just the diagnostic one. There is a need to develop and apply prospective methods of TNA, which are aimed at the description of environmental variables as a means to identify emerging skills (Sparrow & Bognanno, 1994) necessary for workers dealing with the increasing complexity of their tasks stemming from the strategic positioning that organizations choose to take. Some tasks can be sharply designed and it is possible to identify the competence gap easily, but others are so fuzzy and complex that is not possible to define clearly the learning needs by applying reactive TNA, as we see today. Conceptually, the path seems to be much longer since it implies taking up basic questions of definition, precision, as well as the validity of the concepts of needs and the evaluation of needs in the work environment. As such, we hope that this chapter has been a seed of a leafy tree that foresees future knowledge in the area.

Notes

The authors would like to thank all those from Impact Research Group who helped in the great challenge of analyzing the texts.

1   The term isomorphism literally means sameness (iso) of form (morphism). In organizational research, it means that the phenomenon of interest should be measured and interpreted adequately at the level at which it is found, such that the properties are conserved independent of the level of analysis, thus allowing comparisons to be made.

References

Abbad, G., Freitas, I. A. de, & Pilati, R. (2006). Contexto de trabalho, desempenho competente e necessidades em TD&E [Work context, competent performance and needs in TD&E]. In J. E. Borges-Andrade, G. Abbad, & L. Mourão (Eds.), *Treinamento, desenvolvimento e educação em organizações e trabalho: Fundamentos para a gestão de pessoas* (pp. 231–254). Porto Alegre: Artmed.

Abbad, G., & Mourão, L. (2012). Avaliação de Necessidades de TD&E: Proposição de um novo Modelo [TD&E needs assessment: Proposition of a new model]. *Revista de Administração Mackenzie* 13(6), 107–137.

Aelterman, N., Vansteenkiste, M., Van Keer, H., De Meyer, J., Van den Berghe, L., & Haerens, L. (2013). Development and evaluation of a training on need-supportive teaching in physical education: Qualitative and quantitative findings. *Teaching and Teacher Education*, 29, 64–75.

Aguinis, H., & Kraiger, K. (2009). Benefits of training and development for individuals and teams, organizations and society. *Annual Review of Psychology*, 60(1), 451–474. doi:10.1146/annurev. psych.60.110707.163505.

Al-Khayyat, R. M., & Elgamal, M. A. (1997). A macro model of training and development: validation. *Journal of European Industrial Training*, 21(3), 87–101.

Allen, J., Gregory, A., Mikami, A., Lun. J., Hamre, B., & Pianta, R. (2013). Observations of effective teacher–student interactions in secondary school classrooms: Predicting student achievement with the classroom assessment scoring system. *School Psychology Review*, 42(1), 76–98.

Alliger, G. M., Beard, R., Bennett, W., Jr., Symons, S., & Colegrove, C. (2013). A psychometric examination of mission essential competency (MEC) measures used in air force distributed mission operations training needs analysis. *Military Psychology*, 25(3), 218–233.

Alvarez, K., Salas, E., & Garofano, C. M. (2004). An integrated model of training evaluation and effectiveness. *Human Resource Development Review*, 3(4), 385–416.

Asku, A. A. (2005). Defining training needs of five-star hotel personnel: An application in the Antalya region of Turkey. *Managerial Auditing Journal*, 20(9), 945–953. doi:10.1108/02686900510625299.

Baldwin, T., & Magjuka, R. (1997). Organizational context and training effectiveness. In J. K. Ford, S. W. J. Kozlowski, K. Kraiger, E. Salas, & M. S. Teachout (Eds.), *Improving Training Effectiveness in Work Organizations* (pp. 99–128). New York: Psychology Press.

Baumeister, R. F., & Leary, M. R. (1997). Writing narrative literature reviews. *Review of General Psychology*, 1(3), 311–320.

Birdi, K. (2006). Evaluating effectiveness: The taxonomy of training and development outcomes (TOTADO). In *Congresso Brasileiro De Psicologia Organizacional E Do Trabalho (CBPOT)*, 2, Brasília. Anais do 2° Congresso Brasileiro de Psicologia Organizacional e do Trabalho Brasília: Universidade de Brasília, 2006.

Bloom, B. (1956). *Taxonomy Of Educational Objective: The Classification of Educational Goals*. New York: Longmans, Green.

Borges-Andrade, J. E., & Lima, S. V. L. (1983). Avaliação de necessidades de treinamento: Um método de análise de papel ocupacional [Training needs assessment: A method for the analysis of occupational role]. *Tecnologia Educacional*, 12(54), 6–22.

Bowers, C. A., Jentsch, F., Salas, E., & Braun, C. C. (1998). Analyzing communication sequences for team training needs assessment. *Human Factors*, 40(4), 672–679.

Brandão, H. P., Borges-Andrade, J. E., Puente-Palácios, K., & Laros, J. A. (2012). Relationships between learning, context and competency: A multilevel study. *Brazilian Administration Review*, 9(1), 1–22.

Chiu, W., Thompson, D., Mak, W., & Lo, K. L. (1999). Re-thinking training needs analysis: A proposed framework for literature review. *Personnel Review*, 28(1/2), 77–90. doi:10.1108/00483489910249009.

Clarke, N. (2003). The politics of training needs analysis. *Journal of Workplace Learning*, 15(4), 141–153.

Coelho Junior, F. A., & Borges-Andrade, J. E. (2011). Discussão sobre algumas contribuições da modelagem multinível para a investigação de desempenho no trabalho [Discussion on some contributions of multilevel modeling for performance research at work]. *Psico-USF*, 16, 135–142.

Creswell, J. W., Goodchild, L., & Turner, P. (1996). Integrated qualitative and quantitative research: Epistemology, history, and designs. In J. Smart (Ed.), *Higher Education: Handbook of Theory and Research* (vol. 11, pp. 90–136). New York: Agathon Press.

Ferreira, R. R., & Abbad, G. (2013). Training needs assessment: Where we are and where we should go. *Brazilian Administration Review*, 10(1), 77–99.

Ferreira, R. R., Abbad, G., Pagotto, C., & Meneses, P. P. M. (2009). Avaliação de necessidades organizacionais de treinamento: O caso de uma empresa Latino-Americana de administração aeroportuária [Organizational training needs assessment: The case of a Latin American airport administration company]. *Revista Eletrônica de Administração*, 15(2), 1–26.

Fink, L. D. (2003). *Creating Significant Learning Experiences: An Integrated Approach to Designing College Courses*. San Francisco: Jossey-Bass.

Ford, J. K., & Noe, R. A. (1987). Self-assessed training needs: The effects of attitudes toward training, managerial and function. *Personnel Psychology*, 45, 511–527.

Gagné, R. M. (1985). *The Conditions of Learning and Theory of Instruction*. New York: Holt, Richardt and Wilston.

Gould, D., Kelly, D., White, I., & Chidgey, J. (2004). Training needs analysis: A literature review and reappraisal. *International Journal of Nursing Studies*, 41(5), 471–486. doi:10.1016/j.ijnurstu.2003.12.003.

Greene, J. C., Caracelli, V. J., & Graham, W. F. (1989). Toward a conceptual framework for mixed-method evaluation designs. *Educational Evaluation and Policy Analysis*, 11(3), 255–274.

Hauer, J., & Quill, T. (2011). Educational needs assessment, development of learning objectives, and choosing a teaching approach. *Journal of Palliative Medicine*, 14(4), 503–508.

Hicks, C., & Hennessy, D. (1997). The use of a customized training needs analysis tool for nurse practitioner development. *Journal of Advanced Nursing*, 26(2), 389–398.

Hicks, C., & Tyler, C. (2002). Assessing the skills for family planning nurse prescribing: Development of a psychometrically sound training needs analysis instrument. *Journal of Advanced Nursing*, 37(6), 518–531.

Hox, J. (2002). *Multilevel Analysis: Techniques and Applications.* New York: Routledge.

Hox, J., & Roberts, J. K. (2011). *Handbook of Advanced Multilevel Analysis.* New York: Routledge.

Iqbal, M. Z., & Khan, R. A. (2011). The growing concept and uses of training needs assessment: A review with proposed model. *Journal of European Industrial Training,* 35(5), 439–466.

Jacobson, W., Rubin, E. V., & Selden, S. C. (2002). Examining training in large municipalities: Linking individual and organizational training needs. *Public Personnel Management,* 31(4), 485–506.

Jenkins, J. O. (2010). A multi-faceted formative assessment approach: Better recognizing the learning needs of students. *Assessment & Evaluation in Higher Education,* 35(5), 565–576.

Klein, K., & Koslowski, S. W. J. (Eds.) (2000). *Multilevel Theory, Research and Methods in Organizations.* San Francisco: Jossey-Bass.

Koslowski, S. W. J., Brown, K., Weissbein, D., Cannon-Bowers, J., & Salas, E. (2000). A multilevel approach to training effectiveness: Enhancing horizontal and vertical transfer. In K. Klein & S. W. J. Koslowski (Eds.), *Multilevel Theory, Research and Methods in Organizations* (pp. 157–210). San Francisco: Jossey-Bass.

Kraiger, K. (2003). Perspectives on training and development. In W. C. Borman, D. R. Ilgen, & R. J. Klimoski (Eds.), *Industrial and Organizational Psychology, vol. 12 of Handbook of Psychology* (pp. 171–192). Hoboken, NJ: John Wiley & Sons, Inc.

Kreft, I. G. G., & De Leeuw, J. (1998). *Introducing Multilevel Modeling.* London: Sage.

Latham, G. P. (1988). Human resource training and development. *Annual Review of Psychology,* 39, 545–582.

Lazarowitz, R., & Lieb, C. (2006). Formative assessment pre-test to identify college students' prior knowledge, misconceptions and learning difficulties in biology. *International Journal of Science and Mathematical Education,* 4, 741–762.

Ma, A., & Norwich, B. (2007). Triangulation and theoretical understanding. *International Journal of Social Research Methodology,* 10(3), 211–226.

Magalhães, M. L., & Borges-Andrade, J. E. (2001). Auto e hetero-avaliação no diagnóstico de necessidades de treinamento [Self and hetero-assessment in training needs analysis]. *Estudos de Psicologia (Natal),* 6(1), 35–50.

Mager, R. F., & Pipe, P. (1979). *Analysing Performance Problems.* Belmont, CA: Lake Publishing.

Mahler, W., & Monroe, W. (1952). *How Industry Determines the Need for and Effectiveness of Training* (report no. 929). Kentucky: Personnel Research Branch, Department of the Army.

McGehee, W., & Thayer, P. W. (1961). *Training in Business and Industry.* New York: John Wiley & Sons, Inc.

Moore, M. L., & Dutton, P. (1978). Training needs analysis: Review and critique. *Academy of Management Review,* 2, 532–545.

Mossholder, K. W., & Bedeian, A. G. (1983). Cross-level inference and organizational research: Perspectives on interpretation and application. *Academy of Management Review,* 8, 547–558.

Ommani, A. R., & Chizari, M. (2009). Analysis of the training needs of agricultural extension experts associated with environmental security in agriculture. *Research Journal of Environmental Sciences,* 3(5), 594–598.

Onwuegbuzie, A. J., & Teddlie, C. (2003). A framework for analyzing data in mixed methods research. In A. Tashakkori & C. Teddlie (Eds.), *Handbook of Mixed Methods in Social and Behavioral Research* (pp. 351–383). Thousand Oaks, CA: Sage.

Ostroff, C., & Ford, K. (1989). Introducing a levels perspective to training needs assessment. In I. Goldstein (Ed.), *Training and Career Development* (pp. 25–62). San Francisco: Jossey-Bass.

Pilati, R. (2006). História e importância de TD&E [History and importance of TD&E]. In J. E. Borges-Andrade, G. Abbad, & L. Mourão (Eds.), *Treinamento, desenvolvimento e educação em organizações de trabalho: Fundamentos para a gestão de pessoas* (pp. 159–176). Porto Alegre: Artmed.

Powell, L. E., Wallace, T., & Wild, M. R. (2013). Training-the-trainer on assistive technology for cognition (ATC): Current practices. *Perspectives on Neurophysiology and Neurogenic Speech and Language Disorders,* 23(2), 90–94.

Puente-Palácios, K. E. (2003). Multilevel theory, research, and methods in organizations: Foundations, extensions, and new directions [review of *Multilevel Theory, Research, and Methods In*

Organizations: Foundations, Extensions, and New Directions, by K. J. Klein & S. W. J. Kozlowski]. *Revista de Administração Contemporânea*, 7(2), 211–213.

Raubendush, S. W., & Bryk, A. S. (1986). A hierarchical model for studying school effects. *Sociology of Education*, 59, 1–17.

Roberts, K. H., Hulin, C. L., & Rousseau, D. M. (1978). *Developing an Interdisciplinary Science of Organizations*. San Francisco: Jossey-Bass.

Robertson, L. A., Boyer, R. R., Chapman, B. J., Eifert, J. D., & Franz, N. K. (2013). Educational needs assessment and practices of grocery store food handlers through survey and observational data collection. *Food Control*, 34, 707–713.

Rousseau, D. (1985). Issues of level in organizational research: Multi-level and cross-level perspectives. In L. Cummings, & B. Staw (Eds.), *Research in Organizational Behavior* (pp. 1–37). Greenwich: JAI.

Salas, E., & Cannon-Bowers, J. A. (2001). The science of training: A decade of progress. *Annual Review of Psychology*, 52, 471–499.

Snijders, T. A. B., & Bosker, R. (1994). Modeled variance in two-level models. *Sociological Methods and Research*, 22, 342–363.

Sparrow, P. R., & Bognanno, M. (1994). Competency requirement forecasting: Issues for international selection and assessment. In C. Mabey, C. & P. Iles (Eds.), *Managing Learning* (pp. 57–69). London: Routledge.

Tannenbaum, S. I., & Yukl, G. (1992). Training and development in work organizations. *Annual Review of Psychology*, 43, 399–441. doi:10.1146/annurev.ps.43.020192.002151.

Tashakkori, A., & Teddlie, C. (1998). *Mixed Methodology: Combining Qualitative and Quantitative Approaches*. Thousand Oaks, CA: Sage.

Taylor, P., O'Driscoll, M., & Binning, J. (1998). A new integrated framework for training needs analysis. *Human Resource Management Journal*, 8, 29–50.

Vargas, M. R. M., & Abbad, G. (2006). Bases conceituais em treinamento, desenvolvimento e educação – TD&E [Conceptual basis for training, development and education – TD&E]. In J. E. Borges-Andrade, G. Abbad, & L. Mourão (Eds.), *Treinamento, desenvolvimento e educação em organizações de trabalho: Fundamentos para a gestão de pessoas* (pp. 137–158). Porto Alegre: Artmed.

Wellington, J., & Szczerbinski, M. (2007). *Research Methods for the Social Sciences*. London: Continuum.

Wexley, K. N. (1984). Personal training. *Annual Review of Psychology*, 35, 519–551.

While, A., Ullman, R., & Forbes, A. (2007). Development and validation of learning needs assessment scale: A continuing professional education tool for multiple sclerosis specialist nurses. *Journal of Clinical Nursing*, 16, 1099–1108.

Wright, P. C., & Geroy, G. D. (1992). Needs analysis theory and the effectiveness of large-scale government-sponsored training programmes: A case study. *Journal of Management Development*, 11(5), 16–27. doi:10.1108/02621719210014527.

4

Training and Workplace Learning

Karen Evans and Natasha Kersh

Introduction

The issue of learning at work and the significance of different configurations of "learning in, for and through the workplace" (Evans et al., 2006) have been discussed extensively in a number of research publications in recent years (e.g., Aspin et al., 2012; Malloch et al., 2011; Evans et al., 2006; Rainbird, Fuller, & Munro, 2004; Boud, 2006; Guile, 2010a). Aspects such as learning on the job, informal learning and competence development, knowledge management, and the role of digital technologies have been recognized as important areas of research. Rapid changes in economic and social development and the impact of globalization have contributed to the changes in perception of adult and workplace learning and have facilitated the changing nature of the learning space at work. Workplace learning has been recognized as a core component of national and international strategies for lifelong learning, which aim to bring about higher participation in learning by workers as well as expanding the range of learning activities and achievements accessed in, for, or through the workplace.

In this chapter we will start by considering the concept of workplace learning, looking at the workplace through the lens of theoretical approaches to learning at work, specifically drawing on theoretical perspectives developed in Evans et al. (2006), Malloch et al. (2011), and Billett (2011). The complex interdependencies between work, learning, and agency have been underpinned by the interplay between the three scales of workplace learning: *organizational*, *individual*, and *environmental*. This chapter will further consider a range of configurations of these three scales, firstly, looking at the notion of the learning space at work and discussing the ways it facilitates individual engagement and the organizational context in the workplace. The chapter will then discuss the concept of competence development at work, also considering motivational factors within different types of environments. The nature of skills and competences required by contemporary workplaces has been changing gradually. Factors such as the

The Wiley Blackwell Handbook of the Psychology of Training, Development, and Performance Improvement,
First Edition. Edited by Kurt Kraiger, Jonathan Passmore, Sigmar Malvezzi, and Nuno Rebelo dos Santos.
© 2015 John Wiley & Sons Ltd. Published 2020 by John Wiley & Sons Ltd.

development of the knowledge economy and rapidly changing workplace environments underpin the recognition and value of both occupationally specific competences and so-called "softer" transferrable skills, which could be used across different contexts and settings. The chapter will consider the ways in which the acquisition of skills in the workplace is associated with a range of spatial dimensions, also looking at factors that relate to the development of modern technologies. The concluding part will pull together issues considered within this chapter, and will discuss the interpretations and the interplay between the individual, organizational, and environmental dimensions of workplace learning.

The chapter will draw on these key terms that together constitute the concept of workplace learning, looking specifically at their structure, meaning, and affordances. The three scales, namely those of *individual*, *environmental*, and *organizational*, will provide a framework for discussion of learning at work, and will consider the role of individuals and employers within the general context of the contemporary workplace learning space.

Learning in, for, and through the Workplace

"Workplace learning" is a term open to wide-ranging interpretation. As noted by Lee et al. (2004) and Fenwick (2006) there is neither a singular definition nor a unified approach to what workplace learning is, what it should comprise, or for whom it is or should be intended. Definitions, terminology, and perceptions related to learning in the workplace vary between studies, including the use of terms such as work-related learning (Streumer & Kho, 2006), work-based learning (Avis, 2004) or learning at work (Boud & Garrick, 1999). Workplace learning as a concept has been considered through the lens of different theoretical perspectives, such as situated learning (Lave & Wenger, 1998), activity theory (Engestrom, 2001) and social ecology (Evans, Waite, & Kersh, 2011). The body of literature related to issues of human resources and management draws on the concept of workplace learning specifically considering the concept through the theories of knowledge management and organizational learning at work. Cairns and Malloch (2011) suggest that there is a need for a broader conceptualization of workplace learning, arguing that work should be understood and defined as *more than* employment for remuneration, and the concept of workplace learning needs to be considered in the context of three terms: *work*, *place*, and *learning*.

In order to develop our conceptualization of workplace learning, we draw, in the first place, on Unwin and Fuller's (2003) definition that helpfully embraces all types of learning generated from or stimulated by the needs of the workplace, including formal on-the-job training, informal learning, and work-related off-the-job education and training. Evans et al. (2006) have further drawn on this definition in their formulation of workplace learning as that learning which derives its purpose from the context of employment, that is *learning in, for, and through the workplace*. Such a perspective on workplace learning, as Evans et al. (2006) argue, aims to address the needs of a variety of stakeholders: employees, employers, and government. In their approach, *learning in the workplace* relates to different types of learning including both formal and informal learning modes, where some of the learning takes place spontaneously through social interaction, observation, and a range of work activities and experiences. Learning is perceived here as something that "you do continually whilst at work, both out of choice and by necessity" (Gray et al., 2004, p. vii). Similarly, "most of what we learn takes place at work rather than on formal courses. Work activities, the workplace, the supervisor, other workers … are the key learning resources for workers" (Malone, 2005, p. 67). Workers learn through experience in and reflection on their work practice; they share ideas and stories between themselves (Jarvis, 1987; Harris & Chisholm, 2011)

The significance of learning opportunities that are accessed as part of the employment relationship has been further emphasized by Evans et al. (2006), and conceptualized as *learning through the workplace*, which is accessed by employees through their relationships with the employer. Finally, learning for the workplace refers to learning opportunities that may be directly or indirectly related to the job, such as general education or job-specific training, which may take place outside the workplace. The formulation by Evans et al. (2006) of workplace learning as *learning in, for, and through the workplace* brings together and underpins the individual, organizational, and environmental scales of learning at work.

Considering an organizational perspective, Fuller and Unwin (2011) draw attention to the debate about "high-" and "low-"performing work organizations, further concluding that the way work is organized contributes to organizational performance and affects how the workplace is experienced by employees. They caution that high-performance management models need to be tested to distinguish how experiences of employees' groups may differ and to uncover the organizational and sectoral conditions influencing their negative or more positive perceptions (Fuller & Unwin, 2011). Such an argument, as Fuller and Unwin (2011) observe, raises the question of how the workplace could be reconfigured to facilitate more efficient organizational learning, where the learning organization should respond to the demands of both the organization and the individual. Realizing learning in organizations has been perceived as one of the challenges in the area of human resource development (HRD) (Marsick & Watkins, 1999; Jayanti, 2012). Remedios and Boreham (2004, p. 220) argue that a necessary feature for an organization to call itself a learning one is that "mechanisms are put in place to optimize the transfer of knowledge between all levels of employees." A consequence of these mechanisms is the creation of environments where employees recognize that their ideas will be acknowledged and discussed and can influence subsequent working procedures (Remedios & Boreham, 2004, p. 220). The environment is thus integral to the development of work process knowledge in the workforce (Fischer & Boreham, 2004).

This brings us to the discussion of the importance of the *individual level*. The central role and significance of the self and personal agency is now being accounted for within the explanation of workplace learning (Billett, 2011). Within the workplace, personal expectations and goals act as a motivating direction for the future as personal anticipation and hope are also part of the identity formation process (Gnaur, 2010). Issues such as the significance of individual biography (e.g., Hodkinson et al., 2004; Hodkinson, 1995), individual disposition in relation to workplace opportunities (Ecclestone, Biesta, & Hughes, 2009; Evans et al., 2006; Evans, Kersh, & Sakamoto, 2004) and the impact of individual perspective on knowledge and learning at work (Eraut, 2004) have received recognition in the current debate about the workplace learning. Eraut (2004) argues that situational understanding in the workplace is highly dependent on individual experiences. Although, in his work, he draws strongly on the concept of situated learning, Eraut also maintains that Lave and Wenger's (1998) treatment of their own concept overlooks the significance of the individual perspective on knowledge and learning. Billet (2011) notes that workplace participatory practices constitute a means of understanding individual participation and learning in the workplace, and further concludes that they comprise a duality between the affordance of the workplace and the individual engagement with that which they are afforded. The affordances and opportunities provided by the workplace are strongly related to the nature of the environment at work, which influences the way adults learn *in* and *through* the workplace and underpins the interplay between individual agency, learning, work, and organizational structures in the workplace. This interplay, considered through the lens of social-ecological interdependencies, draws attention to the ways – as Evans, Waite, and Kersh (2011) put it – individuals and groups have spaces in which to exercise agency, while also influencing the whole dynamic at work through the interdependencies involved. The *environmental* scale of workplace learning further encompasses the complexities of the nature of environments at work, which could expand or restrict learning (Fuller & Unwin, 2004). Rapidly changing perceptions and the nature of the workplace – as a space for learning, work, and social engagement – have been facilitated by the current drive towards knowledge-based economies and the notion of learning societies in the contemporary world.

Learning Spaces at Work: From Work and Training to Learning?

The interplay between *training* and *learning* at work has received recognition as one of the central tenets of the debate on contemporary workplace skills and competence development. The traditional model of work-based learning was the "one-off, pre-service education and training model" (Hodkinson & Bloomer, 2002). Thus, the traditional view of work-based learning was that it mainly consisted of qualifications or training (such as the apprenticeship model) gained prior to employment or progression in employment. This model is being challenged by the interest in "workforce development" and the changes in the perceptions of the learning spaces at work. The perception of the workplace as a site only for work and organization-specific training is gradually changing, as workplaces are now being acknowledged as sites for learning in various configurations, contributing to lifelong learning, personal development, and social engagement of individuals (Field, Gallacher, & Ingram, 2009; Fuller et al., 2007; Heiskanen & Heiskanen, 2011; Guile, 2010b) as well as the exercise of wider social responsibility in and through learning (Evans, 2009). What employees learn as "learners in the workplace" and in experiences beyond the workplace (Livingstone, 2006) leads to the development of new forms of knowledge and competence, for example, job-specific, occupational, or personal. Evans et al. (2006) distinguish between workplace training and learning by making a point that training implies an intervention that is formally structured and involves a transfer of a body of knowledge, while workplace learning is more encompassing and involves locating learning in social relations at work (Evans et al., 2006). Workplace learning could be further facilitated within a learning organization. Remedios and Boreham (2004) note that a necessary feature for an organization to label itself a learning one is that mechanisms are put in place to optimize the transfer of knowledge between all levels of employees thus creating an environment where employees recognize that their ideas will be acknowledged, discussed and can influence subsequent working procedures.

Different types of learning modes are playing an increasingly prominent role in facilitating employee learning in the workplace, as the search, often policy-driven, for ways of involving adults in continuing learning has emphasized that learning may occur in settings other than the classroom, in a range of formal and informal environments, including workplace sites, virtual learning, home or leisure settings (Evans, Kersh, & Kontiainen, 2004). Different modes of learning embedded in experiential, community-based, and work-based learning have become more prominent in recent years (Kolb, 1984; Beckett & Hager, 2002; Fuller & Unwin, 2004) . Learning and acquiring skills through a range of experiences including learners' own life experiences facilitate links and mutual interaction between learning, work, and leisure. Previous research (Kersh, Evans, & Kontiainen, 2011) has indicated that the concept of the learning space can be considered from various angles and perspectives. Firstly, the learning space can be perceived as a physical space where learning is taking place such as a classroom or any other form of teaching space. O'Toole (2001) notes that the physical surroundings are often overlooked in discussions of learning in the workplace. However, as Peponis argues, it is important to acknowledge that workplace design and layout provide an intelligible framework, and the structure of space supports an organizational culture with cognitive functions (Peponis et al., 2007). Secondly, the learning space can refer to a space where learning occurs unintentionally, such as informal learning, for example, at work where employees learn from each other's experiences (Garrick, 1997; Coffield, 2000; Cross, 2006; McGivney, 2006). Thirdly, the recent expansion of digital technologies has resulted in the development and growth of virtual learning spaces that ultimately change the boundaries of learning spaces, making them more flexible and mobile (Felstead & Jewson, 2012). Finally, the learning space can be perceived as a combination or overlap of a range of components, such as physical space, learning contexts and environments, formal/informal learning, and virtual learning. Recent trends in economic, political, and educational developments have resulted in somewhat blurred boundaries between the spaces in which learning, work, and leisure occur.

Workplace spaces are characterized by being both work and learning spaces where the boundaries between the two are considerably blurred (Solomon, Boud, & Rooney, 2006, p. 6). Situated learning theory further enriches the concept of the learning space by reminding us that learning spaces extend beyond the teacher and the classroom (Kolb & Kolb, 2005). Solomon, Boud, and Rooney (2006) further draw on the term "workplace learning," arguing that this notion has particular meanings and practices because of its location and because that location is not an educational institution. Drawing on the work of Bronfenbrenner (1977, 1979), Kolb and Kolb (2005) refer to four types of learning space. The learner's immediate setting, such as a course or classroom, is defined as the *microsystem*. In this research we also extend the concept of the microsystem to the learner's immediate workplace setting since we consider workplaces as learning sites. Other concurrent settings in a person's life such as other courses or family are called the *mesosystem*. The *exosystem* refers to the formal and informal social structures that influence the learner's immediate environment, for example, institutional policies and procedures and culture. Finally, the *macrosystem* relates to the overarching institutional patterns and values of the wider culture, such as cultural values favoring abstract knowledge over practical knowledge, which influence actors in the person's immediate microsystem and mesosystem.

The significance of the mesosystem, the learners' parallel lives and experience, has been emphasized by our empirical data (Kersh, Evans, & Kontiainen, 2011). One configuration of the mesosystem has been associated with the development of modern technologies that allows learners to extend their learning spaces to a variety of environments, including home and workplace settings. The expansion of digital technologies provides learners with opportunities to access and undertake learning activities in a range of other settings, including home and workplace environments, public libraries and youth centers, and even on trains and buses. Felstead and Jewson (2012) observe that the recent developments in information technology have weakened the spatial fix, with workers becoming increasingly detached from personal cubes of space. The use of devices such as computers, laptops, mobile phones, and netbooks has contributed to the development of the virtual learning space where learning might not be associated with a specific site or specific time. The virtual learning environment provides a degree of flexibility for the learner, enabling them to acquire learning at a time and place convenient for them. The use of new technologies has been gradually changing approaches to and ways of teaching and learning in work-related environments. In this context the concept of mobile learning has been emphasized. As Pachler, Pimmer, and Seipold (2011) stress, mobile learning is not simply about delivering content to mobile devices but, instead, about the processes of coming to know and being able to operate successfully in and across new and ever-changing contexts and learning spaces.

Competence Development and the Workplace

Over the past decade one of the main concerns of governments has been to raise the skills level of the population as a way of increasing competitiveness in the global economy (Guile, 2011). The new debate has highlighted the need to understand better the part played by development of competences in promoting "knowledge-based" economies and societies. Competence is indisputably a complex concept and can be interpreted in a variety of ways (Issit, 1995; Hodkinson, 1995; Eraut, 1994). As Gonczi (1999) notes, the meanings given to competence in everyday life, in vocational education and training settings and in academic settings are quite different. What is more, the meaning is likely to change over time within each of these contexts.

"Workplace competence" is a term that has not been clearly defined and explained, and the terms "competence" and "competency," which are often used interchangeably, are attributed multiple meanings depending on the context and the perspective advocated (Garavan & McGuire, 2001). As similarly noted in one of the CEDEFOP (The European Centre for the Development of Vocational Training) publications, the use of this term is shown to be particularly ambiguous and applicable to various situations with different meanings, specifically, as different countries or regions have their own definition of competence and each sector or occupational family has its own interpretation (Winterton, Delamare-Le Deist, & Stringfellow, 2006; Mulder, 2007). Eraut and Hirsh (2007) acknowledge that the term "competency" has been most commonly used either in a direct performance-related sense (as an element of vocational competence) or simply to describe any piece of knowledge or skill that might be construed as relevant. The former relates to the prevalent conception of "skills" that links it to tasks where performance of that task is subject to subsequent measurement of the intended consequences, or "outcomes," of learning (Oates, 2004; Hyland, 1994; Jessup, 1991). The learning outcomes approach has been adopted as a way to recognize knowledge, skills, and competences across the labor market Europe-wide (Gough, 2013). Eraut's and Hirsh's own definition of the term "competence" emphasizes the significance of links between the individual's capabilities and their competences: competence is "being able to perform the tasks and roles required to the expected standard" (Eraut & Hirsh, 2007, p. 7). In their interpretation, the word "competent," unlike terms such as "knowledge," "learning," and "capability," entails a social judgment, which may vary across contexts and over time and also, sometimes, with the experience, responsibility and reputation of the person concerned. Illeris (2009, 2011) similarly observes that the term "competence" is now perceived as a modern expression for what a person is actually able to do or achieve, and further concludes that, in recent years, the concept of competence has taken a central position, and more or less displaced the concept of qualifications. As a result, the workplace and a range of other work-related learning spaces are seen as primary sites for the acquisition and development of work-related competences (e.g., Ellström, 2001; Eraut, 2000; Evans et al., 2006; Illeris, 2011;

Fuller & Unwin, 2011). Evans et al. (2006) identify different forms of work-related learning that facilitate competence development in its "maximal" sense. Such forms of learning involve *learning in, through,* and *for* the workplace, encompassing activities such as engaging with and mastering changing tasks, roles, and environments (*learning in the workplace*); accessing a range of learning opportunities through the workplace (*learning through the workplace*); and engaging in various opportunities for *learning for the workplace,* which are of particular significance for those who are seeking to re-enter the workplace after a period of absence caused by unemployment or family circumstances. Evans et al.'s view of competences (2006) broadly emphasizes individuals' participation in social situations, also embodying the mental, emotional, and physical processes that are integral to the development and expansion of human capacities. Such an interpretation relates to the conceptualization proposed by Illeris of the concept of competence, which is to use it "as a point of departure for a more nuanced understanding of what learning efforts today are about – with a view of reaching theoretically based and practically tested proposals concerning how up-to-date competence development can be realised for different people in accordance with their possibilities and needs, both within and outside of institutionalised educational programmes" (Illeris, 2011, p. 42).

Supporting Competence Development through "Basic Skills" Programs in the Workplace

Skills such as literacy, numeracy, and information technology have been identified as essential enablers for employees to engage fully in learning and competence development within their workplaces (Evans & Waite, 2009, 2010; Wolf & Evans, 2011). The significance of employing "basic skills" in the workplace has been identified as related both to employees' biographical life experiences and their workplace learning as well as career and life chances. The contemporary workplaces are now increasingly demanding from their employees satisfactory levels of literacy, numeracy, and information technology skills, expecting them to be able to cope with both traditional and online types of paperwork. In the UK the educational and labor market policy context has generated an unprecedented demand for workplace-located basic skills programs as part of a national strategy (Evans, Waite, & Kersh, 2011), which resulted in the setting up of "Skills for Life" courses across all sectors of the economy and public sector starting in 2002. Research (e.g., Evans, Waite, & Kersh, 2011) has indicated that the workplace "Skills for Life" program has been associated with a range of personal and professional outcomes for the employees who took part in these programs. Acquiring or developing relevant basic skills within the workplace has supported some employees into activities that facilitated their competence development (personal or professional) through a range of workplace affordances and life experiences. The extent to which the employees may use, apply, or develop further their skills for life is often integral to the organizational dynamic at work, which either limits or facilitates the workplace environment as a learning space. The research has identified the link between the "Skills for Life" courses and employee motivations and attitudes, specifically related to contrasting the workplace-related provision with school-based learning, which, in some cases, has been associated with negative experiences. Employee engagement in the "Skills for Life" programs in the workplace illustrates the interplay between various configurations of the learning space. Embarking on literacy and numeracy courses in the workplace changes and challenges traditional perceptions of the workplace physical space as a location designated for performing exclusively work activities. At the same time, acquiring a range of "skills for life" enabled employees to use and develop them in other contexts and settings, for example, in their home environments. The interdependencies and interplay in learning between the different contexts and settings are underpinned, in part, by the development of "skills for life" acquired through workplace-located courses.

Rethinking the "Transferability" of Competences: Tacit vs. Explicit

The debate on work-related competences has highlighted the issue of the significance of developing personal competences and abilities that people can use in a variety of settings, including workplace settings (Evans, 2002; Evans, Kersh, & Sakamoto, 2004; Eraut, 2004). The definition of the term "competence" offered by Eraut and Hirsh (2007), quoted above, emphasizes the important links between individuals' capabilities and their competences. All their competences will be, as Eraut and Hirsh (2007) explain, within their capability; but not all their capabilities will be needed for any specific job. Therefore, they will also have *additional capabilities*, which may have a tacit dimension. Such additional capabilities may be helpful both in enhancing one's competences through further learning (Eraut & Hirsh, 2007) and in facilitating the processes by which competences learned in one context can be developed and used in different contexts and settings. Evans' research (Evans, Kersh, & Sakamoto, 2004) develops a model of key competences that has emphasized a broad cluster of capabilities coming together in ways that generate growth, movement, and future development, which are important in negotiating changes of work and learning environments, including the following:

- methodological competences,
- competences related to attitudes and values,
- learning competences,
- social and interpersonal competences, and
- content-related and practical competences.

This clustering of competences is useful as it provides us with a broad framework for categorizing a range of workplace competences, which may be further developed or applied through workplace affordances and opportunities. Boud and Garrick (1999, p. 1) similarly observe that employees are extending their educational capabilities in learning through their work: "opportunities and problems within work are creating the need for new knowledge and understanding. Employees develop skills of expression and communication which spill over into their personal lives. They learn new ways of collaboration and planning which they apply in their families and community organisations to which they belong." The discussion on conceptualizing and understanding work-related competences has underlined the importance of gaining a better understanding of how knowledge and competences are used and developed as people move between different contexts and settings, including both workplace and other informal/formal settings. While the metaphor of "transfer" has been dominant in recent times (Burke & Hutchins, 2007), the current debate has extensively problematized this notion, which often pays insufficient attention to the processes involved in recontextualizing skills and knowledge in order to put them to work in new and changing contexts (see Hager & Hodkinson, 2009; Evans & Guile, 2012). In this context, the role played by tacit skills as well as interdependences and interplay between tacit and explicit dimensions at work have been identified as factors affecting the transferability and use of skills and competences in a range of settings and spaces. Tacit skills are generally thought of as the "hidden" dimensions of the skills and competences that people can learn from a variety of experiences, such as formal education, the workplace, family experience, informal learning. "Tacit skills" is a term that is open to wide interpretation. Definitions and terminology related to those intangible skills varies from study to study, including terms such as "informal skills," "tacit skills," "personal skills," "soft skills," and "interpersonal skills." However, all these terms refer to hidden skills that are difficult to communicate, transmit, and acknowledge. The benefits of capturing such skills for the purpose of recognition and accreditation may be the most relevant measure of progress for a number of different kinds of learners.

The research literature on competence development through workplace learning has recognized the significance of tacit skills in the workplace. (Corno, Reinmoeller, & Nonaka, 1999; Eraut, 2000; Hager, 2000). Various approaches to conceptualizing tacit skills and competences have tended to be shaped by different epistemological stances. Tacit skills conceptualizations and explorations have been discussed within the literatures on knowledge management (e.g., Nonaka & Takeuchi, 1995; McInerney, 2002), scientific knowledge (Polanyi, 1962, 1966), and the knowledge economy (Guile, 2010a). Most of the approaches have drawn on making a distinction between tacit and explicit knowledge and attempted to provide a framework for capturing and identifying tacit knowledge with a primary purpose of making tacit knowledge explicit. Two famous attempts to capture and make tacit knowledge explicit include Nonaka and Takeuchi's cycle of knowledge conversion and Eraut's elicitation method. Their research draws our attention to the role of tacit skills in workplace contexts.

Nonaka and Takeuchi (1995) undertook their research in large Japanese car manufacturing companies (such as Toyota and Honda). The primary focus of their inquiries was the issue of knowledge management and knowledge creation in large companies. Their research led them to argue that the knowledge-creation process is based on a spiraling of interactions between explicit and tacit knowledge and the primary purpose of this process is turning tacit knowledge about products and services into explicit knowledge. Their famous "four steps" model of knowledge conversion (Nonaka & Takeuchi, 1995) demonstrates the way tacit knowledge is converted into explicit knowledge, which ultimately contributes to the process of knowledge creation in an organizational context. Eraut (2004) argued, however, that while Nonaka and Takeuchi demonstrated the value of tacit knowledge and the way it may become shared through the process of interactions at work, most of the knowledge they described was not tacit but rather personal knowledge held by employees, which was not considered relevant to be shared. Therefore their method is useful for providing an approach to share personal knowledge through social interaction at work. The sharing of knowledge through teams and networks is particularly effective for controlling corporate networks and is done through informal task forces and committees, which nurture learning and the development of sharing (Williams, 2011). Capturing tacit knowledge, according to Eraut (2004), requires a more complex approach, which would take into account both past and present experiences of individuals. Eraut's (2000, 2004) exploration of the concept of tacit knowledge led him to call for a greater awareness of the presence of tacit knowledge in the way we do our business and live our daily lives. Drawing on a series of large-scale and small-scale research projects, he concluded that learning occurs informally during normal working processes, and that there could be considerable scope to recognize and enhance such learning if it was sensitively elicited. His "elicitation" approach to uncover tacit skills in the workplace is based on his argument that people need to be supported to bring to the surface their tacit knowledge and skills. Elicitation is achieved by facilitating articulation or identifying (illuminating) instances of the nature of the tacit knowledge that is being considered (Eraut, 2000, p. 119). His approach involved structured elicitation interviewing techniques that supported people into reflecting on their past and present experiences and skills acquired and/or employed within these experiences. Evans and colleagues (Evans, Kersh, & Sakamoto, 2004; Evans et al., 2006) have taken this approach further, specifically demonstrating the way that recognition of employees' tacit skills and personal competences may enhance their motivation and further facilitate their learning attitudes and willingness to take on various workplace learning opportunities. Drawing on the method suggested by Eraut, as a first step that could be used for making tacit skills visible, Evans, Kersh, and Kontiainen's (2004) research suggested an approach that aimed to bring a new dimension to the elicitation process, which would facilitate the recognition of tacit skills through self-reflection and self-awareness. Their research, assisted by the Dynamic Concept Analysis (DCA) modeling method (Kontiainen, 2002) underpins the notion of tacit skills' recognition and self-evaluation, specifically in a range of workplace contexts: such skills have strong tacit dimensions that may become explicit or visible to the holder when deployed or recognized in a relevant context or environment. The elicitation becomes a multifaceted process that involves the learners reflecting on their tacit skills and abilities and relating those to their outcomes, achievements, and learning success. Their approach involved uncovering tacit skills through the DCA graphical modeling, which enables the process of employees' self-evaluation of their tacit skills in a variety of contexts and settings. In particular, research by Evans, Kersh, and Kontiainen (2004) has demonstrated the ways in which adult learners draw on their past experiences and skills acquired in the course of such experiences in their new settings, contexts, and learning spaces. Their research underlines the ways in which tacit skills could be recontextualized and made relevant in a range of activities and/or contexts. The DCA method could be used and applied to uncover, evaluate, and assess adult learners' personal/tacit skills and competences.

The Significance of New Technologies and Skills Development

Factors such as rapid technological development and the expansion of digital technologies have had a profound impact both on the nature of the learning space at work and types of skills and competences that are required by contemporary workplaces. The current debate addresses the need to improve the digital skills of the population in both European and global contexts. Within the US context the public's attainment of twenty-first-century digital literacy skills has been described as essential for the country's economic success in the global environment. Two major federal initiatives – the National Broadband Plan, released in 2010, and the Broadband Technology Opportunities Program, initiated in 2009 – focused national attention on digital inclusion and spurred government agencies to develop a range of policies and programs (Digital Literacy Task Force, 2013). To address opportunities and challenges related to digital literacy and associated national policy conversations, the American Library Association's (ALA) Office for Information Technology Policy (OITP) launched the OITP Digital Literacy Task Force in spring 2011 and brought together literacy experts and practitioners from school, academic, and public libraries (Digital Literacy Task Force, 2013). Similarly, in Europe, the issue of strengthening the competence of the entire European labor force through digital skills proficiency has been emphasized as a critical factor in raising economic productivity. Specifically, it has been highlighted that digital skills underpin both the Europe 2020 strategy for growth and its component plan, the Digital Agenda for Europe (see, e.g., ECDL, 2012; JISC,

2012; Ferrari, 2012). In its communication *E-Skills for the 21st Century: Fostering Competitiveness, Growth and Jobs*, the European Commission underlined the significance of information and communication technology (ICT) skills for business development and growth and called for a greater exploitation of the potential of ICT in this context. Preliminary research (e.g., Kersh, Waite, & Evans, 2012; Kersh & Evans, 2010) has indicated that digital literacy is considered to be one of the most critical factors that help to improve business development and growth across all sectors and to create employment opportunities, in all partners countries (ECDL, 2012; JISC, 2012; Ferrari, 2012). The term "digital literacy" has been widely used in the context of the debate on employment and labor market opportunities, and this notion is often used in a broad sense.

The notion of digital skills and their role in facilitating individuals' life chances and economic productivity has received considerable attention in recent research publications and policy chapters internationally. The literature review has shown that this notion has become a significant concept in the contemporary debate of what types of skills and competences people should have in the knowledge society.

In 2006 the European Union recognized digital competence to be one of the eight key competences for lifelong learning, emphasizing that digital competence involves the confident and critical use of information society technology (IST) and thus basic skills in information and communication technology (European Parliament, 2006). There is a clear demand in society for facilitating transparency and standardization of the notion of digital competences in a European context. This has been underpinned by the European Commision's Joint Research Centre report, which mapped 15 relevant competency frameworks that are currently available across Europe (e.g., ECDL, BECTA, and UNESCO) (Ferrari, 2012). Within the US context, a policy document *Building Digital Communities: A Framework for Action* defined digital literacy as one of seven foundational principles that make up "the basic requirements for creating a digitally inclusive community" (Digital Literacy Task Force, 2013). What unites these definitions employed in different report and policy chapters is that they (in one way or another) have referred to the need to address the capability to make use of digital skills in meaningful ways for life, work, and learning. These definitions may overlap in a number of ways; however, all of them include elements that need to be considered in discussing the problem of digital competence. This suggests that we could consider the term "digital skills/competences" as an "evolving concept" that requires further research and conceptualization, specifically in the contexts of the current demands of the contemporary workplace.

The nature of skills for employment is changing as computer literacy and skills related to the use of technologies are becoming of utmost importance in the context of the modern workplace setting. In order to succeed in the labor market both young and mature employees job seekers need to be computer literate. The expansion of new technologies means that employees are increasingly expected to have good information technology skills. Williams' research makes a point that the emergence of communications technologies and their corresponding access to computer networks are associated with the term "knowledge management" at work (Williams, 2011). There is a growing tendency for "online paperwork." In many organizations it is expected that employees are able to complete or work with various forms (e.g., reports, orders, invoices) online. The need to undertake such tasks may create stress and pressure for some staff in a range of workplaces. The data have indicated that employees who have no or limited IT skills experience difficulties in succeeding in the labor market and feel threatened and demotivated within their workplaces (Kersh & Evans, 2010; Kersh, Waite, & Evans, 2012). What motivates the employees is the fact that their newly acquired information technology (IT) skills might be applied immediately within their workplace settings (Kersh, Waite,

& Evans, 2012). In some cases learners felt that their IT skills really "make a difference" – in other words they enabled them to perform their jobs better. In addition, being computer literate enabled them to expand their learning environments by engaging in many types of "virtual learning" (e.g., through the internet), either tacitly or explicitly. E-learning and modern technologies provide opportunities to facilitate and support teaching practices in the workplace context, in particular by providing flexibility of time and place of delivery, allowing the sharing and re-use of resources, enabling collaborative working, and fostering learning and competence development.

The expansion of new technologies and the development of digital skills of the contemporary workforce have an impact on the concept of the learning space. A range of skills and knowledge can be acquired in so-called virtual settings (e.g., via electronic resources). The notion of the virtual learning space further loosens the boundaries between different types of environment. However, as Kersh et al.'s research concluded (Kersh, Waite, & Evans, 2012), in order to be meaningful, e-learning processes need to be grounded in various workplace activities. Wang et al. (2010) further note that the development of workplace e-learning should consider the alignment of individual and organizational learning needs, the connection between learning and work performance, and communication among individuals. As e-learning becomes embedded in adult learning in workplace settings, it may further contribute to facilitating the development of expansive learning environments for adult learners in both workplace and college contexts. E-learning or modern technologies may provide opportunities to facilitate and support teaching practices in the workplace context, in particular by providing flexibility of time and place of delivery; allowing the sharing and re-use of resources; enabling collaborative working; and fostering learning.

Future Research

The complex interdependencies between work, learning, and agency in the contemporary world call for the exploration of new ideas and directions in the concept of workplace learning. An emerging agenda for researching work, learning, and competence development has been strongly underpinned by issues such as globalization, the knowledge-based economy, and the learning society. The development of ideas about the knowledge economy and the learning society has facilitated the emergence of new approaches towards workplace learning and development. Further research should address a range of innovations and emerging trends that characterize the complex ways we learn "in, for, and through the workplace," such as, for example, the role of workplace learning in employee-driven innovation (Høyrup et al., 2012); an innovative apprenticeship model (Rauner & Smith, 2010), corporate/university partnerships (O'Connor & Lynch, 2011), or a model of lifelong learning that is associated with the model for creating new structures for accreditation of prior learning through reflective practice (Harris & Chisholm, 2011).

A range of international research findings suggests that the current perception of the concept of workplace learning is strongly interrelated with the notion of the learning space, in which individuals and teams work, learn, and develop their skills. The notion of the knowledge society challenges the traditional perception of the learning space, thus encouraging us to develop a better understating of the concept of the workspace and its different configurations as well as the different types of knowledge that are "put to work" as people work and learn (Evans & Guile, 2012) . Although the notion of the learning space at work has been a subject of interest in a number of international studies, the continuous development of the learning society as well as the expansion of digital technologies call for further research to advance our knowledge and understanding of the ways individuals learn "in, through, and for" the workplace within a range of traditional and new learning spaces. The achievement of human agency through environments is another area of research that could be further addressed, specifically by exploring different configurations of the learning space both at the workplace and beyond. The changing nature of workplace competences and the ways individuals acquire and use such competences in different learning spaces provide a basis for an emerging discussion of new types of work-related spaces. Future research can draw upon rich sources of workplace learning theories and approaches in order to expand our knowledge and understanding of the interrelationships between workplaces and individuals in the modern globalized world.

One aspect that should be not overlooked by further research on workplace learning is the international dimension in researching workplace learning. Workplace learning studies in a globalized world are increasingly drawing on the diversity of policies and practices in an international perspective. Chisholm et al. (2012), for example, have shown how transnational explorations of Asian and European research approaches and workplace practices contribute to a better understanding of the notion of learning at work in a comparative perspective and provide an insight into the interrelationships between research and practice. Future approaches to researching work and learning need to take into account a significant challenge of advancing our understanding and conceptualizing the notion of workplace learning internationally. Through a dialogic approach, diverse traditions in researching learning at work (Sawchuk, 2011) can move beyond existing silos to advance theoretical understanding and enhance practice.

Conclusion

The consideration of workplace learning and its different configurations has underpinned the complexities between work, learning, agency, and space. The interdependencies between individual engagement, competence development, and organizational context have been considered through the lens of organizational, individual, and environmental aspects. The complexities of workplace learning have been reflected in the changing requirements for competence development and its interplay with the changing nature of the learning space at work. The interrelations between the individual and environmental scales have been illustrated by the way individuals operate in their workplace environments, and the extent to the which these environments may facilitate or undermine their learning opportunities and life chances. The notion of expansive-restrictive environments (Fuller & Unwin, 2003, 2011) relates to the affordances of the workplace, which is strongly underpinned by the organizational perspective. Organizational and sectoral conditions influence both workplace opportunities and employees' perceptions at work. Making a workplace a learning organization has been considered as one of the challenges of contemporary workplace developments. Support for the continuous competence development of employees has been referred to as one of the factors that facilitates the learning workplace. Work-related competences are now increasingly considered in a broader sense, rather than competences that focus exclusively on performing narrowly defined workplace-related tasks. Individuals are now expected to use a range of competences, including personal skills, and be able to use these as they move between changing contexts, both within and outside their workplaces. The development of work-related competences is strongly influenced by the complexities of learning spaces, including the virtual learning space. As digital technologies have developed, workplace learning has further emphasized the significance of the digital skills of the workforce. The exercise of human agency through the virtual environment has the potential to facilitate learning at work, relating it to other spaces and environments. The perspective of social ecology provides a way into understanding the complexities of factors that impact on learning in the workplace, through the interplay of actors, structures, processes, and environments. This interplay is not restricted to the workplace but involves the overlap of the learning spaces and other contexts that extend way beyond the workplace. The concept of learning *in, for,* and *through* the workplace thus attends to the social processes that shape employees' perceptions and attitudes towards engagement in workplace learning, influencing their professional and personal development and life chances within the workplace and beyond.

References

Aspin, D., Chapman J., Evans, K., & Bagnall, R. (Eds.) (2012). *The Second International Handbook of Lifelong Learning.* Dordrecht: Springer.

Avis, J. (2004). Work-based learning and social justice: "Learning to labour" and the new vocationalism in England. *Journal of Education and Work,* 17(2, June), 197–217.

Beckett, D., & Hager, P. (2002). *Life, Work and Learning: Practice in Postmodernity.* Routledge International Studies in the Philosophy of Education, vol. 14. London and New York: Routledge.

Billett, S. (2011). Subjectivity, self and personal agency in learning through and for work. In M. Malloch, L. Cairns, K. Evans, & B. N. O'Connor (Eds.), *The Sage Handbook on Workplace Learning* (pp. 60–72). Thousand Oaks, CA: Sage.

Boud, D. (2006). Combining work and learning: The disturbing challenge of practice. In R. Edwards, J. Gallagher, & Whittaker, S. (Eds.), *Learning Outside the Academy: International Research Perspectives on Lifelong Learning* (pp. 77–89). London: Routledge.

Boud, D., & Garrick, J. (1999). Understanding of workplace learning. In D. Boud & J. Garrick (Eds.), *Understanding Learning at Work* (pp. 29–44). London: Routledge.

Bronfenbrenner, U. (1979). *The Ecology of Human Development: Experiments by Nature and Design.* Cambridge, MA: Harvard University Press.

Bronfenbrenner, U. (1977). Toward an experimental ecology of human development. *American Psychologist,* 32(7), 513–531.

Burke, L. A., & Hutchins, H. M.(2007). Training transfer: An integrative literature review. *Human Resource Development Review,* 6(3), 263–296.

Cairns, L., & Malloch, M. (2011). Theories of work, place and learning: New directions. In M. Malloch, L. Cairns, K. Evans, & B. N. O'Connor (Eds.), *The Sage Handbook on Workplace Learning* (pp. 3–16). Thousand Oaks, CA: Sage.

Chisholm, L., Lunardon, K., Ostendorf, A., & Pasqualoni, P.-P. (Eds.) (2012). *Decoding the Meanings of Learning at Work in Asia and Europe.* Conference Series. Innsbruck: Innsbruck University Press.

Coffield, F. (2000). Introduction: A critical analysis of the concept of the learning society. In F. Coffield (Ed.), *Differing Visions of a Learning Society: Research Findings* (vol.1, pp. 1–38). Bristol: Policy Press.

Coffield, F. (Ed.) (2000). *The Necessity of Informal Learning.* Bristol: Policy Press.

Corno, F., Reinmoeller, P., & Nonaka, I. (1999) Knowledge creation within industrial systems. *Journal of Management and Governance,* 3, 379–394.

Cross, J. (2006). *Informal Learning: Rediscovering the Natural Pathways That Inspire Innovation and Performance.* San Francisco: Jossey-Bass.

Digital Literacy Task Force (2013). Digital Literacy, Libraries and Public Policies. Report of Office for Information Technology Policy's Digital Task Force. http://www.districtdispatch.org/wp-content/uploads/2013/01/2012_OITP_digilitreport_1_22_13.pdf (accessed August 28, 2013).

Ecclestone, K., Biesta, G., & Hughes, M. (Eds.) (2009). *Transitions and Learning through the Lifecourse.* Abingdon: Routledge.

ECDL (2012). Delivering the Digital Agenda for Europe, March 9. http://www.ecdl.org/media/Delivering%20the%20DAE%20Report_Final_Approved.1.pdf (accessed August 28, 2013).

Ellström, P. E. (2001). Integrating learning and work: Problems and prospects. *Human Resource Development Quarterly*, 12(4), 421–435.

Engestrom, Y. (Ed.) (2001). *Activity Theory and Social Capital*. Helsinki: Centre for Activity Theory and Developmental Work Research.

Eraut, M. (1994). *Developing Professional Knowledge and Competence*. London: Falmer Press.

Eraut, M. (2000). Non-formal learning and tacit knowledge in professional work. *British Journal of Educational Psychology*, 70(1), 113–136.

Eraut, M. (2004). Informal learning in the workplace. *Studies in Continuing Education*, 26(2), 247–273.

Eraut, M., & Hirsh, W. (2007). The Significance of Workplace Learning for Individuals, Groups and Organisations, SCOPE. http://www.skope.ox.ac.uk/sites/default/files/Monogrpah%209.pdf (accessed April 8, 2014).

European Parliament (2006). *Recommendation 2006/962/EC of the European Parliament and of the Council of 18 December 2006 on key competences for lifelong learning*. Official Journal L 394 of December 20, 2006.

Evans, K. (2002). The challenges of "making learning visible." In K. Eans, P. Hodkinson and L. Unwin (Eds.), *Working to Learn: Transforming Learning in the Workplace* (pp. 77–92). London: Kogan Page.

Evans, K. (2009). *Learning, Work and Social Responsibility*. Springer: Dordrecht.

Evans K., & Guile, D. (2012). Putting different forms of knowledge to work in practice. In J. Higgs, R. Barnett, S. Billett, M. Hutchings, & F. Trede (Eds.), *Practice-Based Education: Perspectives and Strategies* (pp. 113–130). Rotterdam: Sense.

Evans, K., Hodkinson, P., Rainbird, H., & Unwin, L. (2006). *Improving Workplace Learning*. New York: Routledge.

Evans, K., Kersh, N., & Kontiainen, S. (2004). Recognition of tacit skills: Sustaining learning outcomes in adult learning and work re-entry. *International Journal of Training and Development*, 8(1), 54–72.

Evans, K., Kersh, N., & Sakamoto, A. (2004). Learner biographies: Exploring tacit dimensions of knowledge and skills. In H. Rainbird, A. Fuller, & A. Munro (Eds.), *Workplace Learning in Context* (pp. 222–241). London and New York: Routledge.

Evans, K., & Waite E. (2009). Adults learning in and through the workplace. In K. Ecclestone, G. Biesta, & M. Hughes (Eds.), *Change and Becoming through the Lifecourse: Transitions and Learning in Education and Life*. Abingdon: Routledge.

Evans, K., & Waite, E. (2010). Stimulating the innovation potential of "routine" workers through workplace learning. *TRANSFER – Journal of the European Trades Union Institute (ETUI)*, 16(2), 243–258.

Evans, K., Waite, E., & Kersh, N. (2011). Towards a social ecology of adult learning in and through the workplace. In M. Malloch, L. Cairns, K. Evans, & B. N. O'Connor (Eds.), *The Sage Handbook on Workplace Learning* (pp. 356–370). Thousand Oaks, CA: Sage.

Felstead, A., & Jewson, N. (2012). New places of work, new spaces of learning. In R. Brooks, A. Fuller, & J. Waters (Eds.), *Changing Spaces of Education: New Perspectives on the Nature of Learning* (pp. 137–158). London: Routledge.

Fenwick, T. J. (2006). Tidying the territory: Questioning terms and purposes in work-learning research. *Journal of Workplace Learning*, 18(5), 265–278.

Ferrari, A. (2012). Digital Competence in Practice: An Analysis of Frameworks, JRC Technical Report, EC. http://ftp.jrc.es/EURdoc/JRC68116.pdf (accessed July 12, 2013).

Field, J., Gallacher, J., & Ingram, R. (Eds.) (2009). *Researching Transitions in Lifelong Learning*. London: Routledge.

Fischer, M., & Boreham, N. (2004). Work process knowledge: Origins of the concept and current developments. In M. Fischer, N. Boreham, & B. Nyhan (Eds.), *European Perspectives on Learning at Work: The Acquisition of Work Process Knowledge* (pp. 12–54). Luxembourg: Office for Official Publications for the European Communities.

Fuller, A., & Unwin, L. (2003). Learning as apprentices in the contemporary UK workplace: Creating and managing expansive and restrictive participation. *Journal of Education and Work*, 16(4), 407–426.

Fuller, A., & Unwin, L. (2004). Expansive learning environments: Integrating organisational and personal development. In H. Rainbird, A. Fuller, & A. Munro (Eds.), *Workplace Learning in Context* (pp. 126–144). London and New York: Routledge.

Fuller, A., & Unwin, L. (2011). Workplace learning and the organization. In M. Malloch, L. Cairns, K. Evans, & B. N. O'Connor (Eds.), *The Sage Handbook on Workplace Learning* (pp. 46–59). Thousand Oaks, CA: Sage.

Fuller, A., Unwin, L., Felstead, A., Jewson, N., & Kakavelakis, K. (2007). Creating and using knowledge: An analysis of the differentiated nature of workplace learning environments. *British Educational Research Journal*, 33(5), 743–759.

Garavan, T., & McGuire, D. (2001). Competencies and workplace learning: Some reflections on the rhetoric and the reality. *Journal of Workplace Learning*, 13(4), 144–164.

Garrick, J. (1997). *Informal Learning in the Workplace*. London: Routledge.

Gnaur, D. (2010). Seizing workplace learning affordances in high-pressure work environments. *Vocations and Learning*, 3, 223–238.

Gonczi, A. (1999). Competency-based learning: A dubious past – an assured future. In D. Boud & J. Garrick (Eds.), *Understanding Learning at Work* (pp. 180–196). London, Routledge.

Gough, M. (2013). New basic skills, non-basic skills, knowledge practices and judgment: Tensions between the needs of basic literacy, of vocational education and training, and of higher and professional learning. In G. Zarifis, & M. Gravani (Eds.), *Challenging the "European Area of Lifelong Learning."* Dordrecht: Springer.

Gray, D., Cundell, S., Hay, D., & O'Neil, J. (2004). *Learning Through the Workplace: A Guide to Work-Based Learning*. Cheltenham: Nelson Thornes.

Guile, D. (2010a). *The Learning Challenge of the Knowledge Economy*. Rotterdam: Sense.

Guile, D. (2010b). Learning to work in the creative and cultural sector: New spaces, pedagogies and expertise, *Journal of Education Policy*, 25(4), 465–484.

Guile, D. (2011). Workplace learning in the knowledge economy: The development of vocational practice and social capital. In M. Malloch, L. Cairns, K. Evans, & B. N. O'Connor (Eds.), *The Sage Handbook on Workplace Learning* (pp. 385–394). Thousand Oaks, CA: Sage.

Hager, P. (2000). Know-how and workplace practical judgement. *Journal of Philosophy of Education*, 34(2), 281–296.

Hager, P., & Hodkinson, P. (2009). Moving beyond the metaphor of transfer of learning. *British Educational Research Journal*, 5(4), 619–638.

Harris, M., & Chisholm, C. (2011). Beyond the workplace: Learning in the lifeplace. In M. Malloch, L. Cairns, K. Evans, & B. O'Connor (Eds.), *The Sage Handbook of Workplace Learning* (pp. 373–385). Thousand Oaks, CA: Sage.

Heiskanen, T., & Heiskanen, H. (2011). Spaces of innovation: Experiences from two small high-tech firms. *Journal of Workplace Learning*, 23(2), 97–116.

Hodkinson, P. (1995). Professionalism and competences. In P. Hodkinson & M. Issit (Eds.), *The Challenge of Competence: Professionalism through Vocational Education and Training* (pp. 58–69). London: Cassell.

Hodkinson, P., & Bloomer, M. (2002). Learning careers: Conceptualising lifelong work-based learning. In K. Evans, P. Hodkinson, & L. Unwin (Eds.), *Working to Learn – Transforming Learning in the Workplace* (pp. 29–43). London: Kogan Page.

Hodkinson, P., Hodkinson, H., Evans, K., & Kersh, N., with Fuller, A., Unwin, L., & Senker, P. (2004). The significance of individual biography in workplace learning. *Studies in the Education of Adults*, 36(1), 6–24.

Høyrup, S., Bonnafous-Boucher, M., Hasse, C., Lotz, M., & Møller, K. (2012). *Employee-Driven Innovation: A New Approach*. Basingstoke: Palgrave.

Hyland, T. (1994). *Competence, Education and NVQs: Dissenting Perspectives*. London: Cassell.

Illeris, K. (2009). *International Perspectives on Competence Development*. Abingdon: Routledge.

Illeris, K. (2011). Workplace and learning. In M. Malloch, L. Cairns, K. Evans, & B. O'Connor (Eds.), *The Sage Handbook of Workplace Learning* (pp. 32–45). Thousand Oaks, CA: Sage.

Illeris, K. (2009). *International Perspectives on Competence Development.* Abingdon: Routledge.

Issit, M. (1995). Competence, professionalism and equal opportunities. In P. Hodkinson & M. Issit (Eds.), *The Challenge of Competence: Professionalism through Vocational Education and Training.* London: Cassell.

Jarvis, P. (1987). *Adult Learning in the Social Context,* London: Croom Helm.

Jayanti, E. (2012). Open sourced organizational learning: Implications and challenges of crowd-sourcing for human resource development (HRD) practitioners. *Human Resource Development International,* 15(3), 375–384.

Jessup, G. (1991). *Outcomes: NVQs and the Emerging Model of Education and Training.* London: Falmer Press.

JISC (2012). Developing digital literacies project. http://www.jisc.ac.uk/developingdigitalliteracies (accessed July 28, 2013).

Kersh, N., & Evans, K. (2010). Facilitating learner's motivation and competence development in the workplace: The UK context. In F. Rauner & E. Smith (Eds.), *Rediscovering Apprenticeship.* Dordrecht: Springer.

Kersh, N., Evans, K., & Kontiainen, S. (2011). Use of conceptual models in self-evaluation of personal competences in learning and in planning for change. *International Journal of Training and Development,* 15(4), 290–305.

Kersh, N., Waite, E., & Evans, K. (2012). The spatial dimensions of workplace learning: Acquiring literacy and numeracy skills within the workplace. In R. Brooks, A. Fuller, & J. Waters (Eds.), *Changing Spaces of Education: New Perspectives on the Nature of Learning* (pp. 182–204). London: Routledge.

Kolb, D. A. (1984). *Experiential Learning.* Englewood Cliffs, NJ: Prentice Hall.

Kolb, A., & Kolb, D. (2005). Learning styles and learning spaces: Enhancing experiential learning in higher education. *Academy of Management Learning and Education,* 4(2), 193–212.

Kontiainen, S. (2002). *Dynamic Concepts Analysis (DCA): Integrating Information in Conceptual Models.* Helsinki: Helsinki University Press.

Lave, J., & Wenger, E. (1998). *Communities of Practice: Learning, Meaning, and Identity.* Cambridge: Cambridge University Press.

Lee, T., Fuller, A., Ashton, D., Butler, P., Felstead, A., Unwin, L., & Walters, S. (2004). *Learning as Work: Teaching and Learning Processes in the Contemporary Work Organisation.* Learning as Work Research Paper No. 2. Leicester: University of Leicester Centre for Labour Market Studies.

Livingstone, D. W. (2006). *Informal Learning: Conceptual Distinctions and Preliminary Findings.* New York: Peter Lang.

Malloch, M., Cairns, L., Evans, K., & O'Connor, B. N. (Eds.) (2011). *The Sage Handbook of Workplace Learning.* Thousand Oaks, CA: Sage.

Malone, S. (2005). *A Practical Guide to Learning in the Workplace.* Dublin: Liffey Press.

Marsick, V., & Watkins, K. E. (1999). *Facilitating Learning Organizations: Making Learning Count.* London: Gower Press.

McGivney, V. (2006). Informal learning: The challenge for research. In R. Edwards, J. Gallagher & S. Whittaker, S. (Eds), *Learning Outside the Academy: International Research Perspectives on Lifelong Learning* (pp. 11–23). London, Routledge.

McInerney, C. (2002). Knowledge management and the dynamic nature of knowledge. *Journal of the American Society for Information Science and Technology,* 53(12), 1009–1018.

Mulder, M. (2007). Competence – the essence and use of the concept in ICVT. *European Journal of Vocational Training,* 40, 5–22.

Nonaka, I., & Takeuchi, H. (1995). *The Knowledge Creating Company.* New York: Oxford University Press.

Oates, T. (2004). The role of outcome-based national qualifications in the development of an effective vocational education and training: The case of England and Wales. *Policy Futures in Education,* 2(1), 53–71.

O'Connor, B. N., & Lynch, D. (2011). Partnerships between and among education and the public and private sectors. In M. Malloch, L. Cairns, K. Evans, & B. N. O'Connor (Eds.), *The Sage Handbook of Workplace Learning* (pp. 420–430). Thousand Oaks, CA: Sage.

O'Toole, K. M. (2001). Learning through the physical environment in the workplace. *International Education Journal* 2(1), 10–19.

Pachler, N., Pimmer, C., & Seipold, J. (Eds.) (2011). *Work-Based Mobile Learning: Concepts and Cases.* Oxford: Peter Lang.

Peponis, J., Bafna, S., Bajaj, R., Bromberg, J., Congdon, C., Rashid, M., Warmels, S., Zhang, Y., & Zimring, C. (2007). Designing spaces to support knowledge work. *Environment and Behaviour*, 39(6), 815–840.

Polanyi, M. (1962). Tacit knowing: Its bearing on some problems of philosophy. *Reviews of Modern Physics*, 34(4), 601–616.

Polanyi, M. (1966). *The Tacit Dimension.* New York: Doubleday.

Rainbird, H., Fuller, A., & Munro, A. (Eds.) (2004). *Workplace Learning in Context.* London: Routledge.

Rauner F., & Smith, E. (Eds.) (2010). *Rediscovering Apprenticeship.* Dordrecht: Springer.

Remedios, R., & Boreham, N. (2004). Organisational learning and employees' intrinsic motivation. *Journal of Education and Work*, 17(2), 219–235.

Sawchuk, P. (2011). Researching workplace learning: An overview and critique. In M. Malloch, L. Cairns, K. Evans, & B. N. O'Connor (Eds.), *The Sage Handbook of Workplace Learning* (pp. 165–180). Thousand Oaks, CA: Sage.

Solomon, N., Boud, D., & Rooney, D. (2006). The in-between: Exposing everyday learning at work. *International Journal of Lifelong Education*, 25(1), 3–13.

Streumer, J., & Kho, M. (2006). The world of work-related learning. In J. Streumer, (Ed.), *Work-Related Learning* (pp. 3–50). Dordrecht: Springer.

Unwin, L., & Fuller, M. (2003). *Expanding Learning in the Workplace: Making More of Individual and Organisational Potential.* NIACE policy discussion paper. London: NIACE.

Wang, M., Ran, W., Liao, J., & Yang, S. J. H. (2010). A performance-oriented approach to e-learning in the workplace. *Educational Technology & Society*, 13(4), 167–179.

Williams, D. (2011). An investigation into tacit knowledge management at the supervisory level. PhD thesis. University of Waikato. http://researchcommons.waikato.ac.nz/handle/10289/5743 (accessed July 30, 2013).

Winterton, J., Delamare-Le Deist, F., & Stringfellow, E. (2006). Typology of knowledge, skills and competences: Clarification of the concept and prototype. European Centre for the Development of Vocational Training. http://www.cedefop.europa.eu/en/Files/3048_EN.PDF (accessed on July 30, 2013).

Wolf, A., & Evans, K. (2011). *Improving Literacy at Work.* Abingdon: Routledge.

5

Transfer of Socialization

Alan M. Saks

Introduction

In the past several decades, a great deal has been learned about the science and practice of training and development and organizational socialization. There have been numerous reviews and meta-analyses in the training (Arthur et al., 2003; Brown & Sitzmann, 2011; Salas, Weaver, & Shuffler, 2012; Tharenou, Saks, & Moore, 2007) and organizational socialization literatures (Chao, 2012; Cooper-Thomas & Anderson, 2006; Saks & Gruman, 2012). As a result, we know a great deal about how to design and deliver effective training programs and how to socialize new hires so that they become effective members of the organization. However, even though both of these important areas of human resources management involve learning as a primary objective, the research on organizational socialization has paid little attention to what has been learned from the training literature. This is unfortunate as research on organizational socialization can benefit a great deal from the training literature, especially in areas such as training design, training evaluation, and most importantly the transfer of training (Saks & Ashforth, 1997).

In this chapter, I focus on the implications of the transfer of training for organizational socialization. I will review the literature on organizational socialization and the transfer of training and then argue that research and practice on organizational socialization can be significantly improved and advanced by applying what we know about the transfer of training to the design and delivery of socialization programs. In the first section I will define training and organizational socialization and describe how similar they are in that learning is the most fundamental and primary objective and outcome of training and organizational socialization. Second, I will review the socialization research on employee orientation and training which are two primary types of formal programs used by organizations to orient and socialize new hires. Third, I introduce a new construct and model to the socialization literature that I refer to as the transfer of socialization, based on a review of the transfer

The Wiley Blackwell Handbook of the Psychology of Training, Development, and Performance Improvement,
First Edition. Edited by Kurt Kraiger, Jonathan Passmore, Sigmar Malvezzi, and Nuno Rebelo dos Santos.
© 2015 John Wiley & Sons Ltd. Published 2020 by John Wiley & Sons Ltd.

of training literature and Baldwin and Ford's (1988) model of the transfer of training process. The chapter concludes with a discussion of future research directions and the implications of the model for socialization practice.

Training and Organizational Socialization

Training and development and organizational socialization are two areas that are closely related and yet they have been studied independently for decades even though the focus of both is learning. Training has been defined as a "formal, planned effort to help employees gain job-relevant knowledge and skills" (Brown & Sitzmann, 2011). These authors note that when training programs are properly designed and delivered they can improve employees' skills and job-related behaviors, reduce accidents, increase innovation, enhance organizational productivity, and increase organizational profits. A key mechanism behind these positive effects is that training helps employees learn to perform their jobs better (Brown & Sitzmann, 2011).

Like training and development, a primary objective of organizational socialization is learning (Klein & Weaver, 2000). Organizational socialization is the process through which newcomers learn "the ropes" of a particular organizational role. It is "the process by which an individual acquires the social knowledge and skills necessary to assume an organizational role" (Van Maanen & Schein, 1979, p. 211). Thus, organizational socialization is primarily a learning process in which new hires must learn new attitudes, behaviors, and ways of thinking (Klein & Weaver, 2000; Saks & Ashforth, 1997).

The importance of learning within the socialization literature has been evident for decades. Fisher (1986) described socialization as primarily a learning and change process. More recently, Cooper-Thomas and Anderson (2006) referred to newcomer learning as the core of organizational socialization. Ashforth, Sluss, and Harrison (2007) argued that learning is central to the socialization process and referred to it as the heart of socialization:

> For socialization to effectively bring the newcomer into the fold, the newcomer should come to know and understand (i.e., learn) the norms, values, tasks, and roles that typify group and organizational membership. As such, newcomer learning lies "at the heart of any organizational socialization model." (p. 16)

Klein and Heuser (2008) also describe socialization as a learning process in which newcomers must acquire a variety of information, attitudes, and behaviors that are necessary to become an effective organizational member.

Many models of organizational socialization treat learning as a key mechanism to explain the effects of socialization practices on work adjustment and socialization outcomes. For example, Saks and Ashforth (1997) developed a multilevel process model of organizational socialization in which cognitive sense-making, uncertainty reduction, and learning intervenes between socialization factors and socialization outcomes. The focus of their model is information and learning, which is consistent with the idea that organizational socialization is primarily a learning process. Similarly, Ashforth, Sluss, and Harrison (2007) developed an integrative model that places learning as a mediating variable between socialization processes and newcomer adjustment. They argue that content is the major linchpin that connects socialization processes to newcomer adjustment. Cooper-Thomas and Anderson (2006) developed a multilevel learning-focused model that describes the relationships between various learning domains and sources of learning and socialization success indicators. Several studies have in fact found that learning mediates the relationship between socialization practices (e.g., orientation, socialization tactics, mentoring, socialization agent helpfulness, and proactive behaviors) and socialization outcomes (Allen, McManus, & Russell, 1999; Ashforth, Sluss, & Saks, 2007; Cooper-Thomas & Anderson, 2002; Klein, Fan, & Preacher, 2006; Klein & Weaver, 2000).

In summary, organizational socialization has been defined and described as a learning process in which newcomers must acquire information and knowledge to become an effective member of an organization (Klein & Weaver, 2000). Thus, learning is considered to be a direct and primary outcome of both training and development and organizational socialization that precedes and predicts other training and socialization outcomes. In the next section, I will review two of the most popular formal means for socializing new hires: new employee orientation and training.

New Employee Orientation and Training Programs

Organizational socialization often consists of formal programs that have their basis in training. Two of the most common formal socialization practices are new employee orientation programs and training programs. Newcomer orientation programs focus on contextual issues such as roles, the organization's history, structure, and culture and are concerned with retention-related outcomes. Training programs for newcomers focus on the technical aspects of the job and are primarily concerned with task performance (Fan, Buckley, & Litchfield, 2012). As described below, orientation and training programs have been found to be related to newcomer learning, adjustment, and socialization outcomes.

New employee orientation programs

The organizational socialization process usually begins with an orientation program. It is during the orientation program that newcomers are introduced to the job, the people they will be working with, and the larger organization (Klein & Weaver, 2000). The orientation period usually lasts from the first day to the end of the first week (Wanous & Reichers, 2000). Onsite orientation sessions are one of the most formal and planned socialization practices used by organizations (Louis, Posner, & Powell, 1983).

Research on orientation programs has found that they are particularly effective for newcomer learning and anxiety reduction. One of the first studies on orientation programs was conducted by Gomersall and Myers (1966) at Texas Instruments where new hires were experiencing anxiety, which was having a negative effect on their work performance. In order to help new employees overcome their anxieties, a one-day anxiety-reduction program was designed to follow the standard two-hour orientation program. Participants who received the anxiety-reduction program were more productive, had better job attendance, and reached higher levels of competence much sooner than a control group that only received the standard two-hour orientation. The program also reduced costs and improved quality and profitability.

Saks (1994a) investigated the effects of an orientation program on seasonal employees of a large amusement park. He found that the accuracy and completeness of the information employees received from the orientation program was positively related to organizational commitment, ability to cope, and met expectations, which were subsequently related to job satisfaction, intention to quit, and job survival.

Klein and Weaver (2000) investigated an organizational-level orientation program on new hire socialization and organizational commitment at a large educational institution.

Newcomers were invited to attend a voluntary three-hour orientation program and asked to complete a survey two months and ten weeks following the orientation program. Compared to a group of newcomers who did not attend the program, newcomers who attended the orientation program had higher scores on several socialization content dimensions (i.e., history, goals/values, people) and reported higher affective organizational commitment. The effect of the orientation program on organizational commitment was mediated by the socialization content dimensions (i.e., goals/values, history).

Wesson and Gogus (2005) compared a traditional (social-based) orientation program to a multimedia, computer-based orientation program in a sample of 261 newcomers from a large technology-based consulting firm. The traditional social-based orientation program was a one-week program that familiarized new hires with the organization and its practices and procedures and created a sense of community and belonging between newcomers and the organization. The orientation consisted of presentations, videos, reading assignments, team-building activities, and question-and-answer sessions. The computer-based orientation program was a self-guided program that covered the same material as the traditional program but involved a multimedia orientation that included written, audio, and video-based sessions and took two to three days to complete.

After two months on the job newcomers who attended the computer-based orientation program had lower scores on the social-related content dimensions of socialization (i.e., people, politics, and organizational goals and values) but not on the more information-based content areas of socialization (i.e., knowledge of the organization's history, language, and performance proficiency). Newcomers in the computer-based orientation program had lower levels of job satisfaction and organizational commitment after four months on the job and their supervisors rated them lower on organizational goals and values socialization and role understanding. The socialization content dimensions (i.e., organization goals and values, politics, and people) mediated the effects of the computer-based orientation program on job satisfaction and organizational commitment.

A problem with orientation programs, however, is that they tend to focus on general facts such as the terms and conditions of employment and are too narrow in focus because they primarily involve imparting information (Fan, Buckley, & Litchfield, 2012; Wanous & Reichers, 2000). Wanous and Reichers (2000) have suggested that orientation programs should be designed to lower the stress of newcomers and should teach newcomers coping skills for the most important stressors they will face and should teach both emotion-focused and problem-focused coping skills. They refer to this kind of orientation program as ROPES – realistic orientation programs for new employee stress.

The focus of a ROPES intervention is to reduce newcomers' stress and anxiety by teaching newcomers how to cope with major entry stressors (Fan, Buckley, & Litchfield, 2012). The basic principles for the design of ROPES involve: (1) provide realistic information that forewarns newcomers about typical disappointments to expect and possible adjustment problems, as well as how to cope by setting goals and taking action; (2) provide general support and reassurance; (3) behavior modeling training that uses models to show coping skills that newcomers rehearse and receive feedback; (4) teach self-control of thoughts and feelings; and (5) target specific stressors for specific newcomers.

Two studies have tested the effects of ROPES-type orientation programs. Waung (1995) investigated new hires in entry-level service jobs at a quick-service food chain and a local hospital. Newcomers in the ROPES condition received self-regulatory training that included cognitive restructuring, positive self-talk, and statements to bolster self-efficacy as well as information about common affective reactions to unpleasant situations. A comparison group received realistic information about the negative aspects of the job and coping behaviors. After the orientation program, participants in the ROPES condition reported higher levels of organizational support but there were no differences in self-efficacy. Four weeks later, the ROPES group had higher job satisfaction and higher turnover. There were no differences for organizational supportiveness, self-efficacy, organizational commitment, anxiety, or intentions to quit. However, new hires in the ROPES group indicated that they were more likely to remain on the job for a year or longer.

Fan and Wanous (2008) compared a ROPES intervention to a more traditional orientation program in a sample of 72 new graduate students from Asia attending a large university in the United States. Based on interviews with international students as well as several pilot tests, a ROPES intervention was designed to teach international students how to cope with three major entry stressors: (1) the fast pace of the academic quarter system (the university has three quarters vs. two semesters); (2) language difficulties; and (3) social interaction difficulties.

Students were randomly assigned to receive the ROPES intervention or a more traditional 3-hour orientation session that focused on students' immediate concerns, such as how to keep legal status in the United States, personal safety issues, how to connect a home phone, and so forth. Students in the experimental condition received a shorter version of the traditional orientation program plus ROPES.

The ROPES participants reported lower pre-entry expectations at the end of the orientation program, and lower stress and higher academic and interaction adjustment six and nine months after the program. ROPES participants also engaged in more adaptive coping behaviors that were taught in the ROPES, had higher adjustment self-efficacy, and higher but nonsignificant retention after two years. The positive effects of ROPES became stronger over time and stress mediated the effect of the ROPES intervention on academic and interaction adjustment (Fan, Buckley, & Litchfield, 2012; Fan & Wanous, 2008).

New employee training programs

In addition to orientation programs, training programs are often a key part of the socialization process. While orientation programs focus on organizational issues, formal training programs focus on the specific knowledge and skills that a new hire requires to perform his/her particular role and tasks. Most newcomers attend some type of formal training when they enter an organization (Feldman, 1989).

According to Feldman (1989), training programs have become the main socialization process for new employees and play "a major role in how individuals make sense of and adjust to their new job settings" (p. 399). Training has become the primary means through which newcomers form perceptions and expectations about the organization, learn the norms for social behavior, and develop their career paths. Thus, training has become synonymous with the socialization process (Feldman, 1989). Several studies have found training to be related to socialization outcomes. For example, in a study on the effects of military recruit socialization training, Tannenbaum et al. (1991) found that training fulfillment (the extent to which training meets or fulfills a trainee's expectations and desires) was positively related to organizational commitment, training motivation, and academic, and physical self-efficacy. Trainee satisfaction with training was positively related to organizational commitment, training motivation, and physical self-efficacy.

Saks (1994b) examined the effects of formal training and tutorial training on the anxiety and stress reactions of newly hired entry-level accountants. He found that the effect of training depended on newcomers' self-efficacy. Formal training lowered the anxiety of newcomers with low technical self-efficacy while tutorial training increased the anxiety for newcomers who had lower academic self-efficacy. Thus, the method of training only mattered for low self-efficacy newcomers who responded best to formal training.

Saks (1995a) investigated the amount of training received by newcomers and the role of self-efficacy. He found that the amount of training received by newly hired entry-level accountants was positively related to post-training self-efficacy, ability to cope, job satisfaction, organizational and professional commitment, and intention to quit the organization and profession. As predicted, newcomers' self-efficacy moderated the relationship between training and adjustment such that training was more strongly related to several of the socialization outcomes for newcomers with lower self-efficacy. In addition, post-training self-efficacy partially mediated the relationships between training and socialization outcomes.

Saks (1996) examined the amount and helpfulness of formal training programs and found that the amount of training newcomers reported receiving during the first six months was significantly related to their ratings of the helpfulness of training. The amount of training received as well as its perceived helpfulness was positively related to job satisfaction, organizational commitment, ability to cope, and negatively related to anxiety and intention to quit. Furthermore, anxiety partially mediated the relationship between training and the socialization outcomes.

Summary

Although research has found both orientation and training programs to be effective in terms of various socialization outcomes, with the exception of research on ROPES, the emphasis has been on whether or not newcomers received orientation or the amount of training they received rather than the content or nature of orientation and training programs. As a result, we really do not know very much about how to make newcomer orientation and training programs more effective especially with respect to learning socialization content. Furthermore, the emphasis in the socialization literature has been on learning with almost no attention on whether or not newcomers actually use and apply what they learn on the job. This is in sharp contrast to decades of research in the training literature on the transfer of training, which is considered to be fundamental for training success and effectiveness. It would seem that the literature on organizational socialization might benefit from what has been learned about the transfer of training.

Therefore, in the following sections I will review the research and literature on the transfer of training and consider its implications for organizational socialization. In particular, I will introduce a new construct to the socialization literature similar to transfer of training that I refer to as transfer of socialization and present a model of the transfer of socialization based on Baldwin and Ford's (1988) model of the transfer of training process.

Transfer of Training

One area of the training literature that has particular relevance for organizational socialization is the transfer of training (Saks & Ashforth, 1997). Transfer of training refers to "the degree to which trainees effectively apply the knowledge, skills, and attitudes gained in a training context to the job" (Baldwin & Ford, 1988). Thus, it extends the learning outcome of training to its use and application in the work environment. As described by Baldwin and Ford (1988), "For transfer to have occurred, learned behavior must be generalized to the job context and maintained over a period of time on the job" (p. 63).

Given that learning is a major objective and outcome of organizational socialization and that newcomers are expected to use and apply what they learn on the job, it stands to reason that the research on transfer of training can be applied to organizational socialization. It would seem especially relevant given that the emphasis in the socialization literature has been on learning socialization content rather than the application of learning. In fact, the whole notion of the application of socialization content is virtually nonexistent in the socialization literature. Rather, it has generally been assumed that newcomers apply what they learn. However, based on what we know about the transfer of training, the extent to which newcomers apply what they learn during socialization is very likely dependent on a number of factors. As noted by Baldwin and Ford (1988), "Training outcomes of learning and retention constitute necessary but not sufficient conditions for generalization and maintenance of skills" (p. 75). Further, while employees might acquire new knowledge and skills from training programs, learning alone is not sufficient for a training program to be considered effective (Grossman & Salas, 2011).

Thus, it would seem that an important but missing variable in the socialization literature is the use and application of what newcomers learn during the socialization process. Based on what we know about the transfer of training, it is very likely that newcomers do not or cannot always use and apply what they learn on the job. In other words, like training, learning is a necessary but not sufficient condition for socialization success. Thus, it is important to consider newcomers' application of what they learn as well as the factors that make it more likely that socialization learning will be used and applied on the job. Like training, newcomers' acquisition of new knowledge and skills alone should not be considered as evidence that socialization is effective.

Therefore, a meaningful extension of the organizational socialization literature is to go beyond the learning of socialization content to its use and application. This suggests a new socialization construct that I will call transfer of socialization. Transfer of socialization can be defined as "the extent to which newcomers effectively apply and make use of the knowledge, skills, attitudes, and behaviors that they acquire during socialization on the job."

The best-known model of the transfer of training is Baldwin and Ford's (1988) model of the transfer of training process. According to Baldwin and Ford (1988), there are two conditions of transfer: generalization and maintenance. Generalization refers to the use of learned material in the job context and maintenance refers to the use of learned material in the job context over a period of time. The model also includes training input factors and training output factors. The training input factors include trainee characteristics, training design, and work environment characteristics. The training outputs refer to the amount of learning that occurs during training and the retention of that learning after a training program has been completed. The model suggests that the training input factors have a direct effect on learning and retention. All of the training input factors have an indirect effect on the conditions of transfer through learning and retention, and trainee characteristics, the work environment, and learning and retention have a direct effect on the conditions of transfer.

The Baldwin and Ford (1988) framework can be used as a model for the transfer of socialization as well as a general model of the organizational socialization process. It is worth noting that the socialization literature has often been described as fragmented (Chao, 2012; Saks & Ashforth, 1997; Saks & Gruman, 2012). This is due in part to research that investigates particular socialization practices independently of other practices. The Baldwin and Ford (1988) model provides a meaningful way to integrate socialization practices and to link them to learning outcomes and the transfer of socialization. It is also a good starting point towards the development of a model of the transfer of socialization, which is described in the next section.

Transfer of Socialization

In this section, I will review the literature on the transfer of training and describe a transfer of socialization model based on Baldwin and Ford's (1988) model of the transfer of training process. I briefly review the main variables in their model and then link them to the transfer of socialization. As shown in Figure 5.1, the model consists of three main types of factors: socialization input factors (newcomer characteristics, socialization design, and the work environment), socialization learning and retention, and transfer of socialization (generalization and maintenance). Following Baldwin and Ford's (1988) model, newcomer characteristics, socialization design, and work environment factors influence socialization learning and retention, and newcomer characteristics, work environment factors, and socialization learning retention influence socialization transfer. Socialization design is indirectly related to socialization transfer through socialization learning and retention.

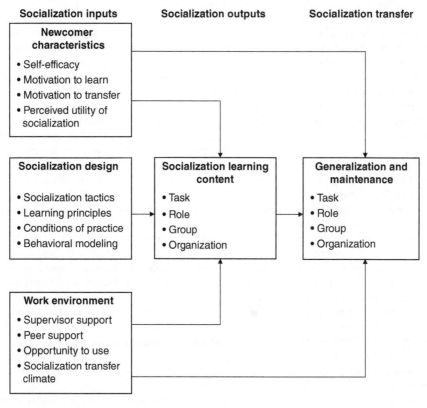

Figure 5.1 A model of transfer of socialization.

Learning and retention

In the socialization literature, the learning of socialization content is usually referred to as socialization content or newcomer learning. It is the substance of what newcomers must learn to be proficient and comfortable members of an organization (Ashforth, Sluss, & Saks, 2007). As indicated earlier, learning is generally considered to be the crux or heart of organizational socialization (Ashforth, Sluss, & Harrison 2007). The different types of learning that occur during organizational socialization have been referred to as learning dimensions or domains (Haueter, Macan, & Winter, 2003).

Fisher (1986) suggested four primary categories or types of learning content: (1) organizational values, goals, culture, and so on; (2) work group values, norms, and friendships; (3) how to do the job and the required skills and knowledge; and (4) personal change and development in terms of identity, self-image, and motive structure. Further, newcomers must first be convinced that learning and adaptation is necessary or what Fisher refers to as preliminary learning. Thus, newcomers must learn "*what* to learn" and "whom to learn from."

Although several measures of socialization content have been developed, there is general agreement that knowledge acquisition and learning includes the job, role, interpersonal and group relationships, and the organization (Ashforth , Sluss, & Saks, 2007). Thus, it is generally believed that new organizational members must acquire information and learn about four main domains or socialization content areas: the task domain, the role domain, the group domain, and the organizational domain (Ostroff & Kozlowski, 1992). The task domain involves understanding task duties, assignments, priorities, how to handle routine problems, and so on. The role domain has to do with learning about the boundaries of one's authority and responsibility as well as the expectations and appropriate behaviors for one's position in the organization. The group domain has to do with learning about group norms and values as well as appropriate co-worker interactions and the normative structure. The organizational domain involves learning about the organization's goals, values, mission, politics, power, leadership styles, and so on (Ostroff & Kozlowski, 1992).

Learning is so central to organizational socialization that several scales have been developed to measure organizational learning content. Chao et al. (1994) developed one of the first such measures. Their scale consists of six dimensions (performance proficiency, people, politics, language, organizational goals and values, and history). Haueter, Macan, and Winter (2003) developed and validated a measure of newcomer socialization called the Newcomer Socialization Questionnaire (NSQ). The scale measures three dimensions of newcomer socialization (the organization, group, and the job/task) and was designed to address some of the shortcomings and concerns of the Chao et al. (1994) scale. The scale items measure factual knowledge as well as knowledge of expected role behaviors. The authors used a content validity approach to develop the scale and then provided evidence of the construct, convergent, and discriminant validity. The scales were also shown to be positively related to newcomers' job satisfaction and organizational commitment.

Klein and Heuser (2008) developed an expanded socialization content typology (i.e., the information and behaviors individuals need to acquire in order to be effective organizational members) that consists of 12 content dimensions that newcomers need to learn for effective socialization. They used an instructional-systems approach to connect the socialization-content dimensions to learning outcomes and they also used the socialization practices (what they refer to as orienting activities) that will be most effective for newcomers to learn the socialization-content dimensions.

As indicated earlier, most measures of newcomer learning/socialization content tend to include components of the task, role, work group, and the organization and they ask newcomers to indicate the extent to which they have learned specific things in each content domain (Ashforth, Sluss, & Saks, 2007). The model in Figure 5.1 upholds the four main dimensions of socialization content (task, role, group, and organization). In addition to comprising the content of learning and retention, each of these domains of learning is also reflected in the conditions of socialization transfer (generalization and maintenance). In other words, just as we can refer to newcomers' learning in each of the four content domains, we can also refer to newcomers' application, use, and maintenance of learning (i.e., transfer of socialization) in each domain. Thus, transfer of socialization means that newcomers must engage in on-the-job behaviors with respect to the performance of their work tasks and roles, their interactions with group members, and the organization's norms, practices, and expectations.

Newcomer characteristics

In the training literature, trainee characteristics have received a considerable amount of attention as predictors of learning and retention as well as transfer (Salas, Weaver, & Shuffler, 2012). Surprisingly, in the socialization literature newcomer characteristics have received limited attention and have not been studied in a systematic manner (Gruman & Saks, 2011). Furthermore, much of the emphasis has been on personality variables such as those from the Five Factor Model, proactive personality, negative affectivity, self-esteem, and general self-efficacy (Chan & Schmitt, 2000; Kammeyer-Mueller & Wanberg, 2003; Li et al., 2011; Saks & Ashforth, 2000; Sluss, Ashforth, & Gibson, 2012; Wanberg & Kammeyer-Mueller, 2000; Weiss, 1977, 1978). Based on the research findings in the transfer of training literature, the following newcomer characteristics are potentially important for predicting newcomer learning and socialization transfer and are included in Figure 5.1 and discussed below: motivation to learn, motivation to transfer, self-efficacy, and socialization utility.

Baldwin and Ford (1988) focused on three types of trainee characteristics: ability, personality (need for achievement and locus of control), and motivation. Although they reported limited support for the effects of ability and personality variables on transfer, in recent years support has been found for cognitive ability and several personality variables. For example, cognitive ability is reported to be the strongest predictor of transfer (Blume et al., 2010; Burke, Hutchins, & Saks, 2013). The problem with cognitive ability and personality traits, however, is that they are not susceptible to change. Furthermore, cognitive ability and personality are often used to make selection decisions, which means that by the time a newcomer begins his/her socialization, cognitive ability and personality have already been taken into account. Therefore, for the purpose of the transfer of socialization, I will focus on newcomer characteristics from the transfer literature that are susceptible to influence and change.

There are a number of trainee characteristics that predict transfer and are susceptible to change. For example, Baldwin and Ford (1988) noted that both motivation to learn and motivation to transfer have been found to predict transfer of training as well as other training outcomes. Motivation to learn refers to the direction, intensity, and persistence of learning-directed behavior in training contexts (Colquitt, Lepine, & Noe, 2000). Motivation to transfer refers to efforts to apply skills and knowledge learned in training to the work situation (Burke, Hutchins, & Saks, 2013). Motivation to learn and motivation to transfer have been found to be related to learning outcomes as well as transfer (Burke & Hutchins, 2007; Burke, Hutchins, & Saks, 2013; Colquitt, LePine, & Noe, 2000). Both of these variables might also be important for newcomer learning and socialization transfer. That is, newcomers who have a higher motivation to learn and motivation to transfer would be expected to learn more of the socialization content and to use and apply what they learn on the job. Thus, just as motivation is a key driver of training effectiveness (Salas, Weaver, & Shuffler, 2012), it is very likely to also be a driver of socialization transfer and success.

Self-efficacy refers to an individual's belief that he/she can successfully perform a task and it has been found to be a strong predictor of learning outcomes and transfer of training (Burke & Hutchins, 2007; Colquitt, LePine, & Noe, 2000; Grossman & Salas, 2011; Salas, Weaver, & Shuffler, 2012). Self-efficacy has also received considerable attention in the socialization literature. As indicated earlier, self-efficacy has been found to be positively related to socialization outcomes and to moderate and mediate the relationship between training and socialization outcomes (Gruman, Saks, & Zweig, 2006; Saks, 1995a). Self-efficacy has also been shown to mediate the relationship between socialization tactics (discussed in the next section) and socialization outcomes (Bauer et al., 2007). Therefore, it is expected that newcomers with higher self-efficacy will be more likely to learn, use, and apply socialization content.

Lastly, training utility or instrumentality, which refers to the extent to which trainees perceive training as useful for enhancing their jobs or careers, has also been found to predict transfer (Burke, Hutchins, & Saks, 2013). Trainees who perceive training as useful and valuable are more likely to apply what they learn in training on the job (Grossman & Salas, 2011). Similar to training utility, *socialization utility* can be defined as the extent to which newcomers perceive their socialization or orientation useful for helping them perform their role and job and in becoming an adjusted and effective member of the organization. Newcomers with higher socialization utility would be expected to learn more socialization content and to use and apply it to a greater extent on the job.

In summary, research on the transfer of training suggests that there are several characteristics of newcomers that are important for learning and socialization transfer and are susceptible to influence. In addition to self-efficacy, newcomers' motivation to learn, motivation to transfer, and perceptions of the utility of socialization are expected to predict newcomer learning and the transfer of socialization.

Socialization design

In the transfer of training literature, training design factors include various learning principles and conditions of practice. Baldwin and Ford (1988) described four such learning principles: identical elements, general principles, stimulus variability, and conditions of practice.

Identical elements involve designing training programs so that the stimulus and response elements in the training setting and the work environment are the same. In effect, identical elements refers to physical and psychological fidelity of training programs and helps to create realistic training environments that contribute to transfer of training (Grossman & Salas, 2011). General principles involve instructing trainees on the general rules and theoretical principles that underlie training content. Stimulus variability involves providing trainees with a variety of relevant stimuli, examples, and experiences during training (Baldwin & Ford, 1988).

Conditions of practice refer to a number of design principles such as massed or distributed training (providing all of the training material in one sitting or breaking it up with rest periods), whole or part training (providing instruction on the entire task at once or breaking it up into sub-tasks), feedback or knowledge of results (providing trainees with information about their performance), and overlearning (continued practice even after trainees have successfully mastered a task). In general, research has found that learning principles have a positive effect on learning, retention, and transfer (Baldwin & Ford, 1988; Kraiger, 2003). Including feedback in the design of training programs is considered to be an especially crucial step for facilitating transfer (Salas, Weaver, & Shuffler, 2012). Several studies have found that receiving feedback regarding one's performance following a training program is positively related to perceptions of training transfer (Van den Bossche, Segers, & Jansen, 2010; Velada et al., 2007).

In addition to the above conditions of practice, there are also prepractice conditions that can be implemented before training such as attentional advice, metacognitive strategies, advance organizers, goal orientation, preparatory information, and prepractice briefs (Cannon-Bowers et al., 1998). Attentional advice refers to providing trainees with information about the task process and general task strategies that can help them learn to perform a task. Metacognitive strategies refer to ways in which trainees can be instructed to self-regulate their learning of a task. Advance organizers are structures or frameworks that can help trainees assimilate and integrate training content. Goal orientation refers to the type of goal that is set during training (e.g., learning goal, performance goal). Preparatory information involves providing trainees with information about what to expect during training and practice sessions. Prepractice briefs are used for team training to help team members establish their roles and responsibilities and performance expectations prior to a team practice session. In general, prepractice conditions have been found to have positive effects on cognitive learning, skill-based learning, and affective learning. With respect to goals, research has found that any pretraining goal is more effective than no goal at all (Mesmer-Magnus & Viswesvaran, 2010).

In addition to learning principles, other training design factors have been found to predict transfer such as behavioral modeling training and post-training interventions such as goal setting and relapse prevention (Burke, Hutchins, & Saks, 2013). Behavioral modeling training has been found to be most strongly related to transfer when models display positive and negative behaviors, trainees set goals, trainees' superiors are trained, and when rewards and sanctions are used (Taylor, Russ-Eft, & Chan, 2005). Behavior modeling is reported to be one of the best methods for transfer of training (Grossman & Salas, 2011).

Although all of these design factors and learning principles are well established in the training literature, they have seldom if ever been considered in the socialization literature. In fact, socialization research has rarely considered the design of socialization programs. As indicated earlier, research on orientation and training simply asks newcomers if they received or attended orientation and training programs or the amount of training they received. Among the various learning principles, only feedback has received some attention in socialization research. Several studies have found that feedback is positively related to socialization outcomes such as job satisfaction and organizational commitment (Colarelli, Dean, & Konstans, 1987). Saks (1995b) found that feedback from co-workers, senior co-workers, and one's manager was positively related to organizational commitment in a sample of entry-level accountants in public accounting firms. Feedback from senior co-workers and the manager was negatively related to intention to quit the organization, and positively related to job performance.

More recently, Li et al. (2011) found that newcomers who received developmental feedback (information that is helpful and useful and enables newcomers to learn, develop, and make improvements on the job) from their supervisor and co-workers exhibited more helping behavior. In addition, supervisor developmental feedback was positively related to newcomer task performance when co-worker developmental feedback was also high.

In addition to feedback, socialization tactics, which have received a considerable amount of attention in the socialization literature, can also be considered design factors since they have to do with the structure of the socialization process or that which Van Maanen and Schein

(1979) refer to as the "structural side" of organizational socialization. Socialization tactics refer to "the ways in which the experiences of individuals in transition from one role to another are structured for them by others in the organization" (Van Maanen & Schein, 1979, p. 230). As indicated by Van Maanen and Schein (1979), socialization tactics can be chosen to achieve particular outcomes as each tactic represents particular events that can influence how a newcomer will respond and perform in their new role and whether they will engage in innovative or custodial role behaviors. Thus, organizations can decide on the most appropriate set of socialization tactics to use in order to obtain the desired response and behaviors from newcomers.

Van Maanen and Schein (1979) identified six socialization tactics dimensions. Each tactical dimension exists on a bipolar continuum with considerable range between the two poles. The six dimensions are: collective–individual, formal–informal, sequential–random, fixed–variable, serial–disjunctive, and investiture–divestiture.

Collective socialization refers to grouping newcomers and putting them through a common set of experiences together. *Individual* socialization involves isolating newcomers from one another and putting them through more or less unique sets of experiences. *Formal* socialization involves segregating newcomers from regular organizational members and putting them through a set of experiences tailored for newcomers. *Informal* socialization does not clearly distinguish a newcomer from more experienced members and learning occurs on-the-job through trial and error. *Sequential* socialization involves a fixed sequence of discrete and identifiable steps leading to the assumption of the role. *Random* socialization involves a number of steps that is ambiguous, unknown, or continually changing. *Fixed* socialization provides a timetable for the steps involved in the assumption of the role and precise knowledge of the time it will take to complete a given passage, which is communicated to newcomers. *Variable* socialization does not provide information about the time it will take to assume the new role. *Serial* socialization involves having experienced members of the organization socialize newcomers and serve as role models. *Disjunctive* socialization does not provide newcomers with experienced role models to show them how to proceed in their new role. Finally, *investiture* socialization confirms the incoming identity and personal characteristics of newcomers. *Divestiture* socialization disconfirms, denies, and strips away newcomers' identity and personal characteristics (Jones, 1986; Van Maanen & Schein, 1979).

Jones (1986) conducted the first empirical study to investigate the relationship between socialization tactics and newcomer adjustment. He organized Van Maanen and Schein's (1979) six socialization tactics into two dimensions. The first dimension he called *institutionalized socialization*, which consists of the collective, formal, sequential, fixed, serial, and investiture tactics. These tactics encourage newcomers to passively accept preset roles and to reproduce the organizational status quo. Institutionalized tactics provide newcomers with information that reduces their uncertainty and reflects a structured and formalized socialization process. The second dimension, which is at the opposite end of the socialization continuum, is individualized tactics that consist of the individual, informal, random, variable, disjunctive, and divestiture tactics. Individualized tactics encourage newcomers to question the status quo and to develop their own unique approach to their roles. Individualized socialization tactics are lacking structure and newcomers are socialized more by default than design (Ashforth, Saks, & Lee, 1998).

Jones (1986) also categorized the tactics into three broad factors: social, content, and context. *Social* tactics consist of the serial–disjunctive and investiture–divestiture dimensions. They are considered to be the most important tactics for newcomers' socialization because they provide social cues and direction that is informative and helpful for learning. The *content* tactics have to do with the content of the information given to newcomers and consist of the sequential–random and fixed–variable dimensions. The *context* tactics have to do with the way in which organizations provide information to newcomers and consist of the collective–individual and formal–informal dimensions.

Institutionalized socialization tactics are believed to have a number of positive effects on newcomers for several reasons. First, institutionalized socialization tactics provide newcomers with information that reduces their uncertainty about the entry-socialization process by providing them with a consistent message about the organization's values and how they should respond to situations (Cable, Gino, & Staats, 2013). Thus, uncertainty reduction theory has often been used to explain the relationship between socialization tactics and newcomer adjustment (Saks, Uggerslev, & Fassina, 2007). Second, institutionalized socialization tactics provide newcomers with greater accessibility to social capital and more frequent interactions and communication with insiders allows them to obtain social resources (e.g., information) that facilitate adjustment and socialization (Fang, Duffy, & Shaw, 2011). And third, there is some evidence that institutionalized socialization tactics send signals to newcomers about how they will be treated in the organization and this leads to increased trust. In other words, trust mediates the relationship between institutionalized socialization tactics and newcomer adjustment (Scott, Montes, & Irving, 2012).

In his study of recent MBA (master of business administration) graduates, Jones (1986) found that institutionalized socialization tactics were negatively related to role ambiguity, role conflict, and intention to quit, and positively related to job satisfaction, organizational commitment, and a custodial role orientation. Self-efficacy moderated the relationship between socialization tactics and role orientation such that institutionalized socialization tactics were more strongly related to a custodial role orientation for newcomers with low self-efficacy. The social tactics were the most strongly related to the outcomes followed by the content tactics and then the context tactics.

Since Jones' (1986) study, there have been over two dozen studies on socialization tactics making this the most researched topic in the socialization literature. Two meta-analyses found that institutionalized socialization tactics are negatively related to role ambiguity, role conflict, and intentions to quit, and positively related to fit perceptions, self-efficacy, social acceptance, job satisfaction, organizational commitment, job performance, and a custodial role orientation (Bauer et al., 2007; Saks, Uggerslev, & Fassina, 2007). Some socialization tactics (i.e., divestiture) have also been found to be positively related to ethical conflict, which is related to higher emotional exhaustion and lower career fulfillment (Kammeyer-Mueller, Simon, & Rich, 2012). Overall, the social tactics have been found to be the most strongly related to socialization outcomes while the weakest relationships were found for the context tactics (Bauer et al., 2007; Saks, Uggerslev, & Fassina, 2007).

Both meta-analyses found that socialization tactics lead to traditional socialization outcomes (e.g., job satisfaction) through more proximal outcomes (e.g., fit perceptions). Furthermore, consistent with the linkage in Figure 5.1, institutionalized socialization tactics have also been found to be positively related to newcomer learning (Ashforth, Sluss, & Saks, 2007). Thus, it would seem that institutionalized socialization tactics are most likely to result in newcomer learning and socialization transfer.

In summary, although socialization research has paid little attention to design factors other than feedback and socialization tactics, the transfer of training literature has identified numerous learning principles and conditions of practice that are important for transfer of training and might also be important for transfer of socialization. Therefore as shown in Figure 5.1, learning principles such as identical elements, general principles, and stimulus variability as well as the conditions of practice are expected to increase the likelihood that newcomers will learn socialization content and use and apply it on the job. The learning principles as well as the conditions of practice can easily be incorporated into existing orientation and training programs. While it may not be necessary or practical to use all of the conditions of practice, it would seem that some should always be considered when designing socialization programs (e.g., attentional advice, metacognitive strategies, advance organizers, preparatory information, and feedback). In addition, more attention should be given to the use of different training methods with particular emphasis on behavioral modeling, which can also improve newcomer learning and socialization transfer.

Work environment

Factors in the work environment have been found to be among the strongest predictors of the transfer of training (Blume et al., 2010). Baldwin and Ford (1988) included support and opportunity to use newly acquired knowledge and skills as work environment characteristics in their model and cited research in which favorable and supportive climates were most likely to result in transfer. They described supervisory support for training as a key work environment variable that affects the transfer process.

Research on the transfer of training has continued to show that both supervisor and peer support have a strong and significant effect on whether or not trainees use their newly acquired knowledge and skills on the job (Cromwell & Kolb, 2004; Grossman & Salas, 2011). In their meta-analysis of the predictors of transfer, Blume et al. (2010) found that supervisor and peer support were among the strongest predictors of transfer. In their review of best practices in training transfer, Burke, Hutchins, and Saks (2013) commented that peer and manager support play a critical role in the successful use of new learning on the job. Furthermore, training professionals identified supervisory support activities as the top-ranked best practice for training transfer (Burke & Hutchins, 2008).

The lack of opportunities to use and practice new skills on the job has consistently been found to be one of the strongest impediments to successful transfer and is considered to be one of the strongest barriers to transfer (Burke, Hutchins, & Saks, 2013; Grossman & Salas, 2011). Thus, it is recommended that the delay between training and application on the job be minimized and that trainees be provided with resources and opportunities to apply their new skills and abilities (Grossman & Salas, 2011). The opportunity to perform has also been ranked by training professionals as one of the best practices for transfer of training (Burke & Hutchins, 2008). Thus, practice is a key factor for successful transfer and performance (Salas, Weaver, & Shuffler, 2012).

Since Baldwin and Ford's (1988) review, a number of other work environment factors have been shown to be important for transfer. One of the most important work environment factors to emerge is the transfer of training climate (Salas, Weaver, & Shuffler, 2012). Transfer of training climate refers to characteristics of the work environment that can facilitate or inhibit the application of learning on the job (Rouiller & Goldstein, 1993). The characteristics of a transfer climate include situational cues such as goals, support, and opportunity to practice, and consequences such as positive and negative feedback. Among the factors in the work environment, the transfer climate has been found to be one of the strongest predictors of transfer (Blume et al., 2010) making it one of the most critical factors for the application and maintenance of learning and new skills on the job (Grossman & Salas, 2011).

Given that the work environment is so critical for trainees to apply their learning on the job and in fact determines whether or not they will exhibit learned behaviors on the job following training (Grossman & Salas, 2011), it seems very likely that the work environment will also play a critical role for newcomer learning and the transfer of socialization. In fact, in the socialization literature social support has received a considerable amount of research attention.

According to Feldman (1989), "A great deal of what new recruits learn is learned through informal interactions with peers, supervisors, and mentors outside the context of formal training" and these informal interactions "play an important role in filling the gaps left by formal training and orientation" (p. 386).

Social support has long been considered a critical factor for the socialization of newcomers (Fisher, 1985; Katz, 1980). Lundberg and Young (1997) found that the critical events newcomers reported most frequently involved supportiveness and caring from co-workers and managers. In one of the earliest studies on social support, Fisher (1985) investigated social support from co-workers and supervisors in facilitating the adjustment of newly graduated nurses working in hospitals. She conceptualized social support as "the number and quality of friendships or caring relationships which provide either emotional reassurance, needed information, or instrumental aid in dealing with stressful situations" (p. 40). Fisher (1985) found that social support from co-workers and the immediate supervisor was negatively related to unmet expectations, stress, turnover intentions, and turnover and positively related to adjustment (i.e., job satisfaction, performance, organizational commitment).

Bauer and Green (1998) found that supportive behavior on the part of managers is important for newcomers' socialization. In particular, manager clarifying behavior was positively related to role clarity and performance efficacy, and manager supporting behavior was positively related to feelings of acceptance by the manager. The relationship between manager behavior and socialization outcomes was mediated by newcomer accommodation.

In a study on supervisor support, Jokisaari and Nurmi (2009) found that newcomers perceived supervisor support declined 6–21 months following organizational entry and resulted in a decrease in role clarity and job satisfaction, and a slower increase in salary. Perceived supervisor support was positively related to initial work mastery and it did not decrease with a decline in perceived supervisor support.

Organizational members that aid newcomers or "socialization agents" provide support to newcomers by providing them with information. Ostroff and Kozlowksi (1992) found that newcomers relied primarily on observation of others followed by interpersonal sources (i.e., supervisors and co-workers) to acquire information and obtaining more information was positively related to job satisfaction and organizational commitment and negatively related to stress and turnover intentions. Klein, Fan, and Preacher (2006) found that newcomers who perceived socialization agents (senior co-workers, supervisors, and administrative assistants) as more helpful for learning about important information had higher affective organizational commitment, job satisfaction, and role clarity and these relationships were mediated by learning socialization content.

Social support can also be provided by organizational members who are formally assigned to mentor newcomers or assume the role of a buddy. For example, Chatman (1991) found that spending time with a mentor was positively related to newcomers' person-organization fit. Ostroff and Kozlowski (1993) found that newcomers who had mentors used them to learn about the organization and their role rather than their task and work group. They learned more about organizational issues and practices than those without a mentor. Newcomers without mentors used co-workers more as a source of information.

Allen, McManus, and Russell (1999) investigated formal peer mentoring in which first-year MBA students were formally assigned a second-year MBA peer mentor. They found that both the psychosocial and career-related mentoring functions were related to overall socialization content. In particular, psychosocial mentoring was related to politics and performance proficiency, and career-related mentoring was related to people socialization content. Both mentoring functions were positively related to protégé beliefs that their mentors helped them reduce and cope with their work-related stress.

Finally, Rollag, Parise, and Cross (2005) found that newcomers who had a "buddy" adjusted more quickly compared to new hires who did not have a "buddy." Further, they found that buddies are more important than mentors and suggest that managers be proactive in helping new hires develop a relationship with at least one co-worker. Having a buddy not only facilitates learning but it also helps newcomers establish relationships with other co-workers (Rollag, Parise, & Cross, 2005). Korte (2009, 2010) also found that building high-quality relationships with co-workers is critical for newcomer learning and adjustment.

Besides social support, other work environment factors are also likely to facilitate socialization learning and transfer. For example, providing newcomers with opportunities to use and practice their learning on the job should be as important for socialization transfer as it is for training transfer. Thus, newcomers should be given time to practice their learning as soon as possible following orientation and training programs. Newcomers who are provided more time to practice using their newly acquired knowledge and skills are more likely to transfer their learning on the job.

Finally, given the importance of the transfer climate for transfer of training (Salas, Weaver, & Shuffler, 2012), a climate for socialization transfer should also be important for socialization transfer. A *socialization transfer climate* can be defined as characteristics in the work environment that can facilitate or inhibit the use and application of socialization learning on the job. Like a transfer of training climate, a socialization transfer climate should consist of cues that remind newcomers to apply what they have learned on the job. They should also be provided with positive consequences such as positive feedback, rewards, and recognition and continuous supervisor and peer support. A positive socialization transfer climate is likely to result in greater learning and transfer of socialization.

Future Research

In the previous section of this chapter, I introduced the construct of the transfer of socialization and described a model of the transfer of socialization process. This opens up many new avenues for future socialization research. An important first step is to develop a measure of transfer of socialization. Most measures of socialization content ask newcomers what they know or understand about each content domain (e.g., Haueter, Macan, & Winter, 2003). Transfer of socialization measures should focus on what newcomers do or the extent to which they have used and applied their learning in each domain on the job. Furthermore, just as the measurement of socialization learning focuses on specific learning or content dimensions, so should a measure of transfer of socialization. As shown in Figure 5.1, it is important to measure the extent to which newcomers have applied what they learned about their task, role, work group, and organization on the job and have done so over a period of time. Thus, transfer of socialization should be measured in each learning domain several times throughout the socialization process in order to measure both the generalization and maintenance of socialization transfer across the four learning content domains.

A second area of research is to examine the relationship between socialization learning and transfer of socialization and to relate both to proximal and distal socialization outcomes. Although I have not included socialization outcomes in the model, it is important to realize that most models of organizational socialization link socialization practices to proximal and distal socialization outcomes and proximal outcomes have been found to mediate the relationship between socialization practices and distal socialization outcomes (Bauer et al., 2007; Saks, Uggerslev, & Fassina, 2007).

Furthermore, learning is believed to precede proximal outcomes. For example, in Saks and Ashforth's (1997) multilevel process model of organizational socialization, socialization factors influence learning and learning results in proximal outcomes (e.g., role clarity), which then leads to distal outcomes. Similarly, Klein and Heuser's (2008) framework of the socialization literature links three socialization practices (organizational tactics and practices, socialization agents, and newcomer proactivity) to learning outcomes, which then lead to proximal outcomes (e.g., role clarity) and then to distal outcomes (e.g., job satisfaction). Therefore, future research should investigate the extent to which transfer of socialization mediates the relationships between learning and proximal and distal socialization outcomes. Given the closer proximity of socialization transfer to socialization outcomes, I would predict that the transfer of socialization is a stronger predictor of both proximal and distal socialization outcomes than is learning and that proximal outcomes will mediate the relationship between socialization transfer and distal socialization outcomes such as job satisfaction, organizational commitment, job performance, and turnover.

Future research is also needed on the social support provided to newcomers, which has not been well developed with respect to the nature and type of support. The literature on the transfer of training provides some suggestions. For example, Baldwin and Ford (1988) describe how supervisory support is a multidimensional construct that can include encouragement, goal setting, reinforcement, and modeling of behaviors. These are all important for socialization and have received limited attention.

Future research should refine measures of supervisor and peer support and investigate various support behaviors such as encouragement, goal setting, recognition, reinforcement, positive feedback, information, rewards, coaching, providing resources, and so on. Thus, while providing support to newcomers should facilitate learning and socialization transfer, there is much to learn about what types of support are most important for newcomer learning and transfer of socialization throughout the socialization process.

A final area of research is to investigate the linkages in Figure 5.1 between the input factors, the output factors, and the transfer of socialization. Most of the variables in the model are new to the socialization literature and have never been studied. This is particularly the case for all of the newcomer characteristics except for self-efficacy; all of the socialization design factors except for feedback and socialization tactics; and all of the work environment factors except for social support. While these variables have been found to be important for learning and the transfer of training, we do not know to what extent they will predict socialization learning and transfer. Furthermore, it is possible that some of these variables will be more important for particular dimensions of socialization learning and transfer. Thus, it would be important to know what input factors best predict each domain of socialization learning and transfer.

The transfer of a socialization model has several important implications for practice. First, it alerts organizations to the fact that learning is not enough for newcomers to become socialized and effective and contributing members of an organization. That is, they need to be able to use and apply what they learn on the job to be successful and effective members of an organization. Therefore, organizations must do more than just provide newcomers with information. They can't assume that newcomers will use and apply their new knowledge and skills acquired through orientation and training programs. Thus, the model alerts organizations to the importance of providing additional programs to help newcomers use and apply what they have learned on the job. In other words, as is the case with the transfer of training, newcomer learning is a necessary but not sufficient condition for the transfer of socialization.

Second, the model indicates the importance of three types of input factors for newcomer learning and socialization transfer. Although this has been evident in the training transfer literature for decades, this has not been the case in the socialization literature. Thus, organizations should focus on newcomer characteristics, the design of socialization programs, and work environment characteristics during the socialization process. Organizations should consider the input factors in each category every time they socialize new hires and plan a strategy that includes all of the input factors.

Third, the model offers clear guidelines as to what organizations can do to improve newcomer learning and socialization transfer. Furthermore, all of the socialization input variables are susceptible to influence. For example, organizations can and should strengthen newcomers' self-efficacy and increase their motivation to learn and transfer and increase their perceived utility of the organization's socialization practices and programs. McNatt and Judge (2008) provide a good example of how a self-efficacy intervention that involved an interview and written communications can be used to increase the self-efficacy of newcomers. Similar interventions can be used to increase motivation to learn and transfer as well as the perceived utility of socialization.

The model also provides numerous ways that socialization programs can be designed to be more effective by incorporating learning principles such as stimulus variability, pre-socialization conditions of practice (e.g., advance organizers, goals), conditions of practice during socialization (e.g., feedback), and the use of behavioral modeling training. These design factors are easy to implement and they have been shown to be effective for learning and transfer in the training literature.

Finally, the model highlights the importance of the work environment for newcomer learning and socialization transfer. Organizations need to ensure that newcomers are provided with support from their supervisors and peers, and that supervisors provide newcomers with opportunities to use and apply their new knowledge and skills on the job soon after they have acquired them. And perhaps most importantly, organizations need to create a positive socialization transfer climate in which newcomers are reminded and encouraged to use and apply what they have learned during their socialization on the job and receive positive consequences for doing so.

Conclusion

In this chapter, I have reviewed the research and literature on organizational socialization and the transfer of training and described how socialization research and practice can benefit from research on the transfer of training. The main implication from the transfer of training literature is that research on organizational socialization should not only focus on what newcomers learn but also on newcomers' application of what they learn on the job or what I have called the transfer of socialization. This represents a shift from an exclusive focus on socialization learning to the application of that learning on the job. This extends and improves our understanding of the socialization process and offers many new directions for socialization research and practice.

Similar to the transfer of training, socialization transfer refers to the extent to which newcomers apply and use what they learn during the socialization process in the work environment. To date, socialization research has simply measured newcomer learning and has not considered whether or not that learning is used on the job.

To understand better how to facilitate the transfer of socialization, I described a model of the transfer of socialization based on Baldwin and Ford's (1988) model of the transfer of training process. This model provides a meaningful way to understand and integrate the socialization literature, which has for decades been described as fragmented (Chao, 2012; Saks & Ashforth, 1997). The three input factors can incorporate all types of socialization variables whether they are characteristics of newcomers, design factors, or work environment characteristics. As a result, it serves as an integrative model of organizational socialization that is more complete than existing models that include only a few socialization variables (e.g., Ashforth, Sluss, & Harrison, 2007). Thus, the transfer of socialization model represents a new framework for understanding and studying organizational socialization. It is particularly noteworthy that it offers many new potential predictors of newcomer learning given calls for more research on the antecedents of newcomer learning (Ashforth, Sluss, & Harrison, 2007).

Finally, I am going to go out on a limb and suggest that the transfer of socialization is perhaps the most important and meaningful outcome of organizational socialization. To be sure, most indicators of newcomer adjustment and socialization are not consistent with the definition and meaning of organizational socialization. Rather, they tend to be work-related attitudes and behaviors such as job satisfaction and turnover. If organizational socialization is really all about learning, then like training, the most important and meaningful indicator of a successful socialization is the use and application of that learning on the job or the transfer of socialization. Socialization research has for decades measured learning without any regard as to whether or not newcomers actually use and apply that learning on the job. It is my contention that transfer of socialization will precede and predict proximal socialization outcomes (e.g., task mastery, social integration) and the more traditional distal socialization outcomes (e.g., job satisfaction, organizational commitment), and that relationships between socialization learning and proximal and distal socialization outcomes will be mediated by the transfer of socialization.

In conclusion, this chapter has suggested a new approach to the study and practice of organizational socialization that shifts the emphasis away from learning to the application of learning and transfer of socialization. It follows then that the often-used phrase that refers to organizational socialization as learning "the ropes," might now be revised to learning and *using* the ropes.

References

Allen, T. D., McManus, S. E., & Russell, J. E. A. (1999). Newcomer socialization and stress: Formal peer relationships as a source of support. *Journal of Vocational Behavior*, 54, 453–470.

Arthur, W. A., Jr., Bennett, W., Jr., Edens, P. S., & Bell, S. T. (2003). Effectiveness of training in organizations. *Journal of Applied Psychology*, 88, 234–245.

Ashforth, B. E., Saks, A. M., & Lee, R. T. (1998). Socialization and newcomer adjustment: The role of organizational context. *Human Relations*, 51, 897–926.

Ashforth, B. E., Sluss, D. M., & Harrison, S. H. (2007). Socialization in organizational contexts. In G. P. Hodgkinson & J. K. Ford (Eds.), *International Review of Industrial and Organizational Psychology* (vol. 22, pp. 1–70). Chichester: John Wiley & Sons Ltd.

Ashforth, B. E., Sluss, D. M., & Saks, A. M. (2007). Socialization tactics, proactive behavior, and newcomer learning: Integrating socialization models. *Journal of Vocational Behavior*, 70, 447–462.

Baldwin, T. T., & Ford, K. J. (1988). Transfer of training: A review and directions for future research. *Personnel Psychology*, 41, 63–105.

Bauer, T. N., Bodner, T., Erdogan, B., Truxillo, D. M., & Tucker, J. S. (2007). Newcomer adjustment during organizational socialization: A meta-analytic review of antecedents, outcomes, and methods. *Journal of Applied Psychology*, 92, 707–721.

Bauer, T. N., & Green, S. G. (1998). Testing the combined effects of newcomer information seeking and manager behavior on socialization. *Journal of Applied Psychology*, 83, 72–83.

Blume, B. D., Ford, J. K., Baldwin, T. T., & Huang, J. L. (2010). Transfer of training: A meta-analytic review. *Journal of Management*, 36, 1065–1105.

Brown, K. G., & Sitzmann, T. (2011). Training and employee development for improved performance. In S. Zedeck (Ed.), *Handbook of Industrial and Organizational Psychology* (vol. 2, pp. 469–503). Washington, DC: American Psychological Association.

Burke, L. A., & Hutchins, H. M. (2007). Training transfer: An integrative literature review. *Human Resource Development Review*, 6, 263–296.

Burke, L. A., & Hutchins, H. M. (2008). A study of best practices in training transfer and proposed model of transfer. *Human Resource Development Quarterly*, 19, 107–128.

Burke, L. A., Hutchins, H., & Saks, A. (2013). Best practices in training transfer. In M. Paludi (Ed.), *The Psychology for Business Success* (vol. 3, pp. 115–132). Santa Barbara, CA: Praeger.

Cable, D. M., Gino, F., & Staats, B. R. (2013). Breaking them in or eliciting their best? Reframing socialization around newcomers' authentic self-expression. *Administrative Science Quarterly*, 58, 1–36.

Cannon-Bowers, J. A., Rhodenizer, L., Salas, E., & Bowers, C. A. (1998). A framework for understanding pre-practice conditions and their impact on learning. *Personnel Psychology*, 51, 291–320.

Chan, D., & Schmitt, N. (2000). Interindividual differences in intraindividual changes in proactivity during organizational entry: A latent growth modeling approach to understanding newcomer adaptation. *Journal of Applied Psychology*, 85, 190–210.

Chao, G. T. (2012). Organizational socialization: Background, basics, and a blueprint for adjustment at work. In S. W. J. Kozlowski (Ed.), *The Oxford Handbook of Organizational Psychology* (vol. 1, pp. 579–614). New York: Oxford University Press.

Chao, G. T., O'Leary-Kelly, A. M., Wolf, S., Klein, H. J., & Gardner, P. D. (1994). Organizational socialization: Its content and consequences. *Journal of Applied Psychology*, 79, 730–743.

Chatman, J. A. (1991). Matching people and organizations: Selection and socialization in public accounting firms. *Administrative Science Quarterly*, 36, 459–484.

Colarelli, S. M., Dean, R. A., & Konstans, C. (1987). Comparative effects of personal and situational influences on job outcomes of new professionals. *Journal of Applied Psychology*, 72, 558–566.

Colquitt, J. A., LePine, J. A., & Noe, R. A. (2000). Toward an integrative theory of training motivation: A meta-analytic path analysis of 20 years of research. *Journal of Applied Psychology*, 85, 678–707.

Cooper-Thomas, H., & Anderson, N. (2002). Newcomer adjustment: The relationship between organizational socialization tactics, information acquisition and attitudes. *Journal of Occupational and Organizational Psychology*, 75, 423–437.

Cooper-Thomas, H., & Anderson, N. (2006). Organizational socialization: A new theoretical model and recommendations for future research and HRM practices in organizations. *Journal of Managerial Psychology*, 21, 492–516.

Cromwell, S. E., & Kolb, J. A. (2004). An examination of work-environment support factors affecting transfer of supervisory skills training to the workplace. *Human Resource Development Quarterly*, 15, 449–471.

Fan, J., Buckley, R., & Litchfield, R. C. (2012). Orientation programs that may facilitate newcomer adjustment: A literature review and future research agenda. In J. J. Martocchio, A. Joshi, and H. Liao (Eds.), *Research in Personnel and Human Resources Management* (vol. 31, pp. 87–143). Bingley: Emerald Group.

Fan, J., & Wanous, J. P. (2008). Organizational and cultural entry: A new type of orientation program for multiple boundary crossings. *Journal of Applied Psychology*, 93, 1390–1400.

Fang, R., Duffy, M. K., & Shaw, J. D. (2011). The organizational socialization process: Review and development of a social capital model. *Journal of Management*, 37, 127–152.

Feldman, D. C. (1989). Socialization, resocialization, and training: Reframing the research agenda. In I. L. Goldstein (Ed.), *Training and Development in Organizations* (pp. 376–416). San Francisco: Jossey-Bass.

Fisher, C. D. (1985). Social support and adjustment to work: A longitudinal study. *Journal of Management*, 11, 39–53.

Fisher, C. D. (1986). Organizational socialization: An integrative review. In K. M. Rowland & G. R. Ferris (Eds.), *Research in Personnel and Human Resources Management* (vol. 4, pp. 101–145). Greenwich, CT: JAI Press.

Gomersall, E. R., & Myers, M. S. (1966). Breakthrough in on-the-job training. *Harvard Business Review*, 44, 62–72.

Grossman, R., & Salas, E. (2011). The transfer of training: What really matters. *International Journal of Training and Development*, 15, 103–120.

Gruman, J. A., & Saks, A. M. (2011). Socialization preferences and intentions: Does one size fit all? *Journal of Vocational Behavior*, 79, 419–427.

Gruman, J. A., Saks, A. M., & Zweig, D. I. (2006). Organizational socialization tactics and newcomer proactive behaviors: An integrative study. *Journal of Vocational Behavior*, 69, 90–104.

Haueter, J. A., Macan, T. H., & Winter, J. (2003). Measurement of newcomer socialization: Construct validation of a multidimensional scale. *Journal of Vocational Behavior*, 63, 20–39.

Jokisaari, M., & Nurmi, J.-E. (2009). Change in newcomers' supervisor support and socialization outcomes after organizational entry. *Academy of Management Journal*, 52, 527–544.

Jones, G. R. (1986). Socialization tactics, self-efficacy, and newcomers' adjustments to organizations. *Academy of Management Journal*, 29, 262–279.

Kammeyer-Mueller, J. D., Simon, L. S., & Rich, B. L. (2012). The psychic cost of doing wrong: Ethical conflict, divestiture socialization, and emotional exhaustion. *Journal of Management*, 38, 784–808.

Kammeyer-Mueller, J. D., & Wanberg, C. R. (2003). Unwrapping the organizational entry process: Disentangling multiple antecedents and their pathways to adjustment. *Journal of Applied Psychology*, 88, 779–794.

Katz, R. (1980). Time and work: Toward an integrative perspective. In B. Staw and L. L. Cummings (Eds.), *Research in Organizational Behavior* (vol. 2, pp. 81–127). Greenwich CT: JAI Press.

Klein, H. J., Fan, J., & Preacher, K. J. (2006). The effects of early socialization experiences on content mastery and outcomes: A meditational approach. *Journal of Vocational Behavior*, 68, 96–115.

Klein, H. J., & Heuser, A. E. (2008). The learning of socialization content: A framework for researching orientating practices. J. J. Martocchio (Ed.), *Research in Personnel and Human Resources Management* (vol. 27, pp. 279–336). Bingley: Emerald Group.

Klein, H. J., & Weaver, N. A. (2000). The effectiveness of an organizational-level orientation training program in the socialization of new hires. *Personnel Psychology*, 53, 47–66.

Korte, R. (2009). How newcomers learn the social norms of an organization: A case study of the socialization of newly hired engineers. *Human Resource Development Quarterly*, 20, 285–306.

Korte, R. (2010). "First get to know them": A relational view of organizational socialization. *Human Resource Development International*, 13, 27–43.

Kraiger, K. (2003). Perspectives on training and development. In W. C. Borman, D. R. Ilgen, & R. J. Klimoski (Eds.), *Handbook of Psychology: Industrial and Organizational Psychology* (pp. 171–192). Hoboken, NJ: John Wiley & Sons, Inc.

Li, N., Harris, T. B., Boswell, W. R., & Xie, Z. (2011). The role of organizational insiders' developmental feedback and proactive personality on newcomers' performance: An interactionist perspective. *Journal of Applied Psychology*, 96, 1317–1327.

Louis, M. R., Posner, B. Z., & Powell, G. N. (1983). The availability and helpfulness of socialization practices. *Personnel Psychology*, 36, 857–866.

Lundberg, C. C., & Young, C. A. (1997). Newcomer socialization: Critical incidents in hospitality organizations. *Journal of Hospitality & Tourism Research*, 21, 58–74.

McNatt, D. B., & Judge, T. A. (2008). Self-efficacy intervention, job attitudes, and turnover: A field experiment with employees in role transition. *Human Relations*, 61, 783–810.

Mesmer-Magnus, J., & Viswesvaran, C. (2010). The role of pre-training interventions in learning: A meta-analysis and integrative review. *Human Resource Management Review*, 20, 261–282.

Ostroff, C., & Kozlowski, S. W. J. (1992). Organizational socialization as a learning process: The role of information acquisition. *Personnel Psychology*, 45, 849–874.

Ostroff, C., & Kozlowski, S.W. J. (1993). The role of mentoring in the information gathering processes of newcomers during early organizational socialization. *Journal of Vocational Behavior*, 42, 170–183.

Rollag, K., Parise, S., & Cross, R. (2005). Getting new hires up to speed quickly. *MIT Sloan Management Review*, 46, 35–41.

Rouiller, J. Z., & Goldstein, I. L. (1993). The relationship between organizational transfer climate and positive transfer of training. *Human Resources Development Quarterly*, 4, 377–390.

Saks, A. M. (1994a). A psychological process investigation for the effects of recruitment source and organization information on job survival. *Journal of Organizational Behavior*, 15, 225–244.

Saks, A. M. (1994b). Moderating effects of self-efficacy for the relationship between training method and anxiety and stress reactions of newcomers. *Journal of Organizational Behavior*, 15, 639–654.

Saks, A. M. (1995a). Longitudinal field investigation of the moderating and mediating effects of self-efficacy on the relationship between training and newcomer adjustment. *Journal of Applied Psychology*, 80, 211–225.

Saks, A. M. (1995b). The relationship between job content and work outcomes for entry-level staff in public accounting firms. *Journal of Accounting & Business Research*, 3, 15–38.

Saks, A. M. (1996). The relationship between the amount and helpfulness of entry training and work outcomes. *Human Relations*, 49, 429–451.

Saks, A. M., & Ashforth, B. E. (1997). Organizational socialization: Making sense of the past and present as a prologue for the future. *Journal of Vocational Behavior*, 51, 234–279.

Saks, A. M., & Ashforth, B. E. (2000). The role of dispositions, entry stressors, and behavioral plasticity theory in predicting newcomers' adjustment to work. *Journal of Organizational Behavior*, 21, 43–62.

Saks, A. M., & Gruman, J. A. (2012). Getting newcomers on-board: A review of socialization practices and introduction to socialization resources theory. In C. Wanberg (Ed.), *The Oxford Handbook of Organizational Socialization* (pp. 27–55). New York: Oxford University Press.

Saks, A. M., Uggerslev, K. L., & Fassina, N. E. (2007). Socialization tactics and newcomer adjustment: A meta-analytic review and test of a model. *Journal of Vocational Behavior*, 70, 413–446.

Salas, E., Weaver, S. J., & Shuffler, M. L. (2012). Learning, training, and development in organizations. In S. W. J. Kozlowski (Ed.), *The Oxford Handbook of Organizational Psychology* (vol. 1, pp. 330–372). New York: Oxford University Press.

Scott, K. A., Montes, S. D., & Irving, P. G. (2012). Examining the impact of socialization through trust: An exploratory study. *Journal of Personnel Psychology*, 11, 191–198.

Sluss, D. M., Ashforth, B. E., & Gibson, K. R. (2012). The search for meaning in (new) work: Task significance and newcomer plasticity. *Journal of Vocational Behavior*, 81, 199–208.

Tannenbaum, S. I., Mathieu, J. E., Salas, E., & Cannon-Bowers, J. A. (1991). Meeting trainees' expectations: The influence of training fulfilment on the development of commitment, self-efficacy, and motivation. *Journal of Applied Psychology*, 76, 759–769.

Taylor, P. J., Russ-Eft, D. F., & Chan, D. W. L. (2005). A meta-analytic review of behavior modeling training. *Journal of Applied Psychology*, 90, 692–709.

Tharenou, P., Saks, A., & Moore, C. (2007). A review and critique of research on training and organizational-level outcomes. *Human Resource Management Review*, 17, 251–273.

Van den Bossche, P., Segers, M., & Jansen, N. (2010). Transfer of training: The role of feedback in supportive social networks. *International Journal of Training and Development*, 14, 81–94.

Van Maanen, J., & Schein, E. H. (1979). Toward a theory of organizational socialization, In B. M Staw (Ed.), *Research in Organizational Behavior* (vol. 1, pp. 209–264). Greenwich, CT: JAI Press.

Velada, R., Caetano, A., Michel, J. W., Lyons, B. D., & Kavanagh, M. M. (2007). The effects of training design, individual characteristics and work environment on transfer of training. *International Journal of Training and Development*, 11, 282–294.

Wanberg, C. R., & Kammeyer-Mueller, J. D. (2000). Predictors and outcomes of proactivity in the socialization process. *Journal of Applied Psychology*, 85(3), 373–385.

Wanous, J. P., & Reichers, A. E. (2000). New employee orientation programs. *Human Resource Management Review*, 10, 435–451.

Waung, M. (1995). The effects of self-regulatory coping orientation on newcomer adjustment and job survival. *Personnel Psychology*, 48, 633–650.

Weiss, H. M. (1977). Subordinate imitation of supervisor behavior: The role of modeling in organizational socialization. *Organizational Behavior and Human Performance*, 19, 89–105.

Weiss, H. M. (1978). Social learning of work values in organizations. *Journal of Applied Psychology*, 63, 711–718.

Wesson, M. J., & Gogus, C. I. (2005). Shaking hands with a computer: An examination of two methods of organizational newcomer orientation. *Journal of Applied Psychology*, 90, 1018–1026.

6

Encouraging Active Learning

Nina Keith and Christian Wolff

Introduction

Traditionally, trainees have been viewed as rather passive recipients of instruction, with the trainer structuring the learning experience. Active learning approaches, in contrast, view trainees as active participants of the learning process. Active learning has in part become popular due to technological developments that facilitate more active engagement of trainees (e.g., e-based training methodologies). Secondly, in modern workplaces – which are characterized by frequent change, uncertainty, and less hierarchy – responsibility for one's learning and development is more and more being shifted to the employees themselves. Apart from these practical reasons and necessities, there are also theoretical considerations and empirical evidence in support of active learning. Active learning approaches may lead to better transfer outcomes than traditional training approaches, particularly when the training goal involves adaptability of trained skills to novel tasks and requirements (i.e., adaptive transfer). At the same time, motivationally, active learning approaches may be more challenging, as trainees may be reluctant to take over responsibility for their own learning, and as learning may become subjectively more demanding.

This chapter explores active-learning approaches as well as benefits and challenges associated with their use in organizational training. We will begin with a discussion of the concept of active learning and an overview of various active-training interventions. Subsequently, we will discuss theory and findings regarding the effectiveness of active-learning approaches as well as cognitive, motivational, and emotional processes that may underlie their effectiveness. We will also present recent evidence on aptitude-treatment interactions (ATI), that is, interactions of training method and person characteristics (e.g., cognitive abilities, personality) that may inform us who benefits most – or least – from active learning. The chapter will close with a discussion of future research directions related to active learning in organizations, which includes research on informal active learning activities in organizations as well as their predictors and outcomes.

The Wiley Blackwell Handbook of the Psychology of Training, Development, and Performance Improvement,
First Edition. Edited by Kurt Kraiger, Jonathan Passmore, Sigmar Malvezzi, and Nuno Rebelo dos Santos.
© 2015 John Wiley & Sons Ltd. Published 2020 by John Wiley & Sons Ltd.

Conceptual Background: What is Active Learning?

Although active learning as a concept is becoming increasingly popular, there is no generally agreed use of the term "active learning." Active learning is usually described as an approach that ascribes the trainee an active role in the learning processes, for example, exploratory training in which trainees explore and experiment with the training tasks. Additionally, active learning is often contrasted with more traditional, more proceduralized, and more structured approaches that view trainees as rather passive recipients of instruction (Bell & Kozlowski, 2010; Keith & Frese, 2005). The lecture may be regarded a prototypical example for traditional instruction; another example is proceduralized training that is based on step-by-step guidance through the training material and tasks. While at first sight the definition of active learning and its differentiation from traditional instruction may appear to be clear cut, there remains some fuzziness about the concept. First, it is not clear what is meant by the term "active" or "activity" in active learning. For example, activity can imply *behavioral* (i.e., observable) activity by the trainees, that is, rather than listening to a one-way lecture or watching a trainer perform correct actions, trainees are required to do something during training themselves (e.g., individual experimentation with the task, a group exercise in class). Other conceptions of active learning focus on *cognitive* (i.e., not directly observable) activities of trainees during training. This conception becomes apparent in cognitive constructivism, which views any learning as active knowledge construction and construction of meaning (e.g., Bruner, 1966). According to this view, knowledge cannot be transmitted from some agent to another (e.g., from the trainer to trainees, from the teacher to students) but needs to be "actively built up" by some "mental activity of learners" (Driver et al., 1994, p. 5). In this chapter, we will primarily focus on active learning involving behavioral activity on part of the trainee – in particular, the activities of exploration and experimentation. We will further propose that cognitive activity – among other processes, such as motivational and emotional processes – function as an important mediator of the effectiveness of active-learning approaches.

Second, there are different conceptions about the setting in which active learning takes place. A useful distinction in this context is between formal and informal learning (Tannenbaum et al., 2010). *Formal learning* refers to planned learning that takes place in a formalized and systematic manner, for example, as part of a training program for employees of an organization. Formal learning activities are usually based on specified learning objectives (i.e., training goals) and have a predefined start and end. *Informal learning* in organizations, in contrast, refers to learning activities that do not have a clearly defined start and end point and that take place in an unsystematic und unstructured way, for example, by observing or asking more experienced colleagues at work or by performing a challenging and new work task (Sonnentag, Niessen, & Ohly, 2004; Tannenbaum et al., 2010). An example for active learning as part of formal training is a training method called error management training (Frese et al., 1991). Error management training is based on the assumption that errors are a natural part of the training processes and may be even useful in learning and mastering a task; trainees are therefore provided with only little structure by the trainer and are encouraged to make errors and learn from them as they explore and experiment with the training tasks (e.g., Heimbeck et al., 2003; Keith & Frese, 2005, 2008). An example of an approach that focuses on active learning as part of informal learning at work (i.e., outside formal training settings) is the job demand-control model by Karasek and Theorell, (1990). This model is much better known for its strain hypothesis, which predicts the development of strain as a reaction to high job demands and low job control. Its *active-learning hypothesis* proposes that high job demands in combination with high job control and support contribute to on-the-job learning and well-being at work (Daniels et al., 2009). Finally, *self-regulated learning* may be positioned somewhat inbetween formal and informal learning. Self-regulated learning implies that learners actively shape their learning experience as they use various cognitive and metacognitive strategies to control and regulate their learning (Zimmermann, 1990). Like formal learning, self-regulated learning is systematic and has a clearly defined goal; unlike formal learning, however, and more like informal learning, it may not have a clear starting and end point and it is not structured by a trainer or the organization but by the learning individual herself/himself.

Finally, a number of group learning approaches or, more specifically, cooperative learning methods are being discussed in educational psychology. These may be termed active learning because individuals actively engage in shaping the learning experience for themselves and for the group. Cooperative learning methods go beyond mere working in groups but assign individuals particular roles within the group. A classical and well-researched example is the jigsaw method (Aronson & Bridgeman, 1979). This method assigns every individual to become an expert on some part of the topic to be learned cooperatively. Experts of every group meet before going back to their groups and teaching their group mates about their area of expertise. Some of the more recent cooperative learning approaches incorporate technological developments (e.g., social interactions in the web, communication via mobile devices) to enhance group learning (e.g., Hsu & Ching, 2013).

Taken together, an array of approaches may be or have explicitly been termed active-learning approaches. While these approaches all have in common the view of the learner – be it the worker, trainee, or student in the classroom – as an active agent of the learning experience, there are considerable differences between these approaches in terms of the setting and type of learning activities. It is conceivable – although ultimately an empirical question – that these differences are paralleled by differences in the psychological processes that are elicited in learners and that may benefit learning. It is beyond the scope of this chapter, however, to provide an overview and integration of these diverse approaches of active learning. Rather, in line with the topic of this volume, we will focus on one class of active-learning approaches, namely, active learning as part of formalized organizational training. To signify this focus, in the remainder of this chapter we will use the more specific term "active *training*" instead of the broader term "active *learning*." The next section will describe in more detail the characteristics of active-training interventions that have been or can be used for training in organizations.

Designing Active Training: An Overview of Active-Training Interventions

All active training interventions engage learners with the training material in some way. Yet, there are considerable differences in how this active engagement of learners is achieved or, in other words, in the design of the training. In this section, we will first propose basic dimensions of active-training interventions. These dimensions describe characteristics of training design that all interventions share although the magnitude may differ (Table 6.1). Second, we will describe supplemental components of active-training interventions which some applications incorporate as an addition to the basic dimensions (Table 6.2).

Basic dimensions of active training interventions

Exploration and experimentation A major ingredient of active training is active exploration and experimentation by trainees during training. In active training, rather than receiving detailed step-by-step guidance about correct procedures as in traditional proceduralized training, participants actively explore the training material on their own. Error management training is an example of an active training intervention that extensively uses exploration during training. For example, in computer software training, participants receive only minimal information on the basic functions of the program and otherwise work independently on training tasks (Frese et al., 1991; Keith & Frese, 2005, 2008). Another way to implement experimentation is to have participants explore simulations. For example, in a study by Oliympiou, Zacharias, and deJong (2013) participants interacted with materials (e.g., a light source) and observed the outcomes of their actions (e.g., shadows or colored light). Finally, a number of studies have used a dynamic decision-making task in which trainees experimented with the task, developed strategies, and tested their effectiveness (Kozlowski et al., 2001).

Amount of information provided Active training interventions often provide only little task information. Rather, trainees are encouraged to explore and infer the information that is necessary to solve the training tasks. For example, in error management training only little information is given to trainees. In an early application of error management training (Frese et al., 1988) novices had to learn how to use a word-processing program without an introduction to the software and without access to a manual but only a list of possible commands. Participants were encouraged to develop and test hypotheses about which commands to use to solve the training tasks. Other studies provided more information to participants, although usually less information than is provided to trainees

Table 6.1 Basic dimensions of training design of active-learning interventions.

Dimension	Description	Typical
Exploration and experimentation	How knowledge is acquired, i.e., • by performing instrumental behavior such as exploration and experimentation	High; exploration and experimentation are core elements of active learning
Amount of information provided	How much information is provided to learners beyond exploration and experimentation	Low; information needs to be acquired through exploration and experimentation
Method of provision of information	How and when information is provided • prior to the active phase (instruction) • permanently during training (permanent access) • as an individualized evaluation of performance and strategy (feedback)	General information is provided at all times; step-by-step instructions are not available at all
Learner control	How much control learners have on the • sequence of tasks • elaboration of strategies • selection of actions	High; learners explore and experiment based on individual choice
Level of difficulty throughout the intervention	How difficult tasks are and whether difficulty changes throughout the training	High

in traditional guided training. Next, we will describe different ways of how and when such information may be provided during the course of training.

Methods of provision of information   In active training, information may be provided (a) prior to the practice phase (instruction), (b) it may be made permanently available during training (permanent access), or (c) it may be delivered in terms of individualized evaluation (feedback).

(a) Instruction. Active training interventions differ in the extent to which they provide pretraining instructions. For example, in a training that taught electronic search skills, participants received sufficient instructions to develop a basic skill level (e.g., overview of the electronic database, description of effective search strategies). An instructor then demonstrated adequate strategies (Wood et al., 2000). A number of studies have used a decision-making simulation called TANDEM (Weaver et al., 1995). These studies usually provided to participants a demonstration of the simulation, an operating manual, and a list of training objectives comprising skills and strategies (e.g., Bell & Kozlowski, 2002, 2008; Ford et al., 1998; Gully et al., 2002; Kanar & Bell, 2013; Kozlowski & Bell, 2006; Kozlowski et al., 2001).

(b) Permanent access. During the practice phase of active training, trainees usually explore and experiment on their own without access to additional task information. Applications of active training may differ in the extent to which they provide access to additional information during the practice phase. In the aforementioned example of early error management training (Frese et al., 1988), participants had access only to a list of commands in a computer software training. As another example, in some electronic search studies, participants received a summary sheet listing the steps of an adequate search strategy that they could use during practice (Debowski, Wood, & Bandura, 2001; Wood et al., 2000). Participants also had access to an online help facility that contained documentation of strategies and solutions. Additionally, a printed version was available on their desk (Debowski, Wood, & Bandura, 2001). In decision-making studies using TANDEM, learners had repeated access to the operating manual as a fixed part of the practice phase (Bell & Kozlowski, 2008).

(c) Feedback. Some training tasks may include task-generated feedback that enables trainees to judge their progress without external guidance. For example, in computer training using modern software packages, the user can usually observe visual changes on the screen that inform him or her whether the goal (e.g., inserting a table in a text) is achieved or not. Accordingly, in error management training of computer skills, no external feedback is provided (cf. Keith & Frese, 2008). In other cases, feedback provided by an external agent (e.g., the trainer) may be necessary. For example, in the aforementioned training of electronic search skills, participants received feedback about performance and strategy. Performance feedback was calculated as the percentage of correctly retrieved search records. Strategic feedback contained expert ratings of several dimensions of their search behavior, that is, breadth, depth, sequence of search, and thesaurus usage (Wood et al., 2000). In the studies mentioned above that used the decision-making simulation, trainees obtained feedback on several important aspects of the task, including basic and strategic performance, after each trial (e.g., Bell & Kozlowski, 2008).

Learner control   Learner control implies that learners are given the opportunity to make "choices in both what and how to learn" (Kraiger & Jerden, 2007, p. 65). These choices may involve aspects such as choice of topic, sequencing of information or tasks, and pacing. At first sight, it may appear that active learning implies learner control because in active learning participants make choices as they independently explore and experiment with the system. While there may be a partial overlap of exploration and choice, the one is not necessarily implied by the other. For example, an instructional software may allow the learner to freely choose the order and pacing of chapters within the instructional program, while each chapter is highly structured and does not allow any exploration. Also, while all active training interventions include exploration to some extent, the degree of unguided exploration and learner control may differ. Some active training interventions reduce learner control, for example, by imposing a given structure on the learner, either in terms of a fixed task sequence (Wood et al., 2000) or a narrow range of choices as a consequence of prescribed strategies (Debowski, Wood, & Bandura, 2001). In a study with particularly high control during exploration (Kamouri, Kamouri, & Smith, 1986), participants were confronted with several technical devices (e.g., an alarm clock). They were instructed to find out how each device worked without receiving any further information. Trainees experimented with the available buttons to discover their corresponding functions. By interacting with the devices, participants explored their functions and inferred the under-lying rules by themselves and without any guidance.

Level of difficulty throughout the intervention Task difficulty during active training varies between studies. In error management training, participants typically work on difficult training tasks, sometimes even with task difficulty increased to levels that render success almost impossible (Frese et al., 1991); the idea of presenting difficult tasks in error management training is to ensure that trainees are actually exposed to errors and setbacks during training – as probably will be the case later in the transfer situation at work – and have the opportunity to develop strategies to deal with them. In a study in which negotiation skills were practiced, confederates intimidated trainees during negotiation to ensure sufficient levels of task difficulty (Stevens & Gist, 1997). Another way to increase difficulty is to include tasks that are both complex and relatively novel for participants (Tabernero & Wood, 1999). Other studies have used relatively easy tasks in the beginning and then progressed to the more difficult ones (Debowski, Wood, & Bandura, 2001).

Supplemental components of active training interventions

In addition to the basic dimensions that characterize active training interventions, some applications have used supplemental instructional components, which will be presented next.

Mastery-goal instructions A mastery- or learning-goal orientation implies that the learner views the training situation as an opportunity to develop task mastery rather than to demonstrate performance to others (i.e., performance-goal orientation; Dweck & Leggett, 1988). In active-training interventions, mastery-goal orientation has been induced by instructions such as "The more practice you have, the more capable you will become" or "Practice makes perfect" (Martocchio, 1994). Participants were informed that skills develop through practice (Nordstrom, Wendland, & Williams, 1998; Tabernero & Wood, 1999), they were instructed to interpret the practice task as an opportunity to improve their skills (Stevens & Gist, 1997; Wood et al., 2000) and to regard their performance score as helpful feedback (Kozlowski et al., 2001). Later research has incorporated lists of explicitly formulated learning goals (referring to skills, principles, and strategies) that were provided to the participants (Kozlowski & Bell, 2006). Those learning goals usually increase in complexity from basic knowledge goals to strategic objectives (Kozlowski et al., 2001).

Table 6.2 Supplemental components of active-learning interventions.

Component	Function	Example
Mastery-goal instructions	• Direct learners' motivational orientation toward the attainment of task mastery • Interpret practice as an opportunity for skill improvement	"Practice makes perfect" (Martocchio, 1994)
Error management instructions	• Encourage making errors • Frame errors positively	"Errors are a natural part of learning. They point out what you can still learn" (Dormann & Frese, 1994)
Emotion-control instructions	• Help individuals manage their negative emotions • Emphasize personal control, i.e., a positive "can do" attitude	"This task may be challenging, but I know I CAN do it" (Bell & Kozlowski, 2008)
Metacognitive instructions	• Enhance deliberate thought processes targeted on solving problems	"What is my problem? What am I trying to achieve?" (Keith & Frese, 2005)
Adaptive guidance	• Provide diagnostic and interpretive information where to direct further effort • Adaptively suggest which skills and strategies need improvement and where proficiency is already high enough	"You have to," "You had better" (controlling) "You can," "if you choose" (autonomy supportive) (Kanar & Bell, 2013)

Error-management instructions   Error-management instructions encourage trainees to make errors during training and to learn from them; errors are positively framed as learning opportunities. The goal of error-management instructions is to turn learners' attention toward the informative aspect of errors and to reduce potential frustration. Most error management training interventions include instructions to supplement exploration and experimentation. In initial studies, questions were asked such as "Why do you think you have made an error and what do you hypothesize to be the right procedure?" Participants were then encouraged to test their hypothesized solutions (Frese et al., 1988). Later studies provided written or orally presented statements during training such as "I have made an error, great because now I can learn something new!" (Frese et al., 1991) or "Errors are a natural part of learning. They point out what you can still learn!" (Dormann & Frese, 1994). In some applications, participants were informed about common errors prior to training (Gully et al., 2002).

Emotion control instructions   Emotion control involves "the use of self-regulatory processes to keep performance anxiety and other negative emotional reactions (e.g., worry) at bay during task engagement" (Kanfer, Ackerman, & Heggestad, 1996, p. 186). Error-management instructions may be regarded as emotion-control instructions because errors are framed positively. This positive view on errors may help trainees to reappraise errors as positive events and negative emotional reactions, thereby, may be reduced before they unfold (Keith & Frese, 2005). Other active-learning interventions have used emotion-control instructions without explicit reference to errors. For example, prior to each practice trial of a simulation, participants were instructed to increase the frequency of positive thoughts and to reduce the frequency of negative emotions (Kanfer & Ackerman, 1990).

As another example, self-dialogue has been introduced to participants as a means to reduce frustration and anxiety. Learners were provided with statements such as "Remember, worry won't help anything" and "This task may be challenging, but I know I CAN do it" or they were encouraged to create their own positive self-statements to control their emotions (Bell & Kozlowski, 2008).

Metacognitive instructions   Metacognition implies that an individual exerts self-regulatory "control over his or her cognitions" (Ford et al., 1998, p. 220) and it involves skills of planning and monitoring as well as evaluation of one's progress during task completion (Brown et al., 1983). Instructions designed to increase metacognition during training may encourage participants to ask themselves questions such as "What is my problem? What am I trying to achieve?" or "What do I know about the program so far that can be useful now?" (Keith & Frese, 2005). Metacognition may further be increased by instigating verbal self-explanation and communication with peers (Roll et al., 2012).

Adaptive guidance   Adaptive guidance provides learners with diagnostic and interpretive information enabling decisions where to direct one's effort. Based on a participant's prior performance, the system adaptively suggests which skills and strategies still need improvement as well as where proficiency is already high so that the learner's attention can be directed accordingly (Bell & Kozlowski, 2002). Adaptive guidance goes beyond performance feedback and reminders about optimal strategies. It combines and supplements both by adaptively directing the learner's attention to the most relevant learning topics with guidance tailored to the individual. Guiding instructions' framing may differ; instructions may be either coercive and controlling ("You have to," "You had better") or emphasize choice and self-initiated behaviors ("You can," "if you choose") (Kanar & Bell, 2013).

Effectiveness of Active Training: The Evidence

The increasing popularity of active learning is often ascribed to characteristics of modern workplaces that are thought to call for active rather than more traditional learning forms (e.g., Bell & Kozlowski, 2008, 2010; Hesketh & Griffin, 2008; Keith & Frese, 2005, 2008). Modern workplaces are characterized by frequent changes, rapid cycles of technological development, uncertainty, and lower hierarchies. There is an increased necessity for continuous learning throughout one's working life, along with a shift of responsibility for one's career and personal development away from the organization to the employee him or herself (Hesketh & Griffin, 2008; Kraiger, 2003). The idea is that active-learning approaches are most suitable – at least better than more traditional approaches – to deal with these workplace characteristics and necessities and, in general terms, to lead to better training outcomes. In the present section, we seek to provide an overview of empirical evidence concerning this claim. Apart from the general question whether active training works or not, we will deal with the question in what situations and for whom active training may be most promising or, conversely, in what situations more traditional guided and structured approaches may be preferred. It should be noted that, because there is no one single form of active learning, our conclusions cannot be generalized across all types of active learning. That being said, we believe that the currently available evidence does permit some theoretically and practically useful conclusions about the scope and boundaries of active training.

Studies evaluating the effectiveness of active training usually compare one (or more) active training conditions with either a no-training condition or with one (or more) alternative (e.g., proceduralized) training conditions. Studies using this evaluation design may yield significantly positive (i.e., in favor of the active training condition), negative (i.e., in favor of the alternative training condition or no-training condition), or nonsignificant effect sizes (i.e., no difference in effectiveness between training conditions). With regard to content domain of active-training interventions, several studies used computer-based decision-making simulations (e.g., Bell & Kozlowski, 2002, 2008; Ford et al., 1998; Gully et al., 2002; Kanar & Bell, 2013; Kozlowski & Bell, 2006; Kozlowski et al., 2001) or computer skills such as software training (e.g., Chillarege, Nordstrom, & Williams, 2003; Dormann & Frese, 1994; Frese et al., 1991; Heimbeck et al., 2003; Keith, Richter, & Naumann, 2010; Nordstrom, Wendland, & Williams, 1998) and electronic or web-based search tasks (e.g., Debowski, Wood, & Bandura, 2001; Lazar & Norcio, 2003; Wood et al., 2000). Other studies used management-related simulations of business administration (Ellington & Dierdorff, 2014), group management (Tabernero & Wood, 1999; Wood & Bandura, 1989), knowledge management (Leemkuil & de Jong, 2012), or production management (Goodman, Wood, & Chen, 2011). Other skills practiced in active-training interventions involved firefighting (Elliott et al., 2007; Joung, Hesketh, & Neal, 2006), a triage procedure (Van Dijk, 2010), hazard handling in a driving simulator (Ivancic & Hesketh, 2000; Wang, Zhang, & Salvendy, 2010), negotiation (Cullen et al., 2013; Gist, Bavetta, & Stevens, 1990; Gist, Stevens, & Bavetta, 1991; Stevens & Gist, 1997), and creative problem solving (Robledo et al., 2012). Finally, some studies used active training in a more academic context, for example, to teach mathematical models (Roll et al., 2012), physical phenomena (Olympiou, Zacharias, & deJong, 2013), environmental phenomena (Barab et al., 2009), and principles of psychological experiments (Schwartz & Bransford, 1998). Recent studies that compared the effectiveness of active training interventions with non-active training comparison conditions are summarized in Table 6.3 (note that the table includes only studies that compared active training with non-active training; it does not include studies that compared different kinds of active-training conditions).

For a subset of active training studies, namely those that used error management training (i.e., active/exploratory training with explicitly positive error management instructions), a meta-analysis is available that was published in 2008 (Keith & Frese, 2008). This meta-analysis included 24 studies that compared error management training with an alternative training condition (e.g., proceduralized step-by-step training, exploratory training without error encouragement). The mean effect size across all studies was 0.44 (Cohen's *d*) and statistically significant, indicating that on average error management training led to better training results than alternative training by 0.44 of a standard deviation. When considering only the more recent studies from Table 6.3 (i.e., studies that were not included in the 2008 meta-analysis), the mean effect size is significant and slightly larger at 0.68 (it remains significant, at 0.36, when the study by Tsai (2011) is treated as an outlier and removed from the study pool). There is, however, a considerable variation among effect sizes (range of –0.73 to larger than 1 in the 2008 meta-analysis) and a number of studies (both in the meta-analysis as well as in two of the studies depicted in the table) do not find any difference in training outcomes between training conditions. The conclusion that active training (or at least error management training as one example of active training) were generally effective and preferable compared to traditional training may therefore be premature. Rather, there may be moderators, that is, factors that relate to the magnitude of the effect size and that may condition the effectiveness of active training. In the following, we will highlight two such moderators that emerge in the literature and that have important implications for theory and practice of active learning (Keith, 2011, 2012; Keith & Frese, 2008). The first moderator refers to the distinction between immediate training performance and post-training transfer performance; the

Table 6.3 Summary of recent studies on the effectiveness of active training that were not included in meta-analysis by Keith and Frese (2008).

Study	N	M_{age} (SD)	Study design	Training content	Active training condition(s)	Comparison condition(s)	Type of transfer measure (time lag where applicable)	Cohen's d (SE)
Barab et al. (2009)	51	undergrad. students	RCT[a]	Environmental phenomena (water quality, fish population)	In a virtual park (an aquatic habitat), students explored the relations underlying the scenario (e.g., influence on how many fish there were) by exploration and experimentation (e.g., talk to virtual characters, conduct water analyses, serve as advisors).	Written information (expository textbook/ simplistic narrative)	Adaptive	0.72 (0.29)*
Carter & Beier (2010)	161	39.7 (13.4)	RCT	Software training (Microsoft Access)	Trainees formulated search queries by experimenting with the software.	Proceduralized instructions	Adaptive (one week)	0.39 (0.16)*
Cullen et al. (2013)	132	24.2 (7.7)	RCT[b]	Negotiation skills	Trainees reviewed transcripts of negotiations to identify the use of strategies and key behaviors. They also identified correct and incorrect behaviors following role plays.	Behavioral modeling[c]	Analogical (three weeks)	0.16 (0.18)
Keith, Richter, & Naumann (2010), Study 1	37	28.4 (7.7)	RCT	Software training (Microsoft Word)	Trainees reproduced a complex table by experimenting with the software.	Proceduralized instructions	Adaptive	0.69 (0.34)*
Tsai (2011)	221	20	Quasi-experimental[d]	Build a website to establish a company	Students worked in small groups on setting up a virtual company by collaboratively exploring their ideas.	Traditional lecture	Analogical (at the end of the semester)	2.40 (0.22)**

(*Continued*)

Table 6.3 (*Continued*)

Study	N	M_{age} (SD)	Study design	Training content	Active training condition(s)	Comparison condition(s)	Type of transfer measure (time lag where applicable)	Cohen's d (SE)
Van Dijk (2010)	49	21.2 (1.9)	RCT	Triage procedure (categorize victims of large-scale accidents)	Trainees learned the procedure by selecting adequate actions and considering the feedback on their behavior. In a virtual environment, they walked from patient to patient and applied the knowledge they had gathered so far.	Worked examples	Analogical (one week)	−0.39 (0.29)
Wang, Zhang, & Salvendy (2010)	32	23.1 (1.7)	RCT	Hazard handling in a driving simulator	Trainees responded to multiple incidents in a driving simulator.	Video-based guided error training	Analogical (one week)	0.81 (0.37)*

Note. RCT = Randomized controlled trial. Positive effect sizes denote performance differences in favor of the active training condition(s).

[a]Participants learned in dyads.

[b]Randomization was groupwise (small groups).

[c]The behavioral modeling condition comprised elements of active training that were not included in the active-training condition such as group discussion of ineffective behaviors.

[d]Quasi-experimental field study in an introductory computer course.

* $p < .05$, ** $p < .01$ (two-tailed).

second moderator refers to the distinction between analogical transfer (i.e., transfer to tasks that are similar to training tasks) and adaptive transfer (i.e., transfer to tasks that are dissimilar from and more complex than training tasks).

Immediate training performance vs. post-training transfer performance

Active training cannot be expected to benefit immediate training performance; rather, it is directed at improving post-training transfer performance. An important but often neglected distinction in training evaluation is between immediate training performance (i.e., completion of training tasks) and post-training transfer performance (i.e., completion of tasks after training, in a transfer phase separate from training itself). This distinction is important because training interventions that benefit immediate training performance may not be effective in promoting transfer in the long run and, conversely, training interventions that may impede immediate training performance may still be effective in the long run (Bjork, 1994; Bjork & Bjork, 2011; Goodman & Wood, 2004; Hesketh, 1997; Keith & Frese, 2005, 2008; Schmidt & Bjork, 1992). A classical study from motor learning demonstrates this point (Shea & Morgan, 1979). In this study, participants learned several movements either in blocked practice or in randomized order. During training, participants of the blocked-practice condition outperformed those of the randomized-order condition but later in a transfer phase after training, the opposite pattern emerged: Randomized-order participants performed better, particularly if transfer tasks were also presented in a randomized order. The phenomenon that introducing difficulties during training may benefit learning and transfer in the long run has been demonstrated across a number of studies using different tasks and interventions, often subsumed under the concept of desirable difficulties. *Desirable difficulties* describe difficulties during learning that, providing learners respond to them successfully, lead to enhanced learning and retention (Bjork & Bjork, 2011). One example is the aforementioned benefit for learning and retention when training in randomized order rather than in blocked practice. Another example is the so-called testing effect (Roediger & Karpicke, 2006), demonstrating that while initially repeated study of the same material may appear to lead to better retention, recall tests are a better method of study in the long run (i.e., worse recall after five minutes but better retention after one week).

The concept of desirable difficulties and the distinction between performance immediately during training vs. after training are relevant for active training for the following reason: Active training, in a way, induces a desirable difficulty, namely, active and independent exploration of the training tasks rather than detailed and guided instructions. The necessity to work independently and without much assistance during training makes the training more difficult for participants of active training. For participants of traditional training, in contrast, who receive guidance and instruction on how to solve the training tasks, no such difficulties arise. As a consequence, their immediate training performance may be better as they follow guiding instructions; long-term learning and performance, however, may suffer (Hesketh, 1997; Ivancic & Hesketh, 1995/6; Keith & Frese, 2005, 2008). In line with this argumentation, the meta-analysis on error management training (Keith & Frese, 2008) found studies that used post-training transfer tasks to evaluate performance to yield larger mean effect sizes than those using training tasks (i.e., significant moderator effect). This finding has two implications for theory and practice of active learning. First, immediate training performance should not mistakenly be used to evaluate training effectiveness or to determine progress of training participants. Merely because participants correctly follow instructions (in guided step-by-step training) this does not mean that they really learned the procedures and will be able to use them outside the training situation. Conversely, merely because participants in training do not immediately find the correct solutions as they explore (in active training), this does not mean they were not learning about the training tasks. Second, motivating participants to actively explore and find solutions on their own may becomes a challenge for trainers. Some participants may simply reject working by themselves and not receiving guidance from the trainer. And even if participants do not entirely reject working independently, there may still be frustrating phases during training in which participants face difficulties and in which they would prefer to receive step-by-step guidance rather than being asked to find task solutions on their own.

Analogical vs. adaptive transfer

Active training may be more suitable to benefit adaptive than analogical transfer of training as compared to traditional guided training. Analogical transfer refers to situations in which transfer tasks are similar to training tasks; analogical transfer tasks can be solved with procedures analogous to those learned during training (Ivancic & Hesketh, 2000). Adaptive transfer, in contrast, implies that new solutions need to be developed to solve the tasks and that procedures be used that have not been taught during training (Ivancic & Hesketh, 2000; a similar distinction is that of near and far transfer, for example, Barnett and Ceci (2002). Training programs may differ as to whether the focus is on analogical or on adaptive transfer. If, for example, the training goal is to learn a clearly definable procedure or set of procedures (i.e., analogical transfer), it makes sense to teach these procedures directly using step-by-step guidance. Using active training in this situation, that is, encouraging trainees to find out about the correct procedures by exploration, may or may not lead to the goal as well, but it certainly is more time-consuming than direct instruction. A different situation arises when during training not all work-related problems and their solutions can be taught and in which, therefore, the training goal is to enable training participants to independently develop solutions to new problems at work (i.e., adaptive transfer). In this case, active training methods may be particularly suitable as they resemble the transfer situation more than guided step-by-step training. While during training there may be a trainer present who can help with the tasks at hand, back at work in the transfer situation the trainee needs to be able to develop solutions without a trainer. In a way, active training is a more realistic representation of the transfer situation than guided training. Trainees of active training may be better prepared to deal with difficulties in the transfer situation because they already learned during training to explore the tasks and to find solutions independently. Also, provided participants had the positive experience during training that they are able to deal with problems without much assistance, they may be more confident and subsequently be more persistent in the transfer situation. This issue is also known as the principle of transfer-appropriate processing, which postulates that those processes required on transfer tasks should be practiced in training (Morris, Bransford, & Franks, 1977).

In line with this reasoning, the meta-analysis on error management training found type of transfer task to moderate training effectiveness. Although for studies using analogical transfer tasks to evaluate training effectiveness a significant mean effect size was found, the magnitude of the effect was small (Cohen's $d = 0.20$). For studies using adaptive transfer tasks, however, the effect size was significantly larger and of large magnitude (Cohen's $d = 0.80$), implying that active training may be particularly beneficial for adaptive transfer tasks. For the practice of active training, this implies that trainers may, before choosing between active training and more guided training methods, consider the particular training goal, that is, whether analogical or adaptive transfer is required back on the job (Hesketh, 1997; Keith, 2011, 2012; Keith & Frese, 2005, 2008; Kozlowski et al., 2001).

Mechanisms of Active Training: What Do We Know about Why it Works?

The previous section dealt with the general question asking whether active training is effective and, additionally, in what situations it may be more beneficial than in others. While the answers to this question already have implications for the application of active training, the present section goes one step further by dealing with the mechanisms and psychological processes that underlie the effectiveness of active training. Identifying the processes both deepens our theoretical understanding of active training and opens up the possibility to design more specific training interventions that purposely address these very processes.

The basic assumption of active-learning theory is that the activity of training participants instigates particular processes that benefit learning; it further assumed that these processes are not, or only to a lesser extent, instigated in participants of nonactive, more traditional training. These processes are then thought to function as mechanisms that explain the effectiveness of active training. But what kind of processes may that be? In the following, we will review a number of processes that have been proposed in the literature as possible pathways of training effectiveness. Where available, we will also describe empirical evidence concerning these processes. These proposed processes may be grouped according to their emphasis either on cognitive, emotional, or motivational processes that may be instigated in active training. Another approach attempts to integrate these views using a self-regulatory perspective. The next paragraphs will be organized along these lines. Where applicable, we will also refer back to the previously described basic dimensions and supplemental components of active training.

Cognitive processes in active training

As outlined above, a basic dimension of active training is active exploration and experimentation during training. In addition, active-training approaches, in contrast to traditional guided training methods, tend to provide trainees with only little task information. As a consequence, much of the knowledge and skills required for successful task completion needs to be developed by participants themselves as they explore the training tasks. In doing so, participants will inevitably make errors and some active-training approaches, most notably error management training, explicitly encourage making errors during training and learning from them. All of these elements of active training may contribute to learning. The active involvement of trainees and the requirement to develop knowledge and skills during independent exploration may lead to deeper cognitive processing of task-related information than under conditions of more passive instruction (Bell & Kozlowski, 2008, 2010; Heimbeck et al., 2003; Keith & Frese, 2005; Ivancic & Hesketh, 1995/6). As participants explore the training tasks, their attention is constantly triggered; they constantly need to reflect on what they are doing and whether their task strategies are successful or need to be changed (Keith, 2011, 2012; Keith & Frese, 2005, 2008). While participants of traditional, more passive forms of instruction may also opt to be attentive and reflective during training, expending this cognitive effort is probably not as essential for task completion as it is in active training. This proposition is in line with action theory (Frese & Zapf, 1994; Hacker, 1973), which posits that active exploration of task solutions may lead to more adequate and richer mental models of the subject under study than more passive forms of instruction. In fact, Dormann and Frese (1994) found the extent of exploration during training to be related to post-training performance on a transfer task. Bell and Kozlowski (2008), who systematically varied several training design elements found exploration during training, as compared to step-by-step guidance, to benefit performance.

Making errors has been proposed to instigate learning (e.g., Frese et al., 1991; Ivancic & Hesketh, 1995/6, 2000; Heimbeck et al., 2003; Keith & Frese, 2005). Errors may improve mental models of the training subject because they pinpoint incorrect assumptions and motivate participants to correct these erroneous assumptions (Keith, 2011, 2012). In line with this proposition, error-related events have been found to be associated with richer mental models than successful ones (Ellis & Davidi, 2005). Errors may also attract attention because they disrupt task completion and participants may then devote their attention to understanding the error and its cause and to finding a solution to the problem (Ivancic & Hesketh, 1995/6, 2000). The literature on error management training (a method of active training which, as described above, combines active exploration with explicit error encouragement) suggests that errors are effective in promoting learning and transfer. In particular, the meta-analysis of 24 studies of error management training found a positive and significant mean effect size in favor of error management training. It should be noted, however, that exploration and making errors are inherently confounded in active training. It is therefore difficult to empirically disentangle the effects of errors and of exploration (cf. Bell & Kozlowski, 2008; Gully et al., 2002).

Motivational processes in active training

Active training may be more motivating for trainees than traditional proceduralized training as they are allowed to work at their own pace and explore tasks on their own rather than following instructions by an external agent (i.e., the trainer). Active training may increase self-determination (Deci & Ryan, 1985) as participants enjoy actively exploring the tasks and decide to spend more effort, which in turn may benefit learning. Instructions to increase mastery- or learning-goal orientation, which are employed in some active training applications, also target participants' motivation during training. The empirical evidence concerning motivation in active training is mixed. For example, a study by Wood et al. (2000) expected intrinsic motivation to mediate effects of enactive exploration (i.e., an active training intervention) in an electronic search task. Contrary to expectations, however, intrinsic motivation was unrelated to performance.

Emotional processes in active training

As mentioned above, active exploration and making errors may at times become frustrating for trainees. To reduce frustration in exploratory training, Frese et al. (1991) introduced so-called error management instructions that aimed to reduce frustration for trainees (e.g., "Say to yourself: I have made an error, great, because now I can learn something new"). It is plausible to assume that these instructions alleviate negative emotions such as anger and frustration during training – emotions that would otherwise distract from the task at hand which in turn would impede learning (Kanfer & Ackerman, 1989). Also, while working on difficult tasks in a later transfer phase, trainees who have previously received error management instructions may be better equipped to deal with potential negative emotions in the face of errors and setbacks. In line with this reasoning, various instructions of error encouragement (i.e., error-management instructions or similar ones) appear to be an effective element of error management training (Bell & Kozlowski, 2008; Heimbeck et al., 2003; Keith & Frese, 2008). Results of studies that directly assessed negative emotions, however, yielded inconsistent results. For example, Nordstrom, Wendland, and

Williams (1998) compared levels of frustration in participants of error management training to that in participants of a traditional proceduralized training method. As expected, frustration decreased in the former and increased in the latter. This effect, however, was not replicated in a similar study (Chillarege, Nordstrom, & Williams, 2003).

Self-regulation of cognitions and emotions in active training

The previous sections have separately considered cognitive, motivational, and emotional processes that may account for the effectiveness of active training. More probably than not, no one single mechanism but rather a combination accounts for the effectiveness of active training. In an attempt to integrate emotional and cognitive perspectives, Keith and Frese (2005) introduced a self-regulatory framework that stresses both emotional and cognitive paths to explain the effectiveness of error management training (for a similar approach, see Bell & Kozlowski, 2008). Self-regulation involves processes "that enable an individual to guide his or her goal-directed activities over time" (Karoly, 1993, p. 25) and serves to reduce discrepancies between goals and performance (Sitzmann & Ely, 2010). Self-regulation may particularly be important for participants in error management training because they work independently and do not receive much guidance during training (cf. Bell & Kozlowksi, 2008; Ford et al., 1998). These self-regulatory skills that participants exert during training may in turn be useful when participants are later confronted with novel tasks that were not introduced during training (i.e., adaptive transfer). Self-regulation can be directed at the "modulation of thought, affect, behavior, or attention" (Karoly, 1993, p. 25).

The two self-regulatory skills investigated by Keith and Frese (2005) were emotion control (i.e., self-regulation of emotions or affect) and metacognition (i.e., self-regulation of cognitions). *Emotion control* is aimed at reducing negative emotional reactions to setbacks and errors (Kanfer, Ackerman, & Heggestad, 1996). Error management training may encourage emotion control through positive framing of errors in error-management instructions. *Metacognition* includes planning, monitoring, evaluation, and revision of task strategies during task completion (Brown et al., 1983). Error management training may be conducive to the development of such skills because "errors prompt learners to stop and think about the causes of the error" (Ivancic & Hesketh, 2000, p. 1968), to come up with potential solutions to the problem, and to implement and test them. In short, Keith and Frese (2005) expected emotion control and metacognitive activities to be stimulated in error management training but not or to a lesser extent in conventional guided training. They further expected these two self-regulatory skills to benefit performance on adaptive transfer tasks and to explain effectiveness of error management training. In line with expectations, emotion control and metacognitive activity during training fully and independently mediated the effect of training method (i.e., error management vs. conventional guided training) on adaptive transfer performance. These results highlight the importance of both emotional and cognitive processes for the effectiveness of error management training (as one particular active training method) and probably for active training in general. They are also in line with the principle of transfer appropriate processing (Morris, Bransford, & Franks, 1977) mentioned above that states that processes that are needed during transfer should be practiced during training. It appears that participants of active training learn to exert self-regulatory skills of emotion control and metacognition during training as they work independently on tasks – skills that prove useful when confronted with novel adaptive transfer tasks that need to be solved without external guidance by a trainer (cf. Keith 2011, 2012).

Evidence on Aptitude-Treatment Interactions (ATI):
Who Benefits Most from Active Training?

The previous sections dealt with the effectiveness of active training and potential mediating mechanisms in general, that is, without consideration of trainee characteristics. It is a common assumption, however, that not all trainees benefit equally from the same training method (Gully & Chen, 2010) – in the present case, from active training. This issue has been termed aptitude-treatment interaction (ATI; Cronbach & Snow, 1977), with "treatment" representing the training method (i.e., active training vs. alternative training) and with "aptitude" encompassing various person aptitudes or attributes such as cognitive abilities, interests, motivation, and personality. Indeed, the many recent studies on active training do not focus on main effects of active training but follow the idea of ATI and specifically address potential interactions of training conditions with various person characteristics. In many cases, the idea is to test who benefits most (or least) from active training, that is, to examine what training method is favorable depending on person characteristics of the trainee. A second approach to ATIs is not to look at levels of person characteristics (e.g., high or low cognitive ability) but on differential effects of them on training outcomes. For example, it is possible that some person characteristic (e.g., cognitive ability) affects training outcomes only for trainees of active learning but not for trainees of structured training or vice versa. In the following, we will refer to and attempt to integrate results of research of both perspectives. It should be noted, however, that integrating results of ATI research to produce a coherent picture is a difficult task. This is because, first, statistical interactions or moderations (in the present case, between training condition and person attributes) are generally more difficult to detect and to replicate and at times results concerning the same person attributes are contradictory. Second, research on active training has only begun to systematically investigate ATIs and the presently available evidence is based on quite heterogeneous task domains, treatments (e.g., active/exploratory with or without error encouragement), comparison training conditions (e.g., different active training conditions or active vs. structured training), and dependent variables. We have also opted to omit, for the sake of clarity of presentation, even more complex findings such as three-way interactions (Carter & Beier, 2010) and interactions on mediating variables (Bell & Kozlowski, 2008). The following overview is organized around potential moderators, namely, cognitive ability, motivation, and personality. Where applicable, we will consider different dimensions and components of active training (e.g., exploration and error encouragement) separately.

Cognitive ability

Exploration   The effect of cognitive ability appears to be reduced in active training as compared to proceduralized training. In terms of levels of cognitive ability, research indicates that for high-ability trainees, the training method (i.e., active vs. proceduralized training) does not matter for performance whereas for low-ability trainees, active training is preferable to proceduralized training (Keith, Richter, & Naumann, 2010). This effect may be explained in terms of resource allocation theory (Kanfer & Ackerman, 1989); the idea is that cognitive resources may be more crucial in less engaging training environments (Keith, Richter, & Naumann, 2010). Note that this finding may be counterintuitive; often it is argued that exploration in active training poses demands on learners that are better met in high-ability trainees (Gully et al., 2002) whereas these findings indicate active training to be beneficial for trainees of all levels of cognitive ability.

Error encouragement With regard to error encouragement, it appears that encouraging errors is particularly effective for individuals with higher, rather than lower, ability. Making errors and dealing with them probably costs cognitive/attentional resources. Encouraging errors may therefore be counterproductive for individuals with lower cognitive ability. In line with this proposition, two studies found higher-ability individuals to benefit more from error encouragement than individuals with lower ability (Gully et al., 2002; Loh et al., 2013). In both studies, the comparison conditions were exploratory training with neutral or with avoidant-error instructions.

Motivation

Exploratory training as compared to proceduralized training appears to reduce the role of motivation in training effectiveness. The pattern is the same as for cognitive ability: while for highly motivated trainees, training conditions did not matter, performance of trainees with low motivation was worse in structured training. Again, this pattern may be explained with reference to resource allocation theory as motivation plays a role in allocation of attentional resources during task completion (Kanfer & Ackerman, 1989). Another study found that during guided exploration, the influence of motivation on performance growth was reduced but only when guiding instructions were phrased in a controlling rather than autonomy-supportive way (Kanar & Bell, 2013). A similar result was found for the construct of goal orientation; while in proceduralized training low performance goal orientation (i.e., prove and avoidance orientation) was detrimental to performance, in active training this motivational person characteristic did not affect performance (Heimbeck et al., 2003). In other words, active training was beneficial for trainees of all levels of motivation.

Personality

Openness to experience and agreeableness Individuals characterized as more open to experience may be expected to be more willing to make mistakes and to learn from them. Results supported this view in that error-encouragement instructions were more beneficial than error-avoidance instructions for individuals higher in openness to experience (Gully et al., 2002; Loh et al., 2013). Similar results were found with respect to agreeableness (Loh et al., 2013). Individuals lower in openness to experience either performed worse (Gully et al., 2002) or no differences between conditions were found (Loh et al., 2013).

Conscientiousness Highly conscientious learners are self-disciplined and effortful in their approach to learning, which may lead to the prediction that they benefit from active training. In line with this prediction, in one study they benefited more form error management training than from a guided-training method (Cullen et al., 2013). On the other hand, one particular facet of conscientiousness – cautiousness – involves a tendency to avoid mistakes. Cautiousness may explain why in one study error encouragement reduced self-efficacy in individuals with higher levels of conscientiousness (Gully et al., 2002).

Extroversion Extroversion may be expected to match active learning as compared to a more guided behavioral modeling approach because extroverts prefer being actively involved rather than being required to passively receive information. In line with this assumption, one study showed that extroverted learners benefited more from error management training whereas introverted trainees benefited more from behavioral-modeling training (Cullen et al., 2013).

Challenges to the Concept of Active Learning

The present chapter has been rather optimistic about active learning. Yet, active learning principles or, more generally speaking, constructivist approaches to learning have not gone uncriticized (e.g., Mayer, 2004). In particular, proponents of cognitive-load theory argue that unstructured and discovery-based training methods may increase what is called extraneous load, that is, cognitive load that does not benefit learning but that poses additional demands on the learner and should be reduced. Indeed, in the context of cognitive load theory, a number of studies and meta-analytical findings indicate that guidance (e.g., worked-out examples of problems) are better for learning than discovery-based methods (e.g., Kirschner, Sweller, & Clark, 2006). We suggest that this apparent contradiction – that active training benefits learning in one set of studies and is detrimental in the other – may be resolved with reference to the type of transfer or respective training goal involved in the studies: while active training is particularly effective for adaptive transfer tasks, many of the studies using guided approaches within the framework of cognitive-load theory probably use an analogical transfer task in which a specific principle taught in training needs to be applied to a similar problem. Another obvious difference between the literature on cognitive-load theory and the presently reviewed active training studies is the sample and setting; while the former focuses on students in school settings, the present chapter only considered studies using adult samples. In any case, a challenge to theory and practice of active training is that the desirable difficulties (Bjork, 1994) induced by active training do not become undesirable difficulties for the learner, that is, pose additional demands on the learners that he or she is not equipped to master. The findings regarding ATIs may be informative in deciding which learners may or may not benefit from active training. It should be noted, however, that at least some of the available studies point out to a seemingly counterintuitive finding (at least not in line with cognitive load theory), namely, that all learners, regardless of their cognitive ability and motivation, benefit from active training while guided training is detrimental to learners of lower ability and lower motivation (Heimbeck et al., 2003; Keith, Richter, & Naumann, 2010). These finding may be explained with reference to the resource allocation theory by Kanfer and Ackerman (1989) but this explanation is somewhat speculative at this point (cf. Keith, Richter, & Naumann, 2010). Future research may investigate in more detail whether this explanation holds and attempt to solve the contradiction between the literatures on cognitive load theory and the presently reviewed active-training studies.

We have suggested exploration in active training to represent a desirable difficulty that may impede immediate training performance but that is beneficial in the long run. An interesting phenomenon in the context of desirable difficulties is that learners often mistake apparent initial learning with actual learning and retention. That is, learners tend to prefer learning strategies that increase apparent learning (e.g., massed practice, repeated study) over strategies that increase actual learning and retention but that may initially slow the learning rate (e.g., distributed practice, testing of studied material) (Kornell & Bjork, 2007). With regard to active training, some trainees may be reluctant to go through the effort of independent exploration when a trainer is available who, in principle, could guide them to correct task solutions. During exploration, trainees may subjectively perceive learning to be less effective and more demanding – and thereby less motivating – than traditional approaches. Likewise, trainers may also be inclined to use more structured training methods that increase apparent learning rather than have trainees struggle to correct task solutions on their own. It may be a challenge for both trainers and trainees to find a balance between the desire for guidance and more effortful but probably more beneficial active exploration.

Future Research

Many of the studies presented in this chapter used active training to train technical skills (e.g., computer skills) or at least computer-based tasks (e.g., computer-delivered decision-making tasks), although more recent studies have applied active training to a diverse set of skills. Also, many of the outcome variables assessed to evaluate training effectiveness were skill-based measures and actual on-the-job performance after training has rarely been assessed. Future research may continue to investigate generalizability of findings to diverse skills and settings and to systematically relate effects of active training to a taxonomy of analogical and adaptive transfer tasks in closed skills (i.e., skills that require the execution of particular procedures) and open skills (i.e., skills that leave latitude in deciding a course of action; cf. Blume et al., 2010). In addition, this chapter has primarily focused on active *training* (as opposed to active *learning* in general), with the most notable characteristic of exploration as opposed to structure and guidance during training. Yet, as mentioned in the beginning of this chapter, many other approaches (e.g., cooperative learning in groups) may be conceived of as active learning approaches. Future research may systematically analyze similarities and differences in diverse active-learning approaches, their underlying mechanisms, and interactions with interindividual difference variables. In this context, investigating informal active learning in organizations may be of particular interest given that much of the learning that takes place in organizations appears to be informal (Kraiger, 2003; Tannenbaum et al., 2010). Indeed, research has shown that so-called deliberate practice activities, that is, self-regulated practice activities at work with the explicit goal of performance improvement, predict performance (Keith & Ericsson, 2007; Sonnentag & Kleine, 2000; Unger et al., 2009). Future research may investigate which characteristics of persons and of the work environment (e.g., job characteristics, organizational culture) are conducive to such active learning of employees at work – along with potential costs associated with learners' effort that is inherent in active learning.

Conclusion

Active learning implies that learners are assigned an active role in the learning process; the responsibility for learning is shifted from external agents (i.e., the trainers or teachers) to the learners themselves. The present chapter gave a brief overview of active-learning approaches in different settings (e.g., informal active learning at work vs. within formalized training; individual learning vs. learning in groups) and then focused on one subset of active-learning approaches, namely, active training, which emphasizes exploration and experimentation during training. Research indicates that active training is beneficial when compared to traditional guided approaches particularly when transfer to novel and complex problems (i.e., adaptive transfer) is the training objective. For transfer to problems that are similar to those taught during training and that need to be performed in some prescribed manner (i.e., analogical transfer), active training might work as well, but guided and structured approaches that directly teach the required skill are probably more efficient. Trainers may therefore consider the training objective before deciding whether to use active training or more guided training methods. Also, trainee characteristics such as cognitive ability or personality of trainees may be considered, although the current evidence suggests that active exploration is beneficial for trainees of all levels of cognitive abilities and motivation. Active-training interventions have been conducted in content domains or used tasks such as decision making, computer skills, management skill simulations, and more specific job-related skills such as firefighting. While it is our hope that this interest of researchers and practitioners in active learning interventions continues, a major challenge may be to design active training such that the desirable difficulties induced in training do not turn into undesirables ones that may impede learning or motivation of trainees.

References

Aronson, E., & Bridgeman, D. (1979). Jigsaw groups and the desegregated classroom: In pursuit of common goals. *Personality and Social Psychology Bulletin*, 5, 438–446.

Barab, S. A., Scott, B., Siyahhan, S., Goldstone, R., Ingram-Goble, A., Zuiker, S. J., & Warren, S. (2009). Transformational play as a curricular scaffold: Using videogames to support science education. *Journal of Science Education and Technology*, 18, 305–320. doi:10.1007/s10956-009-9171-5.

Barnett, S. M., & Ceci, S. J. (2002). When and where do we apply what we learn? A taxonomy for far transfer. *Psychological Bulletin*, 128, 612–637.

Bell, B. S., & Kozlowski, S. W. J. (2002). Adaptive guidance: Enhancing self-regulation, knowledge, and performance in technology-based training. *Personnel Psychology*, 55, 267–306.

Bell, B. S., & Kozlowski, S. W. J. (2008). Active learning: Effects of core training design elements on self-regulatory processes, learning, and adaptability. *Journal of Applied Psychology*, 93, 296–316.

Bell, B. S., & Kozlowski, S. W. J. (2010). Toward a theory of learner-centered training design: An integrative framework of active learning. In S. W. J. Kozlowski & E. Salas (Eds.), *Learning, Training, and Development in Organizations* (pp. 263–300). New York: Taylor & Francis.

Bjork, R. A. (1994). Memory and metamemory considerations in the training of human beings. In J. Metcalfe & A. Shimamura (Eds.), *Metacognition: Knowing about Knowing* (pp. 185–205). Cambridge, MA: MIT Press.

Bjork, E. L., & Bjork, R. A. (2011). Making things hard on yourself, but in a good way: Creating desirable difficulties to enhance learning. In M. A. Gernsbacher, R. W. Pew, L. M. Hough, & J. R. Pomerantz (Eds.), *Psychology and the Real World: Essays Illustrating Fundamental Contributions to Society* (pp. 56–64). New York: Worth Publishers.

Blume, B. D., Ford, J. K., Baldwin, T. T., & Huang, J. L. (2010). Transfer of training: A meta-analytic review. *Journal of Management*, 36, 1065–1106.

Brown, A. L., Bransford, J. D., Ferrara, R. A., & Campione, J. C. (1983). Learning, remembering, and understanding. In J. H. Flavell & E. M. Markman (Eds.), *Handbook of Child Psychology* (vol. 3, pp. 77–166). New York: John Wiley & Sons, Inc.

Bruner, J. S. (1966). *Toward a Theory of Instruction*. Cambridge, MA: Harvard University Press.

Carter, M., & Beier, M. E. (2010). The effectiveness of error management training with working-aged adults. *Personnel Psychology*, 63(3), 641–675. doi:10.1111/j.1744-6570.2010.01183.x.

Chillarege, K. A., Nordstrom, C. R., & Williams, K. B. (2003). Learning from our mistakes: Error management training for mature learners. *Journal of Business and Psychology*, 17, 369–385.

Cronbach, L. J., & Snow, R. E. (1977). *Aptitudes and Instructional Methods: A Handbook for Research on Interactions*. New York: Irvington.

Cullen, M. J., Muros, J. P., Rasch, R., & Sackett, P. R. (2013). Individual differences in the effectiveness of error management training for developing negotiation skills. *International Journal of Selection and Assessment*, 21(1), 1–21. doi:10.1111/ijsa.12013.

Daniels, K. J., Boocock, J. G., Glover, J., Hartley, R., & Holland, J. (2009) An experience sampling study of learning, affect, and the demands control support model. *Journal of Applied Psychology*, 94, 1003–1017.

Debowski, S., Wood, R. E., & Bandura, A. (2001). Impact of guided exploration on self-regulatory mechanisms and information acquisition through electronic search. *Journal of Applied Psychology*, 86, 1129–1141.

Deci, E. L., & Ryan, R. M. (1985). *Intrinsic Motivation and Self-Determination in Human Behavior*. New York: Plenum.

Dormann, T., & Frese, M. (1994). Error management training: Replication and the function of exploratory behavior. *International Journal of Human–Computer Interaction*, 6, 365–372.

Driver, R., Asoko, H., Leach, J., Mortimer, E., & Scott, P. (1994). Constructing scientific knowledge in the classroom. *Educational Researcher*, 23, 5–12.

Dweck, C. S., & Leggett, E. L. (1988). A social-cognitive approach to motivation and personality. *Psychological Review*, 95, 256–273.

Ellington, J. K., & Dierdorff, E. C. (2014). Individual learning in team training: Self-regulation and team context effects. Small Group Research, 45, 37–67.

Elliott, T., Welsh, M., Nettelbeck, T., & Mills, V. (2007). Investigating naturalistic decision making in a simulated microworld: What questions should we ask? *Behavior Research Methods*, 39, 901–910.

Ellis, S., & Davidi, I. (2005). After-event reviews: Drawing lessons from successful and failed experience. *Journal of Applied Psychology*, 90, 857–871.

Ford, J. K., Smith, E. M., Weissbein, D. A., Gully, S. M., & Salas, E. (1998). Relationships of goal orientation, metacognitive activity, and practice strategies with learning outcomes and transfer. *Journal of Applied Psychology*, 83, 218–233.

Frese, M., Albrecht, K., Altmann, A., Lang, J., Papstein, P. V., Peyerl, R., Prümper, J., et al. (1988). The effects of an active development of the mental model in the training process: Experimental results in a word processing system. *Behaviour & Information Technology*, 7, 295–304.

Frese, M., Brodbeck, F. C., Heinbokel, T., Mooser, C., Schleiffenbaum, E., & Thiemann, P. (1991). Errors in training computer skills: On the positive function of errors. *Human–Computer Interaction*, 6, 77–93.

Frese, M., & Zapf, D. (1994). Action as the core of work psychology: A German approach. In H. C. Triandis, M. D. Dunette, & L. M. Hough (Eds.), *Handbook of Industrial and Organizational Psychology* (vol. 4, pp. 271–340). Palo Alto, CA: Consulting Psychologists Press.

Gist, M. E., Bavetta, A. G., & Stevens, C. K. (1990). Transfer training method: Its influence on skill generalization, skill repetition, and performance level. *Personnel Psychology*, 43, 501–523.

Gist, M. E., Stevens, C. K., & Bavetta, A. G. (1991). Effects of self-efficacy and post-training intervention on the acquisition and maintenance of complex interpersonal skills. *Personnel Psychology*, 44, 837–861.

Goodman, J., & Wood, R. E. (2004). Feedback specificity, learning opportunities, and learning. *Journal of Applied Psychology*, 89, 809–821.

Goodman, J. S., Wood, R. E., & Chen, Z. (2011). Feedback specificity, information processing, and transfer of training. *Organizational Behavior and Human Decision Processes*, 115(2), 253–267. doi:10.1016/j.obhdp.2011.01.001.

Gully, S. M., & Chen, G. (2010). Individual differences, attribute-treatment interactions, and training outcomes. In S. W. J. Kozlowski & E. Salas (Eds.), *Learning, Training, and Development in Organizations* (pp. 3–64). New York: Taylor & Francis.

Gully, S. M., Payne, S. C., Koles, K. L. K., & Whiteman, J. A. K. (2002). The impact of error management training and individual differences on training outcomes: An attribute-treatment interaction perspective. *Journal of Applied Psychology*, 87, 143–155.

Hacker, W. (1973). *Allgemeine Arbeits- und Ingenieurspsychologie* [*General work and engineering psychology*]. Berlin: VEB Deutscher Verlag der Wissenschaften.

Heimbeck, D., Frese, M., Sonnentag, S., & Keith, N. (2003). Integrating errors into the training process: The function of error management instructions and the role of goal orientation. *Personnel Psychology*, 56, 333–361.

Hesketh, B. (1997). Dilemmas in training for transfer and retention. *Applied Psychology: An International Review*, 46, 317–339.

Hesketh, B., & Griffin, B. (2008). Selection and training for work adjustment and adaptability. In C. Cooper & S. Cartwright (Eds.), *The Oxford Handbook of Personnel Psychology* (pp. 366–387). New York: Oxford University Press.

Hsu, Y.-C., & Ching, Y.-H. (2013). Mobile computer-supported collaborative learning: A review of experimental research. *British Journal of Educational Technology*, 44, E111–E114.

Ivancic, K., & Hesketh, B. (1995/6). Making the best of errors during training. *Training Research Journal*, 1, 103–125.

Ivancic, K., & Hesketh, B. (2000). Learning from error in a driving simulation: Effects on driving skill and self-confidence. *Ergonomics*, 43, 1966–1984.

Joung, W., Hesketh, B., & Neal, A. (2006). Using "war stories" to train for adaptive performance: Is it better to learn from error or success? *Applied Psychology: An International Review*, 55, 282–302.

Kamouri, A. L., Kamouri, J., & Smith, K. H. (1986). Training by exploration: Facilitating the transfer of procedural knowledge through analogical reasoning. *International Journal of Man-Machine Studies*, 24, 171–192.

Kanar, A. M., & Bell, B. S. (2013). Guiding learners through technology-based instruction: The effects of adaptive guidance design and individual differences on learning over time. *Journal of Educational Psychology*, 105, 1067–1081.

Kanfer, R., & Ackerman, P. L. (1989). Motivation and cognitive abilities: An integrative/aptitude-treatment interaction approach to skill acquisition [Monograph]. *Journal of Applied Psychology*, 74, 657–690.

Kanfer, R., & Ackerman, P. L. (1990). *Ability and Metacognitive Determinants of Skill Acquisition and Transfer* (Air Force Office of Scientific Research Final Report). Minneapolis, MN: Air Force Office of Scientific Research.

Kanfer, R., Ackerman, P. L., & Heggestad, E. D. (1996). Motivational skills and self-regulation for learning: A trait perspective. *Learning and Individual Differences*, 8, 185–209.

Karasek, R. A., & Theorell, T. (1990). *Healthy Work*. New York: Basic Books.

Karoly, P. (1993). Mechanisms of self-regulation: A systems view. *Annual Review of Psychology*, 44, 23–52.

Keith, N. (2011). Learning through errors in training. In D. Hofmann & M. Frese (Eds.), *Errors in Organizations* (pp. 45–65). New York: Taylor & Francis.

Keith, N. (2012). Managing errors during training. In J. Bauer & C. Harteis (Eds.), *Human Fallibility: The Ambiguity of Errors for Work and Learning* (pp. 173–196). New York: Springer.

Keith, N., & Ericsson, K. A. (2007). A deliberate practice account of typing proficiency in everyday typists. *Journal of Experimental Psychology: Applied*, 13, 135–145.

Keith, N., & Frese, M. (2005). Self-regulation in error management training: Emotion control and metacognition as mediators of performance effects. *Journal of Applied Psychology*, 90, 677–691.

Keith, N., & Frese, M. (2008). Effectiveness of error management training: A meta-analysis. *Journal of Applied Psychology*, 93, 59–69.

Keith, N., Richter, T., & Naumann, J. (2010). Active/exploratory training promotes transfer even in learners with low motivation and cognitive ability. *Applied Psychology: An International Review*, 59, 97–123.

Kirschner, P. A., Sweller, J., & Clark, R. E. (2006). Why minimal guidance during instruction does not work: An analysis the failure of constructivist, discovery, problem-based, experiential, and inquiry-based teaching. *Educational Psychologist*, 41, 75–86.

Kornell, N., & Bjork, R. A. (2007). The promise and perils of self-regulated study. *Psychonomic Bulletin & Review*, 14, 219–224.

Kozlowski, S. W. J., & Bell, B. S. (2006). Disentangling achievement orientation and goal setting: Effects on self-regulatory processes. *Journal of Applied Psychology*, 91, 900–916.

Kozlowski, S. W. J., Gully, S. M., Brown, K. G., Salas, E., Smith, E. M., & Nason, E. R. (2001). Effects of training goals and goal orientation traits on multidimensional training outcomes and performance adaptability. *Organizational Behavior and Human Decision Processes*, 85, 1–31.

Kraiger, K. (2003). Perspectives on training and development. In W. C. Borman, D. R. Ilgen, & R. J. Klimoski (Eds.). *Handbook of Psychology: Industrial and Organizational Psychology* (vol. 12, pp. 171–192). Hoboken, NJ: John Wiley & Sons, Inc.

Kraiger, K., & Jerden, E. (2007). A meta-analytic investigation of learner control: Old findings and new directions. In S. M. Fiore, & E. Salas (Eds.), *Toward a Science of Distributed Learning* (pp. 65–90). Washington, DC: American Psychological Association.

Lazar, J., & Norcio, A. (2003). Training novice users in developing strategies for responding to errors when browsing the web. *International Journal of Human-Computer Interaction*, 15, 361–377.

Leemkuil, H., & de Jong, T. (2012). Adaptive advice in learning with a computer-based knowledge management simulation game. *Academy of Management Learning & Education*, 11, 653–665.

Loh, V., Andrews, S., Hesketh, B., & Griffin, B. (2013). The moderating effect of individual differences in error-management training: Who learns from mistakes? *Human Factors*, 55, 435–448.

Martocchio, J. J. (1994). Effects of conceptions of ability on anxiety, self-efficacy, and learning in training. *Journal of Applied Psychology*, 79, 819–825.

Mayer, R. E. (2004). Should there be a three-strikes rule against pure discovery learning? The case for guided methods of instruction. *American Psychologist*, 59, 1–14.

Morris, C. D., Bransford, J. D., & Franks, J. J. (1977). Levels of processing versus transfer appropriate processing. *Journal of Verbal Learning and Verbal Behavior*, 16, 519–533.

Nordstrom, C. R., Wendland, D., & Williams, K. B. (1998). "To err is human": An examination of the effectiveness of error management training. *Journal of Business and Psychology*, 12, 269–282.

Olympiou, G., Zacharias, Z., & deJong, T. (2013). Making the invisible visible: Enhancing students' conceptual understanding by introducing representations of abstract objects in a simulation. *Instructional Science*, 41, 575–596.

Robledo, I. C., Hester, K. S., Peterson, D. R., Barrett, J. D., Day, E. A., Hougen, D. P., & Mumford, M. D. (2012). Errors and understanding: The effects of error-management training on creative problem-solving. *Creativity Research Journal*, 24, 220–234. doi:10.1080/10400419.2012.67 7352.

Roediger, H. L. & Karpicke, J. D. (2006). Test-enhanced learning: Taking memory tests improves long-term retention. *Psychological Science*, 17, 249–255.

Roll, I., Holmes, N. G., Day, J., & Bonn, D. (2012). Evaluating metacognitive scaffolding in guided invention activities. *Instructional Science*, 40, 691–710.

Schmidt, R. A., & Bjork, R. A. (1992). New conceptualizations of practice: Common principles in three paradigms suggest new concepts for training. *Psychological Science*, 3, 207–217.

Schwartz, D. L., & Bransford, J. D. (1998). A time for telling. *Cognition and Instruction*, 16, 475–5223. doi:10.1207/s1532690xci1604_4.

Shea, J. B., & Morgan, R. L. (1979). Contextual interference effects on the acquisition, retention, and transfer of a motor skill. *Journal of Experimental Psychology: Human Learning and Memory*, 5, 179–187.

Sitzmann, T., & Ely, K. (2010). Sometimes you need a reminder: The effects of prompting self-regulation on regulatory processes, learning, and attrition. *Journal of Applied Psychology*, 95, 132–144.

Sonnentag, S., & Kleine, B. M. (2000). Deliberate practice at work: A study with insurance agents. *Journal of Occupational and Organizational Psychology*, 73, 87–102.

Sonnentag, S., Niessen, C., & Ohly, S. (2004). Learning at work: Training and development. In C. L. Cooper & I. T. Robertson (Eds.), *International Review of Industrial and Organizational Psychology* (vol. 19, pp. 249–289). Chichester: John Wiley & Sons, Ltd.

Stevens, C. K., & Gist, M. E. (1997). Effects of self-efficacy and goal-orientation training on negotiation skill maintenance: What are the mechanisms? *Personnel Psychology*, 50, 955–978.

Tabernero, C., & Wood, R. E. (1999). Implicit theories versus the social construal of ability in self-regulation and performance on a complex task. *Organizational Behavior and Human Decision Processes*, 78, 104–127.

Tannenbaum, S. I., Beard, R. L., McNall, L. A., & Salas, E. (2010). Informal learning and development in organizations. In S. W. J. Kozlowski & E. Salas (Eds.), *Learning, Training, and Development in Organizations* (pp. 303–331). New York: Taylor & Francis.

Tsai, C.-W. (2011). Achieving effective learning effects in the blended course: A combined approach of online self-regulated learning and collaborative learning with initiation. *Cyberpsychology, Behavior, and Social Networking*, 14, 505–510.

Unger, J. M., Keith, N., Hilling, C., Gielnik, M. M., & Frese, M. (2009). Deliberate practice among South African small business owners: Relationships with education, cognitive ability, knowledge, and success. *Journal of Occupational and Organizational Psychology*, 82(1), 21–44. doi: 10.1348/096317908X304361.

Van Dijk, V. (2010). Learning the triage procedure: Serious gaming based on guided discovery learning versus studying worked examples. Master's thesis. Universiteit Utrecht.

Wang, Y. B., Zhang, W., & Salvendy, G. (2010). A comparative study of two hazard handling training methods for novice drivers. *Traffic Injury Prevention*, 11, 483–491. doi:10.1080/15389588.2 010.489242.

Weaver, J. L., Bowers, C. A., Salas, E., & Cannon-Bowers, J. A. (1995). Networked simulations: New paradigms for team performance research. *Behavioral Research Methods, Instruments, & Computers*, 27, 12–24.

Wood, R., & Bandura, A. (1989). Impact of conceptions of ability on self-regulatory mechanisms and complex decision making. *Journal of Personality and Social Psychology*, 56, 407–415.

Wood, R. E., Kakebeeke, B. M., Debowski, S., & Frese, M. (2000). The impact of enactive exploration on intrinsic motivation, strategy, and performance in electronic search. *Applied Psychology: An International Review*, 49, 263–283.

Zimmerman, B. J. (1990). Self-regulated learning and academic achievement: An overview. *Educational Psychologist*, 25, 3–17.

7

The Competencies of Effective Trainers and Teachers

Darryl Gauld

Introduction

This chapter includes a review of the literature pertaining to workplace training. It opens by discussing the debate that exists in the literature and then proceeds to examine and present the competencies, processes, and personal characteristics of workplace trainers. The conceptual framework centres on the training model of Knowles (1980). It reaches a conclusion that workplace training is the strategic linchpin of modern productivity, business innovation, and renewed employee commitment that results in higher morale and lower employee turnover.

The changes in workforce demographic/labour market shifts, technology, democratization, governmental regulations, consumers' rising demands, the need for higher quality, the necessity to be more efficient and productive, and competition from intensified globalization of the world economy have made it clear that to compete effectively, businesses must be the best in the world at what they do. Secondly, today's employees expect an environment in which they can contribute and be valued as human beings, otherwise they change jobs, quit the organization, or lapse into postures of apathy and resentment (Walter, 2002). These demands have caused corporations to hone their core competencies towards being world-class, with the concept of the learning organization (Senge, 1990) acting as a trigger for training practices.

Vacant employment positions appearing in recent newspapers seek: "Inspirational Trainer," "Dynamic Trainer," "Training Specialist," "Training Consultant," "Senior Training Presenter," "Learning and Development Professional"; but none of the advertisements is framed using the term "teacher." The distinction between these roles is becoming increasingly untenable. Inquiries into these advertisements reveal that employers have instructed some of the recruitment agents to refer someone to them for employment who has a finance or insurance background, for example, and who can "train." The issue here is that many employers are sending the message that anyone can be a "training specialist" and "inspirational," once they have some knowledge in a particular content area.

The Wiley Blackwell Handbook of the Psychology of Training, Development, and Performance Improvement,
First Edition. Edited by Kurt Kraiger, Jonathan Passmore, Sigmar Malvezzi, and Nuno Rebelo dos Santos.
© 2015 John Wiley & Sons Ltd. Published 2020 by John Wiley & Sons Ltd.

Quite often, training is viewed as a day off work. Providers of the training are more concerned about the content and presentation of the lunch. Consequently, the training function has become a prime candidate for outsourcing that leaves an organization wide open and vulnerable, with its culture potentially at risk. The Canadian Policy Research Networks (2009) published similar results of a workplace training survey.

The unprecedented growth of change, particularly in the nature of work, has lead to a rise in the changing demands for learning. Globalization, new technologies, and international competitiveness have also accentuated this demand, as the need for training has become a management tool, to enhance employer return on investment (ROI) in training. Drucker (1993) sees knowledge as the only meaningful resource. This means that if management wants to increase productivity and utilize resources effectively, it needs to understand what makes an excellent trainer/teacher in the workplace, as presented, below.

Trainer Competencies

The identification of competencies (Olson, 1991, 1993, 1994; Olson & Pachnowski, 1999) and characteristics (Thompson, 2001) of trainers have been previously undertaken by Leach (Leach 1986, 1989a, 1989b, 1991a, 1991b, 1992, 1993, 1996; Leach et al., 1982; Leach & Sandall 1995) with competencies updated by Ireland's Trainers Network in 2009, the Canadian Society for Training and Development, in 2012, and more recently by the ASTD (American Society for Training and Development) in 2013.

Several *names* have been used in reference to generic competencies around the world, including "key competencies" in Australia, "essential skills" in New Zealand, "foundation skills" or "workplace competencies" in the United States, and "core skills" in England, Scotland, Wales, and Germany.

Galbraith (1998) regards questioning as the single most influential teaching behavior, because of its potential to impact learning. In contrast, Stolovich (1999) considers listening to be the most important trainer skill, because it allows the learner to redirect their attention or deepen their thinking; whereas, Wlodkowski (1993) considers timely, sensitive, and relevant feedback to be perhaps the most powerful trainer intervention, yet this competency cannot be initiated until questioning and listening have occurred.

In much the same way that we as humans are quick to form opinions in the first minute or so of meeting someone, Knowles (1980, p. 224) is convinced that, "What happens in the first hour or so of any learning activity, largely determines how productive the remaining hours will be." Creating a positive learning environment by considering the layout of the room and utilizing color and music will also enhance learning (Handley & Lawlor, 1996).

The motivators for learners are internal – ultimately leading to self-actualization (Herzberg, 1966; Maslow, 1970). Herzberg (1966) identified two broad needs of learners – to avoid uncomfortable or dissatisfying situations, and to be involved in something believed to be meaningful. People learn when they are motivated to learn. Because people will not be motivated to learn if they are threatened, it is important for the teacher/trainer to de-power themselves, in order to empower the learner. People need to be convinced in some way to believe that they can learn. This specific transmission of trust is paramount in the initial relationship that is established between the teacher and the learner. If a teacher walks straight into a classroom and starts training, then this important relationship-building process is overlooked, to the point where maximum learning will not occur (Knowles et al., 1985; Ashton & Sung, 2002).

Although there are senior training consultants who warn against the "soft" approach to training, Kinni (2000) asserts that soft skills, such as conflict resolution and stress-reduction techniques, may be intangibles, but they do have value in the workplace and can be measured, indirectly. Nevertheless, Arnott (2000) sees personal development training more as a benefit to the employer, not the employee. He is concerned about the separation from the life-balancing elements of family and community, by the corporate, ideological manipulation of words like, "spirit," "soul," and "fun." Arnott declares that we used to be taught at home how to behave at work; now we learn at work how to behave at home. Bierema (1996) warns of the risk of being distracted from the individual needs of learners if all human resource development efforts and strategies are focused on organizational learning solely as a group process.

For training to facilitate the adoption of a new practice, it must be received by those responsible when they are ready to begin implementing the practice. Bassi et al. (1997) agree that the rapid pace of change requires that workplace learning occurs on a just-in-time, just-what's-needed, and just-where-it's-needed basis. However, the essential "planning and preparation" competency from the perspective of the recipient and provider must not be overlooked.

It is most important that a trainer is aware of and addresses the needs of every student in a training session, regardless of his or her background. "How adult learners are assisted to cope with learning often determines whether they will decide to continue with or abandon the learning process" (Tovey, 1997, p. 20). When it is assumed that someone with experience on the job will make a great teacher, the results are often disastrous for the students, the trainer, and the organization. Rather than just focusing on training employees, a dedicated trainer must show a genuine concern for the learner's needs and resist the temptation to look for instant solutions.

Walter (2002) recalls the story of a Boeing 747 that had an engine fire during take-off from Los Angeles International Airport, in 1998. "The supervisor said the mechanic asked no questions so he assumed the mechanic understood his explanation" (p. 4), about replacing a set of engine fan blades before takeoff. Likewise, from the report by the Australian Transport Safety Bureau into the Qantas "accident" in 1999, when a Boeing 747-400 tried to land in Bangkok in heavy rain and skidded off the runway, "The error was primarily due to the absence of appropriate company procedures and training." Broadwell (1995) draws the analogy from new trainers having to teach a class, before they have had any form of training, to the admonition that, "It's a good thing the airlines don't approach their pilot training that way!"

Communication involves the ability to understand emotions as well as ideas, the body as well as the mind (Lindeman, 1949, in Gessner, 1956) and is another essential competency for effective trainers, including knowing when to cut short the training session.

Training in the area of problem-solving techniques also produces effective results for learners to enhance their ability to locate and solve problems (Bernstein et al., 1957).

Individuals do not learn from experience per se, they learn from reflecting on their experience (Knowles, 1975; Houle, 1996; Thiagarajan & Thiagarajan, 1999). The successful organization in the knowledge economy (Stewart, 1997) welcomes all opportunities to look at itself, for example, through celebration, appraisal, mourning, and nonverbally such as a foyer display and the use of symbols (Bolman & Deal, 1997). Average trainers have a repository of experiences buried away, to call upon for use at a later time, but effective teachers regularly examine them, looking at the lessons they learned, and search for effective ways to express them. Reflection allows us to "know what it is that we know," as well as "knowing what it is that we don't know" and is the basis for effective performance as a trainer.

Unfortunately, "Novice instructors usually pattern their training technique on their past educational experiences; what else have they got to go on?" (Reiss, 1991, p. 4.)

A search of the literature concerning trainer core competencies highlighted a range of competencies that contributes to trainer effectiveness. Table 7.1 lists a compilation

Table 7.1 Trainer competencies.

Trainer competencies	Leach (1996)	Olson (1994)	Thompson (2001)	Pinto and Walker (1978)	Jacobs (1987)	ASTD (2013)	CSTD (2012)	Knowles (1980)	Grabowski (1976)	Lindeman (1926, 1938)	Knox (1979, 1986)	Trainers Network (2009)
Set goals and objectives	☐					☐	☐	☐				☐
Develop lesson plans	☐					☐	☐					☐
Keep current and up-to-date	☐					☐	☐					☐
Conduct needs assessments	☐			☐	☐	☐	☐					☐
Counsel students about other matters	☐			☐		☐	☐					☐
Blend different training techniques	☐						☐		☐			☐
Use questioning to involve participants	☐	☐				☐	☐	☐				☐
Facilitate group learning activities	☐			☐			☐					☐
Attend to individual differences/diversity	☐					☐	☐	☐		☐		☐
Evaluate effects and impact of training	☐	☐					☐	☐	☐			☐
Analyze course materials/learner information				☐		☐	☐	☐				☐
Assure preparation of training site		☐				☐	☐					☐
Establish/maintain trainer credibility		☐	☐		☐	☐	☐	☐				☐

Authors

Possess content knowledge/skill taught	☐								☐	☐		☐
Demonstrate effective communication skills	☐	☐							☐	☐	☐	☐
Demonstrate effective presentation skills	☐	☐	☐						☐	☐	☐	☐
Support learner needs/feedback/transfer of learning	☐							☐	☐	☐	☐	☐
Use media effectively	☐							☐	☐	☐	☐	☐
Evaluate learner performance	☐			☐				☐		☐		☐
Evaluate delivery of training	☐									☐		☐
Report evaluative information	☐									☐		☐
Understand program development	☐		☐	☐	☐			☐	☐	☐		☐
Understand training and development	☐		☐	☐	☐			☐		☐	☐	☐
Apply research skills			☐	☐	☐				☐	☐		☐
Build relationships			☐	☐	☐						☐	☐

of critical competencies for trainers that have been specifically highlighted by a diverse selection of authors and researchers who are highly regarded internationally, in the training profession, in order for trainers to be effective. Although *knowledge in the content area* was included as a trainer competency, it was not seen as influential in determining trainer effectiveness, by one-third of respondents, in this research. In particular, 71.1 percent of the trainers who identified as being formally qualified as a trainer and had been in training positions for over 10 years, did *not* agree that an excellent knowledge of the subject was needed, in order for them to be good at their role.

Accordingly, 73 percent of trainers with less than two *years of experience*, and 69 percent of trainers with less than five years of experience in training positions thought that an excellent knowledge of the subject *was* needed, in order for them to be good at their role. Contrastingly, 43 percent of trainers with over 15 years of experience and 31 percent of trainers with over 10 years of experience in training positions believed that an excellent knowledge of the subject was *not* needed, in order for them to be good at their role.

These findings indicate that an unqualified trainer perceives content knowledge as being detrimental to their role, as opposed to possessing trainer process skills that will override any fear of knowledge lacking in the content area, usually. Considering that the question was positioned at number 16 and was worded negatively among a combination of positively and negatively worded questions and, given the scope for errors, most respondents gave quite clear indications of their stance, based on experience and qualifications that match the literature, under the circumstances outlined.

Many of the trainer competencies presented in the table have been recognized and used in previous studies, as indicated. As a result, these assembled competencies have a very high universal consistency of recognition, among effective trainers.

A common link and consistent theme running through the various fields of literature reviewed is that knowledge in the content area does not imply that a person appointed as a trainer will automatically be competent in imparting that knowledge. This is a reflection of the workplace teaching approach that has been pursued in this study, that is, it is widely reported that subject knowledge is not the overriding factor that determines trainer effectiveness.

In addition to Table 7.1, the updated 2013 ASTD Competency Model highlights the need to foster a culture of connectivity and collaboration in relation to mobile and social technology, learning analytics, and integrated talent management (Arneson, Naughton, & Rothwell, 2013). The best training programs anticipate changes in technology and equip their workers to cope with them, ahead of the competition, if management adopts the right vision.

The literature clearly highlights that those who have ownership of the process almost always have a more positive attitude toward the content. Hence, the next section highlights that trainer processes contribute significantly to trainer effectiveness.

Trainer Processes

Many reasons can be inferred as to why particular process skills are deemed important. For example, trainers who are seen as being able to deliver dry material in a creative and organized way, through understanding knowledge of the target culture, for instance, may be effective in delivering learning outcomes. Communicating the material and expectations in an effective manner can be seen as important, in order for the participant to learn the material (Thompson, 2001). Process skills displayed by trainers are also important to a participant's view of a trainer. Cosmic Blender's motto is: "Teach Don't Train." This training organization then makes the distinction, "You train animals – you teach people" (advertisement in *Training and Development*, 2002, p. 15). Similarly, the Greek philosopher Socrates said "I don't teach, I awaken." The Roman philosopher, Cicero paraphrased the purpose of learning, to enable people to free themselves from the tyranny of the present.

Organizations can no longer afford to leave the educational function to individuals who have little or no understanding of the learning process. Researchers like DiGeorgio (1982, p. 17) and others (Lindeman, 1938; Olson, 1994; Leach, 1996) found that training managers believe that "professional training skills contributed more to success than did content knowledge or skill."

However, Corben and Dunn (1999, p. 3) found that, "industry qualifications (content) seem to be more important than teaching qualifications (process) in the implementation of training packages" in Australia. The results of such findings contributed to the National Skills Standards Council in Australia being established in 2011, to provide advice to the Standing Council on Tertiary Education, Skills and Employment, on national standards for regulation of vocational education and training. This council is very interested to adopt the Effective Trainer Model from this chapter as its core competence approach within the profession.

In a study of workplaces as learning environments in Finland, the workplace trainers wished for closer cooperation with the "teachers" in the future with regard to learning new methods for education, instruction, and guidance (Lasonen, 2000), in order to incorporate the most appropriate training methods to achieve learning objectives. This conclusion is consistent with the findings of Bone, Harris, and Simons (2000), where many workplace trainers believed that formal off-the-job training courses like "train-the-trainer" would be of great benefit. As a result of such studies, formal qualifications to become a trainer are now either mandatory or in the process of becoming so, around the world.

Many authors suggest that trainers need to be more than just subject matter experts. For example, Quick (1991, p. 73) stated that "If trainers don't have a good theoretical and conceptual base, they simply cannot design relevant, realistic, effective training." Also, Reiss (1991, p. 47) found that "subject matter experts with background in education or instructional design [are] quite rare ... with classroom instruction not coming easy for this group." Carnevale, Gainer, and Schulz (1990) also found this observation to be true of workplace trainers in North America. Therefore, it is critical that the trainer understands and can apply principles of adult learning in their delivery of training, for example, engaging learners to identify their own specific learning needs.

Likewise, Leach's 1996 study revealed that less than one-third of the exemplary trainers were subject matter experts in the field(s) for which they provide training, prior to assuming the role of trainer. The majority of the exemplary trainers in Leach's study indicated that they became experts on the content of the training while working in the training department, instead of improving their pedagogical skills as trainers and developing their teaching skills.

Olson's 1994 study found that there was a definite pattern of similar competencies and processes, including presentation and communication skills, group facilitation skills, and adult teaching methods, that are generic for both two-year college instructors and workplace trainers. In contrast, this research and others have found that a lack of process skills will limit and inhibit a trainer's effectiveness; whereas, an effective trainer will find ways to turn changes into positive, energizing events, rather than confusing and demoralizing ones. Such andragogical and pedagogical knowledge of conceptual frameworks for identifying adult learning paradigms better equip a trainer to develop and implement training strategies that promote best practice, to address identified needs.

Some trainers feel threatened by the new workers and refuse to teach them anything at all, in order to retain their "competitive edge" (Walter, 2002). There is also the concern that "consultant trainers" fear a loss of status or displacement (Lave & Wenger, 1991) from sharing their knowledge, as opposed to the traditional/dedicated teacher who sees this as foremost in job satisfaction. The significance of the training problem to management should be a response like, "I'm not really patient about teaching anybody," made by Hatch, the corporate trainer (and winner) on the first international television program, *Survivor* (August 2, 2000). This research has overwhelmingly found that in order to teach an individual, an effective trainer must know that individual.

Training managers believe that, "professional training skills contributed more to success than did content knowledge or skill" (DiGeorgio, 1982, p. 17). The learning process is more important than the content of the course (Hiemstra & Sisco, 1990). Teaching requires more than knowledge of the subject matter (Knowles, 1980; Draves, 1984). It also requires an understanding of how individuals develop and learn (Knowles, 1980; Olson, 1993). "Those having ownership of the process almost always have a more positive attitude toward the content and instructional process" (Hiemstra & Sisco, 1990, p. 14). Accordingly, if a trainer does not apply the processes, not only is the credibility of a trainer doubted, but more importantly, the reputation of the organization is brought into question.

A search of the literature concerning trainer processes highlighted a range of processes that contribute to trainer effectiveness. Table 7.2 lists a compilation of trainer processes from a diverse selection of authors and researchers who are highly regarded internationally, in the training profession. This chapter commenced with the statement that training is the strategic linchpin of modern productivity. Likewise, Dewhurst and Harris (2013) purport that the ultimate goal of training is to contribute to the execution of strategic initiatives. Therefore, "think strategically" is an addition to Table 7.2, as included in the foundational competencies by the ASTD (2013), the Canadian Society for Training and Development (2012), and the Trainers Network (2009).

"Never stop learning" is best highlighted by Lindeman (1945), cited in Gessner (1956, p. 166), who makes the poignant remark, "in some of the best adult classes it is sometimes difficult to discover who is learning most, the teacher or the students." In his son-in-law's tribute (Gessner, 1956, p. 166), Lindeman (1945) also said, "None but the humble become good teachers of adults." Effective trainers constantly refine their experiences as they accumulate new ones and new information. The ability to "know" how to facilitate learning or assess the performance of a learner is often a product of accumulated experience with the trainer drawing upon their experience of learning and what worked best for them.

The trainer processes in Table 7.2 have been recognized and used in previous studies, as indicated. As a result, the processes have a very high universal consistency of recognition, among effective trainers.

Without question, strong knowledge and skill levels are implicit factors in the formula for trainer effectiveness. However, trainers with a repository of knowledge about effective teaching are not always identified as excellent (Leach, 1996). Therefore, the next section discusses personal characteristics of effective trainers that also contribute to their role.

Table 7.2 Trainer processes.

Trainer processes	Authors											
	Leach (1996)	Olson (1994)	Thompson (2001)	Pinto and Walker (1978)	Jacobs (1987)	ASTD (2013)	CSTD (2012)	Grabowski (1976)	Lindeman (1926, 1938)	Apps (1996)	Knox (1979, 1986)	Trainers Network (2009)
Provide positive reinforcement	□	□	□			□	□				□	□
Manage the learning environment		□	□				□					□
Provide motivational incentives/solutions		□	□		□	□	□	□	□			□
Understand adult teaching methods	□	□	□	□	□		□	□	□			□
Use group process skills				□		□	□		□			□
Professional self-development				□	□	□	□			□		□
Never stop learning							□	□				□
Competency identification skills	□	□	□				□					□
Knowledge of target culture						□	□	□	□			□
Demonstrate effective questioning skills	□	□				□	□					□
Think strategically						□	□					□

Trainer Personal Characteristics

Workplace trainers with subject matter expertise and pedagogical knowledge are not always identified as excellent. There is overwhelming evidence in the literature that it takes more than knowledge and skills to define the excellent workplace trainer.

When hiring a trainer, Reiss (1991) suggests looking for personal characteristics such as "sincere," "enthusiastic," and "personable." Murphy (2002, p. 61) also believes that "someone with high social skills ... will be a star trainer." Likewise, Brody (2002) advises that 55 percent of a message is conveyed by your appearance. Consider the politician who grabbed the hand of a young woman, resplendent in a chapeau and frock, among the punters and pumped furiously, only to be confronted with, "Daddy, it's me!" "For just a moment, a look of fear flickered across his [the politician's] face" (McClymont, 2001, p. 26), as he recognized his daughter. A trainer can be taught content, presentation skills, and methodology; but you cannot teach someone personality (Thomas, 1999), which drives and informs someone's customer-service skills. Trainers must want to be trainers and have patience and respect for different learning abilities (Walter, 2002).

Emotional intelligence is "the ability to sense, understand, and effectively apply the power and acumen of emotions as a source of human energy, information, connection, and influence" (Cooper & Sawaf, 1997, p. xiii) that may save an organization from disaster, because it is linked to success and profitability (p. xiv). Decker (in Cooper & Sawaf, 1997, p. 21) recalls how ex-US president Robert Kennedy's "sheer use of personal energy enabled him to connect with the emotions of his listeners. There was energy in his voice and even more in his face, and body language." Other researchers believe that trainers should show their uniqueness to learners and present themselves as "real people," instead of hiding behind a façade of authority (Rogers, 1969; Tough, 1979; Apps, 1981; Heck & Williams, 1984). The more effective trainers are more interested in their students as people and give more helpful support.

Humor (Knowles, 1980; Draves, 1984) is a universal wellspring for boosting energy and busting tension, because it improves work processes such as judgment, problem solving, and decision making (Carnevale & Isen, 1986). Humor is by far the most significant behavior of human intelligence (DeBono, 1991). Philipson (2001, p.1) found that it was more effective to "use a little humour to liven up a talk about business intelligence," instead of relying on PowerPoint that can "dull the message." Although Lindeman, in a 1947 work included in Gessner (1956), does not know whether or not humor is teachable, he feels certain that the adult teacher who is lacking in this quality will make adult education, not a happy adventure of the mind, but rather, a grim despondency of the spirit.

Southwest's CEO Herb Kelleher is renowned for saying, "We can teach the job; we can't teach the attitude" (Chang, in Cortada & Woods, 2002, p. 401). "If the relations of human beings have any significance at all, they are relations which produce ethical results" (Lindeman, in Gessner, 1956, p. 315).

"At the heart of each of us, whatever our imperfections, there exists a silent pulse, a complex of wave forms and resonances, which is absolutely individual and unique, and yet which connects us to everything in the universe" (Leonard, in Cooper & Sawaf, 1997, p. 196). This "pulse" forms fields of energy that react with each in a stimulating, equalizing, or sedating way. "We can experience this upon entering a room filled with people, quickly sensing whether it is permeated with vibrations that are harmonious or discordant" (Klotsche, in Cooper & Sawaf, 1997, p. 197).

According to Knox (1986, p. 43), "teaching tends to be quite intuitive and implicit, largely reflecting the instructor's personal qualities and habits." "The really valuable thing is intuition" (Einstein, in Cooper & Sawaf, 1997, p. 230). "The primary wisdom is intuition. In that deep force, the last fact behind which analysis cannot go, all things find their origin" (Emerson, in Cooper & Sawaf, 1997, p. 232).

Burns (1996) also brought the many labels that get assigned to the generic description of a workplace trainer to the fore. An interesting one, and one that probably comes closest to and more aptly describes the role of a trainer, is the label given to Burns when she was working with prisoners and street kids: "cracker." This seems to be a more precise and accurate down-to-earth title.

Leach's study of industry trainers revealed that although both average and exemplary trainers described themselves as possessing similar personal characteristics, the exemplary trainers seemed to exhibit certain personal characteristics more often than the average trainers, for example, greeting and engaging learners, attending to their social, emotional, and comfort needs. Such trainers create a positive receptivity with learners, to avoid resistance that may interfere with a constructive learning process and discourse that stimulates creative thinking, by managing expressions of prejudice and discrimination without alienating either the individual or group and preventing emotional withdrawal.

From the literature, the assumption is that a trainer who practices and demonstrates these competencies, processes, and personal characteristics will be a more effective trainer, resulting in more competent learners (Leach 1986, 1989a, 1989b, 1991a, 1991b, 1992, 1993, 1996; Leach & Grayslake Lake College, 1982; Leach & Sandall 1995; Olson, 1991, 1993, 1994; Olson & Pachnowski, 1999; Thompson, 2001). Table 7.3 lists a compilation of personal trainer characteristics from a diverse selection of authors and researchers who are highly regarded internationally, in the training profession that contributes to trainer effectiveness.

The unhappiest trainers are those who fail to sense that, "it is their own half-hearted efforts that defraud them" (Melby, 2001, p. 1). Good teaching is not only about motivating students to learn but also teaching them how to learn, in a style that is relevant, meaningful, and memorable.

In summary, "It is tragic that we have not learned how to learn without being taught, and it is probably more important than all of the immediate reasons put together" (Knowles, 1975, p. 15). "It's the acceptance of all that gives power to the teacher" (Melby, 2001, p. 1).

There is a definite need for pedagogical assistance to enhance success in adult education programs and avoid the misguided opinion that "anyone can teach" (Melby, 2001). For example, Lindeman in Gessner (1956) asserts that a true teacher is a person who recognizes that it is the total personality of the student that is to be educated.

Reflecting a similar position, the absence of an appropriate model, which truly signifies the competencies, processes, and ideal personal characteristics of a trainer, has been lamented. Therefore, by identifying threshold competencies, processes, and personal characteristics in the literature, and analyzing the survey data from this research from participating trainers who were identified as being effective in their role as a trainer, who had been in training positions for more than 10 years and were formally qualified as a trainer with at least a bachelor of education degree (any), a profile of an effective trainer was assembled and is presented in Table 7.4. This profile contributes to international best practice.

This Effective Trainer Model is neither exhaustive nor too generalist, but rather includes a commonality of world-class competencies for trainers, recognizing that many other areas of trainer competency exist that are contextually specific. The effective trainer is one who knows a variety of assessment methods and who can identify opportunities and activities that promote the transfer of learning before, during, and after the training process, including a comprehensive evaluation of training effectiveness.

Table 7.3 Trainer personal characteristics.

Trainer personal characteristics	Leach (1996)	Thompson (2001)	Jacobs (1987)	ASTD (2013)	CSTD (2012)	Grabowski (1976)	Lindeman (1926, 1938)	Houle (1956, 1996)	Boag (1989)	Apps (1981, 1996)	Knox (1979, 1986)	Trainers Network (2009)
Responsive	✓			✓	✓							✓
Enthusiastic	✓	✓			✓				✓	✓	✓	✓
Humorous	✓	✓							✓			✓
Sincere	✓	✓			✓							✓
Ethical		✓			✓		✓					✓
Flexible	✓	✓		✓	✓				✓			✓
Tolerant	✓	✓			✓							✓
Confident (high self-esteem)		✓			✓				✓			✓
Pleasant personal appearance				✓	✓			✓				✓
Good speaking ability		✓										✓
Enjoy teaching		✓						✓	✓		✓	✓
Interpersonal skills		✓		✓	✓						✓	✓
Ability to listen		✓		✓	✓	✓				✓		✓

Authors

	C1	C2	C3	C4	C5	C6	C7	C8	C9	C10	C11
Patience	□		□								□
Good personality	□			□					□		□
Empathy	□			□				□	□		□
Approachable	□							□			□
Helpful	□							□	□	□	□
Open-minded	□						□	□	□		□
Concerned	□							□	□		□
Professional	□							□	□	□	□
Ability to work with all ages	□										□
Compassionate	□							□	□		□
Encouraging	□	□	□			□	□	□			□
Innovative	□	□							□		
Unique/human	□	□	□						□		
Leadership skills	□				□			□	□		
Organized	□							□			
Emotional intelligence/critical thinking	□							□	□		□

Table 7.4   Profile of an effective workplace trainer.

Competencies/processes/personal characteristics of an effective workplace trainer	
Bachelor of education qualification	Nine plus years of experience in training positions
Set goals and objectives	Reflect upon work
Evaluate effects and impact of training	Use group skills
Questioning skills and techniques	Self-controlled
Provide positive reinforcement	Facilitate group learning activities
Fair in assessment	Listen actively
Stimulate student interest	Motivate students to do their best work
Understand adult teaching methods/theory	Responsive
Humorous	Sincere
Flexible	Confident (high self-esteem)
Perceptive	Manage time
Enjoy teaching	Conducts a needs assessment
Counsel students	Have competency identification skills
Never stop learning	Have knowledge of the target culture
Enthusiastic	Tolerant
Healthy	Recognize own limitations
Demonstrate vision	Write effectively
Encourage trainees to think for themselves	Ethical
Build relationships	Attend to individual differences in trainees
Know the organization's needs	Foster an environment conducive to learning
Be appreciative of student effort	Understand the qualifications training framework
Keep current and up-to-date	Have research skills
Use appropriate training methods	Encourage open communication
Pleasant personal appearance	Develop lesson plans
Blend different training techniques	Good speaking ability
Excellent knowledge of the subject	Interpersonal skills
Patience	Good personality
Empathy	Approachable
Helpful	Open-minded
Concerned	Professional
Ability to work with all ages	Compassionate
Innovative	Unique/human
Leadership Skills	Organized
Analyze course materials/learner information	Assure preparation of training site
Establish/maintain trainer credibility	Manage the learning environment
Demonstrate effective presentation skills	Use media effectively
Understand training and development	Understand program development
Evaluate learner performance	Evaluate delivery of training
Emotional intelligence/critical thinking	Think strategically
Professional self-development	Support learner needs/feedback/transfer of learning

Future Research

A difficult problem is thinking through how jobs will change in the future and thus, how best to train tomorrow's workforce today, avoiding training workers for jobs that have vanished. Perhaps the toughest aspect of training is that employees' fear of change or failure means they do not always embrace it with open arms. But, studies have shown that workers who are trained earn a higher wage than those who are not and experience fewer bouts of unemployment (Walter, 2002). Training spurs productivity and output.

"Not only do adults need to learn new tricks, they also need to unlearn many of the old habits, beliefs, and facts that are no longer valid" (Birkenholz, 1999, p. 15).

The number of corporate universities is estimated to be more than 5000 in the United States (Allen, 2002) and continues to increase. They aim to differentiate from traditional universities by being strategic in their intent and activities, as opposed to traditional training organizations that are generally tactical in their approach.

Asian organizations appear to embrace a Confucian belief in the educated and self-advancing person, and produce highly skilled and motivated workforces (Stone, 1998). For example, Hitachi's management-developing efforts are based upon the belief that the most important responsibility of a manager is to educate and develop his or her subordinates (Smith, 1990).

Bassi, Cheney, and Van Buren (1997) reminded us that for centuries, the "technology" for transferring skills and knowledge has changed little: one human being teaching another. Generations of classroom trainers have deployed the time-honored, "chalk and talk" approach. Only the overhead projector loomed on the horizon of a training landscape devoid of technology. Now, that landscape is awash with a torrent of new technologies, creating almost limitless possibilities for heightened learning. New developments will remove some of the technical roadblocks, such as bandwidth limitations that will pave the way for unprecedented growth in this area.

The need for employees to commit themselves to "lifelong learning" (Knox, 1979) has been highlighted as a key issue for national prosperity (Stuart, 2000). The term "lifelong learning" was first coined at the University of California Los Angeles in the early 1920s and continues to elicit visionary practices and contribute to competitive standing in the globalized economy.

In a world of accelerating change (the knowledge explosion, the technological revolution, and the information society), learning must be a lifelong process if we are to avoid the catastrophe of human obsolescence. The obsolescence of knowledge is becoming as much a fact of life in the information age as the need for lifelong learning (Birkenholz, 1999). The single most important competence that people must possess to survive is the ability to learn – with or, more importantly, without a teacher (Knowles, 1990).

"If adult education is to produce a difference of quality in the use of intelligence, its promoters will do well to devote their major concern to method and not content" (Lindeman, 1926, p. 179). In the words of futurist Alvin Toffler (1970), "The illiterate of the future will not be the person who cannot read. It will be the person who cannot learn."

Additional challenges will be how to assess the effectiveness of learning technologies and how to determine their useful applications.

Conclusion

It must be remembered that factors such as the information explosion, the changing nature of knowledge, the necessity to be more efficient and productive, competition from intensified globalization of the world economy, consumers' rising demands, increasing organizational complexity, the drive to maintain excellence and to remain competitive, the public's demand for professional accountability, the threat of malpractice litigation, rapid development of new technologies, compliance and shifts in governmental regulatory patterns have all contributed to society's increased awareness of the need for training and to adopt better forms of best practice in the workplace.

The concerns and problems associated with workplace training, raised in this chapter, can be overcome with better management of change and professional recognition appropriated to trainers. Organizations must create and develop a productive workplace teaching culture, seizing the opportunity to fully acknowledge and strengthen their most valuable training asset: the trainer. Just like organizations have adopted "total marketing communications" and the "learning organization," they also need to embrace "the teaching organization."

Regardless of the economies of scale, new technologies must be embraced to transfer information, create knowledge, and build intellectual capital worldwide. Technology appears to be the single most important factor driving changes in today's workplace, making it both a bane and boon to trainers. The speed of change, fierce competition, and the lean organizational style of the previous decades have all helped to drive the demand in more recent times for personal development training. The best training programs anticipate changes in technology and equip their workers to cope with them, ahead of the competition, if management adopts the right vision.

Training serves as a key agent in creating a culture that is receptive to new practices and providing the knowledge to implement the new practices at the workplace. "Winning companies win because they have solid leaders not only at the top, but also at all organizational levels (Cohen & Tichy, 1998, p. 2). Cohen and Tichy found that this was the case because "everyone, including and especially top leaders, were committed teachers" (p. 2).

The andragogical model is expected to be modified, enriched, and superseded by new knowledge about learning in general and learning of adults in particular, as investing in worker education boosts employee loyalty as well as corporate profits. A necessary component in safeguarding precious ongoing and future investment is to ensure the implementation of quality standards within the training profession.

Effective training may become more important as the workforce is reduced and new authority and responsibility are granted to those who remain.

References

Allen, M. (2002). *The Corporate University Handbook*. New York: Amacom.

Apps, J. W. (1981). *The Adult Learner on Campus*. Chicago: Follett.

Apps, J. W. (1996). *Teaching from the Heart*, Malabar, FL: Krieger.

Arneson, J., Naughton, J., & Rothwell, W. (2013). Training and development competencies redefined to create competitive advantage. *Training and Development*, 67(1), 42–47.

Arnott, D. (2000). *Corporate Cults: The Insidious Lure of the All-Consuming Organization*. New York: Amacom.

Ashton, D. N., & Sung, J. (2002). *Supporting Workplace Learning for High Performance Working*. Geneva: International Labour Office.

ASTD. (2013). The ASTD Competency Model. http://www.astd.org/Certification/Competency-Model (accessed April 8, 2014).

Bassi, L. J., Cheney, S., & Van Buren, M. E. (1997). Training industry trends 1997. *Training and Development*, 51(11), 46–59.

Bernstein, B. B., Goldbeck, R. A., Hillix, W. A., & Marx, M. H. (1957). Application of the half split technique to problem solving tasks, *Journal of Experimental Psychology*, 53, 330–338.

Bierema, L. L. (1996). How executive women learn corporate culture. *Human Resource Development Quarterly*, 7(2), 145–164.

Birkenholz, R. J. (1999). *Effective Adult Learning*. Danville, IL: Interstate, Inc.

Bolman, L. G., & Deal, T. E. (1997). *Reframing Organizations.* San Francisco: Jossey-Bass.

Bone, J., Harris, R., & Simons, M. (2000). *More Than Meets the Eye? Rethinking the Role of Workplace Trainer.* Leabrook: NCVER.

Broadwell, M. M. (1995). *The Supervisor and On-the-Job Training.* Reading, MA: Addison-Wesley.

Brody, M. (2002). Test your etiquette. *Training and Development,* February, 64–66.

Burns, S. (1996). *Artistry in Training: Thinking Differently about the Way you Help People to Learn.* Warriewood: Business and Professional Publishing Pty Ltd.

Canadian Policy Research Networks. (2009) http://www.cprn.org/index.cfm (accessed April 8, 2014).

Carnevale, A. P., Gainer, L. J., & Schulz, E. R. (1990). *Training the Technical Work Force.* San Francisco: Jossey-Bass.

Carnevale, P. J. D., & Isen, A. M. (1986). The influence of positive affect and visual access on the discovery of integrative solutions in bilateral negotiation. *Organizational Behavior and Human Decision Processes,* 37, 1–13.

Cohen, E., & Tichy, N. M. (1998). The teaching organization. *Training and Development,* 52(7), 27–33.

Cooper, R., & Sawaf, A. (1997). *Executive EQ: Emotional Intelligence in Business.* London: Orion.

Corben, H., & Dunn, L. (1999). *Influences on the Education of Vocational Education and Training (VET) Practitioners.* Lismore, Australia: Southern Cross University.

Cortada, J. W., & Woods, J. A. (2002). *The 2002 ASTD Training and Performance Yearbook,* New York: McGraw-Hill.

CSTD. (Canadian Society for Training and Development) (2012). *Competencies for Training and Development Professionals.* Canada: CSTD Press.

DeBono, E. (1991). *I am Right, You are Wrong.* New York: Viking.

Dewhurst, D., & Harris, M. (2013). Winning the heads and hearts of leaders. *Training and Development,* 40(4), 4–7.

DiGeorgio, R. M. (1982). Training needs of people who do training. *Training and Development,* 36(6), 16–25.

Draves, W. A. (1984). *How to Teach Adults.* Manhattan, KS: Learning Resource Network.

Drucker, P. F. (1993). *Concept of the Corporation.* New Brunswick, NJ: Transaction.

Galbraith, M. W. (1998). Becoming an effective teacher of adults. In M. W. Galbraith (Ed.), *Adult Learning Methods* (pp. 3–19). Malabar, FL: Krieger.

Gessner, R. (Ed.) (1956). *The Democratic Man: Selected Writings of Eduard Lindeman.* Boston, MA: Beacon Press.

Grabowski, S. (1976). *Training Teachers of Adults: Models and Innovative Programs.* Syracuse, NY: National Association for Public Continuing and Adult Education.

Handley, P., & Lawlor, M. (1996). *The Creative Trainer: Holistic Facilitation Skills for Accelerated Learning.* McGraw-Hill Training Series. London: McGraw-Hill.

Heck, S. F., & Williams, C. R. (1984). *The Complex Role of the Teacher: An Ecological Perspective.* New York: Teachers College Press.

Herzberg, F. (1966). *Work and the Nature of Men,* Cleveland, OH: World Publishing.

Hiemstra, R., & Sisco, B. (1990). *Individualizing Instruction: Making Learning Personal, Empowering, and Successful.* San Francisco: Jossey-Bass.

Houle, C. O. (1956). Professional education for educators of adults. *Adult Education,* 6 (Spring) 131–149.

Houle, C. O. (1996). *The Design of Education.* San Francisco: Jossey-Bass.

Jacobs, R. L. (1987). *Human Performance Technology: A Systems-Based Field for the Training and Development Profession.* Information Series No. 326. Columbus, OH: ERIC Clearinghouse on Adult, Career, and Vocational Education; National Center for Research in Vocational Education, Ohio State University.

Kinni, T. (2000). Self-improvement corporate style. *Training,* 37(5), 57–63.

Knowles, M. S. (1975). *Self-Directed Learning: A Guide for Learners and Teachers.* Chicago: Follett.

Knowles, M. S. (1980). *The Modern Practice of Adult Education from Pedagogy to Andragogy.* Englewood Cliffs, NJ: Cambridge Books.

Knowles, M. S. (1990). *The Adult Learner: A Neglected Species* (4th ed.). Houston: Gulf.

Knowles, M. S., et al. (1985). *Andragogy in Action: Applying Modern Principles of Adult Learning.* San Francisco: Jossey-Bass.

Knox, A. B. (Ed.) (1979). *Enhancing Proficiencies of Continuing Educators.* New Directions for Continuing Education, No 1. San Francisco: Jossey-Bass.

Knox, A. B. (1986). *Helping Adults Learn.* San Francisco: Jossey-Bass.

Lasonen, J. (2000). *Workplaces as Learning Environments Evaluated by Employers, Students, Workplace Trainers and Teachers.* Finland: University of Jyvaskyla, Institute for Educational Research.

Lave, J., & Wenger, E. (1991). *Situated Learning: Legitimate Peripheral Participation.* Cambridge: Cambridge University Press.

Leach, J. A. (1986). An assessment of the importance of selected competencies and perceived ability among training and development professionals. *Journal of Vocational and Technical Education,* 3(1), 45–54.

Leach, J. A. (1989a). Training and development programs in vocational teacher education departments: A preliminary investigation. *Journal of Studies in Technical Careers,* 1(4), 325–332.

Leach, J. A. (1989b). An investigation of trainer certification (preparation) programs in the private sector. Paper presented at the American Vocational Association Convention, Orlando, FL, December.

Leach, J. A. (1991a). *Characteristics of Excellent Trainers in Business and Industry: A Psychological, Interpersonal, Motivational, and Demographic Profile, Working Papers.* Berkeley, CA: National Center for Research in Vocational Education.

Leach, J. A. (1991b). Psychological and interpersonal characteristics of excellent two-year postsecondary vocational-technical instructors. *Journal of Studies in Technical Careers,* 3(1): 61–77.

Leach, J. A. (1992). *Private Sector Instructors: The Nature of Effective Vocational Educators Working in Business and Industry.* Berkeley, CA: National Center for Research in Vocational Education.

Leach, J. A. (1993). Preparing tomorrow's business and industry trainers: Appropriateness of the content of vocational teacher education programs. *Journal of Vocational and Technical Education,* 9(2): 4–16.

Leach, J. A. (1996). Distinguishing characteristics among exemplary trainers in business and industry. *Journal of Vocational and Technical Education,* 12(2), 5–18.

Leach, J. A., & Grayslake Lake College (1982). *Literature Review with Annotated Bibliography. The Accreditation of Training Experiences: Implications for Employment Training Programs.* Grayslake, IL: Project REA, College of Lake County.

Leach, J. A., & Sandall, D. L. (1995). Required business skills for training professionals. *Journal of Industrial Teacher Education,* 32(4), 74–86.

Lindeman, E. C. (1926). *The Meaning of Adult Education.* New York: New Republic.

Lindeman, E. C. (1938). Preparing leaders in adult education. Speech to the Pennsylvania Association for Adult Education, November 18 1938. Reprinted in S. Brookfield (Ed.), *Training Educators of Adults,* New York: Routledge (1988).

Lindeman, E. C. (1945). The sociology of adult education. *Educational Sociology,* 19, September, 4–13.

Maslow, A. H. (1970). *Motivation and Personality* (2nd ed.). New York: Harper & Row.

McClymont, K. (2001). Who's ya daddy. *Sydney Morning Herald,* November 10–11.

Melby, E. (2001). The true teacher accepts all students. http://www.mysdcc.sdccd.edu/Staff/Instructor_Development/Content/HTML/The_True_Teacher_Accepts_All_Students.htm (accessed March 21, 2014). From E. Melby, *The Teacher and Learning.*

Murphy, D. (2002). Got technology? *Training and Development,* June 61.

Olson, S. J. (1991). Postsecondary technical instructor programs and postsecondary technical teacher certification: A national study. *Journal of Studies in Technical Careers,* 13(4), 341–350.

Olson, S. J. (1993). A new source for teachers: Can business and industry fill the gaps in tomorrow's teacher pool? *Vocational Education Journal,* 68(6): 36–37.

Olson, S. J. (1994). Competencies of two-year college technical instructors and technical trainers: similarities and differences. *Journal of Industrial Teacher Education,* 32(1), 65–85.

Olson, S. J., & Pachnowski, L. (1999). An experience in preparing technical instructors for the virtual classroom: Lessons learned. *ATEA Journal,* 26(2), 6–8.

Philipson, G. (2001). Feel the power and miss the point with PowerPoint. *Sydney Morning Herald*, November 6, IT, p. 1.

Pinto, P. R., & Walker, J. W. (1978). *A Study of Professional Training and Development Roles and Competencies*. Madison, WI: ASTD.

Quick, T. L. (1991). *Training Managers So they Can Really Manage: Confessions of a Frustrated Trainer*. San Francisco: Jossey-Bass.

Reiss, C. J. (1991). Turning technicians into trainers. *Training*, 28(7), 47–50.

Rogers, C. R. (1969). *Freedom to Learn*. Columbus, OH: Charles E. Merrill.

Senge, P. M. (1990). *The Fifth Discipline: The Art and Practice of the Learning Organization*. New York: Doubleday/Currency.

Smith, R. M. (1990). *Learning to Learn across the Lifespan*. San Francisco: Jossey-Bass.

Stewart, T. A. (1997). *Intellectual Capital: The New Wealth of Organizations*. New York: Doubleday/Currency.

Stolovich, H. (1999). Adult learning workshop. Training 1999 Conference, Chicago; January.

Stone, R. J. (1998). *Human Resource Management*. Brisbane: John Wiley & Sons, Ltd.

Stuart, K. (2000). Back to school (and stay there). http://www.internetnews.com/bus-news/article.php/469291/Back+To+School+and+Stay+There.htm (accessed March 21, 2014).

Thiagarajan, R., & Thiagarajan, S. (1999). Experiential learning/jolting learners. Training 1999 Conference, Chicago, February.

Thomas, B. (1999). How to hire instructors who love training. *Training and Development*, 53(3), 14–15.

Thompson, K. D. (2001). Adult educator effectiveness with the training context: A study of trainee perception of effective trainer characteristics. PhD thesis. University of Wyoming.

Toffler, A. (1970). *Future Shock*. New York: Random House.

Tough, A. (1979). *The Adult's Learning Projects* (2nd ed.). Austin, TX: Learning Concepts.

Tovey, M. D. (1997). *Training in Australia: Design, Delivery, Evaluation, Management*. Sydney: Prentice Hall of Australia Pty Ltd.

Trainers Network. (2009). Assuring world class competencies for trainers. http://www.trainersnetwork.ie/tnfullrep.pdf (accessed April 8, 2014).

Walter, D. (2002). *Training on the Job*. Alexandria, VA: ASTD.

Wlodkowski, R. J. (1993). *Enhancing Adult Motivation to Learn: A Guide to Improving Instruction and Increasing Learner Achievement*. San Francisco: Jossey-Bass.

8

Training Evaluation

Jonathan Passmore and Maria Joao Velez

Introduction

Training evaluation consists of the systematic collection of data regarding the success of training programs (Goldstein, 1986). While this is considered fundamental in relation to the achievement of intended outcomes of training and whether training objectives have been achieved (Kraiger, Ford, & Salas, 1993) the reality of human resources practice is that training evaluation is often neglected or delivered as an afterthought.

Several models, taxonomies, or frameworks for evaluation exist. This chapter sets out to provide a brief critical review of some of the commonly used training evaluation models, including Kirkpatrick, Phillip's ROI, CIPP, CIRO, Brinkerhoff, IPO, HRD Evaluation and Research, Success Case Method, Dessinger-Moseley Full-Scope (DeSimone, Werner, & Harris, 2002), as well as the SOAP-M evaluation model, a recently proposed model, which seeks to offer a practical framework for use in real world settings (Passmore & Velez, 2012). In reviewing these models the chapter critically reviews research studies that have sought to apply these models in practice.

The Developing Context of Human Resources

As the human resources functions within global organizations have responded to demands to deliver improved people outcomes, so there has been a growing interest in how to improve the measurement and assessment of organizational interventions. This change reflects wider changes both in increasing use of metrics within organizations and a recognition that people management is a critical component in knowledge-based and performance-driven economies (Kumpikaitė, 2007). Kaufman, Keller, and Watkins (1995) have suggested that as a result of these changing factors, there has seen a stronger interest by organizational boards to evaluate each HR intervention for its added value to the business.

The Wiley Blackwell Handbook of the Psychology of Training, Development, and Performance Improvement,
First Edition. Edited by Kurt Kraiger, Jonathan Passmore, Sigmar Malvezzi, and Nuno Rebelo dos Santos.
© 2015 John Wiley & Sons Ltd. Published 2020 by John Wiley & Sons Ltd.

Over the past three decades, an increasing number of human resource training evaluation models have been developed as tools to identify the dimensions or factors of effectiveness (Tzeng, Chiang, & Li, 2007). This has resulted in a plethora of models available to organizations when considering training evaluation.

While for most industrial and occupational psychologists the literature is dominated by a small number of popular models, such as Kirkpatrick, ROI, or the CIRO model, there are a mass of less well known but interesting alternatives.

In this chapter we discuss 11 models (see Table 8.1). The list is not exhaustive and a search of the literature reveals the breadth of interest in this area at an academic level, even if such interest is not matched by the application of such models by practitioners.

A Review of Individual Training Evaluation Models

Kirkpatrick's Model

The most popular and widely known approach to the evaluation of training is Kirkpatrick's framework. The model has served as the primary organizing design for training evaluations in organizations for over 30 years. Kirkpatrick (1979) developed an evaluation model by producing a hierarchical system that indicates effectiveness through four categories of evaluation, from the basic reaction of the participants to training and its impact on the organization: Reaction, Learning, Behavior, and Results (Singh, 2013).

Level 1 includes assessment of training participants' reaction to the training program, especially assessment of affective responses to the quality or relevance of the training. This has been incorporated by most organizations into the frequently used training evaluation questionnaire or "happy sheet." Level 2, learning measures, is harder to measure and is concerned with defining quantifiable indicators of the learning that has taken place during the course of the training. Level 3, behavior outcomes, addresses either the extent to which knowledge and skills gained in training are applied on the job or result in exceptional job-related performance. Finally level 4, outcomes are intended to provide some measure of the impact that training has had on broader organizational goals and objectives (Alliger & Janak, 1989; Bates, 2004; Kirkpatrick, 1979).

Each level builds on the previous and requires more sophisticated data-gathering techniques. Both levels 1 and 2 relate to the value of the training to the individual, while levels 3 and 4 measure the value of the training for the organization (O'Toole, 2009). Bates (2004) underlines the valuable contributions of this model to training evaluation thinking and practice, namely by focusing training evaluation on outcomes; by emphasizing the importance of examining multiple measures of training effectiveness, as well as the importance of the learning process in training effectiveness, through the distinction between learning (level 2) and behavior (level 3).

Kirkpatrick's model of training evaluation and criteria has dominated the evaluation literature. Hilbert, Russ-Eft, and Preskill (1997) review evaluation models in the HRD and psychology literature. Of the 57 journal articles describing evaluation models, 44 (77 percent) included Kirkpatrick's model. One example, Arthur and colleagues. (2003), used this framework to examine the relationship between specified training design and evaluation features and the effectiveness of training in organizations. Results of this meta-analysis suggested that the training method used, the skill or task characteristic trained, and the choice of training evaluation criteria are related to the observed effectiveness of training programs (Arthur et al., 2003). More recently, Lin, Cheng, and Chuang (2011) explored the effect of organizational commitment on employees' reactions to educational training

Table 8.1 Eleven popular evaluation models and their criteria.

Evaluation models	Evaluation criteria
Kirkpatrick's Model	1 Reaction 2 Learning 3 Behavior 4 Results
Kaufman and Keller's Model	1 Enabling and Reaction 2 Acquisition 3 Application 4 Organizational Outputs 5 Societal Outcomes
CIRO Model	1 Contents/Contexts 2 Inputs 3 Reaction 4 Outcomes
CIPP Model	1 Context 2 Input 3 Process 4 Product
Phillips Five-Level ROI	1 Reaction and Planned Action 2 Learning 3 Applied Learning on the Job 4 Business Results 5 Return on Investment
Brinkerhoff's Six-Stage Model	1 Goal Setting 2 Program Design 3 Program Implementation 4 Immediate Outcomes 5 Intermediate or Usage Outcomes 6 Impacts and Worth
IPO Model	1 Inputs 2 Process 3 Outcomes/Outputs
HRD Evaluation and Research Model	1 Learning 2 Individual Performance 3 Organization
Success Case Method	1 Evaluation Focus and Planning 2 Impact Model Creation 3 Administration of a Survey to Gauge Success Rates 4 Conduction of Interviews with Success and Nonsuccess Instances 5 Formulation of Conclusions
Dessinger-Moseley Full-Scope	1 Formative Evaluation 2 Summative Evaluation 3 Confirmative Evaluation 4 Meta-Evaluation
SOAP-M Model	1 Self 2 Other 3 Achievements 4 Potential 5 Meta-Analysis

also using Kirkpatrick's four-level model. According to these authors, Kirkpatrick's model is the most widely accepted and used training-evaluation model, due to its simplicity, clarity, and easiness of application.

A survey conducted by the American Society for Training and Development found that 91 percent of organizations in the United States used the level 1 application of the Kirkpatrick's model, however, only 50 percent of the organizations used level 2 and just 8 percent of respondents claimed to be using level 4 (O'Toole, 2009). According to O'Toole (2009), most organizations never attempt to apply level 4 because it is only possible to use this level in organizations that align training and development programs with objectives that have a measurable output. Besides this, organizational performance also depends on additional factors, for example, motivation, work environment, incentives, rewards, and external constraints.

However, critics have highlighted a series of criticisms of Kirkpatrick's model (Bates, 2004). Guerci and colleagues have suggested that the four levels of evaluation that it proposes lead to an excessively simplified vision regarding the effectiveness of training, particularly because it does not consider the influences of the organizational context (Guerci, Bartezzaghi, & Solari, 2010). A second criticism is based on the causal relations between the levels of evaluation. According to the model it is not possible to achieve positive results at top levels if this did not occur at the lower ones (Alliger & Janak, 1989). There is limited published evidence to support this. A third criticism, offered by Guerci and colleagues, of the hierarchical model is its unitary perspective. The model assumes the point of view of the organization. They argue that the model thus neglects the evaluation needs of all the other stakeholders involved in the training process (Guerci, Bartezzaghi, & Solari, 2010). In this sense Kirkpatrick's framework is a reflection of the time in which it was developed, where organizations were more likely to be hierarchical with a pyramid structure. More recent developments in organizational design have witnessed the growth in the virtual, flat, and matrix-structured organizations.

Kaufman and Keller's Model

Kaufman and Keller (1994) have suggested that Kirkpatrick's four levels are also incomplete and lead to a too narrow focus on the evaluation of training alone (Watkins et al., 1998). Specifically the model fails to take into account estimates of use on the job, organizational performance and the worth of the organizational deliverables (Antos & Bruening, 2006). Watkins et al. (1998) suggest that evaluation should begin by identifying the impact of the intervention outside the organization and only after should analyze the impact of the intervention on organization and on individual performance.

The evaluation framework proposed by Kaufman and Keller (1994) retains the distinctive four-levels from Kirkpatrick's model while adding a fifth evaluation level, aimed at determining societal impact. This addition aims to extend the model to consider the internal and external consequences of all interventions related to performance and organizational improvement. According to these authors, Kirkpatrick's four-level evaluation framework is missing a mega-level evaluation, since it devalues the evaluation of societal impact or the usefulness and availability of organizational resources.

The Kaufman's and Keller's model also presents a more proactive emphasis on continuous or formative evaluation and it does not rely solely on summative data as a guide to improve instruction (Kaufman, Keller, & Watkins, 1995). In this sense, Kaufman and Keller offered four additional aspects (Stokking, 1996, p. 172):

1 Consumer satisfaction and societal contribution as additional evaluation criteria;
2 Evaluation as part of the process of needs assessment and planning;

3   Identification of the desired or expected results and consequences as part of the same process;
4   Availability and quality of resources and efficiency of their use as additional criteria.

Kaufman and Keller further emphasize evaluation planning to anticipate unintended consequences to both the organization and society as a whole (Schankman, 2004).

Stokking (1996), however, is equally critical of the Kaufman's and Keller's model. Stokking (1996) suggests the model lacks clarity in some aspects, such as the distinction between the desired chronology of activities and the aspects of level and importance, or regarding implementation. Implementation and achievement of the learning objectives are integrated into Acquisition (level 2), which should indicate the success of training implementation. Antos and Bruening (2006) have also critiqued the model; while recognizing that this model offers more useful management tools for assessing the organizational success of an intervention, they suggest it fails to constitute a real diagnostic tool for training practitioners interested in improving transfer of training to the workplace.

CIRO Model

An alternative and widely quoted model is the CIRO (Contents/Contexts, Inputs, Reactions, and Outcomes) model proposed by Warr, Bird, and Rackham (1970). The authors argue that before assessing reactions and outcomes, context and inputs should be analyzed. This model, which measures learning/training effectiveness by CIRO elements, both before and after training has been carried out, is currently widely used in business (Tzeng, Chiang, & Li, 2007) as well as in academic contexts. For example, Lee (2012) refers to the Lancashire Business School, which uses CIRO to evaluate its coaching skills workshops aimed at personal tutors who are working to assist student engagement, retention, and examination success. This evaluation was conducted a year after the completion of the program and it underlined the potency of a coaching approach for staff, students, and also for the organization.

CIRO focuses on four general categories of evaluation:

1   Context evaluation refers to collecting information about the operational situation or performance problems, in order to determine training needs and set learning objectives, related to organizational culture and climate, focusing on current operational context. (Roark, Kim, & Mupinga, 2006);
2   Input evaluation involves obtaining and using information about possible training resources to select among alternative inputs for training interventions. At this level, the evaluator determines the training methods or techniques and also decides the best method of delivery, taking into account timescales, in-house resources, level and types of input or financial resources available (Beech & Leather, 2006).
3   Reaction evaluation is similar to Kirkpatrick's reaction level, but with greater emphasis on suggestions. It involves the process of obtaining and using information about the quality of training participants' experiences to improve the training process, based on individual reports or interviews. Trainees' views could reveal extremely useful information if they are collected in a systematic way (Lee & Pershing, 2000);
4   Outcome evaluation is similar to the learning process involved in Kirkpatrick's model. It involves obtaining and using information about the results or outcomes of the evaluation program. This level usually constitutes the most important part of evaluation, since it determines the extent to which training objectives have been achieved. This level is assessed at three levels of outcomes evaluation, corresponding to three levels of training

objectives: immediate evaluation (changes in trainees' knowledge, skills, or attitudes, before job return), intermediate evaluation (impact of training on job performance and transference of learning back into the workplace), and ultimate evaluation (impact of training on departmental or organizational performance) (Hogan, 2007).

The main strengths of the CIRO model is its focus on measurement both before and after the managerial training program and also the effectiveness consideration of objectives (contexts) and training equipment (inputs), which make it formative in nature (Tzeng, Chiang, & Li, 2007).

Tzeng and colleagues have suggested that this model does not measure behavioral changes, nor does it indicate how measurement takes place. They also argue it does not measure the value of the human resources development role to the organizational strategy. For these reasons, this framework does not provide important information regarding the current training situation, which could lead to improvements (Tzeng, Chiang, & Li, 2007).

CIPP Model

Stufflebeam's (2003) systems approach to evaluation is the CIPP Model (Context, Input, Process, Product). The CIPP model shares many of the features of the CIRO model (Roark, Kim, & Mupinga, 2006) but presents a framework around the program objectives, the training content and facilitation, program implementation, and program outcomes.

The CIPP model was initially designed for educational applications, for the use of service providers, such as school principals, college and university administrators, or project staff. The model focuses on the environmental context in which change is supposed to occur and it emphasizes the systematic provision of information for program management (Stufflebeam, 2002). In fact, the CIPP model is a widely known theoretical framework and has often been used for different purposes, such as to evaluate programs in education and administrative organizations (Razack et al., 2007). Schepens, Aelterman, and Vlerick (2009) used the CIPP model as a frame of reference to organize the variables involved in the professional identity formation, in order to examine the interrelationship between the teacher education and professional identity formation.

As previously stated, CIPP stands for context (or planning), input (or structuring), process (or implementing), and product (or recycling) evaluation (Khalid, Rehman, & Ashraf, 2012). According to Stufflebeam (2003), all four components of CIPP evaluation model play essential roles in the planning, implementation, and assessment of a project:

1 Context evaluation (similar to context evaluation in the CIRO model) provides relevant environment and provides situational data (for example, training needs, and opportunities of specific problems), in order to determine program objectives, as well as their relevance to social and organizational culture;

2 Input evaluation (also similar to input phase of the CIRO model) assesses alternative approaches, competing action plans, and the work plans and budgets, in order to determine the strategies used to achieve the outcomes, by examining the capability, resources, and different stages of program development. Levels 1 and 2 can be considered as formative evaluation, since both levels deal with needs analysis and instructional design (Dahiya & Jha, 2011). The results of this type of evaluation include policies, budgets, schedules, proposals, and procedures (Singh, 2013);

3 Process evaluation presupposes information about plans, guidelines, or program implementation, as well as monitoring procedural barriers, identifying needed adjustments, and obtaining additional information for changes, through continuous program

monitoring. Process evaluation includes some techniques, such as reaction sheets, rating scales, on-site observation, participant interviews, questionnaires, case studies of participants, self-reflection sessions, focus groups, or content analysis (Singh, 2013; Zhang et al., 2011).

4   Product involves evaluation of actual outcomes' worth and effectiveness, comparing them to the anticipated outcomes, that is, examines the impact of the program on the target audience, as well as the extent to which the program is sustainable and transferable (Owston, 2008).

The CIPP model guides both evaluators and stakeholders in posing relevant questions at the beginning of a program (context and input evaluation), during its progression (input and process evaluation) and also at its end (product evaluation) (Zhang et al., 2011). In essence, the CIPP model aims to answer key questions: What needs to be done? (Context); How should it be done? (Input); Is it being done? (Process); Did it succeed? (Product) (Owston, 2008).

Stufflebeam (2002) suggested that the model aimed to provide an analytic and rational basis for program decision making, based on a cycle of planning, structuring, implementing, and reviewing decisions. Some advantages of the model include the fact that it provides a systems view of the training being implemented; it facilitates problem areas diagnosis because the model is broken into phases (as opposed to trying to diagnose problems with one large process); and it can be used as a self-assessment tool to make improvements within organizations over time (Stufflebeam, 2002).

However, Bennett (1997) has suggested that the model assumes rationality by decision making and ignores the diversity of interests and multiple interpretations of these agents. Bennett (1997) further suggests the model is overly abstract and hard to implement in practice, which may explain its lack of wider take-up and application among organizational practitioners.

Phillips Five-Level ROI

While Kirkpatrick has been the dominant model for organizational evaluation for three decades Phillips' ROI (return on investment) framework has emerged in the past decade and has entered the organization evaluation lexicon with its focus on return on investment – a popular phrase for those conducting investment decisions.

The model combines the four levels of evaluation developed by Kirkpatrick and adds a fifth level, ROI. This additional level measures success in areas of human resources function, taking into account the steps of the cost–benefit analysis process and the calculation of the ROI ratio (Chmielewski & Phillips, 2002). In order to obtain the ROI, the cost of the training is subtracted from the monetary value of the results.

The five levels of ROI evaluation include (Chmielewski & Phillips, 2002, p. 227):

1   Reaction and Planned Action. Measurement of employee satisfaction with the program and captures planned action;
2   Learning. Measurement of changes in employee knowledge, skills, and attitudes related to the program;
3   Job Applications. Measurement of changes in on-the-job behavior/job processes;
4   Business Results. Measurement of changes in business-impact variables;
5   Return on Investment (ROI). Comparison between benefits and costs.

The model suggests that while the four factors are useful, without a consideration of the monetary value of specific training initiatives, investments should not be considered. The model however has serious limitations, which have largely been ignored in the overt focus on business ROI. One major weakness is the complexity in determining returns on soft aspects of business such as training. In fact we might suggest such efforts are impossible to measure in noncontrolled environments. This is because it is difficult in reality to isolate the effects of the specific intervention, for example training, from other organizational factors that can lead to improvements in performance (Hogan, 2007). These organizational factors can be a change of manager or leadership, to changes to demand for the product or service due to fashion or economic factors, as well as wider the impact of other organizational interventions from a pay rise to a change in office layout. While performance may improve, the training intention may not have contributed anything to the gain.

ROI has been used in several training and coaching evaluations with enthusiasm (see for example McGovern et al., 2001; Phillips, 2007). Phillips (2007) described that ROI methodology was used to evaluate the actual return on investment in terms of organizational performance after the implementation of a structured coaching program designed to improve efficiency, customer satisfaction, and revenue growth for Nations Hotel Corporation. In the McGovern study participants were asked to estimate the value (benefit) of the coaching on key decisions. These estimates were then reduced by 50 percent and compared with costs. Clearly, no serious scientific study to evaluate the efficacy of a drug or therapy intervention would ask clients to estimate the benefit as part of the evaluation. For this reason alone, this study and others using similar ROI methodology, are in our opinion fundamentally flawed. In turn, Hickey (2004) points out that much of Phillip's work is not grounded in empirical findings. In short we might conclude ROI is the "emperor's new clothes" evaluation model.

Brinkerhoff Six-Stage Model

Brinkerhoff (1998) suggests a six-stage approach to evaluation of training that includes the following stages: Goal Setting, Program Design, Program Implementation, Immediate Outcomes, Intermediate or Usage Outcomes, and Impacts and Worth (Kumpikaitė, 2007). Brinkerhoff's model (1988) adds two preliminary levels to Kirkpatrick's model, in order to provide formative evaluation of training needs and the training design (Holton & Naquin, 2005):

- Stage 1 – Goal Setting. Analysis of the organizational needs, problems, and weaknesses, as well as establishment of training goals and determination of the potential value in meeting the assessed needs;
- Stage 2 – Program Design. Assessment of the appropriateness of the training design, through a careful analysis of strategies and materials adequacy;
- Stage 3 – Program Implementation. Training activities monitoring and assessment of participants' satisfaction level (for example, by interviewing, observation, questionnaires and surveys);
- Stage 4 – Immediate Outcomes. Assessment of participants' level of learning and improvement. These are used to revise and refine activities and strategies.
- Stage 5 – Intermediate or Usage Outcomes. Evaluation of actual performance that usually takes place at the workplace. It aims to assess when, where, how well and how often the training and the new skills are actually being applied and how long the effects of training have lasted;
- Stage 6 – Usage Outcomes. Assessment of the worth of the training, by documenting the benefits, assessing their value and comparing them to the cost (time and resources expended) of the training (Otero, 1997).

Brinkerhoff (1988) emphasizes that evaluation is essential to information collecting and posterior decision making. The Six-Stage Model offers a formative evaluation approach and encourages the recycling of evaluative information from and to each of the six stages (Brinkerhoff, 1988). According to Dessinger and Moseley (2006), Brinkerhoff's Six-Stage Model

> evaluates needs and goals that trigger an intervention; the design that addresses responsiveness to needs and goals; operation or the installation and implementation of an intervention in relation to the needs and design; the learning that takes place when interventions are first used; the endurance and sustainability of the intervention over time; and the payoff or the return on investment from the successfully implemented interventions. (p. 317)

For example, Zinser (2003) used Brinkerhoff's evaluation model to evaluate why a community college technical program was not being utilized to its potential and what could be done to improve performance. According to the author, the evaluation process was an opportunity to discuss the study in the larger contexts of trends in occupational education and business partnerships.

The model has a number of limitations, since it consists of both formative and summative evaluation, which is only possible in ideal cases where the employer and the training organizers are closely related, where an evaluation design has already been built during the training process, or where there are no competing deadlines or reduced budgets (Holton & Naquin, 2005).

IPO Model

Bushnell (1990) described the IPO (Inputs, Process, Outputs/Outcomes) Model that sees the evaluation process as cyclical. This model has been widely recognized in the human resources development (HRD) evaluation field, however, the IPO approach is more used in education, vocational, and training areas. For example, IBM developed a global education network evaluation mechanism based on the IPO approach for its training evaluation. IBM considered that the model enabled decision makers to select the package that would optimize the overall effectiveness of a training program and thus deliver organizational value (Bushnell, 1990).

This model includes feedback loops built in critical junctions in the evaluation process, which make the training systems self-correcting (Bushnell, 1990).

This model divides the training process into three main phases, which allow the creation of an evaluation plan, the implementation of the training and evaluation and, finally, the adjustment of the training based on the results of the evaluation (Lea, 2009):

1 Input: Examining of performance indicators or factors that may influence a program's effectiveness (for example, trainees' qualifications, program design, instructors' quality and qualifications, materials quality, facilities, or equipment).
2 Process. Analysis of factors such as planning, design, developing or delivery of the training program.
3 Finally, the evaluation of results is organized into evaluation of outputs (short-term results, that is, data resulting from the training interventions) and evaluation of outcomes (long-term results associated with the sustainability of the training process over time, as well as with improvement in the organizational profitability or competitiveness). Outputs include trainees' reactions, performance or improvement, and outcomes focus on business results (Russ-Eft et al., 2008).

Bushnell (1990) argues that these steps help the instructional designer to define the purpose of the evaluation, create appropriate measurement instruments, define efficient, effective data sources, and then link the results of the evaluation back to the original purpose. Casey (2006) highlights that the main advantage of the model is that it provides a systems view of the training being implemented and facilitates diagnosing problem areas, because the model is divided into phases and it avoids diagnosing problems with one large process. Cox (2011) used Bushnell's model to provide a basis for a framework for nurse educators to plan, implement, and evaluate an intercultural teaching experience, in which the educator continually questioned her/his own effectiveness.

Overall, criticisms of the model are based in its lack of information related to program functioning, or to the specific components that affect the results. For example there is no way to identify at what point the program failed, because no impact is found (Robertson, 2004). On the other hand, a direct evaluation method and performing a full analysis would require a great deal of resources, and thus the model offers some attractions (Casey, 2006).

HRD Evaluation and Research Model

Holton (1996) has proposed the HRD Evaluation and Research Model with a focus on three primary outcomes measures:

1 Learning: Achievement of the learning outcomes desired in an human resources development intervention;
2 Individual performance: Change in individual performance as a result of the learning being applied on the job;
3 Organization: Results at the organizational level as a result of the change in individual performance.

According to Holton (1996), there are three primary influences on learning: trainee reactions, motivation to learn, and ability. In the same way, this model proposed three primary influences on performance outcomes. Learning is expected to lead to individual performance change only when these three influences are at appropriate levels: motivation to transfer (motivation to utilize their learning on the job), transfer conditions (environment), and transfer design (ability). Organizational results are primarily influenced by organizational goals (ability), organizational and individual utility (motivation), and influences of factors outside HRD (environment) (Holton, 1996). This model also proposes secondary intervening variables, such as intervention readiness, job attitudes, personality characteristics, or intervention fulfillment (Holton, 1996).

Holton, Bates, and Ruona (2000) developed the Learning Transfer System Inventory (LTSI) to evaluate the specific factors on those dimensions affecting the transfer of training process. The LTSI includes 16 factors, either facilitators or inhibitors of training transfer. According to Holton, Bates, and Ruona (2000), the LTSI can be used before training as a diagnostic tool to identify unknown and potential transfer problems, as well as leverage points for change. This inventory can also be used as an evaluative tool after the training process to obtain additional information about a training program success or failure. Kirwan and Birchall (2006) used the LTSI to collect quantitative data concerning 72 nurse managers' perceptions of a variety of factors (such as peer support, feedback and coaching, performance self-efficacy, motivation to transfer, manager support, learner readiness, transfer design, perceived content validity, or opportunity to use) likely to affect their transfer of learning from the program these participants attended. Later, Holton (2005) recognized that a full test of initial HRD Evaluation and Research Model is impossible because the majority of the tools to measure the constructs presented in the model did not exist. For these reasons, the author proposed an updated version of the model by delineating specific constructs that should be measured in each of the conceptual categories proposed (Holton, 2005).

Coldwell and Simkins (2010) conclude that

> Holton goes on to develop a more complex model that identifies influences beyond the intervention that are likely to determine: first, whether the intervention will result in learning; second, whether any learning will be transferred into improved participant performance; and third, whether such increased performance will influence organizational results. (p. 145)

In turn, Kirwan and Birchall (2006) pointed out that this model solely "describes a sequence of influences on outcomes occurring in a single learning experience and does not demonstrate any feedback loops" (p. 257) and it doesn't indicate any interaction between factors of the same type. The model also lacks any indication of interaction between factors of the same type (e.g., organizational factors), as well as any mention of how the factors affect transfer. That is, the indicated relationships constitute more a guide to the influences that exist within the model, rather than a real examination of the effects of these factors (Kirwan & Birchall, 2006).

Success Case Method

Brinkerhoff (2003) developed the Success Case Method (SCM) for evaluation. This method has been most frequently used to evaluate staff training and related human resource programs.

An SCM study presents a two-part structure. The first part aims to locate (through surveys, records, reports, performance data, or asking people) potential success cases (individuals or teams) that were successful during a training initiative. The second part of an SCM study presupposes identification of success cases and documentation of the actual nature of success through interviews. These interviews should focus on evidences collection in order to prove the success cases.

According to the author, an SCM study can be used to get answers to any, or all, of four basic questions (Brinkerhoff, 2003):

- What is really happening?
- What results, if any, is the program helping to produce?
- What is the value of the results?
- How could the initiative be improved?

The answers to these questions will give information concerning diverse aspects, such as the way a new innovation is being used; the positive outcomes of a new program or change; identification of organizational units that are using new tools and the success achieved as a result of these new methods; estimation of return on investment; support decision making related to the value a specific program is able to produce, taking into account its current level of impact.

The SCM approach involves two main steps (Brinkerhoff, 2005). During the first step, a brief survey is sent to a large representative sample of all trainees who participated in training. This survey aims to identify the extreme cases from those two ends of the success continuum. In the second step, the successful and unsuccessful trainees are probed in depth, in order to identify the factors that enhance or impede training application. That is, both groups are asked to tell stories about training characteristics and other organizational factors that enhanced or impeded success achievement.

Brinkerhoff (2005) highlights that SCM is relatively simple and can be implemented entirely in a short timeframe, it also can produce concrete evidence of the effect of training, which constitutes always a function of the interaction of training with other performance system factors. "Above all, the SCM is intended to help all stakeholders learn what worked, what did not, what worthwhile results have been achieved, and most important, what can be done to get better results from future efforts" (Brinkerhoff, 2005, p. 90).

Olson, Shershneva, and Brownstein (2011) employed SCM to understand better how three continuous performance-improvement medical-education activities contributed to significant changes in tobacco-cessation practice in nine outpatient practices. These authors concluded that SCM can serve a useful purpose in an evaluation of an educational intervention. However, Olson, Shershneva, and Brownstein also emphasized that SCM limited potential as a case-study method for developing or testing theories or methods applicable to other cases in diverse organizational settings, because "it lacks a means of characterizing the context of change across multiple organizations and systematically exploring how those characteristics mediate or moderate the implementation process" (p. 58). According to Casey (2006), the main disadvantage of SCM is that this model requires some level of judgment regarding what trainers identify as critical success factors on the job, because the model may not identify trainees' problems when returning to work.

Dessinger-Moseley Full-Scope Evaluation Model

More recently, Dessinger and Moseley (2006) developed the Dessinger-Moseley Full-Scope Evaluation Model. This model blends, in an iterative flow, the benefits of performance improvement and evaluation, and it also integrates formative, summative, confirmative, and meta-evaluation (Dessinger & Moseley, 2006):

- Formative Evaluation: Judgment about the merit and worth of the processes involved in the analysis, selection, design, development and implementation of performance interventions, as well the processes outputs and outcomes;
- Summative Evaluation: Judgment about immediate intervention outcomes, such as immediate user competency or immediate intervention effectiveness;
- Confirmative Evaluation: Long-term intervention outcomes (for a year or more), including continuing user competency and intervention efficiency, effectiveness, impact, and value. These data are usually collected through formative and summative evaluation data, organizational impact data, surveys, interviews, observation, or ROI analysis;
- Meta-Evaluation: Judgment about the merit and worth of all evaluation processes and products. Meta-evaluation process includes two distinct types: type 1 meta-evaluation is concurrent and type 2 meta-evaluation only occurs after evaluation is completed and focuses on evaluation process validity and reliability.

In short, the main purpose of the model is to formulate judgments about the merit and worth of any performance improvement intervention.

According to the authors, seven major steps are required to achieve a successful full-scope evaluation (or any evaluation process). Despite the importance of activities indicated below, Dessinger and Moseley (2006) add that "the activities that are most crucial to the success of full-scope evaluation are planning, communicating, documenting, and archiving the evaluation process and results" (p. 321):

1 Plan the evaluation: indicated as the most crucial activity for a successful full-scope evaluation because it guarantees the foundation for why and how the evaluation will be conducted;
2 Design and develop the materials;
3 Collect the data;
4 Analyze the data;
5 Interpret the findings;
6 Communicate the status of the evaluation activities and the findings, with recommendations for action: providing information on the findings with recommendations for action is also critical because stakeholders can use that information to make decisions related to performance improvement;
7 Document and archive information on the evaluation process and results: documenting and archiving what was done (and also what was discovered) can save time and money the next time.

Bishop (2010) notes that the full-scope evaluation model includes practices that should be included in every evaluation process since "evaluation should weave through the entire HPT process, and intervention iterations will result in a more successful final intervention" (p. 9). Additionally, Dessinger and Moseley do not treat evaluation as a separate, on-time process; they spread evaluative activities throughout an ongoing process of developing quality programs. This model also underlines the confirmative processes of analysis and improvement. Outputs of confirmative activities include action plans, data collection through multiple instruments and sources, documentation of findings, an analysis-based report, and, finally action decisions (Schankman, 2004).

Some of the potential weaknesses of the model are noted by the authors themselves. Dessinger and Moseley (2006) refer to the fact that "full-scope evaluation stays around longer than 'regular' evaluation and requires long-term support from the organization and all the stakeholders" (p. 322).

SOAP-M Model for training and coaching evaluation

The SOAP-M (Self, Other, Achievements, Potential, Meta-Analysis) Model for training and coaching evaluation can be implemented within an organization by human resource managers and it aims to fill the gaps of previously described models, as well as to integrate their strengths. This model aims to constitute a practical model, as well as to meet the needs of researchers and academics interested in meta-level assessments of different interventions or training designs (Passmore & Velez, 2012).

This model comprises five levels of analysis which could be used for HR interventions such as training or coaching (Passmore & Velez, 2012):

• Level 1: Self. Like Kirkpatrick's model, this level is based on self-evaluation of the intervention. The self-evaluation process offers benefits to the participant and the organization by offering the opportunity for employees to have a voice and thus providing employee empowerment. Self-evaluation also provides valuable and almost instant feedback for the coach or trainer and allows to the trainer/coach the opportunity of adapting their approach to meet the needs of the audience or individual at the next session. We would argue that the more specific the feedback (evaluation) the more useful the evaluation will be to the trainer or coach.

- Level 2: Other. At this level, the evaluation is completed not by the individual themselves but by others. In this case their line manager, peers, or stakeholders. This evaluation could use either a predefined framework or model such as an internal (or externally designed) competency questionnaire or a psychometric that allows 360 ratings.
- Level 3: Achievements. This level shifts the focus to the impact of these newly acquired behaviors on key tasks. This may include performance against targets set at the annual appraisal or monthly/quarterly goals – such as sales targets or other quantifiable measures. Level 3 can equally be used to assess organizational level goals such as profit, growth in turnover, market share or stock value/share price, where the responsibility for these rests with the individual, such as a chief executive or sales director.
- Level 4: Potential. Coaching or training interventions may impact on potential – helping individuals to develop thinking skills, for example, or emotional maturity. Such aspects are hard to measure through a competence framework for the person's current role and may not be immediately evident in individual achievements, or in self or others assessment of behavior. However, they may be shown up in assessments of the individual's potential. As with previous levels the assessment could take place as pre- and post-assessment, with completion of the questionnaire at T1 (prior to the intervention) and at T2 (a few weeks or months after the intervention).
- Level 5: Meta-Analysis. Meta-studies combine multiple individual studies looking at the impact of an intervention with many different groups, in different organizations and different cultural context. By grouping studies together the significance of local factors can be reduced and a greater focus can be placed on assessing the intervention. At the highest level we see this as a meta-analysis of a number of randomized controlled trials.

The SOAP-M Model offers a framework that could be used at five levels (Self, Other, Achievement, Potential, and Meta-Analysis) by practitioners who aim to think about and design training evaluations at the start of the training intervention.

The model has weaknesses, which include the challenge for using the framework at levels 4 and 5, due to the complexity and cost involved in using a psychometric questionnaire or conducting statistical meta-analysis. Further, lower down the model, at levels 2 and 3, preplanning is required to establish clear goals and to plan evaluation from the start of the intervention.

Future Research

While there has been a continued flow of new models offered by academics, the robust assessment of training interventions has been several steps behind. A few individual studies have been published using the models, but these are comparatively rare and often do not consider an evaluation of the model used.

The gap in our knowledge thus rests with detailed and rigorous assessments of the different evaluation models. In short an evaluation of the evaluation models. Which models work in practice? What are their practical shortcomings? Which is most helpful and in which circumstances?

We would suggest the focus of research might be towards using a number of different evaluation models to evaluate the same training interventions. By undertaking comparative studies academics and researchers could help practitioners develop both a better understanding of how the models can be usefully applied, through detailed case-study descriptions, and which models are most effective at providing information with minimum fuss and disruption to everyday business, by comparing cost, time, and operation factors involved in the planning, data collection, analysis, and reporting.

Conclusion

Our aim in writing this chapter was to review the most popular models offered by writers for use by HR practitioners to help them evaluate HR interventions, such as training or coaching. The changes in HR with increasing data collection mean that evaluation will continue to grow as organizations seek to prove the value of learning and development.

Research developed in 2007 by the Chartered Institute of Personnel and Development (CIPD) aimed to explore the way UK organizations are measuring and reporting the contribution of learning to strategic value. The results identified four main approaches to measuring and reporting on value (CIPD, 2010):

- Learning function efficiency measures
- Key performance indicators and benchmark measures
- Return on investment measures
- Return on expectation measures

According to CIPD, effective evaluation is essential to improve the quality of HR practice. However, to achieve an effective evaluation model it is essential to place learning and development in the centre of the business; to ensure that the used model coincides with the organization's goals and objectives; and, finally, to prove the value of learning with effective measures and metrics (CIPD, 2010).

In our opinion, organizations need to have a range of qualitative and quantitative measures that evaluate financial issues, employees' well-being, turnover, or absenteeism. However, these measures should also help organizations thinking about the impact that HR interventions may be having, always taking into account some contextual changes that are happening in the economy and in the organization, in order to avoid possible contamination factors.

References

Alliger, G., & Janak, E. (1989). Kirkpatrick's levels of training criteria: Thirty years later. *Personnel Psychology*, 42, 331–342.

Antos, M., & Bruening, T. (2006). A model hypothesizing the effect of leadership style on the transfer of training. *Journal of Leadership Education*, 5(3), 31–52.

Arthur, W., Bennett, W., Edens, P., & Bell, S. (2003). Effectiveness of training in organizations: A meta-analysis of design and evaluation features. *Journal of Applied Psychology*, 88(2), 234–245.

Bates, R. (2004). A critical analysis of evaluation practice: The Kirkpatrick model and the principle of beneficence. *Evaluation and Program Planning*, 27, 341–347.

Beech, B., & Leather, P. (2006). Workplace violence in the health care sector: A review of staff training and integration of training evaluation models. *Aggression and Violent Behavior*, 11(1), 27–43.

Bennett, N. (1997). The voices of evaluation. *The Journal of Continuing Education in the Health Professions*, 17, 198–206.

Bishop, B. (2010). The amalgamated process for evaluation (APE): The best of Kirkpatrick, Brinkerhoff, Dessinger & Moseley, and Phillips. http://www.thinkingworlds.com/docs/AmalgamatedProcessForEvaluation_BrianBishop_Jan2010.pdf (accessed January 24, 2012).

Brinkerhoff, R. (1988). An integrated evaluation model for HRD. *Training and Development Journal*, 42(2), 66–68.

Brinkerhoff, R. (2003). *The Success Case Method*. San Francisco: Berrett-Koehler.

Brinkerhoff, R. (2005). The success case method: A strategic evaluation approach to increasing the value and effect of training. *Advances in Developing Human Resources*, 7(1), 86–101.

Bushnell, D. (1990). Input, process, output: A model for evaluating training. *Training and Development Journal*, 44(3), 41–43.

Casey, M. (2006). *Problem-based inquiry: An experiential approach to training evaluation*. PhD thesis. University of Akron.

Chmielewski, T., & Phillips, J. (2002). Measuring return-on-investment in government: Issues and procedures. *Personnel Management*, 31(2), 255–237.

CIPD (Chartered Institute of Personnel and Development). (2010) *Evaluating Learning and Talent Development*. London: CIPD. http://www.cipd.co.uk/hr-resources/factsheets/evaluating-learning-talent-development.aspx (accessed March 21, 2014).

Coldwell, M., & Simkins, T. (2010). Level models of continuing professional development evaluation: A grounded review and critique. *Professional Development in Education*, 37(1), 143–157.

Cox, K. (2011). Evaluating the effectiveness of intercultural teachers. *Nursing Education Perspectives*, 32(2): 102–106.

Dahiya, S., & Jha, A. (2011). Review of training evaluation. *International Journal of Computer Science and Communication*, 2(1), 11–16.

DeSimone, R. L., Werner, J. M., & Harris, D. M. (2002). *Human Resource Development* (3rd ed.). Orlando: Harcourt College.

Dessinger, J., & Moseley, J. L. (2006). The full scoop on full-scope evaluation. In J. A. Pershing (Ed.), *Handbook of Human Performance Technology: Principles, Practices, Potential* (pp. 312–330). San Francisco: Pfeiffer.

Goldstein, I. (1986). *Training in Organizations: Needs Assessment, Design and Evaluation*. Monterey, CA: Brooks/Cole.

Guerci, M., Bartezzaghi, E., & Solari, L. (2010). Training evaluation in Italian corporate universities: A stakeholder-based analysis. *International Journal of Training and Development* 14(4), 291–308.

Hickey, W. (2004). An evaluation of foreign HR consulting company effectiveness in China. *Performance Improvement Quarterly*, 17(1), 81–101.

Hilbert, J., Russ-Eft, D., & Preskill, H. (1997). Evaluating training. In D. Russ-Eft (Ed.), *What Works: Assessment, Development, and Measurement* (pp. 109–150). Alexandria, VA: ASTD.

Hogan, R. L. (2007). The historical development of program evaluation: Exploring the past and present. *Online Journal of Workforce Education and Development*, 2(4), 1–14.

Holton, E. (1996). The flawed four-level evaluation model. *Human Resource Development Quarterly*, 7(1), 5–21.

Holton, E. (2005). Holton's evaluation model: New evidence and construct elaborations. *Advances in Developing Human Resources*, 7(1), 37–54.

Holton, E., Bates, R., & Ruona, W. (2000). Development of a generalized learning transfer system inventory. *Human Resource Development Quarterly*, 11, 333–60.

Holton, E., & Naquin, S. (2005). A critical analysis of HRD evaluation models from a decision-making perspective. *Human Resource Development Quarterly*, 16(2), 257–280.

Kaufman, R., & Keller, J. (1994). Levels of evaluation: Beyond Kirkpatrick. *Human Resource Development Quarterly*, 5(4), 371–380.

Kaufman, R., Keller, J., & Watkins, R. (1995). What works and what doesn't: Evaluation beyond Kirkpatrick. *Performance and Instruction*, 35(2), 8–12.

Khalid, M., Rehman, C., & Ashraf, M. (2012). Exploring the link between Kirkpatrick (KP) and context, input, process and product (CIPP) training evaluation models, and its effect on training evaluation in public organizations of Pakistan. *African Journal of Business Management*, 6(1), 274–279.

Kirkpatrick, D. (1979). Techniques for evaluating training programs. *Training and Development Journal*, 78–92.

Kirwan, C., & Birchall, D. (2006). Transfer of learning from management development programmes: Testing the Holton model. *International Journal of Training and Development*, 10(4), 252–268.

Kraiger, K., Ford, K., & Salas, E. (1993). Application of cognitive, skill-based, and affective theories of learning outcomes to new methods of training evaluation. *Journal of Applied Psychology*, 78(2), 311–328.

Kumpikaitė, V. (2007). Human resource training evaluation. *Engineering Economics*, 5(55), 30–36.

Lea, G. (2009). Final report: Identifying success measurements for default call center agents – Improving training materials via evaluation. *Research in Information and Learning Technologies*, 1–52. http://gregorylea.evitae.org/wp-content/uploads/Documents/FinalReport_GregLea_final.pdf (accessed June 1, 2012).

Lee, A. (2012). *Coaching skills for personal tutors: A key to effective practice and student success*. Paper presented at the What Works? Student Retention and Success Conference, University of York, UK, March.

Lee, S., & Pershing, J. (2000). Evaluation of corporate training programs: Perspectives and issues for further research. *Performance Improvement Quarterly*, 13, 244–260.

Lin, Y., Chen, S., & Chuang, H. (2011). The effect of organizational commitment on employee reactions to educational training: An evaluation using the Kirkpatrick four-level model. *International Journal of Management*, 28(3), 926–938.

McGovern, M., Lindemann, M., Vergara, M., Murphy, S., Barker, L., & Warrenfeltz, R. (2001). Maximizing the impact of executive coaching: Behavioral change, organizational outcomes, and return on investment. *Manchester Review*, 6(1). 1–7. http://www.coachfederation.org/includes/docs/049ManchesterReviewMaximizingImpactofExecCoaching2.pdf (accessed January 29, 2012).

Olson, C., Shershneva, M., & Brownstein, M. (2011). Peering inside the clock: Using success case method to determine how and why practice-based educational interventions succeed. *Journal of Continuing Development in the Health Professions*, 31(1), 50–59.

Otero, C. (1997). *Training as a Development Tool*. Research and Reference Services Project, Document No. PN-ACA-630. United States Agency for International Development – Center for Development Information and Evaluation: Washington, DC. http://pdf.usaid.gov/pdf_docs/PNACA630.pdf (accessed June 1, 2012).

O'Toole, S. (2009). Kirkpatrick on evaluation: Not crazy after all these years. *Training and Development in Australia*, August, 23–25.

Owston, R. (2008). Models and methods for evaluation. In D. Jonassen (Ed.), *Handbook of Research on Educational Communications and Technology* (pp. 605–617). New York: Routledge.

Passmore, J., & Velez, M. J. (2012). SOAP-M: A training evaluation model for HR. *Industrial & Commercial Training*, 44(6), 315–326.

Phillips, J. (2007). Measuring the ROI of a coaching intervention, part 2. *Performance Improvement*, 46(10), 10–23.

Razack, S., Meterissian, S., Morin, L., Snell, L., Steinert, Y., & Maclellan, A. (2007). Coming of age as communicators: Differences in the implementation of common communications skills training in four residency programmes. *Medical Education*, 41(5), 441–449.

Roark, S., Kim, M., & Mupinga, M. (2006). An exploratory study of the extent to which medium-sized organizations evaluate training programs. *Journal of Business and Training Education*, 15, 15–20.

Robertson, M. (2004). *Building program theory for evaluation: The process through a political lens*. PhD thesis. University of Georgia.

Russ-Eft, D., Bober, M., Teja, I., Foxon, M., & Koszalka, T. (2008). *Evaluator Competencies: Standards for the Practice of Evaluation in Organizations* (pp. 3–12). San Francisco: John Wiley & Sons, Inc.

Schankman, L. (2004). *Holistic evaluation of an academic online program*. Paper presented at the 20th Annual Conference on Distance Teaching and Learning, Madison, WI, August.

Schepens, A., Aelterman, A., & Vlerick, P. (2009). Student teachers' professional identity formation: Between being born as a teacher and becoming one. *Educational Studies*, 35(2), 1–38.

Singh, M. (2013). Training evaluation: Various approaches and applications. *The IUP Journal of Soft Skills*, 7(1), 27–34.

Stokking, K. (1996). Levels of evaluation: Kirkpatrick, Kaufman and Keller, and beyond. *Human Resource Development Quarterly*, 7(2), 179–183.

Stufflebeam, D. (2002). CIPP evaluation model checklist. http://www.wmich.edu/evalctr/checklists (accessed June 1, 2012).

Stufflebeam, D. (2003). The CIPP model for evaluation. In D. L. Stufflebeam & T. Kellaghan (Eds.), *The International Handbook of Educational Evaluation* (pp. 31–62). Boston, MA: Kluwer Academic.

Tzeng, G., Chiang, C., & Li, C. (2007). Evaluating intertwined effects in e-learning programs: A novel hybrid MCDM model based on factor analysis and DEMATEL. *Expert Systems with Applications*, 32, 1028–1044.

Warr, P., Bird, M., & Rackham, N. (1970). *Evaluation of Management Training: A Practical Framework, with Cases, for Evaluating Training Needs and Results*. London: Gower Press.

Watkins, R., Leigh, D., Foshay, R., & Kaufman, R. (1998). Kirkpatrick plus: Evaluation and continuous improvement with a community focus. *Educational Technology Research and Development*, 46(4), 90–96.

Zhang, G., Zeller, N., Griffith, R., Metcalf, D., Williams, J., Shea, C., & Misulis, K. (2011). Using the context, input, process, and product evaluation model (CIPP) as a comprehensive framework to guide the planning, implementation, and assessment of service-learning programs. *Journal of Higher Education Outreach and Engagement*, 15(4), 57–84.

Zinser, R. (2003). Evaluating of a community college technical program by local industry. *Journal of Industrial Teacher Education*, 40(2). http://scholar.lib.vt.edu/ejournals/JITE/v40n2/zinser.html (accessed June 14, 2012).

9

Knowledge Transfer and Organizational Learning

Linda Argote

Introduction

Not only do individuals learn from their experience, organizations also learn from their experience. Just as individuals learn vicariously from the experience of others, organizations also learn vicariously from the experience of other organizations. This form of learning indirectly from the experience of others is referred to as knowledge transfer. And just as individuals have memories, organizations also have memories that retain the knowledge acquired through learning. Further, organizations vary in their rates of learning and knowledge transfer and in the extent to which they retain the knowledge they acquire. This chapter presents evidence that characteristics of the organizational context affect organizational learning and knowledge retention and transfer. Factors explaining the variation in organizational learning and knowledge retention and transfer are identified and future research opportunities are described. Because organizational learning, memory, and transfer affect organizational performance, a greater understanding of these factors has the potential to advance both theory and practice.

Although individual learning has received research attention for well over a century, research on organizational learning is a more recent phenomenon. Research on how organizations learn from their experience, retain the knowledge that they acquire and transfer it throughout their establishments are active research areas that emerged in the 1990s (Huber, 1991). The surge of research on organizational learning was fueled by theoretical and methodological developments, which facilitated the study of organizational learning. Levitt and March's (1988) influential *Annual Review of Sociology* article provided the foundation for much of the subsequent work on organizational learning. Developments in statistics for analyzing longitudinal data and ruling out explanations alternative to learning, such as selection, facilitated the analysis and interpretation of data on organizational learning from the field (Miner & Mezias, 1996). Practical concerns, which increased the importance of understanding organizational learning, also contributed to the

The Wiley Blackwell Handbook of the Psychology of Training, Development, and Performance Improvement, First Edition. Edited by Kurt Kraiger, Jonathan Passmore, Sigmar Malvezzi, and Nuno Rebelo dos Santos. © 2015 John Wiley & Sons Ltd. Published 2020 by John Wiley & Sons Ltd.

surge in research on organizational learning. Issues such as concerns about productivity, the anticipated retirement of the baby boom generation, the increased globalization of firms, and the greater use of the multiunit organizational form have increased interest in organizational learning, knowledge retention, and knowledge transfer (Argote, 2012). Further, improved computing technologies have increased the availability of data, which has enhanced opportunities for organizations to learn from experience.

Organizational learning is central to the performance and prosperity of organizations and their members. Balasubramanian and Lieberman (2010) found that rates of organizational learning were linked to the profitability of firms. Organizations that are able to learn, to retain the knowledge they acquire, and to transfer it throughout their establishments are more likely to succeed than their less able counterparts. Indeed, it has been argued that organizational learning is a major source of competitive advantage in firms (Stata, 1989). Firms that are able to learn are able to adapt to changing conditions and prosper.

Organizations vary dramatically in their ability to learn. Many organizations exhibit significant performance improvements with experience while others evidence little or no learning. For example, Argote and Epple (1990) presented data from three truck plants that were part of the same organization and manufactured the same product but differed dramatically in their rates of learning. Similarly, organizations vary in the extent to which they retain (Anand, Gray, & Siemsen, 2012; Argote, 2013) and transfer knowledge successfully (Darr, Argote, & Epple, 1995; Szulanski, 1996).

This chapter argues that characteristics of the organizational context explain variation in organizational learning and knowledge retention and transfer. The organizational context interacts with experience to affect organizational learning and the retention and transfer of knowledge acquired through learning. The organizational context can facilitate or impede the interpretation of experience. Similarly, the context can promote knowledge retention or facilitate knowledge decay. The context can also enable knowledge transfer or enact barriers that impede transfer. The chapter provides an overview of research on organizational learning. Empirical evidence on how the context affects organizational learning and knowledge retention and transfer is reviewed. Fruitful future research directions are discussed.

Organizational Learning: An Overview

Organizational learning is a change in the organization's knowledge that occurs as a function of experience (Fiol & Lyles, 1985). Similar to researchers of individual learning (Hilgard & Bower, 1975; Wingfield, 1979), researchers of organizational leaning assess learning by measuring changes in cognitions and/or behaviors associated with experience (Easterby-Smith, Crossan, & Nicolini, 2000). For example, several researchers have assessed changes in the cognitions of organization members driven by experience (Huff & Jenkins, 2001). Other researchers have studied how organizational routines change as a function of experience (Levitt & March, 1988) or how characteristics of performance, such as its speed or accuracy, change with experience (Dutton & Thomas, 1984). Argote (2013) discussed strengths and weaknesses of various approaches to measuring organizational learning and its retention and transfer. When using the various approaches to measure organizational learning, it is critical to show that the measure changes as a function of experience and to control for alternative explanations.

Learning occurs at different levels of analysis in organizations: individual, group, organizational, and interorganizational (Kozlowski, Chao, & Nowakowski, in press).

For example, in a study of hospital surgical teams, Reagans, Argote, and Brooks (2005) found that learning occurred at the levels of individuals within the team, the team, and the hospital organization. Although learning occurs at the individual level in organizations, in order for organizational learning to occur, the knowledge individuals acquire would have to be embedded in a supra-individual repository so that it persisted when individuals depart the organization. The focus of this chapter is on empirical studies of organizational learning (see Schulz, 2000, for a previous review). Reviews of research on learning at the team or group level can be found in Argote, Gruenfeld, and Naquin (2001) and Edmondson, Dillon, and Roloff (2007). Miner and Haunschild (1995) and Ingram (2002) reviewed research on interorganizational and population-level learning.

Argote and Miron-Spektor (2011) developed a framework for analyzing organizational learning and knowledge. According to their framework, experience interacts with the organizational context to create knowledge. Experience is what occurs in the organization as it performs its task. Experience can be assessed by summing the number of task performances that the organization has attempted in order to arrive at a measure of cumulative experience. For example, the experience of a surgical hospital would be measured by the cumulative number of surgeries performed. The experience of an aircraft manufacturer would be measured by the cumulative number of aircraft produced. The experience of a consulting organization would be measured by the cumulative number of consulting engagements. Through organizational learning processes, experience is interpreted and knowledge is created.

Organizational learning occurs in a context, which affects its processes and outcomes. The context includes the organization's culture, structure, strategy, technology, identity, goals and rewards, and the environment in which the organization is embedded. Argote and Miron-Spektor (2011) distinguished between the active context through which learning occurs and a latent context. The active context includes the basic elements of organizations: members, tools, and tasks and the networks formed by crossing them (Arrow, McGrath, & Berdahl, 2000; McGrath & Argote, 2001). The member–member network is the organization's social network. The task–task and the tool–tool networks specify the interrelationships within tasks and tools, respectively. The member–task network is the organization's division of labor. The member–tool network specifies which tools are used to perform which tasks. The member–task–tool network identifies which members perform which tasks with which tools.

The latent context includes characteristics of the organization such as its culture, structure, reward system, or technology. Dimensions of the latent context affect organizational learning through their effects on the active elements of members, tools, and tasks. The context determines the organization's task and affects the tools available to perform the task. The context also affects which members perform the organization's task and their abilities, motivations, and opportunities.

Organizational learning results in knowledge, which is retained in the basic elements of members, tools, and tasks and their networks. Knowledge can be characterized along several dimensions, such as its tacitness (Nonaka & von Krogh, 2009; Polanyi, 1962), causal ambiguity (Szulanski, 1996), and its demonstrability or ease of showing its correctness and appropriateness (Kane, 2010; Laughlin & Ellis, 1986). These dimensions of knowledge have implications for its storage and transfer.

We turn now to a discussion of how the organizational context affects learning from direct experience, followed by sections on how the context affects knowledge retention and transfer. Each section begins with a discussion of the latent context and concludes with a discussion of the active context.

Learning from Direct Experience

Latent context

This section reviews empirical studies of how organizational learning is affected by dimensions of the organization's latent context, including its structure, culture, resources, goals, feedback system, power distribution, and training systems. Several dimensions of organizational structure have been examined as predictors of organizational learning. Jansen, Van Den Bosch, and Volberda (2006) found that decentralized structures increased explorative learning and formalized structures increased exploitative learning. Densely connected social relations within units were found to enhance both exploration and exploitation. Explorative learning involves pursuing new opportunities while exploitative learning entails refining existing knowledge (March, 1991). Bunderson and Boumgarden (2010) found that specialization, formalization, and hierarchy increased team learning because these structural features increased information sharing and reduced conflict. Specialist organizations, which focus on a narrow range of products or services, have been found to learn more from experience than generalist organizations, which focus on a broad range (Haunschild & Sullivan, 2002; Ingram & Baum, 1997). Vertical integration has been found to slow the rate of learning from direct experience in stable environments and speed the rate of learning in volatile environments (Sorenson, 2003).

Dimensions of an organization's culture have also been found to affect organizational learning. Edmondson (1999) found that a culture where members feel "psychologically safe," or free to take risks and voice their concerns, promoted team learning. Bunderson and Sutcliffe (2003) found that "learning" compared to a "performing" orientation facilitated performance improvements associated with experience. Cohesion (Wong, 2004) and a shared language have also been found to promote learning (Weber & Camerer, 2003).

Organizational slack has been theorized to affect learning and innovation (Cyert & March, 1963). Wiersma (2007) found that slack resources increased experimentation and enhanced organizational learning. Gulati and Nohria (1996) found a nonmonotonic inverted-U relationship between slack and innovation. Slack increased experimentation but decreased discipline. The combination of these forces resulted in an inverted-U relationship between slack and organizational learning: increases in slack initially increased and then decreased organizational learning and innovation.

An organization's goals and aspirations affect learning and innovation. Cyert and March (1963) theorized that search and change are more likely when organizational performance drops below aspiration levels than when it is above aspirations. Empirical research has generally supported their theory (Bromiley, 1991; Lant, 1992).

Performance feedback has been identified as an important contributor to organizational learning (Greve, 2003). Delays in feedback have been found to hinder learning from experience (Gibson, 2000). When behaviors do not have direct payoffs but are part of a sequence with an overall payoff, learning is also impaired, especially when member turnover occurs (Denrell, Fang, & Levinthal, 2004). High feedback specificity has been found to improve learning in the short run but reduce exploration in the long run (Goodman, Wood, & Hendrickx, 2004). Surprisingly, withholding feedback has been found to lead to more meaningful learning than providing feedback (Rick & Weber, 2010). How feedback affects organizational processes might explain the differences in its effect. For example, Rick and Weber (2010) found that not providing feedback led to more meaningful deliberation than providing feedback. By contrast, if feedback leads to thoughtful consideration, providing feedback would be likely to affect learning positively.

There is considerable evidence that power differences negatively affect group and organizational learning (Edmondson, 2002). For example, Loch, Sengupta, and Ahmad (2013) found that differentiated power and status within a group led to overweighting the influence of high-status members and thereby distorted problem solving. Van der Vegt et al. (2010) found that providing feedback at the group level transformed power differences into opportunities for learning.

Training systems in organizations also affect learning (Bell & Kozlowski, 2008; Salas et al., 2012). Several forms of training are especially important for promoting organizational learning. One form is group training in which members of a group or department are trained together. A meta-analysis of the effect of group or team training on team performance found that, on average, team training explained 20 percent of the variance in team performance (see Salas et al., 2008, for a review). Relative to individual training, group training is more likely to lead to the creation of a transactive memory system (Wegner, 1986), which has been shown to improve group performance (Hollingshead, 1998; Liang, Moreland, & Argote, 1995). When group members are trained together, they learn who knows what and who is good at what, which enables them to assign tasks to the most qualified members, to trust each other's expertise, and to coordinate their tasks effectively.

Training that takes the form of apprenticeships and includes opportunities for observation is also especially valuable in organizations. Opportunities for observation enable the transmission of hard-to-articulate tacit knowledge (Nonaka, 1991). Nadler, Thompson, and Van Boven (2003) found that training methods that included opportunities for observation were more effective than methods that did not. Similarly, Salas et al. (2012) concluded that training programs that included demonstrations were more effective than those that did not.

The timing of training is also especially important for organizational learning. Salas et al. (2012) noted that training programs should be designed to minimize skill decay, which occurs when individuals do not have opportunities to utilize the knowledge and skills they had acquired. In a meta-analysis of skill decay studies, Arthur et al. (1998) found that the amount of skill decay increased as the length of time that the skill was not used increased: individuals evidenced little or no skill decay the day after training but after a year of not using the skill had lost over 90 percent of what they had learned. Thus, scheduling training close to the time when individuals have opportunities to use the knowledge and skills is critical. Without practice, the knowledge and skill decay are almost lost one year after training. Further, less decay was found for physical as opposed to cognitive tasks, for speed tasks relative to accuracy tasks, for behavioral as opposed to learning outcomes, and when the training and retrieval contexts are similar.

Active context: Member, tasks, tools, and their networks

Organizational learning is also affected by, and affects, the organization's members, tasks, and tools and the networks formed by crossing these basic elements. Individuals are a key mechanism through which organizational learning occurs. Organizational learning is affected by characteristics of members, such as general cognitive ability (Ree, Earles, & Teachout, 1994). Individual experience, especially the amount of task experience, has also been found to predict individual (see Quinones, Ford, & Teachout, 1995; Tesluk & Jacobs, 1998, for reviews) and team performance (Reagans, Argote, & Brooks, 2005).

Moving members across groups can stimulate organizational learning. Gruenfeld, Martorana, and Fan (2000) found that new knowledge was generated in groups when their members returned from visits to other groups. Choi and Thompson (2005) found that groups whose membership changed were more creative than groups whose membership was stable.

The member-member or the social network also affects knowledge creation. Ties that bridge "structural holes" or unconnected parts of social networks increase exposure to information (Burt, 2004). Tortoriello and Krackhardt (2010) found that bridging ties that span boundaries were especially likely to increase the generation of new knowledge when the ties had a common third-party tie.

Some degree of task heterogeneity is valuable for organizational learning (Haunschild and Sullivan, 2002). Schilling et al. (2003) found that groups learned more from performing tasks that were related than from performing tasks that were either identical or very different. Wiersma (2007) found that organizations with a diverse product mix learned at a faster rate than those with a similar product mix. Diversity in tasks provides individuals with a deeper understanding of the problem space and provides organizations opportunities to transfer knowledge from one task to another, and thereby improve the organization's performance.

Routines specify relationships among tasks and thus are part of the task–task network. Argyris and Schon (1978) showed that defensive routines can prevent learning. Feldman and Pentland (2003) argued that routines can be a source of change as well as stability and demonstrated that differences in how individuals perform routines can lead to changes in them. Loch, Sengupta, and Ahmad (2013) found that groups with a strong identity used their problem-solving routines more consistently than those lacking a strong identity.

Research suggests that tools and the tool–tool network affect the creation of knowledge in organizations. Alavi and Leidner (2001) theorized how information systems facilitate the exchange of ideas and thereby enhance organizational learning. Ashworth, Mukhopadhyay, and Argote (2004) demonstrated that the introduction of information technology in a financial services firm increased the rate of organizational learning.

The member–task network also affects learning from direct experience. A transactive memory system (TMS) is an example of a member–task network. A transactive memory system is a collective system for encoding, storing, and retrieving information (Wegner, 1986). As members acquire experience working together, they learn who is good at what. The knowledge of who is good at what enables the team to assign members to tasks for which they are best qualified. A TMS also facilitates problem solving because members know whom to ask for advice on particular issues. Transactive memory systems have been found to improve group performance (Austin, 2003; Gino et al., 2010; Lewis, 2004; Hollingshead, 1998; Liang, Moreland, & Argote, 1995).

Retaining Knowledge

Knowledge acquired through learning is embedded in the organization's memory. Stein (1995) defined organizational memory as the means through which an organization's past experience affects its current activities. Similarly, Walsh and Ungson (1991) defined organizational memory as stored information from an organization's past. This stored information is embedded in a variety of repositories in organizations. For example, Levitt and March (1988) theorized that knowledge acquired through learning is embedded in an organization's routines, rules, products, processes, technologies, and culture.

The previously discussed conceptualization of the latent context and the active context of members, tasks, tools, and their networks is used as a framework in this chapter for characterizing knowledge repositories. Knowledge can be embedded in individuals through mechanisms such as training, communication, and learning by doing. Knowledge can be embedded in tools, both hardware and software, that are modified as a result of the organization's experience. Knowledge can be embedded in routines or task sequences that are developed through experience.

There is considerable evidence that knowledge embedded in an organization's memory can decay or depreciate. This and related phenomenon has also been referred to as organizational forgetting (e.g., see De Holan & Philips, 2004). Researchers have assessed the extent of depreciation by comparing, in a production function, the effect of measures of cumulative production experience to the effect of measures that allow experience to depreciate (e.g., see Argote, Beckman, & Epple, 1990). Using this approach, researchers have found evidence that knowledge can depreciate in organizations (Benkard, 2000; Darr, Argote, & Epple, 1995). That is, knowledge does not persist indefinitely through time but rather decays. Further, the rate of decay varies across organizations, with some showing significant decay and others showing little or no depreciation (see Argote, 2013, for a review). Jain and Kogut (2014) demonstrated in a simulation that memory is a positive capability that enables organizations to improve their performance, even when knowledge depreciation occurs.

Latent context

The aspects of the latent context that have received the most attention in analyses of knowledge retention are the organization's structure and technology. Structure can buffer the organization from the negative effects of turnover. Turnover has been found to have a less harmful effect in highly structured groups than in less structured groups (Rao & Argote, 2006) because much of the organization's knowledge is embedded in the structure, which is not affected by turnover. Similarly, technology can minimize knowledge depreciation (Ashworth, Mukhopadhyay, & Argote, 2004).

Active context: Member, tasks, and tools and their networks

Using a systems dynamics model, Anderson and Lewis (2013) compared the effects of disrupting knowledge embedded in individuals and knowledge embedded in collective repositories such as routines or shared understandings of who knows what. Disruptions to individual learning were found to benefit organizations in the long run because they prevented overspecialization, whereas disruptions to collective learning were detrimental in both the short and long run.

Empirical research has investigated the effects of disrupting individual knowledge by examining the effect of turnover on organizations. David and Brachet (2011) compared the extent to which member turnover or skill decay caused by inactivity or interference from other tasks contributed to knowledge depreciation and found that the contribution of turnover was twice as strong as the effect of skill decay. Similarly, Lopez and Sune (2013) found that both adding and removing employees contributed to the depreciation of knowledge in a food-processing plant while interruptions in production did not. Thus, member turnover has been found to be a major contributor to knowledge depreciation.

Several reviews and theory pieces have appeared recently on the effect of turnover on organizational performance (Hausknecht & Holwerda, 2012; Park & Shaw, 2013). Based on a meta-analysis, Park and Shaw (2013) concluded that the relationship between turnover rates and performance is significant and negative. Further, they found that the negative relationship between turnover and performance was stronger in small than in large organizations and stronger in commitment-based primary employment systems than in control-based secondary employment systems. While not focusing on learning or changes in performance associated with experience, these reviews indicate that the effect of turnover varies as a function of the organizational context.

In the remainder of this section, we focus on contextual factors that that have been found to moderate the relationship between turnover and learning and knowledge outcomes. The effect of turnover has been found to depend on the member–member network, the task network and the member–task network.

In the context of knowledge retention, the member–member network has been investigated as a variable that moderates the effect of turnover on learning outcomes. For example, although teams learn better and faster than hierarchies, hierarchies are less affected by turnover than teams (Carley, 1992).

An individual's position in a social network also moderates the effect of turnover on organizational learning. For example, whether an employee bridges a structural hole (Burt, 1992) has been found to affect the relationship between turnover and performance. The departure of members who occupy structural holes or bridge unconnected nodes in a network has been found to harm performance more than the departure of members with redundant communication links (Shaw et al., 2005).

The effect of turnover also depends on characteristics of the organization's task. Argote et al. (1995) found that turnover was less harmful on complex tasks that involved innovation than on simple tasks that did not. Thus, if the task involves innovation, the departure of experienced members whose knowledge may have become obsolete can be less harmful than when the task does not involve innovation.

In addition to analyzing tasks as a moderator of the relationship between turnover and learning, researchers have also analyzed task networks as knowledge repositories because knowledge can be embedded in task networks or routines (Cyert & March, 1963; Nelson & Winter, 1982). Cohen and Bacdayan (1994) found that knowledge embedded in routines was not affected by task-performance interruptions. Similarly, Ton and Huckman (2008) found that in organizations where members conformed to task processes, turnover had less of an effect on performance than in organizations where members did not conform to processes. Loch, Sengupta, and Ahmad (2013) found that the retention of routines was enhanced by a strong group identity and impaired by differentiated status. Anand, Gray, and Siemsen (2012) found that mergers appear to cause decay in routines while inspections by regulatory agencies appear to promote the retention of routines. Knott (2001) found that routines of establishments that leave franchises were more likely to decay than the routines of those that remained and further, that drifting from routines hurt the unit's performance.

Embedding knowledge in tools and the tool network also promotes its retention. Alavi and Leidner (2001) indicated that computer storage technology and retrieval techniques can enhance organizational memory. Ashworth, Mukhopadhyay, and Argote (2004) found that the introduction of new information technology at a bank reduced knowledge decay.

A transactive memory system can serve as a knowledge repository because knowledge acquired from experience is embedded in the system (Austin, 2003; Hollingshead, 1998; Lewis, Lange, & Gillis, 2005; Liang, Moreland, & Argote, 1995). Transactive memory systems have been found to improve team performance (see Ren & Argote, 2011, for a review). Transactive memory systems are especially valuable under changing conditions where members might need to consult others for advice (Ren, Carley, & Argote, 2006).

Transferring Knowledge

Knowledge transfer is the process through which one unit is influenced by the experience of another (Argote & Ingram, 2000). Research on knowledge transfer analyzes whether organizational units learn indirectly or vicariously (Bandura, 1977) from the experience of other organizational units. For example, Darr, Argote, and Epple (1995) analyzed whether pizza stores learned from other stores owned by the same franchisee. Bresman (2010) analyzed whether pharmaceutical licensing teams learned from the experiences of other teams. Mechanisms through which one organizational unit learns from another include communication between "donor" and "recipient" units, providing members of recipient organizations training and opportunities to observe donor organizations, and personnel movement between donor and recipient organizations. Providing documents, routines, and templates from the donor organization to the recipient also can facilitate knowledge transfer. Further, interorganizational relationships such as alliances, joint ventures, or consortia can enable knowledge transfer.

Latent Context

Several dimensions of the context have been found to affect knowledge transfer. Perhaps the most fundamental characteristic is whether the contexts of the organizational units involved in the transfer are similar to each other. Knowledge is more likely to transfer across similar than dissimilar contexts (Baum & Berta, 1998; Darr & Kurtzberg, 2000). Knowledge acquired in dissimilar contexts might not be relevant for a focal unit or even harm the unit's performance (Baum & Ingram, 1998; Greve, 1999). Another dimension of the context that has been found to affect knowledge transfer is the geographic distance between organizational units (see Argote, Denomme, & Fuchs, 2011, for a review).

An important dimension of the context that has consistently been found to affect knowledge transfer is whether the organizational unit is part of a multiunit structure such as a franchise or chain. Multiunit structures have been found to facilitate knowledge transfer (Baum & Ingram, 1998; Darr, Argote, & Epple, 1995; Ingram & Simons, 2002). Typically these multiunit structures provide a variety of opportunities for knowledge transfer such as training, opportunities to communicate with and observe other units, and access to templates and routines that promote performance. Winter et al. (2012) found that replicating templates provided by the franchisor was more effective than adapting them.

The quality of relationship between a "donor" and a "recipient" organization has been found to affect knowledge transfer (Szulanski, 1996). Kane, Argote, and Levine (2005) found that groups that shared a superordinate identity through which members felt that they belonged to the same social group were more likely to share knowledge than those lacking a shared social identity. When groups did not share a superordinate identity, they rejected knowledge proposed by a newcomer from another group. By contrast, when groups shared a superordinate identity, they considered the ideas of newcomers from another group and adopted those likely to improve their performance.

The organization's structure and practices have also been found to affect knowledge transfer. Tsai (2002) found that social interaction across organizational units facilitated knowledge transfer while centralized structures impeded transfer. Collins and Smith (2006) determined that commitment-based human resource practices such as group incentives and training were positively related to a climate that included trust, cooperation, and shared language. Further, a firm's social climate affected knowledge transfer, which in turn affected firm performance. Quigley et al. (2007) found that the interaction between the incentive system and norms for sharing knowledge was a significant predictor of the amount of knowledge shared. As one moved from individual to hybrid to group-based incentive systems, the amount of knowledge shared increased when there were norms supporting knowledge-sharing and decreased when those norms were lacking.

Characteristics of organizational units have been found to affect knowledge transfer. Units high in absorptive capacity (Cohen & Levinthal, 1990) are more likely to transfer knowledge successfully than units low in absorptive capacity (Szulanski, 1996). Similarly, previous experience in knowledge transfer increases the success of transfer attempts (Galbraith, 1990). Knowledge developed in a high-status organization is more likely to transfer to other establishments than knowledge created by a low-status organization (Sine, Shane, & DiGrigorio, 2003). Knowledge created by rivals is more likely to transfer when the rival is external rather than internal to the organization (Menon, Thompson, & Choi, 2006), arguably because an external rival is less threatening to the status of members of the focal unit.

Active context: Members, tasks, tools, and their networks

Moving members has been found to be an effective mechanism for transferring knowledge between groups and organizations (e.g., see Almeida & Kogut, 1999). Members have been shown to be an especially effective knowledge transfer mechanism when the organizational units share a superordinate identity (Kane, Argote, & Levine, 2005).

How the member–member or social network affects knowledge transfer has received considerable research attention (see Phelps, Heidl, & Wadhwa, 2012, for a review). Hansen (1999) found that weak ties between members facilitated the transfer of codified or explicit knowledge, while strong ties facilitated the transfer of tacit knowledge. Reagans and McEvily (2003) found that dense internal networks with links to external networks facilitated transfer over and above the effect of tie strength. Tortoriello, Reagans, and McEvily (2012) found that strong ties, network cohesion, and network range all positively affected the amount of knowledge transfer across units.

Moving task networks or routines from one social unit to another is also an effective mechanism for transferring knowledge (Kane, Argote, & Levine, 2005). For example, Darr, Argote, and Epple (1995) found that an innovative routine transferred across the units of fast food franchises.

Knowledge also transfers by moving tools from one context to another (Zander & Kogut, 1995). Transferring knowledge through moving tools enables knowledge to transfer consistently and on a large scale. For example, Ashworth, Mukhopadhyay, and Argote (2004) found that the introduction of new information technology in six geographically distributed units of a bank facilitated knowledge transfer across the units. Moving members along with tools is an approach for transferring tacit knowledge along with explicit knowledge and is generally more effective than moving tools alone (Galbraith, 1990).

A couple of studies have examined the effectiveness of knowledge management systems at transferring knowledge. Haas and Hansen (2005) analyzed a consulting firm's knowledge management system that consisted of document libraries on various topics and industries linked by a search engine. Somewhat surprisingly, the researchers found a negative main effect for the number of documents used from the knowledge management system on consulting team performance. Further, using electronic documents from a knowledge management system was especially likely to impair team performance when the team was experienced and faced a competitive environment.

Kim (2008) also found that the effect of a knowledge management system on performance depended on important contingencies. In contrast to Haas and Hansen's (2005) results, however, Kim (2008) found that the impact of a knowledge management system on the performance of stores in a retail grocery chain was generally positive. Further, the magnitude of the impact of using the knowledge management system on performance was greater for managers with fewer alternative sources of knowledge, for managers who were remotely located, and for those who dealt primarily with products that did not become obsolete quickly.

Research on transactive memory systems has shown that they can serve as knowledge transfer mechanisms. A transactive memory developed in one context can transfer to another as long as the contexts have common elements (Lewis, Lange, & Gillis, 2005).

Future Research

Although significant progress has been made in our understanding of organizational learning, memory, and transfer, additional research would advance our understanding of these important topics. Consistent with members being the media through which organizational learning generally occurs, considerable research has been done on the effects of members on organizational learning, memory, and knowledge transfer. We have made progress understanding the effects of members' abilities and opportunities on organizational learning and knowledge transfer and the effects of their turnover on knowledge depreciation. Although some research has been conducted on the effects of members' motivations (Quigley et al., 2007), identity (Kane, Argote, & Levine, 2005), and emotions (Levin et al., 2010), additional research on these factors is needed. Further, research on aspects of the organizational context in addition to members would also advance our understanding of organizational learning, memory, and knowledge transfer.

More research is needed on the interrelationships between elements of the context. When do the elements of the organization's context substitute for each other as knowledge repositories or knowledge transfer mechanisms and when do they complement each other? For example, moving members can be complementary to moving tools as a knowledge transfer mechanism: members and tools positively reinforce each other. By contrast, transactive memory systems might substitute for tools as knowledge repositories.

Research is also needed on the relationships between organizational learning, memory, and knowledge transfer. For example, Wong (2004) found that learning from direct experience and learning from indirect experience or knowledge transfer seemed to substitute for each other while Bresman (2010) found that learning from direct and indirect experience positively reinforced each other and thus, were complements. Levine and Prietula (2012) theorized that organizational memory and knowledge transfer substituted for each other. We need to determine whether and the conditions under which these processes are substitutes or complements. Further, the factors that enhance learning from direct experience may differ from those that enhance knowledge retention or transfer. For example, personnel movement enhances knowledge creation and transfer but detracts from knowledge retention.

Research is also needed on how organizational learning can lead to the development of organizational capabilities and be a source of competitive advantage for firms. The field of strategic management has increasingly been interested in understanding the micro-foundations of the development of capabilities and competitive advantage in firms (Felin et al., 2012). Argote and Ren (2012) theorized that transactive memory systems provide these micro-foundations. Transactive memory systems have many of the properties that researchers have argued are necessary in order to be a source of competitive advantage. These properties include: being developed or built through experience (Dierickx & Cool, 1989), having many components that fit each other (Rivkin, 2000), and being hard for competitors to imitate (Barney, 1986; Lippman & Rumelt, 1982). Research is needed on whether transactive memory systems, in particular, and organizational learning, in general, are sources of competitive advantage in firms.

Conclusion

A greater understanding of organizational learning and knowledge retention and transfer has the potential to advance practice as well as theory. Lew Platt, a former CEO of Hewlett-Packard, has been quoted as saying, "If Hewlett Packard knew what Hewlett-Packard knows, we would be three times as productive" (Davenport & Prusak, 1998). A greater understanding of organizational learning and knowledge can enable organizations to achieve the increase in productivity that Platt envisioned. Organizations that are able to learn and retain lessons learned from experience can avoid the mistakes of the past and save time and money by not "reinventing the wheel" in the future. Organizations that are able to transfer knowledge throughout their establishments spread the benefits of knowledge acquired by one unit to others. Thus, organizations that are able to learn and manage knowledge effectively are more likely to survive and prosper than their counterparts that are less effective at knowledge management.

References

Alavi, M., & Leidner, D. E. (2001). Review: Knowledge management and knowledge management systems: Conceptual foundations and research Issues. *MIS Quarterly*, 25(1), 107–136.

Almeida, P., & Kogut, B. (1999). Localization of knowledge and the mobility of engineers in regional networks. *Management Science*, 45(7), 905–917.

Anand, G., Gray, J., & Siemsen, E. (2012). Decay, shock and renewal: Operational routines and process entropy in the pharmaceutical industry. *Organization Science*, 23, 1700–1716.

Anderson, E., & Lewis, K. (2013). A dynamic model of individual and collective learning amid disruption. *Organization Science*, 25(2), 356–376.

Argote, L. (2012). Organizational learning and knowledge management. In S. Kozlowski (Ed.), *Oxford Handbook of Industrial and Organizational Psychology* (pp. 933–954). New York: Oxford University Press.

Argote, L. (2013). *Organizational Learning: Creating, Retaining and Transferring Knowledge* (2nd ed.). New York: Springer.

Argote, L., Beckman, S., & Epple, D. (1990). The persistence and transfer of learning in industrial settings. *Management Science*, 36, 140–154.

Argote, L., Denomme, C., & Fuchs, E. (2011). Organizational learning across boundaries: The effect of geographic distribution on organizational learning and knowledge transfer. In M. Easterby-Smith and M. Lyles (Eds.), *Handbook of Organizational Learning and Knowledge Management*. Oxford: Blackwell.

Argote, L., & Epple, D. (1990, February 23). Learning curves in manufacturing. *Science*, 247(4945), 920–924.

Argote, L., Gruenfeld, D., & Naquin, C. (2001). Group learning in organizations. In M. E. Turner (Ed.), *Groups at Work* (pp. 369–411). Mahwah, NJ: Erlbaum.

Argote, L., & Ingram, P. (2000). Knowledge transfer in organizations: A basis for competitive advantage in firms. *Organizational Behavior and Human Decision Processes*, 82, 150–169.

Argote, L., Insko, C., Yovetich, N., & Romero, A. (1995). Group learning curves: The effect of turnover, task complexity and training on group performance. *Journal of Applied Social Psychology*, 25, 512–529.

Argote, L., & Miron-Spektor, E. (2011). Organizational learning: From experience to knowledge. *Organization Science*, 22, 1123–1137.

Argote, L., & Ren, Y. (2012). Transactive memory systems: A micro foundation of dynamic capabilities. *Journal of Management Studies*, 49, 1375–1382.

Argyris, C., & Schon, P. (1978). *Organizational Learning*. Reading, MA: Addison-Wesley.

Arrow, H., McGrath, J. E., & Berdahl, J. L. (2000). *Small Groups as Complex Systems: Formation, Coordination, Development, and Adaptation*. Thousand Oaks, CA: Sage.

Arthur, W., Jr., Bennett, W., Jr., Stanush, P. L., & McNelly, T. L. (1998). Factors that influence skill decay and retention: A quantitative review and analysis. *Human Performance*, 11, 57–101.

Ashworth, M., Mukhopadhyay, T., & Argote, L. (2004). Information technology and organizational learning: An empirical analysis. *Proceedings of the 25th Annual International Conference on Information Systems (ICIS)* (pp. 11–21).

Austin, J. R. (2003). Transactive memory in organizational groups: The effects of content, consensus, specialization, and accuracy on group performance. *Journal of Applied Psychology*, 88(5), 866–878.

Balasubramanian, N., & Lieberman, M. (2010). Industry learning environments and heterogeneity of firm performance. *Strategic Management Journal*, 31(4), 390–412.

Bandura, A. (1977). *Social Learning Theory*, Englewood Cliffs, NJ: Prentice-Hall.

Barney, J. B. (1986). Strategic factor markets: Expectations, luck and business strategy. *Management Science*, 32, 1231–1241.

Baum, J. A. C., & Berta, W. B. (1998). Sources, timing, and speed: Population-level learning by organizations in a longitudinal behavioral simulation. Paper presented at Carnegie-Wisconsin Conference on Knowledge Transfer and Levels of Learning, Carnegie Mellon University, Pittsburgh, PA, June.

Baum, J. A. C., & Ingram, P. (1998). Population-level learning in the Manhattan hotel industry, 1898–1980. *Management Science*, 44, 996–1016.

Bell, B. S., & Kozlowski, S. W. J. (2008). Active learning: Effects of core training design elements on self-regulatory processes, learning, and adaptability. *Journal of Applied Psychology*, 93(2), 296–316.

Benkard, C. L. (2000). Learning and forgetting: The dynamics of aircraft production. *American Economic Review*, 90(4), 1034–1054.

Bresman, H. (2010). External learning activities and team performance: A multimethod field study. *Organization Science*, 21, 81–96.

Bromiley, P. (1991). Testing a causal model of corporate risk taking and performance. *Academy of Management Journal*, 34(1), 37–59.

Bunderson, J. S., & Boumgarden, P. (2010). Structure and learning in self-managed teams: Why "bureaucratic" teams can be better learners. *Organization Science*, 21, 609–624.

Bunderson, J. S., & Sutcliffe, K. M. (2003). Management team learning orientation and business unit performance. *Journal of Applied Psychology*, 88(3), 552–560.

Burt, R. S. (1992). *Structural Holes: The Social Structure of Competition*. Cambridge, MA: Harvard University Press.

Burt, R. S. (2004). Structural holes and good ideas. *American Journal of Sociology*, 110, 349–399.

Carley, K. (1992). Organizational learning and personnel turnover. *Organization Science*, 3(1), 20–46.

Choi, H. S., & Thompson, L. (2005). Old wine in a new bottle: Impact of membership change on group creativity. *Organization Behavior and Human Decision Processes*, 98, 121–132.

Cohen, M. D., & Bacdayan, P. (1994). Organizational routines are stored as procedural memory: Evidence from a laboratory study. *Organization Science*, 5, 554–568.

Cohen, W. M., & Levinthal, D. (1990). Absorptive capacity: A new perspective on learning and innovation. *Administrative Science Quarterly*, 35, 128–152.

Collins, C. J., & Smith, K. G. (2006). Knowledge exchange and combination: The role of human resource practices in the performance of high-technology firms. *Academy of Management Journal*, 49(3), 544–560.

Cyert, R. M., & March, J. G. (1963). *A Behavioral Theory of the Firm*. Englewood Cliffs, NJ: Prentice-Hall.

Darr, E., Argote, L., & Epple, D. (1995). The acquisition, transfer, and depreciation of learning in service organizations: Productivity in franchises. *Management Science*, 44, 1750–1762.

Darr, E. D., & Kurtzberg, T. R. (2000). An investigation of partner similarity dimensions on knowledge transfer. *Organizational Behavior and Human Decision Processes*, 82, 28–44.

Davenport, T., & Prusak, L. (1998). *Working Knowledge: How Organizations Manage What they Know*. Boston, MA: Harvard Business School Press.

David, G., & Brachet, T. (2011). On the determinants of organizational forgetting. *American Economic Journal: Microeconomics*, 3, 100–123.

De Holan, P. M., & Phillips, N. (2004). Remembrance of things past? The dynamics of organizational forgetting. *Management Science*, 50, 1603–1613.

Denrell, J., Fang, C., & Levinthal, D. A. (2004). From t-mazes to labyrinths: Learning from model-based feedback. *Management Science*, 50(10), 1366–1378.

Dierickx, I., & Cool, K. (1989). Asset stock accumulation and sustainability of competitive advantage. *Management Science*, 35(12), 1504–1511.

Dutton, J. M., & Thomas, A. (1984). Treating progress functions as a managerial opportunity. *Academy of Management Review*, 9(2), 235–247.

Easterby-Smith, M., Crossan, M., & Nicolini, D. (2000). Organizational learning: Debates past, present and future. *Journal of Management Studies*, 37(5), 783–796.

Edmondson, A. C. (1999). Psychological safety and learning behavior in work teams. *Administrative Science Quarterly*, 44(2), 350–383.

Edmondson, A. C. (2002). The local and variegated nature of learning in organizations: A group-level perspective. *Organization Science*, 13(2), 128–146.

Edmondson, A. C., Dillon, J. R., & Roloff, K. (2007). Three perspectives on team learning: Outcome improvement, task mastery, and group process. In J. P. Walsh & A. P. Brief (Eds.), *The Academy of Management Annals* (pp. 269–314). Hove: Psychology Press.

Feldman, M. S., & Pentland, B. T. (2003). Reconceptualizing routines as a source of stability and change. *Administrative Science Quarterly*, 48(1), 94–118.

Felin, T., Foss, N. J., Heimeriks, K. H., & Madsen, T. L. (2012). Microfoundations of learning routines and capabilities: Individuals, process and structure. *Journal of Management Studies*, 49, 1351–1374.

Fiol, C. M., & Lyles, M. A. (1985). Organizational learning. *Academy of Management Review*, 10(4), 803–813.

Galbraith, C. S. (1990). Transferring core manufacturing technologies in high-technology firms. *California Management Review*, 32(4), 56–70.

Gibson, F. P. (2000). Feedback delays: How can decision makers learn not to buy a new car every time the garage is empty? *Organizational Behavior and Human Decision Processes*, 83(1), 141–166

Gino, F., Argote, L., Miron-Spektor, E., & Todorova, G. (2010). First get your feet wet: When and why prior experience fosters team creativity. *Organizational Behavior and Human Decision Processes*, 111(2), 102–115.

Goodman, J. S., Wood, R. E., & Hendrickx, M. (2004). Feedback specificity, exploration and learning, *Journal of Applied Psychology*, 89(2), 248–262.

Greve, H. R. (1999). Branch systems and nonlocal learning in populations. In A. Miner & P. Anderson (Eds.), *Advances in Strategic Management* (vol. 16, pp. 57–80). Greenwich, CT: JAI Press.

Greve, H. R. (2003). *Organizational Learning from Performance Feedback*. Cambridge, UK: Cambridge University Press.

Gruenfeld, D., Martorana, P. V., & Fan, E. T. (2000). What do groups learn from their worldliest members? Direct and indirect influence in dynamic teams. *Organizational Behavior and Human Decision Processes*, 82, 60–74.

Gulati, R., & Nohria, N. (1996). Is slack good or bad for innovation? *Academy of Management Journal*, 39(5), 1245–1264.

Haas, M. R., & Hansen, M. T. (2005). When using knowledge can hurt performance: The value of organizational capabilities in a management consulting company. *Strategic Management Journal*, 26, 1–24.

Hansen, M. (1999). The search transfer problem: The role of weak ties in sharing knowledge across organization subunits. *Administrative Science Quarterly*, 44, 82–111.

Haunschild, P., & Sullivan, B. (2002). Learning from complexity: Effects of airline accident/incident heterogeneity on subsequent accident/incident rates. *Administrative Science Quarterly*, 47, 609–643.

Hausknecht, J. P., & Holwerda, J. A. (2012). When does employee turnover matter? Dynamic member configurations, productive capacity and collective performance. *Organization Science*, 24(1), 210–225.

Hilgard, E. R., & Bower, G. H. (1975). *Theories of Learning* (4th ed.). Englewood Cliffs, NJ: Prentice-Hall.

Hollingshead, A. B. (1998). Retrieval processes in transactive memory systems. *Journal of Personality and Social Psychology*, 74, 659–671.

Huber, G. P. (1991). Organizational learning: The contributing processes and the literatures. *Organization Science*, 2, 88–115.

Huff, A. S., & Jenkins, M. (2001). Mapping managerial knowledge. In A. S. Huff & M. Jenkins (Eds.), *Mapping Managerial Knowledge*. Chichester: John Wiley & Sons, Ltd.

Ingram, P. (2002). Interorganizational learning. In J. A. C. Baum (Ed.), *The Blackwell Companion to Organizations* (pp. 642–663). Oxford: Blackwell Business.

Ingram, P., & Baum, J. A. C. (1997). Opportunity and constraint: Organizations' learning from the operating and competitive experience of industries. *Strategic Management Journal*, 18, 75–98.

Ingram, P., & Simons, T. (2002). The transfer of experience in groups of organizations: Implications for performance and competition. *Management Science*, 48, 1517–1533.

Jain, A., & Kogut, B. (2014). Memory and organizational evolvability in a neutral landscape. *Organization Science*, 25(2), 479–493.

Jansen, J. P. J., Van Den Bosch, F. A. J., & Volberda, H. W. (2006). Exploratory innovation, and performance: Effects of organizational antecedents and environmental moderators. *Management Science*, 52(11), 1661–1674.

Kane, A. A. (2010). Unlocking knowledge transfer potential: Knowledge demonstrability and super-ordinate social identity. *Organization Science*, 21, 643–660.

Kane, A. A., Argote, L., & Levine, J. M. (2005). Knowledge transfer between groups via personnel rotation: Effects of social identity and knowledge quality. *Organizational Behavior and Human Decision Processes*, 96, 56–71.

Kim, S. H. (2008). An empirical assessment of knowledge management systems. PhD thesis. Carnegie Mellon University, Pittsburgh, PA.

Knott, A. M. (2001). The dynamic value of hierarchy. *Management Science*, 47(3), 430–448.

Kozlowski, S. W. J., Chao, G. T., & Nowakowski, J. M. (in press). Building an infrastructure for organizational learning: A multi-level approach. In S.W. J. Kozlowski & E. Salas (Eds.), *Learning, Training and Development in Organizations*. Mahwah, NJ: LEA.

Lant, T. K. (1992). Aspiration level adaptation: An empirical exploration. *Management Science*, 38(5), 623–644.

Laughlin, P. R., & Ellis, A. L. (1986). Demonstrability and social combination processes on mathematical intellective tasks. *Journal of Experimental Social Psychology*, 22, 177–189.

Levin, D. Z., Kurtzberg, T., Phillips, K. W., & Lount, R. B., Jr. (2010). The role of affect in knowledge transfer. *Group Dynamics*, 14(2), 123–142.

Levine, S. S., & Prietula, M. J. (2012). How knowledge transfer impacts performance: A multilevel model of benefits and liabilities. *Organization Science*, 23(6), 1748–1766.

Levitt, B., & March, J. G. (1988). Organizational learning. *Annual Review of Sociology*, 14, 319–340.

Lewis, K. (2004). Knowledge and performance in knowledge-worker teams: A longitudinal study of transactive memory systems. *Management Science*, 50(11), 1519–1533.

Lewis, K., Lange, D., & Gillis, L. (2005). Transactive memory systems, learning, and learning transfer. *Organization Science*, 16(6), 581–598.

Liang, D. W., Moreland, R., & Argote, L. (1995). Group versus individual training and group performance: The mediating role of transactive memory. *Personality and Social Psychology Bulletin*, 21, 384–393.

Lippman, S. A., & Rumelt, R. P. (1992). Demand uncertainty and investment in industry-specific capital. *Industrial and Corporate Change*, 1, 235–262.

Loch, C. H., Sengupta, K., & Ahmad, M. G. (2013). The microevolution of routines: How problem solving and social preferences interact. *Organization Science*, 24, 99–115.

Lopez, L., & Sune, A. (2013). Turnover-induced forgetting and its impact on productivity. *British Journal of Management*, 24, 38–53.

March, J. G. (1991). Exploration and exploitation in organizational learning. *Organization Science*, 2, 71–87.

McGrath, J. E., & Argote, L. (2001). Group processes in organizational contexts. In M. A. Hogg & R. S. Tindale (Eds.), *Blackwell Handbook of Social Psychology*, vol. 3: *Group Processes* (pp. 603–627). Oxford: Blackwell.

Menon, T., Thompson, L., & Choi, H. (2006). Tainted knowledge vs. tempting knowledge: People avoid knowledge from internal rivals and seek knowledge from external rivals. *Management Science*, 52(8), 1129–1144.

Miner, A. S., & Haunschild, P. R. (1995). Population-level learning. In L. L. Cummings & B. M. Staw, (Eds.), *Research in Organizational Behavior* (pp. 115–166). Greenwich, CN: JAI Press.

Miner, A. S., & Mezias, S. J. (1996). Ugly duckling no more: pasts and futures of organizational learning research. *Organization Science*, 7, 88–99.

Nadler, J., Thompson, L., & Van Boven, L. (2003). Learning negotiation skills: Four models of knowledge creation and transfer. *Management Science*, 49(4), 529–540.

Nelson, R. R., & Winter, S. G. (1982). *An Evolutionary Theory of Economic Change*. Boston, MA: Belkman.

Nonaka, I. (1991). The knowledge-creating company. *Harvard Business Review*, 69(6), 96–104.

Nonaka, I., & von Krogh, G. (2009). Perspective – tacit knowledge and knowledge conversion: Controversy and advancement in organizational knowledge creation theory. *Organization Science*, 20, 635–652.

Park, T., & Shaw, J. D. (2013). Turnover rates and organizational performance: A meta-analysis. *Journal of Applied Psychology*, 98, 268–309.

Phelps, C., Heidl, R., & Wadhwa, A. (2012). Knowledge, networks and knowledge networks: A review and research agenda. *Journal of Management*, 38(4), 1115–1166.

Polanyi, M. (1962). *Personal Knowledge: Towards a Post-Critical Philosophy*. New York: Harper & Row.

Quigley, N. R., Tesluk, P. E., Locke, E. A., & Bartol, K. M. (2007). A multilevel investigation of the motivational mechanism underlying knowledge sharing and performance. *Organization Science*, 18(1), 71–88.

Quinones, M. A., Ford, J. K., & Teachout, M. S. (1995). The relationship between work experience and job performance: A conceptual and meta-analytic review. *Personnel Psychology*, 48, 887–910.

Rao, R., & Argote, L. (2006). Organizational learning and forgetting: The effects of turnover and structure. *European Management Review*, 3, 77–85.

Reagans, R., Argote, L., & Brooks, D. (2005). Individual experience and experience working together: Predicting learning rates from knowing what to do and knowing who knows what. *Management Science*, 51, 869–881.

Reagans, R., & McEvily, B. (2003). Network structure and knowledge transfer: The effects of cohesion and range. *Administrative Science Quarterly*, 48(2), 240–267.

Ree, M. J., Earles, J. A., & Teachout, M. S. (1994). Predicting job performance: Not much more than g. *Journal of Applied Psychology*, 79, 518–524.

Ren, Y., & Argote, L. (2011). Transactive memory systems: An integrative framework of key dimensions, antecedents, and consequences. *Academy of Management Annals*, 5, 189–230.

Ren, Y., Carley, K. M., & Argote, L. (2006). The contingent effects of transactive memory: When is it more beneficial to know what others know? *Management Science*, 52, 671–682.

Rick, S., & Weber, R. A. (2010). Meaningful learning and transfer learning in games played repeatedly without feedback. *Games and Economic Behavior*, 68, 716–730.

Rivkin, J. W. (2000). Imitation of complex systems. *Management Science*, 46(6), 824–844.

Salas, E., DiazGranados, D., Klein, C., Burke, C. S., Stagl, K.C., Goodwin, G. F., & Halpin, S. M. (2008). Does team training improve team performance? A meta-analysis. *Human Factors*, 50(6), 903–933.

Salas, E., Tannenbaum, S. I., Kraiger, K., & Smith-Jentsch, K. A. (2012). The science of training and development in organizations: What matters in practice. *Psychological Science in the Public Interest*, 13, 74–101.

Schilling, M. A., Vidal, P., Ployhart, R. E., & Marangoni, A. (2003). Learning by doing something else: Variation, relatedness, and the learning curve. *Management Science*, 49(1), 39–56.

Schulz, M. (2002). Organizational learning. In J. A. C. Baum (Ed.), *The Blackwell Companion to Organizations* (pp. 416–441). Oxford: Blackwell Business.

Shaw, J. D., Duffy, M. K., Johnson, J. J., & Lockhart, D. (2005). Turnover, social capital losses, and performance. *Academy of Management Journal*, 48, 594–606.

Sine, W. D., Shane, S., & DiGrigorio, D. (2003). The halo effect and technology licensing: The influence of institutional prestige on the licensing of university inventions. *Management Science*, 49(4), 478–496.

Sorenson, O. (2003). Interdependence and adaptability: Organizational learning and the long-term effect of integration. *Management Science*, 49(4), 446–463.

Stata, R. (1989). Organizational learning: The key to management innovation. *Sloan Management Review*, 30(3), 63–74.

Stein, E. W. (1995). Organizational memory: Review of concepts and recommendations for management. *International Journal of Information Management*, 15, 17–32.

Szulanski, G. (1996). Exploring internal stickiness: Impediments to the transfer of best practice within the firm. *Strategic Management Journal*, 17, 27–43.

Tesluk, P. E., & Jacobs, R. J. (1998). Toward an integrated model of work experience. *Personnel Psychology*, 51(2), 321–355.

Ton, Z., & Huckman, R. S. (2008). Managing the impact of employee turnover on performance: The role of process conformance. *Organization Science*, 19(1), 56–68.

Tortoriello, M., & Krackhardt, D. (2010). Activating cross-boundary knowledge: Simmelian ties in the generation of innovation. *Academy of Management Journal*, 53(1), 167–181.

Tortoriello, M., Reagans, R., & McEvily, B. (2012). Bridging the knowledge gap: The influence of strong ties, network cohesion and network range on the transfer of knowledge between organizational units. *Organization Science*, 23, 1024–1039.

Tsai, W. (2002). Social structure of "coopetition" within a multiunit organization: Coordination, competition and interorganizational knowledge sharing. *Organization Science*, 13(2), 179–190.

Van der Vegt, G. S., de Jong, S. B., Bunderson, J. S., & Molleman, E. (2010). Power asymmetry and learning in teams: The moderating role of performance feedback. *Organization Science*, 21(2), 347–361.

Walsh, J. P., & Ungson, G. R. (1991). Organizational memory. *Academy of Management Review*, 16, 57–91.

Weber, R. A., & Camerer, C. F. (2003). Cultural conflict and merger failure: An experimental approach. *Management Science*, 49(4), 400–415.

Wegner, D. M. (1986). Transactive memory: A contemporary analysis of the group mind. In B. Millen & G. R. Goethals (Eds.), *Theories of Group Behavior* (pp. 185–205). New York: Springer-Verlag.

Wiersma, E. (2007). Conditions that shape the learning curve: Factors that increase the ability and opportunity to learn. *Management Science*, 53(12), 1903–1915.

Wingfield, A. (1979). *Human Learning and Memory: An Introduction*. New York: Harper & Row.

Winter, S. G., Szulanski, G., Ringov, D., & Jensen, R. J. (2012). Reproducing knowledge: Inaccurate replication and failure in franchise organizations. *Organization Science*, 23(3), 672–685.

Wong, S. (2004). Distal and local group learning: Performance trade-offs and tensions. *Organization Science*, 15, 645–656.

Zander, U., & Kogut, B. (1995). Knowledge and the speed of the transfer and imitation of organizational capabilities: An empirical test. *Organization Science*, 6(1), 76–92.

Section II
E-Learning

10

Facilitation in E-Learning

Annette Towler and Tyree Mitchell

Introduction

We are seeing large changes in how we instruct and develop individuals to maximize their learning experiences. Traditional courses are still prevalent yet organizations are developing e-learning courses to cater to the learner. The US military has already moved many traditional, classroom-based courses to e-learning environments (Tucker et al., 2010). Universities are also making substantial inroads in the development of e-learning classes and some predict that this impact of e-learning will lead to a significant reduction in the number of global universities (*Economist*, 2012).

How is e-learning facilitation different from traditional learning facilitation? There is a difference in the amount of social contact between trainees and trainer. Social contact can range from very limited (e.g., email) to distant but rich (e.g., teleconferencing or streaming video). The role of the trainer can be different because the trainer acts as a facilitator rather than a purveyor of knowledge. This can also result in the learner being given more control to choose different training methods and to use different learning strategies.

This chapter will focus on the role that the trainer plays in facilitating e-learning. The chapter will focus on (1) the relationship between the trainer and the trainee within an e-learning environment and (2) the specific trainer behaviors that are conducive for trainee learning. These will include communication style and effective leader behaviors that can facilitate learning before and during training.

In the first section, we focus on the trainer's role and how the trainer can act as an effective guide during the learning process. The trainer can utilize a variety of styles and we draw on the educational psychology literature to talk about the styles that are effective within an e-learning environment. This section also focuses on the relationship between the trainer and the trainees. We discuss how the trainer and trainee can develop a high-quality relationship within an e-learning environment. We utilize the leadership literature to discuss how these high-quality relationships can be developed.

The Wiley Blackwell Handbook of the Psychology of Training, Development, and Performance Improvement,
First Edition. Edited by Kurt Kraiger, Jonathan Passmore, Sigmar Malvezzi, and Nuno Rebelo dos Santos.
© 2015 John Wiley & Sons Ltd. Published 2020 by John Wiley & Sons Ltd.

In the second section, we focus on trainer behaviors that are effective within an e-learning environment. Based on research within the employee training literature, we argue that both trainer delivery and content are important to consider in predicting trainee learning. For example, trainer expressiveness is important because frequently the trainer will narrate instructional content and this can influence the degree to which the trainee is engaged and motivated to learn. We also discuss the content that the trainer uses and focus on how trainer charisma can influence trainee engagement. We also focus on Meyer's multimedia model and discuss the multimedia principles that can engage and influence trainee learning.

Finally, we discuss some new advances that can facilitate e-learning such as the increasing use of pedagogical agents to facilitate training.

The Role of the Trainer

"It is not the technology but the instructional implementation of the technology that determines its effects on learning" (Collis, 1995, p. 146). In contrast to traditional face-to-face classes in which trainers typically direct learning activities and tailor training to accommodate the needs of the average trainee, trainers in an e-learning environment must assume the role of facilitator or coach as opposed to the sole provider of knowledge. As a facilitator, the trainer prepares the learning environment but the trainee is ultimately responsible for their own learning. Though this learner-centered environment may provide trainees with more control over learning, trainees still require a small amount of guidance to help engagement in learning. By encouraging personal growth and emphasizing development of knowledge rather than diffusion of information, trainers can empower trainees to take more control over instructional design elements (e.g., pacing, sequence) and utilize different learning strategies.

Trainer teaching style – particularly, interactions between trainers and trainees – plays a critical role in an e-learning context (Borbely, 1994; Lachem, Mitchell, & Atkinson, 1994; Webster & Hackley, 1997). Learners are more prone to distractions and are more likely to experience difficulty concentrating on course materials in the absence of noticeable trainer–learner interactions (Isaacs et al., 1995). Therefore, it is important that trainers encourage and expect trainees to actively participate in learning activities during training. Moreover, it is important that trainers effectively design interaction mechanisms to improve quality and frequency of interactions in e-learning settings. Research has demonstrated that active participation by the trainer influences student participation in e-learning activities, which, in turn, influences learning through interaction with one another (Jiang & Ting, 1998). This finding is consistent with the view that in an e-learning environment the role of the trainer shifts from a purveyor of knowledge to a facilitator providing scaffolding and support throughout the training process. Much attention has been devoted to the idea that trainers use different instructional styles to accommodate differences in trainee characteristics (Henson & Borthwick, 1984). A simple instructional styles taxonomy identified three teaching styles that focus on how the teacher interacts with the learner: (1) didactic style, which is trainer-controlled; (2) a Socratic style, which is trainer-directed through the use of questions to which the learner respond; and (3) a facilitative style, which allows for more learner control as the trainer prepares the learning environment but the learner is ultimately responsible for their own learning (Jarvis, 1985). Recent research suggests that the trainer should promote an autonomy-driven climate whereby trainees require a small amount of guidance to help engagement in learning (Hutchins, 2009). This area of research is particularly relevant for effective technology-driven instruction because the learner is given more control in contrast to a classroom environment. However, trainees can be passive and reactive during the learning process even within an e-learning environment, particularly if the trainer is reliant on directive methods (e.g., lecture, PowerPoint slides) to facilitate learning. The literature on trainer behaviors that promote trainee engagement is relatively sparse. However, research from the educational literature promotes the importance of the trainer providing a climate that promotes trainee intrinsic motivation. In this model, based on self-determination theory, an effective relationship between the trainer and trainee emerges when trainee individual growth needs are met. Self-determination theory suggests that trainer behavior is on a continuum and can range from a controlling style to an autonomy-supportive style (Deci & Ryan, 1985). A recent study found that when the trainer engaged in autonomy-supportive behavior this was related to student engagement, motivation, and performance (Reeve & Jang, 2006). In this laboratory experiment, students were assigned to either the role of teacher or student and were required to work on a puzzle called Happy Cubes that can be arranged into a variety of shapes. They found that several of the autonomy-supportive trainer behaviors predicted learner autonomy, engagement, and performance. Students felt they were given more autonomy when the trainer allowed the student to work in his or her own way, offered encouragement, and allowed time for students to talk. Learner-perceived autonomy was positively related to learner performance, the degree to which they were engaged in the task, and the extent to which they enjoyed the task.

Trainers' attitudes toward technology and control over the technology also play a critical role in the success of e-learning (Sun et al., 2008; Webster & Hackley, 1997). The view that trainers' attitudes toward technology impacts the success of e-learning is consistent with the social influence model of technology use, which posits that social influences (e.g., supervisor attitudes, work group norms) and behaviors can positively or negatively affect choices, attitudes, and media use (Fulk, Schmitz, & Steinfeld, 1990). Research has shown that when trainers maintain positive attitudes toward the technology, learners are more likely to experience positive learning outcomes (Sun et al., 2008). Additionally, the trainer must demonstrate control over the technology in e-learning settings. Learners can easily become distracted by the use of the equipment (Gowan & Downs, 1994), and become impatient when trainers experience technical problems (Leidner & Jarvenpaa, 1995). However, trainers that demonstrate the capability to control e-learning activities and promptly respond to learners' problems can improve learner satisfaction (Arbaugh, 2002; Thurmond, Wambach, & Connors, 2002).

The relationship between the trainer and trainee

Although the role of the trainer in the learning process has only recently gained attention in the employee training literature, preliminary research has shown several trainer characteristics to be related to training outcomes. For example, trainer organization and expressiveness have been related to trainee performance on a recall test and a problem-solving task, and there is also evidence that these trainer characteristics interact with attributes of the trainee (i.e., learning orientation; Holladay & Quiñones, 2008; Towler, 2009; Towler & Dipboye, 2001). Towler & Dipboye (2001) found that trainees with a high-mastery orientation paid more attention to trainer behaviors than trainees with a low-mastery orientation. This study suggests the quality of the relationship between the trainer and trainee can be influenced by trainee characteristics and trainer behavior. Building a quality relationship is a central theme within the leadership literature because high-quality relationships yield effective outcomes (Graen & Uhl-Bien, 1995). The idea that effective trainers are also effective leaders is not a new one (Kinicki & Schriesheim, 1978). Most models of leadership focus on task-oriented behaviors and person-centered behaviors and are similar to the behaviors demonstrated by educators (Judge, Piccolo, & Ilies, 2004). For example, effective trainers display effective leadership behaviors such as showing consideration for trainees, providing constructive feedback, and conveying high expectations of their trainees. Previous taxonomies have also identified individual consideration and being an effective role model as key indicators of effective instruction (Patrick et al., 2009).

The idea that trainers can develop high-quality relationships with trainees can be further explored through leader–member exchange (LMX) theory, which is based on the idea that leaders develop different relationships with followers as a result of the level of responsibility and interaction between leaders and followers (Liden, Wayne, & Stilwell, 1993). In high-quality LMX relationships, leaders offer resources (e.g., strategic advice, social support, feedback) to followers who respond with cooperation and commitment (Sparrowe & Liden, 2005). Similarly, effective trainers can develop high-quality relationships with trainees by using the technology in e-learning settings (e.g., email, discussion boards, live audio or video) to show consideration for trainees, provide constructive feedback, and convey high expectations. In turn, trainees should respond with increased motivation to communicate with the trainer. Further, because in-group exchanges are typified by trust, liking, and respect (Liden, Wayne, & Stilwell, 1993), learners who perceive an in-group exchange are more motivated to communicate with trainers for relational (desire for interpersonal relationship with trainer), functional (desire to learn course material), participatory (desire to demonstrate comprehension of material), and sycophantic (desire to make a favorable impression) reasons than learners who have an out-group relationship with their trainer (Myers, 2006).

Trainers can also develop a high-quality relationship with trainees through mentoring. The theoretical roots of mentoring can be traced back to Levinson and colleagues' research on the career development of adult men (Levinson et al., 1978). Similar to LMX theory, mentoring relationships are based on reciprocity (Kram, 1985), in which mentors provide vocational (e.g., sponsorship, exposure) and psychosocial (e.g., role modeling, counseling) support functions to protégés. In turn, protégés increase their chances of receiving a higher salary, faster promotion, and experiencing higher levels of career satisfaction by participating in a mentoring relationship (Allen et al., 2004). Like mentors, trainers can provide vocational (e.g., assigning challenging e-learning activities, coaching) and psychosocial support (e.g., expressing confidence in trainees' ability to learn the material) to assist trainees in their learning and development. When trainers provide such support, trainees should respond with increased self-efficacy and motivation to learn, as well as positive reactions to training.

The transformational leadership literature also provides benchmarks for the development of a close relationship between trainer and trainee (Bass, 1990). Transformational leaders empower and motivate their followers to go beyond what is typically expected within the organization. Transformational leadership is composed of four behavioral dimensions: *idealized influence* occurs when leaders foster trust and are effective role models; *inspirational motivation* occurs when the leader communicates to followers that they have high expectations that they can do well and achieve their goals; *intellectual stimulation* occurs when the leader encourages followers to think outside the box and to see the world through other people's perspectives; *individualized consideration* is when the leader responds to the individual needs of others and displays a genuine sense of care and concern (Bass & Avolio, 1990). In the training literature, this model has been applied to understanding and identifying effective trainer behaviors (Beauchamp, Barling, & Morton, 2011). Using a randomized control group design, the intervention was a one-day transformational leadership workshop where physical education teachers learned about the concepts of transformational leadership. The training incorporated lecture, discussion, and watching the movie *Twelve Angry Men*. Then two months after the workshop, the teachers received a booster session that reinforced the principles covered in the earlier workshop. The students of the physical education teachers completed measures of motivation, self-efficacy, and intentions to be physically active, two and four months following the workshop. The findings indicated that the intervention was successful. After two months, the ninth graders rated their teachers as being more transformational, and reported higher levels of self-determined motivation, self-efficacy, and intentions to be physically active than those in the control group. Four months later, these results remained but just for the transformational leadership ratings and self-determined motivation.

Effective Trainer Behaviors

Learning in an asynchronous environment occurs at a trainee's own pace, while a synchronous learning environment requires that trainees and trainers interact online in real time. An asynchronous learning environment can provide trainees with greater flexibility and individualized learning strategies than the traditional classroom environment (Massy & Zemsky, 1995). An asynchronous learning format also allows trainees to self-reflect on their work, which facilitates self-correction, allowing trainees to be more aware of their learning gains (Yamada, 2009). However, a drawback of asynchronous learning environments is that there is minimal social interaction between the trainer and trainee. In particular, the trainer is unable to communicate in real time with the trainee making it more difficult to develop a quality relationship. When designing asynchronous learning environments, instructional designers have focused on creating effective PowerPoint presentations with narration by the trainer (Bersin, 2004). This mode of operating is the most popular format for asynchronous online learning (Jensen, 1999). Trainer communication style becomes an important factor in determining the success of an asynchronous learning environment. An effective trainer communication style can reduce social and psychological distance between trainers and students (Brown, Rietz, & Sugrue, 2005). In particular, the instructional content and the delivery of the material are central elements in ensuring learning occurs. Given the widespread use of PowerPoint slides with narration, trainer expressiveness is an important factor. One quality of trainer delivery considered particularly influential in learning is trainer expressiveness. An expressive trainer is one who shows appropriate vocal intonations and is generally fluent through sounding natural and normal in rate of speaking (Towler & Dipboye, 2001; Abrami, Dickens, Perry, & Leventhal, 1980). When trainees listen to expressive trainers, who deliver information in a well-organized way, they react more positively to the training course, recall more information, and are better problem solvers than trainees who listen to inexpressive trainers (Towler, 2009; Towler & Dipboye, 2001). No expressive delivery can act as "noise" that distracts from the presentation content (Awamleh, & Gardner, 1999; Towler & Dipboye, 2001). Content is also important in online narration. Obviously, the trainer has to impart the necessary technical knowledge but there are other strategies that the trainer can use to enhance trainee learning. Research from the influence literature suggests that trainees respond more positively and perform better when the trainer is charismatic (e.g., Friese, Beimel, & Schoenborn, 2003; Towler, 2003). There is preliminary evidence concerning online learning that a charismatic trainer is effective for recall and transfer of training (Arman et al., 2012). They examined whether charismatic trainer behaviors, including visionary content, intellectual stimulation, and individual attention, influenced affective, cognitive, and skill-based learning outcomes during computer-based training. Using an experimental design, 92 undergraduates were presented with an online Excel training program that contained narration that was either charismatic or noncharismatic. For example, visionary content focused on the importance of IT training to gain a career. Path analysis results indicated that participants who viewed videos narrated by a charismatic trainer (as opposed to a noncharismatic trainer) had positive reactions to the trainer, which was related to positive affectivity. Trainee positive affectivity was subsequently related to recall one week after training, and this recall was related to skill transfer one week after training (Arman et al., 2012).

In the next section we describe several principles that are relevant to instructional content presented in an asynchronous environment. In particular, we draw on the principles of multimedia learning theory that detail factors that facilitate or impede trainee learning (Mayer & Moreno, 2002a, 2002b). Mayer (1997) proposed a three-stage model of technology-driven learning. First, the learner filters and selects instructional information through the verbal route. In selecting information, words are selected and placed in the verbal memory store. This is principally done through auditory or visual channels. In the second stage, when organizing information, the learner selects and filters image-based information, such as graphs or diagrams, and these images are stored in the visual base. In the final stage, the learner integrates visual information and the verbal base to create connections between the two bases and to form a coherent understanding of the training content (Mayer, 1997). These principles are important in helping to consider the importance of the trainer's communication style particularly as the verbal base allows the trainee to create connections to visual information.

Principles of Multimedia Learning

Social perspectives focus on the social relationship between the learner and the instructional environment through emphasizing collaboration and dialogue (Bonk & Wisher, 2000). Both these approaches are necessary in constructing effective technology-driven instruction (TDI) because the trainer's role can change from primary trainer to facilitator of learning. In this section, we provide an overview of Mayer's multimedia theory and then describe basic principles that can be utilized within a multimedia context.

Richard Mayer's multimedia theory provides multiple principles to ensure that learners are engaged in learning. Mayer and his colleagues have formulated a theory of best practices within a multimedia environment, drawing on theories from cognitive psychology including (1) Baddeley's model of working memory, (2) Sweller's cognitive load theory, (3) Paivio's dual-coding theory, and (4) Mayer's personalization theory.

Cognitive perspectives focus on the learner's interpretation and interaction with the instructional material. Social perspectives focus on the social relationship between the learner and the instructional environment through emphasizing collaboration and dialogue (Bonk & Wisher, 2000). Baddeley's theory of working memory (1986) proposed that learners are limited by the amount of material they can retain and transfer to long-term memory. Baddeley (1986) conceived working or short-term memory to be compromised of two separate components, including the phonological loop and the visuo-spatial sketch-pad, each of which are controlled by the central executive. The visuo-spatial pad is assumed to store and maintain visual images, whereas the phonological loop stores and rehearses verbal information. The central executive controls the two systems by deciding what is relevant for information processing. Note that working memory is limited in its ability to retain more than seven items or chunks of information (Miller, 1956). Incorporating effective instructional strategies that enhance trainee motivation will help TDI reach its full potential.

Drawing on the implication that working memory is limited by the amount of information that can be stored, Sweller (1988, 1994) proposed a theory of cognitive load. Cognitive load refers to the total load or stress that performing a particular task imposes on the learner's cognitive resources (Paas & Van Merriënboer, 1994). Capacity for cognitive load is determined primarily by the learner's cognitive ability and the amount of resources devoted to metacognitive or executive processes. This capacity is balanced against the cognitive load created by the difficulty of the material and by task characteristics such as task complexity, use of multimedia, and instructional pace.

A stream of research highlights the importance of regulating cognitive demands on learners so that they are not overwhelmed by the amount of instructional material or the learning interface (e.g., Sweller, 1988, 1994; Van Merriënboer & Sweller, 2005). Cognitive load theory suggests that learners can absorb a limited amount of material into working memory and if they are overloaded with information then they fail to form knowledge schemas that can be transmitted to long-term memory (Sweller, 1988, 1994). Cognitive overload can be created in a number of ways in TDI environments, for example, by separating graphics and text on different web pages, placing too much information on one page, or presenting the same information in several different ways.

The dual coding theory proposed by Paivio attempts to give equal weight to verbal and nonverbal processing. Paivio (1986) argued that humans typically deal with information that is both visual and verbal and so instructional material that promotes both image-based and language-based processing is better remembered because it allows for storage of material in both verbal (specialized for dealing with language) and nonverbal systems (Paivio, 1986; Sadoski, Goetz, & Rodriguez, 2000; Sadoski, Goetz, & Fritz, 1993). Research supports the importance of imagery in cognitive operations (Paivio, 1971). For this reason, Mayer and his colleagues suggest that TDI environments present instructional material in words and pictures rather than just using one mode of presentation (e.g., Mayer & Anderson, 1991, 1992).

Social factors can also play an important role in designing effective TDI platforms. Learners display multiple reactions to the narrator of instructional information depending on whether the speaker is expressive or inexpressive (Towler & Dipboye, 2001). One way in which the narration can affect the learner is through the style that is used to relay information. Mayer's personalization theory proposes that individuals learn better when narration is conducted in a conversational style as opposed to a formal style (Mayer, Fennell, Farmer, & Campbell, 2004). This is normally achieved by addressing the learner in the first person rather than the third person. The personalization effect can maximize transfer of knowledge because the strategy employs a technique that is familiar to learners – the conversational style – to facilitate listening and attention to details. Another aspect of the personalization effect is that cognitive load is reduced for the learner because they are overly familiar with the style used by the narrator and consequently are able to retain more information because they are not distracted by the narrator's style. The type of language that the trainer uses in online training instruction is also important; it appears that trainees learn more when the trainer uses conversational rather than formal language (Mayer & Moreno, 2002a, 2002b).

When engaged in a conversation, the learner typically feels obligated to listen more carefully because of social convention. In a study by Moreno and Mayer (2004), students in a botany TDI program were presented with personalized language (using "I" and "you") or with formal third-person language by a computer-based agent. Learners in the personalized condition experienced the program as both friendlier and more helpful than those in the nonpersonalized condition. In addition, those exposed to personalized language experienced less cognitive load and exhibited more retention and higher performance in a transfer task. Personalization of narration in multimedia training increases the likelihood that trainees will feel like they are in a human-to-human conversation and that they will be more motivated to engage in cognitive processes (Mayer, 2003). Consequently, trainees learn more and are able to apply their knowledge to solve problems (Moreno & Mayer, 2004).

When preparing online material another issue that requires careful consideration is the inclusion of irrelevant content. Frequently, trainers are required to present instructional information that can be dull and mundane for many trainees. Very often it is tempting for trainers to include interesting information that can sometimes be tangential to the central theme of the instructional material. This phenomenon is called the "seductive details effect." Instructional material can be seductive through inclusion of illustrations, text, or oral communication that is interesting and entertaining but tangential to the topic. A common example of a seductive detail in a training context might be a training class that includes Dilbert cartoons on slides containing tips for effective supervision. Although not necessarily relevant to the topic, the cartoons are designed to make the training material more interesting, but the results of multiple studies suggest that their inclusion will harm recall for the primary training content.

Previous research finds that seductive details have a deleterious effect on the amount of information that trainees can recall. In one multimedia training study, college students viewed an animation and listened to concurrent narration explaining the formation of lightning (Mayer, Heiser, & Lonn, 2001). In the seductive details conditions, the experimenters added either interesting but tangential text details to the narration or added tangential video clips within the presentation. Mayer et al. reported that participants in the seductive detail conditions recalled less central information and performed worse on a series of essay questions applying their knowledge to new situations.

However, there is some evidence that within a TDI environment, seductive details might be effective for transfer of training. In a series of studies where trainees learned Microsoft Excel or Microsoft Word in an online environment, seductive details improved performance on transfer of information (Towler et al., 2008). When trainees were asked to apply their knowledge through performing skills they had learned during training, the inclusion of seductive details was effective. Another study (Towler, 2003) also found that trainees who listened to a lecture containing seductive details performed better on a problem-solving test than those who did not hear seductive details. However, this happened only when the trainer was expressive. This finding tends to support the adult-learning theory that adults learn best when they are encouraged to actively process information (Knowles, Holton, & Swanson, 1998). Active processing can occur when material is ill structured or, in this case, contains seductive details that are peripheral to the core material (Towler & Dipboye, 2001). This research on seductive details suggests that trainers should seek to organize information in such a way that interesting, tangential nuggets of information are included as well as core material particularly when trainees are required to transfer their knowledge in a skills-based setting.

Future Research

The effectiveness of pedagogical agents

There are new advances that can facilitate e-learning. The most interesting new development is the increasing use of pedagogical agents to facilitate training. Organizations are increasingly using *animated pedagogical agents* to enhance multimedia learning. Animated pedagogical agents (APA) are frequently seen in TDI programs where they act as virtual trainers, coaches, or guides. Animated pedagogical agents are "computerized characters (either humanlike or otherwise) designed to facilitate learning" (Craig, Gholson, & Driscoll, 2002, p. 428). They reside in learning environments and have the potential to capture trainee attention through mimicking human characteristics such as gazing, gesturing, and providing feedback (Atkinson, 2002). Research also suggests that people ascribe mental states to computers and typically respond to computers in much the same way as they react to other individuals. In general, APAs are relatively socially effective. In terms of nonverbal communication, APAs are as convincing as humans with their ability to be facially expressive and to use gestures in an appropriate fashion (Bickmore & Cassell, 2001). This ability for APAs to be as convincing as humans is referred to as the persona effect, in which the very presence of an agent can have a strong positive effect on learner motivation and engagement (Bates, 1994). However, the evidence regarding their effectiveness has produced mixed results. There is some evidence that although trainees react favorably to APAs, they do not necessarily perform better on learning outcomes. Comparing an APA to a voice-only condition, André, Rist, and Müller (1998) found that participants who experienced the APA reacted more favorably to the training than those in the voice-only condition. However, there was no difference between the two groups on comprehension or recall tasks. In a similar study, an animated agent that pointed to key features on the screen was compared to alternative multimedia such as picture, narration, or animation. There were no differences between the groups on material retention or transfer. Vincent is a pedagogical agent that was specially developed for adult learners in an employee training environment (Paiva & Machado, 1998). The training program focuses on enabling workers in shoemaking factories to learn about production-line control time. The agent was designed to be attractive to this particular group of trainees through being older, extroverted, and a likeable companion. Trainees reacted favorably to Vincent and found the agent to be motivational and engaging. However, they did not examine whether Vincent was effective for trainee learning. Quesnell (2011) examined whether an animated agent displaying charisma (charismatic language, motivate and inspire trainees, and encourage and support trainees) influences trainee learning and transfer task performance during Microsoft Excel training. He also explored the role of subliminal priming on task performance. He found no support for the role of subliminal priming on any of the training outcomes. Trainees who experienced the transformational animated agent had higher positive affect and more positive affective reactions toward the trainer, the course structure, and the training in general compared to a noncharismatic trainer. The charismatic trainer also increased trainee post-training self-efficacy. However, there were no effects of the agent on task performance. Given these mixed findings, there is a need to conduct further research on the effectiveness of pedagogical agents.

Individual differences and context

Learner-focused instructional designs can actively engage the trainee and stimulate curiosity (Bonk & Wisher, 2000). However, these learner-focused designs also require the trainee to expend effort in juggling multiple sources of information. For example, in using multimedia environments, the learner is required to pay attention to both auditory and visual cues within the instruction and, in some cases, control pace, sequencing, and timing of instruction. These strategies can enhance learning but can also increase a learner's cognitive load through requiring increased attention. Learners also vary in the way in which they respond to instructional material. In fact, there are a variety of trainee characteristics that predict the extent to which trainees learn and transfer their knowledge (Gully & Chen,

2010) including cognitive ability, learning styles, personality traits. Instructional material can be tailored or adapted to suit learner characteristics through offering a variety of modalities. In addition, trainees can be encouraged to choose instructional contexts that match their preferences. There is some evidence that individuals' differences do matter within TDI. Klein, Noe, and Wang (2006) conducted a study of students who were engaged in blended learning (a mixture of classroom and online learning). They found that individuals with a learning-goal orientation had higher motivation to learn, which was related to course satisfaction, metacognition, and course grades. There is also evidence that individuals' differences do matter but that training designers need to take context into account. In an unpublished study Mitchell et al. (2014) examined the effects of pedagogical training agents, feedback comparison groups, and performance-approach goal orientation on recall test and transfer task performance. One hundred and sixty-eight participants were randomly assigned to a pedagogical training agent (charismatic vs. noncharismatic) and a feedback comparison standard (i.e., no comparison, peer comparison, national standard). In the charismatic trainer condition, the agent exhibited a number of charismatic behaviors throughout the course of the training (e.g., expressing confidence in trainees' ability to learn material, emphasizing the importance of learning material, altering vocal intonation). In the noncharismatic trainer condition the trainer did not exhibit any charismatic behaviors. In the peer comparison condition, participants were told that scores on recall Test 1 would be compared to the average of DePaul students. In the national standard comparison, participants were told that scores on recall Test 1 would be compared to students on a national average. Participants in the no feedback comparison condition were not told any information about a comparison standard. The participants also completed a measure of performance approach. Individuals with a performance approach are likely to approach achievement situations by seeking to prove their competence and gain favorable comments from others regarding their performance (Dweck & Leggett, 1988). The findings showed a significant three-way interaction of trainer style, feedback comparison, and performance-approach goal orientation on transfer tasks 1 and 2. Results suggest that when high performance approach trainees receive training facilitated by a charismatic training agent, they perform better on transfer tasks when they do not receive a feedback comparison standard, as the peer and national standard distracts trainees from learning the material and leads to a decrement in transfer performance. Additionally, when high performance approach trainees receive training facilitated by a noncharismatic training agent, they perform better on transfer tasks when they receive a feedback comparison standard as the peer and national standard increases trainees' motivation to perform well on transfer tasks.

Facilitating e-learning in crosscultural settings

Organizations are increasing in global operations and are becoming much more boundaryless. Recent developments in the use of computer- and internet-based instruction have enabled organizations to offer training courses to culturally diverse and geographically dispersed workforces. Though modern training texts have advised trainers to take culture into account when designing and instructing training courses, there is scarce empirical research to inform trainers about the specific behaviors they should employ to effectively facilitate computer- and internet-based training in crosscultural settings. For instance, we know that the interaction between the trainer and trainee is typically perceived as a positive characteristic of the learning environment in the United States, while this same type of learning environment may violate expected norms of good instruction in high power–distance cultures such as China. However, we do not know if trainees in high power–distance cultures are more likely to transfer training back on the job if they experience a trainer with a didactic style that is more congruent with their cultural values of good instruction, or if they experience a trainer with a charismatic communication style that uses visionary content to tap into trainees' values and raise their expectations. Seeking out answers to such questions will not only help inform practitioners regarding effective facilitation for training courses in crosscultural settings, but will also inform scholars and researchers regarding theory for facilitation of e-learning.

Training older workers

In recent years, both the European Union and the United States have witnessed an increase in the average age of the workforce – a trend that is only projected to increase in the years to come (Bureau of Labor Statistics, 2010; *Economist*, 2006). The rising age of the workforce has led to an increased focus by researchers and practitioners on training older workers. Considering the significant negative relationship between age and working-memory capacity (Bopp & Verhaeghan, 2005), there is a need for more empirical research that specifies behaviors that trainers should utilize to help reduce demands on working memory and allow trainees to conserve working memory capacity for critical concepts conveyed during training. One potentially fruitful avenue of research in improving working-memory capacity for older workers is examining the effects of trainer communication style on recall ability for older workers. Older workers may benefit from trainers who are organized and expressive in delivering content. Past research has demonstrated that when trainees experience expressive trainers who deliver information in a well-organized way, they tend to recall more information than do trainees who to listen to inexpressive trainers (Towler & Dipboye, 2001). We encourage researchers to investigate how trainer expressiveness and other trainer communication styles can improve recall for older workers.

Conclusion

In conclusion, theory and research has provided some effective benchmarks to aid instructional designers when designing technology-driven courses. Theory and practice suggest that the trainer has an important role to play in TDI through effective communication, individual consideration, and support of trainees. Trainers also need to consider the way in which they convey information to trainees and tailor their behaviors to fit the instructional environment. However, although these benchmarks are useful, more research needs to be conducted to determine how other factors influence the trainer–trainee relationship.

References

Abrami, P. C., Dickens, W. J., Perry, R. P., & Leventhal, L. (1980). Do teacher standards for assigning grades affect student evaluations of Instruction? *Journal of Educational Psychology*, 72, 107–108.

Allen, T. D., Eby, L. T., Poteet, M. L., Lentz, E., & Lima, L. (2004). Career benefits associated with mentoring for protégeé: A meta-analysis. *Journal of Applied Psychology*, 89, 127–136.

André, E., Rist, T., & Müller, J. (1998). Integrating reactive and scripted behaviors in a life-like presentation agent. *Proceedings of the Second International Conference on Autonomous agents* (pp. 261–268). Minneapolis-St. Paul, MN.

Arbaugh, J. B. (2002). Managing the on-line classroom: A study of technological and behavioral characteristics of web-based MBA courses. *Journal of High Technology Management Research*, 13, 203–223.

Arman, G., Quesnell, T., Hoffman, L., & Towler, A. (2012). How charismatic trainers inspire others to learn through positive affectivity. Poster presented at Society of Industrial/Organizational Psychology, San Diego, CA.

Atkinson, R. K. (2002). Optimizing learning from examples using animated pedagogical agents. *Journal of Educational Psychology*, 94, 416–427.

Awamleh, R., & Gardner, W. L. (1999). Perceptions of leader charisma and effectiveness: The effects of vision content, delivery and organizational performance. *Leadership Quarterly*, 10, 345–373.

Baddeley, A. D. (1986). *Working Memory*. Oxford: Clarendon.

Bass, B. M. (1990). From transactional to transformational leadership: Learning to share the vision. *Organizational Dynamics*, 18, 19–31.

Bass, B. M., & Avolio, B. J. (1990). The implications of transactional and transformational leadership for individual, team and organizational development. *Research in Organizational Change and Development*, 4, 231–272.

Bates, J. (1994). The role of emotion in believable agents. *Communications of the ACM* 37(7), 122–125.

Beauchamp, M. R., Barling, J., & Morton, K. L. (2011). Transformational teaching and adolescent self-determined behavior, self-efficacy, and intentions to engage in leisure time physical activity: A randomized controlled pilot trial. *Applied Psychology: Health and Well-Being*, 3, 127–150.

Bersin, J. (2004). Rapid e-learning has arrived. http://www.bersin.com/Blog/post/Rapid-E-Learninge284a2-has-Arrived.aspx (accessed March 24, 2014).

Bickmore, T., & Cassell, J. (2001). Relational agents: A model and implementation of building user trust. In *Proceedings of the ACM CHI-2001 Human Factors in Computing Systems Conference* (pp. 396–403). New York: ACM Press.

Bonk, C. J., & Wisher, R. A. (2000). *Applying Collaborative and E-Learning Tools to Military Distance Learning: A Research Framework* (Technical Report No. 1107). Alexandria, VA: US Army Research Institute for the Behavioral and Social Sciences.

Bopp, K. L., & Verhaughen, P. (2005). Aging and verbal memory span: A meta-analysis. *Journal of Gerontology: Psychological Sciences*, 60B, 223–233.

Borbely, E. (1994). Challenges and opportunities in extending the classroom and the campus via digital compressed video. In R. Mason & P. Bacsich (Eds.), *ISDN: Applications in Education and Training* (pp. 65–82). London: Institution of Electrical Engineers.

Brown, K. G., Rietz, T. A., & Sugrue, B. (2005). The effects of videoconferencing, class size, and learner characteristics on training outcomes. *Performance Improvement Quarterly*, 18, 59–82.

Bureau of Labor Statistics (2010). Occupational outlook handbook; 2010–11 edition. http://www.bls.gov/ooh/About/Projections-Overview.htm (accessed March 24, 2014).

Collis, B. (1995). Anticipating the impact of multimedia in education: Lessons from the literature. *Computers in Adult Education and Training*, 2, 136–149.

Craig, S. D., Gholson, B., & Driscoll, D. M. (2002). Animated pedagogical agents in multimedia educational environments: Effects of agent properties, picture features, and redundancy. *Journal of Educational Psychology*, 94, 428–434.

Deci, E. L., & Ryan, R. M. (1985). *Intrinsic Motivation and Self-Determination Theory*. New York: Plenum.

Dweck, C. S., & Leggett, E. L. (1988). A social-cognitive approach to motivation and personality. *Psychological Review*, 95, 256–273.

Economist. (2006). Turning boomers into boomerangs, 378 (February), 75–77.

Economist. (2012). Learning new Lessons. http://www.economist.com/news/international/21568738-online-courses-are-transforming-higher-education-creating-new-opportunities-best (accessed July 7, 2014)

Frese, M., Beimel, S., & Schoenborn, S. (2003). Action training for charismatic leadership: Two evaluation studies of a commercial training module on inspirational communication of a vision. *Personnel Psychology*, 56, 671–697.

Fulk, J., Schmitz, J., & Steinfield, C. W. (1990). A social influence model of technology use. In J. Fulk & C. Steinfield (Eds.), *Organizations and Communication Technology* (pp. 117–141). Newbury Park, CA: Sage.

Gowan, J. A., & Downs, M. (1994). Video conferencing human–machine interface: A field study. *Information & Management*, 27, 341–356.

Graen, G. B., & Uhl-Bien, M. (1995). Relationship-based approach to leadership: Development of leader–member exchange (LMX) theory of leadership over 25 years: Applying a multi-level, multi-domain perspective. *Leadership Quarterly*, 6(2), 219–247.

Gully, S., & Chen, G. (2010). Individual differences, attribute-treatment interactions, and training outcomes. In S. Kozlowski & E. Salas (Eds.), *Learning, Training, and Development in Organizations* (pp. 3–64). New York: Routledge/Taylor & Francis Group.

Henson, K. T., & Borthwick, P. (1984). Matching styles: A historical look. *Theory into Practice*, 23, 3–9.

Holladay, C. L., & Quiñones, M. A. (2008). The influence of training focus and trainer characteristics on diversity training effectiveness. *Academy of Management Learning and Education*, 3, 343–354.

Hutchins, H. M. (2009). In the trainer's voice: A study of training transfer practices. *Performance Improvement Quarterly*, 22, 69–93.

Isaacs, E. A., Morris, T., Rodriguez, T. K., & Tang, C. (1995). A comparison of face-to-face and distributed presentations. In I. R. Katz, R. Mack, L. Marks, M. B. Rosson, & J. Nelson (Eds.), *Proceedings of the Association for Computing Machinery (ACM) Special Interest Group on Computers and Human Interaction (CHI) 95 Conference* (pp. 354–361). New York: ACM Press.

Jarvis, P. (1985). *The Sociology of Adult and Continuing Education*. Beckenham: Croom Helm.

Jensen, K. K. (1999). Training teachers to use verbal immediacy. *Communication Research Reports*, 16(3), 223–232.

Jiang, M., & Ting, E. (1998). Course design, instruction, and students' online behaviors: A study of instructional variables and student perceptions of online learning. Paper presented at the annual meeting of the American Educational Research Association, San Diego, CA, April 13–17.

Judge, T. A., Piccolo, R. F., & Ilies, R. (2004). The forgotten ones? A re-examination of consideration, initiating structure, and leadership effectiveness. *Journal of Applied Psychology*, 89, 36–51.

Kinicki, A., & Schriesheim, C. A. (1978). Teachers as leaders: A moderator variable approach. *Journal of Educational Psychology*, 70, 928–935.

Klein, H. J., Noe, R. A., & Wang, C. (2006). Motivation to learn and course outcomes: The impact of delivery mode, learning goal orientation, and perceived barriers and enablers. *Personnel Psychology*, 59(3), 665–702.

Knowles, M. S., Holton, E. F., & Swanson, R. A. (1998). *The Adult Learner: The Definitive Classic in Adult Education and Human Resource Development*. Houston, TX: Gulf Publishing.

Kram, K. E. (1985). *Mentoring at Work: Developmental Relationships in Organizational Life*. Glenville, IL: Scott, Foresman and Company.

Lachem, C., Mitchell, J., & Atkinson, R. (1994). ISDN-based videoconferencing in Australian tertiary education. In R. Mason & P. Bacsich (Eds.), *ISDN: Applications in Education and Training* (pp. 99–113). London: Institution of Electrical Engineers.

Leidner, D. L., & Jarvenpaa, S. L. (1995). The use of information technology to enhance management school education: A theoretical view. *MIS Quarterly*, 19, 265–291.

Levinson, D., Darrow, D., Levinson, M., & McKee, B. (1978). *The Seasons of a Man's Life*. New York: Knopf.

Liden, R. C., Wayne, S. J., & Stilwell, D. (1993). A longitudinal study on the early development of leader–member exchanges. *Journal of Applied Psychology*, 78, 662–774.

Massy W. F., & Zemsky, R. (1995). Using information technology to enhance academic productivity (ID: NLI0004). http://www.educause.edu/ELI/UsingInformationTechnologytoEn/159863 (accessed April 21, 2010).

Mayer, R. E. (1997). Multimedia learning: Are we asking the right questions? *Educational Psychologist*, 32, 1–19.

Mayer, R. E. (2003). The promise of multimedia learning: Using the same instructional design methods across different media. *Learning and Instruction*, 13, 125–139.

Mayer, R. E., & Anderson, R. B. (1991). Animations need narrations: An experimental test of a dual-coding hypothesis. *Journal of Educational Psychology*, 83, 484–490.

Mayer, R. E., & Anderson, R. B. (1992). The instructive animation: Helping students build connections between words and pictures in multimedia learning. *Journal of Educational Psychology*, 84, 444–452.

Mayer, R. E., Fennell, S., Farmer, L., & Campbell, J. (2004). A personalization effect in multimedia learning: Students learn better when words are in conversational style rather than formal style. *Journal of Educational Psychology*, 96, 389–395.

Mayer, R. E., Heiser, J., & Lonn, S. (2001). Cognitive constraints on multimedia learning: When presenting more material results in less understanding. *Journal of Educational Psychology*, 93, 187–198.

Mayer, R. E., & Moreno, R. (2002a). Aids to computer-based multimedia learning. *Learning and Instruction*, 12, 107–119.

Mayer, R. E., & Moreno, R. (2002b). Animation as an aid to multimedia learning. *Educational Psychology Review*, 14, 87–99.

Miller, G. A. (1956). The magical number seven, plus or minus two: Some limits on our capacity for processing information. *Psychological Review*, 63, 81–97.

Mitchell, T. D., Brown, S. G., Mann, K. E., & Towler, A. J. (2014). Three to tango: Agent, feedback-comparison, and goal-orientation on training outcomes. Paper presented at the 29th annual conference of the Society of Industrial/Organizational Psychology Conference, Honolulu.

Moreno, R., & Mayer, R. E. (2004). Personalized messages that promote science learning in virtual environments. *Journal of Educational Psychology*, 96, 165–173.

Myers, S. A. (2006). Using leader–member exchange theory to explain students' motives to communicate. *Communication Quarterly*, 54, 293–304.

Paas, F. G., & Van Merriënboer, J. J. (1994). Variability of worked examples and transfer of geometrical problem-solving skills: A cognitive-load approach. *Journal of Educational Psychology*, 86, 122–133.

Paiva, A., & Machado, I. (1998). Vincent, an autonomous pedagogical agent for on-the-job training. *Proceedings of the Fourth International Conference on Intelligent Tutoring Systems* (pp. 584–593). Berlin: Springer.

Paivio, A. (1971). *Imagery and Verbal Processes.* New York: Holt, Rinehart & Winston.

Paivio, A. (1986). Mental representations: A dual coding theory. Oxford: Oxford University Press.

Patrick, J., Scrase, G., Ahmed, A., & Tombs, M. (2009). Effectiveness of instructor behaviours and their relationship to leadership. *Journal of Occupational and Organizational Psychology*, 82(3), 491–509.

Quesnell, T. (2011). Pedagogical training agents, supraliminal priming, and training outcomes. Masters thesis. DePaul University.

Reeve, J., & Jang, H. (2006). What teachers say and do to support students' autonomy during a learning activity. *Journal of Educational Psychology*, 98, 209–218.

Sadoski, M., Goetz, E. T., & Fritz, J. (1993). Impact of concreteness on comprehensibility, interest, and memory for text: Implications for dual coding theory and text design. *Journal of Educational Psychology*, 85, 291–304.

Sadoski, M., Goetz, E. T., & Rodriguez, M. (2000). Engaging texts: Effects of concreteness on comprehensibility, interest, and recall in four text types. *Journal of Educational Psychology*, 92, 85–95.

Sparrowe, R. T., & Liden, R. C. (2005). Two routes to influence: Integrating leader–member exchange and social network perspectives. *Administrative Science Quarterly*, 50, 505–535.

Sun, P.-C., Tsai, R. J., Finger, G., Chen, Y.-Y., & Yeh, D. (2008). What drives a successful e-learning? An empirical investigation of the critical factors influencing learner satisfaction. *Computers & Education*, 50, 1183–1202.

Sweller, J. (1988). Cognitive load during problem solving: Effects on learning. *Cognitive Science,* 12, 257–285.

Sweller, J. (1994). Cognitive load theory, learning difficulty, and instructional design. *Learning and Instruction*, 4, 295–312.

Thurmond, V. A., Wambach, K., & Connors, H. R. (2002). Evaluation of student satisfaction: Determining the impact of a web-based environment by controlling for student characteristics. *American Journal of Distance Education*, 16, 169–189.

Towler, A. J. (2003). Effects of charismatic influence training on attitudes, behavior, and performance. *Personnel Psychology*, 56, 363–381.

Towler, A. (2009). Effects of trainer expressiveness, seductive details, and trainee goal orientation on training outcomes. *Human Resource Development Quarterly*, 20, 65–84.

Towler, A. J., & Dipboye, R. L. (2001). Effects of trainer expressiveness, organization, and trainee goal orientation on training outcomes. *Journal of Applied Psychology*, 86, 664–673.

Towler, A. J., Kraiger, K., Sitzmann, T., Van Overberghe, C., Kuo, J., Ronen, E., & Stewart, D. (2008). The seductive details effect in technology-delivered instruction. *Performance Improvement Quarterly*, 21, 2, 65–86.

Tucker, J. S., Sidman, J., Geyer, A., Mizrahi, G., O'Driscoll, J., & Semmens, R. P. (2010). *Developing a Blended Learning Approach for Army Leader Planning* (Army Research Product 2010-03). Arlington, VA: US Army Research Institute for the Behavioral and Social Sciences. (DTIC No. ADA528755.)

Van Merrienboer, J. J., & Sweller, J. (2005). Cognitive load theory and complex learning: Recent developments and future directions. *Educational Psychology Review*, 17, 147–177.

Webster, J., & Hackley, P. (1997). Teaching effectiveness in technology-mediated distance learning. *Academy of Management Journal*, 40, 1282–1309.

Yamada, M. (2009). The role of social presence in learner-centered communicative language learning using synchronous computer-mediated communication: Experimental study. *Computers & Education*, 52, 820–833.

11

Effective Virtual Learning Environments

Jean-Luc Gurtner

Introduction

Virtual learning environments are nowadays almost ubiquitous in higher education and broadly used in corporate training as well (Mueller & Strohmeier, 2010; Wang, Wang, & Shee, 2007). Virtual learning environments (often abbreviated VLEs) are complex web-based environments designed to afford students interesting opportunities to learn given material without having to be physically present when the material is delivered by the instructor. The complexity of these environments is generally not linked to specific software developments or to any of their interfaces, but rather to the fact that they generally integrate heterogeneous technologies, combine various types of functionalities, and instantiate multiple pedagogical approaches (Dillenbourg, Schneider, & Synteta, 2002). Despite this complexity, VLEs are rather easy to use both for the learner and for the instructor. In North America, the expression "virtual learning environment" is often replaced by "learning management system" (LMS), but both terms relate to a similar category of products. For the sake of simplicity, we will stick to the term VLE, but will include in the discussion many projects and suggestions directly related to such learning management systems.

Each time a new technology is applied to education, the question of its effectiveness is widely discussed and many research projects continue to deal with this issue in various domains and for various kinds of students (Britain & Liber, 2004; Eom, 2012; Green et al., 2006; Haven & Botterill, 2003; Ozkan & Koseler, 2009). Needless to say, no technology is, per se, effective, its effectiveness depending on the way it is used (Evans & Wilkins, 2011). In the present chapter, we will describe various ways VLEs can be used, and analyze the main effects resulting from the use of each of their principal functionalities.

Recently, social issues, such as learner isolation versus group awareness, asynchronous versus synchronous communication, flexible, independent learning versus collaborative learning, have become critical elements of the quality attributed to VLEs as well

The Wiley Blackwell Handbook of the Psychology of Training, Development, and Performance Improvement, First Edition. Edited by Kurt Kraiger, Jonathan Passmore, Sigmar Malvezzi, and Nuno Rebelo dos Santos. © 2015 John Wiley & Sons Ltd. Published 2020 by John Wiley & Sons Ltd.

as learners' satisfaction. These discussions run parallel to both the evolution of learning theories – ranging from instructionism to socioconstructivism – (Kraiger, 2008) as well as new developments enabled by the second generation of the worldwide web (Web 2.0). Other criteria, such as return on investment, are much less discussed in current research.

Virtual Environments, Blended Learning, or Hybrid Systems?

Compared to most other computer-based learning software, VLEs give learners a higher degree of control over their learning process (Kirschner, Sweller, & Clark, 2006; Koller, 2011) and allow greater personalization of instruction (Hudson, Hudson, & Steel, 2007; Xu & Wang, 2006). They also offer larger communication and interaction possibilities between participants as well as between students and their instructor, in some cases even more than the traditional classroom set up (Piccoli, Ahmad, & Ives, 2001).

While some authors restrict the term to platforms commonly used in educational settings, such as Web-CT, Blackboard, Moodle, or Study.NET, others use it in a broader sense to describe various forms of computer-based environments in which the learner can trace out his or her own route through a wide range of resources and learning opportunities and receive support and quick feedback from other users or from the system itself. In this case, the environment may provide tools that are generally not present in conventional VLEs. These include Second Life, diverse forms of social networks, 3D simulations. (Fowler, 2014) They accommodate an increasing diversity of course participants, a current example being massive open online courses (MOOCs) (Mackness, Mak, & Williams, 2010).

To increase teacher–learner contacts and lower the risk of dropout generally observed in independent learning conditions (Keller & Suzuki, 2004), VLEs are rarely used in a fully virtual mode (Sife, Lwoga, & Sanga, 2007). They most often combine online remote learning phases with face-to-face sessions, in so-called blended learning scenarios (Aspden & Helm, 2004; Bonk & Graham, 2006; Garrison & Kanuka, 2004). In blended learning, the proportion of online delivery compared to face-to-face exchange can vary considerably (Thomson NETg, 2003). In its annual report on online education in the United States, the Sloan Consortium calls blended learning all those courses in which the proportion of online delivered content lies anywhere between 30 percent and 79 percent. Courses with a smaller proportion are called web-facilitated, while courses with a higher proportion are called online courses (Allen & Seaman, 2009).

The current evolution of technology and communication software developments offer more and more possibilities to perform operations at a distance that were previously only possible face-to-face, be it interactions between the learner and the instructor or among learners themselves. Assessment is nowadays often integrated in the VLE and increasingly takes on a self-evaluation or peer-evaluation format, allowing the instructor to enroll as many as a 10,000 students in the same course. Just-in-time availability, increased flexibility, cost effectiveness, as well as the possibility to reach a wider audience with the same course all belong to the list of criteria driving organizations and learners to increased use of the virtual mode within blended learning scenarios (Clarke & Hermens, 2001; Moore & Kearsley, 2011).

Other aspects, however, plead for the introduction or the retention of face-to-face phases in the learning process. Well-known examples of activities and processes that can be better achieved in a (small) classroom set up rather than at a distance include motivating students and team or identity building. There are also cognitive reasons such as enabling practice-based experience under the instructor's supervision; analyzing and discussing complicated cases or issues with colleagues; or developing higher-order skills such as leadership or decision-making skills (Cottrell & Robinson, 2003).

In a survey conducted between 2001 and 2005 in the United Kingdom, Jenkins, Browne, and Walker (2005) calculated that the proportion of fully online courses in 2005 remained less than 10 percent, even in the most modern institutions. The proportion of courses in which visiting the platform was optional was still around 50 percent of all courses in British higher-education institutions in 2005, although the figure was decreasing.

Penn State University sees three levels in the mix between onsite and online activities. In the "supplemental model," technology is used to provide documents and resources needed to pass the course, but the course structure and format remain untouched. In the "replacement model," a significant portion of regular classroom activities is carried out online. In class time is then reduced accordingly and used for more interactive learning experiences than in the classic lecture format. In these two models, the pace of the class remains identical for all students and predefined by the instructor. Unlike them, the "emporium model" abandons all lectures and in class activities and replaces them by lab sessions, visits to a learning resource center, and/or meetings with a teaching assistant whose role is to provide individual help based on learners' requests. As a result, students work and learn at their own pace.

Blended learning is often presented as a scenario designed to provide students with the best of both worlds (face-to-face and online instruction). The natural tendency to maximize learning and a constant move towards implementing scenarios based on the emporium model has led more and more scientists to drop the epicurean consumer metaphor, replacing it by a new metaphor in which blended VLEs are nowadays often referred to as hybrid learning environments. In so doing, they borrow the concept of hybridization from genetics, where combining the genes of two parents does not repeatedly produce the same prototype but rather builds new, original, and unique creatures (Olapiriyakul & Scher, 2006). In this vein, more and more authors remark that VLEs and the online delivery of course content have the potential to bring teachers to invent new didactical scenarios, but observe at the same time that most teachers tend to use them in a way quite similar to what they do in traditional lecture formats (Koller, 2011; Lowes, 2007; Martin, 2012).

What is Meant by Effectiveness with Respect to VLEs?

Evaluation of e-learning course effectiveness is vital, but not so easy to do, due to the number of criteria to be considered and the fuzziness of subjective perceptions necessarily included in these criteria (Mueller & Strohmeier, 2011; Tzeng, Chiang, & Li, 2007). Kirkpatrick (1979) suggests four aspects when evaluating training programs: (1) participants' satisfaction with the program (reactions); (2) the principles, facts, or techniques learned (learning); (3) participants' capacity to apply what they have learned in their professional environment (behavior); and (4) the effects these new behaviors have on the overall enterprise performance (success).

Given the high rate of dropout traditionally observed in distance education, the capacity of an online course to retain learners (reactions) can therefore be seen as a first condition of its effectiveness. Student satisfaction with the course is also a key element to consider in evaluating e-learning courses (Levy, 2007; Piccoli, Ahmad, & Ives, 2001). If the quality of the content is often declared by learners as the most valued features of a VLE (Heaton-Shrestha et al., 2007), and by institutions or companies as the most important driving factor for adopting such facilities (Jenkins, Browne, & Walker, 2005), it is not the only significant factor influencing participants' satisfaction (Sun et al., 2008).

Learners' acceptance of and intention to use the technology is also a crucial variable. According to Davis's (1989) technology acceptance model, perceived ease of use and perceived usefulness are necessary conditions for the acceptance of any new technology. Examining participants' responses to a survey related to a company training course, Stonebraker and Hazeltine (2004) observed that besides level of learning, job relevance and feelings of cohesiveness significantly predicted course satisfaction and that course satisfaction was a predictor of course completion.

Wang (2003) also considers the impression of belonging to a learning community as an important determinant of learners' satisfaction, that is, the ease the system affords students to discuss questions with their instructor or other students, to share what they have learnt with others, and access shared content from that community. Comparing a blended learning course with a fully online course, Rovai and Jordan (2004) show that the former leads indeed to a higher feeling of being connected to other learners than the latter and ultimately to better learning.

Participants' learning is inevitably an important objective of all VLEs. But since the learning expected may be of different types (for instance, factual knowledge, procedural know-how, or expertise in the use of a given tool) and because the personal reasons and objectives for joining the course may well be highly different from one participant to another (Kraiger, 2008), the question whether a given VLE is or will be effective with respect to participants' learning is open to different answers.

For instance, while learning about something may result from the provision of good-quality information or explanations given in the form of texts, pictures, graphs, or videos, learning to acquire a specific skill or to become an expert on a certain machine will not be achieved through any of these didactical techniques. In the latter case, learning environments including simulations or games will be much more effective.

Salomon and Perkins (1998) suggest that a clear distinction should be made between the effects of learning *with* a tool and the effects *of* the tool. Assessing learning effects with the tool supposes examining which changes can be evidenced in the functioning of a person and by appreciating the expansion of his or her capabilities while learning to work with that tool. Better skills in a certain domain, improved performances in a particular task, deeper knowledge of a specific subject, are all examples of potential benefits from being allowed to work "with" a specific tool.

On the other hand, having had the chance to use a tool might also affect one's (cognitive) functioning more generally, even in circumstances when and where the tool cannot be used. Such an "impact on one's cognitive arsenal of skills, perspectives, and ways of representing the world" (p. 11) is what the authors have called effects of the use "of" a tool. So if the reference point is the level of mastery or the understanding of a topic one can attain without the VLE, typically using a control group, the difference measured will be an effect *with* the software, while if the reference is the comparison of ways of working observed before or understanding shown before, with those or that present after the course (typically using a pre-post and delayed post-test design) it will attest an effect *of* the VLE.

Using a VLE can also affect other psychological dimensions of the learner, such as his or her self-efficacy beliefs (Bandura, 1997). Shih-Wei and Chien-Hung (2005) show that students trained via a VLE in which learner control was encouraged showed higher self-efficacy beliefs in the field taught (mastery of a basic computer software package) than their counterparts in a traditional classroom. Given that self-efficacy beliefs are significant predictors of behavior, one can reasonably expect that such enhanced beliefs will result in a broader application of the skills and behaviors learned during the course.

Finally, if the literature about the effectiveness of VLEs often puts forward the time learners save, the time and effort spent by the instructor and his or her staff ahead of the course (to conceive the pedagogical scenario, to construct and collect the material, and to put it in the VLE) or during the course (to assist the students) are often underestimated and definitely need to be taken into consideration at the institutional level (Macdonald & Poniatowsky, 2011; Tomei, 2006; Weller, 2007; Wilson, 2012).

Kelly and Ferrell (2005, p. 2) acknowledge that "staff development is crucial to the successful implementation of e-learning. This development includes training in the use of the technology and education in the associated pedagogic models and considerations." Green et al. (2006, p. 393) stress that "the use of a VLE to support student learning is only practical where infrastructure to support such a program is available. Dissatisfaction can arise if infrastructure fails." This is true both for course providers but also for participants, whether they be at home or in their current workplace.

What will be learned in a course also depends on the state of the learner's knowledge, his or her current understanding of the topic when entering the environment, as well as his or her needs, goals, and expectations related to the course (Kraiger, 2008). This point raises the classic discussion in learning sciences about the meaning of learning. Rumelhart and Norman (1978) distinguish three modes of learning: accretion, structuring, and tuning. Accretion is the mode by which new information is entered in an existing schema. This is by far the most common way of learning, but it supposes that the learner has already built an appropriate schema of the topic he or she is confronted with. If no such schema exists, or if the existing schema cannot accommodate the information encountered, no long-lasting learning will occur, or, at least, no real understanding of the new information will happen. For understanding to occur, the learner will first have to engage in ample reflection in order to give sense to the material to be learned. This process, culminating in the forming of a new schema, new conceptualizations of a topic matter, is called structuring. The authors consider this mode as the most difficult and the most significant form of learning.

Tuning is the process the learner engages in so as to improve the adaptation of his or her knowledge to specific situations, making its application more efficient. This process can be seen as a permanent effort to optimize and generalize satisfactory schemata, once they have been set up through the process of structuring. Opportunities to practice become the key to enabling learners to transform their knowledge into automatic skills. Thus, any learning environment will only be seen as effective if it has the potential to stimulate all these processes, depending on the learner's pre-existing knowledge state and reasons for joining a course or a training program.

Finally, from a company's point of view, judging the effectiveness of a course may also be based on other considerations, for instance the "net benefits" or gains it brings to the company, in terms of competitiveness, job performance, or return on investment (Wang, Wang, & Shee, 2007; Wang, Vogel, & Ran, 2011). These aspects, that is, the investment for the educational institution or for the companies, are, however, rarely taken into account in the research on VLEs (Derouin, Fritzsche, & Salas, 2005).

Given that numerous reasons exist for choosing to attend, respectively to offer, a course online, combined with the fact that the same VLE can be used very differently from one course to another, and that the knowledge, expectations, reactions and behaviors of the potential learners are necessarily diverse, it is not possible to assess the effectiveness of VLEs in general. In our review below, we will focus on their specific functionalities, and discuss significant research done with and around each of them.

Features and Functionalities of Effective VLEs

Although they involve different ratios of face-to-face to online activities, all VLEs currently in use present the same core set of functions: course content delivery, information and communication functions between the teacher and the students or among students, a (group) workspace, support to the teacher and to students, and assessment. The mere existence of these functions in a VLE, however, does not imply that they will all be fully exploited either by the instructors or by the students. Also, the presence of such functions in VLEs does not reduce students' use of other technologies, such as search engines, email clients, mobile phones or text messaging, internet telephony, or social networks (De Laat & Conole, 2008). Additional functions are often provided, such as course management tools, student tracking, managing students' records, tracking their study programs, or accessing additional administrative information. As they are not directly related to learning, but more to the management of the courses, and are generally invisible to students, we will not discuss them here.

Content delivery

Using computers to give access to course content is a much older possibility than the development and use of standardized platforms or full VLEs. Nowadays, this function remains a core element of all VLEs, be it to allow students or training participants to catch up when they could not attend lectures, or to ask them to study the material before coming to class so as to be able to discuss it with the teacher, in a so-called "flipped classroom" format (Tucker, 2012).

Goldberg and McKhann (2000) compared student test scores in an introductory neuroscience course in which the course was given in a lecture hall for one half of the class and via a VLE for the others. The groups were switched at the middle of the experiment to rule out possible interference from factors due to the participants. The VLE format included video presentations by the lecturer (the same in both circumstances), a paginated lecture transcript, detailed animations, and an electronic notebook, all provided on a CD-ROM. The internet connection was disabled to avoid students accessing additional resources not available to students in the lecture hall. Student test scores at the end of the course showed a significant impact of the learning conditions on performance which were significantly better for modules studied via the VLE. Moreover, student responses to a questionnaire at the end of the course showed that they considered the VLE more effective and more desirable than the conventional lecture hall for delivering content.

Strayer (2007) compared two college classes, one of which attended the lessons in a traditional lecture/homework format, the other in a flipped format, with course material provided online and the classroom session used to complete active learning projects. Since no learning tests scores are provided, it is not possible to know which format led to better learning. Students from the online "flipped classroom" reported that they appreciated the collaboration and the innovation experienced more than those taught more traditionally. However, they were less satisfied than the normal class students with how the environment oriented them toward course content. This result is attributed to the fact that such innovations put students in a less "comfortable" situation than the more familiar pedagogical format. Martin (2012, p. 27) corroborates this hypothesis, observing that:

> teachers need to be protected from low student evaluation scores. Mazur and others have reported that students give lower evaluations in courses with active learning – even when the evidence shows they have learned more. Students have grown up with conventional lecture teaching, and just like anyone else, they are resistant to change.

Online delivery of the course material is also the cornerstone of massive open online courses (MOOCs), a course format currently being adopted at an impressive rate among the top universities in the world. A MOOC allows thousands of people to attend "big" courses without being enrolled at the corresponding institution (Mackness, Mak, & Williams, 2010). Specialists distinguish between xMOOCs and cMOOCs, where xMOOCs follow a clear instruction-type pattern in which the goals to be attained and material to be studied are predefined by the teacher while in cMOOCs learning goals as well as individuals' pathways across the material are determined by the students themselves (Littlejohn, 2013). Currently, xMOOCs are much more frequent than cMOOCs, a further sign that the delivery of content by an instructor remains a top priority for most online courses.

If most content is usually found directly in the VLE, more peripheral or additional content might be provided to interested students as links to outside resources, to be downloaded from the internet. In many cases, VLEs also take advantage of the libraries of well-established institutions.

Information and communication

If the initial VLEs were essentially conceived as document repositories (Culwin & Marshall, 1996; Sclater, 2008), later developments tended to include more and more communication functions (Kraiger, 2008). Technological, pedagogical, and epistemological reasons lay behind this evolution. Let's mention, for instance, the blossoming of communication tools and social networks, the growing importance taken in education by the socioconstructivist (Palincsar, 1998) and sociocultural learning theories (Rogoff, 1990; Vygotsky, 1978), and the development of the Web 2.0 philosophy (Lambropoulos, Faulkner, & Culwin, 2012). Analyzing the use of technologies among university students, Jones et al. (2010) see communication as the second most frequent purpose to use technologies, both for study and for social life and leisure purposes.

In the literature on virtual learning, two forms of communication are generally distinguished: synchronous and asynchronous (Branon & Essex, 2001; Järvelä & Häkkinen, 2002). VLEs provide both types of communication in various forms and through various tools. Typically, information about a course, its level, objectives, target audience, prerequisites, the name and contacts of the instructor(s), or instructions on how to complete a task or a test are provided in an asynchronous, textual way. Messages to and from students, notifications of work turned in or questions asked by a student, announcements regarding special events, deadlines or face-to-face meetings, as well as topics to be discussed openly, are also mainly conducted asynchronously, offering everybody as much freedom as possible about when to be online. Person-to-person communication is still carried out via email, approximately three times more often than via other communication tools specifically provided by VLEs (De Laat & Conole, 2008).

Analyzing education students' comments on the use of discussion forums and other asynchronous communication tools, Vonderwell (2003, p. 82) reports that students considered computer-mediated communication with the instructor as "more anonymous and you can express your feelings and ask more questions without worrying about what other people think about you." Not being able to meet the instructor however, is seen by students as a real disadvantage of online settings. They also saw asynchronous online communication as a drawback to engaging in collaboration with students they did not know beforehand.

Most modern VLEs also provide or integrate possibilities to interact and communicate synchronously. Tools to achieve this include instant messaging (IM), internet telephony, and conferencing or chat rooms. Jones et al. (2010) notice, however, that students tend to use them much less frequently than asynchronous tools, such as email or text messaging. Timmis (2012) argues however, that the use of IM between peers often goes unnoticed and that it should be acknowledged and encouraged on campus since it can provide motivational, emotional, and practical support to students. Research also shows that the use of IM might increase student participation. Comparing groups that adopted the IM system with groups that did not, Hrastinski (2005) found that the former spent more time working with content and communicating with peers.

Group/collaborative workspace

VLEs are full of information and content provided by instructors. The activity of the learner with and around this content is crucial for his or her learning (Stricker, Weibel, & Wissmath, 2011). Putting together Lee's (2001) model of learner types, click count tracking data and student performances at the end of the course, Maltby and Mackie (2009) observe that there is a high variability in the engagement of students with such platforms and, more importantly, that there is an overall correlation between the number of student clicks and their performance. Compared to other students, those whose performance was high and whose tracking data was considerable, could be characterized as learning-goal oriented, intrinsically motivated, with a high locus of control and a high self-efficacy, but also as granting priority to deep learning rather than surface learning. The authors conclude that VLEs tend to accentuate, rather than reduce differences between student attitudes and behaviors towards learning at school.

To facilitate and optimize the learner's activity, different tools may be provided. While some of them contribute to the development of a private workspace, others create a space in which work can be shared with other participating students. To help learners manage their own learning, VLEs often let them set up a personal archive, a portfolio of submitted tasks, or create a personal learning journal or a learning blog so they can save "lessons" learnt from previous experience and reflect on their learning process.

Nevertheless, current VLEs remain difficult to customize so as to suit the diversity of current learners' styles and approaches. To take the specificity of each learner into account, Xu and Wang (2006) suggest the use of intelligent agents that adapt the environment to the state of a learner's knowledge (learner model), and to his or her learning behaviors (learner profile), as well as providing each learner with a personalized learning plan.

Such propositions go in the direction of so-called personal learning environments (PLEs) (Kesim & Altinpulluk, 2013, p. 1), which "enable learners to organize their learning, provide freedom to choose content, and allow communication and collaboration with others easily. In addition, PLEs enable learners to continue learning after formal courses have ended, and make lifelong learning possible." Vassileva (2008, p. 199) also suggests that "the new social learning technologies should support the learner in finding the right content (right for the context, for the particular learner, for the specific purpose of the learner, right pedagogically)," and hence, becoming able to customize his or her learning to personal objectives and learning style. Wilson et al. (2009) consider that such alternatives will develop in sophistication, making classical VLEs a less attractive option, particularly as we move into a world of lifelong, lifewide, informal, and work-based learning.

But many authors limit the novelty of PLEs to the development of new educational technologies. Fiedler and Väljataga (2011) however, see them as a new approach or concept. They claim that PLEs should "support individuals (and groups) to gain awareness and control over a range of intentional learning activities and their environments, and eventually their overall development as personal (adult) learners living *in* (and not only with) the digital realm."

Instead of trying to design integrated PLEs from scratch, more and more authors suggest exploiting existing Web 2.0 facilities, such as Google search, weblogs, wikis, or specialized repositories such as YouTube or Amazon (Attwell, 2007; Qian, 2010; Sclater, 2008; Žubrinić & Kalpić, 2008). This would make access to learning content easier, requiring less effort than starting with a totally new environment.

Personalization is only one direction of the current development of student workspaces. Facilitating collaborative work within the environment through technology is another direction. Nowadays student workspaces are mostly used to provide collaborative settings and promote social interactions (Dillenbourg, Schneider, & Synteta 2002; Kreijns, Kirschner, & Jochems, 2003). In VLEs, synchronous interaction is achieved through the use of wikis, blogs, interactive whiteboards, and less frequently with simulations, 3D labs, and so on.

Reporting on the deployment of a wiki in a higher-education setting, Su and Beaumont (2010, p. 427–428) note that students quickly became confident in giving and receiving feedback on their work in progress and, as a result, became better at structuring their writing and constructing their arguments. Students admitted that they could avoid mistakes by looking at the tutor's feedback to others. The authors conclude "the wiki's in-situ revision facilities, together with its change-tracking mechanisms promote effective collaboration … and facilitates the development of students as critical learners."

Support and assistance

Most VLEs do provide support and assistance to students as well as the instructor.

Instructors, for instance, will generally get assistance not only in running their courses but also in finding resources or activities to set up a given subject, organizing the course, or constructing tests and assignments. Once the course is launched, activity reports will provide them with useful information on the amount and nature of work done by students (visited links, activities completed so far, etc.) both individually and collectively, allowing the instructor to keep an eye on class progress throughout the course and to take action if student progression does not meet expectations.

Information provided by such user-tracking facilities remains difficult to interpret (Douglas, 2010) and not without risks (Luck, 2010), since it can lead students to anticipate tracking rather than adopting ways of working best suited to their own learning style.

Common VLEs also provide assistance to students in many ways. In case of technical difficulties with the platform, students can often get help by browsing through a set of FAQs (frequently asked questions). The numerous communication facilities available within the platform or outside it can be used to answer technical questions as well as to seek assistance in understanding course content. Finally, to judge how close they are to goals set by the course, students can also evaluate themselves using built-in self-assessment functions. This possibility seems to be especially appreciated by students and particularly useful for those with lower achievement orientation (Hoskins & Van Hooff, 2005). Verpoorten et al. (2009) even suggest taking advantage of the tracking system to give the learner information on his or her learning process, thus producing what they call a "mirroring facility."

Assessments

Modern VLEs include both self-assessment possibilities, often presented as quizzes that are scored automatically, as well as formal assessments allowing the instructor – or the computer – to gauge each student's mastery of course content. De Lange, Suwardy, and Mavondo (2003) show that online assessment facilities score second in the list of the most important determinants of students overall evaluation of a course in accounting based on

Web-CT, just after the availability of lecture notes. Having the possibility to self-assess learning was not significantly related to students' overall evaluation, but there were differences between age groups regarding its importance. Older students (30–40) admitted that self-tests contributed to their learning significantly more than their younger counterparts (under 20 and 20–30).

Both these options increasingly take advantage of peer assessment techniques. Prins et al. (2005, p. 435) however acknowledge that students are not yet used to assessing their peers' work and observe that attempts to use peer assessment in VLEs without making it compulsory run the risks of "limited student participation in peer assessment assignments and of rather low quality assessment products." To avoid these risks, the authors advise tutors to be more active in prompting collaboration among students, and in fostering student reflection on their activities, to give enough time and importance to peer assessment during the course, and to make these assignments part of the marks collected for the course. Davies (2005) goes in the same direction by proposing to create a "mark for marking and commenting."

Formal assessments of students by the instructor can take various formats in VLEs – multiple choices, essays, quizzes, orderings, and so on – and explore various forms of mastery. The grading can be performed automatically in more and more cases, but grading essays will continue to require human marking. Some VLEs even provide item analysis tools for the teacher to assess the quality and the validity of his or her questions. If interested, the instructor can also access the statistics of every action performed by each of his or her students in a given course. Educational data-mining techniques can help make sense of these statistics and so track and assess students' activity level and relevance (Romero, Ventura, & Garcia, 2008).

Psychological and Social Issues

Insufficient opportunities for human interactions have often been attributed to online or virtual learning environments both by researchers and users (Aragon, 2003; Kreijns, Kirschner, & Jochems, 2003, Sit et al., 2005). Kraiger (2008) suggests, however, that insufficiencies might result from a suboptimal exploitation of the learner–learner interaction facilities offered by web-based learning environments, rather than from real technical limitations. To enhance the impression of human interaction, Kreijns et al. (2003) suggest providing nontask contexts and allowing social, off-task communication. Wahlstedt, Pekkola, and Niemelä (2008) go one step further by qualifying current VLEs as learning *spaces*, when what is needed is learning *places*. The distinction between "space" and "place," they argue, is similar to that between a "house" and a "home": a house keeps out the wind and rain, but a home is where we live (p. 1022). "A space becomes a place when meanings, constructed through social interaction, cultural identities and personal involvement are supported and embedded into the environment" (p. 1024). Following Garrison and Cleveland-Innes (2005), they argue that increasing the possibility of social interactions or even stimulating learner participation is not enough. To give people the sense of belonging to a community, social presence, cognitive presence, and awareness of the presence of others are needed.

Finding ways to increase social presence is a very popular topic in literature dealing with computer-based learning environments (Aragon, 2003; Gunawardena, 1995; Richardson & Swan, 2003). By providing both face-to-face meetings and freely managed study periods, blended learning seems to do a better job than online courses in creating a sense of belonging on the part of students. Rovai and Jordan (2004) compared student ratings of connectedness in three situations: full online courses, classroom-only classes, and blended courses. Blended courses were considered as providing significantly higher feelings of connectedness than both other formats.

Besides social presence, cognitive presence and group awareness have also been shown to be important determinants of the level of learner participation (Kimmerle & Cress, 2008; Lambropoulos, Faulkner, & Culwin, 2012). Although they do not see each other, all participants in a collaborative activity should be able, at any time, to evaluate other team members' knowledge and representations of the topic jointly worked on (Roschelle, 1992; Leinonen, & Järvelä, 2006). Dehler et al. (2011) describe and analyze how specific tools can be implemented in computer-supported collaborative scenarios (CSCL) in order to lead students to understand what knowledge they have of a problem, and what knowledge their partners have. Such group knowledge awareness (GKA) tools help partners make better decisions regarding what to ask and what to say to their partners, and hence improve communication and collaboration. While the mere presence of these tools does not induce significant differences in student learning, compared to students solving the same problems without such tools, such tools can prove very useful in the case of conflicting information held by the different partners by helping focus partners' attention on conflicting issues and hence overcome them fruitfully (Buder & Bodemer, 2007).

The possibility of sustaining students' group work certainly represents one strength of current VLEs compared to less complex software. But group awareness remains underdeveloped in the currently available e-learning platforms (Vassileva, 2008).

Besides the lack of social contacts while working, learners studying online will also need special social support from their usual social environment, family, colleagues, and immediate superiors at work. This is even more so for older adults and women (Chu, 2010). Furthermore, since most studying online is done at home, study time is mainly taken at the expense of time spent with the family. A substantial reduction in the time spent with the family has indeed regularly been reported, especially when the time spent on the internet exceeds 10 hours a week (Nie & Erbring, 2002).

Future Research

Research on the use of VLEs is now quite extensive, but the lines of research described in this chapter need to stay abreast of further developments of such environments. Several aspects will need more careful attention in the near future. For instance, if we know precisely what learners (and instructors) should do when they use VLEs, we still lack information on what they actually do, despite the fact that most current platforms keep track of each click or input from users. Recent developments in learning analysis techniques allow the mining of such large data sets and should help detect not only the intensity of use, but also how different types of learners and instructors exploit or neglect the various facilities provided (Agudo-Peregrina et al., 2013). With the increasing diversity of students in higher education and in corporate training such techniques are becoming more and more important.

Obviously, for VLEs to be successful with people of varying age, knowledge, interests and experience, instruction will need to be much more flexible and adaptable than it currently is (Xu & Wang, 2006). Flexibility not only means letting the learner decide when he or she wants to study, but also giving the learner the freedom to study wherever they wish. Mobile technology allows connection anywhere and anytime, but we still do not know how it can best be used for learning. Mobile technologies are conceived as communication rather than learning devices, while desktop computers remain a preferred tool where studying is concerned. Will this change in a near future, or will we maintain a clear distinction between technology for studying and technology for social life, between "technologies for learning" and "technologies for learners" (Halverson & Smith, 2010)? The answer to these questions will not so much depend on technological developments but rather on the way we view how learning occurs. Up to now, VLEs remain heavily centered on a school-based approach to learning. The challenge will be for educational institutions to accept that "Instead of opposing in-school and out-of-school learning, the advent of new learning technologies describes a pluralistic world in which out-of-school learning can complement in-school education" (Halverson & Smith, 2010, p. 52).

Conclusion

To a large extent, the success of VLEs is due to the fact that they seem to allow four interests to merge: that of students to find a way to study without constraints of time and place, that of instructors to avoid endless photocopying of course material, that of educational institutions to distribute knowledge on a large basis (Barajas & Owen, 2000; Littlejohn, 2013) and that of web programmers and educational researchers to popularize their visions about smart computing and powerful learning.

Although they are not yet two decades old, VLEs have already undergone several radical shifts. While the initial VLEs were resolutely *teacher centered*, serving essentially as useful ways to deliver course material to students, to assign work and fix deadlines, and to receive work back once finished, recent developments try to make them more and more *learner centered*. Students are encouraged to raise questions, discuss issues and problems together, and share their reflections while learning.

Based initially on the idea that learning resulted essentially from personal, *independent appropriation of knowledge*, modern VLEs are much more influenced by current representations of learning as the result of sharing ideas, confronting perspectives, working collaboratively, and participating in a *community of learners* (Engle & Conant, 2002). As for the approach to content to be learned, a significant shift is also underway, from *asymmetric* at the beginning of the century to more *symmetry* currently. If the instructor was initially the only person allowed to decide on material made available to students, modern VLEs and especially the so-called personal learning environments give learners an equal possibility to seek and share resources they have personally discovered and found useful. In some environments nowadays, learners even decide on the topic to be focused on (Johnson & Liber, 2008).

Another evolution to be mentioned is the shift from *prevailing commercial products* to the widespread use of *open source solutions*. This evolution also paved the road for numerous adaptations and has made special developments easier.

Finally, over the years, scientific publications on VLEs have tended to be more and more critical, pointing more readily to their *limits* than to their *potential* (Garrison, 2011). Such an evolution is often noted with regards to technologies in education and is certainly a sound attitude, likely to speed up both their technical development and the way they will be used by educational institutions, instructors, and students.

The present chapter has tried to give an overview of the evolution of VLEs in their first 20 years of existence and to sort out what factors are proven contributors to their effectiveness. Given the progress of technologies, the regular emergence of new "hot" themes in education and the ongoing evolution of people's ways of working, the picture might be radically different in 10 or 20 years.

References

Agudo-Peregrina, Á. F., Iglesias-Pradas, S., Conde-Gonzales, M. A., & Hernandez-Garcia, A. (2013). Can we predict success from log data in VLEs? Classification of interactions for learning analytics and their relation with performance in VLE-supported F2F and online learning. *Computers in Human Behavior*, 31, 542–550. doi:10.1016/j.chb.2013.05.031.

Allen, I. E., & Seaman, J. (2009). *Learning on Demand: Online Education in the United States*. Newburyport, MA: Sloan Consortium.

Aragon, S. R. (2003). Creating social presence in online environments. *New Directions for Adult and Continuing Education*, 100, 57–68. doi:10.1002/ace.119.

Aspden, L., & Helm, P. (2004). Making the connection in a blended learning environment. *Educational Media International*, 41, 245–252.

Attwell, G. (2007). Personal learning environments – The future of eLearning? *eLearning Papers*, 2, 1–8.

Bandura, A. (1997). *Self-Efficacy: The Exercise of Control*. New York: Freeman.

Barajas, M., & Owen, M. (2000). Implementing virtual learning environments: Looking for holistic approach. *Educational Technology & Society*, 3, 39–53.

Bonk, C., & Graham, C. R. (Eds.) (2006). *The Handbook of Blended Learning: Global Perspectives, Local Designs*. San Francisco: John Wiley & Sons, Inc./Pfeiffer.

Branon, R. F., & Essex, C. (2001). Synchronous and asynchronous communication tools in distance education. *TechTrends*, 45, 36–36.

Britain, S., & Liber, O. (2004). A framework for pedagogical evaluation of virtual learning environments. University of Bolton: Institutional Repository. http://halshs.archives-ouvertes.fr/docs/00/69/62/34/PDF/Liber-2004.pdf (accessed July 25, 2013).

Buder, J., & Bodemer, D. (2007). Supporting controversial CSCL discussion with augmented group awareness tools. *International Journal of Computer-Supported Collaborative Learning*, 3, 123–139.

Chu, R. J.-C. (2010). How family support and internet self-efficacy influence the effects of e-learning among higher aged adults – Analyses of gender and age differences. *Computers & Education*, 55, 255–264. doi:10.1016/j.compedu.2010.01.011.

Clarke, T., & Hermens, A. (2001). Corporate developments and strategic alliances in e-learning. *Education & Training*, 43, 256–267.

Cottrell, D., & Robinson, R. (2003). Blended learning in an accounting course. *Quarterly Review of Distance Education*, 4, 261–269.

Culwin, F., & Marshall, D. (1996). The design and provision of software engineering education over the web. *Proceedings of the 5th International World Wide Web Conference* (pp. 217–226). Paris.

Davies, P. (2005). Weighting for computerized peer-assessment to be accepted. *Proceedings of the 9th CAA Conference*. Loughborough: Loughborough University. https://dspace.lboro.ac.uk/2134/1988 (accessed July 2, 2013).

Davis, F. D. (1989). Perceived usefulness, perceived ease of use, and user acceptance of information technology. *MIS Quarterly*, 13, 319–339.

De Laat, M., & Conole, G. (2008). Patterns of students' use of networked learning technologies. *Computing*, 19, 85–94.

De Lange, P., Suwardy, T., & Mavondo, F. (2003). Integrating a virtual learning environment into an introductory accounting course: Determinants of student motivation. *Accounting Education: An International Journal*, 12, 1–14. doi:10.1080/0963928032000064567.

Dehler, J., Bodemer, D., Buder, J., & Hesse, F. (2011). Guiding knowledge communication in CSCL via group knowledge awareness. *Computers in Human Behavior*, 27, 1068–1078. doi:10.1016/j.chb.2010.05.018.

Derouin, R. E., Fritzsche, B. A., & Salas, E. (2005). E-learning in organizations. *Journal of Management* 31, 920–940. doi:10.1177/0149206305279815.

Dillenbourg, P., Schneider, D., & Synteta, P. (2002). Virtual learning environments. *Proceedings of the 3rd Hellenic Conference Information & Communication Technologies in Education* (pp. 3–18).

Douglas, I. (2010). Improving the tracking of student participation and effort in online learning. In Y. Kats (Ed.), *Learning Management System Technologies and Software Solutions for Online Teaching* (pp. 1686–1700). Hershey, NY: Information Science Reference.

Engle, R. A., & Conant, F. R. (2002). Guiding principles for fostering productive disciplinary engagement: Explaining an emergent argument in a community of learners classroom. *Cognition and Instruction*, 20, 399–483. doi:10.1207/S1532690XCI2004_1.

Eom, S. B. (2012). Effects of LMS, self-efficacy, and self-regulated learning on LMS effectiveness in business education. *Journal of International Education in Business*, 5, 129–144.

Evans, M. A., & Wilkins, J. L. M. (2011). Social interactions and instructional artifacts: Emergent socio-technical affordances and constraints for children's geometric thinking. *Journal of Educational Computing Research*, 44, 141–171. doi:10.2190/EC.44.2.b.

Fiedler, S. H. D., & Väljataga, T. (2011). Personal learning environments: Concept or technology? *International Journal of Virtual and Personal Learning Environments*, 2, 1–11.

Fowler, C. (2014). Virtual reality and learning: Where is the pedagogy? *British Journal of Educational Technology*. DOI: 10.1111/bjet.12135

Garrison, D. R. (2011). *E-Learning in the 21st Century: A Framework for Research and Practice* (2nd ed.). New York: Taylor & Francis.

Garrison, D. R., & Cleveland-Innes, M. (2005). Facilitating cognitive presence in online learning: Interaction is not enough. *American Journal of Distance Education*, 19, 133–148. doi:10.1207/s15389286ajde1903_2.

Garrison, D. R., & Kanuka, H. (2004). Blended learning: Uncovering its transformative potential in higher education. *The Internet and Higher Education*, 7, 95–105.

Goldberg, H. R., & McKhann, G. M. (2000). Student test scores are improved in a virtual learning environment. *Advances in Physiology Education*, 23, 59–66.

Green, S. M., Weaver, M., Voegeli, D., Fitzsiommons, D., Knowles, J., Harrison, M., & Shephard, K. (2006). The development and evaluation of the use of a virtual learning environment (Blackboard 5) to support the learning of pre-qualifying nursing students undertaking a human anatomy and physiology module. *Nurse Education Today*, 26, 388–395. doi:10.1016/j.nedt.2005.11.008.

Gunawardena, C. N. (1995). Social presence theory and implications for interaction and collaborative learning in computer conferences. *International Journal of Educational Telecommunications*, 1, 147–166.

Halverson, R., & Smith, A. (2010). How new technologies have (and have not) changed teaching and learning in schools. *Journal of Computing in Teacher Education*, 26, 49–54.

Haven, C., & Botterill, D. (2003). Virtual learning environments in hospitality, leisure, tourism and sport: A review. *Journal of Hospitality, Leisure, Sport and Tourism Education*, 2, 75–92.

Heaton-Shrestha, C., Gipps, C., Edirisingha, P., & Linsey, T. (2007). Learning and e-learning in HE: The relationship between student learning style and VLE use. *Research Papers in Education*, 22, 443–464. doi:10.1080/02671520701651797.

Hoskins, S. L., & Van Hooff, J. C. (2005). Motivation and ability: Which students use online learning and what influence does it have on their achievement? *British Journal of Educational Technology*, 36, 177–192. doi:10.1111/j.1467-8535.2005.00451.x.

Hrastinski, S. (2005). Instant messaging use and its effect on student participation in online group work. *Proceedings of World Conference on Educational Multimedia, Hypermedia and Telecommunications* (pp. 701–706).

Hudson, B., Hudson, A., & Steel, J. (2006). Orchestrating interdependence in an international online learning community. *British Journal of Educational Technology*, 37, 733–748. doi:10.1111/j.1467-8535.2006.00552.x.

Järvelä, S., & Häkkinen, P. (2002). Web-based cases in teaching and learning – The quality of discussions and a stage of perspective taking in asynchronous communication. *Interactive Learning Environments*, 10, 1–22.

Jenkins, M., Browne, T., & Walker, R. (2005). VLE surveys. A longitudinal perspective between March 2001, March 2003 and March 2005 for higher education in the United Kingdom. http://www.immagic.com/eLibrary/ARCHIVES/GENERAL/UCISA_UK/U051130J.pdf (accessed June 20, 2013).

Johnson, M., & Liber, O. (2008). The personal learning environment and the human condition: From theory to teaching practice. *Interactive Learning Environments*, 16, 3–15.

Jones, C., Ramanau, R., Cross, S., & Healing, G. (2010). Net generation or digital natives: Is there a distinct new generation entering university? *Computers & Education*, 54, 722–732.

Keller, J. M., & Suzuki, K. (2004). Learner motivation and e-learning design: A multinationally validated process. *Journal of Educational Media*, 29, 229–239. doi:10.1080/1358t65042000 283084.

Kelly, J., & Ferrell, G. (2005). Effective management of virtual learning environments. *JISC infoNet*, UK. 10.1.1.102.1240-3.

Kesim, M., & Altinpulluk, H. (2013). The future of LMS and personal learning environments. http://bildiri.anadolu.edu.tr/papers/bildirimakale/5633_b530m95.pdf (accessed June 20, 2013).

Kimmerle, J., & Cress, U. (2008). Group awareness and self-presentation in computer-supported information exchange. *International Journal of Computer-Supported Collaborative Learning*, 3, 85–97. doi:10.1007/s11412-007-9027-z.

Kirkpatrick, D. L. (1979). Techniques for evaluating training programs. In D. P. Ely & T. Plomp (Eds.), *Classic Writings on Instructional Technology* (vol. 1, pp. 231–241). Englewood: Libraries Unlimited, Inc.

Kirschner, P. A., Sweller, J., & Clark, R. E. (2006). Why minimal guidance during instruction does not work: An analysis of the failure of constructivist, discovery, problem-based, experiential and inquiry-based teaching. *Educational Psychologist*, 41, 75–86.

Koller, D. (2011). Death knell for the lecture: Technology as a passport to personalized education. *New York Times*, December 5.

Kraiger, K. (2008). Transforming our models of learning and development: Web-based instruction as enabler of third-generation instruction. *Industrial and Organizational Psychology*, 1, 454–467.

Kreijns, K., Kirschner, P. A., & Jochems, W. (2003). Identifying the pitfalls for social interaction in computer-supported collaborative learning environments: A review of the research. *Computers in Human Behavior*, 19, 335–353.

Lambropoulos, N., Faulkner, X., & Culwin, F. (2012). Supporting social awareness in collaborative e-learning. *British Journal of Educational Technology*, 43, 295–306. doi:10.1111/j.1467-8535. 2011.01184.x.

Lee, M. G. (2001). Profiling students' adaptation styles in web-based learning. *Computers and Education*, 36, 121–132.

Leinonen, P., & Järvelä, S. (2006). Facilitating interpersonal evaluation of knowledge in a context of distributed team collaboration. *British Journal of Educational Technology*, 37, 897–916. doi:10.1111/j.1467-8535.2006.00658.x.

Levy, Y. (2007). Comparing dropouts and persistence in e-learning courses. *Computers and Education*, 48, 185–204.

Littlejohn, A. (2013). Understanding massive open online courses. CEMCA, EdTech Notes. http://cemca.org.in/ckfinder/userfiles/files/EdTech%20Notes%202_Littlejohn_final_1 June2013.pdf (accessed September 2, 2013).

Lowes, S. (2007). Professional development for online teachers. In C. Cavanaugh & R. Blomeyer (Eds.), *What Works in K-12 Online Learning* (pp. 161–178). Eugene, OR: International Society for Technology in Education.

Luck, M. (2010). Surveillance in the virtual classroom. In A. T. Ragusa (Ed.), *Interaction in Communication Technologies and Virtual Learning Environments: Human Factors* (pp. 160–169). Hershey, PA: Information Science Reference. doi:10.4018/978-1-60566-874-1.ch011.

Macdonald, J., & Poniatowska, B. (2011). Designing the professional development of staff for teaching online: An OU (UK) case study. *Distance Education*, 32, 119–134.

Mackness, J., Mak, S., & Williams, R. (2010). The ideals and reality of participating in a MOOC. *Proceedings of the 7th International Conference on Networked Learning 2010* (pp. 266–275). Lancaster: University of Lancaster.

Maltby, A., & Mackie, S. (2009). Virtual learning environments – Help or hindrance for the "disengaged" student? *Researching Learning Technology*, 17, 49–62. doi:10.1080/09687760802657577.

Martin, F. G. (2012). Will massive open online courses change how we teach? *Communications of the ACM*, 55, 26–28. doi:10.1145/2240236.2240246.

Moore, M. G., & Kearsley, G. (2011). *Distance Education: A Systems View of Online Learning.* Belmont, CA: Wadsworth Cengage Learning.

Mueller, D., & Strohmeier, S. (2010). Design characteristics of virtual learning environments: An expert study. *International Journal of Training and Development,* 14, 209–222.

Mueller, D., & Strohmeier, S. (2011). Design characteristics of virtual learning environments: State of research. *Computers & Education,* 57, 2505–2516. doi:10.1016/j.compedu.2011.06.017.

Nie, N. H., & Erbring, L. (2002). Internet and society: A preliminary report. *IT&Society,* 1, 275–283.

Olapiriyakul, K., & Scher, J. M. (2006). A guide to establishing hybrid learning courses: Employing information technology to create a new learning experience, and a case study. *The Internet and Higher Education,* 9, 287–301.

Ozkan, S., & Koseler, R. (2009). Multi-dimensional students' evaluation of e-learning systems in the higher education context: An empirical investigation. *Computers & Education,* 53, 1285–1296. doi:10.1016/j.compedu.2009.06.011.

Palinscar, A. S. (1998). Social constructivist perspectives on teaching and learning. *Annual Review of Psychology,* 49, 345–375.

Piccoli, G., Ahmad, R., & Ives, B. (2001). Web-based virtual learning environments: A research framework and a preliminary assessment of effectiveness in basic IT skills training. *MIS Quarterly,* 25, 401–426.

Prins, F. J., Sluijsmans, D. M. A., Kirschner, P. A., & Strijbos, J.-W. (2005). Formative peer assessment in a CSCL environment: A case study. *Assessment & Evaluation in Higher Education,* 30, 417–444. doi:10.1080/02602930500099219.

Qian, G. (2010). The web as PLE: Perspective from educational technology and internet psychology. *Education Technology and Computer (ICETC). 2nd International Conference on* (vol. 1, pp. 262–266). IEEE. doi:10.1109/ICETC.2010.5529254.

Richardson, J. C., & Swan, K. (2003). Examining social presence in online courses in relation to students' perceived learning and satisfaction. *Journal of Asynchronous Learning Networks,* 7, 68–88.

Rogoff, B. (1990). *Apprenticeship in Thinking: Cognitive Development in Social Context.* Oxford: Oxford University Press.

Romero, C., Ventura, S., & García, E. (2008). Data mining in course management systems: Moodle case study and tutorial. *Computers & Education,* 51, 368–384.

Roschelle, J. (1992). Learning by collaborating: Convergent conceptual change. *Journal of the Learning Sciences,* 2, 235–276.

Rovai, A. P., & Jordan, H. (2004). Blended learning and sense of community: A comparative analysis with traditional and fully online graduate courses. *International Review of Research in Open and Distance Learning,* 5, 2–13.

Rumelhart, D. E., & Norman, D. A. (1978). Accretion, tuning and restructuring: Three modes of learning. In J. W. Cotton & R. Klatzky (Eds.), *Semantic Factors in Cognition* (pp. 37–60). Hillsdale, NJ: Erlbaum.

Salomon, G., & Perkins, D. N. (1998). Individual and social aspects of learning. *Review of Research in Education,* 23, 1–24.

Sclater, N. (2008). Web 2.0, personal learning environments, and the future of learning management systems. *Research Bulletin,* 13, 2008–2009.

Shih-Wei, C., & Chien-Hung, L. (2005). Learning effectiveness in web-based technology-mediated virtual learning environment: A learner control perspective. *Journal of Computer Assisted Learning,* 21, 65–76. doi:10.1111/j.1365-2729.2005.00114.x.

Sife, A., Lwoga, E., & Sanga, C. (2007). New technologies for teaching and learning: Challenges for higher learning institutions in developing countries. *International Journal of Education and Development using ICT,* 3(2), 57–67.

Sit, J. W. H., Chung, J. W. Y., Chow, M. C. M., & Wong, T. K. S. (2005). Experiences of online learning: Students' perspective. *Nurse Education Today,* 25, 140–147. doi:10.1016/j.nedt.2004.11.004.

Stonebraker, P. W., & Hazeltine, J. E. (2004). Virtual learning effectiveness: An examination of the process. *Learning Organization Journal,* 11, 209–225.

Strayer, J. F. (2007). The effect of the classroom flip on the learning environment: A comparison of learning activity in a traditional classroom and a flipped classroom that use an intelligent tutoring system. PhD thesis. Ohio State University.

Stricker, D., Weibel, D., & Wissmath, B. (2011). Efficient learning using a virtual learning environment in a university class. *Computers & Education*, 56, 495–504. doi:10.1016/j.compedu.2010.09.012.

Su, F., & Beaumont, C. (2010). Evaluating the use of a wiki for collaborative learning. *Innovations in Education and Teaching International*, 47, 417–431. doi:10.1080/14703297.2010.518428.

Sun, P.-C., Tsai, R. J., Finger, G., Chen, Y.-Y., & Yeh, D. (2008). What drives a successful e-learning? An empirical investigation of the critical factors influencing learner satisfaction. *Computers and Education*, 50, 1183–1202. doi:10.1016/j.compedu.2006.11.007.

Thomson NETg. (2003). *Thomson Job Impact Study-final Results – the Next Generation of Corporate Learning: Achieving the Right Blend*. Naperville, IL: NETg.

Timmis, S. (2012). Constant companions: Instant messaging conversations as sustainable supportive study structures amongst undergraduate peers. *Computers & Education*, 59, 3–18. doi:10.1016/j.compedu.2011.09.026.

Tomei, L. (2006). The impact of online teaching on faculty load: Computing the ideal class size for online courses. *Journal of Technology and Teacher Education*, 14, 531–541.

Tucker, B. (2012). The flipped classroom: Online instruction at home frees class time for learning. http://educationnext.org/files/ednext_20121_BTucker.pdf (accessed July 31, 2013).

Tzeng, G.-H., Chiang, C.-H., & Li, C.-W. (2007). Evaluating intertwined effects in e-learning programs: A novel hybrid MCDM model based on factor analysis and DEMATEL. *Expert systems with Applications*, 32, 1028–1044.

Vassileva, J. (2008). Toward social learning environments. *IEEE Transactions on Learning Technologies*, 1, 199–214. doi:10.1109/TLT.2009.4.

Verpoorten, D., Glahn, C., Kravcik, M., Ternier, S., & Specht, M. (2009). Personalisation of learning in virtual learning environments. In U. Dimitrova, V. Cress, & M. Specht (Eds.), *Learning in the Synergy of Multiple Disciplines* (pp. 52–66). Berlin, Heidelberg: Springer.

Vonderwell, S. (2003). An examination of asynchronous communication experiences and perspectives of students in an online course: A case study. *The Internet and Higher Education*, 6, 77–90. doi:10.1016/S1096-7516(02)00164-1.

Vygotsky, L. S. (1978). *Mind in Society: The Development of Higher Psychological Processes*. Cambridge, MA: Harvard University Press.

Wahlstedt, A., Pekkola, S., & Niemelä, M. (2008). From e-learning space to e-learning place. *British Journal of Educational Technology*, 39, 1020–1030. doi:10.1111/j.1467-8535.2008.00821_1.x.

Wang, M., Vogel, D., & Ran, W. (2011). Creating a performance-oriented e-learning environment: A design science approach. *Information & Management*, 48, 260–269. doi:10.1016/j.im.2011.06.003.

Wang, Y.-S. (2003). Assessment of learner satisfaction with asynchronous electronic learning systems. *Information & Management*, 41, 75–86. doi:10.1016/S0378-7206(03)00028-4.

Wang, Y.-S., Wang, H.-Y., & Shee, D. Y. (2007). Measuring e-learning systems success in an organizational context: Scale development and validation. *Computers in Human Behavior*, 23, 1792–1808. doi:10.1016/j.chb.2005.10.006.

Weller, M. (2007). *Virtual Learning Environments: Using, Choosing and Developing your VLE0* Milton Park: Routledge.

Wilson, A. (2012). Effective professional development for e-learning: What do the managers think? *British Journal of Educational Technology*, 43, 892–900. doi:10.1111/j.1467-8535.2011.01248.x.

Wilson, S., Liber, O., Johnson, M., Beauvoir, P., Sharples, P., & Milligan, C. (2009). Personal learning environments: Challenging the dominant design of educational systems. *Journal of e-Learning and Knowledge Society-English Version*, 3, 27–38.

Xu, D., & Wang, H. (2006). Intelligent agent supported personalization for virtual learning environments. *Decision Support Systems*, 42: 825–843. doi:10.1016/j.dss.2005.05.033.

Žubrinić, K., & Kalpić, D. (2008). The web as personal learning environment. *Proceedings of the 31st MIPRO CE*. Opatija, Hrvatska, May 26–30. http://bib.irb.hr/datoteka/357767.576-2219-1-PB-1.pdf (accessed August 5, 2013).

12

Game- and Simulation-Based Approaches to Training

Rebecca Grossman, Kyle Heyne, and Eduardo Salas

Introduction

Increasingly, simulation-based training (SBT) is being recognized as a highly effective approach to training, particularly when targeting complex knowledge, skills, and abilities (KSAs) (e.g., Salas, Wildman, & Piccolo, 2009; Grossman, Spencer, & Salas, 2013). Because it enables trainees to obtain experience enacting target KSAs within a safe environment that mirrors the characteristics of the real environment it serves as a unique mechanism for facilitating learning, administering feedback, and promoting the transfer of training (Salas et al., 2012). Though it is often associated with advanced technology and highly immersive equipment, SBT can come in a variety of forms. Indeed, organizations may shy away from SBT due to the potential costs involved, or in contrast, may overuse it, assuming that the use of cutting edge technology will guarantee effectiveness – in both cases, they would be selling themselves short. Simulations can vary in their degree and type of fidelity, each characteristic proving more or less effective in different contexts. Additionally, the use of simulation alone, regardless of its fidelity, does not guarantee that training will be effective (Oser, et al., 1999b). To work, the design and implementation of SBT must be grounded in the science of training such that it uses systematic procedures and incorporates specific instructional features. The purpose of this chapter is thus to provide an overview of SBT, including a description of what it entails, and what makes it effective. Additionally, we highlight a specific type of SBT – game-based training. This approach is gaining popularity in both research and practice, and may be particularly useful for promoting continuous learning, thus warranting additional discussion.

The Wiley Blackwell Handbook of the Psychology of Training, Development, and Performance Improvement,
First Edition. Edited by Kurt Kraiger, Jonathan Passmore, Sigmar Malvezzi, and Nuno Rebelo dos Santos.
© 2015 John Wiley & Sons Ltd. Published 2020 by John Wiley & Sons Ltd.

What is a Simulation?

A simulation is an artificial scenario or environment that's designed to represent, or *simulate*, some aspect of reality (Bell, Kanar, & Kozlowki, 2008; Galvao, Martins, & Gomes, 2000). Simulations can incorporate different degrees and types of fidelity, or realism, namely, physical, functional, and psychological (Dietz et al., 2013). As its name implies, physical fidelity is the degree to which the simulation recreates the physical elements of the scenario or environment it is meant to represent (Bowers & Jentsch, 2001). If the goal is to simulate flying an airplane, for example, a simulation high on physical fidelity would involve a full-motion simulator that closely mirrors the cockpit and the physical conditions of flying. Functional fidelity involves the recreation of the purpose, meaning, or contextual features of a given scenario or task that is being simulated, such as the goals, responsibilities, and roles (Elliot et al., 2004). A simulation of the job of a manager, for instance, might entail activities such as managing an in-basket (e.g., emails, reports), administering performance feedback, or supervising the amount and quality of others' progress. Finally, psychological fidelity reflects the extent to which the simulation prompts the underlying psychological processes that are relevant to the real world task, scenario, or environment (Kozlowski & DeShon, 2004). In this case, simulations might involve acting out how to deal with a difficult customer, or performing a task under strict time constraints, for example.

The type and amount of fidelity that is most appropriate in different training contexts will depend on the goals of the training. Tasks that are physical in nature (e.g., building a computer) of course will be better served by simulations that are high in physical fidelity, while those that are more heavily grounded in functional (e.g., leading a team) or psychological (e.g., counseling a patient) processes will be best facilitated by their respective types of fidelity. Beyond this, however, the degree of fidelity that is required, meaning the amount of each type (e.g., how much psychological fidelity is incorporated?), and/or the number of types (e.g., are both physical and functional fidelity included?) that are incorporated, may depend on the risks that are involved if one does not appropriately acquire the KSAs being targeted. The medical community, for example, relies heavily upon high-fidelity simulations to train medical personnel to diagnose patients and perform surgical procedures (Dietz et al., 2013; Gordon et al., 2001). Such simulations often involve highly realistic mannequins that are connected to intravenous monitors and are made to react to the actions of the trainee, thus incorporate high degrees of physical, functional, and psychological fidelity. In this case, it is critical for trainees to master the KSAs within the context of the training environment – failing to do so could have life-threatening consequences in the real world. Other training goals, in contrast, may allow more room for error or mastery within the job environment. For a telemarketer who needs to learn a script for making sales calls, for instance, a simple role-playing simulation with a moderate degree of psychological fidelity (e.g., the person playing the role of the customer asks questions that are typical of customers) may be sufficient, as the risks associated with making errors on the job are minimal.

Using simulation therefore does not always mean that advanced technology and expensive equipment are required. Indeed, research has shown that low-fidelity simulations can be equally, if not more, effective than those of higher fidelity (e.g., Jentsch & Bowers, 1998), largely because they tend to incorporate higher degrees of psychological fidelity (Coultas, Grossman, & Salas, 2012). Because of this, and the reduction of costs, lower-fidelity simulations are becoming increasingly prevalent in both research and practice, even for training complex competencies. One emerging approach for doing so is to use computer-based games as a form of simulation. Games, specifically, "serious games," those used for the purposes of training and education (Dietz et al., 2013), provide a rich context for high degrees of psychological fidelity. SimCity, for example, a commercial computer game (SimCity 4: Deluxe Edition, 2004), has been used by researchers to study different organizational phenomena (e.g., Resick et al., 2010). Because the game requires players to utilize different pieces of information to make various choices in the game, and these choices influence their performance outcomes, it serves as a useful platform for simulating individual or team strategic decision making. While it is generally not wise to use off-the-shelf products for training purposes, games can be created or modified to simulate different KSAs being targeted in training. Consistent with these ideas, synthetic task environments (STEs) have also emerged as effective mechanisms for conducting research and implementing training (Dietz et al., 2013). STEs are a special type of simulation or game that emphasizes psychological fidelity by focusing on synthetic tasks, or abstractions of the tasks that need to be performed in the real world (Martin, Lyon, & Schreiber, 1998). In a game like SimCity, for instance, trainees could be prompted to engage in the same types of tasks (e.g., balancing a budget, leading group discussions) they are required to perform in their real jobs. While they have no physical fidelity, and may or may not have functional fidelity, the high psychological fidelity of STEs can make them extremely effective for facilitating learning. As noted earlier, different training goals may call for different types of fidelity, so games and other types of STEs may not always be the most appropriate option.

What is Simulation-Based Training?

As described above, simulations can be used as tools to facilitate the training of various KSAs. Simulations by themselves, however, do not constitute effective training. Training can be defined as a systematic process designed to impart attitudes, concepts, knowledge, rules, or skills in trainees, and to result in improved performance or other organizational outcomes of value (Goldstein, 1991; Salas, Wildman, & Piccolo, 2009). Simulation-based training (SBT), then, is the systematic process of imparting such competencies, primarily by simulating them in some type of synthetic practice environment (Salas, Wildman, & Piccolo, 2009). A key component of this definition is the word *systematic*. To be effective, simulations must be embedded in a broader training system that is grounded in the science of training. Specifically, seven key steps have been identified that, together, make SBT effective (Salas, Wildman, & Piccolo, 2009; Salas et al., 2005, 2006). The first step is to use performance history and skill inventories to ascertain which, and the strength of, the KSAs trainees currently hold. This information will feed into the next step, which is to determine the tasks and competencies that will be targeted in training. In addition to basing this on the information gleaned from step one (i.e., which KSAs trainees are lacking), this also involves conducting a needs analysis to identify which tasks trainees are required to perform on the job, and which KSAs are necessary in order to perform those tasks effectively. Building on the previous steps, step three involves identifying the specific learning objectives that the simulation will be designed to facilitate. At a broad level, learning objectives can be focused on developing outcomes that are cognitive, skill-based, or affective in nature (Kraiger, Ford, & Salas, 1993), and should be grounded in the broader goals of the training, namely, the KSAs that will be targeted. Essentially, they are measurable outcomes that serve as indicators of the degree to which such KSAs have been acquired. For example, if the goal of the training is to improve customer service skills, the learning objectives would involve specific, measurable outcomes that indicate that such skills have been improved, such as increased customer service ratings. In this case, the learning objective would be to increase customer service ratings. Learning objectives can be task-specific (e.g., learn to operate a specific piece of equipment) or task-generic (e.g., improve leadership skills).

Once these things have been established, the simulations can be designed to trigger, or elicit use of the target competencies in the fourth step (Salas, Wildman, & Piccolo, 2009; Salas et al., 2005, 2006). Specifically, the simulation scenarios should be embedded with certain exercises or trigger events that prompt trainees to demonstrate and practice the KSAs being targeted. In addition to these events, simulations should also be embedded with performance measures that are linked to the learning objectives, thus ultimately assess the degree to which the target KSAs are being/have been acquired by the trainee (i.e., step five). For example, a trainer may fill out a subtask checklist or behavioral-rating scale while the trainee performs the simulation, or automated performance measures can be embedded into more high-tech platforms that can then be used to assess his/her level of competence. In this step, performance standards are also established. This involves determining what constitutes "high" or "competent" performance, for instance, in relation to the specific measures that were selected for inclusion. In the sixth step, trainees' performance is diagnosed on the basis of these measures and standards. Performance can be assessed both during and after the simulation period. Essentially, the information that was gathered in step five is used to evaluate the degree to which trainees have achieved learning objectives. This could be done by comparing trainee's post-training scores to those that were measured before training, to the scores of other employees who did not receive the training, or to the performance standards that were established in the previous step. Finally, the performance diagnosis is used to provide feedback to trainees and to conduct a debrief centered on the events that transpired during the simulation (i.e., step seven). Again, this feedback can be administered both within the context of the training, to ensure that trainees acquire target KSAs as they go along, and at the completion of training, to assess the ultimate degree to which the KSAs were acquired, or the training's effectiveness. While the specific features of SBT that help make it effective will be discussed in more detail in subsequent sections, these seven steps represent the broader system in which simulations should be embedded.

What is Game-Based Training?

Game-based training is essentially a form of SBT in which the simulations take place within the context of a serious game. As described earlier, serious games are those used for the purposes of training and education (Dietz et al., 2013). More specifically, Sitzmann (2011, p. 492) defines computer-based simulation games as, "instruction delivered via personal computer that immerses trainees in a decision-making exercise in an artificial environment in order to learn the consequences of their decisions." Such games have been characterized as being interactive, grounded in a set of established rules and constraints, and focused on accomplishing a specific goal (Wouters et al., 2013). Additionally, they provide continuous feedback, through such things as points, scores, or changes in the game, and often involve some form of competitive activity. In the context of training, serious games serve as the platform in which simulations are enacted. Game-based training is particularly valuable because it can facilitate active learning, an approach in which individuals have control of their own learning, and must explore and experiment with the task in order for such learning to occur (Bell & Kozlowski, 2008). Indeed, in a recent meta-analysis, Siztmann (2011) found that game-based training was more effective than other training approaches only when it facilitated active, as opposed to passive, learning. Because serious games have the ability to be actively engaging and motivating, they have great potential to serve as tools for promoting continuous learning opportunities. Specifically, initial evidence suggests employees are willing to use these games on their own time, and that they enhance work-relevant KSAs when they do so (Aldrich, 2007; Jana, 2006). In the meta-analysis mentioned above, game-based training was more effective than other training approaches when trainees were provided with unlimited access to the game, suggesting that individuals do indeed take advantage of opportunities to utilize games to promote learning. Beyond these general characteristics, more specific features that make serious games effective learning tools are further discussed in subsequent sections. Like any other type of SBT, game-based training should be systematic, and should incorporate the seven steps described above.

Is Simulation-Based Training Effective?

SBT has garnered considerable support as an effective approach in the training literature. It has been applied to a variety of settings such as healthcare (e.g., Rosen et al., 2010), the military (e.g., Freeman & Cohen, 1996), management education (e.g., Salas, Wildman, & Piccolo, 2009), and customer service (e.g., Slotte & Herbert, 2008). Empirical research has largely focused on comparing SBT to other training approaches, assessing its effectiveness in different contexts or for training different KSAs, and examining instructional features that render it more or less effective. A variety of studies, for example, have demonstrated its effectiveness within the context of healthcare. It has been used to improve patient care in the high-stakes setting of cardiac surgery (Bruppacher et al., 2010), to enhance residents' performance in advanced cardiac life-support situations (Wayne et al., 2005), and for teaching medical students acute care assessment and management skills (Steadman et al., 2006), to name a few examples. In the latter study, SBT was deemed more effective than problem-based learning, an approach characterized by lower-fidelity scenarios, and less direct forms of feedback.

In a very different setting, Klein et al. (2007) found support for SBT as a promising approach for training the US National Aeronautics and Space Administration's (NASA) space shuttle mission management team. After undergoing SBT, team members had shared beliefs in their abilities to perform as a team, showed increased levels of motivation and readiness, performed at target levels, and had favorable reactions to the training program – they were satisfied with it and believed it was useful for improving their performance. Representing other contexts, Freeman and Cohen (1996) used SBT to improve the decision-making processes of Navy teams, and Slotte and Herbert (2008) found that it facilitated customer service in a sales environment. These examples highlight the value of SBT not only for use in variety of settings, but also for training a variety of competencies. Further emphasizing this, SBT has been used to improve performance in complex decision-making tasks (Fiorella, Vogel-Walcutt, & Shatz, 2012), to increase the speed and accuracy of call center performance (Murthy et al., 2008), and to develop expertise and decision-making skills in teams of low-level workers (DiBello, Missildine, & Struttman, 2009).

Different features have also been shown to facilitate or hinder the effectiveness of SBT. In a study in which video-based SBT was used to train complex decision-making (Fiorella, Vogel-Walcutt, & Shatz, 2012), for example, trainees who received feedback in the form of spoken text performed better than those who received written text. The authors suggested that receiving feedback in a different modality than the training material is less cognitively taxing than receiving both in the same modality, thus facilitates training performance. In another study, SBT was more effective when it was accompanied by metacognitive prompting than when it was not (Fiorella, Vogel-Walcutt, & Fiore, 2012). Metacognitive prompting was described as an external stimulus that serves to activate reflection or strategy with the goal of enhancing learning. Finally, Hochmitz and Yuviler-Gavish (2011) compared SBT high on physical fidelity versus cognitive fidelity (similar to psychological fidelity – the extent to which the cognitive activities encountered in the simulation match those in the real word). They concluded that the two approaches have complementary advantages and should be used in combination to best facilitate training for procedural tasks.

Is Game-Based Training Effective?

As a subset of SBT, game-based training has also generated empirical support in the literature. Orvis, Horn, and Belanich (2009), for example, assessed outcomes such as training satisfaction, ease of using the interface, and training performance within video game-based training, and found that these criteria were influenced by characteristics of the trainees (i.e., prior video-game experience, video-game self-efficacy, and goal orientation). In another study, game-based training was used to facilitate performance relevant to military environments (Morris, Hancock, & Shirkey, 2004). Training was more effective at improving mission performance when it included exposure to a stressful experience, essentially increasing its fidelity, than when it did not. As another important example, Sitzmann (2011) meta-analyzed game-based training relative to a comparison group and found that it was 20 percent more effective for enhancing self-efficacy, 11 percent more for declarative knowledge, 14 percent more for procedural knowledge, and 9 percent more for retention. Additionally, it was particularly effective when the training facilitated active, as opposed to passive, learning, when trainees had unlimited access to the game, and when the game was used in combination with other instructional features rather than independently. In another recent meta-analysis examining the use of serious games in learning contexts (Wouters et al., 2013), results showed further evidence that serious games were more effective for facilitating learning and retention than were more conventional instructional methods. These effects were especially strong when games were supplemented with other instructional methods, when multiple training sessions were incorporated, and when training was conducted in groups.

Features of Simulation-Based Training

In addition to the broader description provided above, simulation-based training has been defined as "a training strategy that uses several aspects of scientific, theory-based training, incorporating information, demonstration, and practice-based methods" (Salas et al. 2006a, p. 36). Simulations provide a platform for the combination of the entire IDPF (Information, Demonstration, Practice, Feedback) framework, features that characterize any effective training program (Salas et al., 2012). SBT is most effective when it is part of such an integrative curriculum (Issenberg et al., 2005; McGaghie et al., 2010). Simulation is only a tool – to be effective, particularly for the training of complex skills, it must be used appropriately (Salas & Burke, 2002). Effective simulations are comprised of core pedagogical features that enable learning to occur, including carefully crafted scenarios that contain trigger events, performance measures that are linked to learning objectives, and feedback that is diagnostic and timely. In addition to these critical features, game-based approaches to SBT also incorporate certain features that are targeted at motivation and the subjective experience of the training program. This section will include a discussion of the core pedagogical features of SBT as well as a subsection describing specific features that contribute to the effectiveness of game-based training. While some of the core pedagogical features were discussed above, in relation to the seven steps of SBT, here they are discussed in further detail. In addition to containing these features, SBT must be embedded within that seven-step process to be optimally effective.

Core pedagogical features

Carefully crafted scenarios   It is important to match training content with a type of presentation that will maximize learning (Bell, Kanar, & Kozlowski, 2008; Mayer & Anderson, 1992). For this reason, SBT is often used to train complex skills or procedures that require significant practice (e.g., teamwork skills, surgical procedures, or flying airplanes). Even within SBT, however, the design of scenarios can make them more or less effective for meeting the goals of the training. In SBT, "scenarios are the curriculum" (Salas et al., 2006b, p. 12), often containing all of the instructional elements typically found in the classroom (Oser et al., 1999a). Therefore, scenarios should be carefully designed and crafted based on the learning objectives to ensure that the requisite competencies are elicited for practice and are appropriately trained (Fanning & Gaba, 2007; Salas et al., 2005, 2006b, p. 12). Broadly, scenario design should focus on the organization and coverage of material, on ensuring that content is complete and presented in a way that optimizes learning, and on anticipating alternative courses of action that trainees might take that could change the course of the simulation (e.g., Alinier, 2011).

More importantly, though, scenarios should be made to contain specific trigger events that are designed to prompt the use of target KSAs, and these events should be embedded within conditions that reflect those that will be encountered in the real world environment (Salas et al., 2002; Salas & Burke, 2002). To accomplish this, scenarios should be grounded in a task or job analysis (i.e., step two of the SBT process) that identifies which tasks need to be performed, the conditions they will be performed under, and the KSAs are necessary to manage these tasks and conditions. As an example, consider the design of a scenario that might be used to enable a medical student to practice diagnosing patients within an emergency room or urgent care setting. Trigger events might involve the patient reporting different symptoms (e.g., pain) or demonstrating different medical conditions (e.g., cardiac arrest), while the surrounding conditions might involve a chaotic environment where multiple patients and doctors are present, and/or where family members are demanding information about the patient while the trainee is in the process of forming the diagnosis. The trigger events would prompt the use of the KSAs that are necessary to diagnose a patient, while the context in which they are embedded would mirror the conditions that will be encountered in the transfer environment, further prompting the use of KSAs that are required to manage those conditions.

The literature has supported the role of scenarios in SBT, largely by demonstrating the importance of practice for facilitating learning and transfer. Issenberg and colleagues (2005), for example, reviewed the literature on SBT within medical education, and identified repetitive practice as a key feature of SBT, suggesting that multiple scenarios should be included, and that scenarios can be utilized more than once. Similarly, the authors of a recent meta-analysis, also within the healthcare domain, concluded that utilizing scenarios that are characterized by a range of difficulty, repetitive practice, and distributed practice, among other things, can be considered "best practices" for enhancing the effectiveness of SBT on the basis of their findings (Cook et al., 2013). More broadly, a wealth of theoretical work has identified scenarios and/or their corresponding trigger events as critical components of effective SBT (e.g., Salas & Burke, 2002; Salas, Wildman, & Piccolo, 2009; Salas et al., 2005, 2006b). For instance, among other conditions, Salas and Burke (2002, p. 119) argue that simulation for training is effective when "carefully crafted scenarios are embedded within the simulation." Importantly, they note that scenarios cannot be created without specific learning objectives in mind if SBT is to be effective.

Performance measures   In order to determine if trained competencies are being learned and applied appropriately, performance measures should be developed and embedded within the practice scenarios (Salas et al., 2006). These metrics allow for the comparison of trainees as well as the provision of timely, informational feedback regarding progression in terms of training benchmarks (Issenberg, 2006). SBT will only be valuable to the extent that it enables target KSAs to be measured and diagnosed (Salas & Burke, 2002; Satish & Streufert, 2002) – without performance measures there is no way of determining whether or not the training was effective. Performance measures can capture both performance processes (the "moment-to-moment actions and behaviors"; Salas & Burke, 2002, p. 119) and performance outcomes – both metrics should be clearly linked to the goals of the training. To obtain the most complete assessment of trainee's abilities, measures should capture both types of performance, and should be included at multiple points throughout SBT, ideally alongside each trigger event that is embedded in the scenarios (Grossman & Salas, 2013; Salas et al., 2009a). For instance, in the emergency room example described above, each trigger event (e.g., the patient reporting pain) could be accompanied by a performance process metric (e.g., did the trainee ask appropriate questions about the pain?), and the appropriateness of the final diagnosis could serve as a performance outcome measure. Performance measures are important not only for assessing the effectiveness of the training upon its completion, but also for diagnosing and providing feedback about trainees' strengths and weaknesses along the way. In line with these ideas, Kraiger (2002) put forth an evaluation framework in which he distinguished between changes in learners, which includes trainees' performance processes, and changes in the organization, which includes trainees' performance outcomes. While both can be important for providing a complete picture of training effectiveness, he argues that the decision about which to focus on should be based on the purpose of the evaluation (e.g., to make organizational decisions; to provide feedback trainees or training designers).

Salas and colleagues (2009a) reviewed the literature and presented a set of best practices for performance measurement within the context of SBT. First, they concluded that *multiple levels of measurement* should be included, meaning that measures should capture multiple dimensions of performance (e.g., behaviors, attitudes), that multiple measures from a variety of sources should be utilized, and that performance should be assessed at multiple levels (e.g., individual, team, organization), if appropriate. Additionally, a plan should be put in place to systematically integrate and interpret the various measures. Like our discussion above, they next argued that measures should *address both processes and outcomes*, such that they capture the processes that contribute to performance, as well as performance outcomes themselves. To make comparisons and evaluations on the basis of these measures, expert models of performance should be utilized. Further, to ease the burden on performance raters, objective, automated measures should be incorporated where possible. Next, the authors suggested that measures should have the capacity to *describe, evaluate, and diagnose performance.* For example, they should be descriptive, comparable, flexible, and diagnostic in the sense that they can provide insight about the causes of performance. Importantly, they noted that observers who are responsible for conducting performance ratings should use specific protocols and should be trained to attain high levels of reliability. Finally, they concluded that measures should provide a basis for remediation, meaning that they have the ability to generate corrective feedback, both in real time and after simulations, and essentially that they support the learning process. These best practices were derived from a review of both theoretical and empirical research, making them a valuable source of information pertaining to performance measurement within SBT contexts.

Feedback   Feedback has been defined as "actions taken by [an] external agent[s] to provide information regarding some aspect[s] of one's task performance" (Kluger & DeNisi, 1996, p. 255) or more specific to training, as "information on performance provided to the learner by the instructor, a peer, or a computer, either during or after the simulation activity" (Cook et al., 2013, p. 868). Feedback is integral to effective SBT (Cook et al., 2013; McGaghie et al., 2010) – it provides trainees with the information and guidance necessary to ensure acquisition of the correct competencies and, as described earlier, can include corrective procedures during the simulation, as well as after-action reviews and debriefs following the simulation (Gaba et al., 2001; Salas, Wildman, & Piccolo, 2009). Feedback can be developmental, remedial, or can be an indicator of progress within the simulation (Issenberg, 2006), serving as a tool for trainees to learn from previous actions and adjust accordingly (Chen & Michael, 2005). To increase its effectiveness, feedback should be task-focused as opposed to person-focused (Kluger & DeNisi, 1996) and should be administered as close to the performance of the task as possible (Salas et al., 2008). When debriefs and after-action reviews – specific types of feedback – are utilized, they should be conducted by individuals who are familiar with the process and should provide opportunities for the trainees to respond to the feedback and provide input of their own (Salas et al., 2008). Additionally, they: should be diagnostic of strengths and weaknesses, providing strategies for improvement; should occur within a comfortable, supportive environment; should be limited in scope, focusing on only a few performance issues; should integrate objective feedback information as well as process-focused feedback; and should be recorded for future reference.

While feedback is an important component of any training (Salas et al., 2012), research has also demonstrated its value in contexts specific to SBT. Cook and colleagues (2013), for example, conducted a meta-analysis on SBT and identified feedback as a key instructional design feature that contributes to training effectiveness. Similarly, feedback was identified as one of 12 features and best practices in a qualitative review of SBT research within the realm of medical education (McGaghie et al., 2010). In another, very specific, meta-analysis, training that incorporated feedback was found to be more effective for training a certain medical procedure than training that didn't incorporate feedback (Johnson et al., 2013). Interestingly, other meta-analytic work found evidence that feedback provided at the end of a simulation may be more effective than that provided concurrently for novice learners (Hatala et al., 2013). The authors suggested that novices may rely too heavily on feedback when it is provided concurrently, leading to a decline in performance once such feedback is taken away. Related to this, feedback does not necessarily need to be provided by an instructor or external source in order for it to be effective. Boet and colleagues (2013), for example, found that teams who underwent SBT showed no significant differences in their training outcomes when debriefings were conducted within the team, versus when they were carried out by an outside instructor. In addition to such empirical findings, theoretical work has also supported the importance of feedback in SBT (e.g., Salas & Burke, 2002; Salas, Wildman, & Piccolo, 2009; Salas et al., 2005, 2006b).

Features specific to game-based training

In addition to the core pedagogical features described above (also see Figure 12.1), SBT that takes place within the context of serious games can also include additional features that serve to engage and motivate the learner, and ultimately to enhance learning outcomes (Wilson et al., 2009). Specifically, within the realm of gaming and video games, researchers focus on constructs like flow, play, and other feelings of subjective enjoyment and engagement (Anderson, 1998; Chen, 2007; Csikszentmihalyi, 1990; Pavlas et al., 2012). Game-based training takes a hybrid design approach, integrating the features of video games that contribute to the subjective experience with the pedagogical features of simulations that emphasize learning. The utility of various features of video games in regards to learning have been thoroughly reviewed (cf. Bedwell et al., 2012; Wilson et al., 2009) and include features like conflict, challenge, control, and mystery. Below, we provide a brief description of some of the primary features that characterize serious games and have been linked to learning outcomes. Interestingly, Sitzmann (2011) coded for some of these features in her meta-analysis on game-based training by considering games with the presence of at least one feature to have "high entertainment value," and those with the absence of any of these features to have "low entertainment value," and did not find an impact of entertainment value on learning. However, the impact of these features may lie more in their ability to enhance trainee's engagement and motivation rather than to enhance learning directly. Indeed, Sitzmann (2011) found that game-based training was more effective when it incorporated other instructional features than when it was used independently, suggesting that the features specific to game-based training themselves are not sufficient for enhancing learning. However, she also found that it was more effective when material was conveyed actively and when trainees were given unlimited access to the game – the features of game-based training can facilitate active learning and can motivate trainees to continue using the game beyond what is required, suggesting that they can ultimately play an important, though less direct role in the learning process.

Conflict/challenge   *Conflict* is the main driver of the plot and action within a game and consists of the "presentation of solvable problems" (Bedwell et al., 2012, p. 732; Crawford, 1984). Problems can vary in the amount of *challenge* present (i.e., "the amount of difficulty and improbability of obtaining goals"; Bedwell et al., 2012, p. 732; Garris, Ahlers, & Driskell, 2002; Owen, 2004). For a game to be challenging, it should incorporate multiple, clearly established goals, a progression of difficulty, and a degree of ambiguity in the information that is presented. Each player possesses different levels of skills and expertise, so the level of difficulty should be *adaptive* and matched to the current player (Bedwell et al., 2012; Prensky, 2001). For example, obstacles of differing levels of difficulty might be presented on the basis of a player's performance rather than on standardized increments.

Game fiction   Game fiction represents the aggregation of two features of video games that can impact the intrinsic motivation of players to engage with a game, as well as learning – fantasy and mystery. Fantasy encourages the player to take on and identify with various fictional roles, and utilizes a "make-believe environment, scenarios, or characters" to engage the imagination and mental imagery of the player for "unusual locations, social situations, and analogies for real-world processes" (Bedwell et al., 2012, p. 732; Garris, Ahlers, & Driskell, 2002; Habgood, Ainsworth, & Benford, 2005; Owen, 2004). Fantasy can be exogenous or endogenous. Exogenous fantasy is a disconnected, direct overlay of game content on learning content, meaning that the skill is necessary for the fantasy, but the fantasy is not necessary for the skill. In contrast, endogenous fantasy is highly connected – there is a critical relationship between the skill being learned and the fantasy context (Bedwell et al., 2012).

Mystery occurs when there is a gap between a player's existing knowledge and knowledge that is unknown (Bedwell et al., 2012). The gap can result from such things as complexity, novelty, surprise, incomplete or inconsistent information, and the violation of expectations. Mystery can invoke a sense of curiosity in the player, causing him/her to be more engaged and motivated throughout the learning process.

Control   Control is defined as "the player's capacity for power or influence over elements of the game" and occurs when the learner has control over some aspects of the game (Bedwell et al., 2012, p. 732; Garris, Ahlers, & Driskell, 2002). Control can be focused directly on the game by interacting with various pieces, representations, equipment, and resources within the game, but can also be thought of as the adaptability and manipulability of a game or the way the game changes in response to the actions of players (Prensky, 2001). Control has the potential to increase intrinsic motivation within players, but

---

Simulation-based training

Design

- **Carefully crafted scenarios** – simulation scenarios should be designed to contain trigger events that prompt the use of target KSAs, and to reflect the contextual characteristics of the real work environment

- **Performance measures** – simulations should be embedded with various performance metrics, particularly in combination with trigger events

- **Feedback** – specific, diagnostic feedback regarding trainees' simulation performance should be incorporated both during and after simulations

Game-based training

- **Conflict/challenge** – the presentation of solvable problems; the amount of difficulty and implausibility associated with obtaining a goal

- **Game fiction** – fantasy (interaction with fictional roles, environments, scenarios, or characters) and mystery (a gap between existing and unknown knowledge)

- **Control** – the degree of power or influence over elements of the game

- **Rules/goals** – clearly stated guidelines that establish the criteria for how a player can win the game

Delivery

- **Role-playing exercises** – trainees act out a certain role, often interacting with other trainees or actors who are also playing a role; often low in physical fidelity

- **Part-task trainers** – the simulation of a specific subset of a desired task or skill

- **Full-motion simulators** – high-tech simulations that mimic the task components and surrounding context of the real world very closely; high fidelity

- **Serious games** – games that are embedded with specific features that make them highly engaging and motivating, and are used for training purposes

---

Figure 12.1   Summary of information about simulation-based approaches to training.

designers need to be careful that the level of control afforded to the player matches their skill and self-efficacy in controlling the game as well as ensuring that the game can be adaptive and respond to various courses of action.

Rules/goals Within a game, rules serve as a foundation for goals and establish the criteria for how a player can win (Bedwell et al., 2012; Blunt, 2007; Garris, Ahlers, & Driskell, 2002; Owen, 2004). Rules and guidelines that are specific and clearly stated are "necessary component[s] for an effective educational game" (Bedwell et al., 2012, p. 733). Three types of rules have been identified: system rules, procedural rules, and imported rules (Bedwell et al., 2012). Systems rules pertain to the functional parameters that are inherent to the game, procedural rules relate to the actions that can be taken within the game to regulate behavior and progress, and imported rules refer to rules that exist in the real world. Consistent with the pedagogical features of SBT, feedback on the player's progression toward following the guidelines and meeting the established goals is necessary for facilitating learning.

Delivery Methods

A variety of delivery methods for SBT exist, including role-playing exercises, part task trainers, full-motion simulators, and, as highlighted throughout this chapter, serious games (Kozlowski & Bell, 2007; Ziv et al., 2003). The decision to utilize a specific delivery method will be informed by the extent to which the method matches the needs of the training, the availability of resources, and the characteristics of the trainees. Here, we provide a brief description of the types of delivery methods that can be utilized.

Role-playing exercises

Role-playing exercises can take place using other trainees or trained actors (e.g., standardized patients in medical simulation) to play the role of a character or individual that is part of the simulated scenario (Salas, Wildman, & Piccolo, 2009). In this approach, trainees learn, practice, and develop skills by interacting with someone who is playing the role of whatever type of individual the trainee is learning to work with, or by playing a role themselves, without necessarily interacting with others. Some examples of interactive role-play include educators role-playing different types of problem students that they will need to interact with, and individuals acting as standardized patients exhibiting symptoms that need to be diagnosed. A trainee acting as a business executive delivering a briefing is an example of role-playing that might not involve interaction with other individuals. These types of exercises are often high in psychological fidelity, and perhaps functional fidelity, but lower in physical fidelity (Dietz et al., 2013).

Part-task trainers

A part-task trainer is a valuable delivery method of SBT that simulates a specific subset of a desired skill (e.g., Cooper & Taqueti, 2008), such as making one surgical incision or building one component of a vehicle. Part task trainers are typically embedded into a larger program of instruction, but can also be utilized after training as practice and for sustaining skill proficiency. Part task trainers, while not as complete as full simulators, are valuable for capturing the portions of a task that require significant practice and placing them within a simulated context. They are typically useful for motor skills that need to be integrated into a larger skill set, and can be a good option in situations where time and other resources are limited.

Full-motion simulators

Full-motion simulators represent the most expensive delivery method, but also the most complete. This delivery method involves mirroring the components of both the task and the surrounding context of the real world environment as closely as possible, creating high degrees of physical, functional, and psychological fidelity (Coultas, Grossman, & Salas, 2012). For example, full-motion simulators used to simulate flying an aircraft would involve a cockpit that has the same appearance and controls as a real cockpit, and that is designed to mimic the physical experience of taking off, being in flight, and landing. These types of simulations avoid the shortcuts taken in other delivery methods (e.g., reduction in some type of fidelity, simplification of learning objectives) but can involve a significant financial commitment in terms of initial development and acquisition costs, as well as maintenance and upkeep to keep the training content up to date. While they can be highly effective, they are not always necessary, particularly if the goals of the training do not require such high fidelity (Coultas, Grossman, & Salas, 2012).

Serious games

As mentioned previously, game-based approaches to SBT, often delivered through computers, focus on the motivational aspects of learning and the subjective experience (Bedwell et al., 2012). Such delivery methods are useful in contexts where some sort of gradual change is desired, a basic skill or set of information is being conveyed, or the designers are trying to prevent the trainees from remaining focused on the fact that they are taking part in training. A potential weakness of game-based simulations is the extent to which the scenarios are able to be played multiple times and still be enjoyable and convey novel information. However, if they are designed to include features that contribute to motivation and learning (e.g., conflict/challenge; Bedwell et al., 2012), they can be a highly valuable delivery method, particularly because they represent a logistic benefit in terms of cost, ease of deployment, and maintenance.

Future Research

As indicated throughout this chapter, much is known about how to utilize simulation-based approaches to training effectively. There is a clear, systematic process that can be followed (i.e., the seven steps; Salas, Wildman, & Piccolo, 2009; Salas et al. 2005, 2006b), and a theoretically and empirically grounded set of features that can be incorporated into SBT to maximize its effectiveness. However, some gaps in knowledge do exist, as well as some unexplored research avenues that should be considered in future efforts. Much of the empirical work on SBT, for example, has come out of the healthcare domain or other settings that can be characterized as high-stakes and/or high-stress (e.g., military, aviation). While SBT has traditionally been utilized in these types of settings because of its ability to provide trainees with experience within relatively risk-free environments, recent work suggests that such experience is becoming necessary even in more typical work settings due to the increasing complexity of the modern workplace (e.g., Grossman, Spencer, & Salas, 2013). Specifically, factors such as globalization and advances in technology are placing increasing demands on everyday workers that require training and expertise in order to manage them, making SBT more and more applicable. While SBT has been used to a degree in management education, and there has been theoretical work aimed to improve its effectiveness in this domain (Salas, Wildman, & Piccolo, 2009), the extent to which the vast majority of SBT findings can be applied to more typical work settings is not currently clear. Thus, research is needed to empirically explore the effectiveness of SBT as a whole, and of its various instructional features within a variety of contexts, particularly those outside of healthcare and other high-stakes settings (e.g., military).

Other gaps in knowledge pertain to the logistics of designing and delivering SBT appropriately. For example, the type and degree of fidelity that is incorporated into a simulation is an important decision that can greatly influence the ability of the training to produce changes in learning and transfer. While there are strong theoretical and practical reasons for selecting the type of fidelity (e.g., the type and amount of fidelity should match the KSA that is being targeted in training; certain types of fidelity require less resources than others), empirical work that specifically compares different fidelities is limited. Specifically, research in which the same KSAs are trained using varying types and degrees of fidelity would help inform knowledge about the specific kinds of simulations that can be used to maximize effectiveness when being used to train different types of KSAs. Additionally, research is needed to gain insight about how the effects of SBT can be sustained over time. Much of the work on SBT has examined its impact on learning outcomes, within the context of the training. To be of significant value, however, such learning needs to be transferred to the real world. While SBT arguably is a primary approach for enhancing transfer due to its ability to closely mirror aspects of the work environment within training (Grossman & Salas, 2011), studies that empirically examine its impact on transfer outcomes are limited in comparison to those examining learning. Thus, research is needed not only to expand on our knowledge of the impact of SBT on the transfer of training, but also to determine if multiple simulations are necessary to facilitate transfer, and if so, how many, how often, and over how long.

Related to these issues is the need for research focusing on the use of simulations for promoting continuous learning within the workplace. As noted above, modern workers are facing increasing demands that are requiring them to continually maintain and expand their repertoires of KSAs in order to perform their jobs effectively. Research is therefore needed to explore potential mechanisms through which these KSAs can be acquired beyond traditional approaches to training. We highlighted game-based training, a particular type of SBT, throughout this chapter because we believe it may be a particularly valuable approach to facilitating such continuous learning. Because serious games can be designed to be highly engaging and motivating (Bedwell et al., 2012), they may be able to serve as enjoyable yet effective ways for trainees to maintain and update their KSAs once the formal training period is over. For example, trainees might be permitted to devote a portion of their work time to playing serious games that have been designed to reinforce learning material and allow for additional opportunities for trainees to practice new competencies. Additionally, feedback can be provided within the game, and followed up by more diagnostic, supervisor feedback so that trainees can be aware of their performance levels and can engage in self-correction when necessary. Such games can even be designed so that multiple workers can play together, enabling trainees to simulate interactive processes such as engaging in teamwork or conducting and delivering performance appraisals to subordinates. Although these ideas are grounded in current knowledge of how SBT functions, at this point they are just that – ideas. Thus, we suggest that future research begins to explore the use of game-based SBT for facilitating continuous learning and practice in the workplace. With this exploration will come a variety of additional questions regarding such things as when and how often such games should be played to optimize effectiveness, who (i.e., what types of trainees) stands to benefit from them the most, what types of KSAs they are best for targeting, and how they can be made to remain engaging and motivating over time. As a final thought, although the broader training literature has provided support for the various steps involved in the training process (e.g., Salas et al., 2012), little if any work has empirically examined them as a whole, particularly in relation to SBT specifically. Future research examining whether SBT is more effective when it is systematic (i.e., utilizes the seven steps) versus when it isn't, or when it only incorporates some of the steps, can provide further support for the importance of the steps and can help illuminate which steps are most critical.

Conclusion

SBT is an increasingly prevalent approach to training, largely due to its ability to develop KSAs that are particularly difficult and/or complex (Salas, Wildman, & Piccolo, 2009; Grossman, Spencer, & Salas, 2013). However, as its name implies, simulations serve as the *basis* for training, not the entire training itself. To be effective, simulations must be embedded within systematic procedures, and must incorporate specific instructional features that are grounded in the science of training. The purpose of this chapter was thus to provide insight into some of this science (a summary of the information we discussed can be found in Figure 12.1). We provided an overview of what SBT is, what we know about it, and the design and delivery approaches that are used to maximize its effectiveness. Additionally, we highlighted a specific type of SBT – game-based training – not only because it is growing in popularity, but also because it may be a particularly powerful approach to promoting continuous learning, something that is increasingly necessary in today's workplace. Finally, we concluded by identifying some avenues for future research efforts, overall, hoping to provide a useful snapshot of the current and future SBT literature.

References

Aldrich, C. (2007). Engaging mini-games find niche in training. *T+D*, 61(7), 22–24.

Alinier, G. (2011). Developing high-fidelity health care simulation scenarios: A guide for educators and professionals. *Simulation & Gaming*, 42(1), 9–26.

Anderson, M. (1998). The meaning of play as a human experience. In D. P. Fromberg & D. Bergen (Eds.), *Play from Birth to Twelve and Beyond: Contexts* (pp. 103–108). New York: Harvard University Press.

Bedwell, W. L., Pavlas, D., Heyne, K., Lazzara, E. H., & Salas, E. (2012). Toward a taxonomy linking game attributes to learning an empirical study. *Simulation & Gaming*, 43(6), 729–760.

Bell, B. S., Kanar, A. M., & Kozlowski, S. W. (2008). Current issues and future directions in simulation-based training in North America. *International Journal of Human Resource Management*, 19(8), 1416–1434.

Bell, B. S., & Kozlowski, S. J. (2008). Active learning: Effects of core training design elements on self-regulatory processes, learning, and adaptability. *Journal of Applied Psychology*, 93(2), 296–316.

Blunt, R. (2007). Does game-based learning work? Results from three recent studies. *Proceedings of the Interservice/Industry Training, Simulation, & Education Conference* (pp. 945–955). Orlando, FL: NDIA.

Boet, S., Bould, M. D., Sharma, B., Revees, S., Naik, V. N., Triby, E., & Grantcharov, T. (2013). Within team debriefing versus instructor-led debriefing for simulation-based education: A randomized controlled trial. *Annals of Surgery*, 258(1), 53–58.

Bowers, C. A., & Jentsch, F. (2001). Use of commercial, off-the-shelf, simulations for team research. In E. Salas (Ed.), *Advances in Human Performance and Cognitive Engineering Research* (vol. 1, pp. 293–317). Amsterdam: Elsevier Science.

Bruppacher, H. R., Alam, S. K., LeBlanc, V. R., Latter, D., Naik, V. N., Savoldelli, G. L., Mazer, D. C., Kurrek, M. M., & Joo, H. S. (2010). Simulation-based training improves physicians' performance in patient care in high-stakes clinical setting of cardiac surgery. *Anesthesiology*, 112(4), 985–992.

Chen, J. (2007). Flow in games (and everything else). *Communications of the ACM* , 50(4), 31–33.

Chen, S., & Michael, D. (2005). Proof of learning: Assessment in serious games. Gamasutra, October 19. http://www.gamasutra.com/features/20051019/chen_01.shtml (accessed March 26, 2014).

Cook, D. A., Hamstra, S. J., Brydges, R., Zendejas, B., Szostek, J. H., Wang, A. T., Erwin, P. J., & Hatala, R. (2013). Comparative effectiveness of instructional design features in simulation-based education: Systematic review and meta-analysis. *Medical Teacher*, 35(1), e867–e898.

Cooper, J. B., & Taqueti, V. R. (2008). A brief history of the development of mannequin simulators for clinical education and training. *Postgraduate Medical Journal*, 84(997), 563–570.

Coultas, C. W., Grossman, R., & Salas, E. (2012). Design, delivery, evaluation, and transfer of training systems. In G. Salvendy (Ed.), *Handbook of Human Factors and Ergonomics* (4th ed., pp. 490–533). Hoboken, NJ: John Wiley & Sons, Inc.

Crawford, C. (1984). *The Art of Computer Design*. Berkeley, CA: Osborne/McGraw-Hill.

Csikszentmihalyi, M. (1990). *Flow: The Psychology of Optimal Experience*. New York: Harper & Row.

DiBello, L., Missildine, W., & Struttman, M. (2009). Intuitive expertise and empowerment: The long-term impact of simulation training on changing accountabilities in a biotech firm. *Mind, Culture, and Activity*, 16, 11–31.

Dietz, A. S., Bedwell, W. L., Oglesby, J. M., Salas, E., & Keeton, K. E. (2013). Synthetic task environments for improving performance at work: Principles and the road ahead. In J. M. Cortina and R. S. Landis (Eds.), *Modern Research Methods for the Study of Behavior in Organizations*. New York: Routledge.

Elliot, L. R., Dalrymple, M. A., Schiflett, S. G., & Miller, J. C. (2004). Scaling scenarios: Development and application to C4ISR sustained operations research. In S. G. Schiflett, L. R. Elliot, E. Salas, & M. D. Coovert (Eds.), *Scaled Worlds: Development, Validation, and Applications* (pp. 119–133). Burlington, VT: Ashgate.

Fanning, R. M., & Gaba, D. M. (2007). The role of debriefing in simulation-based learning. *Simulation in Healthcare*, 2(2), 115–125.

Fiorella, L., Vogel-Walcutt, J. J., & Fiore, S. (2012). Differential impact of two types of metacognitive prompting provided during simulation-based training. *Computers in Human Behavior*, 28(2), 696–702.

Fiorella, L., Vogel-Walcutt, J. J., & Schatz, S. (2012). Applying the modality principle to real-time feedback and the acquisition of higher-order cognitive skills. *Educational Technology Research and Development*, 60(2), 223–238.

Freeman, J. T., & Cohen, M. S. (1996) Training for complex decision-making: A test of instruction based on the Recognition/Metacognition Model. *Proceedings of the 1996 Command and Control Research and Technology Symposium*. Monterey: Naval Postgraduate School.

Gaba, D. M., Howard, S. K., Fish, K. J., Smith, B. E., & Sowb, Y. A. (2001). Simulation-based training in anesthesia crisis resource management (ACRM): A decade of experience. *Simulation & Gaming*, 32(2), 175–193.

Galvao, J. R., Martins, P. G., & Gomes, M. R. (2000). Modeling reality with simulation games for cooperative learning. *Proceedings of the 32nd Conference on Winter Simulation* (pp. 1692–1698). Society for Computer Simulation International, December.

Garris, R., Ahlers, R., & Driskell, J. E. (2002). Games, motivation and learning: A research and practice model. *Simulation & Gaming: An Interdisciplinary Journal*, 33, 441–467.

Goldstein, L. L. (1991). Training in work organizations. In M. D. Dunnette & L. M. Hough (Eds.), *Handbook of Industrial Organizational Psychology* (vol. 2, pp. 507–620). Palo Alto, CA: Consulting Psychologists Press.

Gordon, J. A., Wilkerson, W. M., Shaffer, D. W., & Armstrong, E. G. (2001). Practicing medicine without risk: Students' and educators' responses to high-fidelity patient simulation. *Academic Medicine*, 76, 469–472.

Grossman, R., & Salas E. (2011). The transfer of training: What really matters. *International Journal of Training and Development*, 15(2), 103–120.

Grossman, R., & Salas, E. (2013). Instructional features for training military teams in virtual environments. In C. Best, G. Galanis, J. Kerry, & R. Sottilare (Eds.), *Fundamental Issues in Defence Training and Simulation*. Burlington, VT: Ashgate.

Grossman, R., Spencer, J. M., & Salas, E. (2013). Enhancing naturalistic decision-making and accelerating expertise at work: Training strategies that work. In S. Highhouse, R. Dalal, & E. Salas (Eds.), *The Organizational Frontiers Series: Judgment and Decision Making at Work*. New York: Routledge.

Habgood, M. P. J., Ainsworth, S. E., & Benford, S. (2005). Endogenous fantasy and learning in digital games. *Simulation & Gaming: An Interdisciplinary Journal*, 36, 483–498.

Hatala, R., Cook, D. A., Zendejas, B., Hamstra, S. J., & Brydges, R. (2013). Feedback for simulation based procedural skills training: A meta-analysis and critical narrative synthesis. *Advances in Health Sciences Education*, 19(1), 251–277. doi:10.1007/s10459-013-9462-8.

Hochmitz, I., & Yuviler-Gavish, N. (2011). Physical fidelity versus cognitive fidelity training in procedural skills acquisition. *Human Factors: The Journal of the Human Factors and Ergonomics Society*, 53(5), 489–501.

Issenberg, S. B. (2006). The scope of simulation-based healthcare education. *Simulation in Healthcare*, 1(4), 203–208.

Issenberg, S. B., McGaghie, W. C., Petrusa, E. R., Gordon, D. L., & Scalese, R. J. (2005). Features and uses of high-fidelity medical simulations that lead to effective learning: A BEME systematic review. *Medical Teacher*, 27(1), 10–28.

Jana, R. (2006). On-the-job video gaming. *Business Week*, 3977 (March 27), 43.

Jentsch, F., & Bowers, C. (1998). Evidence for the validity of PC-based simulations in studying aircrew coordination. *International Journal of Aviation Psychology*, 8(3), 243–260.

Johnson, R. L., Cannon, E. K., Mantilla, C. B., & Cook, D. A. (2013). Cricoid pressure training using simulation: A systematic review and meta-analysis. *British Journal of Anaesthesia*, 111(3), 338–346.

Klein, C., Stagl, K. C., Salas, E., Parker, C., & Van Eynde, D. F. (2007). Returning to flight: Simulation-based training for the US National Aeronautics and Space Administration's Space Shuttle Mission Management Team. *International Journal of Training and Development*, 11(2), 132–138.

Kluger, A. N., & DeNisi, A. (1996). The effects of feedback interventions on performance: A historical review, a meta-analysis, and a preliminary feedback intervention theory. *Psychological Bulletin*, 119(2), 254–284.

Kozlowski, S. W., & Bell, B. S. (2007). A theory-based approach for designing distributed learning systems. In S. M. Fiore & E. Salas (Eds.), *Toward a Science of Distributed Learning* (pp. 15–39). Washington, DC: APA.

Kozlowski, S. W. J., & DeShon, R. P. (2004). A psychological fidelity approach to simulation-based training: Theory, research, and principles. In E. Salas, L. R. Elliott, S. G. Schflett, & M. D. Coovert (Eds.), *Scaled Worlds: Development, Validation, and Applications* (pp. 75–99). Burlington, VT: Ashgate.

Kraiger K. (2002). Decision-based evaluation. In K. Kraiger (Ed.), *Creating, Implementing, and Maintaining Effective Training and Development: State-of-the-Art Lessons for Practice* (pp. 331–375). San Francisco, CA: Jossey-Bass.

Kraiger, K., Ford, J. K., & Salas, E. (1993). Application of cognitive, skill-based, and affective theories of learning outcomes to new methods of training evaluation. *Journal of Applied Psychology*, 78(2), 311.

Martin, E., Lyon, D. R., & Schreiber, B. T. (1998). Designing synthetic tasks for human factors research. An application to uninhabited air vehicles. In *Human Factors and Ergonomics Society 42nd Annual Meeting*. Santa Monica, CA: Human Factors and Ergonomics Society.

Mayer, R. E., & Anderson, R. B. (1992). The instructive animation: Helping students build connections between words and pictures in multimedia learning. *Journal of Educational Psychology*, 84, 444–452.

McGaghie, W. C., Issenberg, S. B., Petrusa, E. R., & Scalese, R. J. (2010). A critical review of simulation-based medical education research: 2003–2009. *Medical Education*, 44(1), 50–63.

Morris, C. S., Hancock, P. A., & Shirkey, E. C. (2004). Motivational effects of adding context relevant stress in PC-based game training. *Military Psychology*, 16(2), 135–147.

Murthy, N. N., Challagalla, G. N., Vincent, L. H., & Shervani, T. A. (2008). The impact of simulation training on call center agent performance: A field-based investigation. *Management Science*, 54(2), 384–399.

Orvis, K. A., Horn, D. B., & Belanich, J. (2009). An examination of the role individual differences play in videogame-based training. *Military Psychology*, 21(4), 461–481.

Oser, R. L., Cannon-Bowers, J. A., Salas, E., & Dwyer, D. J. (1999a). Enhancing human performance in technology-rich environments: Guidelines for scenario-based training. *Human Technology Interaction in Complex Systems*, 9, 175–202.

Oser, R. L., Gualtieri, J. W., Cannon-Bower, J. A., & Salas, E. (1999b). Training team problem solving skills: An event-based approach. *Computers in Human Behavior*, 15, 441–462.

Owen, M. (2004). *An Anatomy of Games: A Discussion Paper*. Bristol: Futurelab.

Pavlas, D., Jentsch, F., Salas, E., Fiore, S. M., & Sims, V. (2012). The play experience scale development and validation of a measure of play. *Human Factors: The Journal of the Human Factors and Ergonomics Society*, 54(2), 214–225.

Prensky, M. (2001). *Digital Game-Based Learning*. New York: McGraw-Hill.

Resick, C. J., Murase, T., Bedwell, W. L., Sanz, E., Jimenez, M., & DeChurch, L. A. (2010). Mental model metrics and team adaptability: A multi-method examination. *Group Dynamics: Theory, Research, and Practice*, 14(4), 332–349.

Rosen, M. A., Weaver, S. J., Lazzara, E. H., Salas, E., Wu, T., Silvestri, S., Schiebel, N., Almeida, S., & King, H. B. (2010). Tools for evaluating team performance in simulation-based training. *Journal of Emergencies, Trauma, and Shock*, 3, 353–359.

Salas, E., & Burke, C. S. (2002). Simulation for training is effective when … *Quality and Safety in Healthcare Journal*, 11, 119–120.

Salas, E., Klein, C., King, H., Salisbury, M., Augenstein, J. S., Birnbach, D. J., & Upshaw, C. (2008). Debriefing medical teams: 12 evidence-based best practices and tips. *Joint Commission Journal on Quality and Patient Safety*, 34(9), 518–527.

Salas, E., Oser, R. L., Cannon-Bowers, J. A., & Daskarolis-Kring, E. (2002). Team training in virtual environments: An event-based approach. In K. M. Stanney (Ed.), *Handbook of Virtual Environments: Design, Implementation, and Applications* (pp. 873–892). Mahwah, NJ: Erlbaum.

Salas, E., Priest, H. A., Wilson, K. A., & Burke, C. S. (2006a). Scenario-based training: Improving military mission performance and adaptability. In A. B. Adler, C. A. Castro, & T. W. Britt (Eds.), *Minds in the Military: The Psychology of Serving in Peace and Conflict*, vol. 2, *Operational Stress* (pp. 32–53). Westport, CT: Praeger Security International.

Salas, E., Rosen, M. A., Held, J. D., & Weissmuller, J. J. (2009a). Performance measurement in simulation-based training a review and best practices. *Simulation & Gaming*, 40(3), 328–376.

Salas, E., Tannenbaum, S. I., Kraiger, K., & Smith-Jentsch, K. A. (2012). The science of training and development in organizations: What matters in practice. *Psychological Science in the Public Interest*, 13(2), 74–101.

Salas, E., Wildman, J. L., & Piccolo, R. F. (2009b). Using simulation-based training to enhance management education. *Academy of Management Learning and Education*, 8(4), 559–573.

Salas, E., Wilson, K. A., Burke, C. S., & Priest, H. A. (2005). Using simulation-based training to improve patient safety: What does it take? *Joint Commission Journal on Quality and Patient Safety*, 31(7), 363–371.

Salas, E., Wilson, K. A., Burke, C. S., & Priest, H. A. (2006b). What is simulation-based training? *Forum*, 24, 12.

Satish, U., & Streufert, S. (2002). Value of a cognitive simulation in medicine: Towards optimizing decision making performance of healthcare personnel. *Quality and Safety in Healthcare*, 11, 163–167.

SimCity 4: Deluxe Edition. (2004). Emeryville, CA: EA Games.

Sitzmann, T. (2011). A meta-analytic examination of the instructional effectiveness of computer-based simulation games. *Personnel Psychology*, 64(2), 489–528.

Slotte, V., & Herbert, A. (2008). Engaging workers in simulation-based e-learning. *Journal of Workplace Learning*, 20(3), 165–180.

Steadman, R. H., Coates, W. C., Huang, Y. M., Matevosian, R., Larmon, B. R., McCullough, L., & Ariel, D. (2006). Simulation-based training is superior to problem-based learning for the acquisition of critical assessment and management skills. *Critical Care Medicine*, 34(1), 151–157.

Wayne, D. B., Butter, J., Siddall, V. J., Fudala, M. J., Linquist, L. A., Feinglass, J., Wade, L. D., & McGaghie, W. C. (2005). Simulation-based training of internal medicine residents in advanced cardiac life support protocols: A randomized trial. *Teaching and Learning in Medicine*, 17(3), 202–208.

Wilson, K. A., Bedwell, W. L., Lazzara, E. H., Salas, E., Burke, C. S., Estock, J. L., Orvis, K. L., & Conkey, C. (2009). Relationships between game attributes and learning outcomes review and research proposals. *Simulation & Gaming*, 40(2), 217–266.

Wouters, P., van Nimwegan, C., van Oostendorp, H., & van der Spek, E. D. (2013). A meta-analysis of the cognitive and motivational effects of serious games. *Journal of Educational Psychology*, 105(2), 249–265.

Ziv, A., Wolpe, P. R., Small, S. D., & Glick, S. (2003). Simulation-based medical education: An ethical imperative. *Academic Medicine*, 78(8), 783–788.

Section III

Personal and Professional Development in Organizations

13

Training and Personal Development

Kurt Kraiger and Thomas M. Cavanagh

Introduction

Training and development refer to systematic processes, managed by organizations, that results in a relatively permanent change in the knowledge, skills, or attitudes of its members. In this chapter, we summarize recent evidence of the strategic importance and effectiveness of training, and then identify both established and emerging best practices in training. Eight separate meta-analyses are reviewed. These support the contention that well-designed training works. In terms of established best practices, the classic instructional systems design model still drives needs assessment and training evaluation, although new models emphasize the role of strategic decision-making, promoting transfer, and consideration of special populations. The chapter notes that best practices in maximizing learning outcomes include the promotion of active learning through training techniques that encourage errors, prompting self-regulation, and technology-delivered instruction.

Training as an Investment

The shift towards a global economy made up of lean and efficient organizations has emphasized the central importance of training and development. Both continuous learning and ongoing skill development have become a way of life in organizations of today. Training and development activities allow organizations to be more competitive, to be more efficient and productive, and to adapt and be more innovative. Thus, organizations invest considerable resources into training and development. In the US alone, organizations spent about $171 billion on training and development in 2010, an increase of over 14 percent over the prior year (Green & McGill, 2011). Data available for the European Union shows that while total expenditures on training stayed relatively constant between 2005 and 2010, both worker participation in training and total hours spent in training

The Wiley Blackwell Handbook of the Psychology of Training, Development, and Performance Improvement,
First Edition. Edited by Kurt Kraiger, Jonathan Passmore, Sigmar Malvezzi, and Nuno Rebelo dos Santos.
© 2015 John Wiley & Sons Ltd. Published 2020 by John Wiley & Sons Ltd.

increased over that time – despite worsening economic conditions (European Centre for the Development of Vocational Training, 2010). Organizations invest in training because a skilled workforce is seen as a competitive advantage.

A valuable perspective on the competitive advantage of an organization's human capital is offered by Boudreau and Ramstad (2005). These authors argued that success in three domains leads to a competitive advantage in the marketplace: finance, products or markets, and human capital. Over the past 10 years, economic change and the opening of a global marketplace has reduced differences between organizations in their access to financial capital. Additionally, nearly all organizations can sell to the same global market, with products that are increasingly similar between vendors. Accordingly, the third domain – a skilled and flexible workforce – represents the most sustainable competitive advantage to most organizations (Huselid & Becker, 2011).

In support of this, multiple studies in strategic human resource management have demonstrated direct relationships between investments in human resources and organizational effectiveness. For example, Delaney and Huselid (1996) reported that effective staffing and training practices by organizations were positively correlated with perceived organizational performance. In a study of over 1000 companies, Huselid (1995) found that high performance work practices (which include effective recruitment and selection, compensation systems, and training) were related to both employee retention and individual performance, as well as to corporate financial performance.

A meta-analysis by Arthur et al. (2003) reviewed evidence of the impact of training programs on organizational-level results. Here, the effect size d represents the standardized difference between trained and untrained employees on the criterion of interest. Across 26 studies, the mean d for organizational results criteria was .62 ($N=1748$), indicating that a strong positive effect for training on organizational outcomes (e.g., reduced costs, improved quality and quantity of production). Similarly, in a meta-analysis of managerial training programs, Burke and Day (1986) reported an overall d of .34 for objective learning measures, and .67 objective results criteria. In a meta-analysis of managerial leadership development programs, Collins and Holton (2004) reported an overall mean d of .39, showing a moderately positive effect for such programs.

Salas et al. (2012) more recently summarized the results of eight meta-analyses on training, including the three mentioned above. Their summary also covers meta-analyses of two specific training methods – error management and behavioral modeling training. They also report results of two meta-analyses on team training. With respect to the former, Keith and Frese (2008) report an overall d of .44 for error management training, while Taylor, Russ-Eft, and Chan (2005) report an overall d of 1.09 for procedural knowledge and skills during behavioral modeling training. With respect to the former, Salas, Nichols, and Driskell (2007) reported a d of .29, and Salas et al. (2008) reported a d of .39 for team training on overall performance. While mean effect sizes differed by design, outcome, and type of training, overall Salas et al. (2012) concluded that, collectively, the meta-anayses "strongly support our contention that well-designed training works" (p. 75).

Aguinis and Kraiger (2009) provided several specific examples from European countries of the direct impact of training on organizational performance. For example, Aragón-Sánchez, Barba-Aragón, and Sanz-Valle (2003) investigated the relationship between training and organizational performance through a survey of 457 small- and medium-size businesses in the United Kingdom, Netherlands, Portugal, Finland, and Spain. Organizational performance referred to both effectiveness (i.e., employee involvement, and production or service quality), and profitability (i.e., sales volume and benefits before interest and taxes). The researchers reported that both on-the-job training and in-house training predicted most organizational effectiveness criteria. In another study, Ubeda

García (2005) found that across 78 Spanish organizations, training programs oriented towards human capital development were positively related to employee, customer, owner/shareholder satisfaction as well as sales per employee, an objective measure of organizational performance. Studies such as these demonstrate that investing in sound training practices results in higher employee satisfaction and engagement, as well as organization-level indicators of effectiveness.

In summary it has been widely demonstrated that training is integral to the development of human capital at the organizational and societal levels. Like other human resource operations, training and development projects can be managed effectively or ineffectively. In the subsequent section, we identify best practices for effectively managing training systems and for optimizing learning and transfer.

The Instructional Systems Design Model and Alternatives

When we think of training, we usually think first of the act of instruction, for example, the trainer in front of a room of attentive trainees, or a worker interacting one-on-one with a computer-based training model. However, in work and organizational psychology, training delivery is embedded in a broader instructional system, and the role of the psychologist is to optimize the delivery of training through: (1) managing the instructional system (as a process), (2) conducting a training needs assessment to define training content, (3) training design, (4) delivering training, (5) managing transfer of training back to the job, and (6) evaluating the impact of training and revising the instructional system based on that data. This systems perspective is rooted in Goldstein's instructional systems design (ISD) model (Goldstein, 1974, 1980). This model has proven a useful tool for organizing research on training, as well as actual training applications.

As noted above, the ISD model identifies a series of steps by which training designers move from identification of a potential training problem, through a needs assessment or needs analysis, to training design, training delivery, ensuring training transfers, and, ultimately evaluation of the training and feeding back the results of the evaluation to address whether training needs have been met. From an instructional design perspective, the model is a useful heuristic for planning and managing training projects. Notably however, many modern training applications often circumvent steps (e.g., skip needs assessment or training evaluation). Designers or trainers may have preferred instructional methods so that the "choice" of methods is often not as informed by the needs assessment as the model implies. Nonetheless, the model remains relevant to guide comprehensive thinking about training projects, and it provides a useful organizer for scholarly treatments of training and development. Successful training and development involves needs assessment, design, delivery, evaluation, and transfer; we discuss best practices regarding these topics below.

While the ISD model still dominates discussions of training research, as noted by Kraiger (2003), "modern" training research has been affected by three influential papers published in the late 1980s. Howell and Cooke (1989) introduced training researchers to models of learning from cognitive psychology. Howell and Cooke, followed by Kraiger, Ford, and Salas (1993), helped move us from thinking about *training* as something that organizations *do*, to *learning* as a cognitive activity by individuals. This leads to questions such as: How do we know that something has been learned? How can learning be measured? What can organizations do to make training activities stimulate natural learning behaviors? Baldwin and Ford (1988) discussed the disconnect between what is learned in training and what is applied back on the job. They clarified the distinction between factors that affect what is learned in training and factors that affect transfer. There are similarities, such as trainee motivation, but the organizational context is much greater in questions of transfer. Thus, they helped place training events as part of a broader sociotechnical system. This broader systems focus is also evident in Noe's (1986) training effectiveness model, a model that was later expanded upon by Cannon-Bowers et al. (1995) and Colquitt, LePine, and Noe (2000). Noe's model proposed both within-person variables (e.g., trainee motivation to learn) and organizational-level variables (e.g., whether training is voluntary or mandatory) that influence learning. Like Baldwin and Ford's transfer of training model, the training effectiveness model broadened our understanding of factors that influence training success.

Training needs assessment

According to ISD, the first step in any training design process should be a needs assessment. Needs assessment refers to an ongoing process of gathering data to determine what training needs exist so that training can be developed to help the organization accomplish its objectives (Goldstein, 1974). Needs assessments are conducted in order to identify specific problem areas in the organization that can be solved through training, obtain management support by ensuring that training directly impacts managers and their subordinates, develop baseline data for evaluation, and, finally, determine the costs and benefits of training. Without a proper needs assessment, organizations will often over-train, under-train, or mis-train their employees, making training efforts either minimally useful or completely useless (Brown, 2002).

As noted in several recent reviews (e.g., Aguinis & Kraiger, 2009; Salas et al., 2012), there has been very little empirical research on needs assessment in the past several decades. However, there have been several recent efforts to reframe what is to be learned during the needs assessment process. One example is the recent work of Surface (2012) who proposed a new needs assessment process that explicitly addresses a perceived organizational or job-level need. Surface proposed a four-step needs assessment process. The first step (*needs identification*) explicitly addresses whether a full needs assessment should be conducted. This step determines, from multiple perspectives, the potential impact of analyzing performance issues and implementing training as a solution. The second step (*needs specification*) identifies specific performance gaps and identifies whether or not a learning-based solution can address that gap. If training is a potential solution, the third step (*training needs assessment*) is implemented. This step includes many "classic" needs assessment activities such as organizational, task, and person analyses. At the fourth step (*evaluation phase*), a determination is made of the impact of the decisions during the earlier steps (e.g., did training reduce the performance gap?). Surface's approach is recommended because he transforms the needs assessment process from a series of required steps to a dynamic process that addresses and evolves based on organizational realities.

A second attempt to reconsider the needs assessment process was Kraiger's (2008) "third generation model." The reference to third generation refers to the distinction between instructional models in terms of how knowledge is defined, culled, and translated into training objectives. Since all instructional models include needs assessments, differences among first, second, and third generation models have implications for how training is delivered.

First generation models represent instructional design models prior to about 1980. In these, knowledge is assumed to be objective and is defined by the organization through the needs assessment process. Needs assessment is conducted to determine what knowledge and skills need to be trained, and what are the appropriate behaviors for accomplishing tasks. What is important for performing a job is defined by the organization and the employee is trained to these standards.

Second generation models represent emerging instructional design models between about 1980 and 2000. Rooted in constructivism, these models posit that knowledge is individually constructed; this means that each trainee may form a unique understanding of the knowledge and skills covered in a particular training program. Training is less structured, and the implication for needs assessment is that the training analyst should be less concerned about the "best" way to perform a task, but instead focus on the many ways in which a task can be successfully executed. Training is designed in such a way that it provides different tools or different means for trainees to learn knowledge and skills in a way that best suits them.

Third generation models build on recent views of knowledge as a form of social construction. That is, what is important in training is not that each trainee achieves their own understanding of concepts and skills, but that they learn to socially negotiate the meaning of those concepts and skills. Thus, the outcomes of training are not only a shared meaning of knowledge, but enhanced skills in the negotiation of meaning. For example, customer service training might cover not only technical knowledge of new products, but processes for learning new updates from either the manufacturer or co-workers. During needs assessment, it is important to not only document the breadth of knowledge and skills necessary for performing tasks, but the social skills used to communicate and share emerging knowledge in the workplace. Training based on this approach will not only include opportunities for individualized knowledge, but practice in eliciting and sharing information.

Outcomes of needs assessment

The most important outcomes of a needs assessment are the decisions of whether training should be conducted, and, if so, for whom and on what. While there has been little research on needs assessment as a process, over the past 20 years training researchers have made considerable progress in addressing the "for whom" question. Specifically, research has identified how consideration of individual characteristics of trainees or pretraining motivation to learn can enhance the benefits of training. For example, Tracey et al. (2001) collected data from 420 hotel managers who attended a 2.5-day managerial knowledge and skills training program. Results showed that managers' job involvement, organizational commitment, and perceptions of the work environment (i.e., perceived support and recognition) predicted pretraining self-efficacy, which in turn was related to pretraining motivation. Pretraining motivation was related to post-training measures of utility reactions, affective reactions, declarative knowledge scores, and procedural knowledge scores. Thus, understanding trainees' pretraining motivation can be helpful for understanding whether trainees are ready for training, and can identify the need for organizational interventions to increase motivation (see below). Note that pretraining motivation has also been shown to be related to trainee personality (Wilson, Huang, & Kraiger, 2013), trainee self-efficacy, and training reputation (Switzer, Nagy, & Mullins, 2005), as well as reactions to prior training courses (Sitzmann, Brown, Ely, & Kraiger, 2009).

More generally, Colquitt, LePine, and Noe (2000) summarized 20 years of research on factors affecting trainee motivation. Their meta-analysis showed that training motivation was significantly predicted by individual characteristics (e.g., locus of control, conscientiousness, anxiety, age, cognitive ability, self-efficacy, valence of training, and job involvement), as well as by situational characteristics (e.g., organizational climate).

Within the pretraining environment it is important to consider both situational and individual characteristics. It has been suggested that the way in which training is framed in conjunction with the trainee's abilities or previous experience can influence the outcomes of training. For example, Smith-Jentsch et al. (1996) demonstrated that trainees who had experienced negative pretraining events that could have been helped by the training learned more from training than did those who had not had such prior experience. Other researchers have demonstrated that trainees who perceive their work climate to be supportive are more likely to attend training programs and be motivated to learn (Maurer & Tarulli, 1994; Noe & Wilk, 1993). Further, trainees hold more favorable attitudes toward training when they have input into the design of the training or when they choose to attend training, rather than being assigned (Baldwin, Magjuka, & Loher, 1991; Hicks & Klimoski, 1987). Finally, performance in remedial training is more positive if trainees perceive they were selected fairly (Quiñones, 1995).

Another value of person analysis is that it can identify differences in trainee ability, which in turn can be used to develop different types of training interventions for different ability levels. This would allow for training designers to plan for aptitude by treatment interactions (ATI), The ATI effect refers to the concept that some instructional strategies will differ in effectiveness for particular individuals depending upon levels of specific abilities or individual characteristics (Snow, 1989). Further, the ATI effect suggests that optimal learning will occur when instruction is exactly matched to the aptitudes of the learner.

ATI effects have been documented, and ATI-based instructional programs have been advocated, in a number of different training domains in psychology. This has occurred despite the insistence of Cronbach and Snow (1977) that many ATIs are complex and difficult to demonstrate reliably, and that no particular ATI effect is sufficiently understood to stand as the basis for instructional practice. Research support for ATI effects in education have produced mixed results. Even Cronbach (1975) admitted, "Snow and I have been thwarted by the inconsistent findings coming from roughly similar inquiries. Successive studies employing the same treatment variable find different outcome-on-aptitude slopes."

Kowollik et al. (2010) conducted a meta-analysis of 51 ATI effects from the training literature. Specifically, the researchers looked at the interaction of general mental ability (g) and training structure on multiple training outcomes. Reflecting Cronbach and Snow's pessimism, the authors concluded that the results suggested that the g-structure ATI approach may not be beneficial to organizations as the small gains observed in the literature would likely outweigh the costs of developing and implementing different training programs for different subsets of employees.

One promising area though for ATIs is in the training of older workers. The number of individuals 65 and older is increasing worldwide (Czaja & Lee, 2007; Hedge, Borman, & Lammlein, 2006). By 2018, approximately a quarter of the US workforce will be 55 and older (Toossi, 2009), and in the European Union, the percentage of workers over age 50 is projected to increase by nearly 25 percent over the next 12 years (*Economist*, 2006). Accordingly, organizations are increasingly concerned about how to best train or retrain a graying workforce.

In response, training researchers have begun to examine the challenges of training older adults, and providing prescriptions for interventions to improve training outcomes within this population (e.g., Beier, 2008; Beier, Teachout, & Cox, 2012; Wolfson, Cavanagh, & Kraiger, in press). Are older adults at a disadvantage when it comes to learning in training? Cognitive deficits associated with aging are well-documented (e.g., Bopp & Verhaeghan, 2005; Salthouse, 2004), and a meta-analysis by Kubeck et al. (1996) found that age is positively correlated with training time and negatively correlated with training performance.

Beier (2008) suggested two general approaches to training older workers. One is to simply accommodate older workers by providing more training time and/or allowing self-pacing. In one recent training study, when younger and older learners were given additional time to review materials in a moderated chat room, observed differences in a fixed interval training condition (favoring younger learners) were eliminated (Wolfson, 2013). Alternatively, different training delivery methods may be designed for younger and older learners, essentially treating age as the "aptitude" in a classic ATI paradigm (Snow, 1989). Though there has been little direct research in the training literature, research on elderly populations and automated teller machines (ATM) training has provided support for age-specific training materials (Mead & Fisk, 1998). Another study by Rogers et al. (1996) found that an online tutorial was the most effective type of ATM training for the sample of older adults.

One recent study by Carter and Beier (2010) illustrates nicely the difficulty and complexity of designing appropriate training inventions for younger and older learners. The researchers examined the effectiveness of error management training in both populations while also accounting for the cognitive ability of learners. (Error management training is discussed below.) In general, the error management literature shows that trainees learn better when instructed to make and explore errors (Keith & Frese, 2008). Carter and Beier found that while younger learners did better than older learners in both error management and no error management conditions, for older learners, error management instructions produced better learning outcomes only for trainees with higher cognitive ability. Thus, older adults may be able to achieve learning outcomes similar to younger adults, but only if higher in cognitive ability.

Broadly, needs assessment is the collection of data before the design and delivery of training, so as to make better decisions as to what and how to train. There has been very little empirical work on *how* to do needs assessment, although there have been several new conceptual models offered in recent years (e.g., Kraiger, 2008; Surface, 2012).

Some research has focused on the role of individual differences in trainees that can be identified during a needs assessment, with the hope that such individual differences can predict training outcomes. Motivation to learn and attitudes towards training both show some support in this regard. Traditionally, training and instructional researchers have called for more investigation of ATIs in training contexts, although empirical research suggests that the impact of ATIs is relatively slight. A more potentially fruitful domain for ATIs is in the design of training for older workers, particularly given demographic trends regarding the aging population of the world's workforce.

Having completed a successful training needs assessment, the next step in the ISD model is to design and deliver the training. Other chapters in this volume deal more extensively with specific training topics such as socialization (Saks, Chapter 5, this volume), and knowledge transfer (Argote, Chapter 9, this volume). Still other chapters focus on emerging training media such as e-learning (Towler & Mitchell, Chapter 10, this volume), virtual learning environments (Gurtner, Chapter 11, this volume) and games and simulation-based training (Grossman, Heyne, & Salas, Chapter 12, this volume). Accordingly, we will simply provide an overview of emerging trends in effective training methods.

Effective Training Design – Emerging Training Methods

By drawing on both general learning theory and endemic models of work and organizational psychology, training theory and research has made great advancements in identifying optimal ways of designing and delivering training (Aguinis & Kraiger, 2009;

Salas & Cannon-Bowers, 2001; Salas et al., 2012). Practitioners have demanded evidenced-based prescriptions for the design and delivery of training and, for the most part, science has kept up. Below, we discuss several specific training design features, and how they can be used to improve training outcomes.

Active learning

Traditional, stand-up lectures are an inefficient and ineffective strategy for training new knowledge and skills. As opposed to more passive approaches, such as lecture or video, active learning approaches emphasize trainees' roles in their own development by encouraging trainees to ask questions, explore, seek feedback, and reflect on potential results (Bell & Kozlowski, 2008). Compared to their more passive brethren, these active approaches tend to be more effective for adaptive transfer (the application of skills learned in training to novel situations), even for trainees of relatively low motivation and ability (Keith, Richter, & Naumann, 2010). Adaptive transfer is particularly important because it is often unfeasible – if not impossible – to train for every situation a trainee might encounter.

It is somewhat difficult to confirm empirically that active learning *works* because in practice, active learning can mean different things to different researchers and trainers. For example, Bell and Kozlowski (2008) categorized each of the following training interventions as ones that promote active learning: Exploratory and discovery learning (e.g., Kamouri, Kamouri, & Smith, 1986), guided exploration (e.g., Bell & Kozlowski, 2002); error training and enactive exploration (see below), and mastery training (e.g., Kozlowski & Bell, 2006). Each of these methods includes components of instruction, motivational induction, and emotion control. Further, each is supported by multiple empirical studies. Additionally, other authors have included broader instructional techniques such as collaborative or cooperative learning (e.g., Johnson, Johnson, & Smith, 1998) and problem-based learning (e.g., Norman & Schmidt, 2000). While the examination of the breadth and complexity of active learning is beyond the scope of this chapter, we re-emphasize that work and organizational researchers are increasingly cognizant of the benefits of active learning in training applications. Interested readers are referred to the work of Bell and Kozlowski (2008, 2010) for more detailed theoretical discussions of active learning).

Error management training

One of the most promising active learning techniques is error management training. Error management training is an approach to training in which trainees are encouraged to make errors. Training design has traditionally focused on teaching correct performance methods, and thus avoiding errors. In error management training, however, trainees are encouraged to make errors and engage in reflection to understand the causes of those errors, and strategies to avoid making similar errors in the future. Though errors are avoided in traditional training, errors often occur on the job, and individuals need to learn effective strategies for dealing with them. In addition to increasing knowledge and skill acquisition, error management training minimizes the negative effects of errors on motivation and self-efficacy (Nordstrom, Wendland, & Williams, 1998).

Research has largely supported the effectiveness of error management training for improving performance outcomes. In one study, undergraduates were taught how to use a spreadsheet software program (Heimbeck et al., 2003). In the control condition, trainees were encouraged to avoid errors, whereas in the experimental condition, trainees were provided with explicit instructions to make errors, and encouraged to learn from those errors. As predicted, participants encouraged to make errors performed significantly better than those encouraged to avoid errors. In a follow-up study, error training was combined with metacognitive prompts designed to encourage trainees to explicitly think about what problem they were experiencing and what they were trying to accomplish (Keith & Frese, 2005). Again, these participants performed significantly better than those in the error-avoidant condition. In a similar study, Carter and Beier (2010), found that encouraging errors not only led to improved performance, but also improved self-efficacy, as compared to error-avoidant and no-instruction conditions.

Similar findings have been reported on multiple occasions (e.g., Bell & Kozlowski, 2008; Carter & Beier, 2010; Chillarege, Nordstrom, & Williams, 2003; Frese et al., 1991), supporting the effectiveness of error management training. There is some evidence, however, that individual differences do play a role. Gully et al. (2002), for example, found that the effect of error management training was greatest for participants high in cognitive ability and openness to experience.

Active learning encompasses several techniques that have emerged as an alternative to traditional passive learning techniques, such as participants watching a lecture or video. One of the most promising of these techniques is error management training, during which trainees are encouraged to make and explore errors. Error management training has repeatedly been shown to increase post-training performance, especially when trained skill or knowledge must be applied to novel tasks or situations.

Self-regulation

Self-regulation refers to the extent that trainees monitor and control their own learning processes, including the attention to and active engagement with the training content (Vancouver & Day, 2005). Through monitoring, trainees become aware of whether they understand certain aspects of the training content well or poorly; control allows them to take meaningful action in order to increase understanding when needed. Self-regulation is particularly useful for potentiating adaptive transfer. Chen, Thomas, and Wallace (2005), for example, trained 156 individuals on a flight simulator task, and then examined adaptive performance on subsequent trials. Training participants' self-regulatory processes mediated the effects of training both on task self-efficacy and on their performance across trials. A study by Sitzmann, Bell, Kraiger, and Kanar (2008) provided evidence that, not only does self-regulation facilitate learning, these effects compound over time.

One of the promising aspects of self-regulation is that it requires very few changes to existing training design. Self-regulation by trainees can be increased simply by reminding trainees *before* training of its importance to learning. Moreover, several studies by Sitzmann and colleagues found that simply inserting short prompts into training materials (encouraging self-regulation activity) can increase learning (e.g., Sitzmann et al., 2008; Sitzmann & Ely, 2010). A recent meta-analysis by Sitzmann and Ely (2011) confirmed the effectiveness and robustness of encouraging self-regulation in learning, particularly with respect to self-regulation activities related to goal level, persistence, effort, and self-efficacy.

Technology-delivered instruction

Technology-delivered instruction (TDI) refers to any form of training that is delivered principally via technology (Wolfson, Cavanagh, & Kraiger, in press). This includes web-based instruction, computer-assisted training, intelligent tutoring systems, computer-based simulations, and virtual reality training, delivered through such devices as computers, laptops, tablets, and smartphones. This type of training is increasingly popular in industry

(Miller, 2012). In a meta-analysis, however, Sitzmann, Kraiger, Stewart, and Wisher (2006) found only a small benefit for web-based instruction, a specific form of TDI. Furthermore, even this small benefit disappeared after controlling for instructional principles. This supports Clark's (1994) contention that *the medium doesn't matter*. Well-designed instruction works irrespective of the delivery mode, and cutting-edge technology cannot compensate for poor instructional design. Brown and Ford (2002) suggested that TDI be designed so that (1) information is structured and presented in a meaningful and easy manner, (2) the need for learner control is balanced with guidance to aid learners in knowing what choices to make, (3) opportunities for practice and feedback are provided, and (4) learners are encouraged to be mindful of their cognitive processing and take control of their own learning. Additionally, Kraiger (2008) argued for a number of "side benefits" of TDI based on his third generation learning model. For many learners, the absence of face-to-face contact, the reduced role (and power) of the instructor, and opportunities for reflection and study before being required to produce answers can all combine to increase trainee participation and, ultimately, trainee learning. However, although TDI offers several possible benefits to organizations, trainers must also keep in mind that, in order to be effective, TDI must have a clear purpose and incorporate empirically supported learning principles into the design of the program (Bedwell & Salas, 2010).

One benefit of TDI for organizations is that technology usually allows trainees flexibility in when and where they can access training content. This saves the organization considerable resources in regard to organizing, planning, and scheduling research, a benefit that has become increasingly important in a global economy in which employees may be separated geographically across time zones. One of the potential drawbacks of this flexibility, however, is that trainees are required to assume more control over their own learning, making decisions about what and how to learn (Noe, 2008). Although autonomy in work settings has been linked to higher motivation and superior performance (Spector, 1986), in training, the benefits of learner control have received mixed support. Though originally proposed as a method to improve training, a meta-analysis by Kraiger and Jerden (2007) found little benefit of learning control on learning outcomes, and, in many cases, a negative effect. Learners are often poor judges of what or how much they need to learn or practice, especially when they lack ability or experience (DeRouin, Fritzsche, & Salas, 2004).

One solution to the problems associated with learner control is to combine learner control with adaptive guidance. Adaptive guidance gives learners suggestions on what and how much to practice based upon their performance. Bell and Kozlowski (2002) found that combining adaptive guidance and computer-based training significantly improved trainees' study and practice effort, knowledge acquired, and performance.

Although TDI has yet to demonstrate clear superiority over traditional face-to-face methods, organizations seem eager to adopt it. As technology becomes more complex and sophisticated, so, too, will TDI platforms. Recently, instructional designers have joined forces with game designers to create instruction that is fun, engaging, and educational, in order to achieve organizationally relevant outcomes (Squire, 2008; Wilson et al., 2009). TDI is also being "downsized", that is, delivered through smaller media such as smartphones, and through podcasts and streamed social media (e.g., Bonk, Kim, & Zeng, 2005), allowing trainees to access training materials whenever and wherever they need it. Due to the ubiquity of technology in modern life, and the perceived flexibility and efficiency of TDI, it is likely to continue to be a popular choice in training design for the foreseeable future.

In summary, recent research has focused on the means for increasing learner engagement during training through means such as active learning, error management training, prompting self-regulatory activities, and customizable TDI. Preliminary evidence suggests that each of these has a positive impact on training outcomes.

Measuring Training Outcomes: Baseline and Alternatives

On the back end of the ISD model is the evaluation of training outcomes – did training result in the elimination of gaps in knowledge, skills, and attitudes needed to do the work? More precisely, training evaluation refers to the systematic collection of data in order to answer the question(s) of whether learning objectives were achieved and/or whether accomplishment of those objectives resulted in enhanced performance on the job (Kraiger, Ford, & Salas. 1993). A more detailed review of training evaluation models is provided by Passmore and Velez (Chapter 8, this volume). However, as one of the themes of this chapter has been on how modern views of learning have affected training needs assessment and training design, here we comment briefly on the impact of learning theory on training evaluation.

One of the oldest, and still commonly used, frameworks for assessing training outcomes is Kirkpatrick's (1994) hierarchy. Kirkpatrick's designed his hierarchy in the late 1950s as a response to practitioners who wanted useful techniques for assessing training outcomes. The framework was specifically designed to be practical and applicable, and, due to this, is sometimes criticized for lack of theoretical development (e.g., Salas et al., 2012).

Kirkpatrick (1994) proposed four hierarchical levels by which training can be evaluated. At the lowest level is trainee reactions (essentially a measure of how well trainees liked the training), followed by learning (i.e., declarative knowledge and skills), behavior (changes in job performance), and results (the tangible impact of the training, such as greater profits or fewer errors). Because the framework is hierarchical, higher-level outcomes are not expected to change unless lower-level outcomes are met first, meaning that the evaluation should proceed to higher levels only once changes in lower-level outcomes have been established.

Several alternative training evaluation models have been proposed. Kraiger, Ford, and Salas (1993) proposed a multidimensional learning model that specified cognitive, skill-based, and affective outcomes. Cognitive outcomes refer to the quantity and type of knowledge acquired during training, as well as the relationship between knowledge elements. This includes verbal knowledge, knowledge organization, and cognitive strategies. Skill-based outcomes refer to the development of technical and motor skills. These mainly include compilation, the ability to execute behaviors as a single, fluid action, and automaticity, which enables the accomplishment of tasks without conscious monitoring. Finally, affective outcomes refer to motivation, attitudes, and goals that are relevant to the objectives of the training program, such as self-efficacy and goal orientation, and the link between learning outcomes and evaluation methods.

More recently, Kraiger (2002) proposed a decision-based evaluation model. This model expanded upon the affective, skill-based, and cognitive taxonomy of Kraiger, Ford, and Salas (1993), by both adding additional learning outcomes and greater clarity on linkages between learning outcomes and evaluation measures. More importantly, it connects decisions about what and how to evaluate training to the purpose of evaluation. Evaluation should generally be done to: (1) make a decision about the training (e.g., whether or not to continue an existing training program); (2) provide feedback to trainers, trainees, or training designers; and/or (3) market the training program to future adopters (e.g., other organizational units) or to future trainees. By identifying the evaluation purpose and choosing measures consistent with the purpose(s), there is an increased likelihood that the data can affect change within the organization. Thus, mindful evaluation practice becomes less about moving from one level to another than how to use training evaluation data to drive organizational outcomes.

Planning For and Managing Transfer of Training

The final step in the ISD model is ensuring that learning during training is transferred or applied back on the job. As Kraiger (2002) noted, evaluating training consists of two separate activities. The first is determining whether knowledge and skills covered in training are used back on the job. The second is evaluating whether performance improves as a result. The distinction between behavior change and performance improvement is important, as organizational decision makers sometimes fail to appreciate that as training is applied (new skills are demonstrated), job performance may in fact decrease (at least in the short term). From a theory and research perspective, the antecedents of behavior change and performance improvement differ. As one example, ensuring identical elements between the training and work environments is one way to promote behavior change (e.g., Adams, 1987), but supervisory and upper management support for training encourages repetition and practice that leads to performance change (Tracey et al., 2001).

Baldwin and Ford (1988) define transfer of training as the extent to which trainees effectively apply the knowledge, skills, and attitudes gained from training to the job. This definition blends both the notion of application with the ideas of effectiveness – transfer is said to occur when training is applied and done so effectively. Baldwin and Ford also note the importance of demonstrating that new knowledge or behaviour must be shown to generalize (across tasks) and be maintained over some period of time. As noted above, modern approaches to training effectiveness have moved beyond what happens just within training to considering the broader organizational context. Training is of little value if what is learned is not generalized back to trainee jobs and maintained over time (Kozlowski & Salas, 1997). Applying knowledge, skills, and abilities learned in training to the job is known as transfer. Transfer can be facilitated both through the design of training, and through building a supportive transfer environment once trainees return to their jobs.

There has been considerable research in the areas of instructional and cognitive psychology on factors *within training* that promote or inhibit transfer (e.g., Ellis 1965; Gick & Holyoak, 1987). However, Kraiger (2003) noted that this stream of research should be evaluated carefully before applying them to workplace training. This is because within these realms of basic research, transfer typically is measured in the training context (i.e., immediately after training), and is measured in terms of outcomes such as speed of acquisition of new information.

However, work and organizational psychologists have also conducted considerable research on transfer of training as well. While this research has also examined how training design promotes successful transfer, not surprisingly, work and organizational psychology focuses much more on the impact of the organizational context. There have been multiple reviews of the transfer of training literature including Baldwin and Ford (1988), Burke and Hutchins (2007), and Ford and Weissbein (1997). A recent meta-analysis by Blume et al. (2010) provided estimated effect sizes for a variety of individual, training-level, and organizational-level variables on transfer.

At the organizational level, considerable research has focused on the extent to which workgroup factors such as supervisory and peer support, or other organizational-level factors affect training. For example, at the organizational level, Kontoghiorghes (2004) found support for both transfer climate and and general work environment factors predicted both transfer motivation and actual transfer. In this study, transfer climate included both supervisory and peer support, but also factors such as training accountability and opportunity to perform. Work environment factors included job design factors (e.g., encouraging employee involvement or fostering task autonomy), and a continuous learning environment.

Transfer climate refers broadly to a broad set of organizational variables that affect the extent to which training is applied to the job and leads to better performance (Rouiller & Goldstein, 1993). These variables include both cues (e.g., goals, social factors, and task factors) and intended consequences for behavior (e.g., positive or negative reinforcement, punishment, and extinction; Thayer & Teachout, 1995). While most training researchers agree that transfer climate is important to actual transfer, empirical studies have yielded mixed results. For example, workplace support was found by Richman-Hirsch (2001) to moderate the effectiveness of post-training transfer-enhancing interventions. However, Pidd (2004) found that workplace support affected transfer only when trainees identified with the groups that provided support. Similar mixed results have been found for social support. Chiabura and Marinova (2005) found no effects for supervisory support, but positive effects for peer support, while Van der Klink, Gielen, and Nauta (2001) also found no positive effects for supervisory support. However, Tracey, Tannenbaum and Kavanagh (1995) found that supervisor support did predict transfer. Intuitively, one would expect that the extent to which peers and supervisors offer social cues to apply training, and positive reinforcement for those behaviors would have a strong impact on transfer. In general, research on transfer climate has produced mixed results (e.g., Cheng & Hampson, 2008; Cheng & Ho, 2001), suggesting that there are likely many situational and individual moderators of the relationship.

Other research has examined the efficacy of in-training strategies for improving transfer, again with mixed success. For example, Richman-Hirsch (2001) reported positive effects for a post-training goal-setting intervention, but Brown (2005) reported that trainees given "do your best" goals outperformed those told to set distal goals. In reviewing the effects of in-training and post-training interventions on transfer, Aguinis and Kraiger (2009) concluded that the greatest support lies for the role of interpersonal factors such as supervisory and peer support as moderators of the relationship between training and transfer of training. More distal organizational-level factors such as transfer climate have not received consistent support as important moderators.

Taken across all research on training effectiveness and transfer, some prescriptions emerge for managing training transfer. In order to maximize transfer, training programs should be designed to be as similar to the actual job setting as possible (Baldwin & Ford, 1988; Burke & Hutchins, 2007; Holton & Baldwin, 2003). Note that "similar" can include both physical fidelity and psychological fidelity. The former means that the training environment, work tools, and so forth mirror the work environment, while the latter means that there is considerable overlap in knowledge used and skills practiced in training and those required on the job.

The training program should also introduce variability, to allow trainees to practice under different circumstances. Training designers can vary the stimuli used within the training setting, how often trainees practice, and under which conditions trainees practice (Baldwin & Ford, 1988; Holladay & Quiñones, 2003; Schmitt & Bjork, 1992). Behavioral modeling (Taylor, Russ-Eft, & Chan, 2005) and error management training (Burke & Hutchins, 2007; Heimbeck et al., 2003) have also been shown to promote transfer.

The design of the training program itself, however, is often insufficient to guarantee transfer. To maximize transfer outcomes, training designers should examine facets of the transfer environment (Grossman & Salas, 2011; Tannenbaum et al., 1991). Kraiger and Culbertson (2012) discussed three post-training factors that influence transfer: situational constraints, organizational support, and transfer climate.

Situational constraints include opportunities to use newly acquired knowledge and skills on the job (Ford et al., 1992; Hesketh, 1997; Peters, O'Connor, & Eulberg, 1985). Simply put, the longer the gap between training and when trainees can implement new knowledge or new skills back on the job, the less the transfer of training. Work environments characterized by positive sociotechnical system design factors (e.g., high job involvement and information sharing) and job design variables such as task autonomy are especially effective at promoting transfer (Kontoghioerghes, 2004).

Organizational support refers to providing appropriate prompts for application of trained material, and by making consequences contingent upon successful transfer (Rouiller & Goldstein, 1993). In regard to the consequences of behavior, both formal and informal reinforcement are critical for ensuring that trainees will transfer what they have learned outside the formal training environment (e.g., Chiaburu & Marinova, 2005; Smith-Jentsch, Salas, & Brannick, 2001; Tracey, Tannenbaum, & Kavanagh, 1995). Support can include concrete actions such as encouraging the use of new skills, providing rewards for learning and using new skills, and removing negative contingencies for errors or short-term declines in performance as new skills are practiced.

Finally, transfer climate refers to the extent that trainees perceive their supervisors and peers as supportive of transfer, the extent that they have opportunities to practice and use new knowledge and skills, and that they are held accountable for transfer (Thayer & Teachout, 1995). Supervisors and peers can be antagonistic to transfer, especially when applying new skills leads to an initial drop in performance as those skills are mastered, or when they are committed to performing job tasks the way they have always been performed. Once the transfer climate is established, it facilitates transfer through increased trainee focus, motivation, and transfer intentions (Rouiller & Goldstein, 1993; Tracey, Tannenbaum, & Kavanagh, 1995), and by enhancing trainee self-efficacy and mastery-goal orientation (Chiaburu, Van Dam, & Hutchins, 2010).

While research to date has yet to find consistent support for both in-training and post-training interventions, it is important that such research continues. The ultimate goal of most training programs is not just to improve trainee knowledge and skills, but to improve job performance. To do so, trainees must not just learn training material, they must apply it to their jobs. Both training programs and transfer environments should be designed and managed with this key goal in mind.

Future Research

The future of training research, along with training research needs, is difficult to project. Kraiger and Ford (2007) reviewed the history of training research and concluded that in general, there is a lag of several decades between both basic research in learning and management theory with later applied research in training. Accordingly, they projected that the current interest in decentralized management structures and knowledge management might lead to increased interest in how learners accumulate "packets" of knowledge and combine them to form understanding and develop skills.

Since Ford and Kraiger (2007) the world has changed immensely as a result of technology. Social media and various forms of instant messaging have dramatically changed how individuals are exposed to information. And, there is some thought that the massive amounts of continuous information are also changing how we process information. In a recent *New York Times* bestseller, science blogger Nicholas Carr (2011) argued that our increased use of the internet encourages us to focus on rapid sampling of small information bits from many sources but as we become better at scanning and skimming, we are losing our ability to concentrate and reflect. Certainly, anyone who is a parent to a teen or has taught in a college classroom has noted, at least anecdotally, how adolescents and young adults have greater difficulty focusing on single content and often prefer simultaneous processing of information along multiple channels. While the implications of this are not fully known, when coupled with Kraiger's (2008) argument that knowledge is increasingly socially defined, training researchers must continue to understand how adult learners integrate information from multiple sources, both in structured and on-the-job training.

In addition to this micro-focus, as we outlined before, there is an ongoing need to understand better the social/political/technical environments in which training is delivered and transferred back to the job. Workplace learning is at once a personal event (that occurs in the mind of the trainee), but one occurring in organizational cultures that set expectations, communicate importance, ritualize accomplishments and failures, and continually reinforce both desirable and undesirable behaviors. Thus, we need to continually focus not only on what it means to learn, but how to promote learning before, during, and after training.

Conclusion

The field of training and development has seen remarkable progress over the past 30 years, leading Salas et al. (2012) to proclaim we have achieved a science of training. Training research has continued to embrace the classic ISD model, although new methods have emerged for designing training content and evaluating training success. More importantly, training research has begun to understand how to promote active learning by trainees and much of that research has been translated to practice. As new technology enables more rapid and broad dissemination of training content, it is incumbent on training researchers to ensure learning principles are continued to be integrated into training design, and that new technology be leveraged to increase training effectiveness.

References

Adams, J. (1987). Historical review and appraisal of research on the learning, retention and transfer of human motor skills. *Psychological Bulletin*, 101, 41–74.

Aguinis, H., & Kraiger, K. (2009). Benefits of training and development for individuals and teams, organizations, and society. *Annual Review of Psychology*, 60, 451–474.

Aragón-Sánchez, A., Barba-Aragón, I., & Sanz-Valle, R. (2003). Effects of training on business results. *International Journal of Human Resource Management*, 14, 956 –980.

Arthur, W., Jr., Bennett, W., Jr., Edens, P. S., & Bell, S. T. (2003). Effectiveness of training in organizations: A meta-analysis of design and evaluation features. *Journal of Applied Psychology*, 88, 234–245.

Baldwin, T. T., & Ford, J. K. (1988). Transfer of training: A review and directions for future research. *Personnel Psychology*, 41, 63–105.

Baldwin, T. T., Magjuka, R. J., & Loher, B. T. (1991). The perils of participation: Effects of choice of training on trainee motivation and learning. *Personnel Psychology*, 44, 260–267.

Bedwell, W. L., & Salas. E. (2010). Computer-based training: Capitalizing on lessons learned. *International Journal of Training and Development*, 14, 239–249.

Beier, M. E. (2008). Age and learning in organizations. In G. P. Hodgkinson & J. K. Ford (Eds.), *International Review of Industrial and Organizational Psychology* (vol. 23, pp. 83–105). Chichester: John Wiley & Sons, Ltd.

Beier, M. E., Teachout, M. S., & Cox, C. B. (2012). The training and development of an aging workforce. In J. W. Hedge & W. C. Borman (Eds.), *Work and Aging Handbook* (pp. 436–453). New York: Oxford University Press.

Bell, B. S., & Kozlowski, S. W. J. (2002). Adaptive guidance: Enhancing self-regulation, knowledge and performance in technology-based training. *Personnel Psychology*, 55, 267–306.

Bell, B. S., & Kozlowski, S. W. J. (2008). Active learning: Effects of core training design elements on self-regulatory processes, learning, and adaptability. *Journal of Applied Psychology*, 93, 296–316.

Bell, B. S., & Kozlowski, S. W. J. (2010). Toward a theory of learner-centered training design: An integrative framework of active learning. In S. Kozlowski & E. Salas (Eds.), *Learning, Training, and Development in Organizations* (pp. 263–300). New York: Routledge.

Blume, B. D., Ford, J. K., Baldwin, T. T., & Huang, J. L. (2010). Transfer of training: A meta-analytic review. *Journal of Management*, 36, 1065–1105.

Bonk, C. J., Kim, K. J., & Zeng, T. (2005). Future directions of blended learning in higher education and workplace learning settings. In C. J. Bonk, & C. R. Graham (Eds.), *Handbook of Blended Learning: Global Perspectives, Local Designs* (pp. 550–568). San Francisco: Pfeiffer.

Bopp, K. L., & Verhaughen, P. (2005). Aging and verbal memory span: A meta-analysis. *Journal of Gerontology: Psychological Sciences*, 60B, 223–233.

Boudreau, J., & Ramstad, P. (2005). Talentship, talent segmentation, and sustainability: A new HR decision science paradigm for a new strategy definition. *Human Resource Management*, 44, 129–136.

Brown, K., & Ford, J. K. (2002). Using computer technology in training: Building an infrastructure of active learning. In K. Kraiger (Ed.), *Creating, Implementing, and Managing Effective Training and Development* (pp. 192–233). San Francisco: Jossey-Bass.

Brown T. C. (2005). Effectiveness of distal and proximal goals as transfer-of-training interventions: A field experiment. *Human Resource Development Quarterly*, 16, 369–387.

Burke, L. A., & Hutchins, H. M. (2007). Training transfer: An integrative literature review. *Human Resource Development Review*, 6, 263–296.

Burke, M. J., & Day, R. R. (1986). A cumulative study of the effectiveness of managerial training. *Journal of Applied Psychology*, 71, 232–245.

Cannon-Bowers, J. A., Salas, E., Tannenbaum, S. I., & Mathieu, J. E. (1995). Toward theoretically based principles of training effectiveness: A model and initial empirical investigation. *Military Psychology*, 7, 141–164.

Carr, N. (2011). *The Shallows: What the Internet is Doing to our Brains.* New York: Norton.

Carter, M., & Beier, M. E. (2010). The effectiveness of error management training with working aged adults. *Personnel Psychology*, 63, 641– 675.

Chen, G., Thomas, B., & Wallace, J. C. (2005). A multilevel examination of the relationships among training outcomes, mediating regulatory processes, and adaptive performance. *Journal of Applied Psychology*, 90, 827–841.

Cheng, E. W. L., & Hampson, I. (2008). Transfer of training: A review and new insights. *International Journal of Management Reviews*, 10, 327–341.

Cheng, E. W. L., & Ho, D. C. K. (2001). A review of transfer of training studies in the past decade. *Personnel Review*, 30, 102–118.

Chiaburu, D. S., & Marinova, S. V. (2005). What predicts skill transfer? An exploratory study of goal orientation, training self-efficacy and organizational supports. *International Journal of Training and Development*, 9, 110–123.

Chiaburu, D. S., Van Dam, K., & Hutchins, H. M. (2010). Social support in the workplace and training transfer: A longitudinal analysis. *International Journal of Selection and Assessment*, 18, 187–200.

Chillarege, K. A., Nordstrom, C. R., & Williams, K. B. (2003). Learning from our mistakes: Error management training for mature learners. *Journal of Business and Psychology*, 17, 369–385.

Clark, R. E. (1994). Media will never influence learning. *Educational Technology Research and Development*, 42(2), 21–29.

Collins, D. B., & Holton, E. F., III. (2004). The effectiveness of managerial leadership development programs: A meta-analysis of studies from 1982 to 2001. *Human Resource Development Quarterly*, 15, 217–248.

Colquitt, J. A., LePine, J. A., & Noe, R. A. (2000). Towards an integrative theory of training moti- vation: A meta-analytic path analysis of 20 years of research. *Journal of Applied Psychology*, 85, 678–807.

Cronbach, L. (1975). Beyond the two disciplines of scientific psychology. *American Psychologist*, 30, 116–127.

Cronbach, L., & Snow, R. (1977). *Aptitudes and Instructional Methods: A Handbook for Research on Interactions.* New York: Irvington.

Czaja, S., & Lee, C. C. (2007). The impact of aging on access to technology. *Universal Access in the Information Society*, 5, 341–349.

Delaney, J. T., & Huselid, M. A. (1996). The impact of human resource management practices on perceptions of organizational performance. *Academy of Management Journal*, 39, 949–969.

DeRouin, R. R., Fritzsche, B. A., & Salas E. (2004). Optimizing e-learning: Research-based guide- lines for learner-controlled training. *Human Resource Management*, 43, 147–162.

Economist, The (2006). Turning boomers into boomerangs. 378 (February), 65–67.

Ellis, H. (1965). *The Transfer of Learning.* New York: Macmillan.

European Centre for the Development of Vocational Training. (2010). *Employer-Provided Vocational Training in Europe: Evaluation and Interpretation of the Third Continuing Vocational Training Survey.* Luxembourg: Publications Office of the European Union.

Ford, J. K., Quiñones, M. A., Sego, D. J., & Sorra, J. S. (1992). Factors affecting the opportunity to perform trained tasks on the job. *Personnel Psychology*, 45, 511–524.

Ford, J. K., & Weissbein, D. A. (1997). Transfer of training: An updated review and analysis. *Performance Improvement Quarterly*, 10(2), 22–41.

Frese, M., Brodbeck, F., Heinbokel, T., Mooser, C., Schleiffenbaum, E., & Thiemann, P. (1991). Errors in training computer skills: On the positive function of errors. *Human–Computer Interaction*, 6, 77–93.

Gick, M. L., & Holyoak, K. J. (1987). The cognitive basis of knowledge transfer. In S. M. Cormier & J. D. Hagman (Eds.), *Transfer of Learning: Contemporary Research and Applications* (pp. 9–46). Orlando, FL: Academic Press.

Goldstein, I. L. (1974). *Training in Organizations: Needs Assessment, Development, and Evaluation.* Monterey, CA: Brooks/Cole.

Goldstein, I. L. (1980). Training in work organizations. *Annual Review of Psychology*, 31, 229–272.

Green, M., & McGill, E. (2011). *State of the Industry, 2011: ASTD's Annual Review of Workplace Learning and Developmental Data.* Alexandria, VA: ASTD.

Grossman, R., & Salas, E. (2011). The transfer of training: What really matters. *International Journal of Training and Development*, 15, 103–120.

Gully, S. M., Payne, S. C., Koles, K. L., & Whiteman, J. A. K. (2002). The impact of error training and individual differences on training outcomes: An attribute-treatment interaction perspective. *Journal of Applied Psychology*, 87, 143–155.

Hedge, J. W., Borman, W. C., & Lammlein, S. E. (2006). *The Aging Workforce: Realities, Myths, and Implications for Organizations.* Washington, DC: American Psychological Association.

Heimbeck, D., Frese, M., Sonnentag, S., & Keith, N. (2003). Integrating errors into the training process: The function of error management instructions and the role of goal orientation. *Personnel Psychology*, 56, 533–561.

Hesketh, B. (1997). Whither dilemmas in training for transfer. *Applied Psychology: An International Review*, 46, 380–386.

Hicks, W. D., & Klimoski, R. (1987). The process of entering training programs and its effect on training outcomes. *Academy of Management Journal*, 30, 542–552.

Holladay, C. L., & Quiñones, M. A. (2003). Practice variability and transfer of training: The role of self-efficacy generality. *Journal of Applied Psychology*, 88, 1094–1103.

Holton, E. F., III, & Baldwin, T. T. (2003). Making transfer happen: An action perspective on learning transfer systems. In E. F. Holton III & T. T. Baldwin (Eds.), *Improving Learning Transfer in Organizations* (pp. 3–15). San Francisco: Jossey-Bass.

Howell, W. C., & Cooke, N. J. (1989). Training the human information processor: A review of cognitive models. In I. L. Goldstein (Ed.), *Training and Development in Organizations* (pp. 121–182). San Francisco: Jossey-Bass.

Huselid, M. A. (1995). The impact of human resource management practices on turnover, productivity, and corporate financial performance. *Academy of Management Journal*, 38, 635–672.

Huselid, M. A., & Becker, B. E. (2011). Bridging micro and macro domains: Workforce differentiation and strategic human resource management. *Journal of Management*, 37, 421–428.

Johnson, D., Johnson, R., & Smith, K. (1998). Cooperative learning returns to college: What evidence is there that it works? *Change*, 30(4), 26–35.

Kamouri, A. L., Kamouri, J., & Smith, K. H. (1986). Training by exploration: Facilitating the transfer of procedural knowledge through analogical reasoning. *International Journal of Man-Machine Studies*, 24, 171–192.

Keith, N., & Frese, M. (2005). Self-regulation in error management training: Emotion control and metacognition as mediators of performance effects. *Journal of Applied Psychology*, 90, 677–691.

Keith, N., & Frese, M. (2008). Effectiveness of error management training: A meta-analysis. *Journal of Applied Psychology*, 93, 59–69.

Keith, N., Richter, T., & Naumann, J. (2010). Active/exploratory training promotes transfer even in learners with low motivation and cognitive ability. *Applied Psychology: An International Review*, 59, 97–123.

Kirkpatrick, D. L. (1994). *Evaluating Training Programs: The Four Levels*. San Francisco: Berrett-Koehler.

Kontoghiorghes, C. (2004). Reconceptualizing the learning transfer conceptual framework: Empirical validation of a new systemic model. *International Journal of Training and Development*, 8, 210–221.

Kowollik, V., Day, E. A., Wang, X., Arthur, W., Jr., Schuelke, M. J., & Hughes, M. G. (2010). The interaction between ability and training structure: A meta-analysis. Poster presented at the 25th Annual Conference of the Society for Industrial and Organizational Psychology, Atlanta, GA.

Kozlowski, S. W. J., & Bell, B. S. (2006). Disentangling achievement orientation and goal setting: Effect of self-regulatory processes. *Journal of Applied Psychology*, 91, 900–916.

Kozlowski, S. W. J., & Salas E. (1997). A multilevel organizational systems approach for the implementation and transfer of training. In J. K. Ford, S. W. J. Kozlowski, K. Kraiger, E. Salas, & M. S. Teachout (Eds.), *Improving Training Effectiveness in Work Organizations* (pp. 247–287). Mahwah, NJ: Erlbaum.

Kraiger, K. (2002). Decision-based evaluation. In K. Kraiger (Ed.), *Creating, Implementing, and Maintaining Effective Training and Development: State-of-the-Art Lessons for Practice* (pp. 331–375). San Francisco: Jossey-Bass.

Kraiger, K. (2003). Perspectives on training and development. In W. C. Borman, D. R. Ilgen, & R. J. Klimoski (Eds), *Handbook of Psychology*, vol. 12, *Industrial and Organizational Psychology* (pp. 171–192). Hoboken, NJ: John Wiley & Sons, Inc.

Kraiger, K. (2008). Transforming our models of learning and development: Web-based instruction as enabler of third-generation instruction. *Industrial and Organizational Psychology: Perspectives on Science and Practice*, 1, 454–467.

Kraiger, K., & Ford, J. K. (2007). The expanding role of workplace training: Themes and trends influencing training research and practice. In L. L. Koppes (Ed.), *Historical Perspectives in Industrial and Organizational Psychology* (pp. 218–309). Mahwah, NJ: Erlbaum.

Kraiger, K., Ford, J. K., & Salas, E. (1993). Application of cognitive, skill-based, and affective theories of learning outcomes to new methods of training evaluation. *Journal of Applied Psychology*, 78, 311–328.

Kraiger, K., & Jerden, E. (2007). A new look at learner control: Meta-analytic results and directions for future research. In S. M. Fiore & E. Salas (Eds.), *Where is the Learning in Distance Learning? Towards a Science of Distributed Learning and Training* (pp. 65–90). Washington, DC: APA Books.

Kubeck, J. E., Delp, N. D., Haslett, T. K., & McDaniel, M. A. (1996). Does job-related training performance decline with age? *Psychology and Aging*, 11, 92–107.

Maurer, T. J., & Tarulli, B. A. (1994). Investigation of perceived environment, perceived outcome, and person variables in relationship to voluntary development activity by employees. *Journal of Applied Psychology*, 79, 3–14.

Mead, S., & Fisk, A. D. (1998). Measuring skill acquisition and retention with an ATM simulator: The need for age-specific training. *Human Factors, 40,* 516–523.

Miller, L. (2012). ASTD 2012 State of the Industry Report: Organizations Continue to Invest in Workplace Learning. http://www.astd.org/Publications/Magazines/TD/TD-Archive/2012/11/ASTD-2012-State-of-the-Industry-Report (accessed February 9, 2013).

Noe, R. A. (1986). Trainees' attributes and attitudes: Neglected influences on training effectiveness. *Academy of Management Review, 11,* 736–749.

Noe, R. A. (2008). *Employee Training and Development* (4th ed.). Boston, MA: Irwin-McGraw.

Noe, R. A., & Wilk, S. L. (1993). Investigation of the factors that influence employees' participation in development activities. *Journal of Applied Psychology, 78,* 291–302.

Nordstrom, C. R., Wendland, D., & Williams, K. B. (1998). "To err is human": An examination of the effectiveness of error management training. *Journal of Business and Psychology, 12,* 269–282.

Norman, G., & Schmidt, H. (2000). Effectiveness of problem-based learning curriculum: Theory, practice, and paper darts. *Medical Education, 34,* 721–728.

Peters, L. H., O'Connor, E. J., & Eulberg, J. R. (1985). Situational constraints: Sources, consequences and future considerations. *Research in Personnel and Human Resource Management, 3,* 79–114.

Pidd, K. (2004). The impact of workplace support and identity on training transfer: A case study of drug and alcohol safety training in Australia. *International Journal of Training and Development, 8,* 274–288.

Quiñones, M. A. (1995). Pretraining context effects: Training assignment as feedback. *Journal of Applied Psychology, 80,* 226–238.

Richman-Hirsch, W. L. (2001). Post-training interventions to enhance transfer: The moderating effects of work environments. *Human Resource Development Quarterly, 12,* 105–119.

Rogers, W. A., Fisk, A. D., Mead, S. E., Walker, N., & Cabrera, E. F. (1996). Training older adults to use automatic teller machines. *Human Factors, 38,* 425–433.

Rouiller, J. Z., & Goldstein, I. L. (1993). The relationship between organizational transfer climate and positive transfer of training. *Human Resource Development Quarterly, 4,* 377–390.

Salas, E., & Cannon-Bowers, J. A. (2001). The science of training: A decade of progress. *Annual Review of Psychology, 52,* 471–499.

Salas, E., DiazGranados, D., Klein, C., Burke, C. S., Stagl, K. C., Goodwin, G. F., & Halpin, S. M. (2008). Does team training improve team performance? A meta-analysis. *Human Factors, 50,* 903–933.

Salas, E., Nichols, D. R., & Driskell, J. E. (2007). Testing three team training strategies in intact teams: A meta-analysis. *Small Group Research, 38,* 471–488.

Salas, E., Tannenbaum, S. I., Kraiger, K., & Smith-Jentsch, K. A. (2012). The science of training and development in organizations: What matters in practice. *Psychological Science in the Public Interest, 13,* 74–101.

Salthouse, T. A. (2004). What and when of cognitive aging. *Current Directions in Psychological Science, 13,* 140–144.

Schmidt, R. A., & Bjork, R. A. (1992). New conceptualizations of practice: Common principles in three paradigms suggest new concepts for training. *Psychological Science, 3,* 207–217.

Sitzmann, T., Bell, B. S., Kraiger, K., & Kanar, A. M. (2009). A multilevel analysis of the effect of prompting self-regulation in technology-delivered instruction. *Personnel Psychology, 62,* 697–734.

Sitzmann, T., & Ely, K. (2010). Sometimes you need a reminder: The effects of prompting self-regulation on regulatory processes, learning, and attrition. *Journal of Applied Psychology, 95,* 132–144.

Sitzmann, T., & Ely, K. (2011). A meta-analysis of self-regulated learning in work-related training and educational attainment: What we know and where we need to go. *Psychological Bulletin, 137,* 421–442.

Sitzmann, T., Kraiger, K., Stewart, D., & Wisher, R. (2006). The comparative effectiveness of web-based and classroom instruction: A meta-analysis. *Personnel Psychology, 59,* 623–664.

Smith-Jentsch, K. A., Jentsch, F. G., Payne, S. C., & Salas, E. (1996). Can pretraining experiences explain individual differences in learning? *Journal of Applied Psychology, 81,* 110–116.

Smith-Jentsch, K. A., Salas, E., & Brannick, M. T. (2001). To transfer or not to transfer? Investigating the combined effects of trainee characteristics, team leader support, and team climate. *Journal of Applied Psychology, 86,* 279–292.

Snow, R. E. (1989). Aptitude-treatment interaction as a framework for research on individual differences in learning. In P. L. Ackerman, R. J. Sternberg, & R. Glaser (Eds.), *Learning and Individual Differences: Advances in Theory and Research* (pp. 13–59). New York: Freeman.

Spector, P. E. (1986). Perceived control by employees: A meta-analysis of studies concerning autonomy and participation at work. *Human Relations*, 39, 1005–1016.

Squire, K. (2008). Open-ended video games: A model for developing learning for the interactive age. In K. Salen (Ed.), *The John D. and Catherine T. MacArthur Foundation Series on Digital Media and Learning* (pp. 167–198), Cambridge, MA: MIT Press.

Surface, E. A. (2012). Training needs assessment: Aligning learning and capability with performance requirements and organizational objectives. In M. A. Wilson, W. Bennett, S. Gibson, & G. M. Alliger (Eds.), *The Handbook of Work Analysis: The Methods, Systems, Applications and Science of Work Measurement in Organizations*. New York: Routledge.

Switzer, K. C., Nagy, M. S., & Mullins, M. E. (2005). The influence of training reputation, managerial support, and self-efficacy on pre-training motivation and perceived training transfer. *Applied Human Resource Management Research*, 10, 21–34.

Tannenbaum, S. I., Mathieu, J. E., Salas, E., & Cannon-Bowers, J. A. (1991). Meeting trainees' expectations: The influence of training fulfillment on the development of commitment, self-efficacy, and motivation. *Journal of Applied Psychology*, 76, 759–769.

Taylor, P. J., Russ-Eft, D. F., & Chan, D. W. L. (2005). A meta-analytic review of behavior modeling training. *Journal of Applied Psychology*, 90, 692–709.

Thayer, P. W., & Teachout, M. S. (1995). *A Climate for Transfer Model*. AL/HR-TP-1995-0035, Brooks Air Force Base, TX.

Toossi, M. (2009). Labor force projections to 2018: Older workers staying more active. *Monthly Labor Review*, 30–51.

Tracey, J. B., Hinkin, T. R., Tannenbaum, S., & Mathieu, J. E. (2001). The influence of individual characteristics and the work environment on varying levels of training outcomes. *Human Resources Development Quarterly*, 12, 5–23.

Tracey, J. B., Tannenbaum, S. I., & Kavanagh, M. J. (1995). Applying trained skills on the job: The importance of the work environment. *Journal of Applied Psychology*, 80, 239–252.

Ubeda García, M. (2005). Training and business performance: The Spanish case. *International Journal of Human Resource Management*, 16, 1691–1710.

Van Der Klink M., Gielen E., & Nauta C. (2001). Supervisory support as a major condition to enhance transfer. *International Journal of Training and Development*, 5, 52–63.

Vancouver, J. B., & Day, D. V. (2005). Industrial and organizational research on self-regulation: From constructs to applications. *Applied Psychology: An International Review*, 54, 155–185.

Wilson, C. L., Huang, J., & Kraiger, K. (2013). Personality and the analysis, design, and delivery of training. In N. D. Christiansen & R. P. Tett (Eds.), *Handbook of Personality at Work* (pp. 543–564). New York: Routledge.

Wilson, K. A., Bedwell, W. L., Lazzara, E. H., Salas, E., Burke, C. S., Estock, J., et al. (2009). Relationship between game attributes and learning outcomes: Review and research proposals. *Simulation & Gaming*, 40, 217–66.

Wolfson, N. E. (2013). Shedding light on grey areas: Examining the effect of technology-based collaboration on the learning outcomes of older and younger adults. PhD thesis. Colorado State University.

Wolfson, N. E., Cavanagh, T., & Kraiger, K. (in press). Older adults and technology-based training: Optimizing learning outcomes and transfer. Accepted for publication, *Academy of Management Learning and Education*.

14

The Contribution of Talent Management to Organization Success

David G. Collings

Introduction

Talent management has arguably brought issues around the management of human resources (HR) to the agenda of chief executives and the C-Suite to a far greater degree than has been the case in the past. High-profile advocates such as Jack Welch at General Electric (GE) and consultancies such as McKinsey have lead the discourse around the "War for Talent." They have argued that an organizational culture where talent issues are to the fore are those that are most likely to thrive in the talent economy. Notwithstanding the global economic crisis of 2008, talent issues remain critical in the organizations globally.

For example, a survey of CEOs in 2012 identified developing the leadership and talent pipeline as a key priority of 66 percent of respondents (PWC, 2012). Similarly, a study conducted at Cornell University identified talent as the top priority on CEOs' agenda for HR (Wright, Stewart, & Moore, 2011).

There is very limited empirical evidence of the link between talent and performance. However, a study by Ernst and Young (2010, p. 4) claimed that "superior talent management correlates strongly with enhanced business performance." The study suggests that over a five-year period organizations with talent management programs which are aligned with business strategy deliver a return on investment (measured by return on common equity (ROE)) on average, 20 percent higher than rival companies where strategies are not aligned. Where key elements of their talent management programs are aligned, ROE over a five-year period averages 38 percent higher than competitors without alignment. Clearly, this study has not been peer reviewed in a traditional academic sense, so this correlation needs to be considered with caution.

However the belief in the benefits of talent management are clear. In this chapter, I review the evidence of the impact of talent management on organizational success. Taking a critical stance I examine the intellectual basis of the posited association between effective

The Wiley Blackwell Handbook of the Psychology of Training, Development, and Performance Improvement,
First Edition. Edited by Kurt Kraiger, Jonathan Passmore, Sigmar Malvezzi, and Nuno Rebelo dos Santos.
© 2015 John Wiley & Sons Ltd. Published 2020 by John Wiley & Sons Ltd.

talent management and organizational success and propose some questions that research could usefully address in this important area of contemporary management practice.

Controversies or Consensus

Like any new area of management practice, a key stage of the evolution of the field of talent management has been the establishment of theoretical and conceptual boundaries of the field. However, for scholars working in the field of talent management this has been a rather slow and protracted evolution (Al Ariss, Cascio, & Paauwe, 2014; Dries, 2013a; Lewis & Heckman, 2006; Vaiman & Collings, 2013). Indeed, the term talent management is used in different ways by different authors and practitioners. A key point of departure in any consideration of talent management should be understanding how talent management is defined by authors or practitioners. In this regard one can identify some trends in the evolution of the literature on talent management.

Earlier contributors generally took one of two perspectives on talent management. The first of these was to simply replace the term human resource management with talent management (Lewis & Heckman, 2006). While aspects of HR practice, such as HR planning or leadership development, may have been emphasized by these authors this literature did not advance our understanding of people management in any significant way. Indeed, arguably this stream of literature contributed to the initial skepticism towards talent management among the academic community. Such critics could justifiably classify talent management as nothing more than "old wine in new bottles," with little heuristic value (see Iles, 2011; Preece, Iles, & Chuai, 2011).

The second key approach of early authors strongly resonated with the McKinsey work on the "War for Talent" and practice in high-profile organizations such as GE. This idea clearly resonated with much of the thinking in relation to strategic human resource management (SHRM) that was unfolding at the same time. Jay Barney (1995) and others writing at this time called for organizations to look inside for competitive advantage and insights from the resource-based view, which Barney championed, significantly influenced thinking in SHRM and early approaches to talent management. This line of thinking emphasized the role of a value-creating strategy that competitors could not easily copy in gaining and maintaining competitive advantage. Central to competitive advantage were resources that varied between competing firms and that could not easily obtained or were immobile (Barney, 1991). Human resources represented a key potential source of com-petitive advantage and HRM was identified as having the potential to positively influence an organization's human and organization (structures, systems for planning, monitoring and controlling, social relations within the organization, etc.) resources in the drive for competitive advantage (Schuler & MacMahon, 1984). A central theme in this early talent management literature is that all roles should be filled with "A-performers," referred to as "topgrading" (Smart, 1999). Building on the well publicized "rank and yank" or forced distribution model (Blume, Rubin, & Baldwin, 2013; Grote, 2005), central to the approach was identifying A (top performers), B (solid performers), and C (poor performers) in the organization. It emphasizes the management of "C-players," or consistently poor performers, out of the organization (Michaels, Hadfield-Jones, & Axelrod, 2001). This approach was highly influential, although more recently the idea of forced distribution has been challenged. Clearly, it also helped to create some identifiable distinctions between talent management and traditional approaches to people management. However, for many commentators it was perceived as elitist with many negative implications for employees (Meyers & van Woerkom, 2014; Pfeffer, 2001). I return to this below.

As thinking on talent management evolved, perspectives on talent management arguably became more nuanced and began to offer clearer insights on how organizations could design talent management systems to deliver higher levels of organization performance. For example, the strategic positions perspective emphasizes the identification of key positions that have the potential to differentially impact the competitive advantage of the firm (Boudreau & Ramstad, 2005; Collings & Mellahi, 2009; Huselid, Beatty, & Becker, 2005). The starting point here is identification of key positions rather than talented individuals per se. It stands in contrast to the topgrading perspective outlined above and indeed much of the SHRM literature (c.f. Lepak & Snell, 1999), which adopts a bottom-up focus in theory development positing that employees can contribute to the firm's strategic objective simply by their value and uniqueness (Becker & Huselid 2006). In contrast, Becker and Huselid (2006, p. 904) advocate a top-down focus arguing that "When employees are able to contribute to a firm's strategic objectives they have (strategic) value" but that "not all strategic processes will be highly dependent on human capital." Thus, in certain roles the value added by a high performer may be little more than that added by an average performer. Emphasizing the import of strategic jobs, Huselid, Beatty, and Becker (2005, p. 2) define these "A positions" by their "disproportionate importance to a company's ability to execute some parts of its strategy and second ... the wide variability in the quality of the work displayed among the employees in these positions." It brings talent management systems to the fore by recognizing that there may be little economic value of human capital if it is not deployed effectively (Becker & Huselid, 2006; Boxall & Purcell, 2011).

A second key advancement in the literature improved our understanding of managing talent pools. This approach emphasizes "projecting employee/staffing needs and managing the progression of employees through positions" (Lewis & Heckman, 2006, p. 140). While building on traditional succession planning literatures, this literature adopts a more dynamic perspective that stands in contrast to the static nature of traditional succession planning. For example, organizations such as GE historically had succession plans 30 years into the future (Cappelli, 2010). Clearly, there is increasing recognition that as the business environment is constantly in flux such static conceptualizations of human capital requirements are no longer effective (Cascio & Aguinis, 2008; Cappelli, 2008; Lepak, Takeuchi, & Swart, 2011). For example, Cappelli (2008, p. 77) argues that "how employees advance through development jobs and experiences are remarkably similar to how products move through a supply chain." He uses insights from supply chain management to inform talent management practice. He points to talent failures where there are mismatches between supply and demand of talent. Such mismatches can result in oversupply of talent resulting in employee turnover, or layoffs and restructuring, or an undersupply where key positions cannot be filled and the organization's ability to compete is affected (Cappelli, 2008). More broadly, the talent pool strategy calls for a better understanding of the future value of human capital beyond its present value (Lepak, Takeuchi, & Swart, 2011). It also emphasizes the more proactive identification of talent. In line with insights from supply chain management, this emphasizes predicting future talent requirements and understanding how current human capital stocks might meet those talent requirements. Scenario planning emerges as a key strategic planning tool that provides insights into an organization's talent pool strategy. Scenario planning involves predictions around the alternative "futures" that may evolve for the organization and the consideration of organization responses to these "futures" (Mintzberg, 1994). Clearly the talent requirements are a central consideration of these futures.

Finally, in terms of perspectives on talent management, over the past number of years insights from big data and data analytics have influenced our understanding of talent management. Authors such as Boudreau and Ramstad (2005) pointed to the potential of talent management if it could provide those who ultimately make talent decisions – senior organizational leaders – with the decision framework and data and analysis required to inform key decisions around talent. This again stands in contrast to the historical positioning of HR as having a poor understanding and utilization of qualitative analysis in its decision making (Hammonds, 2005; Fitz-Enz, 2010). As Davenport, Harris and Shapiro (2010, p. 54) argue "if you want better performance from your top employees – who are perhaps your greatest asset and your largest expense – you'll do well to favor analytics over your gut instincts." Further, the deployment of these tools should enhance communication between HR leaders and other organizational stakeholders by reframing HR issues in language and frameworks that these other stakeholders are comfortable with (Boudreau, 2010, p. 11). Further, Davenport and colleagues call for the use of data analytics in ensuring higher productivity, engagement, and retention of top talent. Drawing insights from the wider literature on data analytics Davenport, Harris, and Shapiro (2010) summarize the different uses organizations can make of talent analytics. These range from simple human-capital facts, which include individual-level performance data and enterprise-level data such as head-count, turnover, and recruitment metrics to sophisticated real-time deployment of talent based on quickly changing needs. However, the potential of analytics in understanding which actions have the greatest impact on business performance is also an important category in their typology, which some could argue is the most significant.

There is little doubt that while academics and practitioners alike acknowledge the potential contribution of talent management to organization performance, the lack of consensus over its conceptual and intellectual boundaries has lead to a degree of confusion and indeed skepticism as to its value. However, understanding the differing perspectives at least provides a useful context for the consideration of the potential impact of talent management. For the purposes of the current chapter, I utilize Collings and Mellahi's (2009, p. 305) definition of talent management. They define strategic talent management as:

> activities and processes that involve the systematic identification of key positions which differentially contribute to the organisation's sustainable competitive advantage, the development of a talent pool of high potential and high performing incumbents to fill these roles, and the development of a differentiated human resource architecture to facilitate filling these positions with competent incumbents and to ensure their continued commitment to the organisation.

This definition uses the AMO (ability, motivation, opportunity) theory as an overarching theoretical framework. This reflects the increasing realization that "great systems are often more important than great people" (Beechler & Woodward, 2009, p. 277). Insights from the AMO framework highlight the fact that performance is more complex than simply employing great talent. The AMO framework, proposes that employee performance (P) is a function of the employee's ability (A), motivation (M), and opportunity (O) to perform (Boselie, Dietz, & Boon, 2005; Boxall & Purcell, 2011). Expressed as an equation:

$$P = f(A,M,O)$$

Thus, assuming that ability is taken as a given, as we are considering an organization's key talent, the organization must develop systems that ensure these key talents have the opportunity to perform (though supporting development opportunities and ensuring they are deployed effectively) and are highly motivated (through appropriate human resource policies and supports) to maximize performance. There is a relatively well-established body of empirical study that supports the important of context (opportunity and motivation) in understanding individual performance.

Consistent with Collings and Mellahi's definition of strategic talent management, I propose the ability, motivation, opportunity framework as a very useful frame to consider the linkage between talent management and organization success. Recognizing that simply loading an organization with talented employees is a poor strategy, this approach is premised on the alignment of the highest-performing and highest-potential employees with those roles that have the greatest potential for differential performance.

Having established a working definition of talent management, I now argue that management practice has unfolded based on some flawed assumptions around the relationship between talent management and performance.

Assumptions around Talent and Performance

As noted above a central argument in the current chapter is that not only has research failed to establish a relationship between talent management and organizational performance, but that management practice has unfolded based on some flawed assumptions around the relationship. Reflecting on these is important in charting a way forward for the field of talent management.

The first of these flawed assumptions is that loading an organization full of A-players or "stars" will ensure high levels of organization performance. As outlined above, this view was central to the original McKinsey perspective on the War for Talent (Michaels, Handfield-Jones, & Axelrod, 2001). It raises a number of misconceptions around the link between talent management and organization success. Firstly, it is based on the assumption that organization performance is simply an aggregation of individual performance (Pfeffer, 2001). Indeed, the subsequent failure of a number of the high-profile companies, which were central to the original McKinsey research, points to the implications of this perspective. For example, Enron,[1] which was a key exemplar of the McKinsey approach to talent management, hired 250 MBAs a year from the most prestigious US business schools during the 1990s. It rewarded these individuals inordinately and promoted them rapidly (Michaels, Handfield-Jones, & Axelrod, 2001). However, these talents were given huge levels of autonomy to develop new businesses with little or no organizational oversight or control and failures were glossed over as the individuals had talent (Gladwell, 2002). In an ironic way Enron somehow managed to privilege talent over performance. Indeed, McKinsey's pivotal role in advising Enron has been central to criticism around McKinsey's influence on business practice (McDonald, 2013).

More broadly privileging individual stars risks the creation of a tension between individual performance and reward and the requirement for collaborative effort in most modern organizations owing to the complexity of the issues at hand (See Pfeffer, 2001, p. 249). As Pfeffer (2001) notes, placing too much emphasis on individual performance inevitably diminished teamwork, and creates destructive internal competition in turn retarding knowledge sharing and learning within work groups. Indeed, research shows "that the nearly single-minded focus on individuals that is endemic to companies' strategies for fighting the talent war often backfires and reduces, rather than enhances individuals, teams and organizations" (Beechler & Woodward, 2009, p. 277). This tension is key given that modern organizations can be viewed as highly interdependent "network[s] of workers" (Mailath & Postlewaite, 1990) carrying out interconnected tasks. Indeed, the division of labor (Marengo & Dosi, 2005) and task interdependence in modern organizations have created strong interactions and functional dependencies between individuals

(Galletta & Heckman, 1990; Mailath & Postlewaite, 1990), whereby the effectiveness of high-performing individuals is significantly dependent on colleagues performing complementary and interrelated tasks (Groysberg & Lee, 2008; Groysberg, 2010; Huckman & Pisano, 2006; Hackman, 1987; Graham & Dillon, 1974). Indeed, Groysberg and Lee (2008, p. 1128) found that working with higher-ability individuals may enhance the performance of high-performing individuals and "working with lower-ability individuals may hinder the performance of high-ability individuals." Similarly, Grigoriou and Rothaermel (2013) argue that a sole focus on individual productivity presents an under-socialized view on human capital. In developing the idea of relational stars, they emphasize the importance of individual's embedded relationships in effectively performing knowledge-generating activities (see also Whelan, Collings, & Donnellan, 2010). This body of literature points to the import of the competencies of colleagues and the role of relational capital in facilitating star performance.

In effect the overemphasizing of individual performance risks positioning performance as a zero-sum game, where one individual is designated as a high performer by definition another is designated as not (Pfeffer, 2001). It further, underestimates the importance of teams of performers effectively working together to achieve organization performance.

Relatedly, this perspective implies that that talent designates natural abilities and potential and therefore the role of the organization is to identify, recruit, and hone existing innate talent and not to create talent. It is premised on the idea that talent is fixed and invariant (Pfeffer, 2001). Central to this perspective is the idea that high intelligence, or general mental ability (GMA) is highly correlated with higher levels of performance. The mounting evidence from this literature points to an impressive and uniformly robust positive and direct correlation between GMA and performance. Since Spearman (1904) introduced the concept over a century ago, empirical evidence suggests that GMA has the capacity to predict job performance (Ferris, Witt, & Hochwarter, 2011), in all types of jobs (Hunter, 1986), and that its predictive power of job performance is stronger than any other method (Schmidt & Hunter 1998; Le et al., 2007). Indeed, for many years, scholars (e.g., Schmidt & Hunter, 1998) argued that although g or GMA per se may not predict individual performance in isolation, it sits at the top of the hierarchy of key determinants of outstanding performance. Gottfredson (1986, p. 330) argued that the g-factor is "the single most useful worker attribute for predicting job performance." Similarly, Schmidt, Hunter, and Outerbridge (1986) reported that, ceteris paribus, individuals high in GMA outperform their low-GMA counterparts especially in highly complex tasks.

However, a more nuanced perspective suggests that innate talent is not a sufficient condition for exceptional performance, rather it is a necessary precondition (Meyers, van Woerkom, & Dries, 2013). While these scholars recognize the role GMA plays in enabling high performance, they also recognize that its impact varies in different settings (Ackerman, 1986). As well as recognizing the varying association between GMA and performance from one setting to another, they also recognize that this association changes over time (Simonton, 1999). Murphy (1989), for example, contested the stable GMA performance link across settings and time and argued that its impact on performance may even decline over time. The emphasis is placed upon effective selection to ensure one gets the right talent as organizations may gain very little by investing in the development of talent if individuals do not possess superior raw material of talent. Additionally practices focused on the retention of talent emerge as important (Dries, 2013b; Meyers, van Woerkom, & Dries, 2013; Nijs et al., 2014).

A second flawed assumption around the nature of talent stemming from the A positions literature is that given talent is innate in individuals that talent can easily transfer from one context to another. Insights in this regard can be drawn from the sporting literature and the literature on talent transfer (see Collings & Mellahi, 2013; Meyers, van Woerkom, & Dries, 2013). This literature proposes that talented athletes in one sport can excel in another sport with extensive, high-quality training, other necessary resources, and the possibility to participate in competitions (see Bullock et al., 2009). Indeed, in many instances organizations favor the external market in staffing pivotal roles. For instance, nearly half of CEOs are appointed from outside the organization, an increase from only one in ten in the 1970s (Murphy & Zábojník, 2007). Organizations often pay a significant premium to attract talented individuals under the assumption that they can replicate their past high performance in their new organization (Gibbons & Murphy, 1992; Chevalier & Ellison, 1999). Pfeffer (2001) likens this to the glorification of outsiders while downplaying the talents of insiders, or those already employed by the organization

However, the research evidence points to a number of key limitations on this perspective in a business context. Firstly, as noted above, it costs more to buy talent on the external labor market than develop it internally. For example, a study of some 15,000 employees of a US investment back confirmed that employees recruited externally tended to enjoy a wage premium of 18 percent when compared to internal hires (Bidwell, 2012). This study, also demonstrated that new hires performed significantly less well than promoted employees for two years following joining the organization and were more likely to leave voluntarily or involuntarily. Groysberg's research on the portability of performance also reinforces this challenge. Research on CEOs also points to the challenge of transferring performance from one role to another. For example, a study of former GE executives (a company widely regarded as a standard setter for leadership development) showed that while the stockmarket viewed the hiring of a former GE executive as a CEO as positive, the performance of these new CEOs was far less certain. In about 50 percent of cases, the new hire did not work out and the organization underperformed against the stockmarket by almost 40 percent. When the new hire worked out the positive impact on share price was less than 15 percent. A more recent study of CEOs of the S&P 500 companies found that CEOs with prior CEO experience in other firms performed worse than peers without prior experience as CEO. Hamori and Koyuncu (2013, p. 14) concluded that "Being a prior CEO was negatively and significantly associated with three-year average post-succession return on assets." They traced this to the time taken to unlearn from their prior experience and the tendency to follow shortcuts in decision making based on experience in their past CEO role. They conclude that in effect those with prior CEO experience may be too embedded in the norms, culture, and routines of another organization, which plays out in terms of fixed assumptions about how they should perform their role in the new organization.

More broadly the challenge of transferring performance from one organization to another is well established in this literature. For example, in a large-scale study of stockmarket analysts, Groysberg (2010) demonstrated that despite these individuals' belief that their performance was largely a function of their own talent and independent of the organizations in which they worked, their performance was in fact highly correlated with the organizations for whom they worked. Specifically, almost half (46 percent) of the star performers performed poorly in the year after they changed jobs. Their performance dropped by an average of 20 percent and it took them up to five years to return to their original performance levels. The conclusion drawn from this research is that as little as 30 percent of these stars' performance is determined by the individual; 70 percent is determined by the resources and qualities specific to the firm that developed them. Specific resources might include the reputation of the firm, the IT systems that the analysts use, and the supporting teams around them. Indeed, research on cardiac surgeons confirms the importance of these intangibles on individual performance. Huckman and Pisano's (2006) study showed that surgeon performance was not completely portable across hospitals. They examined the same surgeon performing the same procedure at multiple hospitals and found differences in the mortality rates of patients. Surgeons performed better at hospitals where they performed more procedures. They suggest that this may be traced to the familiarity that a surgeon develops with the assets of a given organization, including other teams members and more broadly the infrastructure in the hospital.

These ideas reinforce the idea that talent management is far more nuanced than a sole focus on A-performers would suggest. Additionally, the research evidence points to the advantages of internal talent development over recruitment in filling pivotal roles. This brings the role of HR systems and processes to the fore in maximizing the contribution of talented employees to organization performance. However, the reality is that many organizations continue to struggle to identify the talent they require. For example, CEOs identified the availability of talent and skills as a key threat to organizations' growth prospects, with talent retention the top priority of HR directors in the same study (PWC, 2013). Indeed, there is a recognition that the HR profession is lacking in the skills required to manage talent effectively. For example, a study by the Boston Consulting Group (BCG, 2009) identified managing talent as one of the five critical challenges facing the HR function through to 2015. However, it was a challenge that the function felt least prepared to deal with effectively. More recently the ability to manage top talent was identified as a key skills gap for HR function by HR directors themselves (PWC, 2013). Indeed, only 31 percent of organizations in the PWC survey had a formal and developed talent management program in place. It seems that in many ways, our understanding has not advanced very much over the decade since Pfeffer and Sutton (2006, p. 90) concluded that "despite the claims in The War for Talent ... and numerous other books on hiring the best people, the talent mind-set is rooted in a set of assumptions and empirical evidence that is incomplete, misleading and downright wrong."

Indeed, over recent years there has been an increasing awareness that "great systems are often more [or at least as] important than great people" (Beechler & Woodward, 2009, p. 277). However, even where systems are in place to manage talent they are often poorly utilized. For example, Wiblen, Dery, and Grant's (2012) study challenges the extent to which managers actually utilize the data from systems and analyses to inform talent decisions. Drawing on the social construction of technology literature, the authors found that the role of IT was contested and marginalized by decision makers. Decisions on whether an individual was designated as talent or not were typically based upon highly subjective interpretation rather than informed by formal measures facilitated through IT. A key implication from this study was that the potential of IT to facilitate better talent-identification decisions was very much under-realized. The process of talent identification has been classified as a two-step process in which largely experience-based (online) performance appraisal evaluations provide input to largely cognition-based (offline) decisions (Mäkelä, Björkman, & Ehrnrooth, 2010). It is in the second stage that decision-makers' biases and the limitation of their cognitive processes come into play in explaining the subjective decisions that they make (see also Mellahi & Collings, 2010). This literature highlights the impact of previous experience and limited cognitive abilities that influence decision criteria and guide decision-makers' search for and choice from available options that result in less than optimal talent decisions.

Thus, significant gaps in our understanding of how best to manage talent remain, with a recent review concluding that "there is a serious gap in our knowledge regarding how talented individuals are managed, especially regarding the processes organizations use to recruit, motivate and reward talent" (McDonnell et al., 2013). The challenge for the more effective management of talent is to institutionalize the expertise in making good judgment in organizations (Conaty & Charan, 2010) and to build effective decision frameworks to inform these decisions (Boudreau & Jesuthasan, 2011). Without these two prerequisites in place it will be very difficult for organizations to build talent management systems to positively impact organizational performance let alone begin to measure the impact.

Further Research

There is little doubt that talent management is a central concern of human resource professionals and organization leaders more generally. Initially, this interest appears to have been sparked by high-profile advocates such as consultancies and high-profile CEOs. Insights from institutional theory would suggest that these early adopters, introduced talent management based on a belief that it would contribute to organizational efficiency and performance. In other words there is reason to believe that these organizations strongly believed in the line of sight between investment in talent management and organizational performance. However, notwithstanding the high-profile failures of a number of the organizations singled out as exemplars of talent management (such as Enron), organizations globally seem to be adopting the philosophy of talent management in their droves. However, in line with institutional theory there is at least some evidence that these organizations are drawn to talent management for reasons of legitimacy rather than performance per se. In effect, managers feel they "should" have talent management programs to be perceived as legitimate organizations with a strong people-management focus. The inability of many managers who claim to practice talent management to articulate how talent management is defined and operationalized in their organizations points to this trend. For example, in a 2006 study by the Chartered Institute of Personnel and Development (CIPD) over 51 percent of HR managers said that their companies practiced talent management, however, fewer than one in five of these managers could define what that meant. Anecdotally at least this points to somewhat of a bandwagon effect whereby managers have adopted the language of talent management in an effort to legitimize their efforts in people management.

As has been illustrated above there are many misconceptions that have underpinned the development of talent management programs in organizations. These misconceptions have arguably retarded the development of talent management practice and reduced the impact of talent management on organization performance. A more mature approach to talent management requires the development of talent-management systems that are closely aligned with the strategy and context of the organization for which they are developed. A nuanced understanding of the current and future talent requirements and availability both internally and externally is a central part of more mature talent management. This allows for a more dynamic approach to human capital within the firm, which is consistent with the fluid organizational and environmental climates in which contemporary organizations operate.

A maturing of talent management in practice will require the academic community to further build the evidence base to inform talent practice and facilitate a greater degree of evidence-based talent management. A number of key questions emerge in this regard. The first is to understand better the relationship between individuals, talent systems, and performance outcomes at the individual, unit, and organizational level. As has been illustrated above these are questions that we do not have a clear evidence base upon which to progress. Closely linked to this question is the question as to whether there is evidence to suggest that there is a universal set of talent management best practices that lead to positive performance outcomes regardless of context or whether the picture is more complex with the requirement to adapt practices to the organizational and national contexts in which they are deployed. While research in the context of multinational organizations suggests that there is indeed evidence of convergence in global talent management practices, at least in leading multinationals (Stahl et al., 2012) we know less about the evidence and impact of such practices in smaller firms and national organizations. Further we do not actually know the impact of the identified best practices on organization performance in the multinational sector. The distance between the dependent variable of organization performance and the independent variables of talent management practices is simply too great to have a clear understanding of the impact of the practices. Similarly despite the pivotal role of global mobility in global talent management programs, the topics have remained largely separate as areas of academic study and debate (cf. Cerdin & Brewster, 2014; Collings, 2014; Sparrow, 2012). In improving organization practice in global mobility management and global talent management, it will be important to further build theoretical and empirical insights to understand better the relationship between these two important areas of practice.

In building this evidence base, researches should draw on insights and theories from the cognate fields of, inter alia, human resource management, industrial and organizational psychology, and strategy. It is also important to consider a pluralistic perspective where the interests of individual employees and other stakeholders are considered in addition to organization concerns (cf. Thunnissen, Boselie, & Fruytier, 2013).

Conclusion

As has been outlined above talent management has gained significant traction as a key area of HR practice and indeed something that senior organization leaders should devote their time to. Arguably it has brought HR issues to the C-Suite in a far more strategic way than has been the case in the past. This chapter has demonstrated that notwithstanding this emphasis on talent management, there is a lack of clarity as to what precisely talent management is and how it should be operationalized. I have argued that this is at least in part owing to the adaptation of talent management in response to institutional pressures and the desire to be perceived as pursuing legitimate people-management strategies as opposed to clear alignment with organization strategy and context.

The development of academic work on talent management has also been retarded by a lack of consensus on the conceptual and intellectual boundaries of talent management. I have classified the different approaches to talent management and presented Collings and Mellahi's (2009) definition as an example of a clearly bounded and theoretically informed definition of talent management that can usefully inform research and practice. Given the lack of clarity around what talent management is and how best to operationalize it, it is unsurprising that it has proven difficult to chart the impact of talent management on organizational performance.

It is also clear that thinking on talent management has been underscored by some key misconceptions around the nature of talent in organizations. First among these is that loading an organization full of A-players or star performers is sufficient to deliver sustained high performance. Beyond the evidence presented above, there is ample evidence from the sporting arena to reinforce the challenges of overly relying on hiring stars to deliver high performance. Such a perspective also creates tensions between individual performance and team dynamics. It also assumes that as talent is innate it cannot be developed and once talent is hired performance will follow. However, the available research evidence suggests that although talent is a necessary precondition of performance, it is not sufficient in itself

(Meyers, van Woerkom, & Dries, 2013). This is illustrated in the challenges of high performers transferring their performance from one organization to another.

All in all, the chapter has outlined the evolution of thinking on talent management, taking a critical stance. Developing a clear line of sight between talent management and organization performance will require the development of an efficient evidence base to inform management practice and the use of this evidence in designing talent management practices in organizations.

Note

1   Enron was a US headquartered company in the energy, commodities, and services area. Prior to its downfall and ultimate bankruptcy in 2001 Enron was regarded as a highly innovative company with revenues of some $101 billion in 2000. However, in 2001 it became clear that the organization's reported financial performance was underpinned by an institutionalized, systematic, and creatively planned accounting fraud. Indeed, the fraud was so significant that it resulted in the dissolution of the company's auditors Arthur Anderson, the imprisonment of senior managers in the firm, and ultimately the introduction of the Sarbanes-Oxley Act of 2002.

References

Ackerman, P. L. (1986). Individual differences in information processing: An investigation of intellectual abilities and task performance during practice. *Intelligence*, 10, 101–139.

Al Ariss, A., Cascio, W. F., & Paauwe, J. (2014). Talent management: Current theories and future research directions. *Journal of World Business*, 49, 173–179. doi: http://dx.doi.org/10.1016/j.jwb.2013.11.001.

Barney, J. (1991). Firm resources and sustained competitive advantage. *Journal of Management*, 17, 99–120.

Barney, J. B. (1995). Looking inside for competitive advantage. *Academy of Management Executive*, 9, 49–61.

BCG (2009). *Creating People Advantage: How to Tackle the Major HR Challenges during the Crisis and Beyond*. Dusseldorf: Boston Consulting Group.

Becker, B. E., & Huselid, M. A. (2006). Strategic human resource management: Where do we go from here? *Journal of Management*, 32, 898–925.

Beechler, S., & Woodward, I. C. (2009). The global "war for talent." *Journal of International Management*, 15, 273–285.

Bidwell, M. (2012). Paying more to get less: The effects of external hiring versus internal mobility. *Administrative Science Quarterly*, 56(3), 369–407.

Blume, B. D., Rubin, R. S., & Baldwin, T. T. (2013). Who is attracted to an organisation using a forced distribution performance management system? *Human Resource Management Journal*, 23, 360–378. doi:10.1111/1748-8583.12016.

Boselie, J. P., Dietz, G., & Boon, C. (2005). Commonalities and contradictions in research on human resource management and performance. *Human Resource Management*, 15, 67–94.

Boudreau, J. (2010). *Retooling HR: Using Proven Business Tools to Make Better Decisions about Talent*. Boston, MA: Harvard Business School Press.

Boudreau, J., & Jesuthasan, R. (2011). *Transformative HR: How Great Companies Use Evidence-Based-Change for Sustainable Advantage*. London: Jossey-Bass.

Boudreau, J. W., & Ramstad, P. M. (2005). Talent, talent segmentation and sustainability: A new decision science paradigm for a new HR paradigm. *Human Resource Management*, 44, 129–136.

Boxall, P., & Purcell, J. (2011). *Strategy and Human Resource Management* (3rd ed.). Basingstoke: Palgrave Macmillan.

Bullock, N., Gulbin, J. P., Martin, D. T., Ross, A., Holland, T., & Marino, F. (2009). Talent identification and deliberate programming in skeleton: Ice novice to Winter Olympian in 14 months. *Journal of Sports Sciences, 27*, 397–404.

Cappelli, P. (2008). *Talent on Demand: Managing Talent in an Uncertain Age*. Boston, MA: Harvard Business School Press.

Cappelli, P. (2010). The rise and decline of managerial development. *Industrial and Corporate Change, 19*, 509–548.

Cascio, W. F., & Aguinis, H. (2008). Staffing twenty-first century organizations. *Academy of Management Annals, 2*, 133–165.

Cerdin, J. L., & Brewster, C. (2014). Talent management and expatriation: Bridging two streams of research and practice. *Journal of World Business, 49*(2), 245–252. doi: http://dx.doi.org/10.1016/j.jwb.2013.11.008.

Chevalier, J., & Ellison, G. (1999). Are some mutual fund managers better than others? Cross-sectional patterns in behavior and performance. *Journal of Finance, 54*, 875–899.

Collings, D. G. (2014). Towards an integration of global mobility and global talent management. *Journal of World Business, 49*, 253–261. doi: http://dx.doi.org/10.1016/j.jwb.2013.11.009.

Collings, D. G., & Mellahi, K. (2009). Strategic talent management: A review and research agenda. *Human Resource Management Review, 19*, 4, 304–313.

Collings, D. G., & Mellahi, K. (2013). Commentary on: "Talent – Innate or acquired? Theoretical considerations and their implications for talent management." *Human Resource Management Review, 24*(3), 322–25.

Conaty, B., & Charan, R. (2010). *The Talent Masters: Why Smart Leaders Put People before Numbers*. New York: Random House.

Davenport, T. H., Harris, J., & Shapiro, J. (2010). Competing on talent analytics. *Harvard Business Review, 88*, pp. 52–58.

Dries, N. (2013a). Talent management, from phenomenon to theory: Introduction to the special issue. *Human Resource Management Review, 23*(4), 267–271.

Dries, N. (2013b). The psychology of talent management: A review and research agenda. *Human Resource Management Review, 23*(4), 272–285.

Ernst and Young. (2010). *Managing Today's Global Workforce: Evaluating Talent Management to Improve Business*. London: Ernst and Young.

Ferris, G. R., Witt, L. A., & Hochwarter, W. A. (2001). Interaction of social skill and general mental ability on job performance and salary. *Journal of Applied Psychology, 86*, 1075–1082.

Fitz-Enz, J. (2010). *The New HR Analytics*. New York: AMACOM.

Galletta, D., & Heckman, R. (1990). A role theory perspective on end-user development. *Information Systems Research, 1*(2), 168–187.

Gibbons, R., & Murphy, K. J. (1992). Optimal incentive contracts in the presence of career concerns: Theory and evidence (no. w3792). Washington, DC: National Bureau of Economic Research.

Gladwell, M. (2002). The talent myth: Are smart people overrated? *New Yorker*, July 22.

Gottfredson, G. D. (1986). An empirical test of school-based environmental and individual interventions to reduce the risk of delinquent behavior. *Criminology, 24*, 705–730.

Graham, W. K., & Dillon, P. C. (1974). Creative supergroups: Group performance as a function of individual performance in brainstorming tasks. *Journal of Social Psychology, 93*, 101–105.

Grigoriou, K., & Rothaermel, F. T. (2013). Structural microfoundations of innovation: The role of relational stars. *Journal of Management, 40*(2), 586–615. doi:10.1177/0149206313513612.

Grote, D. (2005). *Forced Ranking: Making Performance Management Work*. Boston, MA: Harvard Business School Press.

Groysberg, B. (2010). *Chasing Stars: The Myth of Talent and the Portability of Performance*. Princeton, NJ: Princeton University Press.

Groysberg, B., & Lee, L.-E. (2008). The effects of colleague quality on top performance: The case of security analysts. *Journal of Organizational Behavior, 29*(8), 1123–1144.

Hackman, J. R. (1987). The design of work teams. In J. Lorsch (Ed.), *Handbook of Organizational Behavior* (pp. 315–342). Englewood Cliffs, NJ: Prentice Hall.

Hammonds, K. H. (2005). Why we hate HR. *Fast Company*, 97. http://www.fastcompany.com/53319/why-we-hate-hr (accessed January 1, 2014).

Hamori, M., & Koyuncu, B. (2013). The CEO experience trap. *MIT Sloan Management Review*, 55(1), 14–16.

Huckman, R. S., & Pisano, G. P. (2006). The firm specificity of individual performance: Evidence from cardiac surgery. *Management Science*, 52, 473–488.

Hunter, J. E. (1986). Cognitive ability, cognitive aptitudes, job knowledge, and job performance. *Journal of Vocational Behavior*, 29, 340–362.

Huselid, M. A., Beatty, R. W., & Becker, B. E. (2005). "A players" or "A positions"? The strategic logic of workforce management. *Harvard Business Review*, December, 110–117.

Iles, P. A. (2011). Leadership development and talent management: Fashion statement or fruitful direction? In M. Lee (Ed.), *HRD as We Know it: Speeches that have Shaped and Developed the Field of HRD* (pp. 50–66). New York: Routledge.

Le, H., Oh, I., Shaffer, J. A., & Schmidt, F. L. (2007). Implications of methodological advances for the practice of personnel selection: How practitioners benefit from meta-analysis. *Academy of Management Perspectives*, 21(3), 6–15.

Lepak, D. P., & Snell, S. A. (1999). The human resource architecture: Toward a theory of human capital allocation and development. *Academy of Management Review*, 24, 31–48.

Lepak, D. P., Takeuchi, R., & Swart, J. (2011). Aligning human capital with organizational needs. In A. Burton-Jones & J. C. Spender (Eds.), *The Oxford Handbook of Human Capital* (pp. 333–358). Oxford: Oxford University Press.

Lewis, R. E., & Heckman, R. J. (2006). Talent management: A critical review. *Human Resource Management Review*, 16, 139–154.

Mailath, G., & Postlewaite, A. (1990). Workers versus firms: Bargaining over a firm's value. *Review of Economic Studies*, 57, 369–380.

Mäkelä, K., Björkman, I., & Ehrnrooth, M. (2010). How do MNCs establish their talent pools? Influences on individuals' likelihood of being labeled as talent. *Journal of World Business*, 45, 134–142.

Marengo, L., & Dosi, G. (2005). Division of labor, organizational coordination and market mechanisms in collective problem-solving. *Journal of Economic Behavior and Organization*, 58(2), 303–326.

McDonald, D. (2013). *The Firm: The Story of McKinsey and its Secret Influence on American Business*. New York: Simon & Schuster.

McDonnell, A., Collings, D. G., Mellahi, K., & Schuler, R. S. (2013). Talent management: A review of progress and prospects for the field. Unpublished manuscript.

Mellahi, K., & Collings, D. G. (2010). The barriers to effective global talent management: The example of corporate élites in MNEs. *Journal of World Business*, 45, 143–149.

Meyers, M. C., & van Woerkom, M. (2014). The influence of underlying philosophies on talent management: Theory, implications for practice, and research agenda. *Journal of World Business*, 49(2), 192–203. doi: http://dx.doi.org/10.1016/j.jwb.2013.11.003.

Meyers, M. C., van Woerkom, M., & Dries, N. (2013). Talent – innate or acquired? Theoretical considerations and their implications for talent management. *Human Resource Management Review*, 23, 267–271.

Michaels, E., Handfield-Jones, H., & Axelrod, B. (2001). *The War for Talent*. Boston, MA: Harvard Business School Press.

Mintzberg, H. (1994). *The Rise and Fall of Strategic Planning*. New York: Free Press.

Murphy, K. J., & Zábojník, J. (2007). Managerial capital and the market for CEOs. Working paper. Unpublished.

Murphy, K. R. (1989). Is the relationship between cognitive ability and job performance stable over time? *Human Performance*, 2, 183–200.

Nijs, S., Gallardo-Gallardo, E., Dries, N., & Sels, L. (2014). A multidisciplinary review into the definition, operationalization, and measurement of talent. *Journal of World Business*, 49(2), 180–191. doi: http://dx.doi.org/10.1016/j.jwb.2013.11.002.

Pfeffer, J. (2001). Fighting the war for talent is hazardous to your organization's health. *Organizational Dynamics*, 29, 248–259.

Pfeffer, J., & Sutton, R. (2006). *Hard Facts, Dangerous Half Truths, and Total Nonsense: Profiting from Evidence-Based Management*. Boston, MA: Harvard Business School Press.

Preece, D., Illes, P., & Chuai, X. (2011). Talent management and management fashion in Chinese enterprise: Exploring case studies in Beijing. *International Journal of Human Resource Management*, 22, 3413–3428.

PWC (2012). *15th Annual Global CEO Survey*. Belfast: PWC.

PWC (2013). *HR Director Pulse Survey*. Belfast: PWC.

Schmidt, F. L., & Hunter, J. E. (1998). The validity and utility of selection methods in personnel psychology: Practical and theoretical implications of 85 years of research findings. *Psychological Bulletin*, 124(2), 262–274.

Schmidt, F. L., Hunter, J. E., & Outerbridge, A. N. (1986). The impact of job experience and ability on job knowledge, work sample performance, and supervisory ratings of job performance. *Journal of Applied Psychology*, 71, 432–439.

Schuler, R. S., & MacMahon, I. C. (1984). Gaining competitive advantage through HR management practices. *Human Resource Management*, 23, 241–255.

Simonton, D. K. (1999). Creativity as blind variation and selective retention: Is the creative process Darwinian? *Psychological Inquiry*, 10, 309–328.

Smart, B. D. (1999). *Topgrading: How Leading Companies Win by Hiring, Coaching, and Keeping the Best People*. Paramus, NJ: Prentice Hall Press.

Sparrow, P. (2012). Globalising the international mobility function: The role of emerging markets, flexibility and strategic delivery models. *International Journal of Human Resource Management*, 23, 2404–2427.

Spearman, C. (1904). "General intelligence" objectively determined and measured. *American Journal of Psychology*, 15, 201–293.

Stahl, G., Björkman, I., Farndale, E., Morris, S. S., Paauwe, J., Stiles, P., & Wright, P. (2012). Six principles of effective global talent management. *Sloan Management Review*, 53(2), 25–42.

Thunnissen, M., Boselie, P., & Fruytier, B. (2013). Talent management and the relevance of context: Towards a pluralistic perspective. *Human Resource Management Review*, 23, 322–335.

Vaiman, V., & Collings, D. G. (2013). Talent management: Advancing the field. *International Journal of Human Resource Management*, 24(9), 1737–1743.

Whelan, E., Collings, D. G., & Donnellan, B. (2010). Managing talent in knowledge-intensive settings. *Journal of Knowledge Management*, 14(3), 486–504.

Wiblen, S., Dery, K., & Grant, D. (2012). Do you see what I see? The role of technology in talent identification. *Asia Pacific Journal of Human Resources*, 50, 421–438.

Wright, P. M., Stewart, M., & Moore, O. A. (2011). *The 2011 CHRO Challenge: Building Organizational, Functional, and Personal Talent*. Ithaca, NY, Cornell.

15

Action Learning: Approaches, Applications, and Outcomes

Lisa Anderson and Charlotte Coleman

Introduction

Action learning has grown from the simple idea that the task or the problem should take precedence over theory as the basis for learning. In the twenty-first century it has moved into the mainstream of management development and takes a wide range of forms, used in many organizations and educational settings throughout the world. There is a wide range of published work on action learning, ranging from practitioner focused, "how-to" texts to peer-reviewed academic journal papers. However, it is important to say at the outset that while there are a number of approaches to action learning, many of which are described in this chapter, it is often understood and used as a broad term that encompasses any approach to learning that engages learners in some form of activity or in an experiential mode. Here, the focus is on the specifics of action learning rather than the generalities of *active* learning.

This chapter traces the development of action learning and its growth as an approach to developing managers. It sets out the most prevalent approaches to action learning, the contexts in which it is used, the theoretical basis for learning and reflection that underpins it, and the reasons why it is becoming increasingly ubiquitous in management education and development.

The Origins of Action Learning – Reg Revans

Rigg and Trehan (2013) propose that action learning has eschewed simple definition although many exist and indeed, are reproduced in this chapter. However, it is indisputable that action learning was conceived and developed by Reg Revans. As director of education for the National Coal Board (UK) during the early 1950s, Revans, the so-called "Father" of action learning, spent long periods of time with managers in an effort to understand the particular

The Wiley Blackwell Handbook of the Psychology of Training, Development, and Performance Improvement, First Edition. Edited by Kurt Kraiger, Jonathan Passmore, Sigmar Malvezzi, and Nuno Rebelo dos Santos. © 2015 John Wiley & Sons Ltd. Published 2020 by John Wiley & Sons Ltd.

problems they faced and how they might best address them. Revans felt that off-the-shelf knowledge found in books and traditional instruction alone could not help these managers deal with the often intractable problems they faced in an organizational and societal environmental that was significantly different to that of the pre-World War II era. Revans (1979) describes how 22 collieries formed a consortium for their staff to work together on "four common operational problems." This was followed by the Hospitals Internal Communications Project in which 10 large hospitals in London were involved in "mutual study of each others' troubles" (Revans, 1979, p. 4). Through the 1960s and 1970s, action learning began to be widely used throughout the world, including projects in Australia, India and the US (Revans, 1979). Pedler (1996) describes Revans' basic premise: for organizations and individuals to flourish then the rate of learning has to be equal to or greater than the rate of change (expressed as L≥C). Learning has two elements, traditional instruction or *programmed knowledge* (P) and critical reflection or *questioning insight* (Q), giving the learning equation, L = P + Q. Programmed knowledge, however, should only be sought after careful reflection on what knowledge is needed and why. While programmed knowledge can be learned in isolation and as a solitary activity, Revans believed that the development of questioning insight could only happen in the company of others, in a learning community;

> Action learning obliges each to look critically at his own experience, dragging it out for the inspection of his colleagues ... he will constantly be called upon to explain why he is following the course of action he has chosen ... and *will* ... see that the only other persons who can help him are his colleagues, those comrades in adversity who also look to him for help. (Revans, 1980, p. 256– 257)

Revans' emphasis on the importance of exploring the nature of problems through insightful questioning and in a group setting before deciding on a course of action has persisted in all forms of action learning. Learning communities or "sets," as they are more commonly known, bring people together to work on real problems in which managers have a personal stake and that have no easy or obvious solution; to consider the problem from a range of different perspectives and create possibilities for action and then to take that action, which in turn is laid open to question and reflection and as a source of new learning about the problem itself, for the individual who "owns" the problem and about learning itself (Pedler, 1997).

The Development of Action Learning

In the last few years of his life, Revans worked with a group of scholars at Salford University and a number of these, most notably Mike Pedler, have continued to research and write about the practice and philosophy of action learning. They have remained true to Revans' original ideas and see action as the basis for learning, reflection on action, working on organizationally based problems in sets of peers and the primacy of questioning insight (Q) over programmed knowledge (P) (Pedler, Burgoyne, & Brook, 2005).

Pedler's work over the past 20 years (1991, 1996, 1997, 2011) sets out the principles of action learning, provides a guide for practice, and examines the changing nature of action learning in a range of settings. Although Revans' principles and commitment continue under the broad heading of the "scientific school" (Marsick & O'Neil, 1999) or in the "Revansesque tradition" (Anderson & Thorpe, 2004), there are now many ways in which it is conceptualized and practiced. Yorks, O'Neil, and Marsick (1999) offer six definitions, all of which propose that the two central features of action learning are the problem and the development of the individual manager. However, these definitions vary in that they emphasize different features and outcomes of action learning. For example, Pedler includes organizational development as a key element, while McGill and Beatty (1992) specifically mention the need to maintain a focus on action rather than passivity and Mumford (1997) highlights the central role of the facilitator. So there is general agreement that action learning involves individual managers working on a task or a problem in a group with others in order to both find solutions to the problem and, by dint of working in a supportive yet questioning group, to self-develop. However, a range of other purposes, outcomes, and modes of practice are covered in the literature.

Action Learning Review Papers

Cho and Egan (2009) provide a comprehensive and systematic review of the action learning literature from 2000 to 2007. They examine the key themes in the literature derived from 50 empirically based papers published in peer-reviewed journals during the period in question and focus on whether these studies concentrate on either action or learning or if they balance the two elements. Various research areas were covered in the papers under scrutiny: management, education, leadership, engineering, marketing, health policy, and hospitality management as well as HRD and organization development (p. 438). Although Cho and Egan found that action learning was practiced throughout the world, data for this review came mainly from action learning projects based in the UK and Europe and in the public sector. This does not necessarily indicate that action learning is more widely practiced in these locations but perhaps that it is more likely to become the focus of study for those interested in publishing in peer-reviewed journals. This is interesting in itself and the discussion of Marquardt's US-influenced model of action learning, to be found later in this chapter, indicates that the traditional influence of academics on action learning in the UK and Europe (despite Revans' overt disdain for business schools and academics) is countered by a practitioner (or scholar-practitioner) focus in the US and in the Americanized model of action learning practiced elsewhere.

A number of variants of action learning are reported in Cho and Egan's (2009) paper, examples include: business-driven action learning, interorganizational action learning, critical action learning, auto action learning, self-managed action learning, project action learning, developmental action learning, work-based learning, and web-based action learning. Their study also revealed that the balance in action learning is tipped more strongly in favor of learning rather than action. This finding contradicts Raelin's (2008) assertion that action dominates at the expense of learning. However, this can be mitigated by an emphasis on reflection, which according to Raelin (2001, 2008) is a key element of both learning and action. Cho and Egan (2009) also concluded that relatively few studies were concerned with the power, politics, and emotion of action learning. These key ideas of reflection and criticality in action learning are discussed later in this chapter.

Brook, Pedler, and Burgoyne (2012) provide a review of the action learning literature over a 20-year period. They identify the main issues and questions that have emerged:

1   The need to make action learning more critical.
2   The issue of emotion and politics in action learning.
3   The notions and interconnectedness of action and practice.
4   The range of approaches to the practice of learning and the adherence or otherwise to Revans' principles.
5   The individual versus collective focus of action learning.

The opening premise of their paper is that action learning's broad range of definitions is problematic as is the proliferation of types and approaches to its execution. They single out Marquardt's (2004) model as straying significantly from Revans' original principles and identify the use of a coach as the main differentiating factor, pointing out Revans' distaste for facilitators in action learning sets. Brook, Pedler, and Burgoyne (2012) also propose a number of variants of action learning that is much in line with Cho and Egan's (2009) list and examine to what extent they are in line with Revans' classical principles (RCP) namely:

- The requirement for action as a basis for learning.
- Profound personal development resulting from reflection upon action.
- Working with problems (no right answers) not puzzles (susceptible to expert knowledge).
- Problems being sponsored and aimed at organizational as well as personal development.
- Action learners working in sets of peers ("comrades in adversity") to support and challenge each other.
- The search for fresh questions and "Q" (questioning insight) takes primacy over access to expert knowledge (or "P").

(Pedler, Burgoyne, & Brook, 2005, pp. 58–59)

They also consider how these principles may have been diluted by the proliferation and variety of action-learning approaches. Brook, Pedler, and Burgoyne (2012) are concerned too with the relationship between action, learning, and reflection, which is discussed later in this chapter, as are the debates about the nature of criticality in action learning and the influence of politics and emotions.

Marquardt's Model of Action Learning

Michael Marquardt is singled out in Brook, Pedler, and Burgoyne's (2012) piece as the originator of the model of action learning that appears to bear least resemblance to Revans' original ideas about how it should be conceptualized and practiced (see Marquardt, 2000, 2003, 2004; Marquardt & Waddill, 2004; Leonard & Marquardt, 2010; Marquardt & Banks, 2010; Marquardt, Choon Seng, & Goodson, 2010).

Marquardt's (2004) model has six components:

- a problem,
- a diverse group or set,
- reflective inquiry process,
- power to take action,
- commitment to learning, and
- an action learning coach.

(Cited in Brook, Pedler, & Burgoyne, 2012)

Marquardt (2004, p. 6) differentiates between two types of action-learning programs: single-problem, in-company programs; and multiple-problem (open-group or classical) programs. He proposes two ground rules that should underpin action learning:

1 Statements should be made only in response to questions … this helps members make the transition from advocacy to inquiry (p. 8).
2 The action learning coach has power to intervene (p. 9).

Marquardt (2004) also sets out the various stages of action learning:

1 Formation of the group.
2 Presentation of the problem or task to the group ... members ask questions to gather more information.
3 Reframing the problem ... the group, often with the guidance of the action learning coach will reach a consensus as to the most critical and crucial problem to work on and establish the crux of the problem, which may be different from the view of the problem owner.
4 Determining goals – with positive consequences for the individual team and organization.
5 Developing action strategies – identifying and "pilot testing" potential course of action.
6 Taking action – between action-learning sessions.
7 Capturing learnings – the coach may intervene to encourage members to reflect on their performance and to improve how they work as a group (p. 12).

Marquardt (2004) goes onto define the nature of problems best suited to action learning and lists a set of criteria for their selection that includes importance, urgency, feasibility, and potential for learning. He also suggests how to select set members based on a number of features including their commitment, knowledge, power to take action, and diversity. A group of four to eight members is recommended. The power of questions is central to Marquardt's model because "they cause us to think and to learn" (p. 72) and he uses Kolb's (1984) experiential learning model to illustrate how questions encourage learners to reflect and question their assumptions. Marquardt also emphasizes the importance of dialogue over discussion (p. 83) and devotes a section of his book to problem reframing, goal formulation, strategy development, and action taking.

Marquardt's work has a strong appeal to practitioners because it defines action learning in clear terms and explains the process of how sets should operate. Few others have done this in such definitive terms and, in the UK in particular, there is a strong focus on research-led writing that has little appeal to those practitioners who want to learn how to establish and run sets. When it is explained in academic texts and papers, there is far more circumspection and vagueness about how the process should happen than in Marquardt's definitive approach. For example, Anderson and Thorpe (2004, pp. 664–645) explain the process thus:

> Groups on the programme consist of six to eight members and are facilitated by a set advisor. They meet once a month as a set and follow the normal process of "checking-in" (giving a brief résumé of what has happened professionally and personally since the last meeting), deciding on priorities for that meeting (in effect, "carving up" the four-hour time slot) followed by individuals "presenting" their issue ... and other members asking questions about it in order to help that individual's learning. At the end of each student's slot, s/he is invited to reflect, honestly, on their learning from the session and to set objectives based on this.

The Action Learning Coach/Adviser

The role of the coach is central in Marquardt's model and the primary purpose is to focus on learning within the group, encouraging learners to engage in reflection. The coach also acts a role model for effective questioning and listening techniques (Marquardt, 2004, p. 133) and ensures that the rules of action learning are followed. The role of the coach can be rotated around group members or given to a designated person. There is a strong emphasis on maintaining consciousness of the learning process and to keep the conversation focused on individual and group learning. Marquardt (2004) is prescriptive about the behavior of the coach within the group and the power she/he holds:

> The coach never tells set members what to do but through questions, assists them in discovering what they need to do. She does not teach but creates an atmosphere wherein members can learn for and from themselves. (p. 136)
>
> The action learning coach only asks questions unless he is asked a question by the group. (p. 136)
>
> The coach has the power to intervene ... and the group needs to stop working and listen to the questions ... raised by the coach. (p. 137)

In contrast, facilitation is given minimal coverage in the broader literature and the term "set adviser" is used in preference to coach, denoting a softer, less directive approach. David Casey is credited with being the first action-learning practitioner to pay attention to the role of the set adviser and the first sentence of his chapter in Pedler's *Action Learning in Practice* sets his tone on facilitation: "In action learning the prime source of help is the peer group – not the set adviser" (Casey, 2011). However, Casey (2011, p. 58) does go on to suggest that facilitators (or set advisers) have a role to play in action learning and that they have four distinct tasks:

1   to facilitate giving ("generous" questioning that helps others in the set develop);
2   to facilitate receiving (accepting the possibility of receiving help);
3   to clarify the various processes of action learning (processes of change; project management; dealing with the range of people involved, including sponsors and managers of the learners and the process of career development and re-entry of the learner into the workplace); and
4   to help others take over tasks 1, 2 and 3.

Revans (1982) had a dislike for "ambiguous" facilitators and the academy in general. However, as Brook and Aspinwall (2013) conclude, facilitators have now become a necessary part of action learning and particularly in critical action learning. Brook and Aspinwall talk of *context sensitive* facilitation being important where a set advisor has knowledge of the process of action learning and is acutely aware of the sensitivities of the particular environment in which the sets take place.

Self-Managed Action Learning (SMAL)

Bourner (2011) describes an approach to action learning that dispenses with the need for a facilitator, based on the principle that although all sets need some help to become established, after this initial phase the group becomes self-facilitating. This model has the attraction of being less expensive than facilitator-led versions of action learning and thus enables more sets to be established and more people to benefit from action learning and, according to Bourner, it represents a more authentic form of action learning as it is closer to Revans' stance on facilitation. Learners are given training in set participation, facilitation, and management at the beginning of the program although in one of Bourner's (2011) examples of a successful self-managed action learning group, the instigator of the program had just completed a masters degree by action learning and was therefore presumably already well-versed in the processes and philosophy of action learning. Bourner and his colleagues set up a number of successful SMAL programs in a variety of contexts, all involving a foundational workshop for participants, which appears to be crucial to their success.

Other Approaches

Marquardt (2011) reports the use of action learning across the world; in Europe, it is practiced in the UK, Finland, the Netherlands, Italy, and Germany in large organizations such as the BBC, Deutsche Bank, and Nokia. In Asia, there is faster growth in the use of action learning than in any other region (Marquardt, 2011) and its adoption in Korea is particularly notable; Cho and Bong (2010) report that almost all large corporations in Korea use action learning, including Samsung, Hyundai, Korea Electric Power, and Industrial Bank of Korea. In the Middle East, action learning is used in Saudi Arabia, Kuwait, Egypt, and Qatar and there is also growth in Latin America and the Caribbean and in Africa. Marquardt and Yeo (2012) note that hundreds of organizations in the US and Canada have now adopted action learning including the Canadian Food Inspection Service, the US Federal Government, Johnson and Johnson, and as the basis for Boeing's Global Leadership Program.

As action learning has now grown to be a global phenomenon, there are inevitably a range of ways in which it is conceived and practiced. As action learning has developed, so too have the number of varieties. Many of the examples given of successful action learning come from its use in large corporations but there is also a significant literature that deals with action learning in small firms (see, for example, Clarke et al., 2006; Ram & Trehan, 2010; Anderson, Gold, & Gibb, 2011). Pedler's (2011) definitive text on action learning includes chapters on five approaches to action learning. One of these, critical action learning, is discussed in more detail further on in this chapter and we have already considered SMAL. We now turn to two other variations of action learning – business-driven action learning and virtual action learning.

Business-Driven Action Learning (BDAL)

Yury Boshyk has been involved in developing and implementing Business-Driven Action Learning (BDAL) since 1996. During the 1990s a modified version of action learning was created to counter the predominance of learning over action and therefore individual outcomes over organizational achievement. In the early days (Boshyk, 1999, 2002), no connection was made to Revans' classic principles and this Americanized version of action learning (Dixon, 1997) was used to great effect in a large number of companies. BDAL, in common with Marquardt's model, has a set formula and a bespoke terminology that guides its application. According to Boshyk (2011) problems or issues to be resolved are described as "business challenges" (BCs) and these are articulated by the organization's top management; they are normally strategic and have no straightforward solution. A detailed background document informs participants what is expected from them and there may be involvement from internal or external subject-matter experts. BCs are then addressed in business challenge teams. Also included in these teams are a number of external or internal stakeholders who discuss their perspective on the challenge through a series of "outside-ins" – dialogues that are carried out with a subset of the business challenge team and recorded on the program website. Alongside these business challenge teams, participants work on personal challenges (PCs) in learning sets, guided by a more traditional, Revansesque approach. BDAL is now recognized as part of the action learning "family" of approaches and Boshyk has researched and written extensively about Revans' work and philosophy (see Boshyk, 2012).

Virtual Action Learning

Action learning has traditionally been conceived as an activity that takes place face-to-face encouraging mutual support and understanding through dialogue. While it is problematic for some practitioners and researchers to imagine how this can happen in a virtual environment, the pace of technological innovation and the ubiquity of smartphones and tablets in the workplace means that the growth of virtual action learning sets is inevitable. Goodman and Stewart (2011) report that text, visual, and voice media are deployed in virtual action learning and that it occurs both synchronously and asynchronously. There is also evidence of 3D simulation being used. The rules or principles of action learning remain the same, it is simply conducted remotely and using technology. The major advantage of virtual learning is in its ability to bring together participants easily and affordably. Although many workers are now accustomed to working in remote, global teams, Goodman and Stewart (2011) claim that the major disadvantages of virtual action learning lie with the technology itself and cite difficulties with logging on and spending long periods on the telephone as detracting from the learning potential.

Action Learning and Critical Reflection

Marsick and O'Neil (1999) propose a typology of action learning that lists three schools or approaches; scientific, experiential, and critical reflection. The scientific school of action learning encompasses the work of Revans and those writers who most closely adhere to his perspective and are fiercely proud and protective of the tradition of action learning. Marsick and O'Neil choose the label "scientific" because of Revans' assertion that learning is based on a model of problem solving using system alpha, beta, and gamma and on the enduring nature of the $L = P + Q$ equation (discussed earlier in this chapter), which underpins these approaches to action learning. Those writers in the experiential school cited by Marsick and O'Neil (e.g., Lessem, 1991; McGill & Beatty, 1992; Mumford, 1994) explain action learning in terms of Kolb's learning cycle and view action learning as a cyclical process of action, reflection, theorizing, and application. The third approach to action learning proposed by Marsick and O'Neil (1999) is the critical reflection school. They cite Mezirow's (1990, 1991) definition of critical reflection to explain how critical reflection might be understood as an "assessment of the validity of the presuppositions of one's meaning perspectives, and examination of their sources and consequences" (1990, p. xvi).

Since Marsick and O'Neil's (1999) ground-shaping paper, interest in the nature of critical reflection within action learning has grown and the term "critical action learning" has been coined and a discussion of what constitutes criticality in action learning has ensued in the literature. In this section, we consider the nature of reflection, action, and criticality and examine how these are conceptualized and operationalized in the practice of critical action learning.

Reflection and action

Dewey (1933) is the reference point for most commentators on reflection. He defines reflective thought as:

> Active, persistent and careful consideration of any belief or supposed form of knowledge in the light of the grounds that support it and further conclusions to which it leads ... it includes a conscious and voluntary effort to establish belief upon a firm basis of evidence and rationality. (Dewey, 1933, p. 9., cited in Boud, Keogh, & Walker, 1985)

Reynolds (2011, p. 5) distils some of the interpretations of experiential or action learning and extends Dewey's definition within that context:

> Reflection involves thinking about past or ongoing experience of events, situations or actions so as to make sense of them, potentially with a view to informing future choices, decisions or actions. In so doing, we draw on existing ideas – our own or other people's – and in applying them to our experience, may confirm these ideas or develop new ones.

Therefore in an action learning situation, experience rather than theory is the basis of or a starting point for learning and Kolb (1984) would argue that it becomes the basis for the creation of new or amended concepts that in turn become guides for action: "Learning is the process whereby knowledge is created through the transformation of experience" (Kolb, 1984, p. 38).

As Reynolds (2011) points out, this privileging of experience over theory is contrary to the traditions of learning, particularly in further and higher education, where existing knowledge forms the starting point for teachers and learners. Boud, Keogh, and Walker. (1985, p. 19) also discuss an element of learning that is often neglected because of the centrality of theory as the main driver for learning. They emphasize the affective processes involved in reflection: "Those intellectual and affective activities in which individuals engage to explore their experiences in order to lead to new understandings and appreciations."

Here, the expression of feelings in the reflective process, whether this is done as a solitary or collective activity – as in action learning – is seen to be crucial to enhancing learning through reflection. Boud, Keogh, and Walker place a strong emphasis on attending to feelings as a way of producing *rational* reflections on experience, and reflection is directed towards a particular goal or set of outcomes rather than simply being thoughtful. They suggest that learners should work with emotions, find ways of setting them aside, and/ or retain positive emotional responses. They imply that positive emotions are useful in the process of reflection whereas negative responses should be disregarded as part of the process of the rationalization of experience. Although this separation of negative and positive emotions seems rather arbitrary and subjective, this model gives a useful insight into how reflection may lead to change and a commitment to action in the light of a re-evaluation of experience.

Miettinen (2000, pp. 66–67) offers an explanation of the phases of reflective learning and although this was not originally conceived as an illustration of reflection in action learning, it mirrors the stages of the process of problematization, questioning, and action:

1 *The indeterminate situation: the habit does not work*
   Reflective thought starts with some kind of disturbance; something makes the normal flow of action difficult ...
2 *Intellectualization; defining the problem*
   An attempt to define what is wrong in the situation ...
3 *Studying the conditions of the situation and formation of a working hypothesis*
   Analysis and diagnosis of the conditions; a tentative plan to resolve the problem is formed ...
4 *Reasoning – in a narrower sense*
   "Thought experiments"; testing the working hypothesis ...
5 *Testing the hypothesis in action*
   Do the intended consequences inherent in the hypothesis come about in practice? The hypothesis is not always confirmed, "but the hypothesis makes learning possible, because the outcome can be compared to the initial suppositions implied in the hypothesis."

Reflection and practice

Schön (1983, 1987) rejects the technical-rational approach that views practitioners as "instrumental problem solvers" applying well-defined solutions to well-defined problems. In reality, he claims, practitioners are solving novel problems in unique circumstances and they need to experiment and rethink previous practice in order to solve them. They have "reflective conversations" with the situation: reflection entails much more than making thoughtful choices between courses of action (Reynolds, 1998). The main difference between Schön's (1983, 1987) and Kolb's (1984) work is that Schön portrays the learner as being far more engaged with the event or the problem rather than standing back from it. Experience and "reflection-in-action" form the basis of new learning, according to Schön, by providing "exemplary themes" (1987, p. 68) and "Students ... having to learn a kind of reflection-in-action that goes beyond statable rules not only by devising new methods of reasoning ... but also by constructing and testing new categories of understanding strategies of action and ways of framing problems" (1987, p. 39).

Schön's (1987, p. 25) view of knowledge is characterized by "knowing-in-action"; the knowledge that underpins everyday routines and habits, which is often difficult to articulate: "The knowing is in the action. We reveal it by our spontaneous, skillful execution of the performance and we are characteristically unable to make it verbally explicit." This "knowing" is strongly linked to Polanyi's (1967) work on tacit knowledge, cited by Schön. It is significant in that it links reflection, action, and language. Schön (1987) talks of meaning being mediated by a distinctive dialogue between student and coach and of inner dialogues as an element of the process of reflection and in so doing, raises awareness of the value of language in the co-creation of meaning in the learning situation. We return to this idea later in the chapter.

Reflection and "transformative" learning

Cope (2003, p. 432), building on Argyris and Schön's (1978) "theories for action," defines "higher-level" as opposed to "lower-level" learning as "distinguishing between more practical, routine, adaptive learning and more fundamental learning that generates new understandings and new cognitive 'theories for action'." Bateson's (1972) taxonomy of levels of learning (cited in Vince, 1996) also provides a useful way of conceptualizing the differences between different levels of learning. Level 2 suggests that learners become conscious of new ways of approaching problems that are "transferable" and useful to them in the future. Level 3 learning however challenges the whole way they conceive situations and problems and often leads to what Engeström (2001) refers to as expansive learning. This is where individuals begin to gain completely new insights into problems and situations and embrace new possibilities. In this model, level 2 represents reflection or "simple" reflection whereas reflection at level 3 is critical.

What does critical reflection entail?

Reynolds (1997, 1998, 1999) proposes five principles upon which critical reflection is based:

1 Questioning assumptions and taken-for-granteds. "The fundamental task of critical reflection is to identify, question and if necessary, change those assumptions. It is a process of making evaluations, often moral ones, and not simply exercising judgements of a practical, technical nature" (1998, p. 189).

2 It has a collective focus; as an antidote to the "overriding preoccupation with the individual and the personal in adult education" (1998, p. 189).
3 Analyzing power relations – "Perhaps the most notable distinction between reflection and critical reflection" (1998, p. 190).
4 It is concerned with emancipation; "The realization of a more just society based on fairness and democracy" (1999, p. 173).
5 "Confronting spurious claims of rationality and objectivity and revealing the sectional interests which can be concealed by them" (1999, p. 173).

Critical management pedagogy ideally involves radical content (based on critical theory) and process. Radical process is not achieved by taking an experiential approach as in typically constructed management development programs, as their individual focus means that they fail to meet the "collective" ideal (Reynolds, 1999) and also because they are built on a "humanist" perspective, which does not take account of social, political, and cultural forces that provide a context for learning (Reynolds, 1997). For Reynolds and many other critical academics (e.g., Alvesson & Willmott, 1999) critical reflection has its origins in critical social theory. Orthodox critical theory is normally associated with the work of the "Frankfurt School," a diverse group of left-wing intellectuals who worked at the Frankfurt Institute for Social Research during the 1920s and early 1930s. Both Mingers (2000) and Reynolds (1997) refer to and to support Willmott's (1997) proposal that critical action learning presents a useful format for developing criticality and critical reflection in the management classroom and there is an increasing number of published accounts of such practice.

There have been calls for an alternative way of teaching managers, many of which advocate using action learning (McLaughlin & Thorpe, 1993; Willmott, 1994). The critical curriculum is offered as a way of engaging managers more closely in relevant research, which provides them with an opportunity to critique current practice and received wisdom. However, this is often over-politicized and remote from managers' expectations of solution-driven, normative approaches of how-to-do management. While there appears to be a need for managers to examine and critique the norms that drive the practice of the profession, critical theory offers a discourse that can seem remote from a practitioner's experience but there is some consensus that critical or thoughtful reflection and the acknowledgement of the role of tacit knowledge are important factors in transformative management learning.

Critical Action Learning

Calls for the development of a more critically focused version of action learning came in the mid 1990s (McLaughlin & Thorpe, 1993; Willmott, 1994) and were heeded by Rigg and Trehan (2004). In their paper "Reflections on Working with Critical Action Learning", published in the journal instituted at the Revans Centre, *Action Learning, Research and Practice,* they describe how they used critical action learning in an MSc program at a UK university. A fundamental premise of the pedagogy is to use practice as the basis for the creation of new theory; to encourage learners to examine the practice of management and their own practice as managers, learners, and set members having first come to understand a range of critical concepts and ideas. Above all, critical reflection is engendered by learners being encouraged to question their own basic assumptions through the questioning process of the action learning set and in the writing of an autobiographical account of their learning on the program. The illustrations of student learning show how learners questioned their own behavior and practice and pondered its antecedents and consequences by holding themselves up to critique. In particular, issues of power, emotions, and politics came to the fore in these reflections. A powerful example of critical facilitation is also offered in the description of an exchange about racist behavior and attitudes in one of the sets (pp. 157–159). The discomfort of the learners in the illustration comes through strongly and exemplifies the notion that critical reflection involves soul-searching, an examination of conscience, and the laying bare of one's attitudes and feeling. Participants in the sets spoke of personal transformation but, as Rigg and Trehan (2004) concede, there is no way of knowing for sure that this personal disruption persists for any significant duration or has an impact on workplace practice more generally. They also acknowledge the potentially negative consequences of critical reflection and refer to Brookfield's (1994) "dark side" of critical reflection; the way in which it may be emotionally unsettling for students, thus causing "disruption." Brookfield's (1994) "critical" work with adult education teachers resulted in a feeling of "impostorship" among those who were encouraged to critique the work of established management theorists. My own experience of critical action learning has been that emotions often spill over into the set in times of crisis outside it; facilitators need to be conscious of how much discomfort certain individuals and the set itself can reasonably stand (Anderson, Gold, & Gibb, 2011).

Russ Vince's (1996, 2004, 2008) research and practice around action learning is concerned with understanding the emotions and politics involved in the process and is positioned as an antidote to the rational, scientific model presented by Revans. While previous models of action learning emphasized the intellectual and cognitive aspects of action learning, Vince, to some extent in common with Boud, Keogh, and Walker (1985), brings the affective elements of action learning to the foreground. Vince and Martin (1993) see action learning as an anxiety-provoking experience because the normal expectation that learning will be teacher-led is not met and learners have to take responsibility for their own and others' learning. The consequence of the cycle of emotion that is prompted by such anxiety is that learners can choose the route of self-empowerment or, conversely, of self-limitation (Vince & Martin, 1993, p. 211). This stymies the possibilities of working with change in an environment where individuals are more likely to find themselves in a state of *inaction* (Vince, 2008) because of a fear of the consequences of such change either in themselves or in the organization. Vince uses psychodynamic theory to understand and explain how unconscious processes impact on action learning by promoting inaction and limiting reflection on potentially troublesome and problematic organizational processes (Vince 2008, p. 103).

Trehan and Pedler (2011) talk of action learning as being pragmatic yet underpinned by a moral philosophy in that it is concerned with solving organizational problems and business results while at the same time bringing about "transformational learning." It is not, however, always "critical" in the sense that it is underpinned by emancipatory thinking or a radicalized process; neither Boshyk, in his business-driven action learning approach, nor Marquardt would claim to do this. Critical action learning has therefore come to represent those approaches to action learning that bring about critical reflection and that specifically entail questioning basic assumptions. This inevitably leads to an examination of individual emotions and the politics of a given situation.

Evaluating Action Learning

It could be claimed that action learning is akin to motherhood and apple pie – essentially and unquestionably *a good thing*. Very few studies have focused on in-depth evaluations of action learning and most rely on reaction-level evaluation and on qualitative feedback

(Joon, Cho, & Bong, 2012). In 2012, a special issue of *Action Learning* was devoted to papers from a conference that focused on assessing the value of action learning as a technique that has both a personal impact on learners and on business systems more generally. It includes contributions from the UK, Ireland, the Czech Republic, and South Korea (Trehan & Rigg, 2012). Vince (2012) discusses the contradictions of action learning and warns against the overwhelming enthusiasm that many action learning practitioners and scholars have for it. He suggests that we need to be aware of the power relations that underpin any learning activity and how these influence practice and outcomes. Vince is particularly wary of the seemingly equal nature of participants in sets and the discourse that often supports this view during set meetings ("we are all working together") when in fact, power relations are always at play and have a potentially dramatic effect on the outcomes of action learning. Emotions within the group can also lead to self-limiting structures and it is up to facilitators and learners to recognize where these exist and to challenge and question them. Vince's (2012) reminder of the need for criticality in and of the action learning process itself provides a useful backdrop to a discussion of how the effects of action learning might be measured especially as superficial cause and effect claims are likely to be overlaid with more subtle shifts in power distribution both within sets and organizations.

Joon et al. (2012), in the same issue of the journal, present empirical evidence of a dual-action action learning program (DPALP) conducted in South Korea. DPALP requires participants to carry out both an individual and team project as a means of balancing the need for action learners to engage in personal development and for the business objectives of the program to be met. The authors use Cho and Egan's (2009) framework of the four dimensions of action learning and report on a large global IT manufacturing company in South Korea that used action learning as an aid to succession planning in a rapidly growing business. The learners in the project were experienced frontline supervisors and the aim was to develop their leadership competencies. Evaluation of the project was carried out through a 360 degree assessment, learning logs, and judgments made about each group's final report in terms of potential return on investment (ROI) and feasibility. Members of learning sets reported that their skills in meeting facilitation, their understanding of the nature of teams, and their business awareness had all developed as a result of the project. Leadership competences were also shown to have developed, particularly in the areas of performance management, task improvement, and task systematization. Joon et al. (2012) also measured the expected ROI of the projects and these ranged from 20.4 percent to 6783 percent with an average ROI of 1316 percent although the authors concede that their model of ROI forecasting is one of the limitations of the study. It appears that action learning is as subject to the vagaries of evaluation as any other management development technique.

Conklin et al. (2012) evaluate an action learning project in a Canadian healthcare setting, focusing on whether the practice can help to introduce new ideas into a workplace environment. Their findings echo Vince's (2004) ideas about the nature of power and emotionality in action learning sets and particularly how the interplay in a small group setting mirrors that of broader organizational life. This promotes a deeper understanding in action learners of the context in which they are attempting to bring about change.

Clarke et al. (2006) report on an in-depth evaluation of action learning in a wide-scale, longitudinal project to develop owner-managers of small and medium-sized businesses in the north west of England. They report that the opportunity to engage in dialogue with peers led to critical reflection in learners, which enabled them to form networks and alliances outside the action learning set. They also claim that action learning enabled these managers to become more strategic as they shifted their focus away from the day-to-day operational concerns to a broader reflection on the needs of the business.

Published work suggests that action learning has the potential to change both individuals and organizations in a powerful way. Critical reflection and the questioning of basic assumptions, particularly about the nature of power and emotion in organizations, are at the heart of this learning method. However, it is important to note that in any evaluation of a learning activity, the findings are likely to be dictated by the questions asked. The examples of action learning above illustrate how evaluators are likely to shape their findings by the questions they ask, and in many ways the outcome is a self-fulfilling prophecy. Large-scale, independent evaluations such as that conducted by Clarke et al. (2006) are relatively rare in action learning and deliverers are often responsible for their own evaluation. This is the case for many types of training and development activity and emphasizes the need for critical approaches and questions both in the delivery and the assessment of outcomes.

Future Research

The scope of action learning activity and definition has broadened greatly over the past 10 years. This has resulted in a proliferation of research that examines action learning's philosophy, approaches, techniques, methods, and outcomes. Much of this work tends to present descriptions and analysis of individual projects and this has had the effect of producing a broad field of work that illustrates the diverse potential of action learning and the range of ways in which it may be used. Future research could usefully draw together this work and question the various cultural perspectives that underpin the practice of action learning. For example, how does action learning play out differently in an Asian context than in a Western setting and what can we learn from this?

There is also a strong theme of critical action learning (Anderson & Thorpe, 2004; Vince, 2004, 2012; Ram, 2012) that is worthy of further work. The capacity of action learning to enable learners to examine their practice and their organization using deep questioning is something that clearly distinguishes action learning from other, more "technique"-focused approaches to learning and development in organizations. This approach needs to be better understood in a range of contexts as it risks becoming an academic exercise and treatise rather than a philosophy that can be enacted in a real-life context.

It will also be worth re-examining the scope and definition of action learning as a follow-up to work already published (e.g., Brook, Pedler, & Burgoyne, 2012; Cho & Egan, 2009; Pedler, Burgoyne, & Brook, 2005). Action learning has come to mean many things to different people, both philosophically and practically; research that opens up the field to new ideas and possibilities may prove to be more useful than that which attempts to narrow it to a set code and mode.

Conclusion

Over the past 30 years, action learning has become a mainstream management development activity, practiced across the world, albeit in a number of different forms. The main differentiating factors in the philosophy and practice of these different approaches are exemplified in a US-influenced model that emphasizes the primacy of action and positive organizational outcomes over or alongside personal development and a European model that focuses on learning and is increasingly concerned with engendering a critical approach. It is difficult to see how these seemingly philosophically and operationally opposed approaches can be seen as the same practice yet the common themes of action, reflection, and learning tie them together and provide a basis for individual and organizational development that appears likely to stand the test of time.

References

Alvesson, M., & Willmott, H. (1999). Critical theory and management studies: An introduction. In M. Alvesson & H. Willmott (Eds.), *Critical Management Studies.* London: Sage.

Anderson, L., Gold, J., & Gibb, A. (2011). Action learning in SME development. In M. Pedler (Ed.), *Action Learning in Practice.* (4th ed.) Farnham: Gower. pp. 221–231.

Anderson, L., & Thorpe, R. (2004). New perspectives on action learning: Developing criticality. *Journal of European Industrial Training*, 28(8/9), 657–668.

Argyris, C., & Schön, D. A. (1978). *Organizational Learning: A Theory of Action Perspective.* London: Addison-Wesley.

Bateson, G. (1972). *Steps to an Ecology of Mind.* San Francisco: Chandler.

Boshyk, Y. (Ed.) (1999). *Business-Driven Action Learning: Global Best Practices.* London: Palgrave Macmillan.

Boshyk, Y. (Ed.) (2002). *Action Learning Worldwide: Experiences of Leadership and Organization Development.* London: Palgrave Macmillan.

Boshyk, Y. (2011). Business-driven action learning today. In M. Pedler (Ed.), *Action Learning in Practice.* (4th ed.) Farnham: Gower. pp. 141–152.

Boshyk, Y. (2012). History, evolution and some varieties of action learning: A roadmap. Paper presented at New Dimensions in Action Learning: Reinventing Leadership Development MIT Action Learning Conference, August 2, 2012. http://mitsloan.mit.edu/actionlearning/media/documents/conference2012/YuryBoshyk.pdf (accessed March 28, 2014).

Boud, D., Keogh, R., & Walker, D. (1985). *Reflection: Turning Experience into Learning.* London: Kogan Page.

Bourner, T. (2011). Self-managed action learning. In M. Pedler (Ed.), *Action Learning in Practice.* (4th ed.) Farnham: Gower. pp. 113–123.

Brook, C., & Aspinwall, K. (2013). Brief thoughts on facilitating action learning. *Action Learning Research and Practice*, 10(2), 158–159.

Brook, C., Pedler, M., & Burgoyne, J. (2012). Some debates and challenges in the literature on action learning: The state of the art since Revans. *Human Resource Development International*, 15(3), 269–282.

Brookfield, S. (1994). Tales from the dark side: A phenomenography of adult critical reflection. *International Journal of Lifelong Education*, 13(3), 203–216.

Casey, D. (2011). David Casey on the role of the set adviser. In M. Pedler (Ed.), *Action Learning in Practice.* (4th ed.) Farnham: Gower. pp. 55–64.

Cho, Y., & Bong, H. (2010). Identifying balanced action learning: Cases of South Korean practices. *Action Learning: Research and Practice*, 7(2), 137–150.

Cho, Y., & Egan, T. M. (2009). Action learning research: A systematic review and conceptual framework. *Human Resource Development International*, 8(4), 431–462.

Clarke, J., Thorpe, R., Anderson, L., & Gold, J. (2006). It's all action, it's all learning: Action Learning in SMEs. *Journal of European Industrial Training*, 30(6), 441–455.

Conklin, J., Cohen-Schneider, R., Linkewich, B., & Legault, E. (2012). Enacting change through action learning: Mobilizing and managing power and emotion. *Action Learning: Research and Practice*, 9(3), 275–295.

Cope, J. (2003). Entrepreneurial learning and critical reflection: Discontinuous events as triggers for "higher-level" learning. *Management Learning*, 34(4), 429–450.

Dewey, J. (1933). *How We Think* (revised ed.). New York: D. C. Heath.

Dixon, N. M. (1997). More than just a task force. In M. Pedler (Ed.), *Action Learning in Practice* (3rd ed.). Aldershot: Gower. pp. 329–338.

Engeström, Y. (2001). Expansive learning at work: Toward an activity, theoretical reconceptualization. *Journal of Education and Work*, 14(1), 133–156.

Goodman, M., & Stewart, J. (2011). Virtual action learning. In M. Pedler (Ed.), *Action Learning in Practice*. (4th ed.) Farnham: Gower. pp. 153–161.

Joon, H., Cho, Y., & Bong, H. (2012). The impact of a dual-project action learning program: A case of a large IT manufacturing company in South Korea. *Action Learning Research and Practice*, 9(3), 225–246.

Kolb, D. (1984). *Experiential Learning. Experience as the Source of Learning and Development*. London: Prentice Hall.

Leonard, S., & Marquardt, M. (2010). The evidence for the effectiveness of action learning. *Action Learning: Research and Practice*, 7(2), 121–126.

Marquardt, M. (2000). Action learning and leadership. *The Learning Organization*, 7(5), 233–240.

Marquardt, M. (2003). Developing global leaders via Action learning programmes: A case study at Boeing. *Journal of Public Administration*, 3(3), 133–157.

Marquardt, M. (2004). *Breakthrough Problem Solving with Action Learning. Solving Problems and Building Leaders in Real Time*. Yarmouth, ME: Nicholas Brearley.

Marquardt, M. (2011). Action learning around the world. In M. Pedler (Ed.), *Action Learning in Practice*. (4th ed.) Farnham: Gower. pp. 325–337.

Marquardt, M. & Banks, S. (2010). Theory to practice: Action learning. *Advances in Developing Human Resources*, 12(2), 159–162.

Marquardt, M. Choon Seng, N., & Goodson, H. (2010). Team development via action learning. *Advances in Developing Human Resources*, 12(2), 241–259.

Marquardt, M., & Waddill, D. (2004). The power of learning in action learning: A conceptual analysis of how the five schools of adult learning theories are incorporated within the practice of action learning. *Action Learning: Research and Practice*, 1(2), 185–202.

Marquardt, M., & Yeo, R. (2012). *Breakthrough Problem Solving with Action Learning*. Palo Alto: Stanford University Press.

Marsick, V. J., & O'Neil, J. (1999). The many faces of action learning. *Management Learning*, 30(2), 159–176.

McGill, I., & Beatty, L. (1992). *Action Learning: A Practitioner's Guide*. Abingdon: Routledge

McLaughlin, H., & Thorpe, R. (1993). Action learning – A paradigm in emergence: The problems facing a challenge to traditional management education and development. *British Journal of Management*, 4, 19–27.

Mezirow, J. (1990) *Fostering Critical Reflection in Adulthood*. San Francisco: Jossey Bass.

Mezirow, J. (1991). *Transformative Dimensions of Adult Learning*. San Francisco: Jossey-Bass.

Mingers, J. (2000). What is it to be critical? Teaching a critical approach to management undergraduates. *Management Learning*, 31(2), 219–237.

Mumford, A. (1997). *Management Development: Strategies for Action*. London: Chartered Institute of Personnel and Development.

Pedler, M. (1991). *Action Learning in Practice* (2nd ed.). Brookfield, VT: Gower.

Pedler, M. (1996). *Action Learning for Managers*. London: Lemos & Crane.

Pedler, M. (1997). Interpreting action learning. In J. Burgoyne & M. Reynolds (Eds.), *Management Learning; Integrating Perspectives in Theory and Practice*. Sage: London. pp. 248–264.

Pedler, M. (Ed.) (2011). *Action Learning in Practice*. Farnham: Gower.

Pedler, M., Burgoyne, J., & Brook, C. (2005). What has action learning learned to become? *Action Learning Research and Practice*, 2(1), 49–68.

Polanyi, M. (1967). *The Tacit Dimension*. London: Routledge & Kegan Paul.

Raelin, J. (2001). Public reflection as the basis of learning. *Management Learning*, 32(1), 11–30.

Raelin, J. (2008). *Work-Based Learning: Bridging Knowledge and Action in the Workplace*. San Francisco, CA: Jossey-Bass.

Ram, M. (2012). Critical action learning: Extending its reach. *Action Learning Research and Practice*, 9(3), 219–224.

Ram, M., & Trehan, K. (2010). Critical action learning, policy learning and small firms: An inquiry. *Management Learning*, 41(4), 415–424.

Revans, R. W. (1971). *Developing Effective Managers*. London: Longman.

Revans, R. W. (1979). The nature of action learning. *Management Education and Development*, 10, 3–23.

Revans, R. W. (1980). *Action Learning: New Techniques for Management*. London: Blond & Briggs.

Revans, R. W. (1982). *The Origin and Growth of Action Learning*. London: Chartwell Bratt.

Reynolds, M. (1997). Towards a critical management pedagogy. In J. Burgoyne & M. Reynolds (Eds.), *Management Learning; Integrating Perspectives in Theory and Practice*. London: Sage.

Reynolds, M. (1998). Reflection and critical reflection in management learning. *Management Learning*, 29(2), 183–200.

Reynolds, M. (1999). Grasping the nettle: Possibilities and pitfalls of a critical management pedagogy. *British Journal of Management*, 10(2), 171–184.

Reynolds, M. (2011). Reflective practice: Origins and interpretations. *Action Learning: Research and Practice*, 8(1), 5–13.

Rigg, C., & Trehan, K. (2004). Reflections on working with critical action learning. *Action Learning: Research and Practice*, 1(2), 149–165.

Rigg, C., & Trehan, K. (2013). Action learning – reach, range and evolution. *Action Learning: Research and Practice*, 10(1), 1–3.

Schön, D. A. (1983). *The Reflective Practitioner. How Professionals Think in Action*. New York: Basic Books.

Schön, D. A. (1987). *Educating the Reflective Practitioner*. San Francisco: Jossey-Bass.

Trehan, K., & Pedler, M. (2011). Action learning and its impact *Action Learning: Research and Practice*, 8(3), 183–186.

Trehan, K., & Rigg, C. (2012). The impact of action learning: What difference are we making? *Action Learning: Research and Practice*, 9(3): 207–8.

Vince, R. (1996). Experiential management education as the practice of change. In R. French & C. Grey (Eds.), *Rethinking Management Education*. London: Sage.

Vince, R. (2004). Action learning and organizational learning: Power, politics and emotions in organizations. *Action Learning: Research and Practice*, 1(1), 63–78.

Vince, R. (2008). "Learning-in-action" and learning inaction: Advancing the theory and practice of critical action learning. *Action Learning: Research and Practice*, 5(2), 93–104.

Vince, R., & Martin, I. (1993). Inside action learning. *Management Education and Development*, 24, 205–215.

Willmott, H. (1994). Management education: Provocations to a debate. *Management Learning*, 25(1), 105–136.

Willmott, H. (1997). Critical management learning. In J. Burgoyne & M. Reynolds (Eds.), *Management Learning*. London: Sage. pp. 161–176.

Yorks, L., O'Neil, J., & Marsick, V. (1999). Action learning: Theoretical bases and varieties of practice. *Advances in Developing Human Resources*, 1(1), 1–18.

16

Knowledge-Sharing, Cooperation, and Personal Development

Leonor Pais and Nuno Rebelo dos Santos

Introduction

Since the seminal work by Teece (1981) and Nelson and Winter (1982), knowledge has assumed an increasingly legitimate and important role in organization science. The literature produced on this subject has reflected growing understanding of the relationship between organizational processes and results regarding the creation, sharing, and use of knowledge. There has been a search for integrated understanding of the mechanisms where human knowledge has an influence. Going beyond mere conceptualization, the scientific community has attempted to consider questions related to intervention, responding to the needs, problems, and challenges felt by the different organizational actors. This occurs in the domains of knowledge in general, and in the behavioral and social dimensions of its management in organizations, in particular. One of the aspects of those behavioral and social dimensions is knowledge sharing.

This chapter focuses on knowledge-sharing as a cooperative process in organizations and the impact of knowledge-sharing on personal development. We approach the literature on knowledge-sharing highlighting aspects where this is oriented to the importance of people, the interactions they carry out in organizations and which presuppose/involve cooperation and potentially lead to development of the different organizational actors.

Knowledge has its origin and application in the human mind and in organizations it lives in and through people. It is embedded in communities and/or in repositories, and becomes tangible in routines, processes, practices, and organizational norms of action. This "orientation towards action" (Sveiby, 1997) or, in other words, this characteristic of "inducing action," gives knowledge its real meaning and is intimately dependent on knowledge-sharing and the cooperative processes that make this viable. The latter simultaneously and potentially stem from individual development and also lead to it.

The Wiley Blackwell Handbook of the Psychology of Training, Development, and Performance Improvement,
First Edition. Edited by Kurt Kraiger, Jonathan Passmore, Sigmar Malvezzi, and Nuno Rebelo dos Santos.
© 2015 John Wiley & Sons Ltd. Published 2020 by John Wiley & Sons Ltd.

This is followed by a review of knowledge-sharing as a core concept in knowledge management, knowledge-sharing as a cooperative process considered as a social dilemma, and suggestions for future research particularly focused on the expected relationships of these concepts with personal development.

Knowledge-Sharing as a Core Concept in Knowledge Management

Organizational knowledge is a product and determinant of individual behavior and input and output of organizational functioning (Davenport & Prusak, 1998; Denton, 1998; Dixon, 1992, 2000; Grant, 1996; Muñoz Seca & Riverola, 1997; Nonaka, 1990, 1991; Starbuck & Hedberg, 2001; Wei Choo, 1998; Wigg, 1993, 2000). In two definitions widely disseminated in the literature, Davenport and Prusak (1998), consider knowledge to be a "fluid mix of framed experiences, values, contextual information, and expert insight that provides a framework for evaluating and incorporating new experiences and information" (p. 5), while Nonaka and Takeuchi (1995) define it as "a dynamic human process of justifying personal belief toward the truth" (p. 58).

Organizational knowledge is, therefore, a complex, dynamic, and multidimensional combination of elements of a cognitive, emotional, and behavioral order (Earl, 1994; Huber, 1991), about how things are and operate, in relation to what is relevant for organizational functioning. It is a personally and socially constructed "asset" and its orientation towards action makes it a determinant of organizational performance. Considering the fundamental classification of knowledge consensually attributed to Polannyi (1958, 1966), this is present in organizations and may take a more explicit or tacit form, along a continuum (Nonaka, 1991, 1994). In its explicit form, organizational knowledge is easier to access, share, and reproduce, with its tacit form being considerably more discriminative, although its operationalization and management require complex metacognitive processes (Alee, 1997; Brooking, 1996; Dawson, 2000; De Long, 1997; Denton, 1998; Hamel, 1991; Huseman & Goodman, 1999; Prahalad & Bettis, 1986; Prusak, 1997; Snowden, 1999; Sparrow, 1998; Spender, 1993; Starbuck & Hedberg, 2001; Takeuchi, 2001; Teece, 1981, 2001; von Krogh & Roos, 1996; Zack, 1999). Organizational knowledge demands the active and creative role of organizational actors, it is supported by individual action, and in groups and sharing contexts it has essential vectors for its projection in the organization. As an inexhaustible resource, organizational knowledge increases as it is shared and used, forming one of the most important sources of sustainable value for organizations (Andreu & Sieber, 2000; Barney, 1991; Boisot, 1998; Brooking, 1996; Davenport & Prusak, 1998; Denton, 1998; Drucker, 1993; Dyer & Nobeoka, 2000; Grant, 1996; Goodman, 1999; Henderson & Cockburn, 1994; Huseman & Goodman, 1999; Leonard-Barton, 1992, 1995; Nelson, 1992; Nonaka, 1990, 1991, 1994, 1997, 1998; Nonaka & Johansson, 1985; Nonaka & Konno, 1999; Nonaka, Konno, & Kosaka, 1993; Nonaka & Senoo, 1998; Nonaka & Takeuchi, 1994, 1995; Nonaka, Toyama, & Konno, 2001; Quinn, 1992; Starbuck & Hedberg, 2001; Stewart, 1997; Stopford, 2001; Sveiby, 1997; Winter, 1987). It is therefore anchored on individuals who, through their interaction, are the core elements of its creation, sharing, and use. When sharing their knowledge individuals cooperate, through this process they develop, and when they are developed they realize they have to cooperate. These processes are therefore intrinsic, interactive, and dynamically associated.

Two orientations are usually adopted in terms of research and intervention, when what is at stake is to create/capture, share, and use/apply organizational knowledge

(Alvesson & Karreman, 2001; Carter & Scarbrough, 2001; Hansen, Nohria, & Tierney, 1999; Mayer & Remus, 2003; McElroy, 1999, 2000; Metaxiotis, Ergazakis, & Psarras, 2005): one more oriented towards technology and the other towards human resources/people. The first (technology-orientated) stresses the coding and storing of knowledge, so that it can be available to, and used by, any organizational actor, with knowledge being perceived as a separate entity from whoever created, shared, and uses it. The second (people-orientated) focuses above all on the strategies used in terms of human resource management. It sets out from the assumption that knowledge is closely linked to people and that face-to-face contact is the ideal way for it to be effectively shared (e.g., Carter & Scarbrough, 2001; Davenport, 1996; Snowden, 2000).

Currently, there is some consensus among authors in considering that the tasks of conceiving and implementing knowledge-management strategies are difficult to carry out, whether through exclusive use of technology or through recourse to any set of isolated concepts (McElroy, 1999; McDermott, 1999; Bosua & Venkitachalam, 2013). The emphasis is therefore on support for processes of social interaction, in which knowledge is constructed and shared (Carter & Scarbrough, 2001; Nicolini et al., 2008). Questions directly related to communication and the use of language take on an essential role, since it is considered that some of the most effective ways of sharing knowledge that occur in organizations have a social basis, with the content being extremely difficult to formalize. Interpretation and intervention are highlighted, as well as a more integrated and wide-ranging stance, centered on behavioral, social, and cultural dimensions.

The approaches inspired by and centered on people tend to consider that managers can only act indirectly, cultivating contexts (Wenger, McDermott, & Snyder, 2002), stimuli, and conditions that facilitate individual actions (Bhatt, 2002). They also consider that much critical knowledge is tacit, and therefore cannot be easily coded, and so only the interrelationship between the different organizational actors will let it be evoked and encouraged by action. Therefore, they emphasize the relevance of improving the social processes that facilitate personalized communication and sharing of (tacit) knowledge between people (Hansen, Nohria, & Tierney, 1999). Cardoso and Gomes (2011) highlight the importance of managing organizational processes related to tacit knowledge, which emerge essentially from processes of social and discursive interaction involving organizational actors.

Based on the literature produced between 1998 and 2008, Hislop (2010) describes the decline of scientific production focused on IS/IT issues and the increase of that dealing with people-related issues. In doing so, he makes that change tangible and measurable. Nowadays, technology gives users greater potential to create contexts appropriate to the sharing of tacit knowledge. This may spark off renewed interest in these matters. However, the role of the social web, for example, is still unknown and absent from the literature (Panahi, Watson, & Partridge, 2013).

On the other hand, the exponential increase and generalization of technology in all facets of organizational life led to the ironic impact of making people and the product of their action more critical and central than ever in the organizational space (Heil, Bennis, & Stephens, 2000). The devaluation resulting from the amassment and trivialization of data and information gave added value to idiosyncratically human agents and methodologies able to transform information in to knowledge, for its subsequent share and use. The transition of focus in orientations we have alluded to was reflected in the gradual transfer from a vision, mostly based on technology, to a perspective that is closer to the domain of social and human sciences. This is the approach facilitating the focus on knowledge-sharing as a cooperation process, from a perspective of developing organizational actors.

In our understanding, knowledge management "has been defined as a strategy for managing organizational knowledge as a corporate asset and harnessing processes such as creation and acquisition, storage, share and dissemination, retrieval and use of tacit and explicit knowledge. It is about managing the processes and practices that act upon tacit and explicit knowledge" (Cardoso, Meireles, & Peralta, 2012, p. 269). Knowledge management means the possibility of fulfilling organizational objectives, making the knowledge factor productive (Beijerse, 1999) through valuing the active, constructive, and irreplaceable role played by the human factor. According to Birkinshaw and Sheehan (2002), Carrión, González, and Leal (2004) and Snowden (1999), management operates on processes and through processes, which concerning knowledge, can be organized in stages formed by sets of activities/behaviors that focus on different moments of the life-cycle of critical knowledge in a given organizational context (Mayo, 1998).

In 1992, altering and extending the classification by Huber (1991), Dixon presented five fundamental principles that reproduced nonsequential or independent stages regarding how the organization was related to information (acquisition, interpretation, and distribution; making meaning; organizational memory and retrieval) in what was, at the time, his model of organizational learning. Since then, over almost two decades, in the context of approaches to knowledge management, several models have been proposed in the literature (e.g., Alavi & Leidner, 2001; Argote, 1999; Bosua & Venkitachalam, 2013; Cardoso & Gomes, 2011; Conner & Prahalad, 1996; Davenport & Prusak, 1998, 2000; Gold, Malhotra, & Segars, 2001; Grant, 1996; Grover & Davenport, 2001; Hislop, 2010; Lloria (2008); Matayong & Mahmood, 2013; Moustafir & Schiuma, 2013; Kogut & Zander, 1992; Tsoukas & Vladimirou, 2001) with the majority being found to include some (or all) of the following processes: (a) creation and acquisition; (b) sense-making; (c) share and spread; (d) organizational memory; (e) measurement; (f) retrieval; and (g) use.

Despite the convergence of perspectives regarding the existence of a lifecycle for knowledge, investigations stressing the stage of sharing tend to bear more weight than those including the other sub-processes (Aslani, Mousakhani, & Aslani, 2012; Cabrera & Cabrera, 2002; Scholl et al., 2004). This is because creation and use are very dependent on it (Bartol & Srivastava, 2002; Ipe, 2003), as it is a critical process in promoting creativity, absorptive capacity, and innovation (Armbrecht et al., 2001; Foss, Husted, & Michailova, 2010; Sáenz, Aramburu, & Blanco, 2013); and because through it knowledge is expanded from the individual to the group and organizational level. The success of any knowledge management initiative in organizations is therefore intimately related to and dependent on knowledge-sharing (Davenport & Prusak, 1998; Hendriks, 1999; Wang & Noe, 2010). Yang and Farn (2009) take an identical stance, considering that knowledge only has value if used, sharing among organizational members being one of the most important ways to promote its use, and therefore its value. The growing interest shown in this topic can also be explained by the need to analyze and understand the dynamics of knowledge processes in very diverse and increasingly common contexts (e.g., joint ventures, virtual organizations, multinational corporations), where knowledge-sharing acquires a fundamental role (Hislop, 2010).

Different authors adopt different designations in referring to the diverse "movements" that knowledge can take between "supplier and receiver" or, using another metaphor, between "source and recipient" (e.g., Wang & Noe, 2010). In this chapter, adopting a principle also followed by other authors (Cabrera, Collins, & Salgado, 2006; Levin & Cross, 2004), we use the designation of "knowledge-sharing" to designate all behaviors that imply "giving", "receiving", "giving and receiving", "searching for" (when the interlocutor is human), or even "transferring" knowledge. Any of these actions is therefore considered, whether it occurs formally (intentionally) or informally (intentionally or unintentionally). We focus our analysis on knowledge-sharing between individuals, within organizations, knowing that the extent to which this occurs depends on the knowledge spread at the group and organizational levels (Cabrera & Cabrera, 2005; Gupta & Govindarajan, 2000; Tsoukas & Vladimirous, 2001).

Knowledge-sharing occurs when a diverse set of activities of cooperative interaction is carried out to make it viable. These, as mentioned above, have a determinant role of "projection" of individual and group knowledge to the organizational level. These activities can occur intentionally, through carrying out formally established and incentivized behaviors or, even if this is not the case (when there are no formal orientations in this regard), through actions explicitly adopted by the various organizational actors. Included in this context are all activities arising from identification of organizationally valid and instrumental knowledge, which are carried out because they allow for its retention and making it available to the different parties involved in the organization. Holding meetings (Spraggon & Bodolica, 2008), training and development (Dyer & Nobeoka, 2000; Hutchins, Burke, & Berthelsen, 2010), cross-functional teams (Brown & Eisenhardt, 1997), and publication of an internal bulletin/newsletter are some examples of how (formally established) actions can be performed intentionally, potentially leading to knowledge-sharing. Effective use of all available means of communication, namely those which promote and incentivize (individual, group, and organizational)

Table 16.1 Intentional and unintentional knowledge-sharing: Some related activities and enablers.

Intentional sharing	*Related activities*	Identification
		Capture and accumulation
		Integration, systemization, combination
		Formal cooperation/collaboration/
		Training programs/several development actions (e.g., coaching, mentoring)
		Creation of knowledge maps
		Creation of spaces for formal and/or informal sharing (e.g., communities of practice)
		Implementation of infrastructure
		Employee functional rotation
		Availability/spread of knowledge to the whole organization
	Enablers	Shared language
		Face-to-face communication/interaction (individual, group, and collective)
		Virtual communication/interaction (e.g., email, intranets, best practice files, wikis)
		Audio-written-visual means
		Dedicated resources
		Briefing
Unintentional sharing	*Related activities*	Informal interaction/cooperation/collaboration/
		Rotation of work places
	Enablers	Conversations and other occasional communication processes
		Stories, anecdotes and myths
		Taskforces
		Informal work networks
		Shared language

communication, interaction and cooperation in face-to-face and/or virtual situations, serves as an important catalyst of the processes we have been alluding to.

However, organizational knowledge-sharing activities can occur unintentionally (Cardoso & Gomes, 2011; McAdam, Mason, & McCrory, 2007), involving various types of collaboration and cooperation of an informal nature (Hutchinson & Quintas, 2008), through which knowledge is also shared and spread at all organizational levels. To some extent, it can be said that the processes of capture, integration, systemization, combination, making available, and spreading previously mentioned (in the case of intentional sharing) also happen here, although in a register outside the control of the various organizational actors. In an organization, when an individual occupies the place of another (temporarily or permanently), when stories are told about what happens at work, or when chatting about work during the coffee-break, valuable and instrumental knowledge-sharing processes occur. Through the use of a collectively constructed and understood language, the discourse adopted at work and about work takes on a fundamental catalyzing role (Table 16.1).

As we saw, knowledge-sharing is a core process in knowledge management. As a result, the activities we describe are of particular importance, as through them knowledge is multiplied and expanded, allowing it to be used by the whole organization. These activities are characterized, among other aspects, by being essentially collaborative/cooperative. For that reason, the following section will deal with knowledge-sharing as a cooperative process.

Knowledge-Sharing as a Cooperative Process

Knowledge-sharing is in essence a cooperative process. At a first level, those who share knowledge intend it to be shared effectively (one gives and the other receives, these positions possibly being reciprocal and concomitant). The effectiveness of that sharing (as cooperation) will be measured by the quality and quantity of the knowledge effectively shared, considering the resources used to do so. At a second level, we must consider the purpose the shared knowledge will serve.

Although we are already speaking about the process of using knowledge (and no longer of sharing it), they are intimately linked when we look at these phenomena as cooperation. Indeed, the concept of cooperation implies the existence of shared (Argyle, 1991) or interdependent (Johnson & Johnson, 2005) goals, which guide the coordinated action between cooperating members. Therefore, knowledge-sharing always contains two levels of objectives, one consisting of its technical effectiveness and the other consisting of the intended use of the shared knowledge by cooperating members. At the latter level, knowledge can be shared to: (a) follow up cooperating members' common objectives; (b) follow up individual but interdependent objectives; (c) follow up individual and independent objectives; and (d) follow up competitive (negatively associated) objectives. Configuration of objectives as being positively associated (a and b), disassociated (c), or negatively associated (d) characterize the goal structures considered by social interdependence theory (Deutsch, 1973, 1993; Johnson & Johnson, 2005) as being, respectively, cooperative, individualistic, and competitive.

In real knowledge-sharing situations, several competing goals coexist. Furthermore, both levels of objectives present in knowledge-sharing presented above should be considered together. They cross in a complex way in real situations, co-determining the characteristics of the resulting behavior. The instrumental value of knowledge shared (for the individual and for others), the possible loss of power arising from knowledge-sharing, and the effort needed to share it are examples of factors impacting on the resulting motivation to share or not to share knowledge in organizations.

Awareness of the complexity of these processes has led authors to consider that knowledge-sharing is best characterized through the conceptual framework of social dilemmas. The motivations of organizational members, regarding knowledge-sharing, associated with gains and losses, are considered from an individual point of view, as determining aspects of the decision to cooperate or not to cooperate (Cabrera & Cabrera, 2002; Sharma & Bhattacharya, 2013). In these situations, the knowledge-sharing problem is always seen from the prism of contradictory individual motivations, on one hand to share (cooperate), and on the other, not to share (not to cooperate).

The study of social dilemmas has a long tradition in social science, particularly in psychology, and it is prolific in terms of the number of studies it has generated. Countless investigations carried out have been systematized in literature reviews and meta-analysis over the decades (e.g., Balliet, 2010; Balliet, Mulder, & van Lange, 2011; Balliet, Parks, & Joireman, 2009; Pruitt & Kimmel, 1977; Brewer & Kramer, 1986; Van Lange et al., 2013).

In general, social dilemmas are situations where two or more agents are interdependent on the results of interaction according to two conditions:

1   Each party has an individually beneficial short-term strategy that is better than the other strategy, but that individually beneficial strategy has a negative impact on the interests of the other intervening parties. In the case of knowledge-sharing in an organization, this strategy can consist of benefiting from the knowledge shared by others and not sharing one's own knowledge with others (knowledge hoarders, free riders).
2   The collective choice of this strategy (of both parties where they are two, or of a critical majority where there are several), which is usually designated as *noncooperative*, results in something less desirable than the result if all parties had chosen the strategy designated as *cooperative* (Wit & Wilke, 1992). In the case of knowledge-sharing, this would mean that nobody would share knowledge, and therefore, nobody could benefit from the knowledge of others.

The research that approaches knowledge-sharing in organizations as a social dilemma is recent. It is characterized precisely by stressing the contradictory character of the motivations present in the situation. Some authors have approached knowledge-sharing as a dilemma in a different way (Matsuo & Easterby-Smith, 2008). These authors highlight the dilemma of the degree of emphasis given to technology-based systems, knowing that they can inhibit experience-based learning. In this chapter we focus only on the approach of knowledge-sharing as a social dilemma. From this perspective, there are competing motives for individuals sharing their knowledge or not. The insights arising from the theory of social dilemmas have led to considering the importance of its deeper research in studying what to do to promote knowledge-sharing in organizations (Wang & Noe, 2010).

In Table 16.2, we detail the 20 main studies published, indicating their objectives, their variables and core concepts, and their main outputs. As can be seen from the publication dates of these studies, this is a recent approach, although inspired by two very consolidated lines of work, the study of social dilemmas, with many decades of research, and the study of knowledge-sharing which, as a knowledge-management process, became relevant in the second half of the 1990s. Almost half of these papers are theoretical papers without empirical research (Baldwin & Clark, 2006; Bandyopadhyay & Pathak, 2006; Cabrera & Cabrera, 2002, 2005; Cress & Martin, 2006; Ho, Su, & Lin, 2013; Kim, Lee, & Olson, 2006; Riss et al., 2007; Sharma & Bhattacharya, 2013). This can be understood considering the high formulation already reached in research on social dilemmas.

Table 16.2 Papers published on knowledge-sharing as a social dilemma.

Authors/year	Objectives	Core variables/concepts	Main results/outputs
Baldwin & Clark (2006)	To propose a model regarding the effects of structural variables (codebase architecture) on (a) incentives to contribute to the software development and (b) free riding behavior in software development	Code architecture Involuntary altruism Free riding	Codebases that are modular (or have more option value) increase developer's incentives to join and remain involved and decrease the amount of free riding
Bandyopadhyay & Pathak (2007)	To build a model of the knowledge shared between employees from "host" firms and the outsourcing firms	Payoff Outsourcing Complementarity of the knowledge	Better payoffs can be achieved where the degree of complementarity of knowledge between employees is high enough, and top management enforces cooperation between employees
Cabrera & Cabrera (2002)	To analyze knowledge-sharing as a public-good dilemma; To formulate strategies for solving the dilemma based on the literature on public dilemmas	Payoff for contributing Efficacy perceptions Group identity Personal responsibility	3 types of intervention for increasing cooperation: (1) restructuring the payoffs for contributing; (2) increasing efficacy perceptions; (3) making employees' sense of group identity and personal responsibility more salient
Cabrera & Cabrera (2005)	Based on literature to identify people management practices that are most effective in fostering knowledge-sharing	Attitudes towards knowledge-sharing Norms for knowledge-sharing Social ties and shared language Trust Group identification Perceived costs Perceived rewards Self-efficacy Reciprocity	Theoretical propositions on people management practices that foster knowledge-sharing

(Continued)

Table 16.2 (*Continued*)

Authors/year	Objectives	Core variables/concepts	Main results/outputs
Cress & Martin (2006)	To formulate theoretical propositions on contributing knowledge to databases	Knowledge exchange Sharing databases Bonus system for contribution	Rewarding contributions with a cost compensating bonus can increase contribution to shared databases at individual and group level Whether or not a bonus system is self-supporting depends on (1) the critical mass of people needing a contribution, (2) the overlap of people's resources and their interdependency
Cress et al. (2007)	Impact of: (a) rewards for contributing information (b) the individual costs associated with this contribution (c) the prospective meta-knowledge about the importance of one's own information to others (d) retrospective meta-knowledge about how much others contributed to and retrieved from the database on the quality and quantity of databases' content	Prospective meta-knowledge Retrospective meta-knowledge Rewards for contribution Quality and quantity of database content	Meta-knowledge (prospective and retrospective) and use-related reward system influence knowledge-sharing behavior
Cress, Kimmerle, & Hesse (2006)	To analyze the impact of meta-knowledge, use-related bonus system, and contribution cost on information exchange in a shared database	Real information exchange Meta-knowledge on the importance of knowledge Bonus system for contribution	Meta-knowledge enhances the quality of contributions; A use-related bonus system enhances the meta-knowledge effect Increased contribution costs influence the contribution behavior negatively

Author (Year)	Objective	Constructs	Findings
Frost & Morner (2010)	To provide a framework for governance modes and mechanisms according to the public-good characteristics of knowledge resources (case study)	Governance modes (knowledge as resource) Cognitive proximity Procedural adherence	2 actor-oriented characteristics (cognitive proximity and procedural adherence) influence the choice of different governance modes
Ghobadi & D'Ambra (2011)	To test the coopetition model of simultaneous cooperation and competition in knowledge-sharing	Coopetition High-quality knowledge-sharing	Cooperative task orientation, cooperative communication, and cooperative interpersonal relationships influence high-quality knowledge-sharing Competition for tangible resources positively affects cooperative communication of individuals Competition for intangible resources had negative impacts on cooperative communication and task orientations
Ghobadi & D'Ambra (2013)	To find out the underlying mechanisms that generate high-quality knowledge-sharing in software development teams	High-quality knowledge-sharing Cross-functional teams Social interdependence theory Coopetitive model of knowledge-sharing	The research supports the coopetitive model of knowledge-sharing Define structural variables that determine high-quality knowledge-sharing in cross-functional teams
Ho, Hsu, & Lin (2011)	To formulate a model for knowledge-sharing strategies on behavioral dynamics of knowledge-sharing in organizations	ICT platforms Monetary rewards for sharing knowledge Knowledge characteristics: complexity/uniqueness; value to the firm; demand for the knowledge	A new knowledge taxonomy from the perspective of knowledge-sharing dynamics Three hypotheses on ICT platforms, knowledge management, and knowledge characteristics A framework for knowledge-sharing strategies (rewarding according to the type of knowledge)

(Continued)

Table 16.2 (*Continued*)

Authors/year	Objectives	Core variables/concepts	Main results/outputs
Kim, Lee, & Olson (2006)	To analyze the sharing behavior in a community of practice (simulation)	Cooperator Reciprocators Free riders	Cooperator group is positively related to total knowledge contribution and to the reciprocity level Reciprocity level positively affects knowledge contribution
Kimmerle et al. (2011)	To test the following hypotheses: (a) people select their contributions according to the benefit these contributions provide to others (b) the social value orientation of individuals affects their willingness to contribute (c) externally provided behavioral guidelines have an impact on individual behavior	Social value orientation Behavioral guidelines Value of information	People (pro-social and pro-self) avoided contributing such information that would have provided others with a higher benefit than the benefit the contributors themselves received Behavioral guidelines had an impact on the contributions, independent of the value of information
Maciejovsky & Budescu (2013)	To analyze the effect of auction and market structures on knowledge-sharing behavior	Auction mechanisms Structural solutions for dilemmas Knowledge-sharing	Auction mechanisms (rigid set of rules designed to standardize interactions and communication between participants), can prevent some detrimental effects associated with conflict of interest in freely interacting groups Market mechanisms can be used to disseminate knowledge and information in organizations effectively, solving the knowledge-sharing dilemmas

Reference	Objective	Concepts	Findings
Riss et al. (2007)	To compare the case-based task management (CBTM) system and the pattern-based task management (PBTM) system regarding motivational requirements for knowledge-sharing	Process-oriented knowledge management; Human–computer interaction; Personal task management; Task patterns	The PBTM is viewed as the better approach to motivate users to share their work experience by task patterns rather than by cases (emphasizes the collaborative aspect of every contribution and protects the privacy of individual work behavior). It is important to emphasize the social aspect of task patterns
Sharma & Bhattacharya (2013)	How behaviors of organizations' knowledge workers show potential conflicts with what would be optimal for the organization in terms of knowledge flows (game theoretic approach)	4 knowledge dilemmas: (1) Silos of knowledge; (2) Tragedy of the knowledge commons; (3) Knowledge friction; (4) Toxicity of knowledge	Key insights and prescriptive guiding principles in formulating knowledge strategies and policies to combat the major knowledge dilemmas that inhibit effective knowledge flows
Steinel, Utz, & Koningaal (2010)	To analyze the effect of some variables on information-sharing behavior	Information pooling game; Pro-social individuals; Selfish individuals; Information sharedness; Information importance	Information sharing depends on people's pro-social or pro-self motivation; People consider information sharedness and information importance when deciding whether to reveal, withhold, or falsify information; Pro-social individuals honestly reveal their private and important information; Selfish individuals strategically concealed or lied about their private and important information

(Continued)

Table 16.2 (*Continued*)

Authors/year	Objectives	Core variables/concepts	Main results/outputs
Wilkesmann, Wilkesmann, & Virgillito (2009)	How can knowledge transfer be supported?	Organizational culture (involvement and consistency) Intrinsic motivation Direct channels (for interaction)	Requirements for knowledge transfer: direct channels for interaction; organizational culture; intrinsic motivation
Yuan et al. (2005)	To test several hypotheses on the influence of others' behavior and technology-specific competence on the use of intranets	Collective action model Information commons Group-level social influence	The perceived team member behavior (contributions to and retrieval from repositories) and the technology-specific competence are positively related to the individual use of intranets
Zhang et al. (2010)	Case study based on Nash equilibrium on knowledge-sharing situations	Knowledge-sharing situations (Perfect, Free riding, Nonuse, and Dormant)	The following elements facilitate knowledge-sharing: rewards, a quality-evaluating system, extended information technology support, and organizational policy

Overall, these studies allow us to highlight four main aspects that characterize the trend in the knowledge-sharing literature when approached as a cooperative process and a social dilemma where competing drivers play a role:

1 Knowledge-sharing is generally viewed as a desirable practice that organizations have to implement to achieve better performance through organizational knowledge development. However, only a few authors pay attention to the quality of knowledge to be shared and distinguish between desirable and spurious knowledge (Ho, Hsu, & Lin, 2013) and falsified knowledge (Steinel Utz & Koning, 2010). In the literature reviewed, only three articles (Ghobadi & D'Ambra, 2013; Ho, Hsu, & Lin, 2013; Steinel, Uz, & Koningaal, 2010) clearly highlight the possibility of the knowledge shared being of poor quality (useless) or even fake. Therefore, we would like to stress here the evidence that the dark side of knowledge-sharing is under-represented in the literature on the topic. Future research has here an avenue for developing understanding of the negative side of knowledge-sharing processes.

2 Most articles are focused on strategies for promoting knowledge-sharing or on variables that influence it. In some work presented, prescriptions and/or influencing variables are the consequence of the empirical research carried out (Cress et al., 2007; Cress, Kimmerle, & Hesse, 2006; Ghobadi & D'Ambra, 2013; Kimmerle et al., 2011; Maciejovsky & Budescu, 2013; Steinel, Utz, & Koning, 2010; Wilkesmann, Wilkesmann, & Virgillito, 2009; Yuan et al., 2005; Zhang et al., 2010). In other published work, prescriptions and/or influencing variables are based on conceptual and theoretical reflections and deductions (Baldwin & Clark, 2006; Bandyopadhyay & Pathak, 2007; Cabrera & Cabrera, 2002, 2005; Cress & Martin, 2006; Ho, Hsu, & Lin, 2013; Kim, Lee, & Olson, 2006; Sharma & Bhattacharya, 2013; Riss et al., 2007). Among these studies we highlight the proposal of Cabrera and Cabrera (2002) about three types of organizational interventions in line with this vision: (a) interventions focused on management of payoffs arising from sharing (considering them broadly and not just in terms of monetary rewards); (b) improved perception of the effectiveness of sharing and its impact on the organization (what interferes with processes of internal communication); (c) and interventions focused on simultaneous strengthening of group identity and personal responsibility. The three types of interventions are closely linked to human resource management and its policies. Other interesting variables are also put in place, such as individual characteristics which influence knowledge-sharing (e.g., cooperators, reciprocators, and free riders (Kim, Lee, & Olson, 2006); pro-social and pro-self orientations (Kimmerle et al., 2011)), and knowledge characteristics (e.g., complexity/uniqueness, value to the firm, and demand for the knowledge (Ho, Hsu, & Lin, 2013)).

3 The added value that results from knowledge-sharing behavior has been neglected so far. There is no research focused on measuring the results reached through knowledge-sharing. The development of such research evaluating the qualitative and quantitative results of knowledge-sharing should be developed so as to reach a new level in understanding knowledge-sharing as a cooperation process.

4 From the 11 empirical researches reported, four are experimental researches using the framework of social dilemmas. Although simple to operationalize, research on experimental social dilemmas has marked limitations for emulating real knowledge-sharing situations:

(a) In that research, cooperation is operationalized as a choice whose execution is simple. Even if the decision is complex, executing it is simply marking the choice. Therefore, it becomes a very poor emulation of reality where it is necessary to execute actions together or where some coordination is required. This is the case of knowledge-sharing, which sometimes takes place between two people but often between many, with several competing motivators being involved.

(b) Laboratory situations are experienced by subjects differently from that which happens in real life, outside the laboratory. Here, individuals face real knowledge-sharing dilemmas where many more variables intervene simultaneously and the complexity of problems is not reduced to a matrix indicating alternative numerical values. The meaning of choices is variable between subjects and not immediately discernible by the researcher. Agents' dispositional variables of the dilemma situation, such as the social value orientation (Kimmerle et al., 2011), have an expected impact on the meaning of the option (cooperate or not cooperate).

(c) Grzelak and Derlega (1982) consider there is an underlying assumption in social dilemma research: the ideology of the *homo economicus*. In fact, many subjects in experimental research are seen to cooperate more than would be expected if their motivations were centered on their own interests (Andreoni, 1995).

(d) Rabbie (1991) distinguishes *instrumental cooperation* (aiming to produce a result outside the relationship) from *social cooperation* (aiming for a result inherent to the relationship, such as furthering social relationships). We can say that social cooperation is under-represented in social dilemma research. Indeed, subjects do not expect to continue the relationship with their partners in the dilemma, and have little opportunity or expectation to form rich and mutually satisfying relationships with the other participants. Outside the paradigm of social dilemmas, various authors have studied the variables determining knowledge-sharing. For example, Hung et al. (2011) found that the enjoyment in helping others and the reputation feedback were the motives producing the most consistent results (among those considered by the authors) in strengthening sharing behaviors.

(e) By presenting the game situation to the subjects with the respective scores, we assume implicitly that to a certain extent their interests are their own and not those of the partner in the game. Even if the interdependence framework established allows finding a point of balance between the interests of each, they are always presented as the interests of each one considered individually. In other words, cooperation will always look like an interaction where the objectives are positively correlated and never the same shared objective. In many knowledge-sharing situations, what is at stake is a common identity, common objectives, and not only interdependent individual objectives. That is the reason why Cabrera and Cabrera (2002) suggest making employees' sense of group identity (and personal responsibility) more salient, to increase knowledge-sharing.

Although several studies in the framework of these approaches recognize that some individuals repeatedly fall outside this pattern (Caporael et al., 1989) – for example, systematically making *cooperative* choices, despite them not being corresponded – the way the very laboratory situation is constructed and presented implies a vision of individual interests as drivers of decisions, since they are what is equated in the problem posed.

Not all of the empirical research carried out on knowledge-sharing as a social dilemma followed an experimental methodological design (e.g., Frost & Morner, 2010). That is encouraging for the development of other studies that can bring more realism to a paradigm that seems so fertile in setting the problem but has been so sterile in laboratory emulation of the reality it is the intention to study.

Future Research

This section discusses the current research agenda on knowledge-sharing, cooperation, and personal development, stressing the gaps in knowledge that are being discussed and explored, and that are in need of further investigation.

Knowledge-sharing as a cooperative process: new developments

In the framework of social dilemmas, studying knowledge-sharing as a cooperative process can be developed through qualitative studies dealing with real-life situations considering and integrating their complexity. The social dilemma approach is powerful in the clarity with which it equates the contradictory motivations present in the knowledge-sharing process. However, the way research in this domain has been predominantly designed allows researchers great control of the variables, but is removed from the real-life contexts in which the phenomena occur. In addition, qualitative studies will also allow deeper knowledge of the decision process, rather than taking it as an item of data manipulated by the researcher.

Knowledge-sharing as a cooperative process contemplates a dimension of technical effectiveness that is ignored by the theory of social dilemmas. Indeed, in this approach cooperation is an easily executed choice. In real contexts, knowledge-sharing means knowing how to teach and knowing how to learn (absorptive capacity), which requires specific competences that determine the effectiveness of the process. In the theory of social dilemmas, the cooperative or noncooperative choice occurs with clearly established alternatives. This limitation indicates that other approaches to cooperation can significantly expand understanding of these phenomena. One of those approaches is that of cooperative learning (e.g., Bennett, 1991; Cowie, 1995; Brown & Brown, 1995; Kyndt et al., 2013; Sugie, 1995; Huber, 1995; Taylor, 1995; Ovejero, 1990; Hertz-Lazarowitz & Zelniker, 1995; Johnson et al., 1984). Put simply, the dominant research model in these approaches consists of structuring real classroom situations as cooperative, competitive, or individualistic (Johnson & Johnson, 2005). By being real situations, prolonged over time, with real agents, they have total realism. Their results speak highly of cooperative learning techniques. As they are knowledge-sharing situations, it is surprising that research into this phenomenon has not yet adopted the lessons learned from investigations about cooperative learning. So this is a very promising field for future study.

Finally, in studies to be carried out, it is important to integrate the dimension of the time perspective inherent to knowledge-sharing situations in real work contexts, and the fact that these frequently occur without previous planning and preparation by the parties involved. The understanding arising from studying these dimensions could be a valid and expressive contribution to conceptualization and to the management practice of organizational processes related to knowledge-sharing.

Knowledge-sharing and personal development: avenues for future research

It is our assumption that when individuals are prepared to take the risk and share knowledge with each other, they cooperate and this can contribute to their development. At the same time, this development can make them aware of the importance of collaboration and cooperation.

Although this relationship seems obvious, empirical studies of it are scarce. On one hand, research has been focused more on the antecedents of knowledge-sharing (Alavi, 2001; Collins & Hitt, 2006; De Long & Fahey, 2000; Ghobadi & D'Ambra, 2011; Ipe, 2003; Lee, Kim, & Kim, 2006; McDermott & O'Dell, 2001; Rocha, Cardoso, & Tordera, 2008; Wang & Noe, 2010; Witherspoon et al., 2013) than on its results. On the other hand, analysis of the latter shows they do not integrate personal development as an output of sharing. This may arise from the fact that knowledge-sharing is being considered above all in the context of promoting organizational performance or it being mainly at this level that its impacts are expected, assessed, and studied. In fact, knowledge-sharing has not been viewed in the context of its most obvious (and first) impact, which is that of its influence on individuals' development. Not even when focusing on organizational performance is the value of the contribution of individual knowledge/development at that level considered. Priority has been given to outputs at the organizational level, with the individual level being relegated to less-valued aspects. According to Yang and Wu (2008), "few studies include the viewpoint of the economic value of individual knowledge to explore knowledge sharing in an organization" (p. 1130).

Nevertheless, if organizational knowledge arises from the knowledge held by individuals, development of the former depends on development of the latter. The organization as a whole gains with the knowledge they "hold" and with their continuous development and these gains are considered relevant and measurable. So it seems equally relevant to consider and value the gains occurring at the individual level and coming from the knowledge-sharing in which individuals are involved and participate. With these considerations we do not wish to state that individual gains in terms of personal development have been completely ignored, just that they have not been given equitable importance and visibility. Making these gains emerging from sharing processes tangible and explicit, in terms of personal development, can lead to the different organizational actors being more open and willing to cooperate and share their knowledge.

Chalhoub (2009) suggests six components to be considered as key indicators of individuals' development with impact on the organization's performance: participative management, employee training, research and development (R&D) involvement, retention through intellectual advancement, external knowledge management, and market centeredness. These apply to the context of necessarily participative (therefore cooperative) management and let managers identify critical areas of intervention with the potential to facilitate collaborator development. Three of the six indicators – participative management, employee training, and R&D involvement – emerge from organizational processes/practices that are intensive in knowledge-sharing and cooperation. Collaborator development is once again considered above all because it has an impact on organizational performance. However, this study allows identification of at least three drivers of personal development interactively related to knowledge-sharing and cooperation. Through them, managers and their management can foster collaborative development and simultaneously support organizational performance.

In truth, if one of the main objectives of knowledge management initiatives is to improve or facilitate knowledge-sharing by the different organizational actors at work and to work, both individuals (Guechtouli, Rouchier, & Orillard, 2013) and the organization can, through them, learn, grow, and develop (Alavi & Leidner, 2001; Earl, 2001; Nahapiet & Ghoshal, 1998; Mura et al., 2013; Nonaka, 1994; Sveiby, 1997; Yang & Wu, 2008). However, this relationship is rarely considered and stressed, from a logic of personal development, when an individual tries to help another or learn from the other (Aslani, Mousakhani, & Aslani, 2012; Wang & Noe, 2010). Knowledge-sharing can then be seen as an opportunity for learning and growth (Riege, 2005) for either of the parties involved (Wang & Noe, 2010; Wasko & Faraj, 2000) and the more intentional and better it is, the better the learning and (individual and organizational) development arising from it. Also at these levels, there is a need to carry out theoretical and empirical studies.

Conclusion

Based on the literature review carried out, a global view (synthesis) is presented of the interrelationships between knowledge-sharing, cooperation, and personal development. The knowledge-sharing process is one that is intensive in cooperation. Nevertheless, in the dynamics of its functioning competing motivations coexist, which means it can be analyzed as a social dilemma. Intervening on one side are motivations that contribute to the sharing process, while on the other motivations act towards nonsharing. The fact knowledge is a resource that does not diminish when shared does not prevent individuals from feeling that knowledge-sharing is time-consuming and has a cost, as it requires energy, and can correspond to a loss of power. In addition, the others with whom knowledge can be shared are not neutral in the mind of the subjects.

The approach to knowledge-sharing as a cooperative process and at the same time a social dilemma has appeared in the literature since the beginning of the twenty-first century. Theoretical and empirical studies have focused on identifying the variables that can solve the dilemma, making it a nondilemma. Identification of those variables has the potential to contribute to understanding human functioning and to formulating policies and practices of people management that are more effective and compatible with their nature.

In conclusion, we would suggest that if we consider the activities formally carried out in organizations with the aim of facilitating and/or promoting knowledge-sharing, we find that the majority form opportunities for learning and development. So it seems that studying the impact of knowledge-sharing (and related activities) on the learning and personal development of the different organizational actors is fertile and relevant terrain in terms of research. This can be approached from the point of view of the individuals themselves, or those who are their interlocutors in the network of (not only) cooperative relationships occurring at work.

References

Alavi, M. (2000). Managing organizational knowledge. In R. W. Zmud (Ed.), *Framing the Domains of IT Management Research: Glimpsing the Future through the Past* (pp. 15–28). Cincinnati, OH: Pinnaflex Educational Resources.

Alavi, M., & Leidner, D. E. (2001). Knowledge management and knowledge management systems: Conceptual foundations and research issues. *MIS Quarterly*, 25(1), 107–136.

Alee, V. (1997). *The Knowledge Evolution: Expanding Organizational Intelligence*. Boston, MA: Butterworth-Heinemann.

Aliakbar, E., Yusoff, R. B., & Mahmood, N. H. N. (2012). Determinants of knowledge sharing behavior. *International Proceedings of Economics Development and Research*, 29, 208–215. Singapore: IACSIT Press.

Alvesson, M., & Kärreman D. (2001). Odd couple: Making sense of the curious concept of knowledge management. *Journal of Management Studies*, 38(7), 995–1018.

Andreoni, J. (1995). Cooperation in public goods experiments: Kindness or confusion? *American Economic Review*, 85, 891–904.

Andreu, R., & Sieber, S. (2000). La gestión integral del conocimiento y del aprendizaje. *Economía Industrial*, 326, 63–72.

Arce, A., & Long, N. (1992). The dynamics of knowledge: Interfaces between the bureaucrats and peasants. In L. Long, & A. Long (Eds.), *Battlefields of Knowledge: The Interlocking of Theory and Practice in Social Research and Development* (pp. 211–246). London: Routledge.

Argote, L., (1999). *Organizational Learning: Creating, Retaining and Transferring Knowledge.* Norwell, MA: Kluwer.

Argyle, M. (1991). *Cooperation: The Basis of Sociability.* London: Routledge.

Aslani, F., Mousakhani, M., & Aslani, A. (2012). Knowledge sharing: A survey, assessment and directions for future research: Individual behavior perspective. *World Academy of Science, Engineering and Technology,* 6(68), 310–314.

Baldwin, C. Y., & Clark, K. B. (2006). The architecture of participation: Does code architecture mitigate free riding in the open source development model? *Management Science,* 52(7), 1116–1127.

Balliett, D. (2010). Communication and cooperation in social dilemmas: A meta-analytic review. *Journal of Conflict Resolution,* 54(1), 39–57.

Balliet, D., Mulder, L. B., & van Lange, P. A. M. (2011). Reward, punishment and cooperation: A meta-analysis. *Psychological Bulletin,* 137(4), 594–615.

Balliet, D., Parks, C., & Joireman, J. (2009). Social value orientation and cooperation in social dilemmas: A meta-analysis. *Group Processes and Intergroup Cooperation,* 12(4), 533–547.

Bandyopadhyay, S., & Pathak, P. (2007). Knowledge sharing and cooperation in outsourcing projects – A game theoretic analysis. *Decision Support Systems,* 43, 349–358.

Barney, J. (1991). Firm resources and sustained competitive advantage. *Journal of Management,* 17, 99–120.

Bartol, K. M., & Srivastava, A. (2002). Encouraging knowledge sharing: The role of organizational reward systems. *Journal of Leadership and Organization Studies,* 9(1), 64–76.

Beijerse, R. P. (1999). Questions in knowledge management: Defining and conceptualizing a phenomenon. *Journal of Knowledge Management,* 3(2), 94–110.

Bennett, N. (1991). Cooperative learning in classrooms: Processes and outcomes. *Journal of Child Psychology and Psychiatry,* 32(4), 581–594.

Berger, P., & Luckmann, T. (1966). *The Social Construction of Reality.* New York: Penguin.

Bhatt, G. (2000). Organizing knowledge in the knowledge development cycle. *Journal of Knowledge Management,* 1(4), 15–26.

Birkinshaw, J., & Sheehan, T. (2002). Managing the knowledge life cycle. *Management Review,* 44(1), 74–84.

Bogaert, S., Boone, C., & Declerck, C. (2008). Social value orientation and cooperation in social dilemmas: A review and conceptual model. *British Journal of Social Psychology,* 47, 453–480.

Boisot, M. H. (1998). *Knowledge Assets: Securing Competitive Advantage in the Information Economy.* Oxford: Oxford University Press.

Bosua, R., & Venkitachalam, K. (2013). Aligning strategies and processes in knowledge management: A framework. *Journal of Knowledge Management,* 17(3), 331–346.

Brewer, M. B., & Kramer, R. M. (1986). Choice behavior in social dilemmas: Effects of social identity, group size, and decision framing. *Journal of Personality and Social Psychology,* 50, 543–549.

Brooking, A. (1996). *Intellectual Capital.* London: International Thompson Business Press.

Brown, W., & Brown, P. B. (1995). Cooperative learning in Latin America: A perspective from the alternative education experience. *International Journal of Educational Research,* 23(3), 255–266.

Cabrera, A., & Cabrera, E. (2002). Knowledge-sharing dilemmas. *Organization Studies,* 23(5), 687–710.

Cabrera, A., Collins, W. C., & Salgado, J. F. (2006). Determinants of individual engagement in knowledge sharing. *International Journal of Human Resource Management,* 17(2), 245–264.

Cabrera, E., & Cabrera, A. (2005). Fostering knowledge sharing through people management practices. *International Journal of Human Resource Management,* 16(5), 720–735.

Caporael, L. R., Dawes, R. M., Orbell, J. M., & Van De Kragt, A. J. C. (1989). Selfishness examined: Cooperation in the absence of egoistic incentives. *Behavioral and Brain Sciences,* 12, 683–739.

Cardoso, L., & Gomes, D. (2011). Knowledge management and innovation: Mapping the use of technology in organizations. In A. Mesquita (Ed.), *Technology for Creativity and Innovation: Tools, Techniques and Applications* (pp. 237–266). Hershey, PA: IGI Global.

Cardoso, L., Meireles, A., & Ferreira Peralta, C. (2012). Knowledge management and its critical factors in social economy organizations. *Journal of Knowledge Management*, 16(2), 267–284.

Carrión, G. C., González, J. L. G., & Leal, A. (2004). Identifying key knowledge area in the professional services industry: A case study. *Journal of Knowledge Management*, 8(6), 131–150.

Carter, C., & Scarborough, H. (2001). Towards a second generation of knowledge management: The people management challenge. *Education and Training*, 43(4/5), 215–224.

Chalhoub, M. S. (2009). Employee growth and development through knowledge management in the global environment: Effects on the competitiveness of firms in a multinational context. *Journal of Knowledge Globalization*, 2(2), 25–46.

Conner, K., &. Prahalad, C. K. (1996). A resource-based theory of the firm: Knowledge versus opportunism. *Organization Science*, 7(5), 477–501.

Cowie, H. (1995). Cooperative group works: A perspective from the UK. *International Journal of Educational Research*, 23(3), 227–238.

Cress, U., Braquero, B., Schwan, S., & Hesse F. W. (2007). Improving quality and quantity of contributions: Two models for promoting knowledge exchange with shared databases. *Computers & Education*, 49, 423–440.

Cress, U., Kimmerle, J., & Hesse, F. W. (2006). Information exchange with shared databases as a social dilemma: The effect of metaknowledge, bonus systems, and costs. *Communication Research*, 33(5), 370–390.

Cress, U., & Martin, S. (2006). Knowledge sharing and rewards: A game theoretical perspective. *Knowledge Management Research & Practice*, 4, 283–292.

Davenport, T. (1996). Some principles of knowledge management. *CIO Magazine*, July, 1996.

Davenport, T. H., & Prusak, L. (1998). *Working Knowledge: How Organizations Manage What They Know*. Boston, MA: Harvard Business School Press.

Dawson, R. (2000). Knowledge capabilities as the focus of organisational development and strategy. *Journal of Knowledge Management*, 4(4), 320–327.

De Long, D. (1997). *Building the Knowledge-Based Organization: How Culture Drives Knowledge Behaviors*. Center for Business Innovation: Ernst & Young LLP.

Denton, J. (1998). *Organizational Learning and Effectiveness*. London: Routledge.

Deutsch, M. (1973). *The Resolution of Conflict: Constructive and Destructive Process*. New Haven, CT: Yale University Press.

Deutsch, M. (1993). Educating for a peaceful world. *American Psychologist*, 48(5), 510–517.

Dixon, N. (1992). Organizational learning: A review of the literature with implications for HRO professionals. *Human Resource Development Quarterly*, 3(1), 29–51.

Dixon, N. M. (2000). *Common Knowledge: How Companies Thrive by Sharing what they Know*. Boston, MA: Harvard Business School Press.

Donald, H. (2010). Knowledge management as an ephemeral management fashion? *Journal of Knowledge Management*, 14(6), 779–790.

Drucker, P. F. (1993). *The Post-Capitalist Society*. New York: Harper Collins.

Dyer, J. H., & Nobeoka, K. (2000). Creating and managing a high-performance knowledge-sharing network: The Toyota case. *Strategic Management Journal*, 21(3), 345–367.

Earl, M. J. (1994). Approaches to strategic information systems planning: Experience in 21 UK companies. *MIS Quarterly*, 17(1), 1–23.

Foss, N. J., Husted, K., & Michailova, S. (2010). Governing knowledge sharing in organizations: Levels of analysis, governance mechanisms, and research directions. *Journal of Management Studies*, 47(3), 455–482.

Frost, J., & Morner, M. (2010). Overcoming knowledge dilemmas: Governing the creation sharing and use of knowledge resources. *International Journal of Strategic Change Management*, 2(2/3), 172–199.

Ghobadi, S., & D'Ambra, J. (2011). Coopetitive knowledge sharing: An analytical review of literature. *Electronic Journal of Knowledge Management*, 9(4), 307–317.

Ghobadi, S., & D'Ambra, J. (2013). Modeling high-quality knowledge sharing in cross-functional software development teams. *Information Processing and Management*, 49, 138–157.

Gold, A. H., Malhotra, A., & Segars, A. H. (2001). Knowledge management: An organizational capabilities perspective. *Journal of Management Information Systems* 18(1), 185–214.

Grant, R. M. (1996). Prospering in dynamically competitive environments: Organizational capacity as knowledge integration. *Organizational Science*, 7(4), 375–388.

Grover, V., & Davenport, T. (2001). General perspectives on knowledge management: Fostering a research agenda. *Journal of Management Information Systems*, 18(1), 5–22.

Guechtouli, W., Rouchier, J., & Orillard, M. (2013). Structuring knowledge transfer from experts to newcomers. *Journal of Knowledge Management*, 17(1), 47–68.

Hamel, G. (1991). Competition for competence and interpartner learning within international alliances. *Strategic Management Journal*, 12 (Special Issue), 83–103.

Hansen, M. T., Nohria, N., & Tierney, T. (1999). What's your strategy for managing knowledge? *Harvard Business Review*, 77(2), 106–116.

Heil, G., Bennis, W., & Stephens, D.C. (2000). *Douglas McGregor, Revisited: Managing the Human Side of the Enterprise*. New York: John Wiley & Sons, Inc.

Henderson, R., & Cockburn, J. (1994). Measuring competence? Exploring firm effects in pharmaceutical research. *Strategic Management Journal*, 15, 63–84.

Hertz-Lazarowitz, R., & Zelniker, T. (1995). Cooperative learning in Israel: Historical, cultural and educational perspectives. *International Journal of Educational Research*, 23(3), 267–282.

Hislop, D. (2010). Knowledge management as an ephemeral management fashion? *Journal of Knowledge Management*, 14(6), 779–790.

Ho, S. P., Hsu, Y., & Lin, E. (2011). Model for knowledge sharing strategies: A game theory analysis. *Engineering Project Organization Journal*, 1, 53–65.

Huber, G. L. (1995). Cooperative learning in German schools. *International Journal of Educational Research*, 23(3), 201–212.

Huber, G. P. (1991). Organizational learning: The contributing processes and the literatures. *Organization Science*, 2(1), 88–115.

Hung, S.-Y., Durcikova, A., Lai, H.-M., & Lin, W.-M. (2011). The influence of intrinsic and extrinsic motivation on individuals' knowledge sharing behavior. *International Journal of Human–Computer Studies*, 69, 415–427.

Huseman, R. C., & Goodman, J. P. (1999). *Leading with Knowledge: The Nature of Competition in the 21st Century*. Thousand Oaks, CA: Sage.

Hutchins, H. M., Burke, L. A., & Berthelsen, A. M. (2010). A missing link in the transfer problem? Examining how trainers learn about training transfer. *Human Resource Management*, 49(4), 599–618.

Hutchinson, V., & Quintas, P. (2008). Do SMEs do knowledge management? Or simply manage what they know. *International Small Business Journal*, 26(2), 131–154.

Janssen, O., van de Vliert, E., & West, M. (2004). The bright and dark sides of individual and group innovation: A special issue introduction. *Journal of Organizational Behavior*, 25, 129–145.

Johnson, D. W., & Johnson, R. T. (1992). Preparing children to live in an interdependent world. In A. Combs (Ed.), *Cooperation: Beyond the Age of Competition* (pp. 193–202). Amsterdam: Gordon and Breach Science Publishers S. A.

Johnson, D. W., & Johnson, R. T. (2005). New developments in social interdependence theory. *Genetic, Social and General Psychology Monographs*, 131(4), 285–358.

Johnson, D. W., Johnson, R. T., Tiffany, M., & Zaidman, B. (1984). Cross-ethnic relationships: The impact of intergroup cooperation and intergroup competition. *Journal of Educational Research*, 78(2), 75–79.

Kim, J., Lee, S. M., & Olson, D. L. (2006). Knowledge sharing: Effects of cooperative type and reciprocity level. *International Journal of Knowledge Management*, 2(4), 1–16.

Kimmerle, J., Wodzicki, K., Jarodzka, H., & Cress, U. (2011). Value of information, behavioral guidelines, and social value orientation in an information-exchange dilemma. *Group Dynamics: Theory, Research, and Practice*, 15(2), 173–186.

Kogut, B., U., & Zander, U. (1992). Knowledge of the firm, combinative capabilities, and the replication of technology. *Organization Science*, 3(3), 383–397.

Kyndt, E., Raes, E., Lismont, B., Timmers, F., Cascallar, E., & Dochy, F. (2013). A meta-analysis of the effects of face-to-face cooperative learning. Do recent studies falsify or verify earlier findings? *Educational Research Review*, 10, 133–149.

Lee, J. H., Kim, Y. G., & Kim, M. Y. (2006). Effects of managerial drivers and climate maturity on knowledge-management performance: Empirical validation. *Information Resources Management Journal*, 19(3), 48–60.

Leonard-Barton, D. (1992). Core capabilities and core rigidities: A paradox in managing new product development. *Strategic Management Journal*, 13(5), 363–380.

Leonard-Barton, D. (1995). *Wellsprings of Knowledge: Building and Sustaining the Sources of Innovation*. Boston, MA: Harvard Business School Press.

Levin, D. Z., & Cross, R. (2004). The strength of weak ties you can trust: The mediating role of trust in effective knowledge transfer. *Management Science*, 50, 1477–1490.

Lloria, M. B. (2008). A review of the main approaches to knowledge management. *Knowledge Management Research & Practice*, 6, 77–89.

Maciejovsky, B., & Budescu, D. V. (2013). Markets as a structural solution to knowledge-sharing dilemmas. *Organizational Behavior and Human decision Processes*, 120(2), 154–167.

Matayong, S., & Mahmood, A. K. (2013). The review of approaches to knowledge management system studies. *Journal of Knowledge Management*, 17(3), 472–490.

Matsuo, M., & Easterby-Smith, M. (2008). Beyond the knowledge sharing dilemma: The role of customization. *Journal of Knowledge Management*, 12(4), 30–43.

Mayer, R., & Remus, U. (2003). Implementing process-oriented knowledge management strategies. *Journal of Knowledge Management*, 7(4), 62–75.

Mayo, A. (1998). Memory bankers. *People Management*, 2(4), 34–38.

McAdam, R., Mason, B., & McCrory, J. (2007). Exploring the dichotomies within the tacit knowledge literature: Towards a process of tacit knowing in organizations, 11(2), 43–59.

McDermott, R. (1999). Why information technology inspired but cannot deliver knowledge management. *California Management Review*, 41(4), 103–117.

McElroy, M. (1999). Second generation knowledge management. *IBM Knowledge Management Consulting Group*, June, 1–9.

McElroy, M. W. (2000). The new knowledge management. *Knowledge & Innovation: Journal of the KMCI*, 1(1), 43–67.

Metaxiotis, K., Ergazakis, K., & Psarras, J. (2005). Exploring the world of knowledge management: Agreements and disagreements in the academic/practitioner community. *Journal of Knowledge Management*, 9(2), 6–18.

Moustafir, K., & Schiuma, G. (2013). Knowledge, learning, and innovation: Research and perspectives. *Journal of Knowledge Management*, 17(4), 495–510.

Muñoz Seca, B., & Riverola, J. (1997). *Gestión del conocimiento*. Biblioteca IESE de Gestión de Empresas, Universidad de Navarra. Barcelona: Folio.

Mura, M., Lettieri, E., Radaelli, G., & Spiller, N. (2013). Promoting professionals' innovative behaviour through knowledge sharing: The moderating role of social capital. *Journal of Knowledge Management*, 17(4), 527–544.

Nelson, J. E. (1992). Case study: Teaching learning skills as a foundation for technical learning. *Education and Training Technology International*, 29(2), 105–108.

Nelson, R. R., & Winter, S. G. (1982). *An Evolutionary Theory of Economic Change*. Cambridge, MA: Belknap Press.

Nicolini, D., Powell, J., Conville, P., & Martinez-Solano, L. (2008). Managing knowledge in the healthcare sector: A review. *International Journal of Management Reviews*, 10(3), 245–263.

Nonaka, I. (1990). *Chishiki-souzou mo keiei* [A theory of organizational knowledge creation]. Tokyo: Nihon Keizai Shimbun-sha.

Nonaka, I. (1991). The knowledge-creating company. *Harvard Business Review*, 69(6), 96–104.

Nonaka, I. (1994). A dynamic theory of organizational knowledge creation. *Organization Science*, 1(5), 14–37.

Nonaka, I. (1997). A new organizational structure. In L. Prusak (Ed.), *Knowledge in Organizations* (pp. 99–134). Boston, MA: Butterworth-Heinemann.

Nonaka, I. (1998). The knowledge-creating company. *Harvard Business Review on Knowledge Management* (pp. 21–46). Boston, MA: Harvard Business School Press.

Nonaka, I., & Johansson, J. K. (1985). Japanese management: What about the "hard" skills? *Academy of Management Review*, 2(10), 181–191.

Nonaka, I., & Konno, N. (1999). The concept of *ba*: Building a foundation for knowledge creation. In J. W. Cortada, & J. A. Woods (Eds.), *The Knowledge Management Yearbook 1999–2000* (pp. 37–51). Boston, MA: Butterworth-Heinemann.

Nonaka, I., Konno, N., & Kosaka, S. (1993). Chisiki beesu sosiki [The knowledge-based organization]. *Harvard Business Review*, 41(1), 59–73.

Nonaka, I., Reinmoeller, P., & Senoo, D. (1998). The art of knowledge: Systems to capitalize on market knowledge. *European Management Journal*, 16(6), 673–684.

Nonaka, I. (1994). A dynamic theory of organizational knowledge creation. *Organizational Science*, 5(1), 14–37.

Nonaka, I., & Takeuchi, H. (1995). *The Knowledge-Creating Company: How Japanese Companies Create the Dynamics of Innovation*. New York: Oxford University Press.

Nonaka, I., Toyama, R., & Konno, N. (2001). SECI, *ba* and leadership: A unified model of dynamic knowledge creation. In I. Nonaka, & D. Teece (Eds.), *Managing Industrial Knowledge: Creation, Transfer and Utilization* (pp. 13–43). London: Sage.

O'Dell, C., & Grayson, J. C. (1998). *If Only We Knew what We Know: The Transfer of Internal Knowledge and Best Practice*. New York: Free Press.

Panahi, S., Watson, J., & Partridge, H. (2013). Towards tacit knowledge sharing over social web tools. *Journal of Knowledge Management*, 17(3), 379–397.

Polanyi, M. (1958). *Personal Knowledge: Towards a Post-Critical Philosophy*. London: Routledge & Kegan Paul.

Polanyi, M. (1966). *The Tacit Dimension*. London: Routledge & Kegan Paul.

Prahalad, C. K., & Bettis, R. (1986). The dominant logic: A new linkage between diversity and performance. *Strategic Management Journal*, 7, 485–501.

Prusak, L. (1997). *Knowledge in Organizations*. Boston, MA: Butterworth-Heinemann.

Quinn, J. B. (1992). *Intelligence Enterprise: A New Paradigm for a New Era: How Knowledge and Service Based Systems are Revolutionizing the Economy, All Industry Structures, and the Very Nature of Strategy and Organization*. New York: Free Press.

Riege, A. (2005). Three-dozen knowledge-sharing barriers managers must consider. *Journal of Knowledge Management*, 9(3), 18–35.

Riss, U. V., Cress, U., Kimmerle, J., & Martin, S. (2007). Knowledge transfer by sharing task templates: Two approaches and their psychological requirements. *Knowledge Management Research & Practice*, 5, 287–296.

Rocha, F., Cardoso, L., & Tordera, N. (2008). The importance of organizational commitment to knowledge management. *Comportamento Organizacional e Gestão*, 14(2), 211–232.

Sáenz, J., Aramburu, N., & Blanco, C. E. (2012). Knowledge sharing and innovation in Spanish and Colombian high-tech firms. *Journal of Knowledge Management*, 16(6), 919–933.

Scholl, W., König, C., Meyer, B., & Heisig, P. (2004). The future of knowledge management: An international delphi study. *Journal of Knowledge Management*, 8(2), 19–35.

Sharma, R. S., & Bhattacharya, S. (2013). Knowledge dilemmas within organizations: Resolutions from game theory. *Knowledge-Based Systems*, 45, 100–113.

Sirous, P., Jason, W., & Partridge, H. (2013). Towards tacit knowledge sharing over social web tools. *Journal of Knowledge Management*, 17(3), 379–397.

Skok, M. M. (2013). Some characteristics that influence motivation for learning in organisations. *Interdisciplinary Description of Complex Systems*, 11(2), 254–265.

Snowden, D. J. (2000). New wine in old wineskins: From organic to complex knowledge management through the use of story. *Emergence*, 2(4), 50–64.

Sparrow, J. (1998). *Knowledge in Organizations: Access to Thinking at Work*. London: Sage.

Spender, J.-C. (1993). Competitive advantage form tacit knowledge? Unpacking the concept and its strategic implications. Working Paper, Graduate School of Management, Rutgers University.

Starbuck, W. H., & Hedberg, B. (2001). How organizations learn from success and failure. In M. Dierkes, A. B. Antal, J. Child, & I. Nonaka (Eds.), *Handbook of Organizational Learning and Knowledge* (pp. 325–350). Oxford: Oxford University Press.

Steinel, W., Utz, S., & Koningaal, L. (2010). The good, the bad and the ugly thing to do when sharing information: Revealing, concealing and lying depend on social motivation, distribution and importance of information. *Organizational Behavior and Human Decision Processes*, 113, 85–96.

Stewart, T. A. (1997). *Intellectual Capital: The New Wealth of Organizations*. New York: Doubleday Currency.

Stopford, J. M. (2001). Organizational learning as guided responses to market signals. In M. Dierkes, A. B. Antal, J. Child, & I. Nonaka (Eds.), *Handbook of Organizational Learning and Knowledge* (pp. 264–281). Oxford: Oxford University Press.

Sugie, S. (1995). Cooperative learning in Japan. *International Journal of Educational Research*, 23(3), 213–226.

Sveiby, K. E. (1997). *The New Organizational Wealth: Managing and Measuring Knowledge-Based Assets*. San Francisco: Berret-Koehler Publishers, Inc.

Takeuchi, H. (2001). Towards a universal management of the concept of knowledge. In I. Nonaka, & D. Teece (Eds.), *Managing Industrial Knowledge: Creation, Transfer and Utilization* (pp. 315–329). London: Sage.

Taylor, C. A. (1995). Cooperative learning in an African context. *International Journal of Educational Research*, 23(3), 239–254.

Teece, D. (1981). The market for know-how and the efficient international transfer of technology. *Annals of the Academy of Political and Social Science*, November, 81–96.

Teece, D. (2001). Strategies for managing knowledge assets: The role of the firm structure and industrial context. In I. Nonaka, & D. Teece (Eds.), *Managing Industrial Knowledge: Creation, Transfer and Utilization* (pp. 125–144). London: Sage.

Tsai, W. (2002). Social structure of "coopetition" within a multiunit organization: Coordination, competition, and intraorganizational knowledge sharing. *Organization Science*, 13(2), 179–190.

Van der Speck, R., & Spijkevert, A. (1997). Knowledge management: Dealing intelligently with knowledge. In J. Liebowitz, & L. C. Wilcox (Eds.), *Knowledge Management and its Integrating Elements* (pp. 31–59). Boca Raton, Fl: CRC Press.

Van Lange, P. (2008). Logical and paradoxical effects: Understanding cooperation in terms of pro-social and proself orientations. In B. Sullivan, M. Snyder, & J. Sullivan (Eds.), *Cooperation: The Political Psychology of Effective Human Interaction* (pp. 17–34). Oxford: Blackwell.

Van Lange, P. A. M., Joireman, J., Parks, C. D., & van Dijk, E. (2013). The psychology of social dilemmas: A review. *Organizational Behavior and Human Decision Process*, 120, 125–141.

Von Krogh, G., Ichijo, K., & Nonaka, I. (2000). *Enabling Knowledge Creation: How to Unlock the Mystery of Tacit Knowledge and Release the Power of Innovation*. Oxford: Oxford University Press.

Von Krogh, G., & Roos, J. (1996). Conversation management for knowledge development. In G. von Krogh, & J. Roos (Eds.), *Managing Knowledge: Perspectives on Cooperation and Competition* (pp. 218–226). London: Sage.

Wang, S., & Noe, R. A. (2010). Knowledge sharing: A review and directions for future research. *Human Resource Management Review*, 20, 115–131.

Wasko, M. M., & Faraj, S. (2000). "It is what one does": Why people participate and help others in electronic communities of practice. *The Journal of Strategic Information Systems*, 9(2–3), 155–173.

Weber, J. M. (2004). Social dilemmas: A conceptual review of decision making in social dilemmas: Applying a logic of appropriateness. *Personality and Social Psychology Review*, 8(3), 281–307.

Wei Choo, C. (1998). The knowing organization: A process model of knowledge management. *Management & Information*, 6(4), 9–19.

Wenger, E. C., McDermott, R., & Snyder, W. M. (2002). *Cultivating Communities of Practice: A Guide to Managing Knowledge*. Boston, MA: Harvard Business School Press.

Wigg, K. M. (1993). Knowledge management: Where did it come from and where will it go? *Expert Systems with Applications*, 1(13), 1–14.

Wigg, K. M. (2000). Knowledge management: An emerging discipline rooted in a long history. In C. Despres, & D. Chauvel (Eds.), *Knowledge Horizons* (pp. 3–26). Boston, MA: Butterworth-Heinemann.

Wilkesmann, U., Wilkesmann, M., & Virgillito, A. (2009). The absence of cooperation is not necessarily defection: Structural and motivational constraints of knowledge transfer in a social dilemma situation. *Organization Studies*, 30(10), 1141–1164.

Winter, S. G. (1987). Knowledge and competence as strategic assets. In D. Teece (Ed.), *The Competitive Challenge: Strategic for Industrial Innovation and Renewal* (pp. 159–184). New York: Ballinger.

Witherspoon, C. L., Bergner, J., Cockrell, C., & Stone, D. N. (2013). Antecedents of organizational knowledge sharing: A meta-analysis and critique. *Journal of Knowledge Management*, 17(2), 250–277.

Yang, H.-L., & Wu, T. C. T. (2008). Knowledge sharing in an organization. *Technological Forecasting & Social Change*, 75(8), 1128–1156.

Yang, S. C., & Farn, C. K. (2009). Social capital, behavioural control, and tacit knowledge sharing – a multi-informant design. *International Journal of Information Management*, 29(3), 210–218.

Yuan, Y., Fulk, J., Shumate, M., Monge, P. R., Bryant, J. A., & Matsaganis, M. (2005). Individual participation in organizational information commons: The impact of team level social influence and technology-specific competence. *Human Communication Research*, 31, 212–240.

Zack, M. H. (1999). *Knowledge and Strategy*. Boston, MA: Butterworth-Heinemann.

Zhang, X., Chen, Z., Vogel, D., Yuan, M., & Guo, C. (2010). Knowledge-sharing reward dynamics in knowledge management systems: Game theory-based empirical validation. *Human Factors and Ergonomics in Manufacturing & Service Industries*, 20(2), 103–122.

17

Using Competences in Employee Development

Robert A. Roe

Introduction

Until the early 1990s the prevailing idea underlying employee development was that of a lifelong career, unfolding in a rather orderly fashion, largely with the boundaries of a single organization. This idea no longer holds.

> Careers are, for many people, less predictable and more varied than they once were. Work organizations are compelled (and sometimes choose) to change form, strategy, and size in ways which affect the kinds of work roles and careers available. It can be argued that managing careers is difficult yet necessary for both individuals and organizations in these circumstances (Arnold, 2002).

Due to macro-level trends such as globalization, technological innovation, and social change, working populations now flow through external and internal labor markets – "the demographic metabolism of organizations" (Haveman, 1995) – with considerably less inertia and less predictably than in the preceding decades. This reflects in a greater plasticity of individual career paths (Feldman & Ng, 2007) and new career patterns, referred to with terms such as "boundaryless career" and "protean career"(Arthur, 1994; Briscoe & Hall, 2006), which are more dynamic and less often linear (Lichtenstein, Ogilvie, & Mendenhall, 2002; McCabe & Savery, 2007). This does not mean that the conventional "organizational career" has vanished and that people have massively turned to "personal careers" (Guest & Rodrigues, 2012). Today, one finds evidence of both, in a variety of blended forms that vary across national economies and industries.

What has fundamentally changed, though, and is affecting all careers, is *time*. All organizations are confronted with the need to change, and "stable periods" in which the same employees do the same work for the same clients within the same structure, are

The Wiley Blackwell Handbook of the Psychology of Training, Development, and Performance Improvement,
First Edition. Edited by Kurt Kraiger, Jonathan Passmore, Sigmar Malvezzi, and Nuno Rebelo dos Santos.
© 2015 John Wiley & Sons Ltd. Published 2020 by John Wiley & Sons Ltd.

becoming shorter and shorter. The narrowed time perspectives and tighter time constraints of organizations inevitably influence employees. This is well illustrated by data on the organizational tenure of managers. One study reports that the average tenure of CEOs in larger US firms had dropped to less than six years in 2007 (Kaplan & Minton, 2012). Other studies give much lower estimates (Auchterlonie, 2003; Purdum, 2006); a recent study reports 2.4 years for US managers (Dobrev, 2012). How long ordinary employees work for the same firm is not known, due to lack of pertinent research. One study found that high achievers in the US — on average 30 years old, with strong academic records, degrees from elite institutions, and international internship experience — stayed with their employers for just 28 months on average (Hamori, Cao, & Koyuncu, 2012). Considering the fact that employee turnover continues to be a major research issue (50 percent of publications since 1980 are concentrated in the period from 2007) it seems that significant numbers of employees don't follow the careers offered by their employers. Of course, there are still people who are employed by the same organization for ten years or more, but their number is declining, not growing.

The *exchange relationship* between employer and employees is also changing. The former exchange of employment security against loyalty, commitment, and effort seems to have given way to an exchange of employability against effort. Some authors speak of a "new deal," which has surfaced more recently, namely an exchange of expected "employment continuity" – based on opportunities for learning and networking, offered by the employer – against loyalty, commitment, and engagement (M. Clarke, 2013; Guest & Rodrigues, 2012). Such a deal implies a shift in psychological contract, less relational and more transactional. An important part of the new deal pertains to learning. Ongoing changes in work content and closer connections between working and learning that are typical for the knowledge-based economy, require workers to engage in continuous learning (Nijhoff, Simons, & Nieuwenhuis, 2008), something that affects nearly all employees, whether following organizational or personal careers.

The foregoing changes have profound impacts on human resources management. They call for new approaches to recruitment, selection, training, remuneration, for example including employee development. The traditional model in which the organization invests in employee development as part of a HR strategy serving the organization's long-term objectives, is losing ground. With declining certainty about future products, processes, and markets, shorter horizons for planning and decision making, and a less or only temporarily committed workforce, many organizations are *no longer able* to effectively control and manage the careers of employees.

In this chapter, I will examine the possibility of following another approach, based on a redivision of roles between organization and employees. Rooting in the premise of people's ownership of their career and their right and responsibility to shape this career themselves, such an approach should enable them to direct and monitor their development and to optimize their employability – given the opportunities and constraints that organizations are offering. I will focus on the design of an employee development system that is based on the person's agency (Betz & Hackett, 1987; Tams & Arthur, 2010). It should allow people to exercise responsibility for their career and development, decide about the direction of their development, monitor and dynamically readjust their development, and obtain the expertise and methods to do this effectively. I will first discuss the requirements that a contemporary employee development system should meet. Next, I will review some theoretical notions and methods that seem suitable on which to base a new system. After that, I will describe what such a system could look like, including the roles of those involved. This will include practical illustrations from a domain in which these notions have been explored.

Requirements for a System of Employee Development

A key requirement for a system of employee development is a proper framing of contemporary careers and the relations with successive employers implied in them. On the basis of preliminary evidence I propose to describe the personal career as comprising several periods of employment with successive employers, and one or more periods of self-employment. Although the length (and number) of these periods will be different for each person, it seems reasonable to assume that for many younger people it will vary between say two and six years and that it will on average be shorter than the period preferred by the employer.

There is a vast literature discussing alternative career concepts and models that seem to match the current reality better than the traditional "organizational career." Next to the boundary-less career and protean career, which were already mentioned, there are the authentic career, portfolio career, post-corporate career, kaleidoscope career (Briscoe & Hall, 2006; Carbery & Garavan, 2007; Sullivan & Baruch, 2009; Van Dam, Van der Heijden, & Schyns, 2006). While this work describes what forms careers could take, there are also empirical studies proposing ways to operationalize career concepts and investigating how people deal with careers under contemporary conditions (Briscoe, Hall, & Frautschy DeMuth, 2006; Briscoe et al., 2012; Chudzikowski et al., 2009). Publications presenting new approaches to career development invariably emphasize self-directedness (King, 2004; Sturges, 2008).

While a great deal of research has focused on the careers of managers (Carbery & Garavan, 2007; M. Clarke, 2009), the need for novel employee development systems is obviously much broader. It extends to all categories of working people, regardless of their status in the hierarchy of employed people. Building on what was said before, I would suggest that future employee development systems be based on two main propositions. First, *career decisions ought to be taken by – or at least with consent of – the people who "own them,"* that is, individual workers and their families. Secondly, *organizations are no longer in the position to exercise effective control over individual careers.* Organizations may cover part of a person's career, during a limited time period at the beginning of the career or at a later stage, but they cannot span the total career during their employees' lifetime. Therefore, the responsibility for career development should be "transferred to the workers, with the implication being that they now need to be in control of their own career destiny – whether they desired this or not" (Pang, Chua, & Chu, 2008, p. 1384). This idea should be extended to people's development, since learning is no longer limited to prior formal education but narrowly intertwined with activities in the workplaces where people stay during subsequent stages of their career (Watts, 2000).

Emphasizing the person's agency does not imply that individuals can shape careers completely on their own. As Tams and Arthur (2010, p. 633) note, careers remain dependent on employment settings, industries, institutional environments, social networks, and so forth. Individuals continue to be embedded in and dependent on social and material structures, and will always be subject to multiple forces and constraints when choosing their actions. In practical terms no one can build a career without organizations being willing to employ him/her. This implies that people have to be cognizant of and carefully consider the career options that employers are offering, and weigh the benefits and limitations – including such facets as income, working hours, and the duration of engagement. Particularly important in this context are opportunities for learning – in formal training and education as well as informal workplace learning. Nevertheless, people should be able to exercise their freedom to engage or not, enunciate their own values and priorities, and exert greater influence over their career than generations before.

Temporal order is a critical aspect to consider when designing a career development system. Particularly important is the path-dependency inherent in careers. Apart from the fact that people's later decisions and experiences follow from and are constrained by earlier decisions and experiences, there is also path dependency in the process of managing the career. Individuals who have learned to rely on their employer for important career decisions, are unlikely to spontaneously take control later on. Many will lack the skills needed for gathering information, evaluating options, making choices, and so on and therefore be unable to take their own career decisions. Besides, their early experiences can leave traces that affect the satisfaction or disappointment with their entire careers (Baum, 1990). In contrast, those who have learned to take responsibility and manage their career at an early time may profit from their experiences at later moments and avoid such "learned helplessness." Thus, it is important to distinguish between early and later career development, and to realize that the first few years, when workers are beginning their career, are in many ways formative. These years are crucial for learning to understand the challenges of shaping a career and for developing the sense of responsibility and autonomy that is needed later on. Since career development at later stages has much less potential to achieve this, I will focus on employee development during the early career, that is, the first few years after graduation.

The basic requirements for a system of employee development that focuses on employees at an early stage of their career can be described as follows:

1   Self-management: the person shall be able to proactively shape his/her career within a given range of existing opportunities and constraints.
2   Personal direction: the process shall be guided by personal expectations and goals. Combined with requirement 1 this implies self-directedness.
3   Continuous development: the development process shall be continuing from the start till the end of the career, which implies continuing learning.
4   Realism: the person's expectations and goals shall be realistic, given the environment in which he/she is embedded and its changing opportunities and constraints.
5   Adaptability: the process shall allow the person to remain informed about and adapt to developments in the professional environment and the labor market.
6   Employability: during any stage of the career the person shall be able to generate income, either as employee or being self-employed.
7   Delivery: the person shall be able to act in ways that meet employer needs regarding productivity, quality, and innovation, and contribute to organizational learning.
8   Support: the person shall receive support from others, such as coaches, mentors, or members of career communities (e.g, colleagues, alumni; Parker, Arthur, & Inkson, 2004).

An employee development system based on these requirements will differ from conventional employee development programs offered by organizations in some respects. It will have a broader scope, a longer time horizon, and more room for personal choices. Organizational programs are typically limited to high-potential employees, who are seen as candidates for a limited number of functions and they extend over a few years only (e.g., Hurtz & Williams, 2009; Kuvaas & Dysvik, 2009; Lara, 2009; Otto, 2005). Such programs often lack continuity, as they tend to be replaced by other programs within a few years. Although they may require employees to think about their own development and make this explicit in a personal development plan, their prime aim is filling expected vacancies rather than long-term personal development, and they emphasize compliance over personal freedom. Another difference with conventional programs is the absence of a requirement for commitment to a particular organization. The rationale is that, in a person-oriented system, commitment is subordinate to and dependent on the degree to which other requirements are being met. Employees are likely to stay longer with an organization that helps them to realize their career objectives, particularly by providing learning opportunities, than with an organization that emphasizes retention but fails to provide good career support.

Key Notions

The literature offers a number of theoretical notions that help analyzing the above-mentioned requirements and conceiving an employee development system that meets these requirements.

Career self-management

Career management can be defined from an organizational or an individual perspective (e.g., Orpen & Pool, 1995). From an organizational perspective it is typically part of human resources management. It comprises the activities by which HR professionals or managers plan and structure the careers of designated groups of employees – within the brackets of the employment period. Conceived in this way, career management implies that the individual employees agree with and support the organization's interventions. From an individual perspective career management represents the activities that individuals undertake with regard to their personal careers, typically with the help of others. Individual career management, also referred to as "career self-management" (King, 2004), applies to all working people – whether employed or self-employed – and spans the whole of the personal career. During episodes of employment, agreement and support by organizations are assumed. Individuals may profit from organizational career management and vice versa, but there is ample room for discrepancies (Hall, 1986). I will focus on career management from the individual's point of view.

Individual career management comprises a number of recurrent steps. Noe states: "Career management is the process by which individuals collect information about values, interests, and skill strengths and weaknesses (career exploration), identify a career goal, and engage in career strategies that increase the probability that career goals will be achieved" (1996, pp. 119). In the context of employee development a more elaborate description is helpful, comprising the following steps:

1 Situation analysis: based on environmental scanning, aiming to identify opportunities and constraints.
2 Self-exploration: based on a review of personal experiences and qualities, aiming at understanding of oneself.
3 Goal setting: generating new and reviewing previous career goals, and selecting a goal to pursue.
4 Planning: specifying resources and activities in a career plan for a circumscribed period.
5 Implementation: carrying out the plan.
6 Monitoring, documenting, and evaluation against certain criteria.

It is important to consider the temporal facets of these activities. They require different amounts of time, extend over different periods, and may not follow each other in this particular "logical" sequence. Self-exploration and environmental scanning may happen simultaneously, parallel to, or interwoven with everyday work activities. Yet, thorough reflection requires a separate time (and place), just like generating and assessing career goals, choosing a goal, and planning. Implementation can consist of a variety of other activities – including applying for a job, moving to another position, networking, self-promotion, and developmental activities (cf. Sturges, 2008) – that spread over a long period of time. Cycles of career management can very well overlap. For instance, further self-exploration and environmental scanning can happen while implementing an earlier-made career plan. Evaluation of the plan can coincide with generating new goals and provide input for a new career plan.

The view of what defines a successful outcome of career management has evolved over time. In early decades the prevailing notion was "career maturity." It was introduced by Super in the 1950s, and referred "broadly, to the individual's readiness to make informed, age-appropriate career decisions and cope with career development tasks" (Patton & Creed, 2001, p. 336). In later years it was criticized for relying too much on the idea of predictable career stages and career development in adolescents, and being of limited use in understanding adult career development. It was replaced by the notion of "career adaptability," which emphasizes the "continual need to respond to new circumstances and novel situations, ... defined as the readiness to cope with the predictable tasks of preparing for and participating in the work role and with the unpredictable adjustments promoted by changes in work and working conditions" (Savickas, 1997, p. 254). Whereas adaptation and adaptability could be understood in a somewhat passive way, recent publications emphasize the importance of being active and having a sense of control over what happens, as is expressed in notions such as "career decision self-efficacy" (Choi et al., 2012)." Researchers have also proposed defining career success in terms of accomplishment of career goals or aspirations (e.g., Arthur, Khapova, & Wilderom, 2005), either in a subjective sense, such as "career satisfaction" or "perceived marketability" (De Vos, De Hauw, & Van der Heijden, 2011), or in an objective sense, such as mobility, income, or job level (Van Maanen, 1977).

Although many publications have addressed the need for career self-management (King, 2004; Stickland, 1996), there are also studies showing that career self-management is feasible and that it has the potential to produce positive outcomes (e.g., Chiesa, 2011; de Vos, Dewettinck, & Buyens, 2007; Murphy & Ensher, 2001; Orpen, 1994).

Self-development

The function of self-development is similar to that of training and development in traditional career management. It aims at learning processes that prepare the person for a new career achievement, that is a change in responsibility or a transition to another position. However, in the case of self-development control lies in the person's own hands. "Self-development is the process by which individuals: identify their personal development goals; consciously take responsibility for planning and taking appropriate action to reach these goals; develop and use methods of monitoring progress and assess outcomes; and re-assess goals in the light of new experiences" (Delf & Smith, 1978, p. 495). London and Smither (1999) emphasize the importance of the changing environment:

> self-development is important to individuals in today's financially constrained, quality oriented, rapidly changing organizations. Consequently, people need insight into organizational goals, performance requirements, and their ability to meet today's organizational expectations. They also need information about likely organizational directions, implications for future performance requirements, and what they need to do to meet these changing expectations.

They need to consider whether they might be better off finding and preparing for other career directions. They need to engage in continuous learning to keep up with organizational changes and ensure their continued contribution to the organization. (pp. 4–5)

Self-development was first accepted in the area of management development (Boydell & Pedler, 1981), and later in the development of leaders and professionals (Suar, 2001; Van Velsor, Moxley, & Bunker, 2004). However, its general significance for employee development was recognized early on. Already in 1976, Paxton argued that organizations could do more to give employees control over their own development, and that they would draw benefits from this (Paxton, 1976). Over time, the notion of self-development has proven instrumental in redefining the view of employee development in organizations. Its prime significance lies in the recognition that employees need to be in control of their own development and that this can be beneficial for the organization, for example, by contributing to overall organizational learning (e.g., London & Smither, 1999). However, it has profound implications for the way in which employee development is organized and for the role of the organization. For instance, organizations need to make room for self-development, create a positive learning climate, provide the employee with training and on-the-job learning opportunities, and accept that employees pursue their own interest and in doing so may want to pass the borders of their current job. Crucial is that employees receive useful information and feedback from their managers as well as their colleagues and clients (e.g., 360 degree). Self-development also calls for a role of coaches, that is, human development professionals from inside or outside the organizational boundaries.

The process of self-development resembles that of career self-management. It comprises a cycle of similar steps – situational analysis, self-exploration, and so forth. However, its focus is confined to development and cycles may be shorter than in career management. Garofano and Salas (2005) emphasize the importance of continuity in self-development, not only for the individuals involved, but also for the organization. They call for "continuous employee development," which they define "as a cyclical process in which employees are motivated to plan for and engage in actions or behaviors that benefit their future employability on a repetitive or ongoing basis" (p. 282). Again, the person is not completely autonomous and depends on the learning opportunities that organizations are willing to offer. Orvis and Ratwani (2010), speaking about leader self-development, state: "It is important to note that while self-development is inherently voluntarily initiated and completed by the leader, self-development activities do vary along a continuum from completely voluntary and self-initiated to voluntary, yet organization-provided (and perhaps even organization-encouraged)" (p. 658). From the person's viewpoint, this does not need not pose a problem, though. "Aspects of formal management development schemes, such as manpower and succession planning, objective setting, performance appraisal, coaching and counselling etc, will be seen by the self-organised learner as opportunities to exploit in his strategy of self-development" (Delf & Smith, 1978, p. 496).

Actual developmental activities can vary hugely, depending on the person's occupation and organizational environment. For professionals they may include: following training courses or workshops, making assignments, attending conferences, reading books or articles, giving presentations, teaching, coaching others, carrying out self-defined projects. Their focus can be on acquiring new knowledge, applying existing knowledge, developing new routines, changing typical patterns of behavior, building competences, enhancing personal effectiveness, becoming more resilient, improving social relations, networking, and so on. Managers may engage in team projects, case studies, business games, and personal exercises and assignments, including "stretch assignments" that challenge their capabilities (Reichard & Johnson, 2011), with similar learning objectives.

Due to the broad range of activities covered by the label of self-development, its impact is hard to evaluate, but it is generally assumed that self-development pays off for the persons themselves as well as the organization (Delf & Smith, 1978; Orvis & Ratwani, 2010; Pfeffer, 1994).

Self-directed learning

The concept of self-directed learning (SDL) stems from the field of adult education (Candy, 1991), where learning takes place in much less structured environments than in regular training and education, and should satisfy a greater range of learner needs and learning objectives. It allows individualization of the learning process by enabling learners to direct and control their own learning processes. There are several descriptions of SDL in the literature, but the basic underlying notion is that of creating opportunities for self-regulation with regard to learning processes. People are supposed to assess themselves, define their own learning needs, and pursue self-chosen learning goals (Knowles, 1975). SDL has been embraced in various areas, ranging from general and professional education to human resources development and workplace learning (e.g., Ellinger, 2004). It can provide a fertile basis for contemporary employee development (e.g., Smith et al., 2007).

SDL entails a set of principles and techniques from the fields of instructional design and educational research that can help optimize the learning process. These are applied to the particular professional or workplace setting in which learners operate. Bolhuis (2003) underlines the importance of the setting for the learning process: SDL works best when people are already familiar with the concepts, rules, and problems of a particular domain and when they have affinity with it. The social context also matters, since the people with whom the learner interacts help in making sense and in defining the value of what is being learned.

Since it starts from a person's view of the situation and him/herself, derives learning needs from personal experiences and the current knowledge repertoire, and involves a unique learning trajectory, SDL is highly individualized. The process is also highly flexible, as people can change the content and sequence of the learning trajectory and learn at the pace that suits them best. As a self-regulation process, SDL follows essentially the same steps as career self-management and self-development. However, its has a narrower focus and can be considered as a sub-process nested in self-development and career development respectively.

The literature on SDL concentrates on three core processes: self-assessment, task selection, and performance of learning tasks (Kicken, Brand-Gruwel, & Van Merrienboer, 2008; Van Merriënboer & Sluijsmans, 2009). Self-assessment serves to establish whether the person meets a previously set learning goal, and which gap remains to be filled. Selecting learning tasks refers to the defining learning activities that must be undertaken to bridge the gap. Performing learning tasks means that the person acquires new knowledge or skills, or learns to apply them, by studying texts or performing projects. In domains with many degrees of freedom learners can make their own choices, but a supervisor of coach can have an influence on selecting projects or executing them. Thereby they can stimulate that learners focus on application of existing knowledge and skills, or engage in exploration (e.g., Boyer et al., 2012). In settings with complex learning tasks learners may not have the freedom to shape their own learning trajectory, because high cognitive load prevents them from learning. Here, principles from instructional design such as simple-to-complex sequencing and scaffolding may be applied to lower cognitive demand, while allowing the learner to steer the learning process and gain control over the complete cycle of performing, assessing, and selecting learning tasks

(Van Merriënboer & Sluijsmans, 2009). Among the many tools to support SDL, there are *development portfolios,* which allow learners to document and keep track of various aspects of their development (Kicken et al., 2009). In the past these often took the form of paper folders in which the person kept documents with notes on prior experiences, reflections on personal qualities, performance records, pictures, and action plans. Portfolios increasingly take the form of an electronic dossier or ePortfolio (e.g., Kirkham et al., 2009), which opens possibilities for added functionality.

Many studies have demonstrated the effectiveness of SDL in organizations. Among the effects are: increased performance, cost savings in training and development, increased ability for critical thinking and questioning, increased confidence and problem solving, knowledge-sharing and networking, stronger affective commitment, and a sense of meaning at work (see Karakas & Manisaligil, 2012, p. 713). SDL seems suited to broadening the scope of traditional training and development and tuning it to specific needs and interests of learners (Rymell & Newsom, 1981).

Competence acquisition

The concept of competence plays a crucial role in employee development, and combines well with the notions of self-development and self-directed learning. It blends ideas from different theoretical and pragmatics traditions. Its origin lies in pre-World War II Europe (particularly France), where it was used in the context of vocational education and guidance. Here, competence refers to the integration of knowledge, skills, and attitudes distinguishing qualified craftsmen, and enabling them to perform all duties of their profession. In the US the notion of competence (also competency) was mainly used to differentiate good and bad performers (Boyatzis, 1982; McClelland, 1973). When strategy theorists applied the notion to the firm level and portrayed competences as resources that allowed gaining competitive advantage (e.g., Hamel & Prahalad, 1994), it became hugely popular. Due to the improved legitimacy that the link between firm-level competences and employee competences provided to activities such as recruitment, selection, and training, competences became the cornerstone of contemporary HR management (e.g., Nybø, 2004). During the past two decades competences have become widely accepted in other domains as well, including adult education, career development, labor market policy and education.

With its different roots came different ways of understanding, surfacing in the use of the terms competence and competency. Competence, defined according to the European tradition, is an "acquired ability to adequately perform a role, mission or task" (Roe, 2002). Competency in the North American tradition is "an underlying characteristic of a person which is causally related to effective or superior performance in a job or role" (Evarts, 1987). The first definition emphasizes that competences are learned and are specific for particular roles, missions, or tasks. The person who has acquired certain competences *is able* to perform the roles, missions, or tasks in an adequate manner. The second definition refers to personal attributes that are statistically associated with performance. These include learned attributes such as knowledge, skills, attitudes, and more stable attributes such as abilities, personality traits, styles, and values. A person who possesses these attributes *is likely* to perform well.

There are several noteworthy differences between competen*ces* and competen*cies.* For instance, the specificity of competences implies that there are as many competences as there are types of work, and that ongoing learning is needed as job content changes or people move to other positions in the same or other organizations. Using the term competences automatically puts the focus on learning. Competencies lack this specificity; they are general characteristics of people that vary in their relevance for performance. They also lack a consistent reference to learning, with some competencies being considered as learnable and others as nonlearnable. As the notion of competency includes stable attributes of people, there is an implicit reference to recruitment, selection, and placement. Obviously, the notion of competence as defined above makes more sense in the context of employee development. For that reason, I will exclusively use that notion in the remainder of this chapter.

The nature of competences can be elucidated by means of the "architectural model" (Roe, 1999, 2002), shown in Figure 17.1, which distinguishes between stable dispositions, that is abilities, personality traits, and other characteristics; learned qualities, that is knowledge, skills, and attitudes; and lower-order and higher-order competences. The other characteristics include styles, values, and biographical characteristics. The model purports to show that competences are obtained by integrating previously learned knowledge, skills, and attitudes, and all learning is based on or influenced by stable dispositions and other characteristics. The distinction between higher-order and lower-order competences (also: sub-competences or basic competences) is made in order to acknowledge that competences can differ in scope and specificity. Higher-order competences relate to specific tasks practiced in a specific work context, while lower-order competences relate to components of tasks that can be found in different types of work and contexts (e.g., planning or using spreadsheets).

The model uses the metaphor of a Greek temple to visualize the overall structure: a tympanum of competence, resting on the columns of knowledge, skill, and attitude, which have been erected on a stable dispositional basis. The contextual embeddedness should also be noted. The context is displayed as consisting of a proximal layer, the present workplace

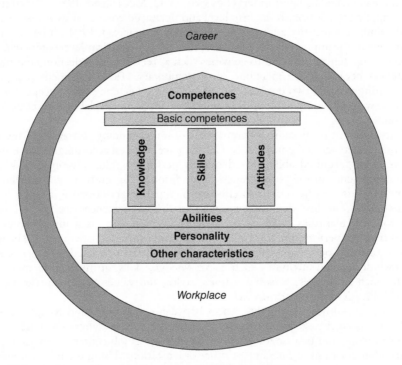

Figure 17.1 Architectural model of competences (after Roe, 1999).

in an organization (at the same time, an industry and a profession) where working and learning take place, and a distal layer, the future career that runs through organizations in the same or another industry, and through the professional field, in a yet unknown manner.

While knowledge and skill are largely acquired through prior learning in scholastic settings, the development of competences requires learning-by-doing in a realistic situation, either at the workplace or in another sphere (e.g., home, hobby, or volunteer work). The process is often described as informal and accidental which means that it occurs as a by-product of other activities that is not explicitly aimed for (Ellström, 2011). Competence acquisition starts from and builds on the person's repertoire of knowledge and learned behaviors and is therefore unique to each person. Two people trying to learn the same professional competence will do so in different ways, because they had different prior experiences and have different knowledge, skills, and so forth. This is one of the reasons why competence development is a unique process. Another reason is that the learning process is moderated by personal factors, such as the abilities, personality traits, and values, in a way that resembles the phenomenon aptitude-treatment interaction, known from the educational literature (Bartram & Roe, 2008). There are more factors that make the learning process idiosyncratic. Among them are the content of the work, the situations in which work tasks are performed, and the support and feedback received from supervisors or coaches. They all are important factors determining the learning-by-doing process. Finally, there is the choice of competences to be developed, which will vary with the learning needs derived from the current competence profile and the person's career choices, and with the preferences of the supervisor.

Although competence acquisition is a natural process that happens as people perform roles, competences can also be learned intentionally, which makes it a powerful instrument in career development. During the past few decades many organizations have recognized this and put in place some system of competence (or competency) management. Such systems focus on the organization's total workforce, or particular segments of it (e.g., managers or professionals). They compare the actual and needed stocks of employees with respect to competencies, using lists of abilities, personality traits, styles, values, and other characteristics, and identify discrepancies that should be bridged by recruitment, selection, and development. In spite of this focus, they often require employees to draw-up a personal development plan, in which they indicate preferences for their own development – in the context of an organizational career.

Competence development can also be part of an individual's career management (e.g., Heilmann, 2011). Being highly idiosyncratic and easy to align with personal goals, it fits well in that context. As mentioned before, it can also be combined with the principles of self-development and self-directed learning (e.g., Hashim, 2008), starting from the person's unique behavior repertoire. The major difference with organizational competence (competency) management is that the learning process aims to bridge gaps between required competences as following from an individual's personal career plan and the competences that are present in the behavior repertoire. Other differences are that the person is making the assessments, setting learning goals and priorities, and deciding how much time and resources to spend on each competence. By departing from the individual's repertoire of learned behaviors, personal competence management opens a richer perspective on learning, allowing it to expand and modify in several directions (Bartram & Roe, 2008; Roe, 2002).

Although its emergence initially had the features of a fashion and the confusion about its meaning and definition has been widely lamented (e.g., Brockmann, Clarke, & Winch, 2009; Le Deist & Winterton, 2005), it is clear that the notion of competence is to stay and that it is of great value in many different domains of policy and action. Especially important in this chapter is that competences have brought new opportunities for career development from a personal perspective, enabling people to define, retain, and advance their human capital, while at the same time addressing the needs of employers for personnel with up-to-date qualifications. It is this capacity to meet the needs of employers and employees and to bridge the gap between their diverging interests that makes competences of interest in contemporary employee development. Its relevance for so many different areas, its ability to link the present to the future and to close the gap between practice and theory (Roe, 2002) make competence a notion of high value in present society.

Competence-Based Employee Development

This section discusses how the foregoing may be integrated in the design of an employee development system that meets the various requirements and acknowledges the lessons drawn from the literature. It proposes an overall structure, introduces tools to fulfill the needed functions, and describes the roles that the organization, the worker, and third parties can play. All this will be illustrated with examples from present-day practice.

Designing a system

A preliminary issue is establishing the *system's boundaries*. Following the argument that a new approach to employee development, based on career self-management and self-development, should be directed towards people at the start of their career, the system can best be focused on starters. Particularly suitable as target group are graduates from vocational or academic education. They are in high demand because of their up-to-date knowledge, eagerness to learn, and low costs, and they are unlikely to stay with the same organization for more than a few years – which means that they need to develop their own career. This target group includes but is not limited to so-called "high-potentials" or "talents." Apart from the fact that the borders between these and others are often quite arbitrary, and that the expected success may not materialize before these persons leave, it is more realistic, socially responsible, and profitable to include starters with a broad range of qualities. It also makes more sense if the aim is to develop competences, that is, to *make* people successful in their careers and deliver value to their employers rather than foretell which of them will likely be successful. As for the system's temporal scope, I suggest to begin with a period of two years – since this seems sufficient for starting the process of shaping participants' careers and their role as employees.

Following the requirements, the key function of the system is to enable people's competence development in the context of self-managed career development, in a manner that is acceptable and beneficial for the organization currently employing them. The realization of this function depends on the design of the system's architecture, which involves the following steps. First, a *definition of the parties (or "users")* and their relationships. These include minimally:

1 A person engaged in developing a personal career, and in the context of this, a set of competences.
2 A supervisor representing the organization that employs the person during the initial years of the career.
3 A coach from inside or outside the organization, who can guide and support.

There may be other parties involved, though, like a HR expert who can help finding opportunities for training and development inside the organization, and people belonging

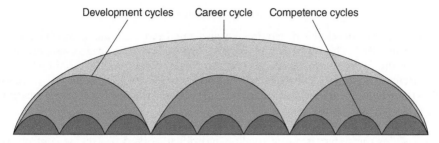

Figure 17.2   Temporal structure of career self-management.

to relevant career communities (like colleagues or other trainees). Yet, it is good to concentrate on the core "triangle" of these three since they need to collaborate intensively and persistently over time in order for the system to fulfill its key function. The second step is defining a temporal structure that determines the *overall process flow*. It consists of dividing the total time period into a nested configuration with larger sections for career management cycles, and smaller sections for self-development cycles, including subsections for acquiring competences. Building this structure is critically important for requirements 1, 2, and 3. The type of structure is visualized in Figure 17.2. It should provide room for developing and implementing career plans, and as part of these learning activities based on personal development plans that include studying, skill learning, and – at the highest level – developing competences.

The third step is defining the *responsibilities of each party and their interaction* via personal encounters and information exchange by other means. This permits structuring their collaboration and arranging them along the timeline in accordance with the temporal structure. Defining the role of the person in charge is crucial for requirements 1 and 2. Collaboration with the supervisor and coach is important for meeting requirements 4, 5, and 6, and the contact with others for requirement 7.

Once the *who does what and when* has been settled, the *how* has to be decided upon – which represents the fourth step. This again depends on principles from career self-management and self-development, as they suggest the precise steps to be taken. It is also the phase where SDL and competence acquisition come in. They help setting up a structure for the learning process, and to provide methods and tools. Competence related methods make it possible to decide *what needs to be learned*, to create the right conditions for learning, and to assess progress and outcomes. SDL principles help structure the learning process to give optimum results. These issues are important for realizing requirements 1, 2, and 3.

A lot of *further detail* comes from the theory of competence acquisition. This draws attention to the need to periodically draw up a profile of required competences, following from career goals, and to assess current competences, evaluate the gap, and plan the further learning process. It follows from the definition of competence (cf. the architectural model) that all this should not be limited to the competences as such, but should also include the knowledge, skills, and attitudes from which competences are built, as well as the requisite personal qualities. In fact, the model has far-reaching implications for the way in which the system deals with content (what to learn) and context (how to handle situations). It calls for multiple foci of development, namely functional development (organization focus), personal development (self-focus), and ultimately career development (career focus) – which require a multiplicity of tools. Identifying these tools and putting them together in well-integrated arrangements will allow realizing requirements 4, 5, and 6.

Participant roles

Effective employee development requires a well-defined and harmonious collaboration of the parties involved. This was so in the times of organizationally managed systems, and it is still so in the days of person-managed systems. Parties cannot do it without each other, and a certain degree of joint management is always needed (Arnold, 2002). This section clarifies the roles of the three parties that make up the core "triangle," and briefly mentions the role of career communities.

The person   As the system is meant to allow individual workers to exercise control over their career and their development, they should be responsible for managing the total process, that is, ensuring that all steps of the successive cycles are taken, including the ongoing monitoring and periodic evaluation. However, people at the start of their career (and even those with several years of experience) are rarely prepared for this when the process begins. Young graduates in their 20s normally have limited experience with self-management and choosing their own direction in matters of career and learning. They also lack the expertise that HR professionals have due to their professional education and training. The average person, therefore, needs to learn what all this requires and how it should be carried out. For this the guidance and assistance of a coach is indispensible. Only after some period of time, as the person has acquired the necessary competences and self-efficacy, he/she may take effective control of the process, while the role of the coach diminishes. Apart from steering and monitoring the process, the person should also carry out the steps of generating, planning, and implementing goals – in recurrent and overlapping cycles. At any stage, the demands on the person will be experienced as high, since the future is ambiguous, career choices are often complex (M. Clarke, 2009), and the person may discover barriers that are hard to overcome (Zikic & Hall, 2009). Also, standards for success are not always obvious and may change as the career unfolds.

The organization   In a system built on the notion of a personal career and self-management, the organization must accept that it is no longer in the position to steer and control the development of "its" employees, and that its role is a complementary and facilitating one. Organizations may not be equally prepared for this and think of their role differently. Some will start from organizational careers, defined by future manpower needs, but make these flexible by creating degrees of freedom that permit employees to make choices. M. Clarke (2013) argues that this enables joint management of development, which may foster balanced relationships as well as longer tenure (i.e., less mobility of employees). Regardless of who is in charge, organizations can contribute to the success of employee development in many ways. With respect to careers, they should generally inform their supervisors and employees about their needs and offerings, and create attractive employment conditions. With respect to development, they should provide opportunities for learning, on the job and in specific training, and for networking activities (McCabe & Savery, 2007; Paxton, 1976). More specifically, they should enable employees to fully utilize their skills and abilities (Holton, 2001), and use delegation to give them room to practice and learn from mistakes (Vinton, 1987). Organizations can also contribute in other, less direct, ways, namely by offering a positive climate for learning (Bartram & Roe, 2008; Park, 2010) and promoting participation in social networks that can function as career communities (Parker, Arthur, & Inkson, 2004).

   In the context of system design the major representative of the organization is the supervisor, typically the employee's manager. This person has a dual role to play, namely directing and controlling the employee's work performance, and providing support to the employee's development. The latter implies: providing information about career and development opportunities in the organization, creating opportunities for learning and networking by finding suitable work tasks and settings, helping to create a positive and safe learning climate, and giving feedback on achievements. All this should help employees in making and executing career and development plans, and realizing learning goals. The manager can also help the employee in monitoring and evaluating the overall process, as in conventional employee development.

The coach There are three main reasons for involving a coach in self-managed employee development. It allows the worker to meet the high demands of managing a career and developing him/herself on top of the work that is being done. It helps the worker to gradually learn how to manage their career and how to develop him/herself ("learning to learn"), and to take control of the process. It leads to a healthier worker–manager relationship, as it helps the worker to reflect on that relationship and learn to improve it, and relieves the manager of duties towards the employee that conflict with his/her remaining duties and for which time is lacking. Coaches can be employed by the same organization (e.g., the HR department) or another organization. The latter has advantages when careers and developmental trajectories reach beyond the organizations' borders; it is also conducive to trust between the worker and the coach, which is beneficial for the effectiveness of the process.

The activities of the coach aim at guiding and monitoring the overall process with an emphasis on the earlier stages; clarifying the career and development process; helping the person in goal setting, making plans, elaborating learning tasks, self-assessment; giving feedback and behavior modeling. The emphasis will generally be on enhancing self-reflection, active exploration, and decision making, but there will be room for identifying and resolving conflicts. All this should be done in a timely manner, by means of regular meetings and other forms of contact, and it should match the overall time structure built into the system. To make the "triangle" work well, the coach should not only meet with the worker but also with the manager, and sometimes with both of them together. Coaching is increasingly recognized as being instrumental in employee development. There are several sources documenting its effectiveness and outlining how it can be improved (e.g., Čiutienė, Neverauskas, & Meilienė, 2010; Trenner, 2013).

Process flow

The preferred process flow should include multiple levels and overlapping iterative cycles as in Figure 17.2. This should enable workers to engage in cycles of career development and self-development, with variable foci on competence, functional, and personal development. A goal-setting cycle, involving situational analysis, generating and choosing goals, planning, and implementation will enable the person to accomplish the development at each level. Regular contact with the coach and supervisor will help performing all steps and getting the most out of the contact time.

Developmental trajectories

The system should support the development of the person along multiple trajectories, which largely unfold in parallel.

Career development This trajectory should allow the person to shape their career by making projections for the next phase and realizing these in a purposeful manner. As described earlier, this includes situation analysis, self-exploration, setting a career goal, planning, and implementation, as well as monitoring and adjusting over time. This is a complex matter that requires a variety of different activities, which call for guidance and support from the coach, the organization, and others.

Situation analysis gives the person ideas about possible career directions. It includes: exploring the world through general sources of vocational and labor market information; databases with advertisements of jobs and traineeships; job markets and recruitment events; or options offered by specific organizations. It is important in career self-management to look beyond the "opportunities of the day" as offered by employers to create a perspective that gives a wide enough picture of the future and allows discerning options that match personal qualities and ambitions. There is a need to explore such directions and identify possible "entry points" for the next phase, considering one's current position. This may be supported by starting from currently known jobs and looking at possible next jobs and the occupational domains embedding them ("zooming out"), or – the other way around – by examining and comparing occupational domains that would be accessible given the person's education and looking for attractive starting jobs ("zooming in"). For instance, one might start from a job as marketer and zoom out to the field of sales and marketing; or one might start comparing fields like finance, sales, communication, choose finance and zoom in to assistant accountant as a possible entry job.

Self-exploration aims at self-discovery, or understanding oneself better. It involves reviewing past workplace experiences in order to learn more about one's expectations, preferences, and motivation. It also involves, reflection on one's performance and feedback received from others, which provides information on abilities, personality, and other characteristics. Self-exploration is a continuing and iterative process that is never completed. Passing thorough different life-stages and reflecting on their experiences, people discover new facets of their personality and keep revising their image of themselves. Since the process is of critical importance at all career stages, it is sometimes set apart and promoted as *personal development* (see below).

Next comes *setting a career goal*, either in terms of a "career direction" one wants to prepare for or a particular position or job one wants to achieve. This builds on the situational analysis but requires gathering of additional information about options, evaluating them with regard to likely outcomes and requirements – particularly learning requirements – and making a choice. An essential part of this is drawing up a preliminary competence profile for each option, and evaluating these in terms of attractiveness and feasibility, considering personal preferences but also knowledge, skills and attitudes, and one's personal dispositions. Initially the emphasis will be on the match between options and the person's personality and abilities, which determine what can be learned and how fast. Later there will be more of a balance between these aspects and the existing repertoire of knowledge and behavior.

The following step is *writing a career plan* that spells out the career goal and the activities that will be undertaken to achieve it. As essential part of the career plan is a complete and detailed competence profile for the chosen career goal. It is an elaborated version of the preliminary competence profile that was used when making a choice. The career plan should also specify practical resources required for learning, including the kind of tasks and work settings needed for learning-by-doing, and courses or tutorials needed to gain more knowledge and skills.

Implementing the career plan takes different forms, depending on the career goal. A person's career goal may involve a change of role or position in the present organization, relocation to another branch office or even expatriation, or a change of employment. Some of these changes will be radical and impact one's personal life (Sturges, 2008). Many changes will imply the need to build a new social network, promote oneself, familiarize oneself with a new organizational environment, or learn new job roles (see *functional development,* below). Of course, there are also changes in the content of the work to be done, such as changes in tasks and task routines, tools being used, interactions with clients, colleagues, and supervisors, and so on. Of special importance in this chapter are learning activities, described below.

Competence development Competence development is a continuing and iterative process that progressively enlarges the person's behavior repertoire through learning activities that focus on a limited number of competences at the same time. Ideally this is done by selecting certain competences that need to be developed, planning the work activities needed to produce the required learning-by-doing, and additional learning to build needed knowledge, skills, and/or attitudes. The model of competences presented above can help structuring the overall process and keep track of progress and outcomes. First, it allows comparing the required competence profile with the person's actual competence profile, and determining which parts of the gap need to be filled in with priority. Second, it allows taking a similar look at required and present knowledge, skills, and attitudes, and deciding which forms of study and practice are needed. These steps result in transparent learning goals and thereby in standards for evaluating progress. The learning goals are also helpful in arranging the needed learning resources and organizing the learning process, in line with the principles of SDL. Clarity about learning goals and the arrangements needed for realizing them is essential for getting support of the organization. It helps informing the manager and HR experts, to negotiate about the conditions, and to get their consent. What follows is a process of working and learning that – if properly monitored and if all goes well – results in the aimed-for outcomes.

Functional development The overall process of career development can benefit from a separate trajectory for functional development. Aiming at getting a good understanding of the job, the immediate work context and the larger organization, it is valuable as a tool for promoting the person's adaptation to the work environment, which is particularly useful when the person moves to another position in the same or another organization. Such a development trajectory does not only have an immediate impact by resolving ambiguities, avoiding conflicts, and promoting positive relations, it also makes the person aware of the importance of successful adaption and one's opportunities for promoting this. Involvement of the coach can make this particularly effective. Functional development can be supported by a record of everyday activities and experiences to stimulate reflection, and a variety of assignments, which include: drawing up an organization chart to describing changes in tasks and jobs; technical innovations; social relationships in the team; and organization change.

Personal development A separate trajectory for personal development is also useful, as it can equip the person with self-exploration skills that are useful throughout the career. The general purpose is to establish and maintain regular self-reflection, by answering such questions as "Who am I?", "How do I feel about things?", "What do I like?", "What do I avoid?", and "Why do I act the way I do?" Reflecting on one's own experiences, comparisons with other people, and feedback from significant others can give a person insight in to one's own personality, capacities, styles, values, attitudes, and preferences. This process does not always produce useful results, either because people are self-defensive and unable to see their weaknesses, or because they are too modest to see their strengths. An independent coach can play an important role in overcoming such limitations. Personal development can be enhanced by psychological assessments, self-assessments, feedback from other people, and assignments that promote personal effectiveness.

Tools for competence-based employee development

This section presents examples of tools that can be used in connection with competence-based employee development. These examples are based on a system developed by Procam BV in the Netherlands for career self-management by young professionals: the Procam Career Management System (PCMS). Its design conforms to the logic outlined in this chapter and its current shape largely meets the aforementioned requirements. The system supports career self-management by graduates at the start of their careers and has modules for functional, personal, and competence development. At the heart of this system lies competence development based on the approach presented earlier. The system has been in use for over 15 years with young professionals in the Netherlands, mainly in the field of informatics, employed by dozens of organizations in computing, banking, infrastructure, energy, and industry – including large global organizations.

Competence profile A useful tool at various stages of career development is the competence profile, a document that gives a description of competences, structured in accordance with the architectural model of competences. Its general structure is described in Table 17.1. The profile has eight sections, that is, competences, sub-competences, knowledge, skills, attitudes, abilities, personality traits, and other characteristics. There are two types of competence profiles, one describing *required competences* corresponding with a particular job or career direction, and one describing a person's *actual competences* at a certain moment. Competence profiles can be drawn up for every single occasion, but it pays off to do this in advance for a whole industry or occupational domain, and to use a standardized terminology as far as possible. Competences are unique to each work domain and they should be updated from time to time, in order to keep track of technological or organizational changes. This also applies to certain knowledge and skills, but many forms of knowledge and skills can be described with standardized terms, just like attitudes. Abilities, personality traits, and other characteristics (including, e.g., styles and values) do not vary with the work domain and are rather stable. They can therefore well be described with standardized terms, based on psychological research. The PCMS includes a competence guide, which gives standardized descriptions of all terms used in the description of competences in a broad range of career directions (Roe, 2012).

Competence profiles are drawn up in a process known as *competence analysis*. It consists of an iterative process with inductive and deductive cycles (Roe, 2001; see also Roe, 2005). It starts with a top-down analysis that follows the logic of task decomposition. It first breaks down the work in tasks and subtasks, focusing on operations, work objects, tools, clients, coworkers, methods, and time aspects. Using information from subject-matter experts (or secondary sources such as O*Net or other industry occupational compendia) it first makes inferences about on-the-job learning experiences that are critical for performing the tasks, next about the knowledge, skills, and attitudes that are needed in this learning process, and finally about abilities, personality traits, and other characteristics that are likely to influence the learning process. Once a draft profile has been made, a behavioral expert conducts a bottom-up analysis to review all aspects and remove those that do not seem critical for learning and performance.

Because of the crucial role of competences as learning targets it is important to avoid confusion about what should be called competence and what not. A simple decision tree involving yes/no answers to four questions can help sorting characteristics (sometimes advanced as "competencies") into the various categories that were mentioned above. This decision tree is depicted in Figure 17.3. A first question is whether the characteristic can be learned or changed by learning; it separates stable dispositions from other characteristics.

Table 17.1 General structure of the competence profile with examples.

Competences – acquired abilities to perform a task
Perform financial analyses
Draw up project proposals
Make a work plan and budget
Determine and clarify client requirements and desires
Evaluate existing financial systems
Advise clients

Subcompetences – acquired abilities to perform a subtask
Set goals
Plan activities
Conduct interviews
Give presentations
Write documentation

Knowledge – what is known, acquired through study
Principles of finance
Econometric models
Accounting techniques
Organization processes
Administration techniques

Skills – what can be done, acquired through practice
Problem analysis
Systematic working
Written expression
Negotiation
Collaboration in teams

Attitudes – typical approaches to people and situations
Precision
Respect for others
Openness to criticism
Quality awareness
Entrepreneurship
Client orientation
Responsibility

Abilities – capacities for problem solving and learning (dispositions)
General mental ability
Numerical ability
Verbal ability
Spatial ability
Creativity

Personality – characteristic behavior tendencies (dispositions)
Energy
Initiative
Decisiveness
Self-confidence
Extroversion
Agreeableness
Cooperativeness

Other characteristics
Goal orientation
Action awareness
Practicality
Criticality
Loyalty

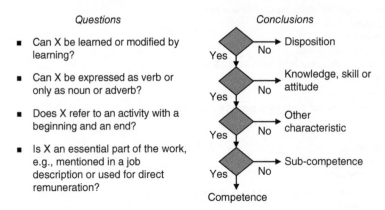

Figure 17.3 Decision tree to identify competences.

The second question is a linguistic one; it checks whether the characteristic refers to an activity, and thereby sets knowledge, skills, and attitudes (as well as some "other" characteristics) apart. The third question is whether the activity has a beginning and an end, or can be dissected into parts with a beginning and an end; which sets remaining "other" characteristics apart and keeps "do-able" competences and subcompetences. The fourth question is whether the activity is an essential part of the work (e.g., would be found in a job description and be a direct basis for remuneration); it separates sub-competences from competences. Thus, only characteristics that refer to discrete activities that can be learned and that are an essential part of the work qualify as competence. For example, designing a sales plan, giving a lecture, or driving a truck are competences, while showing initiative, being persistent, or having impact, are not.

Since competences and all underlying characteristics can vary in the degree to which they are required or present, numerical scales are needed to quantify this. Measurement scales should preferably be standardized and suitable for norm-referenced and criterion-referenced measurement. This requirement may be met for ability and personality traits that can be measured with psychological tests, and for certain knowledge and skills that may be measured with educational achievement tests. Developing such instruments for other attributes is normally not possible because of the excessive time and costs involved. For competences, sub-competences, and knowledge it is even more difficult, because of their unique and dynamic nature. For these attributes rating scales with generic anchors may be used, provided that these anchors are well defined and that users agree about their meaning. When competence profiles are used for orientation it suffices to checkmark the relevant attributes only; when used for learning, more refined scales are needed. An example of a generic scale for measuring competences, used in the PCMS (Roe, 2012), is given in Table 17.2.

The scale anchors reveal that competences are latent attributes and not behaviors. They are residuals of former learning that are not necessarily showing up in behavior and performance all the time. The impact of competence on behavior will only become manifest in an appropriate setting that provides opportunities to show the behavior.

Person description　The person description is a document that covers the stable part of a competence profile only; that is, abilities, personality traits, and other characteristics. It can be used to support self-development, namely by having the person make a self-description with respect to the different characteristics. The process of describing oneself is quite

Table 17.2 Scale for measurement of competences.

Value	Description
1	The person is aware of global task demands and the basic principles for its execution, but is not yet able to carry out the task.
2	The person understands the task demands, knows the basic principles for its execution, and possesses part of the required knowledge, skills, and attitudes, but has no experience with executing the task. He/she can perform a simple task under supervision.
3	The person knows the task demands and the principles for its execution, and possesses the required knowledge, skills, and attitudes, but these are integrated to a limited degree. He/she can perform a simple task independently.
4	The person knows the task demands and the principles, and possesses the knowledge, skills, and attitudes that are needed for executing the task, and these are integrated to a considerable degree. He/she can perform a complex task under supervision.
5	The person knows the task demands, possesses the knowledge, skills, and attitudes that are needed for executing the task, and these are fully integrated. He/she can perform the tasks as required, taking into account all relevant aspects and conditions that may occur. He/she can perform a complex task independently.

demanding and instructive, as it requires integrating various sources of information, such as results of psychological tests, own observations, comparisons with colleagues, notes from feedback by significant others. It can stimulate reflection and self-insight, particularly when done with the help of a coach. Once the description is completed, it can be of use in evaluating career options and choosing a career goal.

Competence profiles of career directions In comparing career directions, as part of the career development cycle, use can be made of reduced competence profiles that summarize the main requirements in terms of competences, as well as knowledge, skills, attitudes, and dispositions. Table 17.3 gives an example of some typical competences in four broad career directions. It is based on complete competence profiles that also include knowledge, skills, and attitudes as well as abilities, personality traits, and other characteristics, that were derived with the help of relevant literature and recent studies of competences in the different areas. The main function of these competence profiles is to help the person orienting himself with regard to relevant parts of the world of work, and to choose a suitable direction or entry job. In that sense they are preliminary and not necessarily in agreement with the career goal that will be chosen at the end of the situation analysis. Analyzing the requirements for competences, knowledge, skills, and attitudes, gives an idea about learning effort that will be needed. Comparing the requirements for abilities, personality traits, and other characteristics with the person description (see above) allows recognizing major discrepancies that might substantially hinder the learning process.

Competence profile of a career goal After a career goal has been chosen, the best fitting preliminary career profile needs to be completed and tailored to the person's intentions. This means that a new competence profile should be drawn up that can be considered as an operational definition of the personal career goal. It is up to the person to ignore items from the preliminary competence profile or to add other items, to honor personal interests or demands from the current organization. Information from the manager and support from the coach are therefore useful in finalizing the profile. The career goal profile is an important tool in the further process, as a source of guidance for the person's

Table 17.3 Examples of competences in four career directions.

Informatics	Finance	Communication	Human resources
• Analyze user requirements and constraints • Make functional analyses • Identify and solve technical problems • Test and evaluate system performance	• Perform financial analyses • Design administrative processes • Advise clients on financial policies • Make budgets and financial reports	• Conduct communication analyses • Design a communication campaign • Choose communication media • Monitor communication effectiveness	• Analyze staffing needs • Design an HR strategy • Elaborate plans for compensation, recruitment, selection, etc. • Compose reports on current workforce and HR development

development and as a standard for monitoring and evaluating the learning process. Since this career goal is going to serve as the basis for subsequent learning activities, it should list all topics that require learning, but there is no need to include the stable dispositions. Thus, the abilities, personality traits and other characteristics that helped in making a career choice can be dropped.

Career plan Once the preparatory steps of situation analysis, self-exploration, and choosing a career goal have been taken, a career plan can be made. The career plan is a document that gives an account of the information and considerations that have led the person to choosing a career goal, a clear description of the career goals, the aimed for development of competences, the practical steps that will be taken, the resources that will be needed, and a time planning with a horizon of two to five years. The primary function of the career plan is to guide the person's actions and to enable self-development. To fulfill this purpose it should include well-defined learning goals. The career plan should include learning goals that are formulated in a SMART manner, that is specific, measurable, attainable, relevant, and time-bound. This gives the coach insight into what the person wishes to achieve and undertake, and how to provide the best possible support. Ideally, the career plan should also be shared with the manager, giving him/her an opportunity to profit from the person's ambitions and to create room for career moves and learning in a way that is beneficial for the organization as well. A career plan can be shaped in different ways. Table 17.4 gives an example of the content that should ideally be covered.

Career plans as referred to here differ from the personal development plans (PDPs) that organizations often ask for (e.g., Beausaert, Segers, & Gijselaers, 2011). The latter require employees to describe their own plans and needs for development, but they tend to have a more confined scope as they are tied to organizational goals and needs. They are more easily aggregated than career plans, allowing organizations to show how the workforce develops with regard to their short- or mid-term objectives, but they fail to show how they relate to the long-term personal goals of those currently employed. Often PDPs focus on competencies rather than competences, which brings ambiguity and makes them less informative with regard to learning activities. The literature gives some examples of PDPs that effectively foster ongoing learning activities in employees, in ways that reach beyond the borders of their current employment (Fenwick, 2003; Taylor & Edge, 1997).

Table 17.4 Content of a career plan.

1 Introduction
  1.1   Personal and contact information
  1.2   Education and additional training
  1.3   Previous positions
  1.4   Current position
  1.5   Time horizon of the career plan
2 Career analysis and goal
  2.1   Self-exploration
  2.2   Career directions and options inside and outside the organization
  2.3   Analysis of required competences
  2.4   Personal career objectives
  2.5   Choice and description of the career goal
3 Development plan
  3.1   Required competence profile (detailed)
  3.2   Current competence profile (detailed)
  3.3   Gap analysis
  3.4   Learning trajectories
  3.5   Needed and available resources
  3.6   Targets, priorities, and timing
4 Conclusion
  4.1   Summary of career goal and development plan
  4.2   View of the coach
  4.3   View of the current employer
5 Appendices
  Including person description, test results, detailed competence profiles files, and results of gap analysis

Progress chart A tool for monitoring progress and outcomes of competence development is the progress chart, of which an illustration is given in Figure 17.4. The progress chart is an extension of the competence profile of the career goal with a time dimension and a scale for measuring the degree of mastery. It lists all competences, knowledge, skills, and attitudes for which further learning is needed, and offers the opportunity to set target dates and an aimed-for degree of mastery. The chart is designed in such a way that one can mark actual learning progress in terms of a level of mastery achieved at successive time moments. The progress chart is an effective tool to support and monitor the overall learning process. Since not all learning tasks can be worked upon at the same time, it calls for establishing sequences and setting priorities – which will reflect the importance assigned by the person and the organization, and available opportunities for learning. The evaluation of progress is not a simple matter; it calls for a thorough analysis of learning efforts and experiences at the level of competences as well as knowledge, skills, and attitudes that helps bringing the principles of SDL into practice. There are additional tools such as development portfolios and a competence analysis scheme that can support this activity.

What to expect?

The transition from organizational careers to personal careers, and from employee development systems managed by organizations to systems relying on self-management, is still underway and it is too early to foretell how the process will unfold and what its effects will be. While many organizations were initially reluctant to give up control over employees'

		Required	Target level	Target data	Ratings by end of quarter to be given by employee and coach (e.g., 3–4)			
Name employee: Mark E. / Name coach: Nancy B. / Period: Year 2015					Level 1 – 2 – 3 – 4 – 5			
					Q1	Q2	Q3	Q4
Competences – *acquired abilities to adequately perform tasks*								
HR1	Analyze staffing needs	3	3	Q1	3–3			
HR6	Advise on compensation and benefits	5	4	Q4	2–2	3–3	4–3	5–4
HR13	Conduct recruitment / selection interviews	3			1–1	1–2		
HR15	Design performance appraisal schemes	3		Q4		1–1	2–2	3–2
HR18	Resolve disputes	N						
Sub-competences – *acquired abilities to adequately perform sub-tasks*								
D2	Plan activities							
D5	Follow procedures			Q2		2–2		
D6	Monitor own achievements			Q3	3–2	3–2	4–3	
D9	Collect information							
D19	Write documentation							

Figure 17.4　Example of a competence development progress chart.

development, there is growing awareness of the need for more flexibility and increasing readiness to accept that employees – at least those in management and certain professional categories – ultimately control their own career and learning activities. It is only realistic for organizations to acknowledge this and to look for ways to align organizational careers with personal careers even if it is for employment episodes of just a few years. A system as outlined above may be useful in this respect, as it redefines the relationship between the person and the organization, and offers tools for information exchange and joint management. Of course, the precise design of the system can vary, depending on how the theoretical principles are used and geared to the specific needs of individuals and organizations. The outcomes will vary with the system's design, its actual implementation and use, the target groups of employees, the specificities of the organization, and the nature of the industry. The time perspective, in terms of a near or remote horizon will also matter. Although the limited experience with new approaches to employee development and the large number of factors involved make it impossible to evaluate their effectiveness, some likely effects may be delineated.

Personal perspective　Using a system that requires employees to devote considerable attention to their own career and development, and, in fact, to take responsibility for their future, is likely to have a number of effects at the personal level. First of all, it will create *greater awareness* of the fact that people's day-to-day activities in education and training as well as in work are part of their career and are shaping the future of that career. It creates a perspective that invites them to reflect on their actions and take control. Secondly, it will *promote self-regulation* with regard to the career, as well as development and work activities. With support of a coach they will learn how to analyze, choose, plan, and implement, how to keep track of their advance, and how to profit from success and failure. They will for instance learn to choose between mobility in their own interest and staying with the organization because of their embeddedness in a social network or investments that were already made (Feldman & Ng, 2007). Likewise, they will develop certain career tactics (Laud & Johnson, 2012). At the level of development they will "learn to learn," which is of potential benefit at all life stages.

Thirdly, it will endow people with *qualities that are important for shaping their future career*. Making their own choices and implementing these, people will develop a sense of control, or career self-efficacy (e.g., Lent & Hackett, 1987). They are also likely to build a (meta-) competence regarding their career, which allows them to asses where they are, where to move, what to do next and what not, what to learn and unlearn, how to overcome career problems, and so forth. People who have learned all this early in the career, will likely be able to profit from it during later years. This competence is important because it may help to identify and overcome career barriers or to keep moving when meeting career plateaus (Zikic & Hall, 2009). This can reduce the likelihood of frustration and bitterness, and promote career satisfaction at later moments in life. Such outcomes are important benefits compared to traditional employee development.

Fourth, it will lead to *more time spent and a deeper engagement in developmental activities* compared to traditional employee development (Birdi, Allan, & Warr, 1997), which likely pays off in the form of greater competence, knowledge, and skill, and more appropriate attitudes and behaviors. The greater investment in self-development can produce better self-insight, enhance self-identity, and "core self-evaluations" (Feldman & Ng, 2007), and lead to greater assertiveness and resilience – making the persons more desired employees. The experiences with PCMS support this expectation: employees that have used this system are generally appreciated for their greater competence, self-awareness, and resilience. Fifth, since competences are a critical prerequisite for effective performance, the competences acquired by using the system raise the value of the persons for the current and later employers. This enhances their *employability and their chances of future career success* (De Vos, De Hauw, & Van der Heijden, 2011). Finally, the system redefines the relationship between employees and employers, reducing the asymmetry between them. This can help in shaping *more realistic psychological contracts*, which are less prone to disruptions because of unfulfilled promises.

Of course, these effects will not happen to the same degree in all persons, but depend on the time and effort they actually invest, and on several other factors, including the support of the organization and the fit between the person, the coach, and the manager.

Organizations Organizations using a system as described above should expect to see the emergence of a different type of employee and a different employment relationship. As mentioned above, employees are likely to be more self-aware, competent, and flexible, compared to other employees, due to the thorough and broad development activities. This has the potential to raise the organization's productiveness and quality, and strengthen its capacity to learn and innovate (London & Smither, 1999). The employment relationship will be influenced by employees' greater sense of self-determination, produced by control over their career, which makes them aware that they are with the employer because they voluntarily chose it. As long as the employees' goals and expectations converge with those of the organization, they will stay; that is, they will show less unwanted turnover and longer tenure. When employees perceive that the organization provides them with training opportunities that meet their development needs, they may reciprocate with greater loyalty and commitment (Benson, 2006; Maurer & Lippstreu, 2008; Tsui et al., 1997). This stands in sharp contrast to the traditional relationship with employees who are present because of a competitive "recruit and retain" strategy. It implies a more realistic relationship, since it recognizes the interests of both parties, and their capacity to end the relationship after a certain time. In spite of the limited duration of each employment period, it is also a more sustainable relationship that generates the maximum returns for both sides.

The different exchange relation has important implications for the organization as well. Longer tenure of employees, particularly high-potentials, reduces costs of replacing early-leavers and enhances return on investment. Since there is no need to bind employees who stay out of their free will, organization can save on retention policies. As self-managing employees are motivated by their own career and development goals, there is less need for actions to motivate them. Financially, one would expect substantial benefits in the long run, even if one takes into account that the additional time taken for learning may suppress productivity to some degree.

The long-term implications for organizations cannot be assessed without considering effects at the collective level. Employees moving from one organization to another after a certain period of time in order to continue their career there, take their capacities and competences with them, allowing the next employer to benefit from the investments made by the previous one. This means, more generally, that the outcomes of employee development represent a collective good, from which all employers profit. Thus, the more employee development through systems as described here, the more each organization will profit from the availability of a more competent, more flexible, and more employable workforce. This adds to the organization's potential for improving performance, competitiveness, and sustainability, but also to their capacity to reduce the negative impact of failed careers, such as an old and immobile workforce, or dissatisfaction, cynicism, or sabotage among employees.

Future Research

In this chapter I have reviewed some concepts and models from the literature, and examined how they might be utilized in building a system for self-managed employee development that can substitute conventional, organization-managed systems. Although there is evidence to suggest that such a system might work well with certain employees and under certain conditions, there are many challenges and open questions that need to be addressed in practical initiatives and scientific research.

While there are extensive literatures on HR management/HR development, labor markets, and careers, the number of publications covering the *intersection between these areas* is very modest in size. Truly alarming is a shocking lack of information on facts. We currently do not know how people pass through organizations in the course of their career, how many positions they fill within the same organization, and how many in different organizations, how many positions they fill during their whole career, how long they stay in each position, and so on – and how all this has changed over time. Evidence on differences between types of employees, larger and smaller organizations and industry sectors, or national populations, is also lacking. Yet, such information is crucial for understanding the magnitude of the issue of developing employees addressed in this chapter. In my view we urgently need research on these basic facts and on the problems emerging from frictions between efforts to steer careers and development from different angles. This also applies to the costs that are incurred – at the organizational and the societal level – due to these problems, and ways in which these costs can be contained.

A second area is the *transition from organizational to personal careers* and finding ways of managing careers and development that do equal justice to the interests of the "owners" of personal careers and those of organizations. I have addressed this area at the level of concepts and methods, and from a design perspective. Although the views and examples that I presented may be useful for exploring new possibilities or changing existing employee development systems, more research and development is needed to turn concepts into practice. Particularly needed are studies on innovative tools for bridging the gap between individuals and organizations, for instance, tools for exchanging information on needs, goals and options, tools for joint assessment or tools for joint management. It would be good to clarify and fully exploit the role of competences – as opposed to competencies – in this context.

Many sources cited in the chapter refer to experiences with new designs and their implementation, but more research – involving a greater variety of employees and work settings – would be welcome. Wanted are pilot studies, simulations, and evaluation studies, involving different target groups and settings. Many readers might wish to see studies describing "best practices," showing the feasibility of certain systems or demonstrating their implementation. There is also a need for research on specific issues, such as the relative effectiveness of introducing career self-management and self-development at the start of people's career (as was chosen in this chapter) or at later stages. It would also be interesting to know what a future employee development system would require from participants, which outcomes it would produce, and how this would translate into costs and benefits for both sides, in a short-term and long-term perspective.

Another issue is how career development and employee development can be *organized and managed*, and what this implies for organizations and individuals interested in making the transition. Several scholars have already written about the change in organizational perspective and routines needed to create room for career self-management or self-development (e.g., N. Clarke, 2006). In effect, the very notion of HR management may have to be revised to allow for such ideas as employment being a transient state and employees crossing organizations and being passers-by. Since these changes are quite profound, much more effort may need to be spent on spreading new ideas, publicizing effective delivery models, and sharing experiences by organizations that have successfully changed.

More research attention is also needed for the *role of the coach*. Although coaching has witnessed a tremendous growth in popularity during the past decade or so, coaching at the crossing of a personal and an organizational career, with due awareness of the diverging interests and different time perspectives, and in the context of a system that is meant to serve many clients simultaneously, is a great challenge that calls for special qualifications and preparation. Coaching for competence development, being heavily entrenched in everyday work activities, also brings special requirements in terms of knowledge of the industry and contact with the organization, which should be carefully balanced with the requirement of independence. These aspects, and the enhanced responsibility of the coach in the initial stage of the process, deserve further research with the aim of determining how coaching can best be done to have optimal effects. Organizing coaching – within a systems context – at a sufficiently wide scale is another important issue. It is hard to imagine that this could be done in a bottom-up manner, upon the initiative of individuals. Finding feasible models for doing this, either departing from agencies providing coaching on a larger scale, or from organizations – either alone, or collaborating at the industry level – is a subject that also requires systematic investigation. This may well combine with exploring ideas about more widely scoped systems spanning multiple organizations and operating in a collective space.

Last but not least is the subject of arranging and *managing the system from the personal perspective*. Many of the notions and methods mentioned in this chapter focus on the individual worker, responsible for and engaged in self-development in the context of his/her personal career. There are many useful ideas in the literature on careers and development that can be exploited in future systems, and there is considerable practical experience (e.g., in the PCMS) with using them to the individual's benefit. Little attention has as yet been devoted to differences between categories of workers (e.g., financial or medical professionals, managers) and to individual differences. A final topic that needs to be explored is the overall organizational arrangement, and the need to safeguard workers' interests when moving towards self-managed employee development at a larger scale.

Conclusion

Fundamental economic, technological, and social changes have produced a new ecology of work in which organizations are no longer able to plan and manage the careers and the development of employees. There is a need for new arrangements that allow individuals to take control of their career and to direct their own learning, in ways that meet personal and organizational requirements in the short run as well as in a longer time perspective. In this chapter, I have examined the requirements for a contemporary employee development system and given suggestions on how it could be put together, starting from the notions of competence and competence acquisition and including the principles of career self-management, self-development, and self-directed learning. I have described how the system could be designed, the roles of workers, supervisors, and coaches, and the types of tools that might be used. Current evidence suggests that self-managed, competence-based employee development is feasible and can be effective, but there are several issues that need to be clarified in further research. Also, more effort will be needed to help organizations make the transition to this type of employee development and to build the infrastructure needed to let all employees take control of their career.

References

Arnold, J. (2002). Careers and career management. In N. Anderson, D. S. Ones, H. K. Sinangil, & C. Viswesvaran (Eds.), *Handbook of Industrial, Work and Organizational Psychology, vol. 2, Organizational Psychology* (pp. 115–132). Thousand Oaks, CA: Sage.

Arthur, M. B. (1994). The boundaryless career: A new perspective for organizational inquiry. *Journal of Organizational Behavior*, 15(4), 295–306.

Arthur, M. B., Khapova, S. N., & Wilderom, C. P. M. (2005). Career success in a boundaryless career world. *Journal of Organizational Behavior*, 26(2), 177–202. doi:10.1002/job.290.

Auchterlonie, D. L. (2003). How to fix the rotating CEO dilemma: Best practices of turnaround management professionals. *Journal of Private Equity*, 6(4), 52–57.

Bartram, D., & Roe, R. A. (2008). Individual and organisational factors in competence acquisition. In W. J. Nijhoff, R. J. Simons, & A. F. Nieuwenhuis (Eds.), *The Learning Potential of the Workplace* (pp. 71–96). Rotterdam: Sense.

Baum, H. S. (1990). *Organizational Membership: Personal Development in the Workplace*. Albany, NY: State University of New York Press.

Beausaert, S., Segers, M., & Gijselaers, W. (2011). The personal development plan practice questionnaire: The development and validation of an instrument to assess the employee's perception of personal development plan practice. *International Journal of Training and Development*, 15(4), 249–270. doi:10.1111/j.1468-2419.2011.00375.x.

Benson, G. S. (2006). Employee development, commitment and intention to turnover: A test of "employability" policies in action. *Human Resource Management Journal*, 16(2), 173–192. doi:10.1111/j.1748-8583.2006.00011.x.

Betz, N. E., & Hackett, G. (1987). Concept of agency in educational and career development. *Journal of Counseling Psychology*, 34(3), 299–308. doi:10.1037/0022-0167.34.3.299.

Birdi, K., Allan, C., & Warr, P. (1997). Correlates and perceived outcomes of 4 types of employee development activity. *Journal of Applied Psychology*, 82(6), 845–857. doi:10.1037/0021-9010.82.6.845.

Bolhuis, S. (2003). Towards process-oriented teaching for self-directed lifelong learning: A multidimensional perspective. *Learning and Instruction*, 13(3), 327–347. doi:10.1016/S0959-4752(02)00008-7.

Boyatzis, R. E. (1982). *The Competent Manager. A Model for Effectice Performance*. New York: John Wiley & Sons, Inc.

Boydell, T., & Pedler, M. J. (Eds.) (1981). *Management Self-Development: Concepts and Practices*. Farnborough: Gower.

Boyer, S. L., Artis, A. B., Solomon, P. J., & Fleming, D. E. (2012). Improving sales performance with self-directed learning. *Marketing Management Journal*, 22(2), 61–75.

Briscoe, J. P., & Hall, D. T. (2006). The interplay of boundaryless and protean careers: Combinations and implications. *Journal of Vocational Behavior*, 69(1), 4–18. doi:10.1016/j.jvb.2005.09.002.

Briscoe, J. P., Hall, D. T., & Frautschy DeMuth, R. L. (2006). Protean and boundaryless careers: An empirical exploration. *Journal of Vocational Behavior*, 69(1), 30–47. doi:10.1016/j.jvb.2005.09.003.

Briscoe, J. P., Henagan, S. C., Burton, J. P., & Murphy, W. M. (2012). Coping with an insecure employment environment: The differing roles of protean and boundaryless career orientations. *Journal of Vocational Behavior*, 80(2), 308–316. doi:10.1016/j.jvb.2011.12.008.

Brockmann, M., Clarke, L., & Winch, C. (2009). Competence and competency in the EQF and in European VET systems. *Journal of European Industrial Training*, 33(8/9), 787–799. doi:10.1108/03090590910993834.

Candy, P. C. (1991). *Self-Direction for Lifelong Learning. A Comprehensive Guide to Theory and Practice*. San Francisco: Jossey-Bass.

Carbery, R., & Garavan, T. N. (2007). Conceptualizing the participation of managers in career-focused learning and development: A framework. *Human Resource Development Review*, 6(4), 394–418. doi:10.1177/1534484307307552.

Chiesa, R. (2011). Career self-management behaviours: The effects on the job satisfaction and job insecurity. *Counseling: Giornale Italiano di Ricerca e Applicazioni*, 4(2), 181–193.

Choi, B. Y., Park, H., Yang, E., Lee, S. K., Lee, Y., & Lee, S. M. (2012). Understanding career decision self-efficacy: A meta-analytic approach. *Journal of Career Development*, 39(5), 443–460.

Chudzikowski, K., Demel, B., Mayrhofer, W., Briscoe, J. P., Unite, J., Milikić, B. B., et al. (2009). Career transitions and their causes: A country-comparative perspective. *Journal of Occupational and Organizational Psychology*, 82(4), 825–849. doi:10.1348/096317909X474786.

Čiutienė, R., Neverauskas, B., & Meilienė, E. (2010). Coaching as a tool to develop employees career. *Economics & Management*, 444–450.

Clarke, M. (2009). Plodders, pragmatists, visionaries and opportunists: Career patterns and employability. *Career Development International*, 14(1), 8–28. doi:10.1108/13620430910933556.

Clarke, M. (2013). The organizational career: Not dead but in need of redefinition. *International Journal of Human Resource Management*, 24(4), 684–703. doi:10.1080/09585192.2012.697475.

Clarke, N. (2006). Why HR policies fail to support workplace learning: The complexities of policy implementation in healthcare. *International Journal of Human Resource Management*, 17(1), 190–206. doi:10.1080/09585190500367589.

De Vos, A., De Hauw, S., & Van der Heijden, B. I. J. M. (2011). Competency development and career success: The mediating role of employability. *Journal of Vocational Behavior*, 79(2), 438–447. doi:10.1016/j.jvb.2011.05.010.

De Vos, A., Dewettinck, K., & Buyens, D. (2007). De professionele loopbaan in goede banen: Het samenspel van loopbaanzelfsturing en het loopbaanbeleid binnen de organisatie. *Gedrag en Organisatie*, 20(1), 21–40.

Delf, G., & Smith, B. (1978). Strategies for promoting self-development. *Industrial & Commercial Training*, 10(12), 494.

Dobrev, S. D. (2012). Career change and the iron cage: Organizations and the early labour market experience of professional managers. *Journal of Management Studies*, 49(5), 843–868. doi:10.1111/j.1467-6486.2011.01038.x.

Ellinger, A. D. (2004). The concept of self-directed learning and its implications for human resource development. *Advances in Developing Human Resources*, 6(2), 158–177. doi:10.1177/1523422304263327.

Ellström, P.-E. (2011). Informal learning at work: Conditions, processes and logics. In M. Malloch, L. Cairns, K. Evans, & B. N. O'Connor (Eds.), *The SAGE Handbook of Workplace Learning* (pp. 105–119). London: Sage.

Evarts, H. F. (1987). The competency programme of the American Management Association. *Industrial & Commercial Training*, 19(1), 3.

Feldman, D. C., & Ng, T. W. H. (2007). Careers: Mobility, embeddedness, and success. *Journal of Management*, 33(3), 350–377. doi:10.1177/0149206307300815.

Fenwick, T. J. (2003). Professional growth plans: Possibilities and limitations of an organization-wide employee development strategy. *Human Resource Development Quarterly*, 14(1), 59–77. doi:10.1002/hrdq.1050.

Garofano, C. M., & Salas, E. (2005). What influences continuous employee development decisions? *Human Resource Management Review*, 15(4), 281–304. doi:10.1016/j.hrmr.2005.10.002.

Guest, D. E., & Rodrigues, R. (2012). Can the organizational career survive? An evaluation within a social exchange perspective. In L. M. Shore, J. A. M. Coyle-Shapiro, & L. E. Tetrick (Eds.), *The Employee–Organization Relationship: Applications for the 21st Century* (pp. 193–222). New York: Routledge/Taylor & Francis Group.

Hall, D. T. (Ed.). (1986). *Career Development in Organizations*. San Francisco: Jossey Bass.

Hamel, G., & Prahalad, C. K. (1994). *Competing for the Future*. Boston, MA: HBR Press.

Hamori, M., Cao, J., & Koyuncu, B. (2012). Why top young managers are in a nonstop job hunt. *Harvard Business Review*, 90(7/8), 28.

Hashim, J. (2008). Competencies acquisition through self-directed learning among Malaysian managers. *Journal of Workplace Learning*, 20(4), 259–271. doi:10.1108/13665620810871114.

Haveman, H. A. (1995). The demographic metabolism of organizations: Industry dynamics, turnover, and tenure distributions. *Administrative Science Quarterly*, 40(4), 586–618.

Heilmann, P. (2011). The dialectics between boundaryless career and competence development findings among Finnish ICT and paper managers. *International Journal of Human Resource Management*, 22(1), 181–196. doi:10.1080/09585192.2011.538981.

Holton, E. F., III. (2001). New employee development tactics: Perceived availability, helpfulness, and relationship with job attitudes. *Journal of Business and Psychology*, 16(1), 73–85. doi:10.1023/A:1007839805642.

Hurtz, G. M., & Williams, K. J. (2009). Attitudinal and motivational antecedents of participation in voluntary employee development activities. *Journal of Applied Psychology*, 94(3), 635–653. doi:10.1037/a0014580.

Kaplan, S. N., & Minton, B. A. (2012). How has CEO turnover changed? *International Review of Finance*, 12(1), 57–87. doi:10.1111/j.1468-2443.2011.01135.x.

Karakas, F., & Manisaligil, A. (2012). Reorienting self-directed learning for the creative digital era. *European Journal of Training & Development*, 36(7), 712–731. doi:10.1108/03090591211255557.

Kicken, W., Brand-Gruwel, S., & Van Merrienboer, J. J. G. (2008). Scaffolding advice on task selection: A safe path toward self-directed learning in on-demand education. *Journal of Vocational Education and Training*, 60(3), 223–239.

Kicken, W., Brand-Gruwel, S., Van Merriënboer, Jeroen J. G., & Slot, W. (2009). The effects of portfolio-based advice on the development of self-directed learning skills in secondary vocational education. *Educational Technology Research and Development*, 57(4), 439–460. doi:10.1007/s11423-009-9111-3.

King, Z. (2004). Career self-management: Its nature, causes and consequences. *Journal of Vocational Behavior*, 65(1), 112–133. doi:10.1016/S0001-8791(03)00052-6.

Kirkham, T., Winfield, S., Smallwood, A., Coolin, K., Wood, S., & Searchwell, L. (2009). Introducing live ePortfolios to support self-organised learning. *Educational Technology & Society*, 12(3), 107–114.

Knowles, M. S. (1975). *Self-Directed Learning: A Guide for Learners and Teachers*. Chicago: Follett.

Kuvaas, B., & Dysvik, A. (2009). Perceived investment in permanent employee development and social and economic exchange perceptions among temporary employees. *Journal of Applied Social Psychology*, 39(10), 2499–2524. doi:10.1111/j.1559-1816.2009.00535.x.

Lara, A. E. (2009). Using competency management as a foundation for employee development in a global information technology company. 70, ProQuest Information & Learning, US. http://search.ebscohost.com/login.aspx?direct=true&db=psyh&AN=2009-99230-541&site=ehost-live&scope=site (accessed April 3, 2014).

Laud, R. L., & Johnson, M. (2012). Upward mobility: A typology of tactics and strategies for career advancement. *Career Development International*, 17(3), 231–254. doi:10.1108/1362043 1211241072.

Le Deist, F. D., & Winterton, J. (2005). What is competence? *Human Resource Development International*, 8(1), 27–46. doi:10.1080/1367886042000338227.

Lent, R. W., & Hackett, G. (1987). Career self-efficacy: Empirical status and future directions. *Journal of Vocational Behavior*, 30(3), 347–382. doi:10.1016/0001-8791(87)90010-8.

Lichtenstein, B. M. B., Ogilvie, J. R., & Mendenhall, M. (2002). Non-linear dynamics in entrepreneurial and management careers. *M@n@gement*, 5(1), 31–47.

London, M., & Smither, J. W. (1999). Empowered self-development and continuous learning. *Human Resource Management*, 38(1), 3.

Maurer, T. J., & Lippstreu, M. (2008). Who will be committed to an organization that provides support for employee development? *Journal of Management Development*, 27(3), 328–347. doi:10.1108/02621710810858632.

McCabe, V. S., & Savery, L. K. (2007). "Butterflying" a new career pattern for Australia? Empirical evidence. *Journal of Management Development*, 26(2), 103–116. doi:10.1108/026217 10710726026.

McClelland, D. C. (1973). Testing for competence rather than for "intelligence." *American Psychologist*, 28(1), 1–14.

Murphy, S., & Ensher, E. (2001). The role of mentoring support and self-management strategies on reported career outcomes. *Journal of Career Development*, 27(4), 229–246. doi:10.102 3/A:1007866919494.

Nijhoff, W. J., Simons, R. J., & Nieuwenhuis, A. F. (Eds.) (2008). *The Learning Potential of the Workplace*. Rotterdam: Sense.

Noe, R. A. (1996). Is career management related to employee development and performance? *Journal of Organizational Behavior*, 17, 119–133.

Nybø, G. (2004). Personnel development for dissolving jobs: Towards a competency-based approach? *International Journal of Human Resource Management*, 15(3), 549–564. doi:10.1080/09585 19042000181250.

Orpen, C. (1994). The effects of organizational and individual career management on career success. *International Journal of Manpower*, 15(1), 27.

Orpen, C., & Pool, J. (1995). The joint effects of individual career planning and organizational career management on employee job performance and job involvement. *Studia Psychologica*, 37(1), 27–29.

Orvis, K. A., & Ratwani, K. L. (2010). Leader self-development: A contemporary context for leader development evaluation. *Leadership Quarterly*, 21(4), 657–674. doi:10.1016/j.leaqua. 2010.06.008.

Otto, S. D. (2005). New methods in employee development: Assessing the relational importance of developing profound strengths. 66, ProQuest Information & Learning, US. http://search.ebscohost.com/login.aspx?direct=true&db=psyh&AN=2005-99020-234&site=ehost-live&scope=site (accessed April 3, 2014).

Pang, M., Chua, B.-L., & Chu, C. W. L. (2008). Learning to stay ahead in an uncertain environment. *International Journal of Human Resource Management*, 19(7), 1383–1394. doi:10.1080/ 09585190802110307.

Park, Y. (2010). The predictors of subjective career success: An empirical study of employee development in a Korean financial company. *International Journal of Training and Development*, 14(1), 1–15. doi:10.1111/j.1468-2419.2009.00337.x.

Parker, P., Arthur, M. B., & Inkson, K. (2004). Career communities: A preliminary exploration of member-defined career support structures. *Journal of Organizational Behavior*, 25(4), 489–514. doi:10.1002/job.254.

Patton, W., & Creed, P. A. (2001). Developmental issues in career maturity and career decision status. *Career Development Quarterly*, 49(4), 336.

Paxton, D. R. (1976). Employee development: A lifelong learning approach. *Training & Development Journal*, 30(12), 24–26.

Pfeffer, J. (1994). *Competitive Advantage through People*. Boston, MA: Harvard Business School Press.

Purdum, T. (2006). Ex-military CEOs shine. *Industry Week/IW*, 255(8), 14.

Reichard, R. J., & Johnson, S. K. (2011). Leader self-development as organizational strategy. *Leadership Quarterly*, 22(1), 33–42. doi:10.1016/j.leaqua.2010.12.005.

Roe, R. A. (1999). Competences, assessment and development 1. Unpublished document.

Roe, R. A. (2001). Competencies and competence management – Critique and proposal for a comprehensive theory-based approach. Paper presented at the 10th European Congress for Work and Organizational Psychology, Prague, Czech Republic.

Roe, R. A. (2002). Competenties– Een sleutel tot integratie in theorie en praktijk van de A&O-psychologie. *Gedrag en Organisatie*, 15(4), 203–224.

Roe, R. A. (2005). The design of selection systems: Context, principles, issues. In A. Evers, O. Smit, & N. Anderson (Eds.), *Handbook of Personnel Selection*. Oxford: Blackwell.

Roe, R. A. (2012). *Competentiegids*. Amersfoort: Procam Holding BV.

Rymell, R. G., & Newsom, R. (1981). Self-directed learning and HRD. *Training & Development Journal*, 35(8), 50.

Savickas, M. L. (1997). Career adaptability: An integrative construct for life-span, life-space theory. *Career Development Quarterly*, 45(3), 247–259.

Smith, P. J., Sadler-Smith, E., Robertson, I., & Wakefield, L. (2007). Leadership and learning: Facilitating self-directed learning in enterprises. *Journal of European Industrial Training*, 31(5), 324–335.

Stickland, R. (1996). Career self-management – Can we live without it? *European Journal of Work and Organizational Psychology*, 5(4), 583–596. doi:10.1080/13594329608414881.

Sturges, J. (2008). All in a day's work? Career self-management and the management of the boundary between work and non-work. *Human Resource Management Journal*, 18(2), 118–134. doi:10.1111/j.1748-8583.2007.00054.x.

Suar, D. (2001). Professionals' self-development through self-renewal. *Psychological Studies*, 46(3), 210–221.

Sullivan, S. E., & Baruch, Y. (2009). Advances in career theory and research: A critical review and agenda for future exploration. *Journal of Management*, 35(6), 1542–1571. doi:10.1177/0149206309350082.

Tams, S., & Arthur, M. B. (2010). New directions for boundaryless careers: Agency and interdependence in a changing world. *Journal of Organizational Behavior*, 31(5), 629–646. doi:10.1002/job.712.

Taylor, D., & Edge, D. (1997). Personal development plans: Unlocking the future. *Career Development International*, 2(1), 21–23. doi:10.1108/13620439710157443.

Trenner, L. (2013). Business coaching for information professionals: Why it offers such good value for money in today's economic climate. *Business Information Review*, 30(1), 27–34. doi:10.1177/0266382113480020.

Tsui, A. S., Pearce, J. L., Porter, L. W., & Tripoli, A. M. (1997). Alternative approaches to the employee–organization relationship: Does investment in employees pay off? *Academy of Management Journal*, 40(5), 1089–1121.

Van Dam, K., Van der Heijden, B. I. J. M., & Schyns, B. (2006). Employability en individuele ontwikkeling op het werk. *Gedrag en Organisatie*, 19(1), 53–68.

Van Merriënboer, J. J. G., & Sluijsmans, D. M. A. (2009). Toward a synthesis of cognitive load theory, four-component instructional design, and self-directed learning. *Educational Psychology Review*, 21(1), 55–66.

Van Velsor, E., Moxley, R. S., & Bunker, K. A. (2004). The leader development process. In C. D. McCauley, R. Moxley & E. Van Velsor (Eds.), *Center for Creative Leadership Handbook of Leadership Development* (2nd ed., pp. 204–233). San Francisco: Jossey-Bass.

Vinton, D. (1987). Delegation for employee development. *Training & Development Journal*, 41(1), 65–67.

Watts, A. G. (2000). The new career and public policy. In A. Collin & R. A. Young (Eds.), *The Future of Career* (pp. 259–275). Cambridge/New York/Melbourne: Cambridge University Press.

Zikic, J., & Hall, D. T. (2009). Toward a more complex view of career exploration. *Career Development Quarterly*, 58(2), 181–192.

18

Personal Development Plan, Career Development, and Training

Simon Beausaert, Mien Segers, and Therese Grohnert

Introduction

The current labor market is characterized by a growing number of short-term contracts, a shortage of skilled workers in various industries, an aging workforce, and increasing employee mobility. Next, organizations are dealing with fast-changing insights and knowledge, globalization and technological innovations. Continuous innovation requires continuous development of employees' expertise and flexibility towards changing circumstances. In addition, companies strong on learning and development policies are often preferred by employees over those offering the greatest rewards (McDowall & Fletcher, 2004). In sum, investment in human capital serves the purpose of the attraction and retention of high-quality employees and is described as a crucial strategic tool for organizations to be competitive in an environment that is characterized by ongoing innovation.

Popular techniques for supporting employees in their learning and development are multisource or 360-degree feedback, self- and peer-assessments, and appraisal or review processes. The latter are often organized around a personal development plan (PDP). In general a PDP can be described as an assessment tool embedded in a larger assessment cycle of development and performance interviews, used to gather and document information about the competencies the employee worked on and is planning to further develop. The PDP is expected to stimulate employees to intentionally undertake learning activities and in turn improve performance (London, 1997; van de Wiel, Szegedi, & Weggeman, 2004). Although there is a trend towards using the tool for performance appraisal (with a summative purpose, i.e., informing high-stake decisions), the power of the tool lies in supporting employees' professional development (so-called formative purpose of assessment) (Darling-Hammond & Snyder, 2000; Smith & Tillema, 2003). Questions which are central in the

The Wiley Blackwell Handbook of the Psychology of Training, Development, and Performance Improvement,
First Edition. Edited by Kurt Kraiger, Jonathan Passmore, Sigmar Malvezzi, and Nuno Rebelo dos Santos.
© 2015 John Wiley & Sons Ltd. Published 2020 by John Wiley & Sons Ltd.

PDP and reflect its formative nature are: On which competencies did you work during the past period? How do you now evaluate your level of proficiency of these competencies? Which evidence informs your assessment? How would you formulate the results of your self-assessment in terms of strengths and points for improvement? Which steps are you going to take further to improve your strengths (learning activities)? The questions are meant to stimulate the employee's reflection on his or her competencies in terms of looking back and looking forward. When an employee reflects on his or her strengths and points for improvement, he or she becomes aware of the competencies he or she still needs to work on in order to reach a certain criterion. In order to fill the gap, the employee starts undertaking formal learning activities (e.g., participating in courses or training programs of different kinds) and/or informal learning activities (e.g., reading a book, looking something up on the internet, having discussions with colleagues, looking for a mentor, ...).

There is a vast amount of literature on PDPs. Most of it is situated within an educational context (students or teachers) or in health services (general practitioners, nurses, dentists, pharmacy assistants, or therapists) in which the tool is often referred to as a portfolio. However, most of the publications are descriptive, describing different cases in which a PDP is effectively used. A literature review presenting a comprehensive overview of the results of empirical research on the use of PDPs revealed 54 relevant references (Beausaert, Segers, van der Rijt, & Gijselaers, 2011). Although most empirical studies indicate that PDP assessment is effective for learning, personal or professional development, and improving professional practice, some studies (e.g. Bunker & Leggett, 2005; Little & Hayes, 2003) do not support these positive findings. It is argued, however hard the evidence, that implementing a PDP does not guarantee positive effects. However the effectiveness is dependent on realizing supporting process conditions (e.g., the support of a supervisor).

In this chapter we will address the use of PDPs as learning and development tools. Five main themes are discussed. First, we define a PDP and its characteristics, referring to the learning and motivation theories on which the use of the tool is grounded. Second, the different purposes of the use of PDPs are outlined. Third, the supporting conditions that make or break the PDP practice are discussed. We distinguish between person- (e.g., being able to reflect) and context-related conditions (e.g., the presence of a supportive supervisor). Fourth, we highlight the feed-forward function of the PDP. In contrast to other assessment tools PDPs should not only be used as feedback tools that look back on the learning that took place. Fifth, a critical perspective is given on how this formal tool can or cannot support informal learning. Although the PDP use is formally organized, the tool should also stimulate informal learning. Finally, suggestions for future research are formulated and conclusions are drawn.

What is a Personal Development Plan?

The PDP can be defined as a tool with four distinct characteristics:

- Gives an overview of the competencies the employee worked on in the past and which competencies the employee is planning to work on in the future.
- Is composed by the employee himself (self-direction by the employee) although the format of the PDP is mostly fixed.
- Is used as basis for, or to structure, the conversations with the supervisor or the coach, who provides the employee with feedback and stimulates the employee's reflection.
- Serves for taking different decisions, going from planning an individual training program to promotion or salary increase.

PDPs are often related to portfolios in general or specific types of portfolio's such as reflective portfolios. In literature, different definitions of the personal development plan, as well portfolio, can be found (for examples of definitions, see Table 18.1). They show a high level of overlap and therefore both concepts are often used interchangeably. Historically, the idea of a purposeful collection of work to evidence competences stems from the arts where portfolios were used as a showcase by photographers, painters, architects, and brokers (Lyons & Evans, 1997; Mathers et al., 1999). Later, they were implemented in secondary schools and higher education to support student learning and to inform certification. One section of the portfolio was dedicated to the professional development of the students, referred to as the PDP (e.g., Driessen et al., 2007). In addition to its use in school settings, professionals such as teachers, nurses, and general practitioners started using portfolios. Portfolios in professional settings are used as a tool to present information about the competencies the employee has been working on and is planning to further develop and are for this reason labeled as PDPs.

The value attached to PDPs is based on different theoretical frameworks. First, different learning theories underpin the relevance of PDPs to stimulate professional development. A PDP requires the user to act as a reflective learner (Schön, 1987). Reflection signifies a critical analysis of previous experiences and aims to intensify cognitive elaboration on those experiences; it is expected to lead to behavioral changes (Anseel, Lievens, & Schollaert, 2009; McMullan et al., 2003; Seng & Seng, 1996; Smith & Tillema, 1998). In other words, reflecting provides insight into the employee's own processes of learning (McMullan et al., 2003). Moreover, Schön makes a distinction between two ways of engaging in reflection: reflection-in-action and reflection-on-action. Reflection-in-action refers to reflecting during the experience, without interrupting it. It allows the reflective practitioner to adjust what he or she is doing while he or she is doing it. To reflect on action means thinking back on what has been done, after the initial experience (Schön, 1987). This reflection on action can be supported by making use of a PDP. Similarly, Kolb

Table 18.1 Definitions of PDPs.

Concept	Definition and reference
Reflective learning portfolio	Cyclical process of professional growth in understanding work experiences (Tillema, 2001, p. 127)
Reflective portfolio	Means of personally driven and directed systematic and continuous reflection on one's work intended toward improved understanding (Tillema & Smith, 2000, p. 194)
Portfolio	Purposeful collection of examples of work collected over a period of time, which gives visible and detailed evidence of a person's competence (Smith & Tillema, 1998, p. 193)
Portfolio	Collection of artifacts or works produced in the course of experiential learning (Austin, Marini, & Desroches, 2005, p. 175)
Personal portfolio	Private collection of evidence, which demonstrates the continuing acquisition of skills, knowledge, attitudes, understanding and achievements. It is both retrospective and prospective, as well as reflecting the current stage of development and activity of the individual (Brown, 1995, p. 3)
PDP	Tool used to gather and document information about the competencies the employee worked on and is planning to further develop (Hagan et al., 2006)

states in his model of experiential learning that learning occurs through "concrete experiences" and the reflection on those experiences (Kolb, 1984), for which a PDP can be used. By thinking about what happened, the learner is able to draw a more general conclusion (abstraction) and build up concepts (conceptualization). Finally, the learner can use previous experiences and what he or she learned from those experiences as a basis for new active experimentation, and, finally, an improved performance. The process of using a PDP mirrors Kolb's circular experiential learning and is thus frequently described as a tool to facilitate this kind of learning from experience (Austin, Marini, & Desroches, 2005).

In this respect, Rouse (2004) compares the process of experiential learning to the process of learning with a portfolio (see Figure 18.1 for an illustration). Instead of starting with concrete experiences, the PDP process begins with the *reflection* stage. This stage involves a careful investigation of personal and organizational goals, an assessment of strengths and weaknesses regarding current competency levels and expected competences. This initial self-assessment serves as a starting point for the creation of a PDP in the second step, *planning*. This step involves the assistance of, e.g., a supervisor or coach to define one's own learning goals in a clear, specific, measurable, achievable, relevant, and time-based manner. The learning goals are to be specified based on the competences described and required by the employer and matched to the self-assessment of personal competencies as identified during reflection. Moreover, the learner needs to specify the activities he or she is planning to undertake in order to reach the defined learning goals. Both the goals and the planned steps to achieve these goals are recorded in the PDP. The next phase is the *concrete experience*: this is where the learner actively engages in learning opportunities, which can be both formal (e.g., classes, workshops, trainings) or informal (discussing with a colleague, feedback-seeking and giving, shadowing a more experienced colleague, etc.) (Smith & Tillema, 2003). Following these active learning experiences is a phase of *evaluation*, both ongoing and scheduled. For a pharmacy context, Rouse (2004) suggested seven elements for evaluating learning:

> (1) if and how well the learning and development objectives were achieved (2) how appropriate and effective the plan was (3) how well the activities undertaken correlated with the plan (4) if the methods of learning were appropriate (5) what impact there has been on knowledge, skills and competence, and confidence (6) if and how practice has changed and (7) if there were improved patient outcomes as a result of the activities. (p. 2073)

These evaluation criteria can be adapted to different contexts. After evaluating the undertaken activities, the cycle begins anew with another reflection and assessment. All activities performed in the circle, including planning, reflecting, and evaluating, are recorded in a PDP. A PDP thus becomes a comprehensive document visualizing and proving an individual's learning effort and performance changes. A PDP should follow a standard format, in which learners can structure their formal and informal evidence, feedback, reflections, thoughts, and ideas (see Figure 18.1). However, as McMullan et al. (2003) emphasize, regarding Kolb's learning cycle, the way an individual works with a portfolio depends on the learner's characteristics. Hence, when a supervisor aims to support an employee in learning with a PDP, he or she should take into account both the format of the PDP as well as individual differences and needs of the employee.

Taking into account learner characteristics and needs is in line with the assumptions of the theory of adult learning (Knowles, 1975): adult learners want to see their previous experiences taken into account as rich resources for their learning. Based on experiences the employee has already gathered a lot of (tacit) knowledge of which he or she is often unaware. By reflection on those experiences the employee's knowledge can be brought to

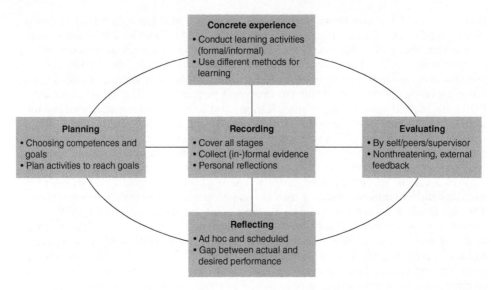

Figure 18.1   The PDP as a tool to support experiential learning (adapted from Rouse, 2004.)

the surface and developed. Knowles (1975) also indicates that adult learners are curious and self-motivated. In line with this assumption, PDPs are theorized to stimulate the employee to take responsibility for his or her own learning (Lyons & Evans, 1997). In other words, a PDP supports a self-directed way of learning, "a process in which individuals take the initiative in evaluating their learning outcomes, diagnosing learning needs, formulating learning goals, and selecting appropriate learning tasks" (Kicken et al., 2008). Next, and in line with Knowles' assumption that adults develop a readiness to learn when looking into real-life situations, the PDP allows the employee to develop readiness to learn from life tasks and problems. By undertaking life tasks and problems the employee is provided with stepping stones to stimulate his learning.

Second, different theoretical perspectives offer indications for a successful implementation of PDPs. First, the self-determination theory (a motivation theory) suggests that, in order to stimulate learning and development, PDPs have to be implemented in a noncontrolling way, empowering self-development and providing the employee with behavioral choices for learning (London & Smither, 1999). This autonomy might lead to an increased intrinsic motivation. Second, research in the domain of transfer of training evidences the importance of supporting and rewarding employees in their learning and development trajectory (e.g., Pham, Segers, & Gijselaers, 2013). Support can be offered by a coach, a mentor, or a supervisor. In organizations the assessment process in which a PDP is used is mostly supported by the supervisor. This is in line with research that found that in using a dossier, training and reflective PDP external feedback was most valued when it was given by a superior (Smith & Tillema, 2003). Furthermore, it was found that employees are more likely to engage in developmental activities such as trainings when they have supervisors that are supportive of their efforts (London, Larsen, & Thisted, 1999). The value of the supportive presence of a supervisor can only be realized when certain conditions are met. First, a supervisor should have sufficient contact with the employee and provide regular feedback (Wasylyshyn, 2003). The lack of interaction with the supervisor is mostly due to time limitations, incompatible work schedules, and physical distance (Noe, 1988).

Additionally, it is evidenced that when the supervisor provides his or her employees with a clear goal, a formal framework (including meetings), specific guidelines and standards, the effects of personal development plan assessment are larger (e.g., Guaglianone, 1995; Noe, 1996; Roberts, 2003). As part of the formal framework, research on feedback stresses the relevance of feedback, feed-up and feed-forward as three phases in the feedback process (Hattie & Timperley, 2007). This implies three core questions guiding the feedback dialogue: Where am I now? (feedback); Where am I going to? (feed-up); and How I am going to realize the next step? (feed-forward). When a discrepancy is detected between the current level of proficiency in terms of competencies and the level aimed for and/or needed within the organization, further learning can be stimulated (Hattie & Timperley, 2007).

Why are PDPs Used?

When it comes to the purposes a PDP is used for, in general a difference is commonly made between professional development (formative assessment) and decision making (summative assessment) (Smith & Tillema, 2001). When a personal development plan is used for professional development, learning takes a central role. Conversely, when a PDP is used for taking high stake decisions (such as promotion, salary increase), presenting oneself is most important. More specifically, a literature review on the use of PDPs (Beausaert, Segers, van der Rijt, & Gijselaers, 2011) resulted in the identification of nine clusters of goals. On the one hand five learning and development purposes were identified: (1) professional development; (2) reflective learning; (3) coaching; (4) stimulating confidence; and (5) organizing. On the other hand four high-stake decision purposes were clustered: (1) providing evidence; (2) documenting; (3) certification, selection, and promotion; and (4) external mobility.

Smith and Tillema (2001, 2003) add the dimension mandatory/voluntary to the formative/summative dimension, resulting in a matrix with four quadrants. They distinguish between the purposes of self-review, self-appraisal, self-evaluation, and self-assessment (Figure 18.2). Each purpose is the response to a specific question an individual might face in a development situation. The *self-review/dossier* approach to a PDP is appropriate in a situation in which an individual needs to attain a certain level of certification in order to remain or advance in an organization. Consequently, a PDP is used to assess whether certain competences were acquired, but not necessarily to give feedback on past and future development of the individual. When an employee chooses to work with a PDP him- or herself in order to gain accreditation, the *self-appraisal* purpose is in place. Compared to self-reviews/dossiers, self-appraisals/reflective portfolios also have a summative purpose, yet are more focused on the learning process, providing deeper insights and greater learning effects (Smith and Tillema, 2001).

Next to the certification purpose, PDPs can also be used for personal development purposes. Employees, who are required by their organization to use a PDP to develop in their job, will use the tool to demonstrate the learning process and it provides a basis for feedback and evaluation interviews – *the self-evaluation purpose*. However, due to the outcome orientation, employees may find it difficult to honestly reflect on their learning experience (Smith & Tillema, 2003). Finally, employees who choose to employ a PDP for their personal development at the workplace profit from a large focus on the learning procedure, due to the formative assessment and process focus of the tool. Moreover, the *self-assessment* purpose allows the learner to make great use of feedback and reflection practices, pushed by personal initiative and motivation (Smith & Tillema, 2003).

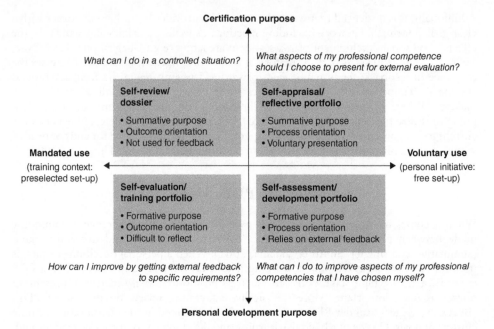

Figure 18.2   Different types of portfolios. (Adapted from Smith & Tillema, 2001, 2003.)

To illustrate the importance of identifying the purpose of a PDP, McMullan et al. (2003) find that a portfolio used for both assessment and development purposes can have adverse effects on the learner. Receiving mixed signals, learners might develop an undesirable focus on their weaknesses and take less ownership of the PDP, which impedes the positive outcomes of PDP use. Beausaert, Segers, and Gijselaers (2011a) researched the influence of the perceived purpose of a PDP on the undertaking of learning activities and performance in a group of experts from an international organization that specializes in medical technology and employees of a regional Dutch governmental organization. The results indicated that although PDPs are valid tools for performance appraisal leading to high-stake decisions, it is a more powerful tool for supporting employees in their professional development. More concretely, the use of a PDP stimulates employees to reflect on the extent to which they possess the competencies necessary for their job and on the learning activities undertaken to enhance the level of proficiency of the job competencies. Furthermore, PDPs lead to a diagnosis of the gaps in job competencies and stimulate employees to plan further learning activities.

These results imply that in order to make employees undertake learning activities and improve their performances by using a PDP, introducing and using the PDP as a tool for learning and development is the most effective. To that end, the supervisor needs to make the learning and development purpose of the PDP explicit to the employee and support the use as a learning tool with appropriate guidance. However, the results also show that, although the impact is smaller, using the tool for high-stake decision making predicts the undertaking of learning activities and employees' performance positively, which leads to the question: How to balance between high-stake decision purpose on the one hand and the learning and development purpose on the other? First, former research in the domain of assessment (Van der Vleuten et al., 2012) has shown the importance of explicitly discerning both purposes. This can be done by, for example, conducting learning and development interviews explicitly separate from performance interviews. Furthermore, it has been argued using different assessors for appraisal interviews serving high-stake decisions purposes and for review techniques with learning and development purposes. In this respect, Brutus, London, and Martineau (1999) researched 360-degree feedback and its relation with setting development goals. They found that ratings given by supervisors are less important than feedback received from subordinates and peers. Moreover, it seems that subordinates and colleagues are better able to influence an employee's learning and development, than is the rating given by the supervisor. Keeping this in mind, supervisors could focus on using the PDP as a certification and selection tool, while the tool could be discussed with coaches, peers, and subordinates in order to reach the learning and development purposes.

What are the Necessary Conditions to Make the PDP Work?

While it is assumed that when the employee works on his or her competencies necessary for the job by using a PDP, his or her performance will improve, a literature review (Beausaert, Segers, van der Rijt, & Gijselaers, 2011) reported inconclusive research findings. While five studies indicated ineffectiveness for learning, providing evidence, reflection, or documenting, the other studies mostly indicated effectiveness for personal or continuing professional development (N studies = 17), stimulating reflection (N studies = 18), and improving professional practice or performance (N studies = 5). However, previous research indicates that it is the way the tool is used and practiced that makes a difference in terms of effects. This section will focus on which conditions are inherently connected to the PDP practice in order to make it work. In general, in literature a distinction is made between conditions related to how the PDP is embedded in the environment (contextual supporting conditions) and those related to the user of the PDP (individual supporting conditions).

Contextual supporting conditions

Table 18.2 gives an overview of the supporting conditions discussed in literature. Concerning the contextual supporting conditions it is indicated that the use of PDPs needs to be backed up by sufficient support. Support can be offered by different key players, such as a coach, a mentor, a supervisor, or a colleague.

Support from a tutor/coach/trainer   To investigate the influence of receiving support in using a PDP, Bullock, Firmstone, Frame, and Bedward (2007) set up an experimental study with a sample of dentists. Participants were divided into an experimental group (N = 42) and a control group (N = 45). The experimental group received support in setting

Table 18.2   Contextual and individual supporting conditions.

Contextual supporting conditions	*Individual supporting conditions*
• Support from a tutor/coach/trainer	• Motivation
• Support from colleagues and peers	• Reflection
• External feedback	• Perceived feasibility
• Clear goals, structure, and guidelines	• Sustained use
• Learning environment	

up a PDP tailored to their needs from a tutor, while the control group set up a PDP by themselves. Results of the study showed that dentists who had received support by a tutor participated in more formal learning activities, such as courses (23 percent versus 18 percent), as well as informal learning activities, for example, discussions with colleagues (43 percent versus 32 percent). Moreover, the experimental group succeeded in fitting their PDP more closely to their learning needs (40 percent versus 32 percent). Finally, dentists in the experimental group reported a higher feeling of impact of these learning activities on their development and practice (40 percent versus 32 percent). Interestingly, this study highlights that the support of a tutor has a stronger impact on undertaking informal learning activities than on the undertaking of formal learning activities. A possible explanation for this finding lies in the tutor's ability to have an outside view and focus the dentists' PDPs on activities that will benefit the individual. This focus can enable individuals to look beyond formal learning.

In this respect, Firssova (2006) highlighted how a PDP shapes the role of the supervisor/tutor/coach. The results of her survey and in-depth interview study indicate that coaches using a PDP with their coachees perceive that it helps to structure their learning and development process as well as increasing efficiency and effectiveness of the coaching process. Moreover, coaches reported that the repertoire of coaching methods they used increased when they used a PDP with their coaches: "The PDP helped to structure the coaching activities, supported preparation of the coach for coaching sessions and served as an additional feedback channel. The coach got broader access to the general background, educational history and viewpoints of the PDP-maker, which provided additional input for coaching activities" (Firssova, 2006, p. 11).

Research by Snadden and Thomas (1998) investigated conditions under which the relationship between trainer and trainee in a medicine setting benefits from the use of a PDP. Specifically, they identified self-confidence by trainees and the perceived trust in the trainer as crucial factors. Through semi-structured interviews, the researchers found that

> confidence was low on entering practice and was one of the factors that acted in a positive way to encourage the adoption of the PDP. ... In addition to this trust, facilitation of the exploration of difficult areas and the generation of a curriculum based on experience between both general practitioners (GPs) and trainer was required. (Snadden & Thomas, 1998, p. 404)

Thus, when the GPs felt that using the PDP could make them more confident in performing their job and they trusted their trainers to help them achieve this goal, using the PDP was successful.

To summarize findings on the importance of tutors, coaches, and trainers, previous research has demonstrated the crucial role a supervisor can play in the learning and development process of an individual, of the trustful relationship between them and of both perceiving the need and benefit of using the tool.

Support from colleagues/peers   Investigating the role of peers in the PDP process, Moore and Bond (2002) and Tigelaar et al. (2006) conducted interviews and also analyzed PDPs in a teacher training setting. They found an overall positive impact of peer support on the use of a PDP. Tigelaar et al. (2006) stated that "most of the teachers found the peer meetings valuable because sharing experiences, hearing different viewpoints, thinking along with others and receiving feedback made them take a fresh look at their own teaching and, in some cases, stimulated them to improve practice" (Tigelaar et al., 2006, p. 375). Often the term "collaboration" is used to point out the interactions with the mentor and/or colleagues, also called peer learning/sharing or collegiality (Seng & Seng, 1996). Hence, next to having a supervisor/trainer or coach, individuals also benefit from discussing their PDPs with peers who can understand their struggles and maybe have insights that help them to maintain focus and stay motivated to undertake learning activities, which a superior or someone not involved in the same learning process may find harder to provide.

Support through feedback   Next to the support provided by supervisors and peers, previous research has identified the crucial role of feedback for benefiting from using a PDP. During conversations with a coach or a colleague, the feedback given plays a crucial role. The coach not only gives guidelines on how to work with the PDP, but also provides constructive, specific, and timely feedback, which is given on a regular basis, in connection to what is written in the PDP. Smith and Tillema (2003) combined semi-structured questionnaires, in-depth interviews and the analysis of PDPs to investigate how far feedback given by different parties can support the learning process. They found that learners who use a dossier/reflective PDP value external feedback most when it is provided by a superior. Linking this finding to the different purposes of PDP uses presented above, feedback by a superior should be directed on the outcome of the learning process and can help the learner to judge whether the PDP is sufficient to fulfill certification criteria. In turn, this finding shows that depending on the purpose the tool is used for, different kinds of feedback (e.g., focused on outcome or process) will be needed by PDP users.

In contrast to other studies Beausaert, Segers, and Gijselaers (2011b) found, by taking questionnaires from 287 employees working in a nonprofit organization in the Netherlands, that the instruction and feedback provided in the context of the PDP did not play a crucial role. More specifically, the following feedback characteristics were evaluated: specificity, timing, constructiveness, and delay. This finding is in line with previous feedback research that indicated that feedback does not always lead to an improvement in performance (e.g., Kluger & DeNisi, 1996). In their meta-analysis Kluger and DeNisi (1996) refer to different factors that influence the effectiveness of feedback such as the source of feedback, timing, and quality of feedback, which might explain the inconclusive results found. They formulate a preliminary feedback intervention theory, which specifies that when the object of feedback is not task learning, or an individual's task motivation, but the individual him- or herself, the effectiveness of feedback decreases. Reasons for this decrease in effectiveness are explained by affective changes that diminish resources available for performing the task at hand (e.g., understanding the feedback, changing behaviors).

In contrast to other assessment tools such as self-assessments, peer-assessments, and 360-degree feedback, using a PDP has the advantage of stimulating the user to not only look back at learning (feedback), but to also discuss future learning and career aspirations (feed-forward). In practice, however, PDPs are often only used as feedback tools. A study conducted by Beausaert et al. (2013) indicated that PDP users undertook more learning activities (in the past) than non-users. However, in contrast to their expectations, users did not plan to undertake more learning activities in the future. They do not plan to undertake further training more often than nonPDP users. This finding might indicate that PDPs are especially used as feedback tools and not as feed-forward tools. In other words, it is expected that the tools are often used for looking back, to discuss learning activities that have been undertaken. They do not serve as a tool to look forward and to get an overview of desired future plans, plan future careers, and plan future learning activities in order to reach set goals. However, in comparison to other assessment tools, such as 360-degree feedback, which put an emphasis on reviewing past performance, the PDP also incorporates the opportunity to look forward at learning and development (Tillema & Smith, 2000). In that perspective, PDPs could be used more often for planning learning activities and career development purposes. Benefits of this feed-forward process within the PDP process could include (1) the ability for the organization to plan ahead with respect to money, time, and planning of learning opportunities for their employees, (2) insight for the supervisors when a certain employee is ready to receive new responsibilities, when to assign a certain employee to a new or existing team and input for evaluation and assessment talks, and (3) a specific plan that employees can follow, possibly connected to certain incentives, such as increased responsibility.

Clear goals, structure, and guidelines   Additionally, introductory sessions that focus on the goal, structure, use (also technical), and assessment criteria have a positive influence on how the employee makes use of a PDP. It is important to provide the employees with this information in advance. However, the tool should not be too highly organized either because that would prevent the employee from taking the responsibility and personalizing the PDP (Tigelaar et al., 2004). Not only the user of a PDP needs support; the mentor or coach who offers the support needs help in his guiding role as well (e.g., Snyder, Pippincott, & Bower, 1998). To strengthen the PDP process mentors need to be supported in understanding their role. They must assist in selecting and developing documentation, in linking the documentation to one or more standards, and in learning from mistakes.

Learning environment   Finally, the learning climate that is characteristic for an organization will influence the way the employee perceives PDP assessment and will have an influence on how they use it. In a school environment, Johnston and Thomas (2005) found the PDP to be perceived as effective for retrospective reflection. However, participants of this study state that the perceived use of the tool was dependent on the kind of support they received within the organization, specifically, when using a PDP was situated in a supportive social network. In this qualitative study, participants named, as example characteristics of such a network, a group they could discuss their portfolio with a place where they could ask for feedback, and a place where they saw opportunities to apply their learning to practice. Consequently, when participants felt these characteristics were lacking in their environment they perceived the tool to be disconnected from practice and as "just one more thing to do" thus impeding learning.

Individual supporting conditions

Next to contextual supporting conditions, several individual supporting conditions are mentioned in the literature. Below an overview of the mostly researched individual supporting conditions is given.

Motivation   In an interview study among 40 GPs, Bahrami, Rogers, and Singleton (1995) demonstrated that learners who are not motivated find composing a PDP very challenging. Specifically, they lack guidance in defining their learning goals and planning appropriate activities to approach these goals. A study by Eisele et al. (2013) demonstrated that how PDP users perceive the contextual supporting conditions is dependent on their goal orientation. This questionnaire study with 48 employees of a Dutch governmental office showed a significant moderation effect of different goal orientations on the relation between PDP use and the tool's effectiveness (in stimulating learning and enhancing job performance). More specifically, employees with a performance orientation, defined as "the desire to prove one's competence and to gain favourable judgments about it" (VandeWalle, 1997, p. 1000) benefitted more from instruction and feedback given in relation to the PDP and preferred an open PDP process that gave them room for choice, while these relations did not hold for mastery-oriented employees, defined as the "desire to develop the self by acquiring new skills, mastering new situations and improving one's competence" (VandeWalle, 1997, p. 1000).

Reflection   The idealized type of PDP user is an employee who is motivated and dedicated to his or her own development, knows how to self-reflect and acts upon that reflection, shows self-directedness, and has confidence in his or her supervisor and the assessment process (Austin, Marini, & Desroches, 2005). In this respect, former research has evidenced that reflection, a vital process for professional development when working with a PDP, is still an unfamiliar skill for PDP users (Smith & Tillema, 1998). Reflection can be conceptualized as a "complex and deliberate process of thinking about and interpreting an experience in order to learn from it" (Boud, Keogh, & Walker, 1985). "It involves the absorption and evaluation of new concepts into personal knowledge structures, relating these concepts to the person's other forms of knowledge and experience" (Anseel, Lievens, & Schollaert, 2009). PDP users may find it hard to reflect on their strengths and weaknesses and to formulate the competencies on which they still need to work. As a consequence, it is possible that PDP users do not show a significant improvement in job competencies because of the lack of reflection and in turn the lack of connection between self-reflection and practice improvement (Austin, Marini, & Desroches, 2005; Orland-Barak, 2005). Therefore, it is important that supervisors or coaches help their employees with reflecting, for example, during interviews in which the PDP is discussed, so that employees can translate their new knowledge into practice. The supervisors or coaches also need to help their employees in connecting reflection with practice improvement further (Austin, Marini, & Desroches, 2005; Orland-Barak, 2005). During meetings in which the supervisor discusses the employee's PDP with the employee attention should go to the future learning of the employee and stimulating his or her reflection on the past learning process. In this way, the supervisor acts as a motivator and a stimulator. A research study among employees in a government office confirmed that employees are far more likely to undertake more learning activities, show more expertise growth and flexibility towards changing circumstances, and perform better if the employee reflects on the PDP and learns from it (Beausaert, Segers, & Gijselaers, 2011b).

Perceived feasibility   According to Smith and Tillema (2003), one major cause for individuals to use PDPs in different ways is perceived feasibility – whether or not an individual feels he or she is able to work with the PDP, for example, by providing the required information. In their mixed-method study with 89 teachers, Smith and Tillema (2003) demonstrated perceived feasibility was higher among teachers who used a PDP type that allowed for self-directed learning.

Sustained use   In a questionnaire and interview study with school principals (N = 35) and managers (N = 14), Smith and Tillema (1998) found that the PDP process can only be successful with sustained use, the maintenance of the PDP, and the ongoing undertaking of reflection, learning activities, and planning. The lack of either contextual or individual supporting conditions can prevent sustained use, such as lack of support by a supervisor, feedback, clear goals or reflection, and perceived feasibility. Moreover, when PDP users perceive an alignment between their learning needs and their day-to-day practice, they will experience increased enthusiasm and satisfaction, which can in turn stimulate personal development (Austin, Marini, & Desroches, 2005; Bahrami, Rogers, & Singleton, 1995; Bullock et al., 2007).

The PDP Paradox: Formalizing the Informal Learning

Formal learning, referring to "learning that occurs in an organised and structured environment … and is explicitly designated as learning" (CEDEFOP, 2008, p. 85) has received the majority of attention by human resource development (HRD) researchers and practitioners in the past. Although it is increasingly evidenced that in many cases formal learning activities do not result in changed behavior in the workplace (low level of transfer of training) (Blume et al., 2010; Ford & Weissbein, 1997), they are still an important measure for HRD, since they are arguably easier to plan and observe than informal learning activities. In this respect, within the context of PDPs, initiatives for taking the next step in competence development often only refer to formal learning activities. In terms of training programs this implies that in practice PDPs are mostly seen as formal learning tools, that is, inside a structure deliberately created for that purpose. However, recently researchers and practitioners start to realize that it is the more (deliberate) informal learning that occurs within or as a result of the PDP practice that determines how much is learned. Informal learning is less prestructured, more in control of the learner, embedded in daily working activities of the employee and therefore often a by-product of some other activity, and may happen unconsciously (cf. Livingstone, 2001; Marsick & Watkins, 2001) or in implicit, reactive, or deliberate ways (Eraut, 2007). Implicit learning is unconscious and not recognized by the learners themselves. He argues that learning from experience mostly has such an implicit component – for example, during the process for (workplace) socialization. Within the PDP practice it can happen that as a result of the questions the supervisor is asking the employee is learning, although he or she is not fully aware of it. However, because of its reflective character and the possibilities it offers for feedback, the PDP is a learning tool in itself, which makes it possible to make implicit learning explicit and thereby overcome the disadvantages of implicit learning. Reactive learning is more conscious. This learning is intended and has a component of reflection. However, it happens in the midst of some other activity, and therefore receives only partial attention. For example, when the employee reflects on a question posed by the supervisor, during a PDP interview, and acquires insight into what he or she learned because of a past experience. Deliberate learning happens in work situations where time is specifically allotted for learning (Tynjälä, 2012); for example, as a follow-up of a PDP interview the PDP user deliberately asks for feedback from his colleague on how he deals with a specific task.

Future Research

Beausaert's literature review on the use of PDPs showed that most studies on their use were conducted by using qualitative research methods (N = 51) or a combination of qualitative and quantitative research methods (N = 23) (Beausaert, Segers, van der Rijt, & Gijselaers, 2011). More specifically, interviews (N studies = 27), portfolio analysis (N studies = 16), and focus groups (N studies = 5) were the most used qualitative research methods. In contrast, questionnaires (N studies = 23) and surveys (N studies = 13) were used less, although they were the most used quantitative methods. Next, studies on PDPs are often based on small sample sizes (e.g., Tigelaar et al., 2006) and therefore do not lead to generalizable results. Furthermore, hardly any studies on the effects of PDPs have been using a control group design and therefore could not draw valid conclusions on the effectiveness of PDPs. Overall, there is a limited amount of empirical research looking into the use of PDPs in a systematic way using control group designs unraveling causal relations.

Given the relative small number of empirical studies, many questions are still unanswered with respect to the design as well as implementation of PDPs in order to be effective. More specifically, future research could look into the issues that follow.

First, future research should not only focus on different definitions and purposes of PDPs, but also on the different formats that are used. Some formats include a proficient analysis of strengths and weaknesses, for instance, while others only focus on defining goals, the way in which the goals are going to be reached, and in which timeframe. Furthermore, some PDPs already indicate the competencies needed for the job profile, while others do not indicate any competency. Next, the implementation and procedure of using and discussing the tool vary a lot between companies. For example, the number of formal meetings in which the PDP is discussed differ. Future research should research the effectiveness of the different procedures.

Second, future research should investigate the effectiveness of PDPs for the undertaking of learning activities and job performance in a broader sample which covers different sectors and professions, ages, levels of expertise, and career possibilities. Furthermore, supporting conditions and effects can differ according to organizational learning culture (Marsick & Watkins, 2003), sectors or disciplines (e.g., Datta, Guthrie, & Wright, 2005), type of organizations (market-oriented or not; Baker & Sinkula, 1999), type of employees (e.g., experienced versus nonexperienced), and organization sizes (small versus large scale; Saru, 2007). Often larger organizations show more sophisticated human resource management (Guthrie, 2001).

Third, it has been demonstrated that a high-quality PDP can only be expected after being used for a longer period of time (Smith & Tillema, 1998). However, so far not many longitudinal studies have been conducted. Studies within a longitudinal design could measure the effectiveness of the PDP in the workplace more accurately. This research design would also allow us to draw conclusions about causality.

Finally, future research should focus on measuring a variety of PDP outcomes in terms of learning and development as well as context-specific performance measures, involving multiraters.

Conclusion

It is not the PDP in itself that makes employees learn and develop; it is the way it is implemented and used that makes the assessment practice work. Research results indicate that assessment tools like PDPs are powerful for supporting learning and development, by looking back, formulating learning goals, and defining steps to take to reach the planned goals. PDPs bridge gaps between formal and informal learning. However, finding the equilibrium between using a PDP to provide a formal framework for learning and using a PDP to stimulate employees to learn informally is a challenge. Because of their reflective nature and the opportunities they create for giving and receiving feedback PDPs incorporate the possibility of making implicit informal learning more explicit, which makes it easier to also make a connection to more formal learning activities.

Evidencing effectiveness of PDP practices asks for measuring both the tool used and the assessment practice around it, characterized by the presence of different supporting conditions. Moreover, future research should look into differences between formats and related practices, be longitudinal in order to look into effects, take into account context-related variables, and involve multiraters.

References

Alsop, A. (2002). Portfolios: Portraits of our professional lives. *British Journal of Occupational Therapy*, 65(5), 201–206.

Anseel, F., Lievens, F., & Schollaert, E. (2009). Reflection as a strategy to enhance task performance after feedback. *Organizational Behavior and Human Decision Processes*, 110, 23–35.

Austin, Z., Marini, A., & Desroches, B. (2005). Use of a learning portfolio for continuous professional development: A study of pharmacists in Ontario (Canada). *Pharmacy Education*, 5, 175–181.

Bahrami, J., Rogers, M., & Singleton, C. (1995). Personal education plan: A system of continuing medical education for general practitioners. *Education for General Practice*, 6, 342–345.

Baker, W. E., & Sinkula, J. M. (1999). The synergistic effect of market orientation and learning orientation on organizational performance. *Journal of the Academy of Marketing Science*, 27, 411–427.

Beausaert, S., Segers, M., Fouarge, D., & Gijselaers, W. (2013). Effect of using a PDP on learning and development. *Journal of Workplace Learning*, 25(3), pp. 145–158.

Beausaert, S., Segers, M., & Gijselaers, W. (2011a). Using a personal development plan for different purposes: Its influence on undertaking learning activities and job performance. *Vocations and Learning*, 4, 231–252.

Beausaert, S., Segers, M., & Gijselaers, W. (2011b). The use of a personal development plan and the undertaking of learning activities, expertise-growth, flexibility and performance: The role of supporting assessment conditions. *Human Resource Development International*, 14(5), 527–543.

Beausaert, S., Segers, M., van der Rijt, J., & Gijselaers, W. (2011). The use of personal development plans in the workplace: A literature review. In P. van den Bossche, W. Gijselaers, & R. Milter (Eds.), *Building Learning Experiences in a Changing World*, vol. 3 of *Advances in Business Education and Training* (pp. 235–265). Dordrecht: Springer.

Biggs, J. (2003). *Teaching for Quality Learning at University*. Maidenhead: McGraw-Hill Education.

Blume, B. D., Ford, J. K., Baldwin, T. T., & Huang, J. L. (2010). Transfer of training: A meta-analytic review. *Journal of Management*, 36(4), 1065–1105. doi:10.1177/0149206309352880.

Boud, D. J., Keogh, R., & Walker, D. (Eds.) (1985). *Reflection: Turning Experience into Learning*. Abingdon: Routledge.

Brown, R. (1995). *Portfolio Development and Profiling for Nurses* (2nd ed.). Lancaster: Quay Publications.

Brutus, S., London, M., & Martineau, J. (1999). The impact of 360-degree feedback on planning for career development. *Journal of Management Development*, 18, 676–693.

Bullock, A., Firmstone, V., Frame, J., & Bedward, J. (2007). Enhancing the benefit of continuing professional development: A randomized controlled study of personal development plans for dentists. *Learning in Health and Social Care*, 6(1), 14–26.

Bunker, A., & Leggett, M. (2005). Teaching portfolios: rhetoric, reality and reflection. Unpublished.

Cayne, J. V. (1995). Portfolios: A developmental influence? *Journal of Advanced Nursing*, 21, 395–405.

CEDEFOP. (2008). *Terminology of European Education and Training Policy*. Luxembourg: Office for Official Publications of the European Communities.

Cross, J. (2007). *Informal Learning*. San Francisco: Pfeiffer.

Darling-Hammond, L., & Snyder, J. (2000). Authentic assessment of teaching in context. *Teaching & Teacher Education*, 16, 523–545.

Datta, D. K., Guthrie, J. P., & Wright P. M. (2005). Human resource management and labor productivity: Does industry matter? *Academy of Management Journal*, 48, 135–145.

Driessen, E. W., van Tartwijk, J., van der Vleuten, C. P. M., & Wass, V. J. (2007). Portfolios in medical education: Why do they meet with mixed success? A systematic review. *Medical Education*, 41, 1224–1233.

Eisele, L., Grohnert, T., Beausaert, S., & Segers, M. (2013) Employee motivation for personal development plan effectiveness. *European Journal of Training and Development*, 37(6), 527–543.

Eraut, M. (2004). Informal learning in the workplace. *Studies in Continuing Education*, 26(2), 247–273. doi:10.1080/158037042000225245.

Eraut, M. (2007). Learning from other people in the workplace. *Oxford Review of Education*, 33(4), 403–422. doi:10.1080/03054980701425706.

Firssova, O. (2006). *ePortfolio* as a coaching support tool for workplace learning of teachers. Paper presented at ePortfolio conference, Oxford, October 11–13. http://www.eifel.org/news/ep2006/programme (accessed September 20, 2007).

Ford, J. K., & Weissbein, D. A. (1997). Transfer of training: An updated review and analysis. *Performance Improvement Quarterly*, 10(2), 22–41.

Guaglianone, C. L. (1995). Portfolio assessment of administrators. Paper presented at the 49th Annual Meeting of the National Council of Professors of Educational Administration, Williamsburg, VA, August 8–12.

Guthrie, J. P. (2001). High-involvement work practices, turnover, and productivity: Evidence from New Zealand. *Academy of Management Journal*, 44, 180–190.

Hagan, C., Konopaske, R., Bernardin, H., & Tyler, C. (2006). Predicting assessment center performance with 360-degree, top-down, and customer-based competency assessment. *Human Resource Management*, 45, 357–390.

Hattie, J., & Timperley, H. (2007). The power of feedback. *Review of Educational Research*, 77, 81–112.

Johnston, M., & Thomas, M. (2005). Riding the wave of administrator accountability: A portfolio approach. *Journal of Educational Administration*, 43(4), 368–386.

Joyce, P. (2005). A framework for portfolio development in postgraduate nursing practice. *Journal of Clinical Nursing*, 14, 456–463.

Kicken, W., Brand-Gruwel, S., van Merriënboer, J., & Slot, W. (2008). Design and evaluation of a development portfolio: How to improve students' self-directed learning skills. *Instructional Science*, 37, 453–473.

Kluger, A. N., & DeNisi, A. (1996). The effects of feedback interventions on performance: A historical review, a meta-analysis, and a preliminary feedback intervention theory. *Psychological Bulletin*, 119(2), 254–284.

Knowles, M. (1975). *Self-Directed Learning: A Guide for Learners and Teachers*. Chicago: Follet.

Kolb, D. A. (1984). *Experiential Learning*. Chicago: Prentice Hall.

Little, P., & Hayes, S. (2003). Continuing professional development (CPD): GPs' perceptions of post-graduate education-approved (PGEA) meetings and personal professional development plans (PDPs). *Family Practice*, 20(2), 192–198.

Livingstone, D. W. (2001). *Adults' Informal Learning: Definitions, Findings, Gaps and Future Research*. Toronto: Centre for the Study of Education and Work, OISE/UT.

London, M. (1997). *Job Feedback: Giving, Seeking, and Using Feedback for Performance Improvement*. Mahwah, NJ: Erlbaum.

London, M., Larsen, H. H., & Thisted, L. N. (1999). Relationships between feedback and self-development. *Group & Organizational Management*, 24, 5–27.

London, M., & Smither, J. W. (1999). Empowered self-development and continuous learning. *Human Resource Management*, 38, 3–15.

Lyons, N., & Evans, L. (1997). Portfolio: A tool for self-directed learning at work. Paper presented at the Self-directed Learning: Past and Future Symposium, Montreal, September 1997.

Marsick, V. J., & Watkins, K. E. (2001). Informal and incidental learning. *New Directions for Adult and Continuing Education*, 89, 25–34. doi:10.1002/ace.5.

Marsick, V. J., & Watkins, K. E. (2003). Demonstrating the value of an organization's learning culture: The dimensions of the learning organization questionnaire. *Advances in Developing Human Resources*, 5(2), 132–151. doi:10.1177/1523422303251341.

Mathers, N. J., Challis, M. C., Howe, A. C., & Field, N. J. (1999). Portfolios in continuing medical education: Effective and efficient? *Medical Education*, 33, 521–530.

McDowall, A., & Fletcher, C. (2004). Employee development: An organizational justice perspective. *Personnel Review*, 33, 8–29.

McMullan, M., Endacott, R., Gray, M. A., Jasper, M., Miller, C. M. L., Scholes, J., & Webb, C. (2003). Portfolios and assessment of competence: A review of the literature. *Journal of Advanced Nursing*, 41, 283–294.

Moore, Z., & Bond, N. (2002). The use of portfolios for in-service teacher assessment: A case study of foreign language middle-school teachers in Texas. *Foreign Language Annals*, 35(1), 85–92.

Noe, R. A. (1988). An investigation of the determinants of successful assigned mentoring relationships. *Personnel Psychology*, 41, 457–479.

Noe, R. A. (1996). Is career management related to employee development and performance? *Journal of Organizational Behavior*, 17, 119–133.

Orland-Barak, L. (2005). Portfolios as evidence of reflective practice: What remains "untold." *Educational Research*, 47(1), 25–44.

Pearson, D. J., & Heywood, P. (2004). Portfolio use in general practice vocational training: A survey of GP registrars. *Medical Education*, 38, 87–95.

Pham, N. T. P., Segers, M. S. R., & Gijselaers, W. H. (2013). Effects of work environment on transfer of training: Empirical evidence from master of business administration programs in Vietnam. *International Journal of Training & Development*, 17, 1–19.

Pitts, J., Curtis, A., While, R., & Holloway, I. (1999). Practice professional development plans: General practitioners' perspectives on proposed changes in general practice education. *British Journal of General Practice*, 49, 959–962.

Roberts, G. E. (2003). Employee performance appraisal system participation: A technique that works. *Public Personnel Management*, 32, 89–98.

Rouse, M. (2004). Continuing professional development in pharmacy. *American Journal of Health-Systems Pharmacy*, 61, 2069–2076.

Saru, E. (2007). Organisational learning and HRD: How appropriate are they for small firms? *Journal of European Industrial Training*, 31(1), 36–51.

Schön, D. A. (1987). *Educating the Reflective Practitioner*. San Francisco: Oxford.

Seng, S. H., & Seng, T. O. (1996). Reflective teaching and the portfolio approach in early childhood staff development. Paper presented at the Joint Conference of the Educational Research Association of Singapore and the Australian Association for Research in Education, Singapore, November 25–29.

Smith, K., & Tillema, H. (1998). Evaluating portfolio use as a learning tool for professionals. *Scandinavian Journal of Educational Research*, 42, 193–205.

Smith, K., & Tillema, H. (2001). Long-term influences of portfolios on professional development. *Scandinavian Journal of Educational Research*, 45, 183–202.

Smith, K., & Tillema, H. (2003). Clarifying different types of portfolio use. *Assessment & Evaluation in Higher Education*, 28, 625–648.

Snadden, D., & Thomas, M. L. (1998). Portfolio learning in general practice vocational training: Does it work? *Medical Education*, 32, 401–406.

Snyder, J., Pippincott, A., & Bower, D. (1998). The inherent tensions in the multiple use of portfolios in teacher education. *Teacher Education Quarterly*, 25(1), 45–60.

Tigelaar, D. E. H., Dolmans, D. H. J. M., De Grave, W. S., Wolfhagen, I. H. A. P., & Van der Vleuten, C. P. M. (2006). Portfolio as a tool to stimulate teachers' reflections. *Medical Teacher*, 28, 277–282.

Tigelaar, D. E. H., Dolmans, D. H. J. M., Wolfhagen, I. H. A. P., & van der Vleuten, C. P. M. (2004). Using a conceptual framework and the opinions of portfolio experts to develop a teaching portfolio prototype. *Studies in Educational Evaluation*, 30, 305–321.

Tillema, H. H. (2001). Portfolios as developmental assessment tools. *International Journal of Training & Development*, 5(2), 126–135.

Tillema, H. H., & Smith, K. (2000). Learning from portfolios: Differential use of feedback in portfolio construction. *Studies in Educational Evaluation*, 26, 193–210.

Tynjälä, P. (2012). Toward a 3-P model of workplace learning: A literature review. *Vocations and Learning*, 6(1), 11–36. doi:10.1007/s12186-012-9091-z.

Van der Heijden, B. I. J. M., Boon, J., Van der Klink, M., & Meijs, E. (2009). Employability enhancement through formal and informal learning: An empirical study among Dutch non-academic university staff members. *International Journal of Training & Development*, 13(1), 19–37. doi:10.1111/j.1468-2419.2008.00313.x.

Van der Vleuten, C. P. M., Schuwirth, L. W., Driessen, E. W., Dijkstra, J., Tigelaar, D., Baartman, L. K., & van Tartwijk, J. (2012). A model for programmatic assessment fit for purpose. *Medical teacher*, 34, 205–214.

Van de Wiel, M. W. J., Szegedi, K. H. P., & Weggeman, M. C. D. P. (2004). Professional learning: Deliberate attempts at developing expertise. In H. P. A. Boshuizen, R. Bromme, & H. Gruber (Eds.), *Professional Learning: Gaps and Transitions on the Way from Novice to Expert* (pp. 181–206). Dordrecht: Kluwer.

VandeWalle , D. (1997), Development and validation of a work domain goal orientation instrument. *Educational and Psychological Measurement*, 8, 995–1015.

Wasylyshyn, K. M. (2003). Executive coaching: An outcome study. *Consulting Psychology Journal: Practice and Research*, 55, 94–106.

19

Leadership Development and Organizational Success

Thomas Garavan, Fergal O'Brien, and Sandra Watson

Introduction

Human resources and in particular leadership resources have been identified as critical to the success to organizations (Mabey, 2013; O'Connell, 2013; Nyberg et al., 2013). Given the importance of leadership skills and behaviors, organizations have made considerable investment in a variety of leadership development practices. These practices are implemented to promote, encourage, and assist in the development of skills, knowledge, and self-awareness to optimize an individual's leadership potential and performance (Garavan, Hogan, & Cahir-O'Donnell, 2009; Martineau, Hoole, & Patterson, 2006). Investment in leadership development is assumed to contribute to organizational performance; however there are many theoretical and empirical questions concerning its effectiveness and numerous researchers have highlighted that little is known about its outcomes and the processes in leadership development that contribute to organizational outcomes (Lockwood, 2006; Brungardt, 1997; Storey, 2011). O'Connell (2013) argues that leadership development lacks a clear definition, its theoretical base is weak and there is relatively little agreement about the key constructs involved. This contrasts with the perspective of leadership development practitioners who argue that it makes business sense as an investment in a key talent group (Conference Board, 2006) and many organizations also believe that it is a valuable activity to invest in given the major growth in the leadership development industry.

The level of expenditure by organizations on leadership development has grown considerably since 2000. Organizations are advised to invest almost half of their training and development budget in leadership development and to spend almost one-third of that budget on the development of first-line leaders (Economist Intelligence Unit, 2011; Corporate Executive Board, 2013). In a review of leadership development Day (2000) observed that "interest in leadership development appears to be at its zenith," however, in the intervening years the level of investment in leadership development has continued

The Wiley Blackwell Handbook of the Psychology of Training, Development, and Performance Improvement,
First Edition. Edited by Kurt Kraiger, Jonathan Passmore, Sigmar Malvezzi, and Nuno Rebelo dos Santos.
© 2015 John Wiley & Sons Ltd. Published 2020 by John Wiley & Sons Ltd.

to grow. A 2003–2004 Leadership Forecast produced by Development Dimensions International noted increased levels of expenditure on leadership development and predicted that spending levels would continue to rise. Lockwood (2006) reported that investment in leadership development had continued to trend upwards to more than $50 billion annually. Bersin (2013) found that annual investment in first-line leader development had grown from $533 in 2009 to $1,761 per supervisor in 2012. Investment in middle- and senior-level leadership development has also grown but not as much as first-line level. In the United States approximately 90 percent of US-based Global 100 firms invested in leadership development (Avolio, Avey, & Quisenberry, 2010) and in the UK 86 percent of organizations invest in leadership development (Jackson & Parry, 2008).

Given the perception that investment in leadership development is a good thing for organizations combined with the need for organizations to be competitive, there is an important gap in our understanding as to whether investment in leadership development impacts organizational outcomes such as performance and financial success. A number of authors have engaged with the task of developing a methodology to assess the financial impact of leadership development (Cascio & Boudreau, 2008; Avolio, Avey, & Quisenberry, 2010) however, leadership development remains one of the least-explored topics within the field of leadership research and theory (Day, Harrison, & Halpin, 2008). Avolio and Luthans (2006) in a review of the literature produced only 201 articles on studies that investigated the impact of leadership development interventions and less than half of these focused on leadership development and organizational performance. The apparent growth in the leadership development industry worldwide should not be taken as a signal that leadership development impacts the business bottom line. It is therefore important for leadership development practitioners and scholars to understand what types of leadership development practices are effective and to develop a strong understanding of the organizational outcomes resulting from investment in leadership development.

To begin the process of answering these two important questions we firstly explore what is understood by leadership development and the different types of leadership development practices found in organizations. The chapter then considers the state of the leadership development–organizational outcomes literature and reviews the studies that have investigated the organizational outcomes of leadership development practices. We categorize leadership development practices into formal leadership development programs, experience-based leadership development programs, and relationship-based leadership development programs and review the organizational outcomes for each of these different sets of practices. The chapter concludes by summarizing an agenda for future research on leadership development and organizational outcomes.

Defining the Scope, Purposes, and Activities of Leadership Development

Leadership development is a widely used term; however it is often understood as a program-based activity (Garavan, Hogan, & Cahir-O'Donnell, 2009; Galli & Muller-Stewens, 2012). The Society of Human Resource Management define leadership development as "Formal and informal training and professional development programs designed for all management and executive level employees to assist them in developing leadership skills and styles required to deal with a variety of situations" (SHRM, 2010, p. 66). Lamoureux (2008) emphasized that leadership development focuses on strategic development of the skills, knowledge, and behaviors of leaders. In a seminal contribution Day (2000) made an important distinction between individual leader development and leadership development.

Individual leader development focuses on the capacity of a leader to participate effectively in leading-following processes. This form of leadership development is premised on the idea that by developing an individual's knowledge, skill, and attitudes more effective leadership will result (Day, 2000; Garavan, Hogan, & Cahir-O'Donnell, 2009). Individual leader development gives primacy to the individual and as a result it ignores the essentially complex, contextual, and interactive nature of the leadership process (DeRue, Sitkin, & Podolny, 2011; Mabey, 2013). Day's second conceptualization, leadership development, emphasizes the development of collective leadership capabilities and the centrality of interpersonal relationships and mutual commitments. The literature on leadership development is strongly biased towards individual leader rather than leadership development. Day (2011) in his attempts to advance leadership development acknowledged that the majority of empirical studies focus upon individual and social psychological variables at the expense of interpersonal relationships and collective processes of leadership. DeRue, Sitkin, and Podolny (2011) have also acknowledged the narrow focus of the leadership development literature on leader development. They concluded that it is necessary to focus on both leader and leadership development in order to achieve a deeper understanding of the processes through which effective leaders are developed. DeRue, Sitkin, and Podolny (2011, p. 67) therefore proposed a definition of leadership development that focuses on preparing "individuals and collectives to engage effectively in leading-following interactions." This definition emphasizes that leader and leadership development are interdependent given that many leadership development interventions inevitably enhance both dimensions.

There are a number of theoretical perspectives that highlight the purposes of leadership development. Adult development theory, for example, indicates that the purpose of leadership development is to enhance a leader's self-awareness, metacognition, and self-motivation and capacity to self-regulate behavior (Chan, Hannah, & Gardner, 2005). Social constructionist perspectives identify the purposes of leadership development as concerned with developing the capacity of a leader to work effectively in a variety of social and situational contexts due to the context-dependent nature of the leadership task in organizations (Porter & McLoughlin, 2006) This challenge requires that leaders develop skills to learn from shared experiences and perform effectively a range of collective tasks such as setting strategic direction, creating strategies and operational alignment, and building commitment towards particular courses of action (Day & Harrison, 2007). Connective values paradigms emphasize the need for leadership development to enhance the skills of leaders to work in different cultural contexts, to adopt multiple perspectives, to develop a multicultural perspective, and to understand the complexity of the global business environment (Engel, 2012; Walumbwa, Lawler, & Avolio, 2007). Leadership development interventions will therefore emphasize the skills to collaborate, to develop social networks, and to coach effectively (Fowler, 2006; Fairholm, 1995). These multiple perspectives on the purposes of leadership suggest that it is a complex activity that is difficult to defend and place boundaries on for the purposes of researching its impact on organizational outcomes.

There is an absence of typologies or frameworks that conceptualize the activities included in leadership development. One such conceptualization is provided by Garavan, Hogan, and Cahir-O'Donnell (2009). They proposed that leadership development interventions can be categorized as: formal development interventions, job-based development interventions, relationship-based interventions, and informal leadership interventions. This categorization is useful as it helps to organize the literatures for the purposes of this chapter. However, the literature on informal leadership is sparse and therefore is not considered in this chapter. The majority of studies focus on formal leadership development interventions, however, studies report outcomes for studies that use a blend of interventions (Conference Board, 2006). Relationship-based interventions in the leadership development context such as coaching and mentoring represent a more recent addition to the literature, however, outcome studies are relatively scarce (DeRue & Ashford, 2010). Experience-based leadership development interventions have grown in popularity with the emergence of international and expatriate job assignments designed to develop global leadership capacities. There are few studies on the outcomes of experience-based leadership development interventions (Ellis et al., 2010). A number of authors make a distinction between individual and collective leadership interventions (Galli & Muller-Stewens, 2012). Individual-focused interventions include multisource feedback, coaching, and mentoring whereas collective practices include action learning, networks, and off-site cross-functional team development activities.

A central premise of the literature on leadership development is the notion that leadership can be learned and developed and it is not just related to the innate qualities of individuals (O'Connell, 2013). Therefore, all individuals have the potential to be leaders provided they receive the necessary development. While there is support for the notion that leaders can be developed there is less agreement about how leadership development should be realized and whether leadership development enhances organizational outcomes. This represents the "elephant in the room" when leadership development specialists go to the top team to secure investment in leadership development activities. The potential of leadership development to impact organizational success is assumed in much of the functionalist discourse (Day, Gronn, & Salas, 2004; Mabey, 2013) however, it is far from proven.

The task of demonstrating that leadership development impacts organizational performance is complicated by a number of important factors. First, leadership development is conducted at multiple levels in organizations with diverse sets of participants ranging from first-line supervisors to executives (Buckingham, 2012). The aims, objectives, and development interventions uses at these different levels will vary as will the anticipated organizational outcomes (Lykins & Pace, 2013). Second, leadership development takes place in a variety of settings including the classroom (Lumpkin & Dess, 2001), the workplace (Mabey, 2002), and through relationships outside of work (Muller-Stewens & Knoll, 2005) thus complicating our understanding of which leadership development practices contribute most to organizational outcomes (Bowman & Helfat, 2001; Martin & Eisenhardt, 2001). Third, leadership development takes place in a diverse set of organizational contexts including multinational companies (MNCs), small-to-medium enterprises (SMEs), not-for-profit organizations, and the public sector (Conference Board, 2006). These different types of organizations make the process of understanding outcomes complex therefore it is not surprising that the academic outcome literature on leadership development is sparse and contradictory.

Theoretical and Methodological Observations on the Leadership Development Outcomes Literature

The firm is the appropriate level of analysis from which to investigate the casual links between leadership development practices and organizational outcomes (Batt & Hermans, 2012). To understand this relationship a number of assumptions need to be made; first it is assumed that top management have considerable discretion in planning how to formulate and execute business strategies, second it is assumed that the policy and strategy formulating process is a rational one and there is a strong link between business strategy and leadership practices. The majority of research in the human resource management (HRM) field considers the firm to be a closed system and there is little consideration of how the external and institutional environment of a firm impinges upon or constrains the level of discretion that managers have in the area of strategy formulation (Gerhart, 2007). Researchers have two choices when investigating the relationship between investment in leadership practices and organizational outcomes; they can focus on the unit or firm-level analysis to understand how leadership development practices impact business outcomes or they can focus on individual-level analysis and identify how leadership development practices impact the behaviors of leaders and employees in an organization. These individual-level outcomes can be aggregated to the unit-level to understand how they affect organizational outcome. This would suggest that individual-level outcomes serve as a mediator of the relationship between investment in leadership development practices and outcomes. However, it is becoming increasingly apparent that to fully understand the impact of leadership development on organizational outcomes it is necessary to utilize a multilevel perspective.

Unfortunately these particular debates are not effectively explored in the leadership development literatures. Efforts to explain the link between leadership development and organizational outcomes are disappointing from theoretical, empirical, and methodological perspectives. The literature on leadership development and organizational outcomes is fragmented and contradictory, and many questions remain unanswered concerning whether leadership development is a valuable investment for organizations to make. This perspective on leadership development takes the view that its primary goal is to enhance stakeholder value. The following section considers the theoretical models used to explain the relationship between leadership development and organizational performance outcomes, the causal models found in the literature, and the methodological problems with existing studies.

Theoretical models explaining the relationship between leadership development and organizational outcomes

The literature on leadership development and strategic HRM identifies a number of theoretical rationales to explain the relationship between investment in leadership development and organizational outcomes. A significant number of studies focus on individual-level outcomes and do not explore how this level of outcomes results in organizational-level outcomes. Therefore while studies seek to demonstrate that leadership development enhances organizational-level outcomes there are significant gaps in terms of theoretical models and models (Avolio, Avey, & Quisenberry, 2010). Consistent with arguments from the strategic HRM literature leadership development practices influence both the leadership human capital pool and the behaviors of leaders (Collins & Holton, 2004).

Four theoretical models are useful in understanding leadership development organizational outcome relationships. Human-capital theory characterizes leaders as "human resources." It is assumed that investments in leadership development will result in a payoff to the organization provided there is a focus on developing firm specific leadership skills. A drawback of this theory is that skilled and well-developed leaders are only of value to the firm provided they are motivated. The resource-based view of the firm argues that an organization's resources are a source of competitive advantage where they possess characteristics that add value to an organization. Therefore where leadership resources are unique, imperfectly imitable, and not substitutable with other resources by competitors they confer competitive advantage. It follows that leadership development is an investment in the human capital of the organization's leadership pool that develops knowledge, behaviors, and abilities. This investment adds value to the organization and enables it to perform activities that enable the achievement of organizational goals resulting in positive organizational outcomes (von Krogh, Nonaka, & Rechsteiner, 2012; Kor & Mesko, 2013)

Behavioral theories focus on the behavior of leaders and argue that the role behavior of the leader will serve as a mediator between the strategy of a firm and organizational performance (Huselid, Jackson, & Schuler, 1997). Following this logic leadership development practices should develop in leaders' behaviors that are necessary to achieve organizational goals. Therefore leadership development should focus on developing the appropriate behaviors that are important to the achievement of strategy (Gentry et al., 2008; Klimoski & Amos, 2012). However, a challenge in this context concerns the amount of time taken to develop these behaviors. Leadership behaviors are incrementally rather than transformationally developed (Dugan et al., 2011) and the evidence suffers that some leadership development practices do not develop these behaviors effectively (Dugan et al., 2011). Another challenge concerns the issue of aligning leadership development practices to develop the behaviors necessary to support the vision, values, and goals of the organization (McCauley, 2008). A major gap in the literature concerns the lack of strong theoretical arguments and empirical research on the mechanisms through which leadership development supports organizational goals and strategies and how strong alignment impacts organizational performance outcomes (Gentry & Leslie, 2007).

Another theoretical perspective, cybernetic theory, postulates that leadership development can be viewed from an input-throughput-output perspective. The inputs in this context consist of the knowledge, skills, and abilities of leaders, the throughput consists of the behaviors of leaders, and the outputs consist of productivity and performance outcomes (Barling, Weber, & Kelloway, 1996). A number of scholars have specified the behavioral outcomes. Mumford, Campion, and Morgeson (2007) developed a leadership skills strataplex that identified four categories of leadership skills requirements: cognitive skills, interpersonal skills, business skills, and strategic skills (Table 19.1). They found that different categories of skill requirements were important at different organizational levels so, for example, cognitive skills were required at all hierarchical levels whereas strategic skills were important at strategic levels in an organization. Dvir et al. (2002), for example, demonstrated that transformational leadership development enhanced a leader's display of transformational leadership behaviors. This in turn impacted the performance of followers. Therefore, consistent with the propositions of cybernetic theory investment in leadership development leads to organizational performance outcomes to the extent that it contributes to the development

Table 19.1 Examples of leadership skills. Adapted from Mumford et al., (2007).

Cognitive skills	*Interpersonal skills*	*Business skills*	*Strategic skills*
Basic cognitive abilities	Negotiating	Planning	Strategic agility
General cognitive abilities	Influencing	Coordinating	Systems thinking
	Conflict management	Resource allocation	Coping with cognitive complexity
Problem solving	Communication skills	Functional expertise	
Information gathering	Empathy	Technical knowledge	Strategic decision making
Investigation skills	Listening	Controlling	
Retrieval skills	Teamworking	Decision making	Managing change
Sensing	Interpersonal understanding		Boundary spanning
	Collaborating		Buffering
	Emotional management		Visioning
	Political skills		Decoupling
	Networking		

of competencies that enable leaders to demonstrate or display the behaviors necessary to achieve desired performance outcomes.

A significant theoretical gap concerns the lack of consideration of the external context in which organizations operate. The majority of leadership development–organizational outcomes research views the organization as a closed system. Many studies start from the assumption that organizations have significant discretion concerning their strategic goals and how they achieve alignment. Batt and Hermans (2012) make a similar observation about the wider HRM-organizational performance literature. Overall, the leadership development–organizational outcomes literature makes two fundamental assertions; first that an organization's leadership talent represent critical strategic human resources and leadership development practices are vital to develop the strategic capability of that pool of leadership talent.

Demonstrating the causal link between leadership development and organizational performance

A variety of approaches are used to connect investment in leadership development to organizational outcomes. One particular approach is to propose direct effects between leadership development and organizational outcomes. However, it is clear that leadership development is only modestly to weakly related to organizational outcomes. Mabey and Ramirez (2005) found evidence of a clear link between leadership development and organizational performance. This impact took the form of outcomes such as employee engagement, product and service quality, increased customer satisfaction, and productivity gains. Two important meta-analysis studies by Burke and Day (1986) and Collins and Holton (2004) examined the overall effectiveness of leadership development and the relative effectiveness of different development practices and found that it makes a positive difference to organizational effectiveness. Both meta-analyses found that studies tended to report fewer instances of system- or organization-level outcomes and more evidence of knowledge outcomes than behavioral outcomes. The methodologies differed significantly, however, which may explain the findings. Burke and Day (1986) included studies that utilized a control/comparison group design whereas Collins and Holton (2004) included studies that utilized a before and after examination of a single training group. Avolio et al. (2009) reviewed 200 studies that manipulated leadership development as an independent variable through training and development. They found that the outcomes of leadership development practices fell between 0.28 and 1.08. Avolio (2010) examined studies that studied developmental experiences and their impact on leadership effectiveness. He found that the average return on investment (ROI) was 44–72 percent for a 1.5-day intervention and 50–87 percent for a three-day intervention. However this outcome depended on the level of the participant and the location of the intervention.

Studies that investigate the direct effects of leadership development can be criticized on a number of fronts. First of all, what is the most appropriate blend of leadership practices to achieve organizational outcomes? Will single leadership practices, for example, be effective? Second, what measures of performance should be used? Existing studies rarely use financial measures and instead focus on broader human resource outcomes such as employee satisfaction, commitment to the organization, and discretionary effort. Third, there are problems around the methodologies that are used to measure direct effects and the lack of objective or company archival data.

An alternative direct model suggests that leadership development will have a direct effect on organizational outcomes but there are important antecedent variables (Hallinger, 2008; Muijs, 2011). This model highlights the importance of antecedent variables such as HRM strategy fit, the role of senior management support for leadership development, the nature of an organization's strategy, and the capital intensity of the firm (Newkirk-Moore & Bracker, 1998; Khatri, 2000). These studies are consistent with a contingent perspective where contextual factors influence or moderate the relationship between investment in leadership development and organizational performance. Other studies have argued for the importance of individual antecedents such as motivation to learn, developmental engagement, and developmental triggers (Avolio, 2005; DeRue & Myers, 2011). However, the current research reports few studies that explore these individual antecedent conditions and their relevance to explaining leadership development outcomes. The configurational approach suggests that issues of fit or alignment are important antecedent variables in explaining leadership development outcomes. The configurational approach emphasizes the role of other HRM practices, learning culture, organizational learning orientation, and strategy alignment (Tharenou, Saks, & Moore, 2007; Faems et al., 2005). The literature provides little in terms of how leadership development practices can be aligned with various organizational characteristics and what value this alignment or fit may have for the organizational outcomes of leadership development.

A third approach to studying leadership development is through its indirect impact on organizational outcomes. This mediation approach is relatively new in the leadership development literature. Consistent with this approach leadership development may create a learning culture or climate that leads to organizational outcomes. Therefore this suggests that effective leaders will exert an influence on the motivation of human resources and the receptiveness of the organization to be innovative (Jiang, Waller, & Cai, 2013). Indirect models are advocated as a way of understanding the "black box" issue in the wider HRM-performance research. However, in the context of leadership development there is an absence of mediation studies and the range of potential mediators is vast. It could include but is not limited to issues such as organization culture, knowledge-management processes, technology processes, and leadership turnover. It should be acknowledged that different mediators will apply depending on the level of analysis being undertaken. Therefore at the individual level mediators of relevance include employee human capital, the opportunities of leaders to perform whereas at the organizational level issues like knowledge-sharing activities, involvement in decision making and the extent of teamwork will have relevance in explaining outcomes. Redman and Wilkinson (2008) have argued that a focus on mediators is complex and difficult where the environment is complex and multiple contingencies cannot be isolated. Furthermore different mediators may be relevant when investigating different leadership development practices and different organizational outcome measures. Hallinger (2008) suggests that there may be support for a reciprocal effects model where leadership development does not simply influence the learning culture and climate leading to organizational outcomes but is also influenced and shaped by the environment in which the leadership development is conducted. However, there are few studies that utilize a reciprocal mediated model to investigate the impact of leadership development outcomes. The predominant focus is on direct models or direct models with antecedents.

Methodological limitations of existing studies

Studies investigating the influence of leadership development on organizational outcomes have a number of methodological limitations in terms of research design, sample size, and the measurement of both leadership development and organizational outcome variables. Simkins (2012) argues that there are significant issues and challenges in measuring the outcomes of leadership development due to concerns about the levels at which to investigate outcomes, the robustness of research designs, and the usefulness of the findings. Studies use a multiplicity of measures however subjective or self-report measures are more common than objective measures. Hayward and Voller (2010) point out that there are pragmatic reasons for the reliance on subjective measures including ease of access, the existence of objective measures that are based on existing assessment processes within the organization but which are not relevant to the issue under investigation, and the difficulties involved in developing measures that are appropriate to identify the organizational impact of leadership development.

The reliance on self-report measures in existing studies is particularity pronounced (Reilly, Smither, & Vasilopoulos, 1996; Seifert, Yukl, & McDonald, 2003; Hayes, 2007). The most common form of research design is a survey of organizational members. These instruments and scales include the supervisory behavior description questionnaire (Tharenou & Lydon, 1990), the multifactor leadership questionnaire (MLQ; Barling, Weber, & Kelloway, 1996), the use of multisource feedback questionnaires (Tyson & Ward, 2004; Parry & Sinha, 2005; Seifert, Yukl, & McDonald, 2003), and leadership competence questionnaires (Dai, De Meuse, & Peterson, 2010). Studies that make use of qualitative methodologies are the exception. Examples include structured interviews (Dexter & Prince, 2007; Parker-Wilkins, 2006), critical incident technique (McGurk, 2009; Watkins, Lysã, & Demarrais, 2011), and grounded analysis of reflective journals (Brown, McCracken, & O'Kane, 2011). These various self-report methods while useful have major limitations when used as the sole means of gathering data on the impact of leadership development. Objective methods where they are used include changes in positions due to promotions (Coloma, 2012; Levenson, Van Der Stede, & Cohen, 2006), the number of personal loans sold (Barling, Weber, & Kelloway, 1996), and enhanced productivity (Olivero, Bane, & Kopelman, 1997). There is also a strong reliance on post hoc measures and few studies are longitudinal. Post hoc questionnaires and interviews are subject to attributional biases such as the attribution of positive outcomes to self and negative outcomes to external factors. Interview methodologies are also subject to self-presentation bias and interviewer expectancy bias where study participants will provide answers that they expect the interviewer wishes to hear. Survey questionnaires are almost invariably cross-sectional in nature and do not allow causality to be established. A small number of studies utilize data from several sources in order to address issues of attributional bias (Tharenou & Lydon, 1990; Walker & Smither, 1999). Studies that utilize pre- and post-measures are relatively uncommon (Bailey & Fletcher, 2002; Seifert, Yukl, & McDonald, 2003; Ciporen, 2010). The use of cross-sectional designs is particularly problematic in the context of demonstrating that leadership development leads to organizational outcomes. Researchers continuously call for the use of longitudinal designs, however, few studies have done so (Batt & Colvin, 2011).

The sample sizes tend to be small (Mean $N = 340$, Median $N = 109$, Range $= 3,434$). This combined with low response rates makes the task of generalizability problematic. The average response rate for the studies that included some form of survey presented in Tables 19.2–19.4 was 62 percent (Median $= 60$ percent) and ranges from a low of 37 percent to 96 percent. A particularly noticeable feature of the studies presented in Tables 19.2–19.4 concerns the inconsistency, across studies of the leadership development measures used. These measures sometimes relate to the amount of leadership development, the nature of the leadership practice or intervention, the mode of learning whether direct or vicarious, the formality of the intervention, the content of the intervention, and the methods of development used. This lack of precision makes it difficult to understand what dimensions of leadership development are related to organizational performance. There is little in the way of guidance concerning the best measures of leadership development and how they may be theoretically linked to organizational performance outcomes. There are additional problems when it comes to measures of organizational-level outcomes. The focus on using subjective measures of organizational outcomes is commonplace in the leadership development literature. These measures are subject to significant inaccuracy and may inflate the effect sizes.

These various limitations make it difficult to make decisive and strong statements about the impact of investment in leadership development on organizational performance. To more fully understand this relationship there is a clear need for longitudinal research designs, greater use of quasi-experimental designs, and more precise definitions of leadership development measures. Where researchers use qualitative methods they also need to utilize longitudinal designs and place more focus on understanding leadership development processes. The bias in existing studies towards studies conducted in the US is pronounced. There is too much reliance on US studies where the cultural context is different and as a result the findings may not apply across countries. Studies conducted in an Asian context are rare and in this context cultural differences may be particularity relevant. There is a tendency to move from research finding to prescription, however, this is dangerous particularly given the biases in current research and where the research base is from a particular country context.

Leadership Development Practices and Organizational Outcomes

Leadership development is not a unitary category or a single leadership development practice. It consists of a multiplicity of practices (Dragoni et al., 2009; Day, Gronn, & Salas, 2004). These practices can be defined as formal leadership development practices such as: classroom-based programs, multisource feedback, and action learning; experience-based development experiences (McCauley et al., 1994) such as job transitions, task-related assignments, managing large projects with both scope and scale, and hardship assignments; and developmental relationship interventions such as mentoring, coaching, and peer mentoring. Studies have investigated these leadership development interventions and their impact on organizational outcomes. Organizational outcomes can be conceptualized in different ways (Tharenou, Saks, & Moore, 2007; Mumford, Campion, & Morgeson, 2007). These outcomes include human resource outcomes such as job satisfaction, motivation, organizational commitment, enhanced human capital, and competencies and retention of employees; organizational performance outcomes such as productivity gains, sales, customer service, and qualification levels; and financial outcomes such as profit/profitability, return on equity, assets and investment, and general financial measures.

Formal leadership development practices and organizational outcomes

The majority of studies have investigated the impact of formal leadership development programs (Table 19.2). However these studies focus on leader rather than leadership development. Formal leadership development programs allow individuals to spend time away from the workplace, to engage in active learning, and reflect on lessons for future leadership behavior (Fulmer, 1997; Belling, James, & Ladkin, 2004). Two meta-analyses (Burke & Day, 1986; Collins & Holton, 2004) found that formal leadership development programs impacted human resource outcomes such as enhanced knowledge and to a lesser extent behavior changes. However, the lack of impact on performance outcomes may be due to transfer barriers such as the lack of managerial support, time constraints, and the lack of opportunities to apply new skills (Belling, James, & Ladkin, 2004; McAlearney,

Table 19.2 Leadership development and organizational success: formal leadership development programs (multisource feedback, formal classroom-based programs, action learning) selected papers.

Study	N	Respondent type	Response rate (N/A where 100% or not known)	Theoretical perspective	Description of leadership development intervention	Method	Type of study	Level of analysis	Scale(s) used	HR outcomes (e.g., low absenteeism and turnover, high motivation, high job performance)	Performance outcomes (e.g., skill, productivity gains, output increases, quality, customer service)	Financial outcomes (e.g., profit, return on invested capital [ROI], return on assets [ROA])
Formal [Action learning, formal course or multisource feedback] [conceptual and skill based, personal growth, feedback-based, action learning or management and leadership education programs]												
Mathieu & Leonard (1987) US	65	Bank managers South-east US	N/A	Human-capital theory	Formal classroom-based intervention	Utility analysis Performance scale = 2 items for each of 9 performance dimensions	Quasi-experimental	Individual	Performance measure (Mathieu & Leonard, 1987)		.16 training effect on individual performance	
Tharenou & Lydon (1990) Australia	100	First-line male supervisors of a state government railway department	N/A	Human-capital theory	22 week formal residential program – lectures, case studies, and role play	[subordinates] 20-item, 5-point SBDQ (supervisor behavior description questionnaire) 4 weeks prior, repeated 2 months after. [leaders] 28-item, 5-point LOQ (leadership opinion questionnaire) 4 weeks prior and 2 months after	Experimental (pre-test, post-test, and control)	Individual	Supervisor behavior description questionnaire (SBDQ; Cook et al., 1981). Leadership opinion questionnaire (LOQ; Cook et al., 1981),		Improvement of 10.08 average for supervisor	

Study	N	Sample	Response rate	Theory	Intervention	Measure	Design	Level	Instrument	Results
Lawrence & Wiswell (1993) US	65	Managers in state agencies	N/A	Human-capital theory	Workshop on feedback skills	26-item SYMLOG leadership values instrument	Experimental field study	Individual and team	The systematic multiple level observation of groups (SYMLOG) (Bales, Cohen, & Williamson, 1979)	Dominance: +1.5 Friendliness: +1.4
Barling, Weber, & Kelloway (1996) Canada	N/A	Bank managers Canada		Human-capital theory; Resource-based theory	Transformational leadership workshop: 1-day introductory classroom-based and 4 booster sessions through group exercises	Subordinates completed MLQ (multifactor leadership questionnaire) and organizational commitment questionnaire. To assess financial performance: number of personal loan sales, as well as the number of credit card sales	Experimental (pre-test, post-test, and control)	Individual	Multifactor leadership questionnaire (MLQ) – Form 5 (Bass & Avolio, 1990) Organizational commitment questionnaire (Mowday, Porter, & Steers, 1982)	Attitudinal variables average +.33 for experimental group and -.05 for control (e.g. intellectual stimulation, charisma)	Personal loan sales = .33 change more effective than control Credit card sales = .25 more effective than control
Reilly, Smither, & Vasipopolous (1996) US	92	Managers worldwide	39%	Human-capital theory; Control theory	Personalized feedback given to managers – interpretive guidelines, comparison between performance categories, summary of strengths, etc.	33-item, 5-point Likert scale	Longitudinal	Individual	Behavioral statements reflecting boss/subordinate relationships (Smither et al., 1995)	Behavioral statements reflecting boss/subordinate relationships (Smither et al., 1995).

(Continued)

Table 19.2 (*Continued*)

Study	N	Respondent type	Response rate (N/A where 100% or not known)	Theoretical perspective	Description of leadership development intervention	Method	Type of study	Level of analysis	Scale(s) used	HR outcomes (e.g., low absenteeism and turnover, high motivation, high job performance)	Performance outcomes (e.g., skill, productivity gains, output increases, quality, customer service)	Financial outcomes (e.g., profit, return on invested capital [ROI], return on assets [ROA])
Rosti & Shipper (1998) US	53	Middle managers in private companies US	88%	Human-capital theory	360-degree feedback based on task cycle model of managerial behavior	Survey of management practices = measure managerial skills (e.g., organizational expertise, functional expertise) 5–6 items per scale, 7-point Likert scale	Experimental (pre-test, post-test, and control)	Individual	The survey of management practices – Form K (Wilson & Wilson, 1991)	Managerial skills improvement Providing feedback	Clarification of goals and objectives Orderly work planning Work facilitating Methods management	
Walker & Smither (1999) US	252	Managers in large companies US	N/A	Human-capital theory	Formal upward feedback program	Multisource feedback	Longitudinal	Individual	Behavioral-based items by Walker & Smither (1999)		Manager's performance improved: .19 improvement from initial to final score	
Sirianni & Frey (2001) US	29	Middle managers US	N/A	Resource-based theory	Action learning	Employee satisfaction ratings Regional scorecard: operator functions (e.g., teller error, business retention)	Experimental	Individual	No published scales used	Employment satisfaction +13.4 (regional; 2.2avg.) Employee turnover -11 compared to previous year.		

(Continued)

| Bailey & Fletcher (2002) UK | 104 | Managers at large service sector private organization UK | N/A | Human-capital theory | Developmental feedback program | At both time points, targets received ratings from one superior, one or more first-level subordinates, and one or more second-level subordinates 50-item, 6-point Likert scale, feedback, corresponded to 4 competency dimensions Measures of self to "other" congruence in ratings were computed by two forms of profile similarity indices (PSIs) – congruence-r and congruence-d (Warr & Bourne, 1999) Performance assessed by: (1) The extent to which the individual had met performance objectives | 50-item feedback scale (Bailey & Fletcher, 2002). Congruence-r and congruence-d (Warr & Bourne, 1999) | .175 average increase in 360-degree feedback rating In comparison to time one, self-assessments and both subordinates' ratings of targets at time two had become more favorable. The increase was statistically significant. Number of items deemed a development need decreased by average of 93% | Significant positive correlations between supervisors' feedback ratings and the annual performance appraisal rating: .51 |

Table 19.2 (*Continued*)

Study	N	Respondent type	Response rate (N/A where 100% or not known)	Theoretical perspective	Description of leadership development intervention	Method	Type of study	Level of analysis	Scale(s) used	HR outcomes (e.g., low absenteeism and turnover, high motivation, high job performance)	Performance outcomes (e.g., skill, productivity gains, output increases, quality, customer service)	Financial outcomes (e.g., profit, return on invested capital [ROI], return on assets [ROA])
						(2) The extent to which the individual met the requirements of the role ("PDR-Com") for the last 12 months preceding assessment						
Seifert, Yukl, & McDonald (2003) Italy and US	21	Mid-level managers from a regional savings bank North-east USA	N/A	Human-capital theory	MSFB 360	Pre-measure: Updated version of 11-item, 5-point, self-report influence behavior questionnaire (Yukl & Tracey, 1992) The multisource raters used the target version of the questionnaire to describe the influence behavior of the focal managers	Experimental	Individual	Influence behavior questionnaire (Yukl & Tracey, 1992).	Enhanced leadership behavior towards subordinates		

Study	N	Sample	Response rate	Theory	Intervention	Measure	Design	Level	Instrument	Outcomes
Tyson & Ward (2004) UK	254	Large public authority UK	51%	Resource-based theory	360-degree feedback, leadership and skills workshops, coaching, "learning exchange" (web-based learning) and self-development guide	Between 1997 and 2001 the senior managers and 50 of the middle managers went through 360-degree feedback twice, as a before and after measure; as well as multiple other sources	Cross-sectional	Individual	No published scales used	Increase in 360-degree feedback scores on competency ratings: Personal impact: +.14 Making things happen: +.15 Communication: +.14 Innovation: +.15 Strategic management: +.16 Developing others: +.13 Managing change: +.16 Inspiration: +.16
Parry & Sinha (2005) Australia and New Zealand	50	Mid-level public and private managers	N/A	Human-capital theory; Resource-based theory; Behavioral theory	Full range leadership development program; formal 3-month executive development–action learning	360 MSFB ratings	Quasi-field experiment	Individual	The multifactor leadership questionnaire (MLQ) (Bass & Avolio, 1990)	Effectiveness of leadership: +1.4% Satisfaction with leadership: 7.2% Extra effort of followers: 8.6%
Dai, De Meuse, & Peterson (2010) US	78	Financial services managers US	N/A	Human-capital theory	360-degree feedback, individual development plans	67-item, 67 leadership competencies	Experimental and longitudinal	Individual	Lombardo & Eichinger (2003) MS feedback instrument	Enhanced competencies

(Continued)

Table 19.2 (*Continued*)

Study	N	Respondent type	Response rate (N/A where 100% or not known)	Theoretical perspective	Description of leadership development intervention	Method	Type of study	Level of analysis	Scale(s) used	HR outcomes (e.g., low absenteeism and turnover, high motivation, high job performance)	Performance outcomes (e.g., skill, productivity gains, output increases, quality, customer service)	Financial outcomes (e.g., profit, return on invested capital [ROI], return on assets [ROA])
Umble et al. (2006) US	N/A	Mid-level managers	N/A	Human-capital theory	Formal seminars, MSFB 360, individual development plans	Self-reported 2–5 multiple choice questions for each course. Self-reported, 2-item skill confidence scale. Self-reported skill development 5-point perceived skill scale. Surveys, interviews, and site visits. Enhanced and forecasted revenue (respondent's estimate of funding probability multiplied by amount of revenue expected)	Experimental (pre- and post-test)			Participants received greater support to apply skills in the workplace	.208 average increase in self-assessed skill levels	$6.045 m total enhanced revenue

Study	N	Sample	Response rate	Theory	Program	Measure	Design	Level	Scale	Outcomes
Dexter & Prince (2007) UK	32	Line managers of a city council organization UK	N/A	Resource-based theory	Postgraduate certificate in management – 6, 10 credit modules [3 on people skills, 2 on operational and quality mgt and 1 on public sector management]	Semi-structured interviews were held with the line managers of 32 of the leading managers from the first three cohorts	Cross-sectional; qualitative	Individual	No published scales used	Customer-focus (outer-directed)—enhanced performance driven by customer focus Enhanced competencies: (1) contribution to better processes and project management; (2) more effective teamworking; (3) developing networks and collaborative working; and (4) improved self-management
Black & Earnest (2009) US	196	leadership development program alumni.	75%	Social-learning theory; Adult learning-theory	Residential workshops, seminars, and personal study	LPOM (leadership program outcomes measure): Self-report questionnaire 5-point: Individual level [12 item] Organizational level [11 item] Community level [8 item]	Experimental	Individual	LPOM (Black, 2006).	Personal outcomes in areas of personal growth, self-confidence group

(*Continued*)

Table 19.2 (Continued)

Study	N	Respondent type	Response rate (N/A where 100% or not known)	Theoretical perspective	Description of leadership development intervention	Method	Type of study	Level of analysis	Scale(s) used	HR outcomes (e.g., low absenteeism and turnover, high motivation, high job performance)	Performance outcomes (e.g., skill, productivity gains, output increases, quality, customer service)	Financial outcomes (e.g., profit, return on invested capital [ROI], return on assets [ROA])
McGurk (2009) UK	18	Middle-managers in an "excellent"-rated local authority adult social services department UK	N/A	Human-capital theory; Resource-based theory	The Diploma in Management. A year-long, taught, part-time management development program, delivered by the in-house corporate training function. (Prescriptive-individual)	26 critical incident semi-structured interviews to give qualitative outcomes	Case study	Individual and organizational	No published scales used		Service improvements Deeper understanding of organizational strategy Greater effectiveness in achieving work objectives	
Ciporen (2010) US	88	Participants attending an executive program	96%	Behavioral theory	Formal executive development program	Pre-program interviews, pre-program 360 reports (2–4 weeks prior), HBDI and LSI during program, post-program interviews (5–7 months), and post-program 360-degree feedback reports (1 year post)	Quasi-experimental (pre-and-post-intervention)	Individual	No published scales used		85% of participants reported evidence of improved leadership skills (leadership style, improved communication with others): The PTL group showed statistically significant change on 11 of the	

Reference / Country	N	Sample	%	Theory	Program	Method of analysis	Design	Level	Scales	Outcomes	Results
Brown, McCracken, & O'Kane (2011) Canada UK New Zealand	75	Utility company employees in a leadership development program Canada UK New Zealand	45%	Behavioral theory	Formal classroom-based leadership development program 1 day with 13 modules	Read through transcripts to determine whether participant displayed competencies of PTL (personally transformative learning) / Grounded analysis of RFJs (reflective learning journals) coded using NVIVO	Longitudinal	Individual	No published scales used	Awareness of individual differences and use these to understand organizational culture / Reflection as improving confidence / Engagement in self-critique	Bringing reflection skills into participant's everyday life / 14 competencies (with exception of communicating with impact, building communities, and managing human networks)
Chochard & Davoine (2011) Switzerland	158	Participants of managerial training programs Switzerland	N/A	Resource-based theory	Several programs	Utility analysis. Average of 7.8 months between program and measurement	Cross-sectional; qualitative	Organizational	Utility analysis method of Morrow, Jarrett, & Rupinski (1997)		.188 variability in job performance average .382 effect size average
Watkins, Lyso, & Demarrais (2011) US and Norway	43	Global healthcare company, US. Corporate network, Norway. Both on executive development/leadership programs	N/A	Behavioral theory	"Leadership of change" program – action learning, 360-degree feedback	Critical incident interviews 6 and 12 months after program	Case studies	Individual and organizational	No published scales used	Competency improvements: more global, innovative, and effective practitioners	68% ROI average (high = 164, low = −55)

(*Continued*)

Table 19.2 (Continued)

Study	N	Respondent type	Response rate (N/A where 100% or not known)	Theoretical perspective	Description of leadership development intervention	Method	Type of study	Level of analysis	Scale(s) used	HR outcomes (e.g., low absenteeism and turnover, high motivation, high job performance)	Performance outcomes (e.g., skill, productivity gains, output increases, quality, customer service)	Financial outcomes (e.g., profit, return on invested capital [ROI], return on assets [ROA])
Coloma (2012) US	103	Middle managers in human service agencies US	72%	Behavioral theory	360-degree feedback, individual development plans, formal workshops, individual journals, coaching, book club, call back training, network opportunities	Follow-up surveys 12 months after intervention – 3-point Likert scale: Reported increases in responsibilities, quality and quantity of work, performance as a leader, and performance as a manager, and the extent to which the program was a factor.	Longitudinal	Individual	Questionnaire based on Kirkpatrick (Coloma, 2012)	21% promoted since program [mean rating was 'between a moderate extent' and 'to a great extent']	Improved quality of work: 2.31 Improved performance as a leader: 2.41 Improved performance as a manager: 2.46 Increase in responsibilities: 2.21	

Author	N	Sample	Response rate	Theory	Program	Method	Design	Level	Instrument/Source	Findings
Harris & Leberman (2012) New Zealand	128	Participants of New Zealand women in leadership program (NZWIL) New Zealand	51%	Behavioral theory; Resource-based theory		Changes in positions (e.g., promotions) and the extent to which the program was a factor. Sent to participant and their supervisor. 1–28 item postal survey (contacting up to 3 years post-completion) 2-Contacted by phone and email requesting feedback similar to questionnaire	Longitudinal case study	Individual	Evaluation of NZWIL program (Harris & Leberman, 2012)	80% reported increased self-confidence 37% gained promotion since program
Strang & Kuhnert (2013) US	67	Management executives US	N/A	Constructive-development theory	Self-awareness leadership development program	Survey, interviews, and multisource feedback instrument	Cross-sectional	Individual	Personality and leadership profile (PLP), a self-report measure of personality (Hagberg Consulting Group, 2002).	Enhancement in leadership performance explained by leadership development level

2006; Gilpin-Jackson & Bushe, 2007). The most common formal leadership development interventions investigated are formal classroom development (Mathieu & Leonard, 1987; Dexter & Prince, 2007; Hayes, 2007), multisource feedback and feedback intensive programs (Reilly, Smither, & Vasilopoulos, 1996; Rosti & Shipper, 1998; Tyson & Ward, 2004), workshops (Lawrence & Wiswell, 1993; Barling, Weber, & Kelloway, 1996; Black & Earnest, 2009), action learning projects (Eden et al., 2000; Sirianni & Frey, 2001; Watkins, Lysã, & Demarrais, 2011), and formal development planning (Dai, De Meuse, & Peterson, 2010; Umble et al., 2006; Hayes, 2007). More recent studies have included multiple development combinations such as feedback processes and development planning and action learning combined with workshops.

The majority of studies that research formal leadership development programs report human resource but not financial performance outcomes. The typical human resource outcomes reported include changes in leadership style (Lawrence & Wiswell, 1993), enhanced employee satisfaction (Sirianni & Frey, 2001), enhanced leadership behaviors (Seifert, Yukl, & McDonald, 2003), enhanced skill levels (Umble et al., 2006), decreased levels of absenteeism (Hayes, 2007), and increased promotions (Harris & Leberman, 2012). Performance outcomes were less frequently reported, however, those studies that reported this type of outcome highlighted individual leader performance improvements (Walker & Smither, 1999; Reilly, Smither, & Vasilopoulos, 1996; Bailey & Fletcher, 2002), increases in customer satisfaction (Hayes, 2007), customer service improvements (McGurk, 2009), and global innovation (Watkins, Lysã, & Demarrais, 2011). Few studies of formal leadership development report financial outcomes, however, the typical outcomes reported include sales (Barling, Weber, & Kelloway, 1996), revenue growth (Umble et al., 2006), and increased ROI (Chochard & Davoine, 2011). Those studies that investigated financial performance outcomes used a combination of objective (Barling, Weber, & Kelloway, 1996) and subjective measures (Umble et al., 2006; Hayes, 2007). Overall investment in leadership development does not appear, based on existing studies, to be strongly related to an organization's financial performance.

Experience-based leadership development practices and organizational outcomes

A relatively small number of studies have investigated the impact of experience-based leadership development interventions on organizational outcomes (Table 19.3). These interventions are given various labels in the literature and reflect a more job-based approach to leadership development. An interesting observation from the practitioner literature on leadership development is the notion that 70 percent of leadership development takes place via on-the-job experiences, however, there is little empirical support for this assertion (McCall, 2010). Most of the research evidence points to the fact that the majority of leadership development activity in organizations consists of formal leadership interventions (O'Leonard, 2010; Klimoski & Amos, 2012). The typical experience-based interventions investigated include expatriation assignments (Earley, 1987; Bonache, 2005; Dickmann & Doherty, 2010), job rotations (Campion, Cheraskin, & Stevens, 1994; Cagliuri & DiSanto, 2001), planned work experience (Dragoni et al., 2011), hardship experiences (Suutari & Makela, 2007), and developmental job assignments (DeRue & Wellman, 2009; Dragoni et al., 2009).

The majority of studies that report the organizational outcomes of experience-based leadership development focus on human-resource and performance outcomes (Earley, 1987; Caligiuri & Tarique, 2009; Jokinen, 2010). Human-resource outcomes make up the majority for existing studies and typically include enhanced job satisfaction (Feldman &

Table 19.3 Leadership development and organizational success: job-based leadership development programs (international assignments for leaders, job rotation, stretch assignments) selected papers.

Study	N	Respondent type	Response rate (N/A where 100% or not known)	Theoretical perspective	Description of leadership development intervention	Method	Type of study	Level of analysis	Scale(s) used	HR outcomes (low absenteeism and turnover, motivation, high job performance)	Performance outcomes (productivity/output, quality, service)
Earley (1987) US	80	Managers in electronic manufacturing company US	N/A	Intercultural theory	Training and expatriation assignment	Performance ratings	Experimental, crossed-factorial	Individual	Perceived intensity of adjustment index Spradley & Phillips (1972)		Performance rating by supervisor = 1.05 average higher rating Self-rating of performance = .9 more effective on average
Feldman & Thomas (1992) US	297	Expatriates in Saudi Arabia, Europe, South America, and Japan	40%	Career-management theory	Expatriation assignment	Performance = 4-item, 5-point Likert scale	Cross-sectional	Individual and organizational		Enhanced career planning, job satisfaction, and mutual influence Greater intention to remain Enhanced skill acquisition	
Campion, Cheraskin, & Stevens (1994) US	255	Large pharmaceutical company	87%	Developmental-experiences theory	Job rotation	Rotation compared to performance metrics (promotion, growth, development, etc.)	Cross-sectional	Individual		Job rotation rate correlated with: Promotion: .37 Salary growth: .29 Personal development: .2 Stimulating work: .23	
Cagliuri & DiSanto (2001) US	163	Managers from multinational companies US	25–55% range	Resource-based theory; Human-capital theory	Job rotation and expatriation assignment	8 scales, self-report questionnaire	Cross-sectional	Individual		.6 average increase in "knowledge of professional contacts worldwide" .63 average increase in knowledge of company's worldwide business structure	

(Continued)

Table 19.3 (*Continued*)

Study	N	Respondent type	Response rate (N/A where 100% or not known)	Theoretical perspective	Description of leadership development intervention	Method	Type of study	Level of analysis	Scale(s) used	HR outcomes (low absenteeism and turnover, motivation, high job performance)	Performance outcomes (productivity/ output, quality, service)
Kraimer, Wayne, & Jaworski (2001) US	583	Expatriates of Fortune 500 companies US	37%	Perceived organizational support (POS); Leader-member exchange (LMX)		6-item job performance scale Black & Stephen's (1989) 14-item scale to assess adjustment to work, general environment, and interactions with host-country citizens	Cross-sectional	Individual	Eisenberger et al.'s (1986) perceived organizational support Liden and Maslyn's (1998) leader-member exchange. Caplan, Cobb, & French . (1975) spousal support subscale Black and Stephen's (1989) scale to assess adjustment Torbiorn's (1982) cultural novelty scale Nicholson's & West's (1988) role novelty Watson, Clark, & Tellegen, (1988) PANAS scale	Better interaction adjustment by expatriate	Enhanced expatriate contextual performance
Stahl, Miller, & Tung (2002) Singapore US Canada	1058	Expatriate managers Germany	47%	Career theory	Expatriation assignment	Self-report questionnaires	Cross-sectional	Individual and organizational		Perceived career impact: 59% highly likely career advancement within the company	

Study	N	Sample	Response rate	Theory	Experience	Measure	Design	Level	Instrument	Findings
Bonache (2005) Spain	1600	Multinational construction company Spain	64.78%	Developmental experiences theory	Expatriate assignment	5-point Likert scales self-report questionnaires	Cross-sectional	Individual		85% demonstration of professional or managerial skills 95% development of intercultural skills. Higher satisfaction with job elements than domestic-Task variety = .33 learning = .37 Likelihood of promotion = .43 Responsibility = .29
Suutari & Makela (2007) Finland	20	Managers, business graduates Finland	N/A	Human-capital theory; Career-capital theory	Expatriation including hardship experience	Structured interview	Cross-sectional	Individual		Increased career capital – increased self-confidence and reliance on their own capabilities. Trust in their employability Development of strong career identity
Caligiuri & Tarique (2009) US	313	Leaders in a diversified firm UK	82%	Human-capital theory; Cross-cultural theory	Cross-cultural leadership development experiences, Global leadership activities	Self-report questionnaire	Cross-sectional	Individual	NEO personality inventory NEO – FFI (Costa & McCrae, 1992).	High contact crosscultural leadership development experience and effectiveness in global leadership activities. r = .35
Derue & Wellman (2009) US	225	Mid- and senior-level managers US	60%	Developmental-experiences theory	Job-based skill development related to developmental challenges	Interviews with supervisors and self-reported produced critical incidents	Cross-sectional/Longitudinal	Individual	Developmental challenge profile (DCP; McCauley et al., 1994). Mumford, Campion, & Morgeson's (2007) taxonomy of leadership skills	Enhanced skill development = 1.45 (but diminishing returns)

(Continued)

Table 19.3 (*Continued*)

Study	N	Respondent type	Response rate (N/A where 100% or not known)	Theoretical perspective	Description of leadership development intervention	Method	Type of study	Level of analysis	Scale(s) used	HR outcomes (low absenteeism and turnover, motivation, high job performance)	Performance outcomes (productivity/output, quality, service)
Dragoni et al. (2009)	445		77%	Developmental experiences theory	Developmental job assignment	(55-item developmental challenge profile) (Spreitzer's measure of competencies)		Individual	DCP; McCauley et al. (1994). VandeWalle's (1997) measure of learning goal orientation Spreitzer, Kizilos, & Nason (1997) measure of competencies		Enhanced end-state competencies ($\beta = .23$, SE = .07, p < .01).
Kraimer et al. (2009) US	190	Repatriated employees of 5 multinational firms US	44%	Developmental-experiences theory; Career theory	Developmental job assignment		Cross-sectional	Individual	Bozeman & Perrewe's (2001) 5-item turnover intentions scale Bolino & Feldman's (2000) measure of perceptions of underemployment. Caligiuri et al.'s (2001) measure for purpose of expatriate assignments. Stahl, Miller, & Tung's (2002) measure of managerial and intercultural competencies. Kraimer & Wayne's (2004) multidimensional perceived organizational support scale	Significant career advancement	

Source	N	Sample/Country	Response rate	Theory	IV	Measures	Design	Level	Scales/Measures	Outcomes	Performance
Stahl et al. (2009) France	1179	International assignees Germany, France, US, Japan, and Singapore	41.4%	Developmental-experiences theory; Resource-based theory	Expatriate job assignment	Career advancement opportunities = single-item, 5-point Likert scale; Choice of 8 objectives for international assignment	Cross-sectional	Individual		Significant career advancement	Enhanced contextual performance
Van der Heijden, Van Engen, & Paauwe (2009) Netherlands	250	In- and expatriates of a MNC operating in the food and personal care industry Netherlands	40%	Support theory; Career theory		Kraimer & Wayne's self-report 9-item scale (2004) Contextual performance = 4 items (contextual performance = activities that are directed at maintaining the interpersonal and psychological environment that needs to exist to allow the technical core to operate)	Cross-sectional	Individual	Kraimer & Wayne's (2004) perceived organizational support scale. Parker & McEvoy's (1993) lack of promotion expectations scale. Wayne, Shore, & Linden (1997) intention to leave. Parker & McEvoy (1993) Perceived career prospects outside the home organization. Expatriate performance was measured using Kraimer & Wayne's (2004) scale		
Dickmann & Doherty (2010) UK	18	Employees of Large MNC (ChocFirm) Europe, Australia, and Asia	N/A	Developmental-experiences theory	Expatriation assignment	Structured interview Interview questions were based on the questionnaire developed by Dickmann & Harris (2005)	Cross-sectional	Individual and organizational		Acquisition of general skills Host and international networks improved, broader perspective, cultural sensitivity and business acumen increased	Higher performance

(Continued)

Table 19.3 (*Continued*)

Study	N	Respondent type	Response rate (N/A where 100% or not known)	Theoretical perspective	Description of leadership development intervention	Method	Type of study	Level of analysis	Scale(s) used	HR outcomes (low absenteeism and turnover, motivation, high job performance)	Performance outcomes (productivity/output, quality, service)
Jokinen (2010) Finland	16	Managers with 2 foreign work experiences Finland	N/A	Career-capital theory; Human-capital theory	Manager expatriation	Semi-structured interviews	Cross-sectional	Individual		Increased career capital	
Dragoni et al. (2011) US	703	Executives who participated in an assessment center	N/A	Developmental-experiences theory; Human-capital theory	Work experience	Assessment centre measurement of leadership competence	Cross-sectional	Individual	Wesman personnel classification test (WPCT; Wesman, 1965) Watson-Glaser critical-thinking appraisal form A (WGCTA; Watson & Glaser, 1980) Global personality inventory (GPI; ePredix, 2001) Leadership experience inventory (LEI; Van Katwyk & Laczo, 2004)	Enhanced strategic thinking competency	
Doherty & Dickmann (2012) UK	3450	Expatriates of 9 MNCs USA, UK, and continental Europe	N/A	Resource-based theory	International assignment	Performance management and appraisal data for expatriated and non-expatriated staff were compared	Action research/Cross-sectional	Organizational		39.9% repatriate promotions after third reporting period	Improved expat performance 28.4% Improved repatriate performance = avg 22.8% over three reporting periods

Thomas, 1992), enhanced social networking (Cagliuri & DiSanto, 2001), better career advancement (Stahl, Miller, & Tung, 2002; Suttari & Makela, 2007), enhanced skills and competencies (Stahl, Miller, & Tung, 2002; DeRue & Wellman, 2009), and enhanced crosscultural awareness (Dickmann & Doherty, 2010). Few studies report enhanced performance outcomes, however, exceptions are Earley (1987) and Doherty and Dickmann (2012) – performance ratings; Kraimer, Wayne, and Jaworski (2001) and Van Der Heijden, Van Engen, and Paauwe (2009) – contextual performance. These performance ratings were based on subjective measures of performance provided by supervisors, and self-ratings. There were no studies that reported financial outcomes of experience-based leadership development.

Relationship-based leadership development practices and organizational outcomes

Recently, there has been an emerging trend towards the study of relational leadership development practices (Table 19.4). DeRue, Sitkin, and Podolny (2011) trace the emergence of this approach to leadership development to leader–member exchange (LMX) theory. A number of studies have investigated the impact of these relational leadership development strategies on organizational outcomes. These studies in the main focus on a specific practice such as coaching (Jones, 2006), executive coaching (Parker-Wilkins, 2006; Smither et al., 2003; Kombarakaren, 2008), and formal mentoring (Levinson, Van Der Stede, & Cohen, 2006) or they are combined with other leadership development practices such as formal classroom development (Olivero, Bane, & Kopelman, 1997). The number of studies is modest, however, the research suggests promise on organizational outcomes. With the exception of one study that demonstrated financial outcomes of leadership development (Parker-Wilkins, 2006) the remaining studies demonstrate both human resource and performance outcomes. Human resource outcomes reported include increased diversity (Parker-Wilkins, 2002), enhanced leadership competencies (Levenson, Van Der Stede, & Cohen, 2006), and enhanced trust (Kombarakaren, 2008). The performance outcomes reported include increased productivity (Olivero, Bane, & Kopelman, 1997; Parker-Wilkins, 2006), enhanced performance (Bowles et al., 2007), and contribution to the company (Kombarkaren, 2008). The measures of both human resource and performance outcomes were essentially subjective with some use of experimental designs with control groups. Overall the evidence suggests that relationship-based leadership development impacts both human resource and performance outcomes, however, the evidence base is small in terms of their impact on financial performance. However, relational-based leadership development practices have the potential to make significant contributions to a number of organizational outcomes.

Future Research

Organizations invest in leadership development to develop their leadership pools in order to optimize the effective performance of the entire organization. It is not solely to increase individual effectiveness in areas such as leadership behaviors (Mumford, Campion, & Morgeson, 2007), affective and motivational characteristics (Ilies, Judge, & Wagner, 2006; Damen, Van Knippenberg, & Van Knippenberg, 2008), and leadership identity and mindset (Yammarino & Atwater, 1993; Shamir and Eilam, 2005). While these are important the ultimate goal is organizational performance. Swanson and Holton (2001) suggested in their results assessment model that organizational performance is characterized as a system of

Table 19.4 Leadership development and organizational success: developmental relationship-based leadership development programs (coaching and mentoring) selected papers.

Study	N	Respondent type	Response rate (N/A where 100% or not known)	Theoretical perspective	Description of leadership development intervention	Method	Type of study	Level of analysis	Scale(s) used	HR outcomes (low absenteeism and turnover, high motivation, high job performance)	Performance outcomes (productivity/ output, quality, service)	Financial outcomes (profit, return on invested capital [ROI], return on assets [ROA])
Olivero, Bane, & Kopelman (1997) US	31	Top and mid-level managers and supervisors at a health agency US	N/A	None specified	Conventional managerial program accompanied by coaching	(Productivity based on PEFs per employee)	Experimental	Individual			Coaching increased productivity by 88%	
Smither et al. (2003) US	1361	Senior managers in a large global organization who received multisource feedback	88%	Human-capital theory	Executive coaching impact on MSFB 360 ratings	Managers who worked with an executive coach more likely than other managers to: set specific goals: d = .16 Solicit ideas for improvement from supervisors: .36 Receive improved ratings: d = .17	Quasi-experimental pre-post control group	Individual		More likely than other managers to set specific (rather than vague) goals (d = .16) to solicit ideas for improvement from their supervisors (d = .36)	Relationship between executive coaching and improvement in direct report and supervisor ratings was positive but small (d = .17)	
Jones, Rafferty, & Griffen (2006) Australia and UK	23	Leaders who volunteered for executive coaching	48%	Human-capital theory	Formal coaching	(9-item individual flexibility scale)	Experimental – repeated measures	Individual			.32 increase in flexibility	

Study	N	Sample	Response rate	Theory	Intervention	Analysis	Design	Level	Findings
Levenson, Van Der Stede, & Cohen (2006) US	1279	Coaches and executives (director level or higher) who received the coaching in four large (Fortune 500 size) firms; and in three industries: consumer products, financial services, and healthcare	63%	Human-capital theory; Resource-based theory	Mentoring about competency system – archival data	Each dimension in the competency system is scored as either "demonstrates" or "does not demonstrate." Promotion to the intermediate level requires consistent demonstration of at least 75% of the competency dimensions in each intermediate-level category	Cross-sectional	Organizational	Impact of mentoring on individual level performance = .16 [$p < .01$]
Bowles, Cunningham, Gabriel, & Picano (2007) US	59	Mid- and executive-level managers within a large recruiting organization involved in US Army recruiting	N/A	Human capital theory	12-month coaching program 8–10 hours of instruction pertaining to the development of a leader plan of action and stress management as well as personal and professional goal setting	Independent samples t-tests comparing quota achievement between previous leaders and coached participants	Experimental	Individual	Both groups of coached participants performed significantly better over the course of coaching than did their uncoached, but experienced counterparts in the previous 12-month period

(Continued)

Table 19.4 (*Continued*)

Study	N	Respondent type	Response rate (N/A where 100% or not known)	Theoretical perspective	Description of leadership development intervention	Method	Type of study	Level of analysis	Scale(s) used	HR outcomes (low absenteeism and turnover, high motivation, high job performance)	Performance outcomes (productivity/output, quality, service)	Financial outcomes (profit, return on invested capital [ROI], return on assets [ROA])
Bowles, Cunningham, Gabriel, & Picano (2007) US (cont'd)											For previous middle managers compared to their coached counterparts this difference was between an average mission achievement of 90.45% and 100.91%, $t(23) = -2.31$, $p < 0.05$, $d = 0.43$.	
Kombarakaren (2008) US	114	Executives in a large multinational corporation	91%	Human-capital theory	Executive coaching	62 closed questions, 3 open-ended questions – self-report questionnaire on 5-point Likert scale	Experimental	Individual		Coaching increased trust in the company .736 Coaching increased work satisfaction .752 Coaching makes the company a better place to work .551	Coaching maximized contribution to the company .758	

Study	N	Sample	Response rate	Theory	Intervention	Method	Design	Level	Measures	Findings
Solansky (2010) US	303	School administrators US	86%	Behavioral theory	Mentoring	360-degree assessment using survey	Cross-sectional	Individual	Posner & Kouzes (1993) leadership practices inventory (LPI).	Enhancement of leadership skills
Chopin et al. (2013) US	260	Executives and future leaders US	N/A	Behavioral theory	Mentoring	Surveys	Cross-sectional	Individual	Murphy's (1992) self-efficacy for leaders. Political skill inventory (Ferris et al., 2005)	No enhancements in self-efficacy of the leader. The quality of the mentoring relationship was related to self-efficacy enhancement. Enhanced political skills

financial outcomes in the form of products or services provided; these are convertible into financial measures. In this review we operationalized organizational outcomes to include human-resource outcomes, performance, and financial outcomes. It is acknowledged that both human resource and performance outcomes are necessary in order to realize financial outcomes. The review of studies reveals that the evidence base does not demonstrate that investment in leadership development leads to enhanced financial performance for the organization. A number of significant hurdles need to be overcome if such a relationship is to be demonstrated.

Broadening the theoretical foundations of the leadership development–organizational outcomes relationship

The over reliance on strategic-type frameworks and concepts to understand the relationship between leadership development practices and organizational outcomes is not beneficial to the development of this area of research. There is a need to investigate more thoroughly the institutional context of these leadership development practices and how this context shapes outcomes. Institutional approaches may provide more insights on sectoral issues, the influence of cultural context, market structures, competitive conditions, and factors that are frequently taken as assumed such as regulatory influences, macro-economic policies, and trade conditions.

Longitudinal studies: does leadership development contribute to organizational outcomes over time?

An important observation from the existing studies is the almost total lack of longitudinal studies examining the leadership development–organizational outcomes relationship. As Simkins (2012) has observed questions of causation are significant if researchers are to make a case for investment in leadership development as something that benefits organizations. Linking leadership development to more distant outcomes such as financial outcomes requires the use of longitudinal designs that utilize robust measures of both leadership development and organizational outcomes. Longitudinal research designs however, present a number of challenges in the context of leadership development. There are significant problems with response rates at future waves of a study and the need to measure both the independent and dependent variables on multiple occasions (Cascio, 2012).

Developing robust measures of both leadership development and organizational outcomes

Existing studies are not particularly insightful when it comes to the identification of both measures of leadership development and organizational outcomes. A central question concerns the dimensions of leadership development and how those dimensions are related to different organizational outcomes. Consistent with the ideas proposed by Shaw et al. (2009) and Gong, Huang, and Farh (2009) there is a need to have more theorizing on different types of leadership development practices and whether they are performance-orientated practices or maintenance-orientated practices. It is likely that these two sets of leadership development practices may have different impacts on outcomes and may operate through different mediating mechanisms. In the existing literature leadership development measures typically focus on the amount of development activity undertaken, the type of leadership development practice, and the level of the development activity. It may also include issues such as the duration of the activity and the number of practices. There is no consensus as to the ideal number of practices or for that matter the most effective mix of practices. It may be appropriate to utilize context-specific practices because they have greater reliability and internal validity. An important issue concerns the coverage of leadership development practices in an organization. Measures of leadership development may over-report the practice where it is confided to an exclusive talent group, for example, or where it is only utilized on a sporadic basis. As a consequence many existing studies focus on specific interventions and as a result the sample of respondents is small.

The choice of organizational measures is also of importance. In the literature on leadership development, the focus of attention has not been on financial measures but on collective human-resource outcomes and to a lesser extent performance outcomes, which is in contrast to the HRM literature. The use of financial measures in the leadership development–organizational outcomes literature would enhance the field of study because where such measures are objective it will reduce the probability of common method variance. There are numerous financial measures that can be used in the leadership development context such as net profits, share price, return on assets, and return on sales. Net profits are considered to be an effective measure of financial performance (Singh et al., 2012).

Future research questions on the leadership development–organizational outcomes relationship

Many questions remain unanswered on the relationship between investment in leadership development and organizational outcomes. The field of leadership development has not travelled far when it comes to understanding its impact on organizational outcomes. There are numerous research questions that remain unanswered. The most fundamental one concerns its relationship with financial performance. The existing studies provide little in the way of answers to this question. The leadership development literature argues that investment in leadership development can contribute to an organization's profitability; however, based on the existing evidence, it cannot plausibly make that claim. There is a need to understand the host of internal and external factors that potentially impact that relationship and to explore the influence of relevant mediators of that relationship. These questions need to be answered using a broader theoretical foundation and there needs to be an increased use of longitudinal designs. We need to understand these relationships in different types of organizations, including SMEs, public sector organizations, and MNCs. We need to achieve a better understanding of the leadership development–organizational outcomes relationship in non-US settings and in particular Asian and European organizations.

Conclusions

This chapter reviewed the current state of knowledge on the relationship between investment in leadership development and organizational outcomes. Over the past 20 years or so researchers have sought to define what constitutes leadership development and explore its relationship with organizational outcomes. Progress to date is limited with few studies that have investigated the impact on financial performance. The majority of the research is firm- and intervention-centric with little research that investigates sets of leadership development practices. There is also a closed-system bias in the few studies that have investigated the impact of external factors on the relationship between leadership development and organizational outcomes. There is a need therefore to broaden the theoretical foundations to explore this relationship and to utilize more sophisticated methodologies that provide researchers and practitioners with the confidence that investment in leadership development is worthwhile.

References

Avolio, B. J. (2005). *Leadership Development in Balance: Made/Born*. Mahwah, NJ: Erlbaum.

Avolio, B. J., Avey, J. B., & Quisenberry, D. (2010). Estimating return on leadership development investment. *Leadership Quarterly*, 21(4), 633–644.

Avolio, B. J., & Luthans, F. (2006). *The High Impact Leader: Moments Matter in Accelerating Authentic Leadership*. New York: McGraw-Hill.

Avolio, B. J., Reichard, R. J., Hannah, S. T., Walumbwa, F. O., & Chan, A. (2009). A meta-analytic review of leadership impact research: Experimental and quasi-experimental studies. *Leadership Quarterly*, 20(5), 764–784.

Bailey, C., & Fletcher, C. (2002) The impact of multiple source feedback on management development: Findings from a longitudinal study. *Journal of Organizational Behavior*, 23, 853–867.

Bales, R. F., Cohen, S. P., & Williamson, S. A. (1979). *SYMLOG: A System for the Multiple Level Observation of Groups*. New York: Free Press.

Barling, J., Weber, T., & Kelloway, E. K. (1996). Effects of transformational leadership training on attitudinal and financial outcomes: A field experiment. *Journal of Applied Psychology*, 8(6), 827–832.

Bass, B. M., & Avolio, B. J. (1990). The implications of transactional and transformational leadership for individual, team, and organizational development. *Research in Organizational Change and Development*, 4, 231–272.

Batt, R., & Colvin, A. J. (2011). An employment systems approach to turnover: Human resources practices, quits, dismissals, and performance. *Academy of Management Journal*, 54(4), 695–717.

Batt, R., & Hermans, M. (2012). Global human resource management: Bridging strategic and institutional perspectives. *Research in Personnel and Human Resources Management*, 31, 1–52.

Belling, R., James, K., & Ladkin, D. (2004). Back to the workplace: How organizations can improve their support for management learning and development. *Journal of Management Development*, 23(3), 234–255.

Bersin (2013). *Predictions for 2013: Corporate Talent, Leadership and HR – Nexus of Global Forces Drives New Models for Talent*. Oakland, CA: Bersin by Deloitte.

Black, A. (2006). Leadership program outcomes measure – LPOM. Paper presented at International Leadership Association Conference, Chicago, IL.

Black, A. M., & Earnest, G. W. (2009). Measuring the outcomes of leadership development programs. *Journal of Leadership & Organizational Studies*, 16, 184–196.

Black, J. S., & Stephens, G. K. (1989). The influence of the spouse on American expatriate adjustment in overseas assignments. *Journal of Management*, 15, 529–544.

Bolino, M. C., & Feldman, D. C. (2000) The antecedents and consequences of underemployment among expatriates. *Journal of Organizational Behavior*, 21(8), 889–911.

Bonache, J. (2005). Job satisfaction among expatriates, repatriates and domestic employees: The perceived impact of international assignments on work-related variables. *Personnel Review*, 34, 110–124.

Bowles, S., Cunningham, C. J. L., Gabriel, M., & Picano, J. (2007). Coaching leaders in middle and executive management: Goals, performance, buy-in. *Leadership & Organization Development Journal*, 28, 388–408.

Bowman, E. H., & Helfat, C. E. (2001). Does corporate strategy matter? *Strategic Management Journal*, 22(1), 1–23.

Bozeman, D. P., & Perrewe, P. L. (2001). The effect of item content overlap on organizational commitment questionnaire-turnover cognitions relationships. *Journal of Applied Psychology*, 86(1), 161–173.

Brown, T., McCracken, M., & O'Kane, P. (2011). "Don't forget to write": How reflective learning journals can help to facilitate, assess and evaluate training transfer. *Human Resource Development International*, 14(4), 465–481.

Brungardt, C. (1997). The making of leaders: A review of the research in leadership development and education. *Journal of Leadership Studies*, 3(3), 81–95.

Buckingham, M. (2012). Leadership development in the age of the algorithm. *Harvard Business Review*, 90(6), 86–92.

Burke, M. J., & Day, R. R. (1986). A cumulative study of the effectiveness of managerial training. *Journal of Applied Psychology*, 71(2), 232.

Caligiuri, P., & DiSanto, V. (2001). Global competence: What is it, and can it be developed through global assignments? *Human Resource Planning*, 24(3), 27.

Caligiuri, P., Phillips, J., Lazarova, M., Tarique, I., & Burgi, P. (2001). The theory of met expectations applied to expatriate adjustment: The role of cross-cultural training. *International Journal of Human Resource Management*, 12, 357–372.

Caligiuri, P., & Tarique, I. (2009). Predicting effectiveness in global leadership activities. *Journal of World Business*, 44(3), 336.

Campion, M. A., Cheraskin, L., & Stevens, M. J. (1994) Career-related antecedents and outcomes of job rotation. *Academy of Management Journal*, 37(6), 1518–1542.

Caplan, R. D., Cobb, S., & French, J. R. (1975). Relationships of cessation of smoking with job stress, personality, and social support. *Journal of Applied Psychology*, 60, 211–219.

Cascio, W. F. (2012). Methodological issues in international HR management research. *International Journal of Human Resource Management*, 23(12), 2532–2545. doi:10.1080/09585192.2011.561242.

Cascio, W. F., & Boudreau, J. W. (2008). *Investing in People: Financial Impact of Human Resource Initiatives*. New Jersey: FT Press.

Chan, A., Hannah, S. T., & Gardner, W. L. (2005). Veritable authentic leadership: Emergence, functioning, and impacts. In W. L. Gardner, B. J. Avolio, & F. O. Walumbwa (Eds.), *Authentic Leadership Theory and Practice: Origins, Effects and Development* (pp. 227–250). Oxford: Elsevier.

Chochard, Y., & Davoine, E. (2011). Variables influencing the return on investment in management training programs: A utility analysis of 10 Swiss cases. *International Journal of Training & Development*, 15, 225–243.

Ciporen, R. (2010).The role of personally transformative learning in leadership development: A case study. *Journal of Leadership & Organizational Studies*, 17(2), 177–191.

Collins, D. B., & Holton, E. F. (2004). The effectiveness of managerial leadership development programs: A meta-analysis of studies from 1982 to 2001. *Human Resource Development Quarterly*, 15(2), 217–248.

Coloma, J., Gibson, C., & Packard, T. (2012). Participant outcomes of a leadership development initiative in eight human service organizations. *Administration in Social Work*, 36, 4–22.

Conference Board (2006). *Are They Really Ready to Work? Employers' Perspectives on the Basic Knowledge and Applied Skills of New Entrants to the 21st Century US Workforce*. New York: The Conference Board, Inc., the Partnership for 21st Century Skills, Corporate Voices for Working Families, and the Society for Human Resource Management.

Cook, J. D., Hepworth, S. J., Wall, T. D., & Warr, P. B. (1981). *The Experience of Work*. San Diego: Academic Press.

Corporate Executive Board. (2013). Leadership development: Two-thirds of execs say it's broken. http://www.executiveboard.com/blogs/leadership-development-two-thirds-of-execs-say-its-broken/ (accessed April 11, 2014).

Costa, P. T., Jr., & McRae, R. R. (1992). *Revised NEO Personality Inventory (NEO-PI-R) and NEO Five-Factor Inventory (NEO-FFI) Professional Manual*. Odessa, FL: Psychological Assessment Resources, Inc.

Dai, G., De Meuse, K., & Peterson, C. (2010). Impact of multi-source feedback on leadership competency development: A longitudinal field study. *Journal of Managerial Issues*, 22, 197.

Damen, F., Van Knippenberg, B., & Van Knippenberg, D. (2008). Affective match in leadership: Leader emotional displays, follower positive affect, and follower performance 1. *Journal of Applied Social Psychology*, 38(4), 868–902.

Day, D. (2011). Leadership development. In A. Bryman, D. Collinson, K. Grint, B. Jackson, & M. Uhl-Bien (Eds.), *The SAGE Handbook of Leadership* (pp. 37–50). London: Sage.

Day, D. V. (2000). Leadership development: A review in context. *Leadership Quarterly*, 11(4), 581–613.

Day, D. V., & Harrison, M. M. (2007). A multilevel, identity-based approach to leadership development. *Human Resource Management Review*, 17, 360–373.

Day, D. V., Harrison, M. M., & Halpin, S. M. (2008). *An Integrative Approach to Leader Development: Connecting Adult Development, Identity, and Expertise*. New York: Routledge.

Day, D. V., Gronn, P., & Salas, E. (2004). Leadership capacity in teams. *Leadership Quarterly* 15(6), 857–880.

DeRue, D. S., & Ashford, S. J. (2010). Power to the people: Where has personal agency gone in leadership development? *Industrial and Organizational Psychology*, 3(1), 24–27.

DeRue, D. S., & Myers, C. G. (2011). What is your motivation for learning? Cultural differences and the impact on leader development. Paper presented at the 2011 Annual Meeting of the Academy of Management.

DeRue, D. S., Sitkin, S. B., & Podolny, J. M. (2011). Teaching leadership – Issues and insights. *Academy of Management Learning & Education*, 10, 369–372.

DeRue, D. S., & Wellman, N. (2009). Developing leaders via experience: The role of developmental challenge, learning orientation, and feedback availability. *Journal of Applied Psychology*, 94, 859–875.

Dexter, B., & Prince, C. (2007). Evaluating the impact of leadership development: A case study. *Journal of European Industrial Training*, 31, 609–625.

Dickmann, M., & Doherty, N. (2010). Exploring organizational and individual career goals, interactions, and outcomes of developmental international assignments. *Thunderbird International Business Review*, 52, 313–324.

Doherty, N. T., & Dickmann, M. (2012). Measuring the return on investment in international assignments: An action research approach. *International Journal of Human Resource Management*, 23(16), 3434–3454.

Dragoni, L., Oh, I.-S., VanKatwyk, P., & Tesluk, P. E. (2011). Developing executive leaders: The relative importance of cognitive ability, personality and the accumulation of work experience in predicting strategic thinking competency. *Personnel Psychology*, 64, 829–864.

Dragoni, L., Tesluk, P. E., Russell, J. E. A., & Oh, I. S. (2009). Understanding managerial development: Integrating developmental assignments, learning orientation, and access to developmental opportunities in predicting managerial competencies. *Academy of Management Journal Archive*, 52, 731–743.

Dugan, J. P., Bohle, C. W., Gebhardt, M., Hofert, M., Wilk, E., & Cooney, M. A. (2011). Influences of leadership program participation on students' capacities for socially responsible leadership. *Journal of Student Affairs Research and Practice*, 48(1), 63–82.

Dvir, T., Eden, D., Avolio, B. J., & Shamir, B. (2002). Impact of transformational leadership on follower development and performance: A field experiment. *Academy of Management Journal*, 45, 735–744.

Earley, P. C. (1987). Intercultural training for managers: A comparison of documentary and interpersonal methods. *Academy of Management Journal*, 30(4), 685–698.

Economist Intelligence Unit (2011). *Leaders of Change: Companies Prepare for a Stronger Future*. London: Economist Intelligence Unit, Ltd.

Eden, D., Geller, D., Gewirtz, A., Gordon-Terner, R., Inbar, I., Liberman, M., et al. (2000). Implanting Pygmalion leadership style through workshop training: Seven field experiments. *Leadership Quarterly*, 11(2), 171–210.

Eisenberger, R., Huntington, R., Hutchison, S., & Sowa, D. (1986). Perceived organizational support. *Journal of Applied Psychology*, 71, 500–507.

Ellis, S., Ganzach, Y., Castle, E., & Sekely, G. (2010). The effect of filmed versus personal after-event reviews on task performance: The mediating and moderating role of self-efficacy. *Journal of Applied Psychology*, 95, 122–131.

Engel, A. M. (2012). On global citizenship. *American Theatre*, 2902, 10–11.

ePredix (2001). *Global Personality Inventory Technical Manual*. Minneapolis, MN: ePredix.

Faems, D., Sels, L., DeWinne, S., & Maes, J. (2005). The effect of individual HR domains on financial performance. *International Journal of Human Resource Management*, 16, 676–700.

Fairholm, G. W. (1995). Values leadership: A values philosophy model. *International Journal of Value-Based Management*, 8, 65–77.

Feldman, D. C., & Thomas, D. C. (1992) Career management issues facing expatriates. *Journal of International Business Studies*, 271–293.

Ferris, G. R., Treadway, D. C., Kolodinsky, R. W., Hochwarter, W. A., Kacmar, C. J., Douglas, C., & Frink, D. D. (2005). Development and validation of the political skill inventory. *Journal of Management*, 31, 126–152.

Fowler, S. M. (2006). Training across cultures: What intercultural trainers bring to diversity training. *International Journal of Intercultural Relations*, 30, 401–411.

Fulmer, R. M. (1997). The evolving paradigm of leadership development. *Organizational Dynamics*, 25(4), 59–72.

Galli, E. B., & Müller-Stewens, G. (2012). How to build social capital with leadership development: Lessons from an explorative case study of a multibusiness firm. *Leadership Quarterly*, 23(1), 176–201.

Garavan, T. N., Hogan, C., & Cahir-O'Donnell, A. (2009). *Developing Managers and Leaders: Perspectives, Debates and Practices in Ireland*. Dublin: Gill & Macmillan Ltd.

Gentry, W. A., Harris, L. S., Baker, B. A., & Leslie, J. B. (2008). Managerial skills: What has changed since the late 1980s. *Leadership & Organization Development Journal*, 29, 167–181. doi:10.1108/01437730810852506.

Gentry, W. A., & Leslie, J. B. (2007). Competencies for leadership development: What's hot and what's not when assessing leadership – implications for organization development. *Organization Development Journal*, 25, 37–46.

Gerhart, B. (2007). Horizontal and vertical fit in human resource systems. In C. Ostroff & T. Judge (Eds.), *Perspectives on Organizational Fit* (pp. 317–348). New York: Erlbaum.

Gilpin-Jackson, Y., & Bushe, G. R. (2007). Leadership development training transfer: A case study of post-training determinants. *Journal of Management Development*, 26(10): 980–1004.

Gong, Y., Huang, J. C., & Farh, J. L. (2009). Employee learning orientation, transformational leadership, and employee creativity: The mediating role of employee creative self-efficacy. *Academy of Management Journal*, 52(4), 765–778.

Hagberg Consulting Group (2002). *Personality and Leadership Profile*. San Mateo, CA: Author.

Hallinger, P. (2008). Methodologies for studying school leadership: A review of 25 years of research using the Principal Instructional Management Rating Scale. Paper presented at the Annual Meeting of the American Educational Research Association, New York, April.

Harris, C. A., & Leberman, S. I. (2012). Leadership development for women in New Zealand universities. *Advances in Developing Human Resources*, 14, 28–44.

Hayes, J. (2007). Evaluating a leadership development program. *Organization Development Journal*, 25, 89.

Hayward, I., & Voller, S. (2010). How effective is leadership development? The evidence examined. *Ashridge Journal*, Summer, 8–13.

Huselid, M. A., Jackson, S. E., & Schuler, R. S. (1997). Technical and strategic human resource management effectiveness as determinants of firm performance. *Academy of Management Journal*, 40, 171–188.

Ilies, R., Judge, T., & Wagner, D. (2006). Making sense of motivational leadership: The trail from transformational leaders to motivated followers. *Journal of Leadership & Organizational Studies*, 13(1), 1–22.

Jackson, B., & Parry, K. (2008). *A Very Short, Fairly Interesting and Reasonably Cheap Book About Studying Leadership*. Thousand Oaks, CA: Sage.

Jiang, L. A., Waller, D. S., & Cai, S. (2013). Does ownership type matter for innovation? Evidence from China. *Journal of Business Research*, 66(12), 2473–2478.

Jokinen, T. (2010). Development of career capital through international assignments and its transferability to new contexts. *Thunderbird International Business Review*, 52, 325–336.

Jones, R. A., Rafferty, A. E., & Griffin, M. A. (2006). The executive coaching trend: Towards more flexible executives. *Leadership & Organization Development Journal*, 27, 584–596.

Khatri, N. (2000). Managing human resources for competitive advantage. *International Journal of Human Resource Management*, 11, 336–365.

Klimoski, R., & Amos, B. (2012). Practicing evidence-based education in leadership development. *Academy of Management Learning and Education*, 11(4), 685–702.

Kombarakaran, F. A., Yang, J. A., Baker, M. N., & Fernandes, P. B. (2008). Executive coaching: It works! *Consulting Psychology Journal: Practice and Research*, 60, 78–90.

Kor, Y. Y., & Mesko, A. (2013). Dynamic managerial capabilities: Configuration and orchestration of top executives' capabilities and the firm's dominant logic. *Strategic Management Journal*, 34(2), 233–244.

Kraimer, M. L., & Wayne, S. J. (2004). An examination of POS as a multidimensional construct in the context of an expatriate assignment. *Journal of Management*, 30, 209–237.

Kraimer, M. L., Wayne, S. J., & Jaworski, R. A. A. (2001). Sources of support and expatriate performance: The mediating role of expatriate adjustment. *Personnel Psychology*, 54, 71–99.

Lamoureux, K. (2008). Developing leaders. *Leadership Excellence*, 25(7), 11–12.

Lawrence, H. V., & Wiswell, A. K. (1993). Using the work group as a laboratory for learning: Increasing leadership and team effectiveness through feedback. *Human Resource Development Quarterly*, 4(2) 135–148.

Leonard, H. S., & Goff, M. (2003). Leadership development as an intervention for organizational transformation: A case study. *Consulting Psychology Journal: Practice and Research*, 55(1), 58.

Levenson, A. R., Van Der Stede, W. A., & Cohen, S. G. (2006). Measuring the relationship between managerial competencies and performance. *Journal of Management*, 32, 360–380.

Liden, R. C., & Maslyn, J. M. (1998). Multidimensionality of leader-member exchange: An empirical assessment through scale development. *Journal of Management*, 24, 43–73.

Lockwood, N. R. (2006). Leadership development: Optimizing human capital for business success. *HR Magazine*, 51, A1–12.

Lombardo, M., & Eichinger, R. (2003). *The Leadership Architect Norms and Validity Report*. Minneapolis: Lominger Limited, Inc.

Lumpkin, G. T., & Dess, G. G. (2001). Linking two dimensions of entrepreneurial orientation to firm performance: The moderating role of environment and industry life cycle. *Journal of Business Venturing*, 16(5), 429–451.

Lykins, L., & Pace., A. (2013). Mastering millennial leadership development. *T+D*, 43–45.

Mabey, C. (2002). Mapping management development practice. *Journal of Management Studies*, 39(8), 1139–1160.

Mabey, C. (2013). Leadership development in organizations: Multiple discourses and diverse practice. *InternationalJournalofManagementReviews*,15,359–380.doi:10.1111/j.1468-2370.2012.00344.x.

Mabey, C., & Ramirez, M. (2005). Does management development improve organizational productivity? A six-country analysis of European firms. *International Journal of Human Resource Management*, 16(7), 1067–1082.

Martin, J. A., & Eisenhardt, K. M. (2001). Exploring cross-business synergies. *Academy of Management Proceedings*, 2001(1), H1–H6.

Martineau, J., Hoole, E., & Patterson, T. (2006). Leadership development: Is it worth the money? *Global Focus. European Foundation for Management Development*, 3(3), 44–47.

Mathieu, J. E., & Leonard, R. L. (1987). Applying utility concepts to a training program in supervisory skills. *Academy of Management Journal*, 30, 316–335.

McAlearney, A. S. (2006). Leadership development in healthcare: A qualitative study. *Journal of Organizational Behavior*, 27(7), 967–982.

McCall, M. W., Jr. (2010). Peeling the onion: Getting inside experience-based leadership development. *Industrial and Organizational Psychology: Perspectives on Science and Practice*, 3(1), 61–68.

McCauley, C. D. (2008). *Leader Development: A Review of Research*. Greensboro, NC: Center for Creative Leadership.

McCauley, C. D., Ruderman, M. N., Ohlott, P. J., & Morrow, J. E. (1994). Assessing the developmental components of managerial jobs. *Journal of Applied Psychology*, 79, 544–560.

McGurk, P. (2009). Outcomes of management and leadership development. *Journal of Management Development*, 29, 457–470.

Morrow, C. C., Jarrett, M. Q., & Rupinski, M. T. (1997). An investigation of the effect and economic utility of corporate-wide training. *Personnel Psychology*, 50, 91–119.

Mowday, R., Porter, L., & Steers, R. (1982). *Employee–Organization Linkages: The Psychology of Commitment, Absenteeism, and Turnover*. New York: Academic Press.

Muijs, D. (2011). Leadership and organizational performance: From research to prescription? *International Journal of Educational Management*, 25(1), 45–60.

Müller-Stewens, G., & Knoll, S. (2005). Erfolgreiches Management von Cross-Business-Synergien ? Die Bedeutung des organisatorischen Kontextes. In H. Hungenberg & J. Meffert (Eds.), *Handbuch Strategisches Management* (pp. 791–814). Wiesbaden: Gabler.

Mumford, T. V., Campion, M. A., & Morgeson, F. P. (2007). The leadership skills strataplex: Leadership skill requirements across organizational levels. *Leadership Quarterly*, 18, 154–166.

Murphy, S. E. (1992). The contribution of leadership experience and self-efficacy to group performance under evaluation apprehension. PhD thesis. University of Washington, Seattle.

Newkirk-Moore, S., & Bracker, J. S. (1998). Strategic management training and commitment to planning. *International Journal of Training & Development*, 9, 82–90.

Nicholson, N., & West, M. A. (1988). *Managerial Job Change: Men and Women in Transition*. Cambridge: Cambridge University Press.

Nyberg, A. J., Moliterno, T. P., Hale, D., & Lepak, D. P. (2013). Resource-based perspectives on unit-level human capital: A review and integration. *Journal of Management*. doi:10.1177/014920 6312458703.

O'Connell, P. K. (2013). A simplified framework for 21st century leader development. *Leadership Quarterly*, 25(2), 183–203

O'Leonard, K. (2010). *The Corporate Learning Factbook 2009: Benchmarks, Trends and Analysis of the US Training Market*. Oakland, CA: Bersin & Associates.

Olivero, G., Bane, K. D., & Kopelman, R. E. (1997). Executive coaching as a transfer of training tool: Effects on productivity in a public agency. *Public Personnel Management*, 26, 461–470.

Parker, B., & McEvoy, G. M. (1993). Initial examination of a model of intercultural adjustment. *International Journal of Intercultural Relations*, 17, 355–379.

Parker-Wilkins, V. (2006). Business impact of executive coaching: Demonstrating monetary value. *Industrial and Commercial Training*, 38, 122–127.

Parry, K. W., & Sinha, P. N. (2005). Researching the trainability of transformational organizational leadership. *Human Resource Development International*, 8(2), 165–183.

Porter, L. W., & McLaughlin, G. B. (2006). Leadership and the organizational context: Like the weather? *Leadership Quarterly*, 17, 559–576.

Posner, B., & Kouzes, J. (1993). Psychometric properties of the leadership practices inventory – updated. *Educational and Psychological Measurement*, 53, 191–198.

Redman, T., & Wilkinson, A. (Eds.) (2008). *Contemporary Human Resource Management: Text and Cases*. London: Pearson Education.

Reilly, R. R., Smither, J. W., & Vasilopoulos, N. L. (1996). A longitudinal study of upward feedback. *Personnel Psychology*, 49, 599–612.

Rosti, R. T., Jr., & Shipper, F. (1998). A study of the impact of training in a management development program based on 360 feedback. *Journal of Managerial Psychology*, 13(1–2), 77–89.

Seifert, C. F., Yukl, G., & McDonald, R. A. (2003). Effects of multisource feedback and a feedback facilitator on the influence behavior of managers toward subordinates. *Journal of Applied Psychology*, 88, 561–569.

Shamir, B., & Eilam, G. (2005). "What's your story?" A life-stories approach to authentic leadership development. *Leadership Quarterly*, 16(3), 395–417.

Shaw, J. D., Dineen, B. R., Fang, R., & Vellella, R. F. (2009). Employee-organization exchange relationships, HRM practices, and quit rates of good and poor performers. *Academy of Management Journal*, 52(5), 1016–1033.

SHRM (Society of Human Resource Management). (2010). *Glossary of Human Resource Terms*. Alexandria, VA: Society of Human Resource Management.

Simkins, T. (2012). Understanding school leadership and management development in England retrospect and prospect. *Educational Management Administration & Leadership*, 40(5), 621–640.

Sirianni, P. M., & Frey, B. A. (2001). Changing a culture: Evaluation of a leadership development program at Mellon Financial Services. *International Journal of Training & Development*, 5(4) 290–301.

Smither, J. W., London, M., Flautt, R., Vargas, Y., & Kucine, I. (2003). Can working with an executive coach improve multisource feedback ratings over time? A quasi-experimental field study. *Personnel Psychology*, 56, 23–44.

Smither J. W., London, M., Vasilopoulos, N. L., Reilly, R. R., Millsap, R. E., & Salvemini, N. (1995). An examination of the effects of an upward feedback program over time. *Personnel Psychology*, 48, 1–34.

Solansky, S. T. (2010). The evaluation of two key leadership development program components: Leadership skills assessment and leadership mentoring. *Leadership Quarterly*, 21(4), 675–681.

Spradley, J. P., & Phillips, M. (1972). Culture and stress: A quantitative analysis. *American Anthropologist*, 74, 518–529.

Spreitzer, G. M., Kizilos, M. A., & Nason, S. W. (1997). A dimensional analysis of the relationship between psychological empowerment and effectiveness, satisfaction, and strain. *Journal of Management*, 23(5), 679–704.

Stahl, G. K., Chua, C. H., Caligiuri, P., Cerdin, J. L., & Taniguchi, M. (2009). Predictors of turnover intentions in learning-driven and demand-driven international assignments: The role of repatriation concerns, satisfaction with company support, and perceived career advancement opportunities. *Human Resource Management*, 48(1), 89–109.

Stahl, G. K., Miller, E. L., & Tung, R. L. (2002). Toward the boundaryless career: A closer look at the expatriate career concept and the perceived implications of an international assignment. *Journal of World Business*, 37, 216–227.

Storey, J. (Ed.) (2011). *Leadership in Organizations*. London: Routledge.

Suutari, V., & Mäkelä, K. (2007). The career capital of managers with global careers. *Journal of Managerial Psychology*, 22, 628–648.

Swanson, R. A., & Holton, E. (2001). *Foundations of Human Resource Development*. San Francisco: Berrett-Koehler.

Tharenou, P., & Lyndon, J. T. (1990). The effect of a supervisory development program on leadership style. *Journal of Business and Psychology*, 4, 365–373.

Tharenou, P., Saks, A. M., & Moore C. (2007). A review and critique of research on training and organizational-level outcomes. *Human Resource Management Review*, 17(3), 251–273.

Torbiorn, I. (1982). *Living Abroad: Personal Adjustment and Personnel Policy in the Overseas Setting*. New York: John Wiley & Sons, Inc.

Tyson, S., & Ward, P. (2004). The use of 360-degree feedback technique in the evaluation of management development. *Management Learning*, 35, 205–223.

Umble, K. E., Orton, S., Rosen, B., & Ottoson, J. (2006). Evaluating the impact of the Management Academy for Public Health: Developing entrepreneurial managers and organizations. *Journal of Public Health Management and Practice*, 12, 436–445.

Van Der Heijden, J. A. V., Van Engen, M. L., & Paauwe, J. (2009). Expatriate career support: Predicting expatriate turnover and performance. *International Journal of Human Resource Management*, 20, 831–845.

Van Katwyk, P., & Laczo, R. M. (2004). *The Leadership Experience Inventory Technical Manual*. Minneapolis, MN: Personnel Decisions International.

VandeWalle, D., & Cummings, L. L. (1997). A test of the influence of goal orientation on the feedback-seeking process. *Journal of Applied Psychology*, 82(3), 390–400.

von Krogh, G., Nonaka, I., & Rechsteiner, L. (2012). Leadership in organizational knowledge creation: A review and framework. *Journal of Management Studies*, 49(1), 240–277.

Walker, A. G., & Smither, J. W. (1999). A five-year study of upward feedback: What managers do with their results matters. *Personnel Psychology*, 52(2), 393–423.

Walumbwa, F. O., Lawler, J. J., & Avolio, B. J. (2007). Leadership, individual differences, and work-related attitudes: A cross-culture investigation. *Applied Psychology: An International Review*, 56(2), 212–230.

Watkins, K. E., Lysä, I. H., & Demarrais, K. (2011). Evaluating executive leadership programs. *Advances in Developing Human Resources*, 13, 208–239.

Watson, D., Clark, L. A., & Tellegen, A. (1988). Development and validation of brief measures of positive and negative affect: The PANAS scales. *Journal of Applied Psychology*, 54, 1063–1070.

Watson, G., & Glaser, E. (1980). *Watson–Glaser Critical Thinking Appraisal*. London: Psychological Corporation.

Wesman, A. G. (1965). *Personnel Classification Test Manual* (revised ed.). New York: Psychological Corporation.

Yammarino, F. J., & Atwater, L. E. (1993). Understanding self-perception accuracy: Implications for human resource management. *Human Resource Management*, 32, 231–247.

Yukl, G., & Tracey, J. B. (1992). Consequences of influence tactics used with subordinates, peers, and the boss. *Journal of Applied Psychology*, 77, 525–535.

20

Structured Actions of Intentional Development

Nuno Rebelo dos Santos and Leonor Pais

Introduction

Several structured actions for professional and personal development are available for human resources and organizations. Those actions are frequently made available in organizations, which is important considering employee development is one of the most powerful motivators for high performers. It is through people development that organizations reach good performance. This chapter presents a revision of the conceptual definitions of some of those structured actions which are based, like training, on the interaction and relationships between two or more individuals who interrelate for at least one of them to develop in one or several dimensions of personal or professional fields. The criteria used to choose which actions to include in our comparative analysis are: (a) structured actions, meaning there is a prescribed way (with varying degrees of flexibility) to carry them out; (b) based on interpersonal interaction and relationships; (c) having conceptual developments and some associated research, so they have an identity; (d) used for promoting the development of people in organizations; and (e) having as the main guiding thread the practice of real people, being a way of reflection-on-action (Schön, 1996). Some of these characteristics are shared by several actions, such as training, but we exclude training from our chapter considering it is dealt with thoroughly in other chapters of this handbook.

Following the criteria referred to above, we will compare the following structured actions in this chapter: (a) Balint Groups; (b) supervision; (c) communities of practice; and (d) mentoring. Each one is unique and can be considered when human resource management defines the developmental strategy for people and for the organization. This comparative description is also helpful for researchers as it can inspire research questions. These research questions might be, for instance, related to the variables that determine the preference for and adjustment to each structured action, the diversity in operationalization, and the effectiveness and corresponding outputs.

The Wiley Blackwell Handbook of the Psychology of Training, Development, and Performance Improvement,
First Edition. Edited by Kurt Kraiger, Jonathan Passmore, Sigmar Malvezzi, and Nuno Rebelo dos Santos.
© 2015 John Wiley & Sons Ltd. Published 2020 by John Wiley & Sons Ltd.

The chapter presents each structured action in a section, starting with its purpose and definition, and its characterization according to the guiding thread that defines the content and sequence of activities along the process. The boundary clarity and institutional implementation are also presented, as well as who the main participants are and their relationships when the action is put into place. At the end of each section, a general characterization of the research carried out is also presented. The chapter terminates with a comparative analysis of the four structured actions, proposals for future research, and a conclusion.

Balint Groups

Definition and purpose

Balint Groups (BGs) are considered here as an educational practice for professionals whose job has interpersonal relationships as an important core dimension. We consider BGs as a structured action aimed at the development of interpersonal relationship competence within a framework of professional performance (ACGME, 2007). The psychoanalyst Michael Balint worked with groups of general practitioners (GPs) at the Tavistock Clinic in London in the 1950s. He was the pioneer and created Balint Groups that became used worldwide (Balint, 1985; De Lambert, 2010; Johnson, 2001; Lakasing, 2005; Rüth, 2009). The main objective of BGs is to improve understanding of the relationship between a professional (helper) and his or her clients/users/patients. Having started with general practitioners, BGs spread to other professionals such as nurses and social workers (defined here as helpers). All those helpers need to develop their communication and relationship skills to achieve optimal levels of performance (Simpson et al., 1991) and to prevent burnout and distress (Benson & Magraith, 2005). A Balint Group consists nowadays of a small group of helper-practitioners who meet regularly and in a structured framework to discuss their cases, with a focus on the psychological aspects of the professional–client/user/patient relationship (Lustig, 2004). The relationship with the patient's family might be included when appropriate (Shorer et al., 2011). Each meeting lasts about 1.5 hours, and usually takes place once a week or once a fortnight. Some authors describe a lower frequency of meetings. For instance, Shorer et al. (2011) indicate meetings occur every three or four weeks. Group members have a relationship of mutual consultation as equals (Jablonski, 2003). Through new understanding and through the role model offered by other participants, the strengthening of interaction (or interplay) competence is expected. BG attendance can also improve relationships with colleagues (Rabin et al., 2009) and deepen self-awareness, as shown by several authors (Rüth, 2009; Shorer et al., 2011). Finally, BGs are seen as good tools for preventing burnout, distress, and other health problems suffered by helpers (Rabin et al., 2005).

Guiding thread

The line followed in BG meetings is formed by the sequence of cases participants bring for discussion. Cases should be discussed in a nonjudgmental atmosphere. There is no given structure of contents to be followed. The BG progresses from case to case and the same BG may last for two or three years, or even more.

Participants

There are two distinct roles in Balint Groups: regular participants and the leader or coordinator. The role of coordinator is held throughout the Balint Group work by the same person, who should be a qualified BG leader (recognized by the International Balint Federation). The leader's function is to keep the group working according to the guidelines of Balint work. According to the results of Johnson et al. (2004), effective BG leadership is characterized by creating a safe environment and moving the group on for a new understanding of the doctor–patient relationship. Those leaders protect presenters in BGs from being interrogated, promote speculation, tolerate silence and uncertainty, and avoid premature solutions. These results were obtained from experienced BG leaders and the characteristics mentioned have emerged in the convergence of all sets of data gathered.

The other participants are usually helpers in the same profession (GPs, social workers, psychologists, or nurses) who wish to develop their competence in professional relationships (or interaction, or even interplay) with clients (Jablonski, 2003). The original idea was that BG members were free to leave the group, as they joined on a voluntary basis, but some groups report mandatory group attendance when this is included in regular helper training (Das et al., 2003). All participants are treated as equals, but the group leader has the specific role mentioned. He or she is someone with psychological training and experience as a Balint Group member. These are the conditions for being an accredited BG leader. BG participants present a case for group discussion, one at a time (Jablonski, Kjeldmand, & Salinsky, 2013). The role of presenter shifts from session to session.

Boundary clarity and institutional implementation

Although BGs' work can be described and has a strong identity, the boundaries with other forms of group work are blurred (Jablonski, 2003). Since there is an international institution hosting national associations, which defines the criteria for being considered a BG, the sharpness of a BG is defined by these criteria. BGs have spread worldwide and more than 20 countries have national associations that regulate Balint work and train group leaders to coordinate Balint Group meetings. The International Balint Federation consists of more than 20 national associations, and Balint Groups operate in at least 28 countries.

Research on Balint Groups

A substantial amount is published on Balint Groups, but little refers to empirical research. Small samples were used in most work published (e.g., Kjeldmand, Jablonski, & Salinsky, 2013; Turner & Malm, 2004). There is no meta-analysis carried out on Balint Groups as a structured action of intentional development. Nevertheless, results reinforce the idea that BGs are appropriate for developing professionals regarding interpersonal dimensions. Fitzgerald and Hunter (2003), in pre-experimental design research, showed the improvement resulting from Balint Group attendance as a means of training in psychotherapy. There was no comparison group and once again the sample was very small. Yakeley et al. (2011) compared BGs with other methods of developing knowledge about the doctor–patient relationship. They found good achievements with all three methods but their research sample was small.

Cataldo et al. (2005) found no association between BG attendance and work satisfaction. However, Kjeldmand and Holmström (2008) got the opposite result, as the

GPs interviewed reported the joy of being a physician through the sense of security and competence. Balint Group attendance allowed an expanded perception of competence (regarding the relationship with clients and coping strategies for dealing with stress) that strengthened professional identity (Kjeldmand & Holmström, 2008). Also Andersson, Lindberg, and Troein (2002) found that BGs help when working with depressed patients. Turner and Malm (2004) compare Balint and non-Balint trainees, and their results show that BG members obtain better results in psychological dimensions such as psychological medicine skills, abilities, and confidence.

Regarding empathy, although BGs were supposed to improve this (Hojat, 2009), BG attendance does not seem to relate to higher levels of empathy when compared to non-attendance (Cataldo et al., 2005). However, those authors found that BG attendees state more than nonattendees that they would choose the same specialty if they could start again, showing they are more satisfied with being GPs. We have to consider that this research was correlational and therefore causal relations cannot be stated.

Improvement of the relationship with clients is also reported in research on BGs: attentive listening, mindfulness, sincerity and genuineness, compassion, intimacy, and modesty (Matalon et al., 2005). Graham et al. (2009) also identify a better understanding of the case dynamics, an awareness of own feelings and the ability to cope with them, and an understanding others' feelings.

Balint Groups have some problems as developmental tools. Kjeldmand (2006) and Kjeldmand and Holmström (2010) found three types of issues in BG participation: (a) when the physician has needs, vulnerabilities, and defenses that emerge during the process and do not match the BG work; (b) the existence of hidden agendas and interpersonal issues; and (c) contextual or environmental constraints that cause problems for BG work. The low level of attendance at Balint Groups led Launer (2007) to suggest the importance of moving on from BGs to other structured actions that bring together the best of several other practices under the umbrella of supervision. Regarding the differences between BG attendees (for two years) and those who left the BG after six months, Johnson, Brock, and Hueston (2003) found the only significant difference in personality dimensions measured (using the Myers-Briggs personality inventory – MBTI) is in the *intuitive* dimension.

Summarizing, BGs seem to be appropriate for improving professional relational competences and as a way to strengthen the professional identity of helpers, although they are not suitable for all people (Kjeldmand, Jablonski, & Salinsky, 2013). More empirical research is needed, including larger samples and measurement of the results of GP attendance at Balint Groups on their patients.

Supervision

Definition and purpose

The word *supervision* is widely used among others in the psychological, educational, and management literature, with quite different meanings. In the management literature, *supervision* means a hierarchical relationship where one person (supervisor) occupies a position of authority over another (supervisee), and has to ensure the supervisee performs according to accepted procedure (e.g., Bono et al., 2007; Hannah et al., 2013). This can be carried out either through guiding behaviors (before or during the performance) or by evaluation (after the performance). In higher-education literature, supervision means the guiding behavior that a senior researcher adopts to help a junior researcher to learn how to carry out research and become an autonomous researcher (McCallina & Nayar, 2012).

This kind of supervision is usually found in postgraduate programs and in doctoral projects (e.g., Firth & Martens, 2008; Halse, 2011; Vanstone et al., 2013). In lower educational levels *supervision* is also widespread (e.g., Kalule & Bouchamma, 2013) and has a similar meaning to the one found in psychological literature: a senior professional (supervisor) interacts regularly with a less experienced one (supervisee) aiming for the performance and competence development of the supervisee through discussion of the real practice brought by the latter.

In psychological literature, *supervision* (usually called clinical supervision) is hardly defined as a sharp concept clearly distinct from others in a consensual way. Rather, it is possible to describe its core elements, but the boundaries are unclear and blurred. We found a similarity in the literature between supervision and other structured actions of intentional development, like mentoring and coaching (Gray, 2010). However, Milne (2007) wrote a very precise definition, which we propose to use here: "the formal provision by senior/qualified [...]/ [experienced staff] of an intensive [...] relationship-based education and training that is case-focused and which supports, directs and guides the work of colleagues (supervisees)" (p. 440). Therefore, the goal of the education and training offered in supervision is the competence and performance development of the supervisee.

Supervision started in the late nineteenth century with social workers and psychoanalysts, spreading later to other helpers. At that time, the concept was the practice of reflection on the real cases professionals brought for discussion with colleagues. By the 1950s, supervision had evolved through the introduction of new approaches beyond the classical psychodynamic one. After the 1970s, supervision became clearly focused on practice and therefore on whatever influences it, which includes the professional, the client, and the organizations involved in the professional service delivered (Carroll, 2007). Nowadays, supervision is focused on the case presented by the junior professional (supervisee), on the relationship and interaction between the professional and his or her client/user, and on the organizational context where the supervised work takes place. In this chapter, we consider only the psychological meaning of the word *supervision*, considering it is that meaning that best fits the concept of an intentional developmental structured action.

Traditionally, (clinical) supervision has been applied to the helping professions such as social work, counseling, psychotherapy, psychology, and teaching. Nowadays, other professional areas are finding supervision a worthwhile developmental practice. A wealth of literature has been published on (clinical) supervision in the past decades (e.g., Barker & Hunsley, 2013; Robiner & Schofield, 1990) in several professional areas, namely psychiatry (e.g., MacDonald, 2002), nursing (e.g., Davis & Burke, 2012; Koivo, Hyrkäs, & Saarinen, 2011), coaching (e.g., Moyes, 2009; Passmore & McGoldric, 2009), management (e.g., Sirola-Karvinen & Hyrkas, 2006), social work (e.g., Chiller & Crisp, 2012), psychology (e.g., Kaslow, Falander & Grus, 2012), counseling (e.g., Robiner & Schofield, 1990), and psychotherapy (e.g., Guest & Beutler, 1988).

Having a developmental purpose, several functions of supervision have been described, all related to developmental aspects. Fieldon (2008) proposes that supervision helps an experienced, autonomous, decision-making practitioner, to become an internal supervisor. Also Sirola-Karvinen and Hyrkas (2006) in their literature review summarize the functions of supervision in managers' professional development: the normative function (related to the intensification and clarification of activities and actions as well as improving the quality of care), the formative function (related to leadership skills development, professional development, innovative and problem-solving skills development, and better functionality in teams/work and society), and the restorative and support function (related to self-management, internal management, self-knowledge, self-awareness development, the improvement of interaction and cooperation skills, and coping better at work). Hoge et al. (2011) describe the four core functions of supervision as (a) quality of care, (b) administrative aspects, (c) professional development, and (d) support. Summarizing, the functions of supervision are closely related to professional development, whether referring to the development of skills for individuals' performance in their organizational and social systems, or the strengthening of professional identity. Those functions are also partially expressed in the questionnaires by Zarbock et al. (2009) (supervisor and supervisee) for evaluating supervision results. They identified three dimensions: relationship (the support aspect of supervision joined with interpersonal relationship competences), problem solving, and clarifying (competence development).

Guiding thread

The content of the supervision process is determined by the supervisee's professional practice. He/she is responsible for bringing cases or events that will be subject to reflection in the interaction with the supervisor. It is a kind of reflection-on-action (Schön, 1996). Competency-based supervision (Falender & Shafranske, 2007) is an example of a peripheral concept of supervision, as it brings to the guiding thread the knowledge, skills, and values that have to be achieved through the practice. Therefore, competency-based supervision is close to training, where the guiding thread is partly provided from outside.

Participants

The typical supervision process concerns a one-to-one relationship where there are two different roles: the supervisor, who is the experienced/senior/expert, and the supervisee who is the less experienced/junior/learner. Supervision exists for the supervisee's professional learning and development. So one-to-one supervision is not a relationship of parity. Two other forms of supervision should also be mentioned: (a) group supervision, where the supervisor has a small group of supervisees at the same time and they have the opportunity to learn from each other as well as from the supervisor's contributions; and (b) peer supervision, where supervisors are also supervisees and they only learn from each other. Peer supervision was defined as "a structured, supportive process in which counselor colleagues (or trainees), in pairs or in groups, use their professional knowledge and relationship expertise to monitor practice and effectiveness on a regular basis for the purpose of improving specific counseling, conceptualization, and theoretical skills" (Wilkerson, 2006, p. 62). In the present chapter we consider one-to-one supervision as the core of our analysis. The required competencies and training for the role of supervisor have been subject to reflection. According to Falender et al. (2004), the clinical supervisor role should be based on the knowledge, skills, values, and meta-knowledge (including self-awareness) required for effective performance.

Boundary clarity and institutional implementation

Considering that the word *supervision* has a diversity of meanings, as mentioned above, the boundaries between this developmental practice and others in its neighborhood are blurred. Nevertheless, the Association of National Organizations for Supervision in Europe that represents 22 countries in Europe and more than 80 training organizations. National bodies of several professional areas like psychology and psychotherapy also regulate supervision requirements (e.g., American Psychological Association, British Psychological Society, Conselho Federal de Psicologia, Psychology Board of

Australia). The conditions for being a supervisor depend on the specific criteria used by these professional bodies for their specific area.

Research on supervision

Empirical evidence of the effectiveness of clinical supervision has been considered weak (Dilworth et al., 2013; Wright, 2012). But there is research on the positive results of supervision. We present some examples below. In social work, Chiller and Crisp (2012) found supervision to be one reason why social workers stay in the same job/profession instead of changing career. In coaching supervision, we highlight research by Passmore and McGoldric (2009) into the perceived benefits of coaching supervision outputs related to professional development, both regarding professional identity (as the sense of belonging) and competence development (as insights that show the supervisee's blind spots). In nursing, supervision seems to promote well-being among nurses (Koivo, Hyrkäs, & Saarinen, 2011). Other authors have found more uneven results. Livni, Crowe, and Gonsalvez (2012) found no positive effects of supervision on burnout, well-being, and satisfaction, but in their research, supervisory alliances were strongly correlated with perceived supervision effectiveness (supervisees' perspective). Supervision is also seen as a learning and support tool, but at the same time having negative effects, such as being time consuming, possibly having confidentiality issues, and triggering negative feelings (Davis & Burke, 2012). When comparing different tools for professional development, Tulinius and Hølge-Hazelton (2010) researched general practitioners. They found supervision as the preferred practice in terms of learning afforded, when compared with ePortfolio, written material, and teaching days. The small sample and the specific subject of the learning (children in need) were two important weaknesses of this research.

In general, research on the results of supervision suffers from the problem of small samples. The variety of professional areas where supervision is carried out is an additional problem that has to be addressed. Results from one area might not be transferable to others. It is perhaps more important to think in terms of the critical incidents that bring learning and development to the supervisee. The quality of supervision varies and it is important to know what determines the high quality supervision in order to improve it as a tool for professional development. Future research can address these issues.

Communities of Practice

Definition and purpose

Some researchers have published what are considered seminal works on the concept of community of practice (CoP). We can refer here to Lave and Wenger (1991), Brown and Duguid (1991), Wenger (1998), and Wenger, McDermott, and Snyder (2002). CoPs have no historic point of origin and theorizing on the topic is recent.

In their seminal work, Lave and Wenger (1991) proposed the term "community of practice" (CoP) as a central element in their theory of "situated learning". For these authors, learning is more than a process of acquiring knowledge, being about an identity change, involving a complex relationship between a novice and an expert, where peripheral participation has an important role. Learners are socialized into the practice and develop an identity within the community, through a learning process that facilitates knowledge integration. According to Brown and Duguid (1991), a community of practice is an informal group of individuals in an egalitarian relationship, doing the same or similar jobs. The relation between the community and the organization is a central issue in their approach and has increased value in the concept's definition, setting it more directly in the organizational context. Sharing identity, unity of purpose, and meaning are central questions for Malhotra (1997). Wenger (1998), refining the concept, emphasized knowledge creation and sharing coming from the interaction between individuals. Three important dimensions were proposed to define an existing CoP: joint enterprise, mutual engagement, and shared repertoire. Later, in 2002, Wenger, McDermott, and Snyder contributed to a more complex and wide definition, considering a CoP as a managerial tool, within which groups of people work together to share knowledge, innovate, and improve organizational performance. Considering CoP as a managerial tool was an important step in expanding the possibilities for organizations to foster employees' development and, according to Cox (2005), was an essential redefinition of the concept. For this author, there was also a change in terms of what kind of people/workers would participate in a CoP, to include also "knowledge workers" that managers need to manage. However, a CoP can only be fostered (or cultivated) by management and not managed by management (Cox, 2005). This chapter only considers the CoP definition that includes it as an intentional structured developmental practice. In a community of practice, groups of people share interests, concerns, and problems, deepening their knowledge and expertise by interacting on a permanent basis. They develop a set of unique and shared perspectives, as well as a common body of knowledge, practices, and methods. At the same time, they learn together better ways of interacting and develop a common sense of identity (Rivera, 2011). As Wenger, McDermott, and Snyder (2002) said, "communities of practice create value by connecting the personal development and professional identities of practitioners to the strategy of the organization" (p. 17).

In close connection with evolution of the definition, the objectives pursued through development of a CoP also evolved. For Lave and Wenger (1991), the initial purpose was the socialization of newcomers into knowledge through a learning process. Improving new knowledge was the principal aim according to Brown and Duguid (1991), whereas the focus in Wenger (1998) was the development of individual identity. Since Wenger, McDermott, and Snyder (2002) and the resulting change to a more managerial approach, the emphasis has been placed on finding solutions to new problems and no longer on the acquisition of pre-existing knowledge. Following this, CoPs are also promoted, inter alia, as drivers of knowledge management, to spark off innovation and improve organizational performance (Ranmuthugala et al., 2011). According to Barnett et al. (2012), in the field of business, online CoPs (including a mix of face-to-face and online support) contribute to decreased cost and promote innovation through workers' cooperation and knowledge sharing.

Summarizing, we would say that the main objectives of CoPs are: (1) socializing newcomers and improving learning through socialization; (2) creating, developing, and sharing knowledge; (3) developing identity; (4) developing workers' capabilities and their professional development; (5) finding solutions to new problems; (6) improving performance quality; and (7) stimulating creativity and innovation.

Guiding thread

The guiding thread of a CoP could be diverse, such as perplexities, doubts, questions, concerns, interests, goals, and experiences of the participants, and is driven by the task in which they are involved (Cox, 2005). As opposed to training, the guiding thread is not provided from an external source. It is provided at every moment by the participants, who share their knowledge and their questions, and find answers and support from their colleagues, strengthening the feeling of belonging and professional identity.

Participants

When a CoP is hosted by a specific organization, organizational members can enroll voluntarily, usually determined by expertise, interest, or a passion for the topic(s). If the CoP is not hosted in a specific organization but includes members of several organizations, there might be some requirements for participation, but enrolment is always voluntary. Some members may be experts and others apprentices, but there are no formal roles and learning is two-way. Members can take turns at being learner and provider. Wenger, McDermott, and Snyder (2002) suggested that an ideal CoP group should include a leader(s)/champion(s), a facilitator(s), a core group of experts who regularly interact with the group, and a dedicated group of members with varying levels of expertise. But there are no compulsory rules to be followed in this respect. That is only a preferred configuration. The social interaction in CoPs is informal and situated, and all participants will interact intensely with each other (Cox, 2005).

Boundary clarity and institutional implementation

The boundaries of CoPs are blurred. The use of the term *community* does not "imply necessarily co-presence, a well-defined, identifiable group or socially visible boundaries" (Cox, 2005). There is no international federation of CoPs, but several international organizations have named some kind of internal organizational units as "communities of practice," for instance, the case of the International Coach Federation, which replaced the concept of special interest group with that of CoPs.

Research on CoPs

Six literature reviews were considered to systematize the research topics that have been studied by authors engaged in the study of CoPs. These reviews cover the period from 1991 to 2012 and their authors are: Cox (2005), Li et al. (2009), Riviera (2011a, 2011b), Ranmuthugala et al. (2011), and Barnett et al. (2012). The main topics of research at their origin now follow.

Cox (2005) reviews four seminal works on communities of practice, namely: Lave and Wenger (1991), Brown and Duguid (1991), Wenger (1998), and Wenger, McDermott, and Snyder (2002). This is a theoretical review and an important reference for those who want to understand the emergence and development of the concept.

Li et al. (2009), looked for studies published between 1991 and 2005. Their objective was to compare the definition and use of CoP in two different sectors (business and health) and evaluate their effectiveness in the health sector in terms of improving best practices and mentoring new practitioners. Most of the studies were qualitative and the authors found that the structure of CoP varied widely, with four characteristics identifying CoPs and their effectiveness in the health sector remaining unclear.

Riviera published two studies in 2011 on the topic of communities of practice. Both of them are literature reviews. The first covers the period between 1995 and 2004 and the second focuses on papers published between 1998 and 2009. In the first case, the author compares CoPs to knowledge management and concludes that publications in the field of CoPs integrate technological, managerial, and psychosocial aspects differently to the structure of those related to knowledge management. In the latter the author considers the approach is more technological and popular. The second study published by this author describes what CoPS are and why they work as an effective tool in knowledge management. Aligned with the conclusions of the first study described above, the author concludes that the literature reviewed on communities of practice integrates the relevant technological, managerial, and behavioral factors, being conceptually more solid than those of knowledge management, which highlight a more technological and popular approach. These conclusions must be read contextually, considering the various frameworks of knowledge management and the different kinds of interventions organizations can put into action in this field.

Ranmuthugala et al. (2011) conducted a systematic review of the literature on CoPs in the healthcare sector focusing on papers published between January 1, 1990 and September 30, 2009. Their aim was to analyze how and why CoPS were established and if they had improved healthcare practice. The results show that in earlier publications the focus was on learning and exchanging information and knowledge while in more recent papers CoPs were considered more as a tool to develop clinical practice and to enable the implementation of practice based on evidence. The authors conclude that CoPs in the healthcare sector differ in form and aims and a deeper understanding is needed on how to form and sustain CoPs to make best use of them and improve healthcare services.

Barnett et al. (2012) also focus on the health sector, reviewing papers published on virtual communities of practice (VCoP) in GP training. Considering the reduced number of studies on this specific topic, the authors gathered data without time restrictions. Twenty-three articles met the inclusion criteria defined by authors but none was on VCoP in GP training. The results showed that the framework established by Probst is reflected in the health literature, albeit with some variations, and there was less use of measurements in health VCoPs. Virtual communities of practice seem to be a potential way of overcoming isolation and pressure for GP trainees.

In summary, CoPs have been the subject of much published literature, most of this being conceptual papers. The role of CoPs in knowledge management and the specificities of CoPs in designated sectors were also researched. However, it is clear that empirical research is lacking and deserves more attention from researchers.

Mentoring

Definition and purpose

The concept of mentoring has blurred boundaries and overlaps with others. In fact, mentoring is different from, but overlaps with, other kinds of developmental relationships such as role model–observer, teacher–student, advisor–advisee, supervisor–subordinate, and coach–client (Eby, Rhodes, & Allen, 2007). However, this is not an important problem because, according to Haggard et al. (2011), it might be not possible or even desirable to reach a total agreement among all researchers on one specific, comprehensive definition of mentoring. Kram (1985) in his seminal work recognized that even the word *mentor* could have several meanings for different people. In spite of this absence of consensus, the conceptualization of mentoring and of mentoring relationships has had a notable development in the past few decades (e. g., Eby, Rhodes, & Allen, 2007; Haggard et al., 2011; Kram & Ragins, 2007; Noe, Greenberger, & Wang, 2002; Wanberg, Welsh, & Hezlett, 2003). We agree with Haggard et al. (2011) when they say that most scholars share a general view that a mentor is a more senior person who offers various types of personal and career support to a less senior or less experienced person (the "protégé" or "mentee"). Currently, we can identify three distinct areas of mentoring: youth, academic, and workplace in different developmental phases (Eby et al., 2013).

However, in this chapter we focus mainly on workplace mentoring as a structured action of intentional development. In fact, if in the beginning mentoring became associated with Levinson's et al. (1978) seminal study of human development, later on Kram's (1985) research on the influence of mentoring on employees' personal and professional development extended scholarly study of mentoring to the organizational field. In organizational settings, mentoring is oriented to help the protégé develop personally and professionally (Kram, 1985), supported by his or her mentor. Mentors can also offer support that builds trust, intimacy, and interpersonal nearness serving as a role model (Kram, 1985; Ragins & McFarlin, 1990). Regarding this kind of role and according to McDowall-Long (2004), considering the profusion of research on the positive functions and outcomes associated with mentors and their role models it is relevant to be able to identify the characteristics of their effectiveness as mentors and role models. For those authors, these characteristics fall into two categories: interpersonal skills (friendly, approachable, understanding, and patient) and expertise (teaching skills, professional skills, organization, communication skills, and self-confidence). These can be applied to high-quality mentors in both formal and informal mentoring relationships. However, it is important to emphasize that while the primary goal of workplace mentoring is protégé development, mentors can also benefit from these relationships. Effectively, mentoring has been deemed a "learning partnership" (Eby, Rhodes, & Allen, 2007), a concept that stresses both the reciprocal and the developmental components of workplace mentoring. Greengard (2002), among other authors, mentioned this phenomenon as "reverse mentoring," meaning the process developed with the intent that the protégé provides developmental support to the mentor. This situation typically involves the use of technology and/or information and knowledge sharing, and it may happen in the case of young, well-educated entry-level workers, who have more knowledge about technology than their mentors.

Related to the use or role of technology, we have to refer to electronic mentoring, or e-mentoring, within which technology is used to foster developmental relationships. Ensher and Murphy (2007) defined e-mentoring as a reciprocally beneficial relationship between a mentor and a protégé, which offers new learning as well as career and emotional support, through electronic means (e.g., email, chat rooms, social networking spaces). They emphasize that e-mentoring can succeed or fail depending on whether technological means are used exclusively or not.

Haggard et al. (2011), based on their literature analysis, proposed three core attributes of workplace mentoring that differentiate mentoring from other types of work-related relationships, namely: reciprocity, developmental benefits, and regular/consistent interaction over a period of time.

To finish this conceptual approach to mentoring, it is relevant to refer to some organizational outcomes arising from it: it helps organizations directly by maintaining skilled employees and an internal culture, and improves the fit between managers and organizations (Parnell, 1998). Mentoring is associated with better career advancement, more career development opportunities, higher levels of career maturity, and higher overall job satisfaction among protégés. So the mentoring relationship produces *developmental benefits* linked to the protégés' work and/or career, which often go beyond the strictly job-related skills or protégé benefits required by the organization (Haggard et al., 2011). However, mentoring is not only related to the development of mentee goals. It may also focus on organizational objectives. According to McDowall-Long (2004), formal mentoring programs are developed by organizations in order to meet both organizational and employee development objectives. In contrast, informal mentoring relationships have been developed for a number of reasons, such as mutual attraction and liking

(Ragins & Cotton, 1999; Covan, 2000), the aspiration of experienced professionals to be at the origin of innovation in their professions or organizations (Genser, 1998; Covan, 2000), and interpersonal comfort (Ragins & Cotton, 1999). Nevertheless, formal mentoring relationships can fail in many of these aspects, leading to lower levels of interpersonal exchange.

Guiding thread

The mentoring process moves on along three possible guiding tracks: (a) the required competencies for performing a specific job within the specific organization; (b) the professional opportunities and wishes of the mentee considering his or her future career; and (c) the professional characteristics of the mentee.

Participants

As we we exclude group mentoring from our analysis (Kaye & Jacobson, 1995), the main participants of workplace mentoring are mentor and mentee (or protégé). The mentor is in charge of helping the mentee in their developmental process. The mentee is the object of the intervention, being helped by the mentor. Where there is a formal mentoring process, someone from the human resource department can have a management role checking schedules and participating in the evaluation of the results. In long-lasting mentoring relationships, mentee and mentor roles can become blurred and reciprocity of learning occurs. Reverse mentoring is an example. According to Haggard et al. (2011), mentoring requires the willingness to develop a *reciprocal* relationship. Implying mutuality of social exchange, mentoring is something more than a one-way relationship. This relationship is predominantly a mentor–mentee relationship and can take several forms (e.g., formal/informal, peer, supervisory) and different kinds of interaction modalities (e.g., face-to-face, telephone, virtual). At the same time, mentoring involves *regular/consistent interaction* between the mentor and the protégé over time. Finally, also according to the authors cited, we have to consider the context in which the relationship occurs and how this context influences mentoring relationships and their outcomes. We emphasize this aspect, because these types of *developmental relationships* can lead to both positive and negative outcomes for participants, may be very effective, very ineffective, and even dysfunctional. Another important aspect is the formal or informal nature of the relationship. McDowall-Long (2004) identified a clear difference between formal and informal mentor–protégé relationships, with informal mentoring relationships being longer in duration and focused on long-term goals.

Boundary clarity and institutional implementation

Mentoring has unclear boundaries and overlaps with other developmental practices. For instance, scholars claim there are several common aspects between mentoring and coaching (Ruru et al., 2013). International institutions join mentoring and coaching together (e.g., European Mentoring and Coaching Council), and several academic journals are focused on both developmental practices (e.g., *International Journal of Evidence Based Coaching and Mentoring*; *International Journal of Mentoring and Coaching*).

Research on mentoring

Allen et al. (2008), based on their research, concluded that mentoring research carried out so far was of a predominantly quantitative, correlational, cross-sectional nature. Data were collected from a single source, most of the time from the protégé, and a single method was used for collection. However, the authors also said that more complex types of study were emerging, such as longitudinal and multisource. Regarding the content of the research developed, they highlight the importance given to the study of the predictors and outcomes of mentoring, to theory and measurement development, as well as to research review.

A few years later, Haggard et al. (2011) stressed that research on mentoring has focused on several questions. Among them, we emphasize those devoted to the concept of mentoring and its nuclear dimensions, the influence of mentoring on the protégé's career, the study of the protégé and/or mentor perspective/characteristics, and the process of mentoring, its phases and the type/quality of the relationship between mentor and protégé.

Recently, Eby et al. (2013), in their meta-analysis, summarized research developed in this field on the antecedents, correlates, and consequences of instrumental and psychosocial support and the quality of the relationship according to protégé perceptions. Researchers interested in mentoring belong to different and diverse disciplines (e.g., psychology, sociology, education, health) and, according to the authors, methodological limitations may explain the results found. As noted earlier, there still seems to be a need to develop this field of research.

Comparing Structured Actions of Intentional Development

The developmental practices presented here are typical ways of reflection-on-action (Schön, 1996) and are seen to be unique in their identity and at the same time blurred in their boundaries. All of them are focused on the real practice of the individual who is the target of the developmental process carried out. The guiding threads are the criteria used for the sequence of the various steps in the process of each structured action of intentional development (SAoID). In supervision and Balint Groups, the guiding threads are the cases brought by the practitioner that are considered to deserve special attention. In CoP there is no specific structure for bringing practice for reflection: questions, doubts, ideas, tips that can be shared by CoP members. In mentoring, the reflection on action is structured according to the expected tasks that have to be performed in the specific job and organization, and also guided by the future projects and career prospects of the mentee. Although the guiding thread in the four SAoIDs is the actual practice of the individual who is the subject of developmental intervention, there is a different way of bringing that practice for reflection and discussion. Balint Groups have the most structured way of doing so. Members present their cases, one at a time, and their colleagues discuss the case almost without the intervention of the presenter. The most open way of bringing practice for discussion occurs in CoPs, as members present their questions, answers, and comments as they think best, without specific structured guidelines. Regarding the level of structuring, mentoring, and supervision can be put in the middle as the guidelines for reflection on action are less strict than in the BGs, but stricter than in CoPs.

Concerning the focus of the SAoID, BGs concentrate on understanding the practitioner–client relationship. That means emotional and communication dimensions are core aspects of the reflection that should take place. In supervision the focus is on understanding the case, the practitioner–client relationship, and the organization where the service occurs (Carroll, 2007). CoPs have a less defined focus, as everything related to the professional area of the CoP is a possible subject to be approached and discussed. Finally, workplace mentoring focuses on the tasks that are part of the role in a specific organization, and so mentoring has to do with both contextual and task performance (Motowidlo, 2003). The interests and professional aspirations of the mentee are also put on the table to design developmental strategies.

Regarding duration, three out of the four SAoIDs presented here vary greatly, from a few weeks to several years, each session lasting between one and two hours. CoPs are the exception as no duration or length of session is defined. Some rules can be agreed for each specific CoP.

Considering institutional implementation, three of the four SAoIDs are supported by international institutions, which take care of accreditation, training, and definition of the ethical principles and code of conduct for the specific developmental practice. CoPs are mentioned within several professional bodies that promote them internally but they have no international institution for member affiliation.

Finally, regarding definitions of the SAoIDs, we presented a core definition of each one, knowing that there are blurred boundaries and some overlapping, namely regarding some variants of each. In Table 20.1, we present the main characteristics of the four SAoIDs through their definitions, keeping the identity of each one clear, and also their overlapping and blurred boundaries. As can be seen, we bring contributions from several authors.

SAoIDs are structured actions, which means that to be considered as such, they have a specific way (with varying degrees of flexibility) to be carried out. They are also based on interpersonal interaction and relationships, whether between peers (BGs and CoPs) or between more experienced/qualified professionals and less experienced/qualified professionals (CoPs, supervision, and mentoring). As we have shown throughout this chapter, all SAoIDs have been the focus of conceptual developments and empirical research, which has strengthened the identity of each. They are all focused on promoting the development of professionals through reflection on action (Schön, 1996) for skills development, identity reinforcement, and emotional support. This last point (emotional support) stands out particularly in BGs. Finally, we have to consider that while BGs and supervision are focused on relationship competencies (and are therefore appropriate for helping professionals), CoP and mentoring cover all professional areas.

Future Research

Although the four SAoIDs presented have a strong conceptual identity and have been used worldwide for the personal and professional development of practitioners, research comparing them was not found. They are all developmental practices that have been the focus of specific empirical research and conceptual writings.

Besides being a developmental practice, BGs have also been considered a method of research on their own (Hull, 1996). That can explain why most research on BGs is qualitative and has small samples, as well as their implementation often being described in qualitative research. Future developments need larger samples. A better understanding of the characteristics of those who benefit most from BG attendance is needed. Clear consolidation of the outputs that emerge from BG enrolment and attendance is important, to justify the time and energy required from all participants.

Table 20.1 Main conceptual definitions of structured actions of intentional development

SAoID	Balint Groups	Supervision	Communities of practice	Mentoring
What	A formal reciprocal provision	A formal provision	A nonformal reciprocal (or not) provision	A formal provision
By whom	By peers professionals	By a qualified/ experienced professional	By professionals interested and experienced in specific subjects	By a qualified/ experienced professional
To whom	To peers professionals	To less experienced professionals	To less experienced professionals (or to peers)	To less experienced professionals
Structured by	An accredited leader	An experienced professional (supervisor)	The community as a self-regulated group	An experienced professional (mentor)
When	Intensive	Intensive	Variable	Intensive
Based on	Relationship/ interaction based (periodic meetings)	Relationship/ interaction based (periodic meetings)	Relationship/ interaction based	Relationship/ interaction based (periodic meetings)
What content	For reflection on practice (case-focused) as helper (professional relationships)	For reflection on practice (case-focused) as helper	For reflection on practice	For reflection on practice and career
What is done	Supports, directs, and guides	Supports, directs, and guides	Supports, directs, and guides	Supports, directs, and guides
Intention	The work of others (peers) and them as professionals	The work of others (supervisees) and them as professionals	The work of others (novices or peers) and them as professionals	The work of others (mentees) and them as professionals
Inspiring authors	Balint (1985) De Lambert (2010) Jablonski, Kjeldmand, & Salinsky (2013) Johnson (2001) Lakasing (2005) Lustig (2004, 2007) Rüth (2009)	Carroll (2007) Chiller & Crisp (2012) Davis & Burke (2012) Guest & Beutler (1988) Jones (2006) Kaslow, Falander, & Grus (2012) Koivo, Hyrkäs, & Saarinen (2011) Milne (2007) MacDonald (2002) Moyes (2009) Robiner & Schofield (1990) Sirola-Karvinen & Hyrkas (2006)	Brown & Duguid (1991) Cox (2005) Lave & Wenger (1991) Wenger, McDermott, & Snyder (2002) Li et al. (2009) Rivera (2011, 2011a) Barnett et al. (2012)	Eby, Rhodes, & Allen (2007) Haggard et al. (2011) Kram (1985) Kram & Ragins (2007) McDowall-Long (2004) Noe, Greenberger, & Wang (2002) Wanberg, Welsh, & Hezlett (2003)

Regarding supervision, empirical evidence of the effectiveness of clinical supervision has been considered weak (Dilworth et al., 2013; Wright, 2012). We presented some evidence of the following outcomes of supervision: strengthening professional identity (Passmore & McGoldric, 2009), staying in the same profession (Chiller and Crisp, 2012), professional and competence development (Passmore & McGoldric, 2009), and well-being (Koivo, Hyrkäs, & Saarinen, 2011). Other results are less positive: no positive effects on burnout, well-being, and satisfaction. Livni, Crowe, and Gonsalvez (2012) found no positive effects of supervision on burnout, well-being, and satisfaction, and it was perceived as time-consuming, triggering negative feelings, and possibly threatening confidentiality (Davis & Burke, 2012). Future developments can consolidate the effects of supervision as a developmental tool and the factors that determine its differential suitability for individuals and professional areas.

Regarding CoPs, several suggestions were made by different authors (Cox, 2005; Li et al., 2009), such as: to examine how existent CoPs deal with technological, strategic, and behavioral problems in their implementation and development; to analyze and compare different companies that have communities of practice and other forms of knowledge management; to develop specific indicators that expand the characteristics of a CoP already identified (allowing to distinguish "CoPs" from "non-CoPs" and identify the stage of development of a CoP); to study thoroughly the expectations, roles, and responsibilities of the various participants within CoPs and the power relationships between them; to research the relationship between the internal characteristics of CoPs (in different stages of development) and the structural forces present when they operate; to study the role of virtual CoPs in overcoming isolation in geographically dispersed participants; to validate the theoretical framework that supports the implementation of CoPs in different kinds of organizations and contexts; to assess the effectiveness of CoPs in different sectors of activity and compare the results.

Similar research challenges can be considered for mentoring, namely confirmation of its outcomes, the differential suitability of mentoring for different people, and the developmental stages of the mentoring process. The quality of the relationship between mentor and mentee is also a challenge for further research. Finally, careful descriptions of the function that BGs, supervision, CoPs, and mentoring can have in the personal and professional development of practitioners would be welcome, in order to include them as one structured action of intentional development among others.

Comparative research can clarify which developmental practices fit which individuals and contexts, as well as what results to expect from each. That kind of work helps human resource managers, systematically, to have a diversity of tools available, for developing people within organizations, and design the human resource development strategy according to informed criteria.

Conclusion

This chapter summarizes four intentional developmental practices (Balint Groups, supervision, communities of practice, and mentoring), all of them being structured ways of reflection on action (Schön, 1996) through which people can develop personally and professionally. All have been implemented for several decades, have a conceptual identity, and empirical research has been carried out on them. Interaction between people is the common means by which learning and reflection takes place. However, they have also blurred boundaries that bring complexity to understanding their differential effects and the sharp distinction of the diversity of their aims. The chapter has presented the dominant definition of each SAoID, its purpose, guiding thread, participants, institutional implementation, and the main research topics found for each of them. The chapter ends with suggestions for further research. These are forms of personal and professional development that can be used by human resource departments and individuals who want to develop their skills and competencies.

References

ACGME (2007). Competencies and Balint Training: Competencies taught by Balint work. http:// balintaustralianewzealand.org/articals/abs%20ACGME.pdf (accessed April 10, 2014).

Allen, T. D., Eby, L. T., O'Brien, K. E., & Lentz, E. (2008). The state of mentoring research: A qualitative review of current research methods and future research implications. *Journal of Vocational Behavior*, 73, 343–357.

Andersson, S. J., Lindberg, G., & Troein, M. (2002). What shapes GPs' work with depressed patients? A qualitative interview study. *Family Practice*, 19(6), 623–631.

Balint, E. (1985). The history of training and research in Balint-groups. *Psychoanalytic Psychotherapy*, 1(2), 1–9.

Barker, K. K., & Hunsley, J. (2013). The use of theoretical models in psychology supervisor development research from 1994 to 2010: A systematic review. *Canadian Psychology*, 54(3), 176–185.

Barnett, S., Jones, S. C., Bennett, S., Iverson, D., & Bonney, A. (2012). General practice training and virtual communities of practice – a review of the literature. *BMC Family Practice*, 13, 87–99. doi:10.1186/1471-2296-13-87.

Benson, J., & Magraith, K. (2005). Compassion, fatigue and burnout: The role of Balint Groups. *Australian Family Physician*, 34(6), 497–498.

Bono, J. E., Foldes, H. J., Vinson, G., & Muros, J. P. (2007). Workplace emotions: The role of supervision and leadership. *Journal of Applied Psychology*, 92(5), 1357–1367.

Brown, J. S., & Duguid, P. (1991). Organizational learning and communities of practice: Toward a unified view of working, learning and innovation. *Organization Science*, 2(1), 40–57.

Carroll, M. (2007). One more time: What is supervision? *Psychotherapy in Australia*, 13(3), 34–40.

Cataldo, K., Peeden, K., Geesey, M., & Dickerson, L. (2005). Association between Balint training and physician empathy and work satisfaction. *Family Medicine*, 37(5), 328–331.

Chiller, P., & Crisp, B. R. (2012). Professional supervision: A workforce retention strategy for social work? *Australian Social Work*, 65(2), 232–242.

Covan, E. K. (2000). Revisiting the relationship between elder modelers and their protégées. *Sociological Perspectives*, 43(4), S7–S20.

Cox, A. M. (2005). What are communities of practice? A comparative review of four seminal works. *Journal of Information Science*, 31(6), 527–540.

Das, A., Egleston, P., El-Sayeh, H., Middlemost, M., Pal, N., & Williamson, L. (2003). Trainee's experiences of a Balint Group. *Psychiatric Bulletin*, 27, 274–275.

Davis, C., & Burke, L. (2012). The effectiveness of clinical supervision for a group of ward managers based in a district general hospital: An evaluative study. *Journal of Nursing Management*, 20, 782–793.

De Lambert, L. (2010). Postscript to Balint work increases the ability to think one's own thoughts. *Group Analysis*, 43, 86–89.

Dilworth, S., Higgins, I., Parker, V., Kelly, B., & Turner, J. (2013). Finding a way forward: A literature review on the current debates around clinical supervision. *Contemporary Nurse*, 45(1), 22–32.

Eby, L. T., Allen, T. D., Hoffman, B. J., Baranik, L. E., Sauer, J. B., Baldwin, S., et al. (2013). An interdisciplinary meta-analysis of the potential antecedents, correlates, and consequences of protégé perceptions of mentoring. *Psychological Bulletin*, 139(2), 441–476.

Eby, L. T., Rhodes, J. E., & Allen, T. D. (2007). Definition and evolution of mentoring. In T. D. Allen & L. T. Eby (Eds.), *The Blackwell Handbook of Mentoring: A Multiple Perspectives Approach* (pp. 7–20). Oxford: Blackwell.

Ensher, E. A., & Murphy, S. E. (2007). E-mentoring: Next-generation research strategies and suggestions. In B. R. Ragins & K. E. Kram (Eds.), *The Handbook of Mentoring at Work: Theory, Research, and Practice* (pp. 299–322). Thousand Oaks, CA: Sage.

Falender, C. A., Cornish, J. A., Goodyear, R., Hatcher, R., Kaslow, N. J., Leventhal, G., et al. (2004). Defining competencies in psychology supervision: A consensus statement. *Journal of Clinical Psychology*, 60, 771–785. doi:10.1002/jclp.20013.

Falender, C. A., & Shafranske, E. P. (2007). Competence in competency-based supervision practice: Construct and application. *Professional Psychology: Research and Practice*, 38, 232–240.

Fielden, K. (2008). From novice to expert therapist: The role of clinical supervision in the transition. PhD thesis. Roehampton University.

Firth, A., & Martens, E. (2008). Transforming supervisors? A critique of post-liberal approaches to research supervision. *Teaching in Higher Education*, 13(3), 279–289.

Fitzgerald, G., & Hunter, M. D. (2003). Organising and evaluating a Balint group for trainees in psychiatry. *Psychiatric Bulletin*, 27, 434–436.

Genser, E. S. (1998). Finance professionals benefit from mentoring. *Healthcare Financial Management*, 52(12), 70–72.

Graham, S., Gask, L., Swift, G., & Evans, M. (2009). Balint-style case discussion groups in psychiatric training: An evaluation. *Academic Psychiatry*, 33, 198–203.

Gray, D. E. (2010). Towards the lifelong skills and business development of coaches: An integrated model of supervision and mentoring. *Coaching: An International Journal of Theory, Research and Practice*, 3(1), 60–72.

Greengard, S. (2002). Moving forward with reverse mentoring. *Workforce*, 81, 15.

Guest, P. D., & Beutler, L. E. (1988). Impact of psychotherapy supervision on therapist orientation and values. *Journal of Consulting and Clinical Psychology*, 56(5), 653–658.

Haggard, D. L., Dougherty, T. W., Turban, D. B., & Wilbanks, J. E. (2011). Who is a mentor? A review of evolving definitions and implications for research. *Journal of Management*, 37(1), 280–304.

Halse, C. (2011). Becoming a supervisor: The impact of doctoral supervision on supervisors' learning. *Studies in Higher Education*, 36(5), 557–570.

Hannah, S. T., Schaubroeck, J. M., Peng, A. C., Lord, R. G., Trevino, L. K., Kozlowski, S. W. J., et al. (2013). Joint influences of individual and work unit abusive supervision on ethical intentions and behaviors: A moderated mediation model. *Journal of Applied Psychology*, 98(4), 579–592.

Hoge, M. A., Migdole, S., Farkas, M. S., Ponce, A. N., & Hunnicutt, C. (2011). Supervision in public sector behavioral health: A review. *The Clinical Supervisor*, 30, 183–203.

Hojat, M. (2009). Ten approaches for enhancing empathy in health and human services cultures. *Journal of Health and Human Services Administration*, 31(4), 412–450.

Hull, S. A. (1996). The method of Balint group work and its contribution to research in general practice. *Family Practice*, 13, S10–S12.

Jablonski, H. (2003). Defining Balint work – Is there a heartland? And which are the neighbouring countries? In J. Salinsky & H. Otten (Eds.), *The Doctor, the Patient and their Well-Being – World Wide*. Proceedings of the Thirteenth International Balint Congress, Berlin. The International Balint Federation.

Jablonski, H., Kjeldmand, D., & Salinsky, J. (2013). Balint Groups and peer supervision. In L. S. Sommers & J. Launer (Eds.), *Clinical Uncertainty in Primary Care: The Challenges of Collaborative Engagement* (pp. 73–93). New York: Springer.

Johnson, A. (2001). The Balint movement in America. *Family Medicine*, 33(3), 174–177.

Johnson, A. H., Brock, C. D., & Hueston, W. J. (2003). Resident physicians who continue Balint training: A longitudinal study 1982–1999. *Family Medicine*, 35(6), 428–433.

Johnson, A. H., Nease, D. E., Milberg, L. C., & Addison, R. B. (2004). Essential characteristics of effective Balint group leadership. *Residency Education*, 36(4), 253–259.

Kalule, L., & Bouchamma, Y. (2013). Teacher supervision practices: What do teachers think? *International Studies in Educational Administration (Commonwealth Council for Educational Administration & Management (CCEAM))*, 40(3), 91–104.

Kaslow, N. J., Falender, C. A., & Grus, C. L. (2012). Valuing and practicing competency-based supervision: A transformational leadership perspective. *Training and Education in Professional Psychology*, 6(1), 47–54.

Kaye, B., & Jacobson, B. (1995). Mentoring: A group guide. *Training & Development*, 49(4), 23–27.

Kjeldmand, D. (2006). The doctor, the task and the group: Balint groups as a means of developing new understanding in the physician–patient relationship. Acta Universitatis Upsaliensis. Digital Comprehensive Summaries of Uppsala Dissertations from the Faculty of Medicine 157. Uppsala.

Kjeldmand, D., & Holmström, I. (2008). Balint Groups as a means to increase job satisfaction and prevent burnout among general practitioners. *Annals of Family Medicine*, 6(2), 138–145.

Kjeldmand, D., & Holmström, I. (2010). Difficulties in Balint Groups: A qualitative study of leaders' experiences. *British Journal of General Practice*, 60, 808–814.

Kjeldmand, D., Jablonski, H., & Salinsky, J. (2013). Research on Balint groups. In L. S. Sommers & J. Launer (Eds.), *Clinical Uncertainty in Primary Care: The Challenges of Collaborative Engagement* (pp. 95–116). New York: Springer.

Koivo, A., Hyrkäs, K., & Saarinen, P. I. (2011). Who attends clinical supervision? The uptake of clinical supervision by hospital nurses. *Journal of Nursing Management*, 19, 69–79.

Kram, K. E. (1985). *Mentoring at Work: Developmental Relationships in Organizational Life.* Glenview, IL: Scott, Foresman.

Kram, K. E., & Ragins, B. R. (2007). The landscape of mentoring in the 21st century. In B. R. Ragins & K. E. Kram (Eds.), *The Handbook of Mentoring at Work: Theory, Research, and Practice* (pp. 659–692). Thousand Oaks, CA: Sage.

Lakasing, E. (2005). Michael Balint – An outstanding medical life. *British Journal of General Practice*, 55, 724–725.

Launer, J. (2007). Moving on from Balint: Embracing clinical supervision. *British Journal of General Practice*, 57, 182–183.

Lave, J., & Wenger, E. (1991), *Situated Learning: Legitimate Peripheral Participation.* Cambridge: Cambridge University Press.

Levinson, D. J., Darrow, C. N., Klein, E. B., Levinson, M. H., & McKee, B. (1978). *Seasons of a Man's Life.* New York: Knopf.

Li, L. C., Grimshaw, J. M., Nielsen, C., Judd, M., Coyte, P. C., & Graham, I. G. (2009). Use of communities of practice in business and health care sectors: A systematic review. *Implementation Science*, 4(27), 1–9.

Livni, D., Crowe, T. P., & Gonsalvez, C. G. (2012). Effects of supervision modality and intensity on alliance and outcomes for the supervisee. *Rehabilitation Psychology*, 57(2), 178–186.

Lustig, M. (2004). Generating a reflective space for GPs: Working with Balint Groups. *Australasian Journal of Psychotherapy*, 23, 66–85.

Lustig, M. (2007). From psychoanalytic psychotherapy to Balint groups: What do leaders need to know? *Australasian Journal of Psychotherapy*, 26(1), 40–46.

MacDonald, J. (2002). Clinical supervision: A review of underlying concepts and developments. *Australian and New Zealand Journal of Psychiatry*, 36, 92–98.

Malhotra, Y. (1997). Knowledge management in inquiring organizations. *Proceedings of 3rd Americas Conference on Information Systems* (pp. 293–295). Indianapolis, IN.

Matalon, A., Rabin, S., & Maoz, B. (2005). Communication, relationships and Balint groups. *Proceedings of the 14th International Balint Congress.* Stockholm, Sweden.

McCallina, A., & Nayar, S. (2012). Postgraduate research supervision: A critical review of current practice. *Teaching in Higher Education*, 17(1), 63–74.

McDowall-Long, K. (2004). Mentoring relationships: Implications for practitioners and suggestions for future research. *Human Resource Development International*, 7(4), 519–534.

Milne, D. L. (2007). An empirical definition of clinical supervision. *British Journal of Clinical Psychology*, 46, 437–447.

Motowidlo, S. J. (2003). Job performance. In W. Borman, D. Ilgen, & R. Klimoski (Eds.), *Handbook of Psychology*, vol. 12, *Industrial and Organizational Psychology* (pp. 39–53). Hoboken, NJ: John Wiley & Sons, Inc.

Moyes, B. (2009). Literature review of coaching supervision. *International Coaching Psychology Review*, 4(2), 162–173.

Noe, R. A., Greenberger, D. B., & Wang, S. (2002). Mentoring: What we know and where we might go. *Research in Personnel and Human Resources Management*, 21, 129–173.

Parnell, J. A. (1998). Improving the fit between organizations and employees. *SAM Advanced Management Journal*, 63(1), 35–43.

Passmore, J., & McGoldric, S. (2009). Super-vision, extra-vision or blind faith? A grounded theory study of the efficacy of coaching supervision. *International Coaching Psychology Review*, 4(2), 145–161.

Rabin, S., Maoz, B., Shorer, Y., & Matalon, A. (2009). Balint groups as "shared care" in the area of mental health in primary medicine. *Mental Health in Family Medicine*, 6, 139–143.

Rabin, S., Matalon, A., Maoz, B., & Shiber. A. (2005). Keeping doctors healthy: A salutogenic perspective. *Families, Systems and Health*, 23, 94–102.

Ragins, B. R., & Cotton, J. L. (1999). Mentor functions and outcomes: A comparison of men and women in formal and informal mentoring. *Journal of Applied Psychology*, 84(4), 529–549.

Ragins, B. R., & McFarlin, D. B. (1990). Perceptions of mentor roles in cross-gender mentor relationships. *Journal of Vocational Behavior*, 37, 321–340.

Ranmuthugala, G., Plumb, J. J., Cunningham, F. C., Georgiou, A., Westbrook J. I., & Braithwaite J. (2011). How and why are communities of practice established in the healthcare sector? A systematic review of the literature. *BMC Health Services Research*, 11 (273), 1–16.

Rivera, J. C. A. (2011a). Las comunidades de práctica y la gestión del conocimiento: Un estúdio descriptivo. *Revista Internacional Administracion & Finanças*, 4(1), 83–100.

Rivera, J. C. A. (2011b). Communities of practice: Improving knowledge management in business. *Business Education & Accreditation*, 3(1), 101–111.

Robiner, W. N., & Schofield, W. (1990). References on supervision in clinical and counseling psychology. *Professional Psychology: Research and Practice*, 21(4), 297–312.

Ruru, D., Sanga, K., Walker, K., & Ralph, E. (2013). Adapting mentorship across the professions: A Fijian view. *International Journal of Evidence Based Coaching and Mentoring*, 11(2), 70–93.

Rüth, U. (2009). Balint work increases the ability to think one's own thoughts: Classic Balint Group work and the thinking of W. R. Bion. *Group Analysis*, 42(4), 380–391.

Schön, D. A. (1996). *Educating the Reflective Practitioner: Toward a New Design for Teaching and Learning in the Professions*. San Francisco: Jossey-Bass.

Shorer, Y., Biderman, A., Levy, A., Rabin, S., Karni, A., Maoz, B., et al. (2011). Family physicians leaving their clinic – The Balint Group as an opportunity to say good-bye. *Annals of Family Medicine*, 9, 549–551.

Simpson, M., Buckman, R., Stewart, M., Maguire, P., Lipkin, M., Novack, D., et al. (1991). Doctor–patient communication: The Toronto consensus statement. *British Medical Journal*, 303, 1385–1387.

Sirola-Karvinen, P., & Hyrkas, K. (2006). Clinical supervision for nurses in administrative and leadership positions: A systematic literature review of the studies focusing on administrative clinical supervision. *Journal of Nursing Management*, 14, 601–609.

Tulinius, C., & Hølge-Hazelton, B. (2010). Continuing professional development for general practitioners:Supporting the development of professionalism. *Medical Education*, 44, 412–420.

Turner, A. L., & Malm, R. L. (2004). A preliminary investigation of Balint and non-Balint behavioral medicine training. *Family Medicine*, 36(2), 114–122.

Vanstone, M., Hibbert, K., Kinsella, E. A., McKenzie, P., Pitman, A., & Lingard, L. (2013). Interdisciplinary doctoral research supervision: A scoping review. *Canadian Journal of Higher Education*, 43(2), 42–67.

Wanberg, C. R., Welsh, E. T., & Hezlett, S. A. (2003). Mentoring research: A review and dynamic process model. *Research in Personnel and Human Resources Management*, 22, 39–124.

Wenger, E. (1998). *Communities of Practice: Learning, Meaning, and Identity*. Cambridge, UK: Cambridge University Press.

Wenger, E., McDermott, R., & Snyder, W. (2002). *Cultivating Communities of Practice*. Boston, MA: Harvard Business School Press.

Wilkerson, K. (2006). Peer supervision for the professional development of school counselors: Toward an understanding of terms and findings. *Counselor Education & Supervision*, 46, 59–67.

Wright J. (2012). Clinical supervision: A review of the evidence base. *Nursing Standard*, 27(3), 44–49.

Yakeley, J., Shoenberg, P., Morris, R., Sturgeon, D., & Majid, S. (2011). Psychodynamic approaches to teaching medical students about the doctor–patient relationship: Randomised controlled trial. *The Psychiatrist Online*, 35, 308–313. doi:10.1192/pb.bp.110.033704.

Zarbock, G., Drews, M., Bodansky, A., & Dahme, B. (2009). The evaluation of supervision: Construction of brief questionnaires for the supervisor and the supervisee. *Psychotherapy Research*, 19(2), 194–204.

21

Informal Learning
and Development

Valéria Vieira de Moraes and Jairo Eduardo
Borges-Andrade

Introduction

Work-related learning happened mostly through the observation of more experienced performers and by doing, over long periods of apprenticeship in workshops, until the industrial revolution. Industrial plants as the work *locus* came along with the requirement of quite narrowly defined task performances and clear labor division processes. An approach to manage those plants and these processes was needed. As a result structured methods and techniques were developed for efficient learning. The promotion of this fast learning process often occurred outside the workplace under the auspices of plant owners or government. It may be argued that these structured methods and techniques have become panaceas. However, they often fail to take into account the context (i.e., collective learning) as a predictor of training effectiveness (Mourão & Borges-Andrade, 2013), as well as individual characteristics (i.e., motivation to learn and to apply and satisfaction with learning), moderated by the cognitive complexity of training (Pilati & Borges-Andrade, 2008).

Contemporary transformations taking place in the nature of work (Frese, 2008; Sonnentag, Niessen, & Ohly, 2004) demand more flexible and reflective workers capable of keeping up-to-date with constantly changing technology. Behavioral (i.e., seeking help in written online materials and help from co-workers) and cognitive (i.e., intrinsic and extrinsic reflection) learning strategies, used by these workers, may predict the development of innovative competencies (Isidro-Filho et al., 2013). Information and communication technologies allow for work in virtual teams, in which their perceived performance may depend on the use of behavioral learning strategies such as reading and personal study (Gondim, Puente-Palacios, & Borges-Andrade, 2011). Focus shifts to unstructured learning activities that happen along with work itself, as they are credited to contribute more significantly to the development of skills (Day, 1998; Bierema & Eraut, 2004; Eraut, 2004; Tynjälä, 2008). Carefully designed training and development programs

The Wiley Blackwell Handbook of the Psychology of Training, Development, and Performance Improvement,
First Edition. Edited by Kurt Kraiger, Jonathan Passmore, Sigmar Malvezzi, and Nuno Rebelo dos Santos.
© 2015 John Wiley & Sons Ltd. Published 2020 by John Wiley & Sons Ltd.

may be less important for the prediction of management competencies, than the use of cognitive learning strategies by managers plus their collective perception of a company's performance management practices (Brandão et al., 2012).

In the context of modern organizations and workplaces, in which the workers are expected to be flexible, up-to-date, and to think about what they do, structured and unstructured learning approaches are necessary. Training effectiveness at work may be highly dependent on the ex-trainee's own use of strategies for the transfer of learning and these spontaneous actions may be dependent on the existence or perception of the organization's support for learning transfer (Pilati & Borges-Andrade, 2012). Performance expected from workers can vary from the very simple and clearly defined list of steps of a certain task to a broad range of behaviors included in the notion of competence. Tasks and competences may be the object of a careful instructional design or they may be expected to be learned by an autonomous worker. In order to encompass those two approaches, often referred to as formal and informal learning, the concept of workplace learning may be useful. It has been receiving growing attention in the scientific literature, in countries in Africa, America, Asia, Europe, and Oceania (Malloch et al., 2011).

The objective of this chapter is to describe informal learning and its role for the development of individuals in workplaces. It is structured around a comprehensive workplace learning model, which may serve as a reference background for understanding the informal learning that happens between individuals at work. Before the presentation of this model, a brief critical analysis is made of the concept of workplace learning and of its formality, ending with a look at the different levels of analysis of learning, according to the current literature. Afterwards, two sections are dedicated to a typology of learning based on the induction of learning opportunities at the workplace and to its possible outcomes. The chapter finally draws on some research studies and concludes with suggestions for future investigation.

Workplace Learning Theory

The concept and what it means

The verb "to learn" is adverbial. It represents a description of something that needs to be completed: to learn ... "a word," "a concept," "a principle," "a belief," "a value," "a norm," "how to operate a machine," "how to solve a problem." Therefore, it needs a "content" (learn what, learn how). This content is acquired, processed, and retained and this is done for some purpose. The verb "to learn" is an open disposition. It synthesizes what happened (some past experience) and what may be predicted (some action in the future). Therefore, it needs "places," where the experience has happened and where the action may be shown. This verb is bipolar: learning may happen or learning may not happen. References to "unlearning" are somewhat senseless. Instead, people may forget, or may not have learned. A thorough critical analysis of the concept of learning has been made by Coelho and Borges-Andrade (2008), by discussing some of its most common daily uses, following recommendations made by Ryle (2000). This analysis of daily concepts allows the extraction of the major ideas they represent. They argue that the polysemous nature of this concept and the diversity of meanings attached to it may explain its attractiveness and its generalized use. However, they also argue for caution on this use, since the absence of a unique meaning may result in contradictory definitions and, therefore, in a useless multiplication of theories.

Learning is a process that may have provided some advantage to some animal species, during evolution. This is especially true for human beings, since they were not the fastest or the strongest animals and did not have the sharpest nails or teeth. Learning is quite useful, when contexts change and human beings need to try new ways of environmental functioning and, if these ways work, to teach them to other member of their species (or group). This usefulness is probably one of the reasons why learning became so popular, in workplaces, even before the industrial revolution. The rapid contemporary transformations of work, in the different places where it may be done, have increased the idea of this usefulness, until a point in which workplace learning may have been turned into a panacea, or a remedy for all diseases. It is highly valued, under the supposition that the performance of workers, and their organizations, may be improved by learning that takes place in schools and in training and development centers, or as those workers act. However, it must be taken into account that the mentioned performances may also be jeopardized by learning.

The major features of human learning are (mostly based on Illeris, 2011):

1   It is an individual acquisition process of knowledge, skills, and attitudes (KSAs).
2   This process results from the social interaction of the person with the environment.
3   The social interaction may be mediated by people or texts, images, and sounds produced by people.
4   That acquisition process is situated in terms of content, over which those KSAs are built.
5   That acquisition process is situated in terms of context, places in which those KSAs may be demonstrated.

These places may be the house, the street, the school, the community, the disco, the church, the prison, an agricultural field, the industrial plant, or the office. But they may be virtual, instead of physical places, such as a chat, an organizational intranet or the internet. They may be interpersonal (school or working peers, family or church members, friends) or even intrapersonal (the learner's own working memory). Human learning needs these spaces, in which experiences happen and in which individuals may later apply what they have acquired. These spaces are workplaces when the individual intentional action produces a recognized outcome that involves effort and persistence and when these are demanded, as an obligation or challenge. This action is called work. Thus, workplace learning is an individual process, in which KSAs are acquired as a consequence of social interaction in spaces where work occurs. The acquisition results in changes of behaviors, in these contexts, and may or may not be induced, by activities designed and organized in order to promote KSAs. This definition is based mainly on psychological theories. There might be others, from management or economical theories, for example.

Formality, informality, and other possibilities

The approach to the learning phenomenon derives from three main different basic research lines in the scientific literature about learning related to work. From a behaviorist point of view, the focus is on behavioral change resultant of an individual's interactions with the environment. On the other hand, the cognitive approach postulates that an intrapsychic process mediates those changes in behavior. Both lines have the individual as the focal point of analysis. However, the context is taken into account in more historically recent production, mostly as a *container* of social and material environments, including other people, objects, and technologies, in which the learner moves (Fenwick, 2008). Finally, the socioconstructivists argue that learning is the construction of knowledge through the social interaction of the individual directly with others or indirectly by means of socially constructed artifacts. In this case, the context is a "relational mesh, [where] there is no discernible individual separable from particular actions, cultural norms and practices" (Fenwick, 2008).

Theory construction on workplace learning is faced with the existence of tension between the first two cognitive approaches against the context-considering third one (Hager, 2011). A claim for an integrated view of the phenomenon is also present in a number of texts (Clarke, 2004; Marshall, 2008; Illeris, 2003). More recently, another approach underpinning research (Armson & Whiteley, 2010; Toiviainen, Lallimo, & Hong, 2012) points to another key issue: the temporal change that characterizes learning (Hager, 2011). In this case, learning is said to be *emergent*, an ongoing process creatively transforming and being transformed by the context. In this view, the two metaphors related to the traditional approaches, *acquisition* and *participation*, should be replaced by terms such as *engagement, (re)construction, emergence*, or *becoming*.

Another recurrent distinction in the literature opposes two types of learning: formal and informal (Marsick & Volpe, 1999; Clarke, 2004). Formal learning is typically highly structured, institutionally supported, and occurs in classrooms, according to Marsick & Watkins (2001). Instructional actions planned in organizations such as training, courses, seminars, and workshops are included in this category, as well as other more contemporary actions like formal mentoring and job rotation.

Informal learning at work, on the other hand, provides a simple contrast to formal learning suggesting more flexibility and freedom to learners, as pointed out by Eraut (2004). It also includes the notion of social interaction and can occur in various contexts. The main features of informal learning are noted by Marsick & Volpe (1999): it is integrated in work and daily routines, it is initiated by an internal or external jolt, it is not very conscious, it has no direction, it is influenced by chance, it is a process induced by reflection, action, and by others. Also according to these authors, this type of learning is predominantly unstructured, experiential, and noninstitutional as well as directed by the choices, preferences, and intentions of individuals. Informal learning is undertaken by the individual or by a collective, without any imposed external criterion or presence of institutionally approved instructor (Livingstone, 1999).

Formal learning actions, in their classical form (instructions in classroom, computer trainings, seminars, workshops, etc.), represent a minor portion of what employees need to learn about work (Conlon, 2004). These are quite uncomfortable figures when one considers the volume of resources allocated to these actions. In contrast informal learning is responsible for 80–90 percent of learning at work (Tinjälä, 2008; Hicks et al., 2007), probably because formal learning is often disconnected from the reality of work, thus missing relevance from the point of view of the employee (Clarke, 2004). Nonetheless, there are allegations of potential drawbacks related to informal learning: "its narrow, contextual focus; learning bad habits or wrong lessons; accreditation challenges; and the fact that such learning is so well integrated with work that it may not be recognized" (Marsick, 2009). Furthermore, in the day-to-day reality of work, employees sometimes oppose the positive learning discourse (Järvensivu & Koski, 2012).

There is a strong tendency to view formal and informal learning as separate and antagonistic entities. A literature review to identify the criteria and establish ideal types of formal and informal learning was conducted by Malcolm, Hodkinson, & Colley (2003). However, their goal was not achieved, since the criteria were too numerous, varied, and disputed for the intended purpose. They argue that this polarization is not desirable, since the meaning of the terms may vary according to their application. In addition, attributes of informality and formality may be present in all types of learning. To sum up, they make four propositions: (1) all (or almost all) learning situations contain attributes of formality/informality, but the balance between them may vary significantly in each situation; (2) these attributes are also interrelated in different ways in different learning situations; (3) these attributes and their interrelationships influence the nature and effectiveness of learning in all situations; and (4) these interrelationships and effects can only be properly understood if learning is examined in relation to the broader contexts in which it occurs. They propose the association of the attributes with four aspects related to learning: the process taking place, the location and context where it occurs, the purpose of learning, and finally the content to be learnt. These distinctions are also used by Sonnentag, Niessen, and Ohly (2004), referring to characteristics of the environment. They propose the use of "learning in formal/informal contexts."

In order to avoid the blurred limits of this distinction, the expression "workplace learning" is used in the literature to include both forms (Jacobs & Park, 2009), as "learning in work can involve formal or informal teaching" (Fenwick, 2008), although it often refers specifically to informal learning. It is particularly useful, as deliberate interventions to foster learning opportunities are increasingly adopted by human resources as development tools. This trend has led to another category in line with the dichotomy formal/informal appearing more recently, which is non-formal learning. It "consists of all education that takes place outside of the school [educational sector]" (Kyndt, Dochy, & Nijs, 2009). It must be noted, however, that workplace learning is a quite an ambiguous expression itself. The concept of work, as highlighted before, is going through significant changes (Billet & Choy, 2013) and place can also be interpreted in a variety of meanings and concepts. Five different ideas and situations, to which place may refer when it comes to learning, may be: intrapersonal, physical, interpersonal, spiritual, and virtual (Cairns & Malloch, 2011).

Parallel to the formal/informal typology there are also other possible classifications of learning. The concept of incidental learning is suggested by Marsick and Watkins (2001) and covers unintentional situations. Conlon (2004) has offered a similar concept in his own work. In other cases, authors focus on differences in learning content or outcome, often trying to account for the differences between learning the routine and learning to innovate. This has lead to the concepts of implicit, reactive, and deliberative learning (Eraut, 2004); adaptive or reproductive and developmental learning (Ellström, Ekholm, & Ellström, 2008); expansive learning (Engëstrom, 1997); and single and double loop learning (Argyris & Schön, 1996).

Each typology is useful in grasping important aspects of learning. However, from a human resources development point of view, the need is for some kind of general model of workplace learning that takes into consideration the many factors at stake in the interplay of two human ventures: work and learning. There are remarkable efforts to depict the process of workplace learning, rooted in the different approaches mentioned here (Marsick & Volpe, 1999; Nonaka & Takeuchi, 1995; Engëstrom, 1997). However, a heuristic model such as the one proposed by Illeris (2004, 2011), which encompasses both the intrapsychic and the context arguments, may be more suitable to this need. The next section contains a detailed description of this model. A typology based on it is derived afterwards.

A comprehensive model of work-related learning

There is a general model of learning that integrates the notion of an individual's cognitive process, which leads to permanent changes not related to maturation, with the idea of a sociocultural construction derived from the relationship of the individual with the environment. This model has been built by Illeris (2004, 2011). He postulates two processes (acquisition and social interaction), both integrated and necessarily active before learning occurs. These two processes are co-determinants of learning. Three dimensions (content, dynamics, and social) are the components of the model. The acquisition process concerns both the cognitive and the emotional aspects, while the interaction process is related to the context, which is social and cultural in nature and obeys a sociohistorical logic. The content or rational dimension of the acquisition process refers to knowledge and skills. The emotional dimension includes emotions, feelings, motivation, and volition. Learning is always about these three integrated dimensions, which relate in a dynamic way: the cognitive, the emotional, and the social. The model strengthens the notion of constant interaction between the three dimensions.

In order to situate these learning processes and dimensions in the workplace, Illeris (2004) uses another model, proposed by Jørgënsen and Warring (2000), which describes the conditions in which learning occurs in working life.

Workplace learning happens at the encounter of the learning environment and the individual's processes, which are influenced by worker's characteristics (work experience, education and training, social history), within professional practice, for these authors. The concept of learning environment relates to learning opportunities present in the material and social environment. It is the learning process of the individual, through his/her readiness to learn, that finds and explores the learning opportunities of the environment in a dynamic relationship between the environment and the learner's characteristics.

The learning environment refers to learning opportunities embedded in the material and social context. It subdivides in two specific environments, the technical-organizational and the sociocultural. They both compete and interact dynamically and are subject to influences from outside the organization, arising from the market and the social, cultural, and political-institutional conditions.

The technical-organizational environment determines the qualifications required of the employee. Market forces and the organizational and technological changes mainly influence their development. From the point of view of learning, it is important to identify their qualities in terms of the experiences provided to the worker. Thus, it is possible to distinguish four aspects, each influencing the level of learning opportunities offered by the environment: division of work and work content; autonomy and application of skills; possibility of social interaction; and strain and stress. These aspects describe the physical, technical, operational, and organizational work process. They define the learning processes in the workplace and encompass both resources and limitations for learning.

The learning opportunities, in the second dimension of the environment, relate to social and cultural issues. In this case, there are three types of communities: working, political, and cultural. The first focuses on the implementation of collective tasks. Learning within these communities relates, most of the time, to being able to perform the tasks expected with the quality standards set by the community, although it also includes the ability to innovate. On the other hand, political communities are established based on the struggle for control, power, status, and influence in the workplace. Learning in this case is about solidarity and community behaviors, as well as standards and language of the community. Finally, cultural communities emerge based on values, norms, and shared perceptions. Learning consists of being able to get on within the business culture and its various subcultures.

In order to combine the three-dimensional learning model with the explanatory model of learning in the workplace, Illeris (2004, 2011) merges the two into a holistic representation of learning at work.

This heuristic model integrates the main variables intervening in the work-related learning process and may be useful to guide research as well as planned learning interventions. It also offers an opportunity to suggest a typology of learning. It is the space of professional practice that characterizes workplace learning. Competencies, that include combined learning content and learning dynamics, may be developed in this space, as the individual brings previous experiences and interacts with the technical-organizational and social-cultural environments. Professional practice represents the dimension of learning through which the individual interacts with the learning opportunities available in the workplace. From this point emerges the differentiation that may be useful for the management of learning interventions in organizations, or to take advantage of opportunities, in the workplace, in order to induce individual learning.

Inducing learning opportunities – a typology

An alternative typology to the previous classifications of workplace learning is grounded in a few assumptions, namely: (1) learning refers exclusively to internal psychological processes, and thus belongs to an individual; (2) learning is inextricably linked to the interactions an individual has with the environment; (3) although learning can occur in any situation, the focus is on the specific case of its occurrence related to work in organizations, where the goal is to ensure that these results translate into significant performance improvement; and (4) in order to attain a better management of learning outcomes in organizations, it is important to set these outcomes in advance.

The proposed typology is based on the source of the initiative to generate learning opportunities, featuring three modes of learning: induced by the organization, induced by the individual, and not induced. Training, seminars, workshops, and the more recent practices of mentoring, coaching, and job rotation are examples of learning situations induced by the organization. These situations may be systematically managed by organizations, based on effectiveness models (Borges-Andrade et al., 2013).

In individual-induced learning, it is the learner himself/herself who plays the major role in promoting learning opportunities, as when he or she decides to seek further information on the internet about a subject or asks a colleague how to perform a given task. These situations may also be systematically managed by organizations, as Abbad et al. (2013) have proposed. Finally, the third case includes those situations in which learning occurs without any previous deliberation from the individual or the organization. The acquisition of tacit knowledge by the individual is often the case. Table 25.1 summarizes the proposed typology.

The underlying rationale in this typology is that if learning happens as learning opportunities are available for individuals, then it is important to deliberately induce these learning opportunities, adhering to the prescription of Marsick, Volpe, & Watkins (1999) that "the first step to improve someone's learning is to become more intentional about it." This means that human resource development professionals' main task in this case is to plan and execute workplace learning actions and, simultaneously, promote the conditions for employees to reflect on and meet their own learning needs. Those actions and the intervention on these conditions may result in learning outcomes, or competencies, that may be useful for performance in organizations.

Table 25.1 Induction typology of workplace learning.

Types of workplace learning	*Characteristics*
Induced by the organization	Learning occurs as a consequence of the organization deliberately promoting a learning opportunity
Induced by the individual	Learning occurs as a consequence of the individual deliberately promoting a learning opportunity
Not induced	Learning occurs without any deliberate action to promote it

Learning outcomes

Measuring formal learning outcomes, despite the supposed control over these planned activities, is not a simple task (Salas & Cannon-Bowers, 2001), despite the volume of research and practice on the subject (Alvarez, Salas, & Garofano, 2004; Aguinis & Kraiger, 2009). This research has resulted in several measurement scales and other evaluation procedures that have been systematized for professional practice, as does the book published by Abbad et al. (2012). The difficulty involved in measuring learning significantly increases when addressing informal learning outcomes, as "informal learning can occur anytime, anywhere and with anyone" (Livingstone, 1999). Given its nature, measurement of informal learning outcomes can represent significant problems, since it often is ad hoc (Clarke, 2004).

The diversity in the conceptualization of the phenomenon, as discussed earlier, may bring considerable confusion at the practice level. He also discloses the existence of two contrasting points of view on how learning in organizations should be measured: the learning perspective, which is focused on strengthening the capacity of individuals and organizations to learn; and the performance perspective, which ensures that learning is translated into behavior associated with the achievement of organizational goals. These points are similar to the two types of approaches described by Alvarez, Salas, and Garofano (2004), for formal learning: effectiveness models (with a focus on the prediction of training and development effects); and evaluation models (with a focus on these effects at the individual, team, or organizational performance levels).

Assessment of workplace learning tends to follow the learning perspective, therefore, covering mechanisms that supposedly facilitate it. One of the problems of this approach to evaluation is that there is no judgment on the relevance of what is learned, be it associated with the content or dynamics dimensions, or with a combination of them. But it is important, nonetheless, to assess which practices can stimulate learning, be they in the technical-organizational or in the social-cultural dimensions, or in both. Some examples of research on these features can be found in Clarke (2004), Antonello (2005, 2006), and Skule (2004).

Workplace learning is frequently not recognized as learning, as individuals associate learning situations with training in classrooms and consequently do not attribute the acquired contents to learning outcomes (Eraut, 2004). Those individuals understand that learning and work are two separate activities that are never combined, although research results show that the majority of work-related learning occurs while work is accomplished.

The revealed difficulties suggest an area that still needs to be explored, which could explain the higher incidence of qualitative studies focusing on learning conditions rather than quantitative outcome measures associated with learning conditions. Nevertheless, efforts have been made to identify learning outcomes related to work. Some of the typologies previously presented are based on the type of learning outcome that can be expected: knowledge of procedures; knowledge of propositions, values, attitudes; and skills are some of the results inferred from the proposed typologies of learning (Smith, 2003). Following the same line, there is increasing concern about the development of accreditation methods of prior learning in order to shorten educational paths and/or to promote progression in employment (Berglund & Andersson, 2012).

The reference to competence building as a workplace learning outcome is frequent (Conlon, 2004; Illeris, 2011; Larsen, 2004). As Brandão and Borges-Andrade (2007) highlight, "learning represents the process by which one acquires competence, while the person's performance at work represents an expression of his/her skills, a manifestation of what the individual has learned throughout his/her life."

There are different conceptualizations of competence in areas such as education, linguistics, psychology, and organizational theory, as noted by Lima and Borges-Andrade (2006). In the perspective of human resource development in organizations, they report a fundamental agreement around the idea of an individual attribute that encompasses knowledge, skills and attitudes, motivation, beliefs, and behaviors, which are required for an adequate performance in one area or on one task.

An integrative and cognitive approach, more widely accepted, defines competence as "synergistic combinations of knowledge, skills and attitudes expressed by job performance within an organizational context, which add value to individuals and organizations" (Brandão & Borges-Andrade, 2007). The notion of competence means "a complex totality of traditional and up-to-date knowledge, orientation and overview, combined with professional and everyday life skills and a broad range of personal qualities such as flexibility, openness, independence, responsibility, creativity, etc." (Illeris, 2011).

These definitions reveal the challenges faced when it comes to learning at work. In the early days of Taylorism, the main concern was to ensure mastery of the restricted knowledge and skills required to perform a narrow and repetitive task. Eliciting such knowledge and skills and training them was feasible and could meet the needs of acquisition and transfer. Now, in the information economy, organizations expect the worker to yield sophisticated performance to respond to unpredictable and complex situations, as shown by Illeris's (2011) competence definition. It requires specific ways of being and acting in face of these situations, demanding much more than restricted or isolated knowledge and skills that are frequently used at work.

Hence, the appropriate construct to reflect this new order of demands on workers is the notion of competence, which adds attitudes to the two other elements. Therefore, this notion takes into account the interaction between the previously mentioned learning content and learning dynamics dimensions. Furthermore, the construct definition postulates that this combination of elements must be synergistic and value adding. Therefore, it is not enough to know *what* and *how*; the worker also needs to be able to adequately combine these two elements, which ultimately means *know what to be* (what the organization expects).

Workplace learning with all the dimensions and interconnections of the previously presented model is more likely to withstand the challenge underneath this construct. "Workplace learning is not just about learning to do a job; it is about personal development and the acquisition of knowledge, skills and attitudes that transcend particular settings and roles that parallel the wider society or learning and working" (Walkington & Vanderheide, 2008).

Organizational learning and learning organizations

A relevant issue related to the debate about workplace learning is the consideration of the level of occurrence of the phenomenon, which appears more consistently in the field of "organizational learning." In this case, learning is described as an individual as well as a collective or organizational phenomenon (Shipton, 2006). Here the debate takes place around the learner – the individual, psychological view, or the organization, within the administration.

These different lines also span a continuum ranging from prescription to description. The descriptive dimension is typically associated with academic research stemming from various epistemological approaches. The prescriptive dimension originates from reports of practical intervention cases conducted by consultants and management professionals and is commonly associated with the expression "learning organization" (Easterby-Smith & Araujo, 2001).

Some of these views on learning are not antagonistic, according to Antonello and Godoy (2010). In one of them, organizational learning is seen as an analogy of individual learning. From this perspective, knowledge about individual learning processes can be used to understand the process of organizational learning. According to another view, individual learning is the basis for the organizational learning, so that increasing organizational knowledge – an indicator of organizational learning – is based on individual knowledge acquisition in the organization.

Learning at the organizational level is mainly associated with the acquisition of best practices, technologies, and processes. It is also related to organizational change and abandonment of concepts, processes, knowledge, and practices outside the scope of the organization's needs as well as those that are obsolete or inadequate. Its effects are significantly perceived in the performance of organizations (Ho, 2008; Khandekar & Sharma, 2006). In any of these approaches, however, learning processes in the organization start at the individual level (Antonello, 2005; Nonaka & Takeuchi, 1995). But individual acquisition only effectively turns into organizational change when it is applied at work and when it is shared between workers, spreading through the organization. Otherwise, KSAs learned by individuals are always lost with staff rotation.

Arguments against the "learning organization" are mostly based on the disregard of the psychological character of the learning phenomenon. The right expression should be "effectively and qualitatively developing organization" or "organization where learning is promoted" (Illeris, 2003), following the same line of Senge's (1990) propositions about it. The former author argues that, apart from being a kind of verbal theft, the expression indicates an inadequate approach because it doesn't address the issues concerning why employees learn or fail to learn what is intended by management, from a psychological point of view.

To sum up, there is a lack of theoretical and methodological integration between these two levels of analysis of the learning phenomenon. Additionally, gaps in the specification of how individual learning becomes organizational learning are associated with high risks of anthropomorphism (Bastos, Gondim, & Loiola, 2004; Easterby-Smith & Araújo, 2001; Lipshitz, 2000).

Together, the three-dimensions model, the induction typology of workplace learning, and the comprehension of the different analysis levels provide a framework to guide human resource development professionals in planning and executing learning interventions, taking into account all the factors influencing the process and the challenges concerning the expected outcomes. The next section summarizes the research findings that sustain the role of each dimension in the previously described model of workplace learning.

Research Findings on Workplace Learning

Most research on workplace learning adopts a qualitative methodological approach, using a diverse set of techniques (interviews, reflective journals, field notes, focal groups, "complete this sentence" activities, scenarios, grounded theory, etc.). Therefore, relationships between elements of the workplace learning model and even the attribution of results to this type of learning presented in these studies are mostly dependent on self-assessment and perceptions. Only a few of them report statistically tested variables interrelations and effects. Therefore, data summarized next are essentially situated and context-related. Nonetheless, as sites and subjects are extremely diverse, recent examples may be useful in clarifying field boundaries.

The content dimension

The examples of research studies grouped in this section are those that answer the question *What is being learned through workplace learning?*

Two longitudinal research projects involving almost 200 early and mid-career workers from business and accounting, engineering, and healthcare were reported by Eraut (2011). Data collected led to a typology of workplace learning trajectories, comprised of eight learning pathways that individuals progress along, many of them simultaneously: task performance; awareness and understanding; personal development; academic knowledge and skills; role performance; teamwork; decision making and problem solving; and finally judgment. The significance and the importance of these categories change considerably over time as workers deal with more difficult and complex problems, widen the range of competence, and acquire greater responsibility.

There are also reports pointing to complex contents such as learning to change patterns of socialization and emotions (Shan, 2012), coping with crisis (Mano, 2010), general knowledge and understanding about the area (Goldman et al., 2009), as well as specific procedures (Goldman et al., 2009). A study dealing with the recognition of prior learning, or validation, is also noteworthy (Cameron, 2012).

The dynamics dimension

This section exemplifies studies dealing with the question *How is the required knowledge being learned?* This refers to the emotions, attitudes, strategies, volitions, and other individual aspects that shape learning dynamics.

A study of 73 employees in the ICT-department of a large company in Flanders tested the influence of an individual characteristic (self-directed learning orientation) and three contextual characteristics (job demands, job control, and social support) on the work-related learning behavior of the workers (Gijbels et al., 2012). Although job demands and job controls showed to be moderately and positively linked, only self-directed learning orientation predicted work-related learning behavior. Another study with two teachers from the same school has shown that workplace conditions are not objective nor a given fact, determining teacher's behavior and teacher's learning in a one-directional manner. In fact, they are mediated by the way individuals perceive these conditions (Hoekstra et al., 2009).

Asking questions and observing colleagues read and monitor situations and take decisions about them are actions undertaken by workers in order to learn (Eraut, 2011). In this same vein, a report of eight different ways of learning was obtained with 30 knowledge workers, novice and senior, in a multinational company: formal learning (classroom blended, self-paced, and online); learning by doing; learning by discussing with others; coaching/mentoring; learning by teaching others; vicarious learning (learning by observation); learning by trial and error; and self-study (e.g., reading professional literature) (Milligan, Margaryan, & Littlejohn, 2013). Another study also mentions drawing upon past experience, collaboration and inquiry with colleagues, and trial and error (Wofford, Ellinger, & Watkins, 2012). Learning from error was reported by Gola (2009).

The social dimension

According to the description of the learning environments in Illeris's model of workplace learning, this section gathers research findings that relate to factors enabling or preventing the emergence of learning opportunities.

In an encouraging quantitative research, the effects of management practices on workplace learning were studied by Matsuo and Nakahara (2013). They report on a survey of 641 employees of a Japanese fire and marine insurance company testing on-the-job-training (OJT) practices' (direct supervision, empowerment), plan-do-check-action (PDCA) practices, and reflective communication's influence on workplace learning, ultimately resulting in higher performance. Results showed that OJT direct supervision has a negative impact on workplace learning, while empowerment, PDCA practices, and reflective communication are learning enhancing.

Other practices and sources of learning related to the environment of workplaces present in the literature were: challenges, informal social interactions and exchange of knowledge with colleagues (Lundgren, 2010); relationships (formal and informal mentoring, peer relationships); job enlargement (temporary job changes, cross-training, stretch assignments) or redesigning and enrichment (acting management opportunities, full-time temporary assignments, on-the-job opportunities); planning processes (defining clear performance parameters, matching employees and assignments, recognizing individual needs, and using the departmental skills database); active learning and modeling (defining general career maps, developing active learning networks, encouraging proactive behaviors, encouraging supportive relationships) (Cunningham & Hillier, 2012); and the right level of challenge (Eraut, 2011).

The relationship between workload, autonomy, and learning opportunities was tested in a sample drawn from the Flemish Workability Monitor survey of years 2004 and 2007, of 11,099 and 9,738 Belgian wage-earning respondents respectively (van Ruysseveldt & van Dijke, 2011). Results showed that the relationship between workload and workplace learning opportunities is influenced by the level of workload itself, in the sense that too high levels of workload hinders its challenging potential. It was also influenced by the level of autonomy, as insufficient autonomy leaves the employee with too little opportunity for flexible adjustment and active engagement in problem solving at work.

The competitiveness–reinforcing partnership structure and the pervasiveness of time-billed targets are learning inhibiting, according to interviews made with members of a firm in the law sector (Watson & Harmel-Law, 2010). Learning opportunities are also dependent on characteristics of the leadership and professional relationships in the workplace (Jurasaite-Harbison, 2009).

Future Research

The predominance of qualitative research findings in the previous section shows that the field as a whole needs more investigation in order to build robust knowledge about workplace learning. This trend is also acknowledged by Marsick (2003) who relates it to the difficulties encountered by researchers in quantitatively addressing the construct due to its unconscious and somewhat opportunistic quality. She claims that this type of learning may only be understood using both qualitative and quantitative strategies. In addition, better measures of acquisition and transfer of KSAs are needed.

The model proposed by Illeris (2004, 2011) describes a close relationship between learning content and learning dynamics, at the individual level. Research results have been described where motivation and volition are used as instances of learning dynamics. However, more systematic studies are needed, when emotions and feelings are used as instances of learning dynamics.

At the environmental level, this model describes a close relationship between the technical-organizational learning dimension and the sociocultural learning dimension.

Studies seldom collect and aggregate data, on this latter dimension, at the group or organizational levels. This is more frequently done for the technical-organizational dimension. As a consequence of this lack of balance in research studies' levels of analysis, there is not much evidence to support the hypothesized relationship between these two environmental dimensions of workplace learning.

There are several studies that support the hypothesized relationship between: learning environment variables and the individual dimensions of learning content (knowledge and skills); and learning dynamics (especially motivation and commitment). But, in most cases, they have been done after training and development activities. There have been very few attempts to investigate individual acquisition, which has not been promoted by such activities, nor its relationships with aggregated data on both dimensions of the learning environment: technical-organizational and sociocultural.

Given human resources development practitioners' needs, it is important to explore the influence of contextual factors that can systematically build up a learning-supporting environment, notably through management practices. Research findings presented were consistent with the hypothesized relationships described in the workplace-learning model, suggesting it may have value for generating future research questions. However, contextual variables should not be used at the individual level of analysis. They may be collected at this level, but they should be aggregated to other levels (i.e., collective values or believes), such as teams and organizations, or they should be collected at these other levels of analysis (i.e., size of teams, level of centralization in organizations).

Conclusion

Formal and informal learning should be taken into account, in order to develop individual competencies at work. However, the needed knowledge, in order to foster informal learning, is far behind what is known about the design and promotion of formal learning, despite the fact that this may be less effective in several circumstances. Measurement difficulties have been a major problem in the study of informal learning at work. As a result, most research reports are descriptive and there is not much information on relationships between the antecedents and consequences of informal learning. This hinders the possibilities for prescribing human resources development practices aimed at the improvement of informal learning. The lack of knowledge may have been one of the reasons for the abundance of workplace learning models, as compared to the fewer training and development effectiveness models. Adopting one of these models, in order to organize research results, may be the first step for advancing knowledge in this area. The next step should be to improve measurements and test hypothesized relationships.

References

Abbad, G. S., Mourão, L., Menezes, P. P. M., Zerbini, T., & Borges-Andrade, J. E. (2012). *Medidas de Avaliação em Treinamento, Desenvolvimento e Educação: Ferramentas para a Gestão de Pessoas.* Porto Alegre: Artmed.

Abbad, G. S., Souza, E. R. L. C., Zerbini, T., & Borges-Andrade, J. E. (2013). Aprender em organizações e no trabalho. In L. O. Borges & L. Mourão (Eds.), *O Trabalho e as Organizações: Atuações a partir da Psicologia* (pp. 465–496). Porto Alegre: Artmed.

Aguinis, H., & Kraiger, K. (2009). Benefits of training and development for individuals and teams, organizations, and society, *Annual Review of Psychology*, 60, 451–474.

Alvarez, K., Salas, E., & Garofano, C. M. (2004). An integrated model of training evaluation and effectiveness. *Human Resource Development Review*, 3(4), 385–416.

Antonello, C. S. (2005). Articulação da aprendizagem formal e informal: Seu impacto no desenvolvimento de competências gerenciais. *Revista Alcance*, 12(2), 183–209.

Antonello, C. S. (2006). Aprendizagem na ação revisitada e sua relação com a noção de competência. *Comportamento Organizacional e Gestão*, 12(2), 199–220.

Antonello, C. S., & Godoy, A. S. (2010). A encruzilhada da aprendizagem organizacional: Uma visão multiparadigmática. *RAC: Revista de Administração Contemporânea*, 14(2), 310–332.

Argyris, C., & Schön, D. (1996). *Organizational Learning II – Theory, Method, Practice*. Reading: Addison-Wesley.

Armson, G., & Whiteley, A. (2010). Employees' and managers' accounts of interactive workplace learning: A grounded theory of "complex integrative learning." *Journal of Workplace Learning*, 22(7), 409–427.

Bastos, A. V. B., Gondim, S. M. G., & Loiola, E. (2004). Aprendizagem organizacional versus organizações que aprendem: Características e desafios que cercam essas duas abordagens de pesquisa. *RAUSP: Revista de Administração*, 39(3), 220–230.

Berglund, L., & Andersson, P. (2012). Recognition of knowledge and skills at work: In whose interests? *Journal of Workplace Learning*, 24(2), 73–84.

Bierema, L. L., & Eraut, M. (2004). Workplace-focused learning: Perspective on continuing professional education and human resource development. *Advances in Developing Human Resources*, 52(6), 52–68.

Billet, S., & Choy, S. (2013). Learning through work: Emerging perspectives and new challenges. *Journal of Workplace Learning*, 25(4), 264–276.

Borges-Andrade, J. E., Zerbini, T., Abbad, G. S., & Mourão, L. (2013). Treinamento, desenvolvimento e educação: Um modelo para sua gestão. In L. O. Borges & L. Mourão (Eds.), *O Trabalho e as Organizações: Atuações a partir da Psicologia* (465–496). Porto Alegre: Artmed.

Brandão, H. P., & Borges-Andrade, J. E. (2007). Causas e efeitos da expressão de competências no trabalho: Para entender melhor a noção de competência. *Revista de Administração Mackenzie*, 8(3), 32–49.

Brandão, H. P., Borges-Andrade, J. E., Puente-Palacios, K. E., & Laros, J. A. (2012). Relationships between learning, context and competency: A multilevel study. *Brazilian Administration Review*, 9(1), 1–22.

Cairns, L., & Malloch, M. (2011). Theories of work, place and learning: New directions. In M. Malloch, L. Cairns, K. Evans, & B. N. O'Connor (Eds.), *The SAGE Handbook of Workplace Learning* (pp. 3–16). London: Sage.

Cameron, R. (2012). Recognising workplace learning: The emerging practices of e-RPL and e-PR. *Journal of Workplace Learning*, 24(2), 85–104.

Clarke, N. (2004). HRD and the challenges of assessing learning in the workplace. *International Journal of Training and Development*, 8(2), 140–156.

Coelho, F. A., Jr., & Borges-Andrade, J. E. (2008). Uso do conceito de aprendizagem em estudos relacionados ao trabalho e organizações. *Paidéia*, 18(40), 221–234.

Conlon, T. J. (2004). A review of informal learning literature, theory and implications for practice in developing global professional competence. *Journal of European Industrial Training*, 28(2–4), 283–295.

Cunningham, J. & Hillier, E. (2013). Informal learning in the workplace: Key activities and processes. *Education & Training*, 55(1), 37–51.

Day, N. (1998). Informal Learning. *Workforce*, 77 (6), 30–34.

Easterby-Smith, M., & Araújo, L. (2001). Aprendizagem organizacional: Oportunidade e debates atuais. In M. Easterby-Smith, J. Burgoyne, & L. Araújo (Eds.), *Aprendizagem Organizacional e Organização de Aprendizagem: Desenvolvimento na Teoria e na Prática* (pp. 15–38). São Paulo: Atlas.

Ellström, E., Ekholm, B., & Ellström, P. (2008). Two types of learning environment: Enabling and constraining a study of care work. *Journal of Workplace Learning*, 20(2), 84–97.

Engström, Y. (1997). *Learning by Expanding: An Activity-Theoretical Approach to Developmental Research*. Helsinki: Orienta-Konsultit.

Eraut, M. (2004). Informal learning in the workplace. *Studies in Continuing Education*, 26(2), 247–273.

Eraut, M. (2011). Informal learning in the workplace: Evidence on the real value of work-based learning (WBL). *Development and Learning in Organizations*, 25(5), 8–12.

Fenwick, T. (2008). Understanding relations of individual collective learning in work: A review of research. *Management Learning*, 39(3), 227–243.

Frese, M. (2008). The changing nature of work. In N. Chmiel (Ed.), *An Introduction to Work and Organizational Psychology* (pp. 397–413). Oxford: Blackwell.

Gijbels, D., Raemdonck, I., Vervecken, D., & van Herck, J. (2012). Understanding work-related learning: The case of ICT workers. *Journal of Workplace Learning*, 24(6), 416–429.

Gola, G. (2009). Informal learning of social workers: A method of narrative inquiry. *Journal of Workplace Learning*, 21(4), 334–346.

Goldman, E., Plack, M., Roche, C., Smith, J., & Turley, C. (2009). Learning in a chaotic environment. *Journal of Workplace Learning*, 21(7), 555–574.

Gondim, S. M. G., Puente-Palacios, K. E., & Borges-Andrade, J. E. (2011). Performance and learning in virtual work teams: Comparing Brazilians and Argentineans. *Revista de Psicología del Trabajo y de las Organizaciones*, 27(1), 31–41.

Hager, P. (2011). Theories of workplace learning. In M. Malloch, L. Cairns, K. Evans, & B. N. O'Connor (Eds.), *The SAGE Handbook of Workplace Learning* (pp. 17–31). London: Sage.

Hicks, E., Bagg, R., Doyle, W., & Young, J. D. (2007). Canadian accountants: Examining workplace learning. *Journal of Workplace Learning*, 19(2), 61–77.

Ho, L.-A. (2008). What affects organizational performance? The linking of learning and knowledge management. *Industrial Management & Data Systems*, 108(9),1234–1254.

Hoekstra, A., Korthagen, F., Brekelmans, M., Beijaard, D., & Imants, J. (2009). Experienced teachers' informal workplace learning and perceptions of workplace conditions. *Journal of Workplace Learning*, 21(4), 276–298.

Illeris, K. (2003). Towards a contemporary and comprehensive theory of learning, *International Journal of Lifelong Education*, 22(4), 396–406.

Illeris, K. (2004). *Learning in Working Life*. Frederiksberg: Roskilde University Press.

Illeris, K. (2011). Workplace and learning. In M. Malloch, L. Cairns, K. Evans, & B. N. O'Connor (Eds.), *The SAGE Handbook of Workplace Learning* (pp. 32–45). London: Sage.

Isidro-Filho, A., Guimarães, T. A., Perin, M. G., & Leung, R. C. (2013). Workplace learning strategies and professional competencies in innovation contexts in Brazilian hospitals. *Brazilian Administration Review*, 10(2), 121–134.

Jacobs, R. L., & Park, Y. (2009). A proposed conceptual framework of workplace learning: Implications for theory development and research in human resource development. *Human Resource Development Review*, 8(2), 133–150.

Järvensivu, A., & Koski, P. (2012). Combating learning. *Journal of Workplace Learning*, 24(1), 5–18.

Jorgënsen, C. H., & Warring, N. (2000). Workplace learning and learning environments. Working paper 77, Working Knowledge: Productive Learning at Work Conference, University of Technology, Sydney.

Jurasaite-Harbison, E. (2009). Teachers' workplace learning within informal contexts of school cultures in the United States and Lithuania. *Journal of Workplace Learning*, 21(4), 299–321.

Khandekar, A., & Sharma, A. (2006). Organizational learning and performance: Understanding Indian scenario in present global context. *Education and Training*, 48(8–9), 682–692.

Kyndt, E., Dochy, F., & Nijs, H. (2009). Learning conditions for non-formal and informal workplace learning. *Journal of Workpklace Learning*, 21(5), 369–383.

Larsen, H. H. (2004). Experiential learning as management development: Theoretical perspectives and empirical illustrations. *Advances in Developing Human Resources*, 6(4), 486–503.

Lima, S. M. V., & Borges-Andrade, J. E. (2006). Bases conceituais e teóricas de avaliação de necessidades em TD&E. In J. E. Borges-Andrade, G. S. Abbad, & L. Mourão (Eds.), *Treinamento, Desenvolvimento e Educação em Organizações de Trabalho: Fundamentos para a Gestão de Pessoas* (pp. 199–215). Porto Alegre: Artmed.

Lipshitz, R. (2000). Chic, mystique and misconception: Argyris and Schön and the rhetoric of organizational learning. *Journal of Applied Behavioral Science*, 36(4), 456–473.

Livingstone, D. W. (1999). Exploring the icebergs of adult learning: Findings of the first Canadian survey of informal learning practices. *Canadian Journal for the Study of Adult Education*, 13(2), 49–72. (The Research Network on New Approaches to Lifelong Learning, Ontario Institute for Studies in Education of the University of Toronto, Toronto.)

Lundgren, S. (2010). Learning opportunities for nurses working within home care. *Journal of Workplace Learning*, 23(1), 6–19.

Malcolm, J., Hodkinson, P., & Colley, H. (2003). The interrelationships between informal and formal learning. *Journal of Workplace Learning*, 15(7–8), 313–318.

Malloch, M., Cairns, L., Evans, K., & O'Connor, B. N. (2011). *The SAGE Handbook of Workplace Learning*. London: Sage.

Mano, R. C. (2010). Past organizational change and managerial evaluations of crisis: A case of double-loop learning effects in non-profit organizations. *Journal of Workplace Learning*, 22(8), 489–507.

Marshall, N. (2008). Cognitive and practice-based theories of organizational knowledge and learning: Incompatible or complementary? *Management Learning*, 39, 413–435.

Marsick, V. J. (2003). Invited reaction: Informal learning and the transfer of learning: How managers develop proficiency. *Human Resource Development Quarterly*, 14(4), 389–395.

Marsick, V. J. (2009). Toward a unifying framework to support informal learning theory, research and practice. *Journal of Workplace Learning*, 21(4), 265–275.

Marsick, V. J., & Volpe, M. (1999). The nature and need for informal learning. *Advances in Developing Human Resources*, 1(1), 1–9.

Marsick, V. J., Volpe, M., & Watkins, K. E. (1999). Theory and practice of informal learning in the knowledge era. *Advances in Developing Human Resources*, 80(1), 80–95.

Marsick, V. J., & Watkins, K. E. (2001). Informal and incidental learning. *New Directions For Adult and Continuing Education*, 89(Spring), 25–34.

Matsuo, M., & Nakahara, J. (2013). The effects of the PDCA cycle and OJT on workplace learning. *International Journal of Human Resource Management*, 24(1), 195–207.

Milligan, C., Margaryan, A., & Littlejohn, A. (2013). Learning at transition for new and experienced staff. *Journal of Workplace Learning*, 25(4), 217–230.

Mourão, L., & Borges-Andrade, J. E. (2013). Impact evaluation of T&D at the societal level. *Journal of Workplace Learning*, 25(8), 505–520.

Nonaka, I., & Takeuchi, H. (1995). *The Knowledge-Creating Company*. New York: Oxford University Press.

Pilati, R., & Borges-Andrade, J. E. (2008). Affective predictors of the effectiveness of training moderated by the cognitive complexity of expected competencies. *International Journal of Training and Development*, 12(4), 226–237.

Pilati, R., & Borges-Andrade, J. E. (2012). Training effectiveness: Transfer strategies, perception of support and worker commitment as predictors. *Revista de Psicología del Trabajo y de las Organizacione*, 28(1), 25–35.

Ryle, G. (2000). *The Concept of Mind*. Harmondsworth: Penguin.

Salas, E., & Cannon-Bowers, J. A. (2001). The science of training: A decade of progress. *Annual Review of Psychology*, 52, 471–499.

Senge, P. (1990). *The Fifth Discipline: The Art and Practice of the Learning Organization*. New York: Doubleday.

Shan, H. (2012). Learning to "fit in": The emotional work of Chinese immigrants in Canadian engineering workplaces. *Journal of Workplace Learning*, 24(5), 351–364.

Shipton, H. (2006). Cohesion or confusion? Towards a typology for organizational learning research. *International Journal of Management Review*, 8(4), 233–252.

Skule, S. (2004). Learning conditions at work: A framework to understand and assess informal learning in the workplace. *International Journal of Training and Development*, 8(1), 8–20.

Smith, P. J. (2003). Workplace learning and flexible delivery. *Review of Educational Research*, 73(1), 53–88.

Sonnentag, S., Niessen, C., & Ohly, S. (2004). Learning at work: Training and development. In C. L. Cooper & I. T. Robertson (Eds.), *International Review of Industrial and Organizational Psychology* (vol. 19, pp. 249–289). Hoboken, NJ: John Wiley & Sons, Inc.

Toiviainen, H., Lallimo, J., & Hong, J. (2012). Emergent learning practices in globalizing work: The case of a Finnish-Chinese project in a Finnish technology consulting firm. *Journal of Workplace Learning*, 24(7–8), 509–527.

Tynjälä, P. (2008). Perspectives into learning at the workplace. *Educational Research Review*, 3, 130–154.

van Ruysseveldt, J., & van Dijke, M. (2011). When are workload and workplace learning opportunities related in a curvilinear manner? The moderating role of autonomy. *Journal of Vocational Behavior*, 79(2), 470–483.

Walkington, J., & Vanderheide, R. (2008). Enhancing the pivotal roles in workplace learning and community engagement through transdisciplinary "cross talking." *Engaging Communities, Proceedings of the 31st Higher Education Research and Development Society of Australasia Annual Conference* (pp. 361–370). Rotorua: HRDSA.

Watson, S., & Harmel-Law, A. (2010). Exploring the contribution of workplace learning to an HRD strategy in the Scottish legal profession. *Journal of European Industrial Training*, 34(1), 7–22.

Wofford, M. G., Ellinger, A. D., & Watkins, K. E. (2012). Learning on the fly: Exploring the informal learning process of aviation instructors. *Journal of Workplace Learning*, 25(2), 79–97.

Section IV
Performance Management

22

Performance Appraisal and Development

Jeffrey R. Spence and Patricia L. Baratta

Introduction

Many organizations utilize a formal performance appraisal system where once or twice a year employees are evaluated on predetermined dimensions of performance (DeNisi & Pritchard, 2006; Seldon, Ingraham, & Jacobson, 2001). The expectations of employee performance appraisals can be presented in a deceptively simple manner: (a) performance ratings are expected to be accurate and (b) the performance of those being rated is expected to improve on account of being evaluated and given feedback. Within this simple breakdown, performance appraisals can be seen to possess the properties of a Janus head, having multiple faces within organizations. Traditionally, appraisals had a face of allocating rewards and recognition to employees, but have more recently been recognized as a tool for employee motivation, legal defense for selection tools, and strategic planning at the organizational level (Woodford & Mayes, 2002). Performance ratings can also be the focus of litigation and have their veracity challenged in court (Arvey & Murphy, 1998; Bernardin & Tyler, 2001; Werner & Bolino, 1997). The great conundrum of appraisals is that they are needed to fulfill a number of important personnel and organizational needs, yet they have a reputation for being futile (Bowman, 1994). The negative view of performance appraisals is not restricted to academic circles. A recent survey of human resource professionals revealed that 45 percent of respondents thought that annual performance appraisals were not accurate assessments of performance (Society of Human Resource Management & Globoforce, 2012). Over several decades of scientific investigation, researchers have explored different strategies to increase the quality of performance ratings as well as the performance outcomes of ratings.

In the current chapter, we review performance appraisal theory and research to examine the expectations that (a) performance ratings are accurate and (b) performance improves as a result of receiving feedback. We provide a critical analysis of the performance appraisal literature and identify successes and challenges in living up to these expectations. We

The Wiley Blackwell Handbook of the Psychology of Training, Development, and Performance Improvement,
First Edition. Edited by Kurt Kraiger, Jonathan Passmore, Sigmar Malvezzi, and Nuno Rebelo dos Santos.
© 2015 John Wiley & Sons Ltd. Published 2020 by John Wiley & Sons Ltd.

organize our review in two major sections. The first major section reviews predominant strategies and challenges to improve the quality of ratings. The second major section reviews research on performance feedback, focusing on the characteristics of feedback that are likely to lead to employee development. Other chapters in this volume concentrate on designing feedback to improve performance (London & Mone, Chapter 23, this volume), using 360 feedback for developing employees (Fletcher, Chapter 24, this volume), the use of social networks for feedback (Van den Bossche, Van Waes, & van der Rijt Chapter 25, this volume), and the process of informal learning and development (Vieira de Moraes & Borges-Andrade, Chapter 21, this volume).

Strategies for Improving the Quality of Performance Ratings

Subjective performance appraisals, where a rater observes an employee, evaluates his/her performance, and records the evaluation on an appraisal form, have been criticized for their poor quality (Arvey & Murphy, 1998). At a conceptual level, performance ratings are criticized because they do not reflect the target's true level of performance (Murphy, 2008). Operationally, this means that the association between a performance rating and actual performance ("true performance") is low. Although this perspective is generally accepted in performance appraisal research, the resoluteness of this stance has been criticized for being too strong a position given the type of evidence there is to support it (Woehr, 2008). Specifically, Woehr (2008) noted that the magnitude of the association between performance and ratings is not known, but only inferred from indirect evidence. Indirect evidence for the magnitude of the relation between true performance and performance ratings is found by looking at the psychometric characteristics of ratings: characteristics of performance appraisal data and that data's association with other variables. The distribution of appraisal ratings tend to be negatively skewed – indicating that more people score at the upper end of the scale than at the lower or middle end – and range restricted ratings demonstrate little variability with most employees receiving similar ratings (Saal, Downey, & Lahey, 1980). In addition to these distributional properties, ratings can have low levels of reliability (Pearlman, Schmidt, & Hunter, 1980; Rothstein, 1990; Viswesvaran, Ones, & Schmidt, 1996) and dimensions that are highly related and lack discriminability (Cooper, 1981; Landy & Farr, 1980; Saal, Downey, & Lahey, 1980). These types of characteristics are referred to as psychometric error. Two of the major attempts to improve the psychometric quality of ratings include developing better appraisal formats and training raters. In the next sections, we provide an overview and an analysis of these two approaches.

Building a better mouse trap: appraisal formats

The tactic of changing appraisal formats in order to improve performance ratings occurred largely between 1950 and 1980 (Arvey & Murphy, 1998; Farr & Levy, 2007). Advancements during this era were largely focused on developing rating scales that produced more valid and reliable ratings. Many of the new formats that were developed focused on the assessment of employee *behavior*. The evaluation of employee behavior marked a shift from rating formats that asked raters to assess employee traits or qualities (Farr & Levy, 2007). The behavioral emphasis of the rating formats developed during this time is reflected in the format names: *behaviorally* anchored rating scales (BARS; Smith & Kendall, 1963), *behavioral* expectation scales (BES; Smith & Kendall, 1963), *behavioral* discrimination scales (BDS; Kane & Lawler, 1979), and *behavioral* summary scales (BSS;

Borman, 1979). Although this period led to the development of a number of different rating formats, efforts in this area were largely abandoned after they were criticized for being ineffective (Austin & Villanova, 1992; Borman, 1979; Landy & Farr, 1980; Murphy & Cleveland, 1995).

Nevertheless, attempts to improve ratings by changing the way employee performance is evaluated and recorded are still being tried. However, recent developments have not been as subtle as previous attempts and have made more dramatic changes to the process and format through which performance is rated (e.g., Borman et al., 2001). For example, Borman et al. (2001) applied computational and technical sophistication to the rating of performance by developing a computer adaptive rating scale (CARS) for contextual performance. Inspired by item response theory, raters complete a paired comparison rating scale wherein items are scaled (based on an algorithm) from the rater's response to previous items. The CARS strategy is intended to more precisely pinpoint an employee's actual level of performance through an iterative and adaptive process. CARS has been shown to be effective in increasing the validity and reliability of ratings (Borman et al., 2001). In this seminal investigation, CARS was applied to the domain of contextual performance (Borman et al., 2001) and it has since been successfully applied to the assessment of task performance (Schneider et al., 2003).

Another technique developed in an attempt to improve the quality of performance ratings through altering the appraisal format and structure is the 360-degree or multi-source performance ratings (MSPR) system. In a MSPR system, performance ratings are provided to employees from raters occupying different roles. The different sources of ratings are most commonly supervisors, subordinates, peers, and the self. The receipt of ratings from multiple sources deviates from the conventional arrangement wherein ratings are provided by a manager who is rating his/her direct reports.

MSPR are a relatively contemporary development and were unearthed by researchers during the mid to late 1990s (Latham & Mann, 2006). By the late 1990s and early 2000s, the majority of organizations in North America were utilizing some form of a multisource rating system (Brutus & Derayeh, 2002; Church & Bracken, 1997; Latham & Mann, 2006). MSPR systems are largely used for developmental purposes (Timmreck & Bracken, 1997), but are also used as an assessment tool (DeNisi & Kluger, 2000; Toegel & Conger, 2003). Fletcher's chapter on 360-degree feedback (Chapter 25) in this volume provides a review of multisource feedback's use for development purposes. MSPR systems that are used for dual purposes, both administrative and developmental, have come under criticism (Ghorpade, 2000; Toegel & Conger, 2003). These criticisms are largely based on the idea that different appraisal purposes activate different rater goals and that it becomes difficult to get honest and valid ratings when raters have competing goals (Toegel & Conger, 2003). The significance of rater goals in the performance rating process will be discussed in more detail in the "Rating context and rater motivations" section below.

Like more traditional appraisal formats, the utility of MSPR systems are contingent on the validity of performance ratings (London & Smither, 1995). As a result, research has investigated the psychometric qualities of MSPR (Conway & Huffcutt, 1997; Diefendorff, Silverman, & Greguras, 2005; Hoffman & Woehr, 2009; Scullen, Mount, & Judge, 2003). The results of research on the psychometric quality of MSPR have been somewhat mixed. Correlations between different sources are generally low (Conway & Huffcutt, 1997; Hoffman & Woehr, 2009), with research finding a correlation of .18 between self and supervisor ratings, a correlation of .22 between self and peer ratings, and a correlation of .25 between supervisor and peer ratings (Smither, London, & Reilly, 2005). At the same time, research suggests that ratings from different sources are valid measures of performance with peer ratings accounting for a significant amount of variance in objective measures of performance

(Conway, Lombardo, & Sanders, 2001). However, the patterns of associations are not consistent across ratings from different sources. Ratings from different sources have been shown to correlate differently with external constructs (Hoffman & Woehr, 2009), suggesting that ratings from different sources are not measuring the same content.

It has been suggested that low levels of agreement between different rating sources are due to rating sources having different conceptualizations of what job performance is (Campbell & Lee, 1988). When investigating this question, some research has found evidence that raters from different sources have the same conceptualization of performance (Diefendorff, Silverman, & Greguras, 2005; Scullen, Mount, & Judge, 2003), whereas other research has found that there are small differences across sources in their conceptualization of performance (Bynum et al., 2013). Bynum et al. (2013) also concluded that although rater idiosyncrasies (variance due to the rater) explained 83 percent of the variance in MSPR ratings, ratings from the same source are more similar than ratings from different sources. Given this pattern of results, it has been suggested that different sources may be better suited to evaluate different skills or activities (Hoffman & Woehr, 2009).

Based on the evidence to date, it does not appear as though ratings generated by MSPR systems are of unequivocally better quality than more traditional single source ratings. MSPR are still susceptible to the factors that affect traditional ratings and the implementation of a MSPR system alone is not enough to improve the quality of ratings. It has been suggested that MSPR systems be combined with other strategies, such as rater training programs, to increase the psychometric quality of ratings (Bynum et al., 2013).

Rater training

One of the oldest approaches to improve the quality of performance ratings has been to train those who are providing the ratings (Bittner, 1948). Over the years, there have been a number of approaches to rater training. These approaches have worked to improve rating quality from different perspectives. Principal approaches to rater training include: (a) rater error training, (b) performance dimension training, (c) behavioral observation training (BOT), and (d) frame of reference (FOR) training. *Rater error training* attempts to teach raters about common forms of rating errors, such as leniency, halo, central tendency, and contrast errors (Smith, 1986). Raters are then encouraged to try to avoid making these types of errors when rating performance (Bernardin & Pence, 1980; Borman, 1975). *Performance dimension training* teaches raters about the performance dimensions that are going to be rated ahead of time. This can be done by reviewing the rating scales with the raters or by having raters participate in the scale's development (Smith, 1986). Providing raters with information about what is going to be rated was believed to enable raters to form better judgments about performance when observing employee behavior (Woehr & Huffcutt, 1994). BOT is focused on training raters on what behaviors to observe. Different researchers have developed different approaches to BOT (see Noonan & Sulsky, 2001, for a review), with some systems incorporating a form of rater error training wherein raters are taught which errors to be aware of and to avoid (e.g., Latham, Wexley, & Pursell, 1975; Thornton & Zorich, 1980). The core aspects of BOT focus on training raters on what behavioral episodes are relevant performance behaviors and on encouraging raters to record or keep track of these episodes whenever possible (Noonan & Sulsky, 2001). Focusing on the observation of behavior is believed to enable raters to detect, perceive, and recall specific events more effectively, which then leads to a reduction in rating errors, such as halo and leniency (Woehr & Huffcutt, 1994). FOR training was developed to increase rating accuracy (Bernardin & Buckley, 1981) and aims to provide raters with an effective theory of performance. A theory of performance contains explanations of dimensions of performance, which behaviors coincide with each dimension of performance, how to judge behaviors with respect to their effectiveness, and how to combine these judgments into performance ratings (Sulsky & Day, 1992). An effective or useful theory of performance is one that is in line with the organization's theory of performance (Woehr & Huffcutt, 1994). By providing raters with an appropriate theory of performance, ratings are thought to be less influenced by raters' idiosyncrasies and are less susceptible to rating errors (Stamoulis & Hauenstein, 1993; Sulsky & Day, 1994; Woehr & Huffcutt, 1994).

In one of the best-known and most cited investigations of rater training, Woehr and Huffcutt (1994) conducted a meta-analysis to examine the efficacy of these different training strategies. The results of their meta-analysis indicated that FOR training was the most effective training method for improving the quality of ratings, compared to rater error training, dimensional training, and BOT. Specifically, FOR training resulted in the largest increase in rating accuracy (effect size, $d = .83$) and demonstrated moderate effect sizes for increasing observational accuracy and decreasing halo and leniency. FOR trained raters were also significantly better than raters who did not receive any training in that they recalled significantly more behaviors and used more appraisal dimensions (Woehr & Huffcutt, 1994). Despite the efficacy of FOR training, at the time of Woehr and Huffcutt's (1994) study, rater error training was the most frequently studied training approach, with twice as many studies investigating rater error training as FOR training.

Recently, this trend has reversed and FOR training is the most studied method (Roch et al., 2012). FOR training has also spilled over into other contexts where it has been applied to improve an array of different evaluations in domains such as competency modeling (Lievens & Sanchez, 2007), assessment centers (Schleicher et al., 2002), and job analysis (Aguinis, Mazurkiewicz, & Heggestad, 2009). Although research on the lasting effects of FOR training is limited (Roch et al., 2012), some research has shown that FOR training can improve the quality of ratings beyond training (e.g., Roch & O'Sullivan, 2003; Sulsky & Day, 1994). In these studies, however, the length of time between training and follow-up has been somewhat limited with two weeks being the longest timeframe (Roch & O'Sullivan, 2003).

Roch et al. (2012) updated Woehr and Huffcutt's (1994) study by including more articles and by expanding the number of research questions that were investigated. The results were largely consistent with the 1994 investigation. Roch et al. (2012) found that FOR training improved the accuracy of ratings with an average effect size of .50 across all operationalizations of accuracy of ratings (see Sulsky & Balzer, 1988, for a review on different types of accuracy). FOR training was also found to have a large effect size on the accuracy of observations ($d = .88$). Overall, the body of evidence on rater training indicates that FOR training is the most effective for increasing accuracy (Roch et al., 2012; Woehr & Huffcutt, 1994). Moreover, the results indicate that FOR training has become the rater training method of choice with other training methods (e.g., rater error training) declining in popularity (Roch et al., 2012).

To date, the evidence for the efficacy of FOR training is clear and is supported by the results from two meta-analyses (Roch et al., 2012; Woehr & Huffcutt, 1994). In these two studies, FOR training was shown to have sizable effects on the accuracy of ratings and observations. A wide range of research studies have demonstrated that FOR training is the most effective training method and is thought to increase accuracy by helping raters understand which employee behaviors correspond to certain levels of performance for specific dimensions and by presenting raters with performance prototypes during the training process. It is a cognitively oriented training program as these prototypes help counteract memory failures by enabling raters to easily categorize behaviors based on these prototypes

(Roch et al., 2012; Sulsky & Day, 1992, 1994; Woehr, 1994). When a specific theory of performance is provided, raters can be trained to apply this theory to the task of rating, which increases the accuracy of ratings.

Other considerations

Despite the effectiveness of FOR training and rating formats such as CARS, there are other notable factors that influence the quality of performance ratings. These factors reveal themselves when the assumptions of the different improvement approaches are contemplated. This section reviews challenges that underlie rater training and rating format development approaches by highlighting two assumptions of the performance rating process: (a) that raters are impartial observers who want to provide accurate ratings and (b) that true performance is a single knowable construct that is normally distributed.

Rating context and rater motivations Marking a departure from format and training perspectives, research has considered the organizational context and rater volition as a source of rating variance (Levy & Williams, 2004; Murphy & Cleveland, 1995). The organizational context and raters' motivations during the appraisal process have been increasingly recognized by researchers as an important source of rating error (Levy & Williams, 2004; Murphy & Cleveland, 1995; Spence & Keeping, 2011). Although the notion that raters are autonomous and react to the appraisal context is not new (Banks & Murphy, 1985; McGregor, 1957), recent work has developed these ideas further by empirically establishing that motivations can alter appraisal ratings (Murphy et al., 2004; Spence & Keeping, 2010; Wang, Wong, & Kwong, 2010; Wong & Kwong, 2007), by uncovering and classifying different motivations (Harris, 1994; Longenecker, Sims, & Gioa, 1987; Murphy & Cleveland, 1995; Spence & Keeping, 2011), and by developing theory outlining how raters' intentions are related to other sources of appraisal error (Spence & Keeping, 2013).

Rater training and measurement format changes have been targeted at reducing psychometric errors (Kline & Sulsky, 2009). From these perspectives, sources of rating errors were primarily the result of cognitive lapses (Landy & Farr, 1980) and these errors were manifest in the accuracy of appraisal ratings as well as the accuracy of raters' observations (Woehr & Huffcutt, 1994). However, when one considers the social context and the sovereignty of raters, (a) new sources of error become apparent (e.g., intentional distortions) and (b) the definition of what an effective or quality rating is begins to change.

To understand the implications of the organizational context and rater volitions on performance ratings, an implicit assumption of rater training and measurement perspectives needs to be outlined. Strategies for training raters in order to improve ratings have concentrated on cognitive processes (e.g., FOR training, BOT) and assume that raters are trying to provide the highest quality ratings possible or are indifferent to the prospect of providing inaccurate ratings. Researchers have identified that this can be a tenuous starting point as the organizational context is not a disinterested environment (Banks & Murphy, 1985; Spence & Keeping, 2011). Moreover, appraisals are typically done so that the ratings can be used to make decisions that affect the salary and career opportunities of the employees receiving the ratings (DeCottis & Petit, 1978; Jawahar & Williams, 1997; Taylor & Wherry, 1951).

When viewed from this perspective, the organizational context and raters' responses to the context can be a source of variance in performance ratings. That is, cognitive errors in attention, observation, and memory are not the only source of error variance. One illustration of the impact that the organizational context can have on performance ratings can be seen in the well-documented effect of appraisal purpose on the magnitude of performance ratings (Jawahar & Williams, 1997). The most common distinction in appraisal research is between performance appraisals that are conducted for administrative purposes and appraisals that are conducted for developmental purposes. Appraisals done for administrative purposes are used to make personnel decisions such as pay increases, promotions, and retention whereas appraisals done for developmental reasons are used to identify strengths, weaknesses, and training needs. These two categories are not exclusive as appraisals may also be done for research purposes or be used for dual purposes (Boswell & Boudreau, 2002; Prince & Lawler, 1986). Research on the effects of appraisal purpose on ratings indicates that when ratings are provided for administrative purposes they tend to be higher than when provided for developmental purposes or research purposes (Jawahar & Williams, 1997). Different appraisal purposes are thought to activate different motivations in raters, such as wanting to attain positive consequences (i.e., pay increases, performance improvement), resulting in the different ratings (Murphy & Cleveland, 1995). The different implications and consequences created by the rating context may generate a response from raters in the form of altered performance ratings.

The appraisal purpose is only one example. Researchers have identified a number of contextual and motivational factors that can influence performance ratings (Murphy et al., 2004; Spence & Keeping, 2011). For example, raters are thought to alter performance ratings in order to avoid conflicts with ratees (Longenecker, Sims, & Gioia, 1987; Murphy & Cleveland, 1995), to maintain harmonious relations (Murphy et al., 2004; Wang, Wong, & Kwong, 2010; Wong & Kwong, 2007), to comply with organizational norms (Bernardin, Orban, & Carlyle, 1981; Tziner et al., 1996), to look more successful (Harris, 1994; Villanova & Bernardin, 1989), to motivate employees (Harris, 1994; Villanova & Bernardin, 1989), and to promote fairness (Murphy et al., 2004; Wang, Wong, & Kwong, 2010; Wong & Kwong, 2007). These motivations can be in addition to, or in lieu of, a motivation to rate accurately (Harris, 1994; Kane, 1994; Spence & Keeping, 2013). As a result, the interpretation of whether or not a rating was useful or effective can be viewed in reference to the intention (or intentions) the rater had when rendering the ratings. Therefore, a second implication of organizational context and raters' responses to the organizational context is that the standard of accuracy may not be the only standard for judging the quality of performance ratings. More specifically, if a performance rating had the effect of motivating a ratee and procuring him/her desirable resources, it may be legitimately seen as an effective rating even though it did not accurately reflect the employee's actual level of performance.

The rating context, rater motivation, and rater training From the perspective of rater training, these additional motivational factors may be seen as impediments to training effectiveness. It has been recognized that contextual variables can influence individuals' motivation to expend cognitive resources on information processing (Feldman, 1994; Schleicher & Day, 1998). As a result, rater training that focuses on cognitive processes, such as FOR training, needs to consider whether or not trainees are motivated to rate accurately. A lack of motivation to rate accurately has been considered in the context of FOR training with respect to raters disagreeing with the theory of performance that is presented (Schleicher & Day, 1998). The rater intentions outlined above and the organizational context may have a similar effect on rater motivation in that a rater may not be motivated to provide accurate ratings because he or she is compelled by other ideas.

If one considers the possibility that raters can simultaneously possess several, possibly competing, intentions (Spence & Keeping, 2013), it becomes important to not only consider the extent to which raters are motivated to provide accurate ratings (Banks & Murphy,

1985; Harris, 1994; Murphy & Cleveland, 1995), but to also consider the extent to which raters lack other rating intentions. That is, a rater in a training program may be motivated to rate accurately, but may also be motivated to avoid conflict and to comply with organizational norms. In this context, the efficacy of training may be masked by the presence of other demands that erode the program's effectiveness over time. Even if raters are motivated to rate accurately and are devoid of other motivations at the time of training, the social context can make it difficult for training programs, such as FOR training, to have continued effectiveness given that after the training, raters will be immersed in an environment in which they will face pressures from subordinates and peers that may conflict with the theory of performance they learned in training. Over time, raters may adopt an alternate theory of performance or revise the theory of performance they learned from FOR training as a result of their social environment.

To address the influence of rater motivations, rater training could incorporate interventions designed to increase motivation to rate accurately and reduce competing motivations. In order for raters to be effective, researchers have argued that raters must take the appraisal process seriously (Latham & Latham, 2000), which they can do by making connections between what they do as raters and positive outcomes (Latham & Latham, 2000). Making meaningful connections between work and desirable outcomes, even when the outcome is distal, has been found to increase motivation and performance in other domains (Grant, 2008; Grant & Parker, 2009). Thus, changing training to incorporate information that explicitly maps connections between the performance ratings and outcomes at individual and organization levels could prove effective.

As outlined earlier, not every outcome of the appraisal process is positive. Some by-products such as conflict, low ratings, and demotivated employees can be negative. As a result, initiatives that develop rater self-efficacy and confidence to deal with negative outcomes may also be beneficial (Brutus, Donia, & Ronen, 2013; Tziner, Murphy, & Cleveland, 2001). Training programs may be developed that can teach raters effective techniques for delivering negative feedback and handling the fallout of employees being upset after receiving negative feedback. If raters feel equipped for these situations, they may feel more confident about rendering accurate ratings that convey negative information. Theoretical frameworks from clinical or counseling psychology have also been identified as a potential means to increase the effectiveness of appraisal systems (Latham & Mann, 2006). Some of these clinical or counseling psychology frameworks may be effective for coaching raters to be more committed to rating accurately.

The nature of performance and performance ratings   In addition to contextual and motivational factors, the nature of performance itself can pose unique challenges to initiatives aimed at improving the quality of performance ratings. As reviewed earlier, psychometric error refers to performance ratings that have restricted variance, are negatively skewed, and are comprised of dimensions that are highly related (Jacobs, Kafry, & Zedeck, 1980; Landy & Farr, 1980). An accepted interpretation of psychometric error has been that these characteristics are not a result of error, but instead are a reflection of actual job performance (Cooper, 1981; Roch et al., 2012). This idea has implications for how we understand accuracy and error in performance ratings (Murphy & Balzer, 1989), but the negative skew also suggests that true performance may not correspond to a normal distribution. The distributional properties of "true" performance can be an explicit part of appraisal systems, such as forced distribution. Forced distribution systems categorize employee performance in a predetermined performance distribution, which typically approximates a normal distribution (Berger, Harbring, & Sliwka, 2013; Canter, 1953; Schleicher, Bull, & Green, 2009). As a result, the distributional properties of performance can have both conceptual and practical implications for the rating of performance.

Recent research on the distribution of performance suggests that performance does not follow a normal distribution or a negatively skewed distribution, but instead corresponds to a Paretian (power) distribution (O'Boyle & Aguinis, 2012). Examining data from 198 samples with a total sample size of 633, 263, the authors found that individual performance fit a Paretian distribution better than a normal distribution. A Paretian distribution is positively skewed and allows for more extreme values than a normal distribution (O'Boyle & Aguinis, 2012). Data points that would be considered outliers in a normal distribution would be expected under a Paretian distribution. To illustrate, Paretian distributions have been characterized with the Pareto Principle or 80/20 principle where 80 percent of a characteristic is accounted for by 20 percent of the sample (e.g., 80 percent of wealth is held by 20 percent of people; Juran, 1975; Pareto, 1897). In the case of performance, it would be expected that 80 percent of the performance would be the result of 20 percent of people. O'Boyle and Aguinis (2012) found support for this idea and presented data across a range of occupations that revealed that a large proportion of performance outcomes were attributable to small sets of high performers. The Paretian distribution is opposite to the types of distributions found in discussions of psychometric error, which find that most performers are at the top of the distribution. As a result, the conclusion that negatively skewed ratings are a reflection of actual performance and are not the result of error may need to be re-examined. Moreover, a rater's ability to appropriately differentiate a few exceptionally high-performing employees from the rest of the group may be limited or impossible in some appraisal systems. There may be an insufficient arrangement of categories to recognize these individuals. Rater training programs and appraisal format improvement techniques may need to incorporate ideas about the underlying distribution of performance, allowing for more extreme performers in order to be more effective.

Separate from the distribution of performance, attention has also been given to the dynamic nature of performance. That is, job performance is not a singular static entity that employees achieve and maintain indefinitely, but can be viewed as a dynamic construct that exhibits variability within individuals over time (Fisher, 2008; Stewart & Nandkeolyar, 2006; Thoresen et al., 2004; Zyphur, Chaturvedi, & Arvey, 2008). Within-person variability in employee performance has been examined at different intervals of time ranging from the duration of an employee's tenure with an organization (Deadrick, Bennett, & Russell, 1997) to changes in performance within a single day of work (Beal et al., 2005).

Not unlike trying to hit a moving target, the dynamic nature of performance can pose unique challenges to raters when trying to rate performance. Raters are required to aggregate performance episodes over a defined period of time to single ratings. In addition to being cognitively demanding, these changes and the nature of these changes can introduce other sources of rating variability. When evaluating performance over time, different patterns of performance change have been found to influence ratings (Lee & Dalal, 2011; Reb & Cropanzano, 2007; Reb & Greguras, 2010). Reb and Cropanzano (2007) had participants rate the performance of fictitious employees over a 26-week period and found that, irrespective of the mean level of performance, the performance trends exhibited by employees were a significant source of rating variability. For example, an improving performance trend was rated more positively than a flat trend, and a flat trend was rated more positively than a deteriorating trend. Additionally, a U-shaped trend was rated similarly to a flat trend and an improving trend, and an inverted U-shaped trend was rated higher than a deteriorating trend (Reb & Cropanzano, 2007). Although work in this area is relatively new, it has uncovered other sources of rating variability and highlights that raters make use of a variety of performance characteristics when rating performance.

In addition to highlighting the importance of understanding how raters make use of dynamic performance information, these investigations raise conceptual questions about the nature of true performance. That is, is true performance simply the average level of performance across a given period of time or should other performance information be incorporated in the definition? Specifically, do consistency and progress have a place in the true performance construct? For example, if two employees have the same mean level of performance over a year, but one has been steadily improving while the other has been erratic with peaks and valleys, are these equivalent employees with the same level of true performance? Disentangling these questions can have implications for appraisal research and our understanding of error. At a practical level, if these definitional considerations are made explicit, they could be incorporated into theories of performance in FOR training programs and appraisal formats could be designed to quantify them accordingly (e.g., questions about the stability or variability of performance).

Developing Employees through Appraisals and Feedback

Irrespective of rating quality, performance appraisals are often conducted to further employee development (DeNisi, 2011; Dusterhoff, Cunningham, & MacGregor, 2014; Fletcher, 2008b; Nurse, 2005; Pichler, 2012). There is doubt, however, as to whether or not performance appraisals are actually effective in this regard (DeNisi & Sonesh, 2011; Tuytens & Devos, 2012) and some researchers go so far as to recommend the cessation of performance appraisals altogether (Coens & Jenkins, 2000). In this section, we examine the relationship between appraisals and employee development. We outline the importance of ratee reactions to feedback and the characteristics of feedback in determining if ratee behavior will change following an appraisal.

Performance feedback

The rendering of performance feedback is perhaps the most important component of performance appraisals (Jawahar, 2010). Performance feedback has been defined as quantitative and/or qualitative information regarding an individual's performance (Prue & Fairbank, 1981). At minimum, performance feedback consists of performance ratings, but may also include more descriptive or qualitative information regarding performance. Though performance feedback has been hypothesized to promote development, such as through improved performance, (Ilgen, Fisher, & Taylor, 1979; Murphy & Cleveland, 1995), research yields mixed findings regarding its efficacy. For example, while some studies indicate that performance feedback leads to improved performance, others report no effect of feedback on subsequent performance (see Balcazar, Hopkins, & Suarez, 1986, for a review; see Kluger & DeNisi, 1996, for a meta-analysis). These discrepant findings hold across different performance appraisal systems, including upward feedback or feedback from direct reports/subordinates (e.g., Atwater et al., 2000; Heslin & Latham, 2004; Jhun, Bae, & Rhee, 2012) and multisource or 360-degree feedback (see Seifert, Yukl, & McDonald, 2003, for a review; Smither, London, & Reilly, 2005). These inconsistent findings have led researchers to investigate which feedback-related aspects of the performance appraisal system influence the efficacy of feedback.

Some researchers assert that performance ratings based on competencies should be instrumental in enabling employee development (e.g., Abraham et al., 2001; Fletcher,

1995; Fletcher, 2008a). Competencies can include behaviors, abilities, and/or skills (Stevens, 2013) and, when used for employee development, should focus on malleable qualities for which improvement is possible (Rupp et al., 2006). Past research has demonstrated that performance ratings based on behavioral competencies predict performance and career advancement within organizations, suggesting that performance feedback that identifies competencies may be helpful in fostering development (Bondy et al., 1997; Catano, Darr, & Campbell, 2007). Few organizations, however, use competencies as part of their performance ratings. Results of one survey found that although organizations indicate that certain competencies are critical for job performance in specific domains, many do not evaluate these competencies during the performance appraisal (Abraham et al., 2001).

A separate line of research suggests that performance appraisal systems used for developmental purposes are more likely to foster employee development than appraisals used for administrative purposes. Indeed, Fletcher (1995) argues that appraisals that emphasize development are instrumental in motivating employees to modify their behavior. Appraisals used for developmental purposes emphasize employee development by identifying strengths and weaknesses, whereas appraisals used for administrative purposes are used for personnel decisions, such as promotions and salary increases (Stephan & Dorfman, 1989). Research investigating the role of appraisal purpose on development following ratings, however, is fairly limited as most research focuses on how appraisal purpose influences *raters* and not *ratees* (Greguras et al., 2003; Jawahar & Williams, 1997). Furthermore, the few studies that have investigated the efficacy of both administrative and developmental appraisals are field experiments and often are unable to account for confounding variables making it difficult to draw causal conclusions regarding the effect of appraisal purpose (Jhun, Bae, & Rhee, 2012). Experimental research, however, provides some evidence of the advantages of using performance appraisals for developmental purposes. Stephan and Dorfman (1989) found that both developmental appraisals, emphasizing strategies for improvement, and administrative appraisals, emphasizing results, led to increased performance on a related task, but only developmental appraisals led to improved performance on an unrelated task for which feedback was not given. Similarly, Lam and Schaubroeck (1999) found that participants performed better on a task following a developmental appraisal that emphasized understanding compared to an administrative appraisal that stressed results. These findings suggest that developmental appraisals may be more helpful than administrative appraisals in providing individuals with the necessary skills to further their development.

Performance appraisals used for developmental purposes are likely to be advantageous because they provide ratees with practical feedback that enables them to alter their behavior. Indeed, research suggests that providing individuals with suggestions or recommendations on how to improve leads to a boost in subsequent performance (Duijnhouwer, Prins, & Stokking, 2012; Haynes, 1973; Jawahar, 2010; Smither et al., 2004). These findings are mirrored by research on the effect of feedback on development within the context of developmental assessment centers (DACs). DACs focus on developing potential through the provision of feedback regarding one's strengths and weaknesses and developmental needs (Rupp et al., 2006; Woo et al., 2008). Participants typically complete a number of tasks, such as in-basket exercises and role plays, and later meet with an assessor who provides them with feedback much like a typical performance appraisal (Arthur & Day, 2011). Research in this area suggests that developmental feedback provided within the context of DACs predicts future job performance and career advancement within the organization (Engelbrecht & Fischer, 1995; Jones & Whitmore, 1995; Rupp et al., 2006). Thus, providing individuals with feedback that underscores the competencies on which they can improve as well as recommendations on how they can hone these competencies positively contributes to their development at work.

In developmental appraisals, ratees are often provided with information in addition to a simple rating or ranking. As a result, there may be advantages to providing employees with qualitative information regarding their performance. Past research has largely ignored the impact of qualitative feedback on development, focusing solely on performance ratings (Brutus, 2010; Smither & Walker, 2004). This is surprising given that feedback recipients attend to qualitative information more than quantitative information (Ferstl & Bruskiewicz, 2000; Rose & Farrell, 2002) and may even perform better when given qualitative feedback regarding their performance (Kilduski & Rice, 2003). Cannon and Witherspoon (2005) reported that managers call for an increase in the use of qualitative feedback as they believe that this kind of feedback is crucial to their development. London and Mone's chapter (Chapter 23) in this volume on designing feedback to improve performance elaborates some of the benefits of using qualitative feedback.

Providing qualitative feedback in and of itself, however, is not likely to lead to better performance unless it includes information that can be acted upon. Finney (2010) asserts that specific, detailed feedback that targets tasks or behaviors and directs recipients towards a desired outcome is most effective for eliciting behavioral change. Past research, however, indicates that most comments provided during performance appraisals do not provide useful information (Louis-Slaby & Helland, 2004) and few include developmental suggestions (Rose & Farrell, 2002). This variability in how managers provide feedback, with some managers emphasizing performance ratings and others qualitative feedback, may provide some indication as to why research yields inconsistent findings regarding the effect of feedback on development. That is, both within and across organizations, managers differ in the feedback they give and how they deliver it, making it difficult to detect a consistent, stable relationship between feedback and development. When viewed in conjunction with the variability in how performance appraisal systems are designed – appraisals for developmental purposes versus administrative purposes – it becomes clearer as to why research has shown that performance feedback does not uniformly lead to development among feedback recipients. It also needs to be recognized that in addition to differences in the purpose and content of feedback, employees receiving performance feedback can differ in their reactions.

Ratee reactions to appraisals and feedback

In evaluating the efficacy of performance appraisals, ratee reactions to appraisals are perhaps the best indication of whether or not appraisals will be effective in fostering employee development (e.g., Bernardin & Beatty, 1984; Cardy & Dobbins, 1994; Cawley, Keeping, & Levy, 1998; Keeping & Levy, 2000). Ratee reactions to the appraisal and their perceptions of the appraisal system are crucial to the success of the appraisal system. That is, if individuals are dissatisfied with the appraisal system or view it as unfair, do not accept the feedback they receive, or believe the feedback to be inaccurate or not useful, they will be unlikely to use the feedback regardless of how well the performance appraisal system is designed (Cardy & Dobbins, 1994; Cawley, Keeping, & Levy, 1998; Ilgen, Fisher, & Taylor, 1979; Kinicki et al., 2004; Levy & Williams, 2004; Murphy & Cleveland, 1995). The fact that not all individuals react to the appraisal or feedback in the same way may provide some insight into why previous research has shown that performance feedback does not uniformly lead to improvement (Kluger & DeNisi, 1996).

In their review of the ratee reactions literature, Levy and Williams (2004) identify satisfaction, perceptions of justice (or fairness), and the acceptability, perceived accuracy, and perceived utility of feedback as commonly studied reactions to performance appraisals. Research in this area has proliferated since the 1990s (Levy & Williams, 2004) with most research focusing on what aspects of the performance appraisal system, process, and/ or feedback affect ratee reactions. With respect to development, researchers assert that individuals who respond favorably to the appraisal and/or feedback – that is, by experiencing the reactions outlined above – should subsequently improve as a consequence of these positive reactions (e.g., Anseel & Lievens, 2006; Dusterhoff, Cunningham, & MacGregor, 2014; Tuytens & Devos, 2012).

A number of studies have shown that when ratees participate in the performance appraisal process, they experience increased satisfaction with both the appraisal system and the appraisal session in addition to perceiving the feedback as fair and useful (see Cawley, Keeping, & Levy, 1998, for a meta-analysis; Dewettinck & van Dijk, 2013; Douthitt & Aiello, 2001; Kavanagh, Benson, & Brown, 2007; Tuytens & Devos, 2012). Other research has found that individuals are more likely to be satisfied with their feedback and perceive it as accurate, useful, and fair when they receive feedback from an individual high in credibility, expertise, or trustworthiness (Bannister, 1986; Brett & Atwater, 2001; Facteau et al., 1998; Jawahar, 2010; see Levy & Williams, 2004, for a review; Steelman & Rutkowski, 2004). In addition, performance appraisal systems that follow a due process model, by providing adequate notice, fair hearing, and judgment based on evidence, are more likely to elicit feedback acceptance, satisfaction, and perceptions of accuracy and fairness in those being rated (see Levy & Williams, 2004, for a review).

Most research on appraisal and feedback characteristics has focused on feedback valence with most researchers contending that individuals tend to respond more favorably to positive feedback than they do to negative feedback (e.g., Ilgen, Fisher, & Taylor, 1979; Belschak, & Den Hartog, 2009). Indeed, research suggests that positive feedback is perceived as more accurate, useful, and satisfying (Anseel & Lievens, 2006; Brett & Atwater, 2001), whereas negative feedback is perceived as less accurate and is less likely to be accepted (Brett & Atwater, 2001; Coleman, Jussim, & Abraham, 1987; Ilgen, Fisher, & Taylor, 1979; Stone & Stone, 1985). Other research, however, suggests that individuals only react favorably to feedback that is consistent with their self-perceptions regardless of its valence (Jussim, Yen, & Aiello, 1995; Tonidandel, Quinones, & Adams, 2002). For instance, in one study, individuals accepted positive feedback and were more satisfied with this feedback when they thought that they had performed well whereas individuals who thought that they performed poorly only accepted negative feedback (Tonidandel, Quiñones, & Adams, 2002).

A limiting factor of ratee reactions research is that it often concentrates on ratee reactions to appraisal and feedback characteristics and does not investigate if or how these reactions translate into subsequent behavior. Researchers (Ilgen, Fisher, & Taylor, 1979) have proposed a model that outlines that perceptions of performance feedback influence how one behaviorally responds to this feedback. Understanding this causal relationship is important as, within the context of employee development, it seems impractical to attempt to understand how to foster favorable employee reactions during the appraisal process without first understanding whether or not these reactions affect behavior.

Researchers have only recently begun to investigate how ratee reactions relate to development. Most research focuses on performance as a gauge of development and indicates that positive reactions to performance appraisals and/or feedback lead to improved performance (e.g., Jawahar, 2010; Selvarajan & Cloninger, 2011). For instance, research has shown that perceived accuracy, feedback acceptance, satisfaction with the appraisal system, satisfaction with feedback, and perceptions of justice are positively related to one's motivation to improve performance (Anseel, & Lievens, 2009; Burke, Weitzel, & Weir,

1978; Roberson & Stewart, 2006; Selvarajan & Cloninger, 2011; Steelman & Rutkowski, 2004). Similarly, longitudinal research has shown that perceived accuracy and satisfaction with feedback predict future performance (Jawahar, 2010; Jawahar 2006). Thus, when individuals believe that feedback reflects their actual performance, accept the feedback, are satisfied with it, and perceive it as fair, they are more likely to use this feedback to improve their performance.

Research on the perceived utility of feedback shows mixed results with respect to development or performance. Perceived utility of feedback is commonly operationalized as the extent to which one believes that performance feedback provides clear direction and is helpful in improving one's performance (Greller, 1978). Whitaker and Levy (2012) found that feedback quality, which is defined as the extent to which one perceives performance feedback as useful and meaningful and is thus analogous to how perceived utility is typically defined, was positively correlated with supervisor ratings of task performance. This finding was replicated by Steelman and Rutkowski (2004), who found that feedback quality was positively correlated with motivation to improve performance. Other research has found that the perceived helpfulness of performance appraisals is positively correlated with self-reports of performance, but only when individuals receive feedback regularly (Kuvaas, 2011). The results of longitudinal research suggest a different relationship between perceived utility and future performance. Specifically, Jawahar (2010) found that perceiving performance feedback as useful during the initial semi-annual performance appraisal did not predict ratings of job performance given for the second performance appraisal. Thus, it is unclear whether or not perceiving performance feedback as useful is instrumental in improving performance. The results of longitudinal research are seemingly inconsistent with the finding that developmental feedback – has a positive impact on future performance (e.g., Duijnhouwer, Prins, & Stokking, 2012; Jawahar, 2010). Perhaps this relates to the distinction between the objective versus the subjective utility of feedback. That is, perceiving one's feedback to be helpful is unlikely to enable one to improve performance if such feedback contains irrelevant or impractical information.

Though the overall findings seem to support the notion that reacting favorably (i.e., perceptions of accuracy, satisfaction, etc.) to the appraisal system, process, and/or feedback enables individuals to develop through performance improvement, research on this topic is limited. Most studies are cross-sectional (e.g., Roberson & Stewart, 2006; Selvarajan & Cloninger; 2011; Steelman & Rutkowski, 2004; Whitaker & Levy, 2012), with very few employing longitudinal designs (e.g., Jawahar, 2010; Jawahar, 2006), making it difficult to determine whether or not ratee reactions actually lead to changes in performance. In addition, most researchers do not measure actual performance and instead measure indices of performance, such as motivation to improve performance (e.g., Roberson & Stewart, 2006; Selvarajan & Cloninger; 2011; Steelman & Rutkowski, 2004) or self-reports of performance (e.g., Kuvaas, 2011; Kuvaas, 2006). The theoretical assumption that these constructs relate to actual performance has received little empirical attention. Kinicki et al. (2004) did find that one's intended response to performance feedback was positively related to actual performance 11 months later. Interestingly, however, though the authors found that appraisal reactions (i.e., perceived accuracy) were positively related to one's intended response, they did not investigate the extent to which appraisal reactions related to future performance. We suggest that future research address the limitations outlined above by examining the causal relationship between ratee reactions and actual performance in order to provide a coherent and comprehensive understanding of the role of performance appraisals in improving performance.

Future Research

Past research has pointed towards specific, behavior-oriented, developmental feedback for fostering employee development (e.g., Catano, Darr, & Campbell, 2007; Duijnhouwer, Prins, & Stokking, 2012; Lam & Schaubroeck, 1999). Future research could use interventions to understand better this relationship as few organizations evaluate behaviors or competencies during the performance appraisal or provide ratees with recommendations and/or suggestions for improvement, making it difficult to study this relationship (Abraham et al., 2001; Louis-Slaby & Helland, 2004; Rose & Farrell, 2002). In addition, when looking at appraisals for developmental purposes, researchers could focus on how these impact *ratees* and not just *raters*. Research on DACs addresses these concerns, though participants in DACs tend to be high-performing individuals who have been identified as having potential for managerial positions. Thus, future research may want to investigate if this developmental feedback is as effective for less motivated or capable employees.

In addition to the content of feedback, researchers have identified ratee reactions as important components of the appraisal process (e.g., Levy & Williams, 2004). Future research should aim to understand better the role of ratee reactions by focusing on the relationship between reactions and development. As indicated above, most research focuses on which aspects of appraisals and feedback elicit favorable ratee reactions without first understanding whether or not reactions relate to actual behavior. We recommend that future research investigate this relationship through the use of longitudinal designs and observable outcomes, such as performance ratings or career advancement, instead of variables that only approximate these outcomes (e.g., motivation to improve).

As outlined earlier in this chapter, future research can work to develop and test the efficacy of rater training programs that address motivations in order to improve the quality of ratings. Research and theory suggests that rater volitions can be an important determinant of rating quality. As a result, developing and testing the efficacy of interventions that are designed to increase a rater's motivation to rate accurately and reduce competing motivations could prove fruitful. Current research and theory suggests that self-efficacy training or training that outlines the importance of the task of rating performance may prove effective (Grant, 2008; Grant & Parker, 2009; Latham & Latham, 2000). Latham and Mann (2006) also discussed the option of applying theoretical frameworks from clinical or counseling psychology to increase the effectiveness of appraisal systems. Such clinical or counseling psychology frameworks may provide novel insights for helping raters to be more committed to rating accurately.

In addition to rater training, research should continue to advance our understanding of the nature of performance itself. Both the distribution of performance and its dynamic nature have direct implications for how we understand the quality of performance ratings. Developing appraisal systems that are able to accommodate Paretian distributions may prove effective at combating certain types of rating errors. Also, continued work in understanding how raters process and evaluate dynamic performance can provide insights into what factors beyond average performance level are considered. Highlighting how raters incorporate ideas around improvement and consistency can inform conceptual questions about the nature of true performance.

Conclusion

In the current chapter, we reviewed the performance appraisal literature by examining factors that influence the quality of performance appraisals and the utility of appraisals for enabling employee development. Overall, singular attempts to improve the quality of ratings, whether they are format changes or select training programs (e.g., rater error training, BOT), are not entirely effective. Given the complexity of the task of rating, the organizational context, and the nature of performance, a silver-bullet strategy to improve rating quality is unlikely. However, despite the challenges and criticisms of performance rating quality and techniques to improve ratings, FOR training is an effective technique to improve the quality of ratings. Moreover, FOR training may prove particularly effective if it incorporates dynamic performance information and is combined with techniques that address rater motivations.

The use of performance appraisals to promote employee development is as difficult, if not more difficult, as improving the quality of ratings. It is clear that the provision of feedback alone is not enough for development. However, this appears to be where much of the consensus ends. Feedback that provides constructive ideas on how to improve is effective, provided recipients react favorably to the feedback and the system that was used to create the feedback. Despite research revealing that the valance and quality (e.g., accuracy, fairness) of feedback can predict reactions, our understanding of the effectiveness of feedback in fostering development is restricted by a lack of research linking feedback characteristics to actual performance outcomes. Much of the research is cross-sectional and uses attitudes and justice perceptions as proxies for development.

References

Abraham, S. E., Karns, L. A., Shaw, K., & Mena, M. A. (2001). Managerial competencies and the managerial performance appraisal process. *Journal of Management Development*, 20, 842–852.

Aguinis, H., Mazurkiewicz, M. D., & Heggestad, E. D. (2009). Using web-based frame-of-reference training to decrease biases in personality-based job analysis: An experimental field study. *Personnel Psychology*, 62, 405–438.

Anseel, F., & Lievens, F. (2006). Certainty as a moderator of feedback reactions? A test of the strength of the self-verification motive. *Journal of Occupational and Organizational Psychology*, 79, 533–551.

Anseel, F., & Lievens, F. (2009). The mediating role of feedback acceptance in the relationship between feedback and attitudinal and performance outcomes. *International Journal of Selection and Assessment*, 17, 362–376.

Arthur Jr., W., & Day, E. A. (2011). Assessment centers. In S. Zedeck (Ed.), *APA Handbook of Industrial and Organizational Psychology* (vol. 2, pp. 205–235). Washington, DC: APA Press.

Arvey, R. D., & Murphy, K. R. (1998). Performance evaluation in work settings. *Annual Review of Psychology*, 49, 141–168.

Atwater, L. E., Waldman, D. A., Atwater, D., & Cartier, P. (2000). An upward feedback field experiment: Supervisors' cynicism, reactions, and commitment to subordinates. *Personnel Psychology*, 53, 275–297.

Austin, J. T., & Villanova, P. (1992). The criterion problem: 1917–1992. *Journal of Applied Psychology*, 77, 836–874.

Balcazar, F. E., Hopkins, B. L., & Suarez, Y. (1986). A critical, objective review of performance feedback. *Journal of Organizational Behavior Management*, 7, 65–89.

Banks, C., & Murphy, K. (1985). Toward narrowing the research-practice gap in performance appraisal. *Personnel Psychology*, 38, 335–345.

Bannister, B. D. (1986). Performance outcome feedback and attributional feedback: Interactive effects on recipient responses. *Journal of Applied Psychology*, 71, 203–210.

Beal, D. J., Weiss, H. M., Barros, E., & MacDermid, S. M. (2005). An episodic process model of affective influences on performance. *Journal of Applied Psychology*, 90, 1054–1068.

Belschak, F. D., & Den Hartog, D. N. (2009). Consequences of positive and negative feedback: The impact on emotions and extra-role behaviors. *Applied Psychology: An International Review*, 58, 274–303.

Berger, J., Harbring, C., & Sliwka, D. (2013). Performance appraisals and the impact of forced distribution – An experimental investigation. *Management Science*, 59, 54–68.

Bernardin, H. J., & Beatty, R. W. (1984). *Performance Appraisal: Assessing Human Performance at Work*. Boston, MA: Kent.

Bernardin, H. J., & Buckley, M. R. (1981). Strategies in rater training. *Academy of Management Review*, 6, 205–212.

Bernardin, H. J., Orban, J., & Carlyle, J. (1981). Performance ratings as a function of trust in appraisal and rater individual differences. *Proceedings of the Academy of Management Meetings*, 311–315.

Bernardin, H. J., & Pence, E. C. (1980). Effects of rater training: New response sets and decreasing accuracy. *Journal of Applied Psychology*, 63, 60–66.

Bernardin, H. J., & Tyler, C. L. (2001). Legal and ethical issues in multisource feedback. In D. W. Bracken, C. W. Timmreck, & A. H. Church (Eds.), *The Handbook of Multisource Feedback* (pp. 447–462). San Francisco: Jossey-Bass.

Bittner, R. H. (1948). Developing an industrial merit rating procedure. *Personnel Psychology*, 1, 403–432.

Bondy, K. N., Jenkins, K., Seymour, L., Lancaster, R., & Ishee, J. (1997). The development and testing of a competency-focused psychiatric nursing clinical evaluation instrument. *Archives of Psychiatric Nursing*, 11, 66–73.

Borman, W. C. (1975). Effects of instructions to avoid halo error on reliability and validity of performance evaluation ratings. *Journal of Applied Psychology*, 60, 556–560.

Borman, W. C. (1979). Format and training effects on rating accuracy and rater errors. *Journal of Applied Psychology*, 64, 410–421.

Borman, W. C., Buck, D. E., Hanson, M. A., Motowidlo, S. J., Stark, S., & Drasgow, F. (2001). An examination of the comparative reliability, validity, and accuracy of performance ratings made using computerized adaptive rating scales. *Journal of Applied Psychology*, 86, 965–973.

Boswell, W. R., & Boudreau, J. W. (2002). Separating the developmental and evaluative performance appraisal uses. *Journal of Business and Psychology*, 16, 391–412.

Bowman, J. S. (1994). At last, an alternative to performance appraisal: Total quality management. *Public Administration Review*, 129–136.

Brett, J. F., & Atwater, L. E. (2001). 360° feedback: Accuracy, reactions, and perceptions of usefulness. *Journal of Applied Psychology*, 86, 930–942.

Brutus, S. (2010). Words versus numbers: A theoretical explanation of narrative comments in performance appraisal. *Human Resource Management*, 20, 144–157.

Brutus, S., & Derayeh, M. (2002). Multisource assessment programs in organizations: An insider's perspective. *Human Resource Development Quarterly*, 13, 187–202.

Brutus, S., Donia, M. B., & Ronen, S. (2013). Can business students learn to evaluate better? Evidence from repeated exposure to a peer-evaluation system. *Academy of Management Learning & Education*, 12, 18–31.

Burke, R. J., Weitzel, W., & Weir, T. (1978). Characteristics of effective employee performance review and development interviews: Replication and extension. *Personnel Psychology*, 31, 903–919.

Bynum, B. H., Hoffman, B. J., Meade, A. W., & Gentry, W. A. (2013). Reconsidering the equivalence of multisource performance ratings: Evidence for the importance and meaning of rater factors. *Journal of Business and Psychology*, 28, 203–219.

Campbell, D. J., & Lee, C. (1988). Self-appraisal in performance evaluation: Development versus evaluation. *Academy of Management Review*, 13, 302–314.

Cannon, M. D., & Witherspoon, R. (2005). Actionable feedback: Unlocking the power of learning and performance improvement. *Academy of Management Executive*, 19, 120–134.

Canter, R. R. (1953). A rating-scoring method for free-response data. *Journal of Applied Psychology*, 37, 455–457.

Cardy, R. L., & Dobbins, G. H. (1994). *Performance Appraisal: Alternative Perspectives*. Cincinnati, OH: South-Western Publishing.

Catano, V. M., Darr, W., & Campbell, C. A. (2007). Performance appraisal of behavior-based competencies: A reliable and valid procedure. *Personnel Psychology*, 60, 201–230.

Cawley, B. D., Keeping, L. M., & Levy, P. E. (1998). Participation in the performance appraisal process and employee reactions: A meta-analytic review of field investigations. *Journal of Applied Psychology*, 83, 615–633.

Church, A. H., & Bracken, D. W. (1997). Advancing the state of the art of 360-degree feedback: Guest editors' comments on the research and practice of multirater assessment methods. *Group & Organization Management*, 22, 149–161.

Coens, T., & Jenkins, M. (2000). *Abolishing Performance Appraisals: Why they Backfire and What they Do Instead.* San Francisco: Berrett-Koehler.

Coleman, L. M., Jussim, L., & Abraham, J. (1987). Students' reactions to teachers' evaluations: The unique impact of negative feedback. *Journal of Applied Social Psychology*, 17, 1051–1070.

Conway, J. M., & Huffcutt, A. I. (1997). Psychometric properties of multisource performance ratings: A meta-analysis of subordinate, supervisor, peer, and self-ratings. *Human Performance*, 10, 331–360.

Conway, J. M., Lombardo, K., & Sanders, K. C. (2001). A meta-analysis of incremental validity and nomological networks for subordinate and peer rating. *Human Performance*, 14, 267–303.

Cooper, W. H. (1981). Ubiquitous halo. *Psychological Bulletin*, 90, 218–244.

Deadrick, D. L., Bennett, N., & Russell, C. J. (1997). Using hierarchical linear modeling to examine dynamic performance criteria over time. *Journal of Management*, 23, 745–757.

Decotiis, T., & Petit, A. (1978). The performance appraisal process: A model and some testable propositions. *Academy of Management Review*, 3, 635–646.

DeNisi, A. S. (2011). Managing performance to change behavior. *Journal of Organizational Behavior Management*, 31, 262–276.

DeNisi, A., & Kluger, A. (2000). Feedback effectiveness: Can 360-degree appraisals be improved? *Academy of Management Executive*, 14, 129–139.

DeNisi, A. S., & Pritchard, R. D. (2006). Performance appraisal, performance management and improving individual performance: A motivational framework. *Management and Organization Review*, 2, 253–277.

DeNisi, A. S., & Sonesh, S. (2011). The appraisal and management of performance at work. In S. Zedeck (Ed.), *APA Handbook of Industrial and Organizational Psychology* (vol. 2, pp. 255–281). Washington, DC: APA Press.

Dewettinck, K., & van Dijk, H. (2013). Linking Belgian employee performance management system characteristics with performance management system effectiveness: Exploring the mediating role of fairness. *International Journal of Human Resource Management*, 24, 806–825.

Diefendorff, J. M., Silverman, S. B., & Greguras, G. J. (2005). Measurement equivalence and multisource ratings for non-managerial positions: Recommendations for research and practice. *Journal of Business and Psychology*, 19, 399–425.

Douthitt, E. A., & Aiello, J. R. (2001). The role of participation and control in the effects of computer monitoring on fairness perceptions, task satisfaction, and performance. *Journal of Applied Psychology*, 86, 867–874.

Duijnhouwer, H., Prins, F. J., & Stokking, K. M. (2012). Feedback providing improvement strategies and reflection on feedback use: Effects on students' writing motivation, process, and performance. *Learning and Instruction*, 22, 171–184.

Dusterhoff, C., Cunningham, J. B., & MacGregor, J. N. (2014). The effects of performance rating, leader-member exchange, perceived utility, and organizational justice on performance appraisal satisfaction: Applying a moral judgment perspective. *Journal of Business Ethics*, 119, 265–273.

Engelbrecht, A. S., & Fischer, A. H. (1995). The managerial performance implications of a developmental assessment center process. *Human Relations*, 48, 387–404.

Facteau, C. L., Facteau, I. D., Schoel, L. C., Russell, J. E. A., & Poteet, M. L. (1998). Reactions of leaders to 360-degree feedback from subordinates and peers. *Leadership Quarterly*, 9, 427–448.

Farr, J. L., & Levy, P. E. (2007). Performance appraisal. In L. L. Koppes (Ed.), *Historical Perspectives in Industrial and Organizational Psychology* (pp. 311–327). Mahwah, NJ: Erlbaum.

Feldman, J. M. (1994). On the synergy between theory and application: Social cognition and performance appraisal. In R. S. Wyer, Jr., & T. K. Srull (Eds.), *Handbook of Social Cognition* (2nd ed., vol. 2, pp. 339–397). Hillsdale, NJ: Erlbaum.

Ferstl, K. L., & Bruskiewicz, K. T. (2000). Self–other agreement and cognitive reactions to multi-rater feedback. Paper presented at the 15th annual conference of the Society of Industrial and Organizational Psychology, New Orleans, LA, April.

Finney, T. G. (2010). Performance appraisal comments: The practitioner's dilemma. *The Coastal Business Journal*, 9, 60–69.

Fisher, C. D. (2008). What if we took within-person performance variability seriously? *Industrial and Organizational Psychology*, 1, 185–189.

Fletcher, C. (1995). New directions for performance appraisal: Some findings and observations. *International Journal of Selection and Assessment*, 3, 191–196.

Fletcher, C. (2008a). *Appraisal, Feedback and Development: Making Performance Review Work* (4th ed.). New York: Routledge/Taylor & Francis Group.

Fletcher, C. (2008b). Performance appraisal: Assessing and developing performance and potential. In N. Chmiel, (Ed.), *An Introduction to Work and Organizational Psychology: A European Perspective* (2nd ed., pp. 76–96). Malden, MA: Blackwell.

Ghorpade, J. (2000). Managing five paradoxes of 360-degree feedback. *The Academy of Management Executive*, 14, 140–150.

Grant, A. (2008). The significance of task significance: Job performance effects, relational mechanisms, and boundary conditions. *Journal of Applied Psychology*, 93, 108–124.

Grant, A., & Parker, S. (2009). Redesigning work design theories: The rise of relational and proactive perspectives. *Academy of Management Annals*, 3, 317–375.

Greguras, G. J., Robie, C., Schleicher, D. J., & Goff, III, M. (2003). A field study of the effects of rating purpose on the quality of multisource ratings. *Personnel Psychology*, 56, 1–21.

Greller, M. M. (1978). The nature of subordinate participation in the appraisal interview. *Academy of Management Journal*, 21, 646–658.

Harris, M. (1994). Rater motivation in the performance appraisal context: A theoretical framework. *Journal of Management*, 20, 737–756.

Haynes, M. E. (1973). Do appraisal reviews improve performance? *Public Personnel Management*, 2, 128–132.

Heslin, P. A., & Latham, G. P. (2004). The effect of upward feedback on managerial behavior. *Applied Psychology: An International Review*, 53, 23–37.

Hoffman, B. J., & Woehr, D. J. (2009). Disentangling the meaning of multisource performance rating source and dimension factors. *Personnel Psychology*, 62, 735–765.

Ilgen, D. R., Fisher, C. D., & Taylor, M. S. (1979). Consequences of individual feedback on behavior in organizations. *Journal of Applied Psychology*, 64, 349–371.

Jacobs, R., Kafry, D., & Zedeck, S. (1980). Expectations of behavioral expectation scales. *Personnel Psychology*, 33, 595–640.

Jawahar, I. M. (2006). An investigation of potential consequences of satisfaction with appraisal feedback. *Journal of Leadership & Organizational Studies*, 13, 14–28.

Jawahar, I. M. (2010). The mediating role of appraisal feedback reactions on the relationship between rater feedback-related behaviors and ratee performance. *Group & Organization Management*, 35, 494–526.

Jawahar, I. M., & Williams, C. R. (1997). Where all the children are above average: The performance appraisal purpose effect. *Personnel Psychology*, 50, 905–925.

Jhun, S., Bae, Z., & Rhee, S. (2012). Performance change of managers in two different uses of upward feedback: A longitudinal study in Korea. *International Journal of Human Resource Management*, 23, 4246–4264.

Jones, R. G., & Whitmore, M. D. (1995). Evaluating developmental assessment centers as interventions. *Personnel Psychology*, 48, 377–388.

Juran, J. M. (1975). The non-Pareto principle: Mea culpa. *Quality Progress*, 8, 8–9.

Jussim, L., Yen, H., & Aiello, J. R. (1995). Self-consistency, self-enhancement, and accuracy in reactions to feedback. *Journal of Experimental Social Psychology*, 31, 322–356.

Kane, J. (1994). A model of volitional rating behavior. *Human Resource Management Review*, 4, 283–310.

Kane, J. S., & Lawler, E. E. (1979). Performance appraisal effectiveness: Its assessment and determinants. In B. Staw (Ed.), *Research in Organizational Behavior* (vol. 1, pp. 425–478). Greenwich, CT: JAI.

Kavanagh, P., Benson, J., & Brown, M. (2007). Understanding performance appraisal fairness. *Asia Pacific Journal of Human Resources*, 45, 132–150.

Keeping, L. M., & Levy, P. E. (2000). Performance appraisal reactions: Measurement, modeling, and method bias. *Journal of Applied Psychology*, 85, 708–723.

Kilduski, N. C., & Rice, M. S. (2003). Qualitative and quantitative knowledge of results: Effects on motor learning. *American Journal of Occupational Therapy*, 57, 329–336.

Kinicki, A. J., Prussia, G. E., Wu, B., & McKee-Ryan, F. M. (2004). A covariance structure analysis of employee's responses to performance feedback. *Journal of Applied Psychology*, 89, 1057–1069.

Kline, T. J., & Sulsky, L. M. (2009). Measurement and assessment issues in performance appraisal. *Canadian Psychology*, 50, 161–171.

Kluger, A. N., & DeNisi, A. (1996). The effects of feedback interventions on performance: A historical review, a meta-analysis, and a preliminary feedback intervention theory. *Psychological Bulletin*, 119, 254–284.

Kuvaas, B. (2006). Performance appraisal satisfaction and employee outcomes: Mediating and moderating roles of work motivation. *International Journal of Human Resource Management*, 17, 504–522.

Kuvaas, B. (2011). The interactive role of performance appraisal reactions and regular feedback. *Journal of Managerial Psychology*, 26, 123–137.

Lam, S. S. K., & Schaubroeck, J. (1999). Total quality management and performance appraisal: An experimental study of process versus results and group versus individual approaches. *Journal of Organizational Behavior*, 20, 445–457.

Landy, F. J., & Farr, J. L. (1980). Performance rating. *Psychological Bulletin*, 87, 72–107.

Latham, G. P., & Latham, S. D. (2000). Overlooking theory and research in performance appraisal at one's peril: Much done, more do to. In C. Cooper & E. A. Locke (Eds.), *International Review of Industrial Organizational Psychology* (pp. 199–215). Chichester: John Wiley & Sons, Ltd.

Latham, G. P., & Mann, S. (2006). Advances in the science of performance appraisal: Implications for practice. In G. P. Hodgkinson & J. K. Ford (Eds.), *International Review of Industrial and Organizational Psychology* (vol. 21, pp. 295–337). Chichester: John Wiley & Sons, Ltd.

Latham, G. P., Wexley, K. N., & Pursell, F. D. (1975). Training managers to minimize rating errors in the observation of behavior. *Journal of Applied Psychology*, 60, 550–555.

Lee, H., & Dalal, R. S. (2011). The effects of performance extremities on ratings of dynamic performance. *Human Performance*, 24, 99–118.

Levy, P. E., & Williams, J. R. (2004). The social context of performance appraisal: A review and framework for the future. *Journal of Management*, 30, 881–905.

Lievens, F., & Sanchez, J. I. (2007). Can training improve the quality of inferences made by raters in competency modeling? A quasi-experiment. *Journal of Applied Psychology*, 92, 812–819.

London, M., & Smither, J. W. (1995). Can multi-source feedback change perceptions of goal accomplishment, self-evaluations, and performance-related outcomes? Theory-based applications and directions for research. *Personnel Psychology*, 48, 803–839.

Longenecker, C., Sims Jr., H. & Gioia, D. (1987). Behind the mask: The politics of employee appraisal. *The Academy of Management Executive*, 1, 183–193.

Louis-Slaby, M. R., & Helland, K. R. (2004). The role of open-ended comments in multisource feedback programs. Paper presented at the 19th Annual Conference of the Society for Industrial and Organizational Psychology, Chicago, IL, April.

McGregor, D. (1957). An uneasy look at performance appraisal. *Harvard Business Review*, 35, 89–94.

Murphy, K. R. (2008). Explaining the weak relationship between job performance and ratings of job performance. *Industrial and Organizational Psychology*, 1, 148–160.

Murphy, K. R., & Balzer, W. K. (1989). Rater errors and rating accuracy. *Journal of Applied Psychology*, 74, 619–624.

Murphy, K. R., & Cleveland, J. N. (1995). *Understanding Performance Appraisal: Social, Organizational, and Goal-Based Perspectives.* Thousand Oaks, CA: Sage.

Murphy, K., Cleveland, J., Skattebo, A., & Kinney, T. (2004). The roles of rater goals and ratee performance levels in the distortion of performance ratings. *Journal of Applied Psychology*, 95, 546–561.

Noonan, L. E., & Sulsky, L. M. (2001). Impact of frame-of-reference and behavioral observation training on alternative training effectiveness criteria in a Canadian military sample. *Human Performance*, 14, 3–26.

Nurse, L. (2005). Performance appraisal, employee development and organizational justice: Exploring the linkages. *International Journal of Human Resource Management*, 16, 1176–1194.

O'Boyle, Jr., E., & Aguinis, H. (2012). The best and the rest: Revisiting the norm of normality of individual performance. *Personnel Psychology*, 65, 79–119.

Pareto, V. (1897). *Le cours d'economie politique.* London: Macmillan.

Pearlman, K., Schmidt, F. L., & Hunter, J. E. (1980). Validity generalization for tests used to predict job proficiency and training success in clerical occupations. *Journal of Applied Psychology*, 65, 373–406.

Pichler, S. (2012). The social context of performance appraisal and appraisal reactions: A meta-analysis. *Human Resource Management*, 51, 709–732.

Prince, J. B., & Lawler, E. E. (1986). Does salary discussion hurt the developmental performance appraisal? *Organizational Behavior and Human Resource Decision Processes*, 37, 357–375.

Prue, D. M., & Fairbank, J. A. (1981). Performance feedback in organizational behavior management: A review. *Journal of Organizational Behavior Management*, 3, 1–16.

Reb, J., & Cropanzano, R. (2007). Evaluating dynamic performance: The influence of salient Gestalt characteristics on performance ratings. *Journal of Applied Psychology*, 92, 490–499.

Reb, J., & Greguras, G. J. (2010). Understanding performance ratings: Dynamic performance, attributions and rating purpose. *Journal of Applied Psychology*, 95, 213–220.

Roberson, Q. M., & Stewart, M. M. (2006). Understanding the motivational effects of procedural and informational justice in feedback processes. *British Journal of Psychology*, 97, 281–298.

Roch, S. G., & O'Sullivan, B. J. (2003). Frame-of-reference rater training issues: Recall, time and behavior observation training. *International Journal of Training and Development*, 7, 93–107.

Roch, S. G., Woehr, D. J., Mishra, V., & Kieszczynska, U. (2012). Rater training revisited: An updated meta-analytic review of frame-of-reference training. *Journal of Occupational and Organizational Psychology*, 85, 370–395.

Rose, D., & Farrell, T. (2002). The use and abuse of comments in 360-degree feedback. Paper presented at the 18th Annual Conference of the Society for Industrial and Organizational Psychology, Toronto, ON, April.

Rothstein, H. R. (1990). Interrater reliability of job performance ratings: Growth to asymptote level with increasing opportunity to observe. *Journal of Applied Psychology*, 75, 322–327.

Rupp, D. E., Gibbons, A. M., Baldwin, A. M., Snyder, L. A., Spain, S. M., Woo, S. E., et al. (2006). An initial validation of developmental assessment centers as accurate assessments and effective training interventions. *Psychologist-Manager Journal*, 9, 171–200.

Saal, F. E., Downey, R. G., & Lahey, M. A. (1980). Rating the ratings: Assessing the psychometric quality of rating data. *Psychological Bulletin*, 88, 413–428.

Schleicher, D. J., Bull, R. A., & Green, S. G. (2009). Rater reactions to forced distribution rating systems. *Journal of Management*, 35, 899–927.

Schleicher, D. J., & Day, D. V. (1998). A cognitive evaluation of frame-of-reference rater training: Content and process issues. *Organizational Behavior and Human Decision Processes*, 73, 76–101.

Schleicher, D. J., Day, D. V., Mayes, B. T., Mayes, B. T., & Riggio, R. E. (2002). A new frame for frame-of-reference training: Enhancing the construct validity of assessment centers. *Journal of Applied Psychology*, 87, 735–746.

Schneider, R. J., Goff, M., Anderson, S., & Borman, W. C. (2003). Computerized adaptive rating scales for measuring managerial performance. *International Journal of Selection and Assessment*, 11, 237–246.

Scullen, S. E., Mount, M. K., & Judge, T. A. (2003). Evidence of the construct validity of developmental ratings of managerial performance. *Journal of Applied Psychology*, 88, 50–66.

Seifert, C. F., Yukl, G., & McDonald, R. A. (2003). Effects of multisource feedback and a feedback facilitator on the influence behavior of managers toward subordinates. *Journal of Applied Psychology*, 88, 561–569.

Seldon, S. C., Ingraham, P. W., & Jacobson, W. (2001). Human resource practices in state government: Findings from a national survey. *Public Administration Review*, 61, 598–614.

Selvarajan, T. T., & Cloninger, P. A. (2011). Can performance appraisals motivate employees to improve performance? A Mexican study. *International Journal of Human Resource Management,* 23, 3063–3084.

Smith, D. E. (1986). Training programs for performance appraisal: A review. *Academy of Management Review,* 11, 22–40.

Smith, P. C., & Kendall, L. M. (1963). Retranslation of expectations: An approach to the construction of unambiguous anchors for rating scales. *Journal of Applied Psychology,* 47, 149–155.

Smither, J. W., London, M., & Reilly, R. R. (2005). Does performance improve following multi-source feedback? A theoretical model, meta-analysis, and review of empirical findings. *Personnel Psychology,* 58, 33–66.

Smither, J. W., London, M., Reilly, R. R., Flautt, R., Vargas, Y., & Kucine, I. (2004). Discussing multisource feedback with raters and performance improvement. *Journal of Management Development,* 23, 456–468.

Smither, J. W., & Walker, A. G. (2004). Are the characteristics of narrative comments related to improvement in multirater feedback ratings over time? *Journal of Applied Psychology,* 89, 575–581.

Society of Human Resource Management & Globoforce (2012). Employee Recognition Survey Winter 2012 Report: The Impact of Recognition on Employee Engagement and ROI. http://go.globoforce.com/rs/globoforce/images/SHRMWinter2012Report.PDF (accessed June 12, 2013).

Spence, J. R., & Keeping, L. M. (2010). The impact of non-performance information on ratings of job performance: A policy-capturing approach. *Journal of Organizational Behavior,* 31, 587–608.

Spence, J. R., & Keeping, L. M. (2011). Conscious rating distortion in performance appraisal: A review, commentary, and proposed framework for research. *Human Resource Management Review,* 21, 85–95.

Spence, J. R., & Keeping, L. M. (2013). The road to performance ratings is paved with intentions: A framework for understanding managers' intentions when rating employee performance. *Organizational Psychology Review,* 3(4), 360–383.

Stamoulis, D. T., & Hauenstein, N. M. A. (1993). Rater training and rating accuracy: Training for dimensional accuracy versus training for ratee differentiation. *Journal of Applied Psychology,* 78, 994–1003.

Steelman, L. A., & Rutkowski, K. A. (2004). Moderators of employee reactions to negative feedback. *Journal of Managerial Psychology,* 19, 6–18.

Stephan, W. G., & Dorfman, P. W. (1989). Administrative and developmental functions in performance appraisals: Conflict or synergy? *Basic and Applied Social Psychology,* 10, 27–41.

Stevens, G. W. (2013). A critical review of the science and practice of competency modeling. *Human Resource Development Review,* 12, 86–107.

Stewart, G. L., & Nandkeolyar, A. K. (2006). Adaptation and intraindividual variation in sales outcomes: Exploring the interactive effects of personality and environmental opportunity. *Personnel Psychology,* 59, 307–332.

Stone, D. L., & Stone, E. F. (1985). The effects of feedback consistency and feedback favorability on self-perceived task competence and perceived feedback accuracy. *Organizational Behavior and Human Decision Processes,* 36, 167–185.

Sulsky, L. M., & Balzer, W. K. (1988). Meaning and measurement of performance rating accuracy: Some methodological and theoretical concerns. *Journal of Applied Psychology,* 73, 497–506.

Sulsky, L. M., & Day, D. V. (1992). Frame-of-reference training and cognitive categorization: An empirical investigation of rater memory issues. *Journal of Applied Psychology,* 77, 501–510.

Sulsky, L. M., & Day, D. V. (1994). Effects of frame-of-reference training on rater accuracy under alternative time delays. *Journal of Applied Psychology,* 79, 535–543.

Taylor, E. K., & Wherry, R. J. (1951). A study of leniency in two rating systems. *Personnel Psychology,* 4, 39–47.

Thoresen, C. J., Bradley, J. C., Bliese, P. D., & Thoresen, J. D. (2004). The big five personality traits and individual job performance growth trajectories in maintenance and individual stages. *Journal of Applied Psychology,* 89, 835–853.

Thornton, G. C., & Zorich, S. (1980). Training to improve observer accuracy. *Journal of Applied Psychology*, 65, 351–354.

Timmreck, C. W., & Bracken, D. W. (1997). Multisource feedback: A study of its use in decision making. *Employment Relations Today*, 24, 21–27.

Toegel, G., & Conger, J. A. (2003). 360-degree assessment: Time for reinvention. *Academy of Management Learning & Education*, 2, 297–311.

Tonidandel, S., Quiñones, M. A., & Adams, A. A. (2002). Computer-adaptive testing: The impact of test characteristics on perceived performance and test takers' reactions. *Journal of Applied Psychology*, 87, 320–332.

Tuytens, M., & Devos, G. (2012). The effect of procedural justice in the relationship between charismatic leadership and feedback reactions in performance appraisal. *International Journal of Human Resource Management*, 23, 3047–3062.

Tziner, A., Latham, G., Price, B., & Haccoun, R. (1996). Development and validation of a questionnaire for measuring perceived political considerations in performance appraisal. *Journal of Organizational Behavior*, 17, 179–190.

Tziner, A., Murphy, K. R., & Cleveland, J. N. (2001). Relationships between attitudes toward organizations and performance appraisal systems and rating behavior. *International Journal of Selection and Assessment*, 9, 226–239.

Villanova, P., & Bernardin, J. (1989). Impression management in the context of performance appraisal. In R. Giacalone & P. Rosenfeld (Eds.), *Impression Management in the Organization* (pp. 299–314). Hillsdale, NJ: Erlbaum.

Viswesvaran, C., Ones, D. S., & Schmidt, F. L. (1996). Comparative analysis of reliability of job performance ratings. *Journal of Applied Psychology*, 81, 557–574.

Wang, X. M., Wong, K. F. E., & Kwong, J. Y. (2010). The roles of rater goals and ratee performance levels in the distortion of performance ratings. *Journal of Applied Psychology*, 95, 546–561.

Werner, J. M., & Bolino, M. C. (1997). Explaining US court of appeals decisions involving performance appraisal: Accuracy, fairness, and validation. *Personnel Psychology*, 50, 1–24.

Whitaker, B. G., & Levy, P. (2012). Linking feedback quality and goal orientation to feedback seeking and job performance. *Human Performance*, 25, 159–178.

Woehr, D. J. (1994). Understanding frame-of-reference training: The impact of training on the recall of performance information. *Journal of Applied Psychology*, 79, 525–534.

Woehr, D. J. (2008). On the relationship between job performance and ratings of job performance: What do we really know? *Industrial and Organizational Psychology*, 1, 161–166.

Woehr, D. J., & Huffcutt, A. I. (1994). Rater training for performance appraisal: A quantitative review. *Journal of Occupational and Organizational Psychology*, 67, 189–205.

Wong, K. F. E., & Kwong, J. Y. Y. (2007). Effects of rater goal on rating patterns: Evidence from an experimental field study. *Journal of Applied Psychology*, 92, 577–585.

Woo, S. E., Sims, C. S., Rupp, D. E., & Gibbons, A. M. (2008). Development engagement within and following developmental assessment centers: Considering feedback favorability and self–assessor agreement. *Personnel Psychology*, 61, 727–759.

Woodford, K., & Mayes, J. D. (2002). Employee performance evaluations: Administering and writing them correctly in the multi-national setting. *Equal Opportunities International*, 21, 1–8.

Zyphur, M. J., Chaturvedi, S., & Arvey, R. D. (2008). Job performance over time is a function of latent trajectories and previous performance. *Journal of Applied Psychology*, 93, 217–224.

23

Designing Feedback to Achieve Performance Improvement

Manuel London and Edward M. Mone

Introduction

This chapter examines ways to increase the value of job feedback for performance management and improvement. Other chapters in this volume focus on feedback from multiple vantage points, specifically, 360-degree feedback for development (Fletcher, Chapter 24), how employees support each other and encourage development through feedback in social networks (Van den Bossche, Van Waes, & van der Rijt, Chapter 25), and how feedback contributes to learning (Valéria Vieira de Moraes & Jairo Eduardo Borges-Andrade, Chapter 21). These elements are incorporated in applications of feedback. Feedback is not a standalone event but part of a performance management process that includes (a) articulation of the department's mission and alignment of the employee's job and strengths with department and company goals, (b) ongoing discussions about expectations, (c) developmental experiences, including challenging assignments and mentoring, (d) regular discussions about performance, (e) clear standards of performance, (f) job training and training in how to seek and use feedback (and for managers, give feedback), and (g) surveys to track satisfaction and perceptions of the job, supervisor, and opportunities for development. Our chapter establishes the foundation for understanding why feedback is important and how it can be structured and delivered to be accurate, accepted, and, most importantly, used to improve job performance. We show how feedback can be beneficial and also how it can be detrimental to performance and the employee's sense of self-esteem. We consider the value of feedback to the individual employee, the team, and the organization, and the role of all of these perspectives to understanding how feedback is structured and operates. We begin by examining what we know about feedback from research and theories of learning and development that determine the effectiveness of feedback interventions.

The Wiley Blackwell Handbook of the Psychology of Training, Development, and Performance Improvement,
First Edition. Edited by Kurt Kraiger, Jonathan Passmore, Sigmar Malvezzi, and Nuno Rebelo dos Santos.
© 2015 John Wiley & Sons Ltd. Published 2020 by John Wiley & Sons Ltd.

What We Know about Feedback

London (2003) summarized major findings about giving, seeking, and using feedback for performance improvement: overall, feedback improves performance by keeping employees goal directed. However, people are generally apprehensive about giving and receiving feedback. Feedback can be constructive or destructive depending on how it is presented by the giver and interpreted by the receiver. People tend to overrate themselves unless they have objective information about their performance and are held accountable for improving their performance. Multisource (360-degree) feedback surveys have become a popular method for giving feedback, especially for development but also for making decisions about people. Coaches can help people process feedback survey results mindfully and use the information to change their behavior (Smither et al., 2003; Peltier, 2010). Some people are more ready to seek and accept feedback than others (a concept called feedback orientation) especially in an environment that supports feedback and development. In this section, we review feedback in relation to goal setting, consider types of feedback, particularly, autonomic feedback and 360-degree feedback, consider the mindful processing of feedback, and recognize the diminishing returns of increasing levels of feedback.

Goal setting and feedback

Goal specificity and difficulty together with feedback about performance increase task performance and informal citizenship performance-related behaviors, such as helping others perform better (Vigoda-Gadot & Angert, 2007). Difficult/ambitious, yet achievable/realistic goals and clearer/more specific goals increase individual effort and persistence (Locke & Latham, 1990). However, goal setting alone is insufficient to calibrate performance. Feedback is necessary to performance maintenance and continuous improvement (Erez, 1977).

There is a debate about the importance of feedback compared to goal setting (Kayes & Kayes, 2011; Latham & Locke, 2006). One side of the argument is that goal setting is key to guiding and motivating performance. Feedback may be ignored if it provides negative information – that is, suggests that the goal is not being achieved or may not be met. Feedback contributes to performance by helping evaluate progress toward goal accomplishment, but behavior is directed by focusing on the goal. Goal setting is important when effort and energy produce positive results, but more may be needed, such as skills, knowledge, and the right conditions and resources. The other side of the argument is that goal setting can be counterproductive. People who set goals unrealistically high are likely to misrepresent or outright lie about their performance (cf., Schweitzer, Ordonez, & Douma, 2004). Goal setting may also increase risk taking or maintaining commitment to a course of action that is unlikely to bear fruit (Ross & Staw, 1993; Kayes, 2006; Knight, Durham, & Locke, 2001). Feedback too can be dysfunctional if not presented in a constructive way and in line with the recipient's openness to learning (Kluger & DeNisi, 1996). We will say more about this below.

Goal setting and feedback are related to informal helping behaviors on the job as well as task job performance. Having more difficult goals requires extra effort, which leaves less energy to help others do their work (that is, engaging in altruistic organization citizenship behavior (OCB) (Wright et al., 1993; Vigoda-Gagot & Angert, 2007). Clear and difficult goals help determine how much effort is necessary. Feedback indicates how close one is to the goals and whether there is indeed extra energy left to help others. Feedback helps others understand what behaviors are necessary, how well one is doing, how well others are doing, and the value of helping others to one's own and the team's performance as well as one's relationship with others (Klein, 2003).

Autonomic feedback

Although we typically think of feedback coming from sources outside the individual, feedback can be from the autonomic nervous system – for instance, your heart racing from stress, burnout, and nervousness (Klein & Verbeke, 1999). Experiencing more intense autonomic reactions may affect job outcomes. Levels of feedback may impair performance on complex tasks or under time pressure, and individual differences in autonomic feedback, and sensitivity to this feedback (being sensitive to one's body reaction), may affect behaviors positively or negatively. Sensitivity to autonomic feedback increases feelings of burnout from stress and negatively affects extra-role performance and job satisfaction (Klein & Verbeke, 1999).

360-degree feedback

As we noted above, Fletcher (Chapter 24, this volume) covers 360-degree feedback in depth. Given the pervasiveness of this method of feedback collection and delivery, it deserves brief mention here. The notion behind 360-degree surveys is that ratings from different sources provide a more balanced and complete view of performance than can be obtained from supervisor ratings and feedback alone. The method is used to give managers suggestions for development and in some cases, to make administrative decisions about them, such as promotion, termination, and developmental assignments. Best practices from a benchmark survey of 211 feedback programs across 30 industries in the US and Canada provide guidelines for designing a 360-degree feedback process that improves performance (3D Group, 2013). The survey found that common design features are anonymous raters, coaching to help recipients use the results, training for raters, graphics to display results clearly, and presenting results along with comparisons to company norms and previous year's scores.

A concern is that the meaning of performance dimensions and their relationships may be different for different sources, and this needs to be examined within an organization to determine how the feedback ratings were used at any given time. That is, the survey can be factor analyzed for each rater group (peers, supervisors, subordinates, customers) at each collection time to demonstrate areas of equivalence or difference in meaning. When factor structures differ between raters, this can be used to help recipients understand how to interpret ratings from different sources. For example, if subordinates do not distinguish between dimensions of performance and rate them all similarly, subordinate ratings may be a reflection of overall perception and not useful in pinpointing areas for behavior change. If supervisors and peers have the same factor structure, this would suggest that their ratings on dimensions of performance can be compared. Such analyses would be needed in each company each time the survey is administered since meaning of performance dimensions may change.

Coaching for mindful processing of feedback

When feedback is negative and inconsistent with self-perceptions, it tends to prompt a negative reaction – possibly withdrawing, ignoring, or disputing the feedback. Coaches and others (supervisors, co-workers) can assist the recipient in reflecting on the meaning of the feedback and ultimately accepting and using it (Sargeant et al., 2009). Reflection is the process of interpreting feedback, accepting it, and identifying ways to change behavior and improve performance. Reflection helps evaluate progress toward a goal (Bandura, 1986). A component of experiential learning, reflection allows conceptualizing meaning and experimenting with alternative behaviors (Kolb, 1984). The feedback recipient examines, analyzes, and integrates the feedback, test assumptions, considers alternative behaviors, tries them, and plans to act differently in the future (Dahling et al., 2012).

Qualitative feedback

Just as coaching matters, narrative comments, or qualitative feedback, in a performance appraisal is another way to expand on ratings and help the recipient process performance feedback and results mindfully. Narrative comments may be used in conjunction with ratings so raters can provide explanations for their evaluations. Narratives may be a sole source of information, skipping the ratings entirely. This is especially valuable after organizational downsizings when the most valuable employees remain in the organization. Quality of narrative comments that supervisors and other raters may write are more effective in improving performance when they are both directive and motivational. Directive comments are substantive in length and specificity and include goals. Motivational comments are positive and high in interactional justice – fair and equitable (David, 2012).

Informal ongoing feedback

Feedback should not be an event that occurs once or twice a year, but part of a performance management process (London, 2003). Performance that drives results includes setting clear expectations for employees, helping employees solve problems, providing work assignments that allow employees to use their strengths rather than weaknesses, addressing development needs, and giving regular, informal feedback (Meyrowitz et al., 2012). Goals may be SMART (specific, measurable, attainable, relevant, and time-bound) and associated with key performance measures that employees and supervisors can track daily, weekly, or monthly. Formal feedback entails the supervisor evaluating performance outcomes and giving employees the rationale for their evaluation. More regular, informal feedback can be developmental. This feedback happens spontaneously – in the moment and in time to change behavior. It examines what went right and wrong, and what can be done differently. Moreover, it relies on two-way conversation between the supervisor and employee – a real discussion about actions that can improve performance. Unfortunately, supervisors often are not skilled at giving feedback. They avoid performance discussions and even are shy about praising positive behaviors and results. Their feedback tends to be superficial and not of much use (Meyrowitz et al., 2012).

Feedback can induce voluntary behaviors to improve performance. Tay (2012) conducted a meta-analysis of research that examined how feedback interventions influence voluntary environmentally sensitive behaviors (e.g., energy conservation) in the workplace and at home. The results showed that the most effective feedback was provided over a short period of time following behaviors, was given frequently, even daily, used objective measures of behaviors, and encouraged setting future goals. Goal setting together with objective indicators of performance improves task performance (Fante, Davis, & Kempt, 2013).

Diminishing returns

Increased feedback is desirable up to a point, but may have diminishing returns. More feedback may have little new information and may desensitize the recipient to the feedback. Similarly, feedback seeking has diminishing returns (Trinh & Mitchell, 2009). If the feedback environment is unsupportive and there is already high leader-member exchange, feedback seeking will be unnecessary. In contrast, feedback seeking will be more important to improving performance when the feedback environment is less supportive and leader-member exchange is low (Bolino & Turnley, 2009; Lam, Peng, & Wong, 2012).

Summary

Feedback is part of a performance management process. It unfolds over time as one obtains performance information, relates the feedback to performance goals and expectations, and acts differently to improve future performance, which in turn should be reflected in subsequent feedback. Goal setting and feedback are mutually reinforcing but can be dysfunctional. Feedback informs both formal task performance and informal helping behaviors. Feedback comes from inside as well as outside the individual, meaning that people have feelings about the goodness or value of their behaviors and performance and this also influences how they change their actions. Feedback – whether quantitative or qualitative – needs to be provided in ways that are constructive and do not impose limitations or barriers to performance accomplishment. Coaching for support in processing feedback and recognizing the ongoing nature of the feedback process are important in understanding how to use and design feedback processes that improve performance. Finally, more feedback is not necessarily better; an absence of feedback is likely to prompt employees to find their own sources of feedback. Next, we turn to theoretical underpinnings of feedback to understand better ways to design and leverage feedback processes to improve performance.

Theoretical Underpinnings

Research and associated theory development and testing have guided feedback design. Feedback intervention theory, building on self-enhancement theory, demonstrates the importance of a constructive approach to giving feedback and the potential dysfunctional consequences of feedback that threatens the recipient's self-image.

Feedback intervention theory

Kluger and DeNisi (1996) formulated feedback intervention theory based on a meta-analysis of 131 studies and 470 estimated effect sizes from 12,652 participants and 23,663 observations. They found that the average effect size was .38 (SE = .09), and 32 percent of the effects were negative. The effect of feedback depended on the direction of the feedback relative to task performance. Feedback was most effective in producing learning and performance improvement when it provided information on correct rather than incorrect behaviors and when it showed change in outcomes from previous learning trials (Kluger & DeNisi, 1996; Hattie & Timperley, 2007). Essentially, the theory and data argue that improvement does not always occur in response to performance feedback (Carr, 2006). The effectiveness of feedback diminishes and becomes counterproductive (dysfunctional) when the feedback moves the recipient's attention up the task–self hierarchy closer to a focus on self and away from specific task behavior (Kluger & DeNisi, 1996). As such, feedback should not threaten the recipient's self-image or else it can have deleterious effects. Threatening feedback addresses the recipient's personality or ability, which is tied to the person's self-concept and is not easily changeable, criticizes, and/or attributes blame for a negative result.

More specifically, according to feedback intervention theory, performance goals are arrayed hierarchically in three levels: (1) task learning, which relates goals to task elements and behaviors needed to perform each element, (2) task, which relates goals to task performance, and (3) self (the highest level), which relates goals to self-concept (DeNisi & Kluger, 2000). Feedback that is meant to address task learning or performance that is interpreted as reflecting one's self-image, or that is meant to threaten one's self-image is likely to evoke negative emotions and divert attention from the task and associated behaviors. However, coaching from an external source, the supervisor or others, that can help recipients interpret unfavorable feedback at the task learning level not as criticism of the "self," decreases emotional reactions and distress and is likely to produce behavior change and learning. Generalized critical feedback, though, can lead to self-doubt, anger, or frustration (Sargeant et al., 2008). Feedback that focuses on behaviors that need to be learned and that can be improved produces mindful reflection and results in learning. Having a process for collection of feedback that asks about behaviors that are important to performance and that is clear about who provided feedback and how they were asked prevents perceptions that the process was unfair (cf. Gielen, Dochy, & Dierick, 2003; Sargeant et al., 2008).

Elaborating on the Kluger and DeNisi feedback intervention model, Hattie and Timperley (2007) outlined a model of feedback to enhance learning in an educational setting. They proposed that the purpose of feedback is to reduce discrepancies between current performance and a desired goal. The student can reduce the discrepancy by increasing effort, changing strategy to one that will be more effective, or abandoning, lowering, or blurring the goal. The teacher (coach) can reduce the discrepancy by providing challenging and specific goals (cf. Locke & Latham, 1990) and helping students reach the goals through effective learning strategies such as explanation, demonstration, and feedback. Feedback addresses how close the student is to the goal and what the student might do next to improve the likelihood of achieving the goal. These elements of feedback can be at the level of task behavior, the level of desired performance outcomes, self-perceptions relative to ability to perform (self-efficacy), and self-regulation to monitor, direct, and alter one's actions.

Negative feedback that is not accompanied by discussion and coaching is likely to be avoided or ignored by the subordinate (DeNisi & Kluger, 2000), and without coaching, feedback is likely to be worthless, particularly when there are behavioral areas for improvement. For instance, in a study of 189 newly hired supervisors who participated in a developmental assessment center, those who performed poorly in the center, especially on interpersonal dimensions, were less likely to initiate a scheduled telephone call with an assigned coach to receive feedback (Abraham, Morrison, & Burnett, 2006). In other words, those who needed the improvement the most avoided the discussion about what they realized was poor performance. They sensed how they performed on the different assessment exercises and preferred to avoid the feedback discussion. Participants who did well were more likely to initiate the call, perhaps because they knew they had performed well and this would be a self-affirming discussion.

Research also shows that unfavorable ratings may not lead to performance improvement. For example, in another study, 78 managers in a financial services firm received 360-degree feedback – reports from their supervisor, peers, and subordinates (Bailey & Austin, 2006). The assumption of feedback is that managers who receive lower ratings than their self-ratings would use this information to improve (London & Smither, 1995). However, the study found that subsequent performance ratings three months after the initial feedback became more favorable when the initial feedback was favorable rather than unfavorable (Bailey & Austin, 2006). Receiving unfavorable feedback resulted in lower changes in performance. Moreover, those who were more confident in their capabilities (that is, had higher self-efficacy) responded more positively to favorable ratings, particularly from peers and others. Those who were less confident in their capabilities responded more positively to favorable ratings from their immediate supervisor.

In short, constructive feedback focuses on strengths (Bouskila-Yam & Kluger, 2011). Aguinis, Gottfredson, and Joo (2012) recommended that supervisors focus on employees' strengths and link any negative feedback to employees' knowledge and skills instead of inherent talents. Whoever provides the feedback – supervisor, coach, or co-worker–should be familiar with the employee and the employee's position. They also recommended that the provider of feedback select an appropriate setting for giving feedback, be considerate, and be as specific and accurate as possible. Also, the feedback should be tied to important consequences and valued outcomes. In addition, the feedback provider should be sure to follow up, speaking to the employee over appropriate time periods about the employee's efforts to improve and build on strengths.

In summary, negative feedback and lack of support for interpreting and applying feedback results produce unfavorable outcomes. Conversely, constructive, strengths-based feedback, supported by coaching, can build self-image while focusing on change-able behaviors. Underlying these processes is the notion that people want to enhance their self-image.

Self-enhancement theory

Self-esteem affects performance by influencing analytic thinking and goal setting. High self-esteem individuals set goals that are challenging and doable; low self-esteem individuals set easy goals or goals that are unachievable, thereby affirming their self-image (Wood & Bandura, 1989). Self-esteem that is situation-specific refers to a person's desire to maintain a positive image about his or her ability to perform a task and do better than others. It is not one's beliefs about absolute ability in all situations but one's perceptions of one's relative standing among one's peers. People are motivated to do better than others, and so they work harder.

With this idea in mind about self-esteem and motivation, Kuhnen and Tymula (2012) studied the effects of expectations to receive feedback for subjects working on multiplication problems – tasks that require little previous advanced knowledge and minimal learning effects. In an experimental setting, people worked harder and expected to rank better than others when they were told they would learn their ranking compared to cases when people did not expect to receive feedback. Those who ranked better than they expected then decreased their output (they felt they didn't need to work harder) yet they expected to rank more highly in the future. Those who ranked worse than expected increased their output but expected lower future ranks, perhaps to protect their self-image. Kuhnen and Tymula (2012) concluded that feedback contributes to a ratcheting up effect in productivity because people are motivated to achieve dominance over others.

This suggests that organizations can improve productivity by increasing the likelihood of feedback, being sure there is a meaningful reference group (e.g., other learners – those with equivalent experience), and a clear explanation about what the feedback means – its information value for calibrating performance and effort-performance relationships. The referent group may affect how people react to feedback. If someone is surrounded by more or less productive peers, those peers set the standard for comparison for calibrating one's performance, estimating one's ability in relation to others, providing public recognition and status, and setting goals for improvement. If others are performing better, are held in high regard, and do not appear to have higher ability, the feedback recipient is likely to be motivated to try harder (cf., White, Kjelgaard, & Harkins, 1995). If others are perceived as having higher ability, they are essentially setting a standard that the individual believes he or she cannot achieve. This lowers self-efficacy relative to the task and is likely to reduce effort and possibly induce withdrawal behavior or seeking alternative attributions to save face and explain the lower performance (e.g., not having the resources others had). Individuals judge their expectation that effort will lead to performance, in this case, achieving at the level of others. Higher expectancy increases the likely value of expending the effort needed to perform at that level (Vroom, 1964; also see Staw & Boettger, 1990).

Feedback recipients who are high in core self-evaluations (individuals' core beliefs about themselves and their ability to function in the world; Judge, Locke, Durham, & Kluger, 1998) take feedback to heart, particularly feedback that differs from their self-evaluations, and are more committed to developmental goals several months after receiving the feedback (Bono & Colbert, 2005). Core self-evaluations are a function of such individual characteristics as self-esteem, internal locus of control, and emotional stability (Judge & Bono, 2001). However, recipients who are low in core self-evaluations are more committed to developmental goals when the feedback is consistent with their self-evaluations.

Other research found that feedback recipients who are low in explicit self-concept of intelligence and high in implicit self-concept intelligence (for instance, defining themselves in positive terms but not responding as such when asked directly about their self-image) are more likely to improve their performance following negative feedback compared to those who are high in explicit self-concept intelligence or low in both explicit and implicit self-concept intelligence (Gerstengerg et al., 2013). Those who are high in explicit self-concept intelligence or low in both are likely to be frustrated or outraged by the negative feedback whereas those who are low in explicit and high in implicit break only after self intelligence don't ruminate about the feedback but set out to use the information to increase their achievement.

The process of evaluating one's own performance, particularly when individuals feel responsible for their performance, is as much an evaluation of oneself as a capable individual as it is an evaluation of outcomes (Jordan & Audia, 2012). Individuals' motives may be to assess themselves accurately and improve their performance in the future. Also, their motives may be to verify or confirm their pre-existing self-image as effective (or ineffective) (cf., Swann, 1983), and enhance their self-image – to see themselves as effective no matter what their actual performance (Pyszczynski & Greenberg, 1987). People tend to process positive information about themselves more easily and take credit for their successes, blaming outside influences for their failures (the classic attribution error; Sedikides & Strube, 1997). The self-enhancement motive is likely to be stronger when there is a threat to self-image for instance, because performance is lower than aspirational levels (cf. Baumeister, Smart, & Boden, 1996; Gramzow, 2011) and there is a perception of personal accountability for that performance (Audia & Brion, 2007). In developing their model of learning from feedback, Jordan and Audia (2012) indicated that people will observe their performance feedback and adopt a problem-solving mode when their performance is above aspiration levels. The desire to protect one's self-image when performance is low causes a switch in attention from missing a goal to one of surviving the threat to their self-image (March & Shapira, 1992).

Organizations can reduce decision-makers' latitude to portray low performance positively by implementing formal control systems, for instance, requiring top managers who face difficult tasks to commit to specific standards for evaluation in advance so that they cannot later redefine the standards in ways that puts their performance in a positive light (Jordan & Audia, 2012). Setting unambiguous criteria for evaluation in advance reduces later escalation of commitment to a failed decision, presumably by reducing self-enhancing interpretation of performance (Simonson & Staw, 1992). Individuals who are working toward well-defined goals evaluate their performance more modestly than when they are working toward more ambiguous goals (cf., Mento, Locke, & Klein, 1992).

When problems are highly complex and performance criteria naturally vague, informal control mechanisms, such as the organization's culture, shared values, and norms, can reduce the feelings of threat from low performance, making failure and learning from failure acceptable (Chatman & Cha, 2003). Such a culture emphasizes that people can learn and improve their abilities (cf., Dweck, 2006), and an organizational culture that supports this view reduces defensive self-enhancing behavior. Individuals can describe their own mistakes to others, recognize these are inevitable and key to their growth and performance improvement, and are models for others to learn from, for instance, teams collecting data to identify types and sources of problems and experimenting with changes to improve outcome quality – the foundation for continuous quality improvement (London, 1988). (For more information about research on the role of feedback in learning, see Valéria Vieira de Moraes & Jairo Eduardo Borges-Andrade, Chapter 21, this volume.)

In summary, feedback intervention theory indicates methods for constructive feedback that provide the recipient with useful information to change behavior without threatening the individual's self-image. A coach may be needed to help recipients process feedback mindfully and avoid tendencies to see only positive elements of performance and ignore unfavorable results. Clear goals, structured tasks, and informal control mechanisms such as norms for seeking feedback and making continuous strides to improve can decrease defensiveness and self-enhancement biases and improve the value of feedback. This suggests the need to consider factors that affect reactions to feedback.

Understanding Reactions to Feedback

Reacting to feedback takes emotional energy. As we will see, people who are motivated to learn and advance their careers and who are ready to change are more likely to value feedback than those who are low on these characteristics.

Emotional labor in responding to feedback

Cognitive and emotional dynamics affect how we react to feedback, making it more painful and less useful than it should be. People have trouble recognizing how their own emotional dynamics interfere with their ability to gain value from feedback and how their reactions interfere with the ability of feedback providers to give useful feedback (Cannon & Witherspoon, 2005). People manage their emotional expressions – a concept called "emotional labor" (Hochschild, 1979; Zapf, 2002; Zhong et al., 2012). Their emotional labor strategies may be surface acting – suppressing felt emotions and faking desired emotions; or deep acting – modifying inner feelings and actually experiencing desired emotions (cf., Diefendorff, Croyle, & Gosserand, 2005). Zhong et al. (2012) suggested that people who are high in neuroticism would act in ways that require little mental effort to regulate their emotions and so would have difficulty implementing a deep acting strategy. These individuals are likely to perceive feedback negatively and avoid or reject feedback in order to cope with the stress of negative emotions.

In interpreting feedback, people follow a ladder of inference (Argyris, 1982). This starts with available information. The feedback recipient selectively perceives information and selects information to interpret, perhaps paraphrasing it from one's own standpoint. They name what's happening, giving it a label based on their interpretation or what they want to believe. They develop an explanation for the feedback and alternative courses of action, and then decide what to do. The source of the information also selects what information to provide. How the feedback is given will influence how the recipient "climbs" the ladder of inference, sometimes with the help of the feedback provider or coach.

Sargeant et al. (2009) developed a model of reflection and decision making in regard to multisource feedback. If the feedback is consistent with expectations and one's self-perceptions, the recipient's emotional response is likely to be positive and accepting, the reflective period is likely to be comparatively short, the recipient accepts the feedback, and either takes no action, or continues to pursue the current mode of activity, since the feedback confirmed the behavior. If the feedback was inconsistent with the recipient's self-perceptions, the emotional response is likely to be negative surprise. These are likely to be strong feelings accompanied by feelings of long-lasting distress (Sargeant et al., 2008). The recipient is likely to take a long time to make sense of the feedback. He or she may decide to accept the feedback and take action to improve (resulting in learning) or reject the feedback and take no action to improve, other than perhaps to question the review method or sources (Sargeant et al., 2009).

Motivation to use feedback to improve performance

Developmental feedback provides useful information to guide and improve performance in the future (Zhou, 2003). Unlike evaluative feedback, developmental feedback provides information and focuses particularly on improvement. Developmental feedback to new-comers from their supervisor and co-workers together positively affect newcomers' job performance and their helping behavior on the job (Li et al., 2011). As such, develop-mental feedback is likely to increase newcomers' intrinsic motivation and feelings of self-efficacy. It increases newcomers' interest in the work and organization and increases their desire to learn and improve (Li et al., 2011). Since this type of feedback is providing information (e.g., how to do the task) the sign of the feedback does not matter as much as the content. Feedback from co-workers can be especially valuable to newcomers because co-workers know the job well. Feedback from supervisors is valuable because supervisors clarify newcomers' role expectations and help newcomers set reasonable goals. Negative feedback (what newcomers are doing wrong) may send negative signals, but it should motivate them to improve in the future. Moreover, developmental feedback may have social as well as task components, for instance, how to get along with others or information about organizational norms – "the way we do things around here." It helps to socialize newcomers into their jobs and the organization. This is all the more the case for new-comers who are self-motivated, proactive learners (Li et al., 2011). Proactive learners take the initiative to produce positive change, build networks, and overcome situational bar-riers (cf., Fuller & Marler, 2009).

Feedback helps employees take advantage of developmental experiences such as training, challenging assignments, formal and informal mentoring and coaching, and assessment data (Cannon & Witherspoon, 2005; Kuchinke, 2000). Feedback specificity needs to match the complexity of the task and it must be available when there is time for recipients to pro-cess the feedback mindfully and take action to improve their performance (Korsgaard & Diddams, 1996). Feedback provides a basis for anticipating the likely effect or outcome of one's actions or decisions. Making a decision and then receiving a projection of the likely outcome based on a simulation model, for instance, produces better decisions (decisions that more closely match objective criteria of performance effectiveness) over time than not receiving a projection of a likely outcome. Moreover, having information about others' decisions and having a chance to interact to improve understanding of the problem as well as one's own and a simulation-based projection of a likely outcome produces even better decisions (Škraba, Kljajić, & Borštnar, 2007).

Employees respond differently to feedback depending on the purpose. Ratings that are purely for developmental purposes and are not used to make administrative decisions may not garner the recipient's attention sufficiently to be processed mindfully and change behavior. However, if told that performance results would be linked to disciplinary action, employees are more likely to take notice and change their actions to improve their performance (Ludwig & Goomas, 2009; Smither & Walker, 2004). Ratings themselves are affected by purpose, with administrative ratings reflecting the average performance during the rating period and development ratings reflecting perceptions of performance change over time (Reb & Greguras, 2010).

Recipients' readiness to change

Being able to learn quickly and respond flexibly is important in complex, dynamic work environments (London & Sessa, 2006). Feedback is important for learning agility – the ability to learn from experience and change one's behavior fast and flexibly to produce more positive outcomes for oneself, one's team, and the organization (DeRue, Ashford, & Myers, 2012; DeMeuse, Dai, & Hallenbeck, 2010). There are four dimensions of learning agility: people, results, mental, and change (Lombardo & Eichinger, 2000). People agility refers to knowing oneself well, being able to learn from experience, and do so in a way that shows resilience under pressures for change. Results agility refers to producing results under difficult circumstances and building confidence and inspiring others along the way. Mental agility refers to thinking through problems and being open to fresh perspectives that help deal with complex and ambiguous situations, and being able to explain their thinking clearly. Change agility refers to being open to learning, having a passion for, and curiosity about, new and different ideas, and being willing to try new behaviors and learn new skills. DeRue, Ashford, and Myers (2012; Ashford & DeRue, 2012) incorporated feedback and feedback seeking into a model of learning agility. Their model indicated that individual differences include the motivation to learn, reflect, and be open to new experience.

Feedback orientation

Individual change in response to feedback requires individual and organizational precursors. Individual factors that make a person responsive to feedback include self-awareness and awareness of performance expectations, resources, and rewards, a recognition that performance improvement is important, confronting change, being willing to seek feedback, and desiring to learn and develop (Silverman, Pogson, & Cober, 2005). Feedback orientation is an individual's receptivity to seeking, listening to, interpreting, and using feedback (London & Smither, 2002). Understanding an individual's feedback orientation determines how employees are likely to respond to feedback. Knowing this can help supervisors and coaches understand a feedback recipient's reactions to feedback or, better yet, to shape feedback in a way that will help the individual be more receptive.

Feedback seeking

An important behavior associated with feedback is not just reacting to it but actually seeking it. Feedback-seeking refers to taking action to request or view performance results, obtain guidance about how to perform better, and judge potential for promotion or any other decision that might be made about the employee or opportunities that might be available to the employee (Ashford & Cummings, 1983, 1985). Feedback seekers consider the source of information, the type of information sought, and how they ask (seeking strategy). Unlike formal feedback during a performance review, feedback-seeking is informal, meaning sought by employees any day when they feel they want information about their performance. They may also be proactive during formal reviews to ask for more details from the supervisor to clarify the supervisor's meaning and suggestions for improvement.

Anseel et al. (2013) conducted a meta-analysis of 115 studies of the antecedents and consequences of feedback-seeking behavior published between 1983 and 2011. People seek feedback by monitoring their own performance from objective information and interpreting others' reactions to their behavior and performance. They may also inquire directly, asking supervisors and co-workers, "How am I doing?" Individuals who seek feedback tend to be those who have high self-esteem, often receive positive feedback, and have a high-quality relationship with the feedback provider. They are likely to be motivated to learn and enhance their performance (performance goal orientation) as opposed to avoid failure. Also, they are high in transformational style of leadership. Surprisingly, the more uncertain the situation, the less people seek feedback, suggesting that some people may avoid knowing. People who are likely to seek feedback are likely to be younger and have less tenure on the job or with the organization.

Feedback seeking has an element of impression management. Employees ask for feedback when they see a need to promote themselves. They may be trying to manage what they anticipate will be a negative performance review by asking for feedback before formal feedback is needed, thereby hoping to lessen the supervisor's criticism by asking for it early (cf., Morrison & Bies, 1991, and Larson, 1989, cited in Krasman, 2011). Impression management is not foolproof. For instance, employees may be seen more negatively by others because they sought feedback. Also, a strategy of asking for feedback directly may have different results than asking for feedback indirectly in a roundabout or joking way (Miller & Jablin, 1991). Employees may ask for feedback in a way that implies they only want to hear positive results (e.g., asking, "I'm sure I did well, don't you think?" rather than asking, "How can I improve?"). Generally, employees who proactively seek feedback are likely to have higher job performance, be more satisfied with their jobs, indicate they plan to stay with the company, help co-workers, and give others feedback (cf., Kudisch, Fortunado, & Smith, 2006; Whitaker, Dahling & Levy, 2007). And they are viewed more positively by others (Williams et al., 1999).

Summary

Emotional energy, the motivation to perform better, perhaps as a step toward career advancement or other positive outcomes, and readiness to change are individual characteristics and processes that influence reactions to feedback. Together, these and other individual differences comprise feedback orientation. Some people are more proactive than others when it comes to seeking feedback. Now that we have considered individual differences affecting how feedback influences performance improvement, we consider how the organizational environment affects feedback processes and outcomes.

Feedback Environment and Positive Organizational Support

Taking an active role in feedback seeking reduces uncertainty about one's behavior and performance outcomes (Whitaker, 2011; Ashford & Cummings, 1983). However, employees are likely to decrease feedback seeking if they perceive too many costs, for instance, calling attention to errors, taking time and energy, the lack of supervisor openness, poor relationships with co-workers (Whitaker, Dahling, & Levy, 2007). Organization support theory argues that employees develop beliefs about the extent to which their organization and supervisor are concerned for their well-being and value their contributions (Eisenberger et al., 1986; Whitaker, 2011). This includes providing resources to do their jobs and meeting their socio-emotional needs for emotional support, affiliation, esteem, and approval. This construct is called "perceived organizational support" (POS; Eisenberger et al., 1986). POS stems from feelings of being treated fairly, receiving support from one's supervisor, gleaning rewards from the organization, and generally favorable job conditions (Rhoades & Eisenberger, 2002). Favorable POS invokes a norm of reciprocity that encourages an employee to repay positive treatment by being more involved in the job, help co-workers (citizenship behaviors), and show loyalty – all behaviors that improve the organization's performance and reduce behaviors that may hurt organizational performance (e.g., tardiness and absenteeism). Employees who are high in job involvement will try to achieve goals and seek feedback to calibrate how well they are doing and determine what more they can do to improve their performance and contribute to desired organizational outcomes. As such, Whitaker (2011) proposed that individuals who psychologically identify more closely with their work and have a stronger desire to help the organization to be successful will be more likely to seek feedback. Seeking feedback becomes a way to guide and improve their performance for highly job-involved individuals. Since their high job involvement stems from a perception of favorable organizational support, the environment is likely to be conducive to receiving constructive feedback that will indeed help them improve their performance.

Silverman, Pogson, and Cober (2005) identified characteristics of organizations and feedback itself that affect the value of feedback. Organizational factors include alignment of the employee's job and skills with the organization, an environment in which supervisors and others provide performance information, opportunities for learning, including formal training and developmental job assignments, measuring improvement in performance, and a compensation system that rewards performance. Important elements of the feedback itself include:

- Source credibility (e.g., supervisor and/or co-workers are familiar with employee's performance);
- Feedback quality (e.g., specific, behaviorally oriented information);
- Feedback delivery (e.g., supervisor and/or co-workers consider subordinate's feelings when giving feedback);
- Favorable feedback (e.g., supervisor and/or co-workers praise employee's positive performance and frequently give positive feedback);
- Unfavorable feedback (e.g., supervisor and/or co-workers are clear when employee's performance does not meet standards);
- Source availability (e.g., supervisor and/or co-workers are available when employee seeks performance feedback);
- Encouragement for feedback seeking (e.g., supervisor and/or co-workers give performance information as soon as employee asks for it and encourage employee to ask for feedback).

A positive feedback environment can improve task performance and organization citizenship behavior (OCB; Norris-Watts & Levy, 2004; Rosen, Levy, & Hall, 2006; Whitaker, Dahling, & Levy, 2007) and reduce deviant, counterproductive behavior (Peng, 2012). Providing clear and frequent information about goals and performance can increase an employee's ability and motivation to meet expectations and increase employees' perceptions that their supervisor and the organization values and supports them. This feeling of support promotes a tighter bond between leader and subordinate (leader-member exchange) and induces voluntary helping behaviors beyond job performance (Peng, 2012).

Whitaker (2011) considered how the feedback environment affects feedback seeking, drawing on organizational support theory, the norm of reciprocity, and extant research. Analyzing data from 202 supervisor-subordinate dyads, he showed that employees' perceived organizational support and felt job involvement were important in linking the feedback environment to feedback seeking, as measured by supervisor observations. The feedback environment includes the amount and availability of positive and negative information about performance from various sources (cf., Herold & Parsons, 1985). More broadly, the feedback environment includes a range of social and situational factors that influence the availability of feedback on a daily basis (Whitaker, 2011). The feedback environment consists of characteristics of co-workers (peers, supervisors, and others with whom the employee interacts) as feedback sources. Potentially relevant dimensions of these sources include their credibility, the quality of the feedback, how the feedback is delivered, their availability, the valence of the information – favorable feedback and unfavorable feedback – and encouragement for feedback seeking (Steelman, Levy, & Snell, 2004).

In summary, both individual's feedback orientation and positive organizational support for feedback influence feedback-related behaviors directed toward improved performance. Next, we consider how feedback operates at the level of teams and the organization as a whole.

A Multilevel View: Feedback to Teams and Organizations

Feedback to teams

From the perspective of a collection of individuals, feedback is "information about the actual performance or actions of a system used to control the future actions of a system" (Nadler, 1979, p. 310). The system can be an individual, team, and/or organization. Feedback for teams can shape individual team members' behavior as well as the task process, interpersonal interactions, and team outcomes (London & Sessa, 2006; London, 2007). The source of feedback to teams can be team members, team leader, team facilitator, and/or observers. Public feedback in a team setting can affect the team's learning goals and regulatory responses (e.g., team members' confidence in the team's ability to accomplish its goals (DeShon et al., 2004)). Feedback can affect the team's mental model of how it can and should operate, the ability of the members to learn new ways to interact and be productive, and readiness to share ideas internally and seek new ideas, information, and members from outside the team (Fiore, Salas, & Cannon-Bowers, 2001).

As teams assess their performance, the assessment (feedback) helps them adjust to the task requirements, reinforces a feeling of interdependence among members, helps members develop an accurate view of the team's performance, and increases the members' feelings of being accountable for helping the team achieve its goals (Breugst et al., 2012; also see Freeman & Greenacre, 2011; Volkema, 2010).

Breugst et al., (2012) offered a multilevel model of a team's perception of its own performance drawing on self-enhancement theory (Bettencourt & Dorr, 1998) and construal level theory of psychological distance (Trope & Liberman, 2010). Team members individually and as a group are more objective and hence accurate in evaluating their performance when there is relationship conflict in the team. Breugst et al. (2012) reasoned that team members who experience relationship conflict are more likely to want to distance themselves from the team. The team's performance is less tied to their self-image and implicit desire to enhance their own image by their connection with the team. Although relationship conflict may diminish task performance (cf., Langfred, 2007; Mohammed & Angell, 2004), it improves the team's ability to assess its performance accurately, and thereby in the long run, help it correct its performance, or at least recognize that performance cannot be improved easily because of the relationship conflict.

Feedback is especially important in teams that have high autonomy. Studying 109 teams with a total of 1023 individuals in a private sector firm in South Korea, Gonzalez-Mule, Courtright, and Seong (2012) found that team feedback moderated the relationship between team autonomy and performance. Feedback included team members' perceptions that they received feedback on the quality of their work, on how well they are doing, and on that the way that they do their jobs is assessed. When autonomy was low, feedback did not affect performance. When autonomy was high, however, high feedback improved performance significantly, and low feedback depressed performance. Autonomy and feedback provided the right combination of stimuli to motivate goal generation and goal striving (Chen & Kanfer, 2006).

Teams that take the time to reflect on their work processes and performance – to think about and discuss what is working and what needs improvement – learn from their mistakes and improve their performance (Schippers, Homan, & Knippenberg, 2013). Taking time to reflect, not surprisingly, is especially important when the team is not doing well and has considerable room for improvement. Reflection is most valuable, however, when the team members are in a positive mood conducive to consider their process and performance, and the leader's performance, accurately and without rancor or disgruntlement (Kollee, Giessner, & van Knippenberg, 2013).

Feedback to organizations

Krasman (2011) examined the extent to which feedback seeking is influenced by structural factors in the organization. In a survey of part-time MBA students, he found that when the work is standardized and performance needs meet certain criteria, employees need feedback to calibrate how they are doing and what they need to do to improve. So they are more likely to seek feedback from their supervisor, peers, and objective indicators of performance. However, the wider their supervisor's span of control (the more subordinates the supervisor manages), the less accessible the supervisor is, and the less the supervisor knows about the subordinate's performance. So wider spans of control decrease feedback seeking. Krasman (2011) also found that the availability of formal feedback from documentation increases the employee's likelihood of using it as a source of feedback. Doing so is less risky than seeking feedback from someone who will form an impression of the subordinate by the way and frequency with which the subordinate asked for feedback. In addition, Krasman (2011) found that subordinates are more likely to seek feedback from co-workers and supervisors who have less power to influence decisions that affect their jobs.

Feedback signals the success of an organizational strategy. Feedback may be a social comparison, for instance, comparing return on assets to the average return on assets of other active firms in the same industry in the same year. Positive feedback (performance above an aspiration level relative to other firms) signals success and reinforces current decisions and reduces the likelihood of changing strategy and experimenting with risky options. Negative feedback signals a failing strategy and motivates experimentation and strategic adjustments for deploying resources (cf. Bromiley, 1991; March, 2010; Levintahl & March, 1981; Grohsjean, Kretschmer, & Stieglitz, 2012). Expanding this concept, moderately negative feedback stimulates an "immune response" in organizations, which prompts decision makers to maintain a course of action and exert extra effort to maximize success. However, strongly negative or moderately positive feedback do not stimulate this activation effect, which in turn decreases the likelihood of maintaining the current course of action (Wohlgezogen, Stern, & Galinsky, 2012).

In summary, feedback processes apply to individuals, teams, and organizations. Of course, in teams and organizations, the feedback may be at the unit level (that is, how well the team as a whole, or the organization as a whole, performed), but it is up to the leader and the members to process the feedback and determine ways to change their behavior and relationships as well as different decisions they may need to make to improve performance. Many of the same principles and findings from individual feedback apply at the team and organization level to encourage deliberate examination of the feedback and prompt action rather than withdrawal or ignoring feedback (e.g., the "immune response").

Future Research

Future research should examine antecedents and consequences of feedback processes, including seeking, accepting, and applying feedback. Feedback is not a one-time event but a process that unfolds over time. We need to understand feedback seeking and reactions in relation to self-motives, organizational support, and level of aggregation (individual, team, and/or organization). Here we consider initial progress that has been made in areas that are ripe for research on feedback. In particular, metacognitive training can help employees to process feedback. Technology provides alternative modes for collecting, delivering, and tracking performance results. How feedback is perceived and the extent to which it is valued may depend on contextual factors, such as national culture and profession.

Metacognitive training

Employees can be trained to process feedback mindfully. Called metacognitive training, employees can learn to answer questions that prompt them to monitor their progress and identify performance problems and areas for improvement (Ford et al., 1998). Questions that prompt mindful processing may focus on self-evaluation (e.g., "Describe your current performance"), reflection about strategies ("What strategies did you use?"), reflection, and evaluation ("What is the relationship between your performance and outcomes?"), reasoning and retrospective analysis ("How could you have done things differently?"), planning ("What are your goals for the next performance cycle?"), and predictions of behavior and outcomes ("What do you plan to do next and what is the likely outcome?") (cf., Wong, Wood, & Goodman, 2012). These questions are particularly useful when feedback is specific and needs to be interpreted (Wong, Wood, & Goodman, 2012).

Technology for performance ratings and monitoring

Electronic technologies provide methods for monitoring performance and providing employees with objective data about their behaviors and outcomes. Communications methods (e.g., do-it-yourself surveys) are ways employees can seek feedback when they need it, and co-workers can provide performance evaluations anonymously if desired.

Also, employees can use the internet to search for information about others' performance for comparative purposes (comparing one's career progress to former college classmates). Information is often readily available about standards and methods for various tasks. However, communicating with colleagues electronically (e.g., through email, instant messages, and online surveys) can be a barrier to developing closer relationships or, conversely, can be open to more direct and honest feedback. These are the potential problems and advantages of "virtual distance" (Sobel-Lojeski & Reilly, 2008).

The internet has increased the capability of collecting and disseminating feedback from many sources with low cost. However, people may be tempted to provide performance ratings when asked to do so without spending the time and effort to reflect or not having observed the target employee's behavior and performance. An open question is how to improve rating accuracy and honesty. When objective measures of performance are available, this information can be provided to raters after their ratings to help them understand their perceptions and calibrate their evaluations. Still, conflicts of interest may lead raters to distort their true opinions – for instance, to make themselves look good. Recognizing these rater errors, Miller, Resnick, and Zeckhauser (2005) suggested that ratings could be improved by rewarding honesty. This is more difficult when objective measures of performance are not available. In such cases, ratings from others can be used as a basis for comparison and rating improvement. However, if raters are compared with each other, a rater may not provide unfavorable ratings thinking that others probably had a different experience with the person rated. Miller, Resnick, and Zeckhauser (2005) suggested that raters can be compared not in their level of agreement per se but on the extent to which their ratings predict others' ratings and the agreement of that prediction with others' actual ratings. They also suggested creating a reward structure for more accurate ratings, but this is likely to be difficult to do in performance contexts. Raters may be given feedback that their ratings were not useful, and this might give them more initiative to provide careful ratings in the future or to not provide a rating for a performance dimension they cannot evaluate.

Email can be perceived as an important and useful means of delivering feedback (Balsor & Weatherbee, 2010), however, not necessarily for negative feedback. Kurtzberg, Belkin, and Naquin (2006) found that mixing both positive and negative feedback was perceived more negatively if it was sent by email rather than given face-to-face. Email is viewed as an informal mode of communicating and not viewed as an appropriate social norm for feedback (Moser & Axtell, 2013).

National culture

Multinational companies may be tempted to implement the same performance management and support systems across the company in an effort to build a common corporate culture and ensure alignment between business units. However, appraisal and feedback methods and performance dimensions may have different meaning in different cultures varying with differences in cultural values, norms, and expectations. The concept of a leader and managerial performance may be different in different cultures (Leung et al., 2005). For instance, Gillespie (2005) demonstrated this in a study of 360-degree feedback ratings from 1833 leaders of a US-based transportation company with employees in four nations (Great Britain, Hong Kong, Japan, and the US). The results showed differences in the factor structure, suggesting that the constructs and their relationships differ across cultures. This suggests that in addition to accurate, clear, and comparable translations, survey items should be pretested for measurement equivalence to show which aspects of performance have the same meaning across cultures or whether some aspects of performance need to be customized and results examined separately for corporate units in different countries. A global company can generate country norms for each performance dimension to provide a clearer measure for them to understand and compare their performance (Gilespie, 2005).

Differences between professions

An individual's profession may affect the content of the feedback and reactions to feedback from different sources. For instance, the *Physician Achievement Review* provides physicians with performance assessment data from surveys completed by medical colleagues, co-workers (e.g., nurses and technicians), and patients on five practice domains: consultation communication, patient interaction, professional self-management, clinical competence, and psychosocial management of patients (Sargeant et al., 2011). The *Review* provides physicians with a confidential report aimed at practice improvement. Interestingly, feedback from fellow physicians tends to be perceived as lacking specificity and credibility compared to feedback from patients and co-workers. This may be because physicians are less likely to trust their medical colleagues' viewpoints, perhaps because they feel that their colleagues do not have direct knowledge of the situation or reasons for medical treatment decisions. Indeed, they may use a variety of sources of information to make their assessment, including medical records, referral letters, third-hand information from others, and speaking to the patients, whom they might share. The *Review* improved the value of the ratings from physicians by identifying behavioral anchors indicative of high- and low-scoring performance for each of the five practice domains. For example, a sample of high-scoring psychosocial management would be: "Considers psychosocial issues in treatment plan," and a sample of low-scoring performance would be: "Does not manage patient psychosocial concerns; has attitude: 'if you have mental problems, go see a psychiatrist'" (Sargeant et al., 2011, p. 92).

Conclusion

Research and theory offer directions for using feedback to improve performance. Feedback helps calibrate goals; however, both goal setting and feedback can be dysfunctional if they focus behavior on producing the wrong or narrow set of outcomes, limit flexibility, and/or provoke defensiveness. Feedback can come from natural, autonomic sources, qualitative evaluations from supervisors and co-workers, and/or structured feedback processes such as 360-degree feedback surveys. Coaching helps feedback recipients process feedback results mindfully. However, feedback is also an informal, ongoing process that requires attention to track and use. Feedback intervention and self-enhancement theories recognize that people are likely to protect their self-image, and so feedback is constructive when it focuses on behaviors, recognizes situational conditions, and does not impugn an individual's character. Givers of feedback need to understand and consider how reactions to feedback are affected by the recipient's emotional energy, motivation to use the information, and readiness to change behavior. Feedback orientation is the extent to which an individual is open to feedback, seeks it, is ready to comprehend the information and its implications, and wants to change behaviors to improve performance. A feedback-oriented environment is one that supports the use of feedback whether by training supervisors to coach subordinates, expecting that coaching and developing others is part of the management job, or incorporating feedback collection and delivery processes into performance management systems. Feedback content can address individual, team, and organizational performance. Feedback at the team and organization level challenges individuals to focus on shared goals and try different ways of working together. Overall, feedback has considerable potential, indeed is necessary, to improve performance by keeping people aware of the consequences of their behavior and decisions for themselves and others. People can learn to accept, interpret, and apply feedback. Finally, we highlighted some potentially fruitful areas for future research, including metacognitive training, technology-mediated feedback, and differences in the use of feedback in different national cultures and professions.

References

3D Group (2013). *Current Practices in 360 Degree Feedback: A Benchmark Study of North American Companies.* Emeryville, CA: 3D Group.

Abraham, J. D., Morrison, J. D., Jr., & Burnett, D. D. (2006). Feedback seeking among developmental assessment center participants. *Journal of Business and Psychology,* 20, 383–394. doi:10.1007/s10869-005-9008-z.

Aguinis, H., Gottfredson, R. K., & Joo, H. (2012). Delivering effective performance feedback: The strengths-based approach. *Business Horizons,* 55, 105–111. doi:10.1016/j.bushor.2011.10.004.

Anseel, F., Beatty, A., Shen, W., Lievens, F., & Sackett, P. R. (2013). How are we doing after 30 years? A meta-analytic review of the antecedents and outcomes of feedback-seeking behavior. Unpublished paper. Department of Personnel Management, Ghent University.

Argyris, C. (1982). *Reasoning, Learning, and Action.* San Francisco: Jossey-Bass.

Ashford, S. J., & Cummings, L. (1983). Feedback as an individual resource: Personal strategies of creating information. *Organizational Behavior and Human Performance,* 32, 370–398.

Ashford, S. J., & Cummings, L. (1985). Proactive feedback seeking: The instrumental use of the information environment. *Journal of Occupational Psychology,* 58, 67–79.

Ashford, S. J., & DeRue, D. S. (2012). Developing as a leader: The power of mindful engagement. *Organizational Dynamics,* 41, 146–154.

Audia, P. G., & Brion, S. (2007). Reluctant to change: Self-enhancing responses to diverging performance measures. *Organizational Behavior and Human Decision Processes,* 102, 255–269.

Bailey, C., & Austin, M. (2006). 360 degree feedback and developmental outcomes: The role of feedback characteristics, self-efficacy and importance of feedback dimensions to focal managers' current role. *International Journal of Selection and Assessment,* 14, 51–66.

Balsor, M. R., & Weatherbee, T. G. (2010). Email and the performance feedback: An exploratory study of e-feedback. *Workplace Review,* 7, 47–63.

Bandura, A. (1986). *Social Foundations of Thought and Action: A Social Cognitive Theory.* Englewood Cliffs, NJ: Prentice Hall.

Baumeister, R. F., Smart, L., & Boden, J. M. (1996). Relation of threatened egotism to violence and aggression: The dark side of high self-esteem. *Psycholgoical Review,* 103, 5–33.

Bettencourt, B., & Dorr, N. (1998). Cooperative interaction and intergroup bias: Effects of numerical representation and cross-cut role assignments. *Personality and Social Psychology Bulletin,* 24, 1276–1293.

Bolino, M. C., & Turnley, W. H. (2009). Relative deprivation among employees in lower-quality leader-member exchange relationships. *Leadership Quarterly,* 20, 276–286.

Bono, J. E., & Colbert, A. E. (2005). Understanding responses to multi-source feedback: The role of core self-evaluations. *Personnel Psychology,* 58, 171–203.

Bouskila-Yam, O., & Kluger, A. N. (2011). Strength-based performance appraisal and goal setting. *Human Resource Management Review,* 21(2), 137–147.

Breugst, N., Patzelt, H., Shepherd, D. A., & Aguinis, H. (2012). Relationship conflict improves team performance assessment accuracy: Evidence from a multilevel study. *Academy of Management Learning & Education,* 11, 187–206.

Bromiley, P. (1991). Testing a causal model of corporate risk taking and performance. *Academy of Management Journal*, 34, 37–59.

Cannon, M. D., & Witherspoon, R. (2005). Actionable feedback: Unlocking the power of learning and performance improvement. *Academy of Management Executive*, 19, 120–134.

Carr, S. (2006). The Foundation Programme assessment tools: An opportunity to enhance feedback to trainees? *Postgraduate Medical Journal*, 82, 576–579. doi:10.1136/pgmj.2005.042366.

Chatman, J. A., & Cha, S. E. (2003). Leading by leveraging culture. *California Management Review*, 45, 20–34.

Chen, G., & Kanfer, R. (2006). Towards a systems theory of motivated behavior in work teams. *Research in Organizational Behavior*, 27, 223–276.

Dahling, J., Ritchie, S., Chau, S., Schoepfer, R., & Dwight, S. (2012). A multilevel model linking managerial coaching effectiveness to sales performance. Paper presented at the Annual Meeting of the Academy of Management, Boston.

David, E. (2012). Examining the role of narrative performance appraisal comments on performance. Paper presented at the Annual Meeting of the Academy of Management, Boston.

DeMeuse, K. P., Dai, G., & Hallenbeck, G. S. (2010). Learning agility: A construct whose time has come. *Consulting Psychology Journal: Practice and Research*, 62, 119–130.

DeNisi, A. S., & Kluger, A. N. (2000). Feedback effectiveness: Can 360-degree appraisals be improved? *Academy of Management Executive*, 14, 129–139.

DeRue, D. S., Ashford, S. J., & Myers, C. G. (2012). Learning agility: In search of conceptual clarity and theoretical grounding. *Industrial and Organizational Psychology: Perspectives on Science and Practice*, 5, 258–279. doi:1754-9426/12.

DeShon, R. P., Kozlowski, S. W. J., Schmidt, A. M., Milner, K. R., & Wiechmann, D. (2004). A multiple-goal, multilevel model of feedback effects on the regulation of individual and team performance. *Journal of Applied Psychology*, 89, 1035–1056.

Diefendorff, J. M., Croyle, M. H., & Gosserand, R. H. (2005). The dimensionality and antecedents of emotional labor strategies. *Journal of Vocational Behavior*, 66, 339–357.

Dweck, C. S. (2006). *Mindset: The New Psychology of Success*. New York: Ballantine Books.

Eisenberger, R., Huntington, R., Hutchison, S., & Sowa, D. (1986). Perceived organizational support. *Journal of Applied Psychology*, 71, 500–507.

Erez, M. (1977). Feedback: A necessary condition for the goal setting–performance relationship. *Journal of Applied Psychology*, 62, 624–627.

Fante, R., Davis, O. L., & Kempt, V. (2013). Improving closing task completion in a drugstore. *Journal of Organizational Behavior Management*, 33, 77–83.

Fiore, S. M., Salas, E., & Cannon-Bowers, J. A. (2001). Group dynamics and shared mental model development. In M. London (Ed.), *How People Evaluate Others in Organizations* (pp. 309–336). Mahwah, NJ: Erlbaum.

Ford, J. K., Smith, E. M., Weissbein, D. A., Gully, S. M., & Salas, E. (1998). Relationships of goal orientation, metacognitive activity, and practice strategies with learning outcomes and transfer. *Journal of Applied Psychology*, 83, 218–233.

Freeman, L., & Greenacre, L. (2011). An examination of socially destructive behaviors in group work. *Journal of Marketing Education*, 33, 5–17.

Fuller, B., & Marler, L. E. (2009). Change driven by nature: A meta-analytic review of the proactive personality literature. *Journal of Vocational Behavior*, 75, 239–345. doi:10.1016/j.jvb.2009.05.008.

Gerstenberg, F. X. R., Imhoff, R., Banse, R., Altstotter-Gleich, C., Zinkernagel, A., & Schmitt, M. (2013). How implicit-explicit consistency of the intelligence self-concept moderates reactions to performance feedback. *European Journal of Personality*, 27(3), 238–255. doi:10.1002/per.1900.

Gielen, S., Dochy, F., & Dierick, S. (2003). Evaluating the consequential validity of new modes of assessment: The influence of assessment on learning, including pre-, post-, and true-assessment effects. In M. Sigers, F. Dochy, & E. Cascallar (Eds.), *Optimizing New Modes Of Assessment: In Search of Qualities and Standards* (pp. 37–54). Dordrecht: Kluwer.

Gillespie, T. L. (2005). Internationalizing 360-degree feedback: Are subordinate ratings comparable? *Journal of Business and Psychology*, 19, 361–382.

Gonzalez-Mule, E., Courtright, S. H., & Seong, J. Y. (2012). Channeled autonomy: Joint effects of autonomy and feedback on team performance through goal clarity. Paper presented at the Annual Meeting of the Academy of Management, Boston.

Gramzow, R. H., (2011). Academic exaggeration: Pushing self-enhancement boundaries. In M. D. Alicke & C. Sedikides (Eds.), *Handbook of Self-Enhancement and Self-Protection* (pp. 455–471). New York: Guilford Press.

Grohsjean, T., Kretschmer, T., & Stieglitz, N. (2012). Performance feedback, firm resources, and strategic change. Paper presented at the Annual Meeting of the Academy of Management, Boston.

Hattie, J., & Timperley, H. (2007). The power of feedback. *Review of Educational Research*, 77, 81–112. doi:10.3102/003465430298487.

Herold, D., & Parsons, C. (1985). Assessing the feedback environment in work organizations: Development of the job feedback survey. *Journal of Applied Psychology*, 70, 290–305.

Hochschild, A. R. (1979). Emotion work, feeling rules, and social structure. *American Journal of Sociology*, 85, 555–575.

Jordan, A. H., & Audia, P. G. (2012). Self-enhancement and learning from performance feedback. *Academy of Management Review*, 37, 211–231. doi:10.5465/amr.2010.0108.

Judge, T. A., & Bono, J. E. (2001). Relationship of core self-evaluations traits – self-esteem, generalized self-efficacy, locus of control, and emotional stability – with job satisfaction and job performance: A meta-analysis. *Journal of Applied Psychology*, 86, 80–92.

Judge, T. A., Locke, E. A., Durham, C. C., & Kluger, A. N. (1998). Dispositional effects on job and life satisfaction: The role of core evaluations. *Journal of Applied Psychology*, 83, 17–34.

Kayes, A. B., & Kayes, D. C. (2011). *The Learning Advantage: Six Practices of Learning Directed Leadership*. Basingstoke: Palgrave-Macmillan.

Kayes, D. C. (2006). *The Destructive Goal Pursuit: The Mount Everest Disaster*. Basingstoke: Palgrave-Macmillan.

Klein, D. J., & Verbeke, W. (1999). Autonomic feedback in stressful environments: How do individual differences in autonomic feedback relate to burnout, job performance, and job attitudes in salespeople? *Journal of Applied Psychology*, 84, 911–924.

Klein, W. M. P. (2003). Effects of objective feedback and single other or average other social comparison feedback on performance judgments and helping behavior. *Journal of Personality and Social Psychology*, 29, 418–429.

Kluger, A. N., & DeNisi, A. (1996). The effects of feedback interventions on performance: A historical review, a meta-analysis, and a preliminary feedback intervention theory. *Psychological Bulletin*, 119, 254–284. http://doi.org/gtw.

Knight, D., Durham, C. D., & Locke, E. A. (2001). The relationship of team goals, incentives, and efficacy to strategic risk, tactical implementation, and performance. *Academy of Management Journal*, 44, 326–338.

Kolb, D. (1984). *Experiential Learning*. Englewood Cliffs, NJ: Prentice-Hall.

Kollee, J. A. J., Giessner, S. R., & van Knippenberg, D. (2013). Leader evaluations after performance feedback: The role of follower mood. *Leadership Quarterly*, 24, 203–214.

Korsgaard, A. M., & Diddams, M. (1996). The effect of process feedback and task complexity on personal goal, information searching, and performance improvement. *Journal of Applied Social Psychology*, 26, 1889–1911.

Krasman, J. (2011). Taking feedback-seeking to the next "level": Organizational structure and feedback-seeking behavior. *Journal of Managerial Issues*, 23, 9–30.

Kuchinke, P. K. (2000). The role of feedback in management training settings. *Human Resource Development Quarterly*, 11, 381–401.

Kudisch, J., Fortunado, V., & Smith, A. (2006). Contextual and individual difference factors predicting individuals' desire to provide upward feedback. *Group & Organization Management*, 31, 503–529.

Kuhnen, C. M., & Tymula, A. (2012). Feedback, self-esteem, and performance in organizations. *Management Science*, 58, 94–113. doi: 10.1287/mnsc.1110.1379.

Kurtzberg, T. R., Belkin, L. Y., & Naquin, C. E. (2006). The effect of e-mail on attitudes towards performance feedback. *International Journal of Organizational Analysis*, 14, 4–21.

Lam, L. W., Peng, K. Z., & Wong, C. S. (2012). Is more feedback always better? LMX moderates the relationship between FSB and performance. Paper presented at the Annual Meeting of the Academy of Management, Boston.

Langfred, C. W. (2007). The downside of self-management: A longitudinal study of the effects of conflict on trust, autonomy, and task interdependence in self-managing teams. *Academy of Management Journal*, 50, 885–900.

Larson, J. (1989). The dynamic interplay between employees' feedback-seeking strategies and supervisors' delivery of performance feedback. *Academy of Management Review*, 14, 408–422.

Latham, G. P., & Locke, E. A. (2006). Enhancing the benefits and overcoming the pitfalls of goal setting. *Organizational Dynamics*, 35, 332–340.

Leung, K., Bhagat, R. S., Buchan, N. R., Erez, M., & Gibson, C. B. (2005). Culture and international business: Recent advances and their implications for future research. *Journal of International Business Studies*, 36, 357–378.

Levinthal, D. A., & March, J. G. (1993). The myopia of learning. *Strategic Management Journal*, 14, 95–112.

Li, N., Harris, B., Boswell, W. R., & Xie, Z. (2011). The role of organizational insiders' developmental feedback and proactive personality on newcomers' performance: An interactionist perspective. *Journal of Applied Psychology*, 96, 1317–1327. doi:10.1037/a0024029.

Locke, E. A., & Latham, G. P. (1990). *A Theory of Goal Setting and Task Performance*. Englewood Cliffs, NJ: Prentice Hall.

Lombardo, M. M., & Eichinger, R. W. (2000). High potentials as high learners. *Human Resource Management*, 39, 321–330.

London, M. (1988). *Change Agents: New Roles and Innovation Strategies for Human Resource Professionals*. San Francisco: Jossey-Bass.

London, M. (2003). *Job Feedback: Giving, Seeking, and Using Feedback for Performance Improvement* (2nd ed.). Mahwah, NJ: Erlbaum.

London, M. (2007). Performance appraisal for groups: Models and methods for assessing group processes and outcomes for development and evaluation. *Consulting Psychology Journal: Practice and Research*, 59, 175–188.

London, M., & Sessa, V. I. (2006). Group feedback for continuous learning. *Human Resource Development Review*, 5, 303–329.

London, M., & Smither, J. W. (1995). Can multi-source feedback change perceptions of goal accomplishment, self-evaluations and performance related outcomes? Theory based applications and directions for research. *Personnel Psychology*, 48, 803–839.

London, M., & Smither, J. W. (2002). Feedback orientation, feedback culture, and the longitudinal performance management process. *Human Resource Management Review*, 12, 81–100.

Ludwig, T. D., & Goomas, D. T. (2009). Real-time performance monitoring, goal-setting, and feedback for forklift drivers in a distribution centre. *Journal of Occupational and Organizational Psychology*, 82, 391–403.

March, J. G. (2010). *The Ambiguities of Experience*. Ithaca, NY Cornell University Press.

March, J. G., & Shapira, Z. (1992). Variable risk preferences and the focus of attention. *Psychological Review*, 99, 172–183.

Mento, A. L., Locke, E. A., & Klein, H. (1992). Relationship of goal level to valence and instrumentality. *Journal of Applied Psychology*, 77, 395–405.

Meyrowitz, M., Mueller-Hanson, R., O'Leary, R., & Pulakos, R. (2012). *Building a High-Performance Culture: A Fresh Look at Performance Management*. Alexandria, VA: Society for Human Resource Management.

Miller, N., Resnick, P., & Zeckhauser, R. (2005). Eliciting informative feedback: The peer-prediction method. *Management Science*, 51, 1359–1373. doi:10.1287/mnsc.1050.0379.

Miller, V., & Jablin, F. (1991). Information seeking during organizational entry: Influences, tactics, and a model of the process. *Academy of Management Review*, 16, 92–121.

Mohammed, S., & Angell, L. C. (2004). Surface- and deep-level diversity in workgroups: Examining the moderating effects of team orientation and team process on relationship conflict. *Journal of Organizational Behavior*, 25, 1015–1039.

Morrison, E. W., & Bies, R. J. (1991). Impression management in the feedback-seeking process: A literature review and research agenda. *Academy of Management Review*, 16, 522–541.

Moser, K. S., & Axtell, C. M. (2013). The role of norms in virtual work: A review and agenda for future research. *Journal of Personnel Psychology*, 12, 1–6. doi:10.1027/1866-5888/a000079.

Nadler, D. A. (1979). The effects of feedback on task group behavior: A review of experimental research. *Organizational Behavior and Human Performance*, 23, 309–338.

Norris-Watts, C., & Levy, P. (2004). The mediating role of affective commitment in the relation of the feedback environment to work outcomes. *Journal of Vocational Behavior*, 65, 351–365.

Peltier, B. (2010). *The Psychology of Executive Coaching: Theory and Application*. New York: Routledge.

Peng, J. C. (2012). The relationship between supervisor feedback environment and voluntary work behavior. Paper presented at the Annual Meeting of the Academy of Management, Boston.

Pyszczynski, T., & Greenberg, J. (1987). Toward an integration of cognitive and motivational perspectives on social inference: A biased hypothesis-testing model. *Advances in Experimental Social Psychology*, 20, 297–340.

Reb, J., & Greguras, G. J. (2010). Understanding performance ratings: Dynamic performance, attributions, and rating purpose. *Journal of Applied Psychology*, 95, 213–220.

Rhoades, L., & Eisenberger, R. (2002). Perceived organizational support: A review of the literature. *Journal of Applied Psychology*, 87, 698–714.

Rosen, C. C., Levy, P. E., & Hall, R. J. (2006). Placing perceptions of politics in the context of the feedback environment, employee attitudes, and job performance. *Journal of Applied Psychology*, 91, 211–220.

Ross, J., & Staw, B. M. (1993). Organizational escalation and exit: Lessons from the Shoreham nuclear power plant. *Academy of Management Journal*, 36, 701–732.

Sargeant, J., Macleod, R., Sinclair, D., & Power, M. (2011). How do physicians assess their family physician colleagues' performance? Creating a rubric to inform assessment and feedback. *Journal of Continuing Education in the Health Professions*, 31, 87–94.

Sargeant, J., Mann, K., Sinclair, D., van der Vleuten, C., & Metsemakers, J. (2008). Understanding the influence of emotions and reflection upon multi-source feedback acceptance and use. *Advances in Health Sciences Education*, 13, 275–288.

Sargeant, J. M., Mann, K. V., van der Vleuten, C. P., & Metsemakers, J. F. (2009). Reflection: A link between receiving and using assessment feedback. *Advances in Health Science Education*, 14, 399–410. doi:10.1007/s10459-008-9124-4.

Schippers, M. C., Homan, A. C., & Knippenberg, D. V. (2013). To reflect or not to reflect: Prior team performance as a boundary condition of the effects of reflexivity on learning and final team performance. *Journal of Organizational Behavior*, 34, 6–23. doi:10.1002/job.1784.

Schweitzer, M. E., Ordonez, I., & Douma, B. (2004). Goal-setting as a motivator of unethical behavior. *Academy of Management Journal*, 47, 422–432.

Sedikides, C., & Strube, M. J. (1997). Self-evaluation: To thine own self be good, to thine own self be sure, to thine own self be true, and to thine own self be better. *Advances in Experimental Social Psychology*, 29, 209–269.

Silverman, S. B., Pogson, C. E., & Cober, A. B. (2005). When employees at work don't get it: A model for enhancing individual employee change in response to performance feedback. *Academy of Management Executive*, 19, 135–147.

Simonson, I., & Staw, B. (1992). Deescalation strategies: A comparison of techniques for reducing commitment to losing courses of action. *Journal of Applied Psychology*, 77, 419–426.

Škraba, A., Kljajić, M., & Borštnar, M. K. (2007). The role of information feedback in the management group decision-making process applying system dynamics models. *Group Decision and Negotiation*, 16, 77–95. doi:10.1007/s10726-006-9035-9.

Smither, J. W., London, M., Flautt, R., Vargas, Y., & Kucine, I. (2003). Can executive coaches enhance the impact of multisource feedback on behavior change? A quasi-experimental field study. *Personnel Psychology*, 56(1), 23–44.

Smither, J. W., & Walker, A. G. (2004). Are the characteristics of narrative comments related to improvement in multirater feedback ratings over time? *Journal of Applied Psychology*, 89, 575–581.

Sobel-Lojeski, K. S., & Reilly, R. R. (2008). *Uniting the Virtual Workforce: Transforming Leadership and Innovation in the Globally Integrated Enterprise.* Hoboken, NJ: John Wiley & Sons, Inc.

Staw, B. M., & Boettger, R. D. (1990). Task revision: A neglected form of work performance. *Academy of Management Journal, 33,* 534–559.

Steelman, L., Levy, P., & Snell, A. F. (2004). The feedback environment scale (FES): Construct definition, measurement, and validation. *Educational and Psychological Measurement, 64,* 165–184.

Swann, W. B., Jr. (1983). Self-verification: Bringing social reality into harmony with the self. In J. Suls & A. G. Greenwald (Eds.), *Psychological Perspectives on the Self* (vol. 2, pp. 33–66). Hillsdale, NJ: Erlbaum.

Tay, J. K. (2012). The impact of feedback activators on environmentally significant behaviors: A review. Paper presented at the Annual Meeting of the Academy of Management, Boston.

Trinh, K. C. W., & Mitchell, W. (2009). Talk, think, read (if absolutely necessary): The impact of social, personal, and documentary knowledge on task performance. *European Management Review, 6,* 29–44.

Trope, Y., & Liberman, N. (2010). Construal-level theory of psychological distance. *Psychological Review, 117,* 440–465.

Vigoda-Gadot, E., & Angert, L. (2007). Goal setting theory, job feedback, and OCB: Lessons from a longitudinal study. *Basic and Applied Social Psychology, 29,* 119–128.

Volkema, R. J. (2010). Designing effective projects: Decision options for maximizing learning and project success. *Journal of Management Education, 34,* 527–550.

Vroom, V. H. (1964). *Work and Motivation.* San Francisco: Jossey-Bass.

Whitaker, B. G. (2011). Linking the feedback environment to feedback seeking through perceptions of organizational support and job involvement. *International Journal of Organization Theory and Behaviour, 14,* 383–403.

Whitaker, B. G., Dahling, J. J., & Levy, P. (2007). The development of a feedback environment and role clarity model of job performance. *Journal of Management, 33,* 570–591.

White, P. H., Kjelgaard, M. M., & Harkins, S. G. (1995). Testing the contribution of self-evaluation to goal-setting effects. *Journal of Personality and Social Psychology, 69,* 69–79.

Williams, J., Miller, C., Steelman, L., & Levy, P. (1999). Increasing feedback seeking in public contexts: It takes two (or more) to tango. *Journal of Applied Psychology, 84,* 969–976.

Wohlgezogen, F., Stern, I., & Galinsky, A. D. (2012). Immunizing joint ventures: How negative feedback positively influences retention decisions. Paper presented at the Annual Meeting of the Academy of Management, Boston.

Wong, M. W. K., Wood, R. E., & Goodman, J. S. (2012). Metacognitive training, feedback specificity, metacognitive activity, and transfer of training. Paper presented at the Annual Meeting of the Academy of Management, Boston.

Wood, R., & Bandura, A. (1989). Impact of conceptions of ability on self-regulatory mechanisms and complex decision making. *Journal of Personality and Social Psychology, 56,* 407–415.

Wright, P. M., George, J. M., Farnsworth, S. R., & McMahan, G. C. (1993). Productivity and extra-role behavior: The effects of goals. *Journal of Applied Psychology, 78,* 374–381.

Zapf, D. (2002). Emotion work and psychological well-being: A review of the literature and some conceptual considerations. *Human Resource Management Review, 12,* 237–268. doi:10.1016/S1053-4822(02)00048-7.

Zhong, J. A., Cao, Z. L., Huo, Y., Chen, Z., & Lam, W. (2012). The mediating role of job feedback in the relationship between neuroticism and emotional labor. *Social Behavior and Personality, 40,* 649–656.

Zhou, J. (2003). When the presence of creative coworkers is related to creativity: Role of supervisor close monitoring, developmental feedback, and creative personality. *Journal of Applied Psychology, 88,* 413–422. doi:10.1037/0021-9010.88.3.413.

24

Using 360-Degree Feedback as a Development Tool

Clive Fletcher

Introduction

Multisource, multirater (MSMR) feedback, also known as 360-degree feedback (the terms will be used interchangeably here) was scarcely heard of before 1980 and went through an explosive growth in use from the 1990s onwards, to the point where it is now a commonplace feature of the HR scene in the UK, the US, and many other countries. Essentially, such feedback refers to a process whereby an individual (usually referred to as the focal manager) completes a self-rating on behaviors associated with each of several competencies, and is also rated on those same behaviors by bosses, peers, subordinates, and team members – and in some instances by customers or other stakeholders too. These colleagues may also add written comments as well as ratings. All this data is pulled together in a report that allows the focal manager to see how their colleagues view them and how this contrasts with their self-view. Originally, the aim of this was in most cases a development exercise for the focal manager, but increasingly it has been used as an input to the formal appraisal process (Fletcher, 2001).Whilst this chapter focuses on MSMR feedback as an aid to development, that development can come from such feedback being used for varying reasons – including appraisal – and in varying ways. Moreover, much of what might be said about it applies to the study of feedback processes in general, as can be seen in Chapter 23 by London and Mone (this volume). They give an excellent account of the theoretical perspectives on feedback, so the present chapter will not seek to repeat that but instead will address itself to what the research tells us, both directly and indirectly, about the more practical aspects of using 360-degree feedback in development.

Underlying the use of 360-degree feedback is the assumption that a single perspective on an individual's behavior and performance – as embodied in traditional top-down performance appraisal schemes – is unlikely to be sufficient for a full and accurate picture to be formed. The reasons for this are not just the possibility of bias in a single rater, but the belief that an individual may behave differently with different groups of colleagues

The Wiley Blackwell Handbook of the Psychology of Training, Development, and Performance Improvement,
First Edition. Edited by Kurt Kraiger, Jonathan Passmore, Sigmar Malvezzi, and Nuno Rebelo dos Santos.
© 2015 John Wiley & Sons Ltd. Published 2020 by John Wiley & Sons Ltd.

(peers, team members, etc.). A boss's view of how a manager supervises his team may be quite different from that of the team members themselves, who have a more direct and lengthy exposure to the manager and his/her supervisory style, and possibly also a different set of priorities. For example, Salam, Cox, and Sims (1997) found that managers who were seen as challenging the status quo and encouraging their staff to take independent action were rated higher by the latter and lower by the manager's own bosses.

Hence, to capture these different perspectives and to arrive at a more rounded and fairer assessment on which to base development steps, MSMR feedback is needed. Perhaps the first question, then, is whether differing views of an individual do really emerge from such feedback processes. The answer to this is a resounding "yes." In fact, the differences between rater groups have often been found to be so large as to raise questions about the justification for using the same rating dimensions for each group (Hoffman et al., 2010). However, studies such as those of Facteau and Craig (2001) and Guenole et al. (2011) have demonstrated that even with such differences, the use of the same rating dimensions across different groups is valid. This leads us to some of the complexities of understanding how 360-degree feedback and its effects on development can be evaluated. In particular, what criteria can we use in assessing the impact of feedback and the changes it might lead to in those receiving it? The next section addresses this.

Measuring Change and Development Post-Feedback

The measures of the impact of MSMR feedback essentially come down to:

1 Development activity taking place as a result of feedback;
2 Changes in ratings from colleagues on successive feedback episodes; are focal managers seen to improve following feedback?
3 Reduced discrepancy between self-ratings and others' ratings over time – do those receiving feedback become more self-aware as a result and modify their self-view?

The first of these is the most clear-cut as a criterion for assessing development as it relies on some tangible evidence of development activity taking place. But it is also probably the least researched outcome measure. There are two reasons for this. The first is that it is surprisingly difficult to track development activities – many may take place in the immediate context of the job and thus not be formally recorded (as opposed to going on a course, which HR are likely to be involved in). Moreover, in many cases, organizations simply provide the feedback report to the focal manager and to nobody else, so there is no formal follow-up or review of development action implied as necessary by the feedback or subsequently taken as a result of it. The second reason is that it may be difficult to tie the development activities to the feedback – the question is not just whether development takes place, but whether it was triggered by the feedback and whether the specific activity was related to the nature of the feedback (e.g., if the feedback highlighted a development need in communications skills, was the development action that followed clearly addressing that need?). This requires a considerable degree of detailed follow-up to establish.

Most studies on the effects of MSMR feedback have utilized the situation where a sample of managers have been through the feedback process twice, usually with around a year or so between each occasion, and have focused on changes in ratings made by all parties involved in the second feedback administration compared to the first. The implication is that if ratings improve, this indicates development has taken place as a result of the first feedback and performance has improved. The problem here is that a change in ratings may arise through factors other than improved performance (Fletcher & Baldry, 1999). Firstly, different staff may be involved in giving feedback across the two occasions. Secondly, different groups of colleagues may have different perspectives on what if anything has changed, so an overall measure of rating change may not make this clear. Thirdly, those giving feedback may expect change and be more likely to report it as a result.

All of these issues relating to using ratings change as a criterion apply to the third measure mentioned above: reduced self–other discrepancy. In theory, greater similarity between self-ratings and the ratings given by colleagues after successive feedbacks is a positive outcome. Quite apart from the desirability of people having a more "realistic" view of themselves (defined here as one that is in greater accord with how they are seen by those who work with them), there is actually ample evidence that this – often called self-awareness – is consistently associated with good performance, and lack of it with poor performance (Atwater et al., 2005; Fletcher, 1997). However, even where reduced self–other discrepancy is found, care has to be taken in analyzing what kind and degree of change has taken place. For example, in a longitudinal study by Bailey and Fletcher (2002a), greater congruence between focal managers' self-assessments and subordinates' ratings of them over time was found to arise from the latter group, rather than the focal managers, changing their ratings. Thus, subordinates perceived change (or at least, changed their ratings) but the individuals they were giving feedback to did not, remaining largely the same in their self-view, which calls into question whether any real development had taken place. Moreover, the focal managers' bosses in this study saw very little in the way of development needs for these individuals in the first place, which meant that there was little scope for showing an improvement on this measure over subsequent feedbacks. This kind of "ceiling" effect is another potential limit on using rating change as a criterion.

Finally, very few if any studies include a control group. In other words, if we see a change in behavior from one feedback administration to another, is this due to the feedback or to some other influence – would it have happened without the feedback? To answer this properly, one would need a control group who were assessed on the same dimensions over a similar period but without receiving any feedback. Methodologically desirable as this is, to arrange it is very difficult for organizations to do.

This section has outlined the kind of criteria that are typically used in researching the impact of 360-degree feedback on development, and the kinds of problems that can arise with them. Nonetheless, they remain the best measures available – it is simply that they have to be interpreted with care. With that caveat in mind, we can look at some of the evidence for the effects of MSMR feedback processes on development. Space limitations preclude describing all the studies done in this realm, but the ones outlined below are representative of the field.

The Effectiveness of 360-Degree Feedback in Improving and Developing Recipients

One cannot assume that feedback will automatically bring about development that in turn will lead to better performance. Indeed, Kluger and DeNisi (1996) in their review of feedback effects concluded that in a third of cases performance did not simply fail to improve, it actually declined – though it should be emphasized that this is based on many different kinds of feedback process and a wide range of situations. So it is imperative that we evaluate the effectiveness of 360-degree feedback, and fortunately a number of studies have attempted to do that. One of the best is that reported by Dai, De Meuse, and Peterson (2010), a particular strength being that in this longitudinal research, competencies specifically selected by managers for development were identified and compared in terms of changes resulting from several applications of 360-degree feedback to other competencies that were not targeted. In effect the non-targeted competencies formed a kind of control group. In addition, using an established systematic procedure, the "developmental difficulty" of various competencies was assessed to determine if this influenced potential improvement. The results showed clearly that participants improved significantly more on competencies selected for development than on competencies not selected, and this improvement was sustained over the successive feedback episodes. The researchers also found that managers improved more on competencies classed as developmentally less difficult than on harder ones.

Tyson and Ward (2004) carried out a large UK study where 360-degree feedback was itself a measure of the effectiveness of a management development program, with participants being assessed through the 360 process before and after the development interventions. Substantial improvements in the ratings were observed from time one to time two, and 85 percent of the senior managers involved felt that the feedback had significantly contributed to their development in its own right, quite apart from its use as a measure of change. Another slightly indirect piece of evidence is provided by Atwater and Brett (2006) who found that after managers had been through a 360 process, their staff showed improved attitudes and engagement – presumably as a result of the managers changing their behavior in response to the feedback.

Although most research on 360 effects has been done with managerial samples in industrial, commercial, or civil service-type organizations, some have been done in educational or medical contexts. For example, Violato, Lockyer, and Fidler (2008) tracked changes in the performance of doctors following MSMR feedback over five years, and reported mostly "small to moderate" improvements. On the other hand, Malling et al. (2009) looking at MSMR feedback with senior medics, concluded from their research that it was "not sufficient to foster plans for the development of leadership performance." Nor is this the only negative finding; Pfau and Kay (2002), quoted in Dai, De Meuse, and Peterson (2010), actually reported a decrease in performance following 360 feedback. Maurer, Mitchell, and Barbeite (2002) found few relationships between feedback ratings and subsequent involvement in development activities. So, whilst most of the research findings reported are generally positive in relation to the impact of such feedback, there is undeniably a good deal of variation in what has been observed, as was noted by Smither, London, and Reilly (2005) in their comprehensive review of the evidence to that point,

Smither, London, and Reilly (2005) conducted a meta-analysis – a statistical technique that makes it possible to aggregate the results of many different studies in such a way as to facilitate a common measure of outcome that summarizes all of them. They brought together the results of 24 longitudinal studies that tracked changes in ratings given to focal managers over two or more 360 feedback exercises. Whilst they found that nearly all the changes reported by peers, bosses, and direct reports were positive (i.e., they rated the focal managers higher on successive feedbacks), there was substantial variation in the results and overall the degree of behavior change seen by these groups was small. Further analyses of these findings led them to assert that practitioners should not expect large, wide-scale performance improvement after feedback without taking into account a number of factors that impacted on that. In particular, improvement was only likely to occur when feedback indicated that change was necessary, when those receiving it had a positive attitude to feedback and reacted constructively to it, saw a need to change their behavior and felt that change was feasible, set appropriate goals and took the right development action. In other words, there is little point in asking a question as simple as "does 360-degree feedback bring about development in those receiving it? " The only sensible questions are whether such feedback, *when properly designed, applied, and resourced*, brings about specified changes in individuals receiving it, and what attributes of those individuals are likely to affect their response to feedback and post-feedback actions. The next section will look at these factors in some detail.

Factors Impacting on the Value of 360-Degree Feedback in Development

To consider every factor that has been postulated or found to affect responses to 360-degree feedback would take a book in itself, but some of the most salient ones are described here under four headings – system factors, feedback characteristics, personality and other attributes of the focal manager, and cultural influences.

System factors

The most fundamental issue here is the purpose of the feedback – whether it is for appraisal or for development. In general, it can be said that MSMR feedback produces more positive gains in terms of performance change when it is used for development (Smither, London, & Reilly, 2005). When it is used for appraisal, there is evidence to suggest that the feedback given is of lower quality in various respects and more lenient, that is unduly favorable (Greguras et al., 2003; Fletcher, 2008). All this is probably due to the concern that less positive feedback may have an impact on the recipients' rewards and prospects in the organization – a concern that makes feedback givers more cautious and reluctant to give low ratings while simultaneously making focal managers more defensive about the whole process.

Another crucial factor here, and one that is often overlooked, is the quality of the feedback questionnaire. Although many organizations employ external consultants or buy off-the-shelf packages to run their feedback process, others simply design the feedback questionnaire themselves. Whichever way it is sourced, there is a tendency to think that the feedback questionnaire is somehow automatically valid as a measure of the competencies being assessed. Unfortunately, evidence suggests this is not the case, and that some questionnaires being used are not in fact assessing the competencies they claim to be assessing (Fletcher, Baldry, & Cunningham-Snell, 1998). In which case, any development activity based on them runs the risk of being wrongly directed. Clearly, organizations should check the validity of their feedback questionnaires.

Putting these two points together – potential for reluctance to give feedback and design of the feedback questionnaire – brings us to the question of the rating scales used. The writer has frequently noted how relatively short scales, equally balanced between positive and negative ratings, often lead to only favorable feedback being given. It seems that feedback givers are loath to give "below average" or "poor" ratings. The use of positively skewed response alternatives (e.g., excellent/very good/good/ average/below average/ poor), particularly where most of the positive ratings carry with them a secondary descriptor suggesting that development is still relevant to bring about improvement (e.g., "Very good: generally achieves high standards in this respect but could still develop this strength further"), seems to help feedback givers to spread their ratings across a broader range. This is also true of self-ratings (Jones & Fletcher, 2002, 2004).

A 360 questionnaire may be a sound measure but still not cover competencies seen to be those that are most important to feedback recipients in terms of their role and how they are assessed; perceived relevance of the feedback dimensions is important (Bracken & Rose, 2011; Bailey & Austin, 2006). This is something that should normally be dealt with in the consultation phase before a 360-feedback system is introduced – both focal managers and feedback givers need to be briefed thoroughly about the process and how it will work, and indeed be allowed to comment on it before it is finalized. Without that kind of consultation and chance for participants to air concerns and ask questions, 360-feedback systems are likely to run into problems, not least a reluctance of colleagues to give meaningful feedback to focal managers, and reluctance by the latter to accept such feedback that they do get.

Two other factors should be mentioned under this heading. The first has already been referred to earlier, namely that some competencies or feedback dimensions are easier to do development work on than are others; for example, "timely decision-making" might be considered an easier attribute to improve on than "innovation management." Dai, De Meuse, and Peterson (2010) found that more improvement took place on developmentally easier competencies following feedback. The second – although not strictly speaking a feature of the 360-degree system itself – is the level and quality of development resource available to focal managers post-feedback. This will inevitably have an effect on the amount and type of development activity that they embrace.

Feedback characteristics

One influence dominates this above all others – the sign of the feedback; what motivates improvement more, receiving negative or positive messages? The research findings in the context of 360 feedback have not been altogether consistent or positive. For example, Brett and Atwater (2001) found that managers receiving unfavorable (critical) feedback were discouraged and consequently unmotivated to change their behavior. This should not cause great surprise, given that the potentially demotivating effects of critical comments in an appraisal context were demonstrated many years ago (Meyer, Kay, & French, 1965). On the positive side, though, other studies run counter to this; for example, Walker and Smither (1999) found that managers who initially received less favorable ratings put more effort into subsequent development activities than those who got higher ratings. Mostly, though, this is a subject that has to be examined in the light of other factors, principally those concerning the characteristics of the feedback recipient, which will be dealt with in the next section.

Before that, however, we should consider the other side of the equation, namely the source of the feedback, and specifically its credibility. As indicated in by London and Mone (Chapter 23, this volume), this has been found to be a key determinant of response to feedback generally and not just in the 360-feedback context (e.g., Bastos & Fletcher, 1995; Kluger & DeNisi, 1996). If feedback recipients do not feel the feedback giver has a valid position from which to comment on them, or feels they are not competent to comment in other ways, they will take little or no notice of the feedback on offer. Hence, allowing individuals to choose their own feedback givers, or at least most of them, is usually considered wise. The concern is often raised here that focal managers will nominate their "buddies" in an attempt to get better ratings. Where 360 feedback is being used for development purposes, this would seem to be a self-defeating strategy – for development, one wants useful, objective feedback. Moreover, research indicates that irrespective of whether the feedback is being collected for development or for appraisal, focal managers select their feedback givers on the basis of familiarity, not liking (Brutus, Petosa, & Aucoin, 2005). Familiarity is entirely appropriate in this context – you cannot assess someone's competence if you are not familiar with them.

There is one feedback source, though, whose credibility in terms of accuracy of judgment is not correlated with the perceived value of its feedback – the focal manager's boss. Bailey and Fletcher (2002b) found that feedback from the boss was perceived to be the most important even where it was viewed as inaccurate. This is entirely understandable, as (a) the boss often has the power to determine the individual's rewards in terms of promotion, merit pay, and so forth, and, given that, (b) if the boss has a view of the individual that the latter believes to be wrong, it is all the more important to get the feedback and to then seek to challenge or correct it. Some practitioners believe that the boss's influence in feedback can be too powerful and reduce attention given to feedback by other colleagues, and as a result they do not include the boss in the process (whereby it presumably becomes 270-degree feedback!). However, as we will see below, there are very strong arguments for keeping the boss as an input to the process.

An aspect of feedback characteristics that has attracted rather little attention from an academic viewpoint but a good deal of discussion among practitioners is the relative merit of quantitative versus qualitative feedback. Many MSMR systems combine both – they invite feedback givers to make quantitative ratings and also some qualitative ones. The latter are often structured around questions such as "What would you like X to do more of, and what would you like them to do less of?" In other cases the feedback giver is simply invited to add any free written comments either to elucidate their ratings or to comment on something that is important but seemingly not covered by the rating dimensions. Indeed, some 360-feedback processes are entirely qualitatively based. Typically, this is where a coach working with a senior manager on an individual basis collects feedback from selected colleagues, usually by interviewing them, gathers the resulting observations together, and talks them through with the focal manager. Qualitative feedback has attracted very little research – it does not lend itself to quantitative analysis to the extent that ratings do. This paucity is all the more to be regretted as Antonioni (1996) found that focal managers value written feedback more than ratings. Atwater and Brett (2006), on the basis of their research, suggest that combining ratings and textual feedback is the most effective approach. Nonetheless, there are pros and cons in terms of practical application that need careful consideration (Antonioni & Woehr, 2001), not least of which revolve around the potential impact of negative or destructive comments, which will be discussed later in this chapter.

Personality and other attributes of the focal manager

Characteristics of the focal manager may influence not only what feedback ratings they get but also how they respond to them. From a developmental perspective, the important thing here is the extent to which self-ratings diverge from feedback ratings and what factors seem to be associated with the degree of divergence. A discrepancy between self and others' ratings can be a reflection of self-ratings being low and feedback ratings being high, or vice versa. So we may have three groups – people who over-rate themselves, people who under-rate themselves and people who rate themselves much as others rate them (who might thus be deemed "accurate" self-raters). Where the wide divergence is in the direction of focal managers markedly and consistently rating themselves higher than they are rated by others, this is associated both with poorer performance and an indication of a potentially larger developmental need to be addressed. Evidence suggests that people's self-rating styles are consistent, that this in effect is a personality factor, a trait of self-awareness (Church, 1997; Fletcher & Baldry, 2000). Clearly, this has an effect on how feedback is received. Habitual over-raters are likely to get feedback that portrays them in a less favorable light than they perhaps expect, while under-raters will tend to have feedback that suggests they are better performers than they give themselves credit for. The former may react defensively and reject the feedback, the latter may be pleasantly surprised and encouraged – unless, that is, they see it as reflecting expectations of them that they feel they cannot live up to, and/or feel discomforted by the dissonance with their existing self-image, becoming anxious as a consequence. This has been found to affect responses to developmental feedback outside the MSMR domain also. For example, Halman and Fletcher (2000) found that over-raters' self-assessments – and high levels of self-esteem – remained unchanged after going through a development centre (DC) and receiving feedback, a finding echoed in the later work of Woo et al. (2008). They noted that individuals whose self-ratings were higher than the ratings they received in a DC subsequently showed less engagement in the program than did under-raters. Findings such as these suggest that the rather disappointing level of development activity and behavior change that has been noted following DC attendance (Carrick & Williams, 1999) might be attributable to the influence of habitual over-raters who do not respond to the feedback and reduce any overall or mean scores on measures of post-DC development activity. The same is likely to be true of 360-degree feedback – some focal managers may receive ratings that are lower than they have given themselves and respond positively by seeking to improve, but there may well be another, possibly larger, group (habitual over-raters showing a deficit in self-awareness) who remain stubbornly resistant to such feedback.

Going beyond self-awareness, another personality characteristic demonstrated to be important in responses to 360-degree feedback is self-efficacy (Bandura, 1977) – the individual's judgment either of their ability to perform some specific task or achieve some objective, or of their general capability to perform effectively (Maurer, Mitchell, & Barbeite, 2002; Bailey & Austin, 2006). If a focal manager receives feedback suggesting a need to improve in some direction, whether that improvement takes place is likely to be dependent in part on his or her belief that they are capable of doing it, that is, their self-efficacy. Whilst high self-efficacy cannot guarantee success in tackling a development objective, it does mean that the individual is more likely to attempt it. In similar vein, Bono and Colbert (2005) related focal managers' responses to feedback with their core self-evaluations. The latter was based on a composite of personality measures covering self-esteem, generalized self-efficacy, locus of control, and (low) neuroticism. They found that commitment to post-feedback developmental goals is higher in focal managers who had high (positive) core self-evaluations when there was a discrepancy between self and others' ratings. In contrast, focal managers with low core self-evaluations were most committed to development when there was agreement between self and others' ratings. What the results of this longitudinal study are telling us is that individuals who are psychologically strong are able and motivated to change their behavior if they find that others see them differently from the way they see themselves, whereas focal managers who are more brittle and vulnerable in their self-image are only likely to commit to development action when they have the psychological comfort of seeing that they have a self-view that is congruent with their feedback – though of course how well directed their development efforts are, and how long sustained, is open to question. A general point from this study is that an individual's satisfaction with the feedback received was not itself the predictor of commitment to development.

A whole host of other attributes have been found to exert some influence on focal managers' response to 360-degree feedback. In a large-scale study, Ostroff, Atwater, and Feinberg (2004) found that women, whites, younger managers, and those with higher educational levels tended to show more agreement between self-ratings and feedback ratings in 360 feedback. Smither, London, and Reilly (2005) cite studies showing that high Conscientiousness is associated with participation in post-feedback development and both that and Openness to Experience correlate with post-feedback performance improvement. It is worth noting that personality can also be an influence in the ratings an individual receives, as there is ample evidence to show that personality characteristics of the person making the assessment are correlated with the ratings they make. Bernardin, Tyler, and

Villanova (2009) found that raters who were more Agreeable and less Conscientious made more lenient and less accurate assessments. Randall and Sharples (2012) also found rater Agreeableness to impact ratings in a similar fashion.

Culture as an influence in responses to multisource, multirater feedback

Given that there are considerable cultural variations in performance appraisal and other HR practices generally (Fletcher & Perry, 2001; Peretz & Fried, 2012) it would be surprising if 360-degree feedback did not show some differences when used across international and cultural boundaries. Much of the work done on this topic has been grounded in Hofstede's groundbreaking research (Hofstede, 1980, 2001) and in particular has looked at two of his dimensions of cultural difference – power distance (PD) and individualism/collectivism (I/C). In high-PD cultures, there is an acceptance of unequal distribution of power, and greater distance between people at different hierarchical levels. Individualistic cultures value personal identity and striving, whereas collectivist cultures emphasize group values and well-being over individual goals and needs. Typically, it has been hypothesized that subordinates in a high-PD culture might feel inhibited in giving feedback – especially critical feedback – to their superiors. And while collectivist cultures might seem suited to multiple feedback sources being involved, assessment and feedback might be viewed as posing a risk to group harmony and cohesion. Also, collectivist cultures may feel that the emphasis of feedback should be on the group rather than on the individual, and that one should show modesty in one's self-assessment.

Such research as there is on cultural differences in this domain tends to support these and other hypotheses that would flow from the distinctions implied by the PD and I/C dimensions. For example, Varela and Premeaux (2008) looked at 360-degree feedback in Venezuela and Colombia, both countries that are collectivist and high-PD cultures. They found that – in contrast to studies in the US and western Europe (mostly low-PD and individualist cultures) – subordinate ratings of their bosses were the most positive of all the ratings given. In another study (Gentry, Yip, & Hannum, 2010), self-ratings made as part of 360 feedback in Asian countries characterized by high collectivism were lower than for Asian countries classed as high on individualism. They also found greater discrepancy between self and others' ratings in Asian countries displaying a high-PD culture compared to those low on PD. Certainly, looking at the variations in how 360-degree feedback is applied in different countries (Brutus et al., 2006) one can see the influence of PD and I/C at a more macro level. For example, such schemes in China (high-PD) are less likely to allow focal managers to choose their own raters and instead have them nominated by superiors.

Whilst these dimensions are helpful in thinking about possible cultural differences in response to feedback, there are many complications. Cultures can change rapidly and caution is needed in making assumptions about them; and the influence of organizational culture, especially with multinationals, can sometimes be sufficiently strong to overlay and overcome the influence of national culture (Bailey & Fletcher, 2008). Perhaps the biggest challenge is where there is a multicultural workforce working together in the same country and organization. This can result in different combinations, such as bosses coming from a low-PD culture, subordinates from a collectivist background, the focal manager from a high-PD country, and peers from a mixture of all of them!

On a slightly different note, Gillespie (2005) studied 360-degree feedback ratings with employees of the same company across four countries (Great Britain, Hong Kong, Japan, and the US) and found differences in the factor structure of those across cultures. This suggests that – quite apart from making sure the translation of the feedback questionnaire is correct when it is used in countries with different languages – organizations need to ensure that the questions asked have the same meaning across cultures and whether they need to be adapted for particular languages/countries. Finally, on the theme of corporate culture, Brutus, Fleenor, and London (1998) examined differences in 360-feedback ratings across differing work sectors and industries. Among other things, they found a leniency bias in educational institutions and that inter-rater agreement was lowest in government agencies and highest in education and manufacturing organizations. They suggested that feedback of this kind may work differently across different organizations. That said, in my own experience of implementing and researching 360-degree feedback, I have sometimes been struck by how differently it seems to work, for no apparent reason, in what are on the face of it very similar schemes in almost identical organizations!

Reflections on the Research

It is not within the scope of this chapter to go into detailed consideration of coaching methods or approaches that may be helpful in using multisource feedback on an individual basis; there are helpful accounts of these elsewhere (see for example Kwiatkowski, 2006; McDowall & Kurtz, 2008; Nowack, 2009). However, there are many implications and lessons that can be drawn from the research reviewed above. What do these research findings lead us to conclude? Firstly, that, because of various methodological issues it is not easy to evaluate the impact of such feedback on development. Second, that although there is much research evidence that feedback of this kind can bring about changes in behavior and performance, its impact is highly variable and one is by no means guaranteed to achieve positive developmental action and outcomes as a result of it. Many different factors play a part in determining how effective a feedback system is and what results it leads to. This section will seek to pull together the lessons we can take from research and experience on how to build and apply 360-degree feedback systems for maximum developmental effect.

The findings on system factors described above show the importance of designing a feedback questionnaire that (1) provides a valid measure of the competencies to be covered, (2) uses a rating scale that allows feedback givers to choose from a range of responses implying a need for development without sounding overly critical, and (3) deals with competencies seen by focal manages as relevant to their role. All of these are issues to be addressed in the design and planning of MSMR feedback, and in the way it is introduced. For example, there should be little danger of competencies being seen as not relevant if plans for the scheme and how it will operate have been discussed with participants in advance, a step which is also usually necessary to allay fears or concerns of both feedback givers and receivers.

The other obvious – but still sometimes neglected – issue in designing such systems is that if you set up something to promote development, the resources to facilitate that development need to be put in place. Which brings us to the downfall of many 360-degree feedback systems. Even if the resources are in place, and no matter how detailed the feedback report or how much guidance it tries to give in how to use the feedback, those being developed (the focal managers) may need some help in choosing and implementing the appropriate development activities for them. Now, it is frequently the case that when used specifically for development, the view taken is that the feedback report should go to the focal manager and nobody else. The individual then has the choice as to whether they share some or all of it with their line manager, their feedback givers, HR, or possibly an external coach. We know from research (London & Smither, 1995) that those who discuss their feedback show more improvement in performance over time than those who do not.

For example, Smither et al. (2003) found that focal managers who worked with a coach to review feedback and set development goals improved more than those who did not. Tyson and Ward (2004) also emphasize the need to build coaching into the follow-up on feedback. However, it may well be that some of those who get the most negative feedback and/or who are habitual over-raters – are reluctant to share it. Or perhaps to even remember it: Smither, Brett, and Atwater (2008) found that focal managers, when asked to recall feedback they received months earlier, tend to remember the positive messages more than the less positive

The question, then, is whether feedback systems should *ever* be implemented on a basis of just "share it if you want to." If we take the answer to this as being "no," then who should the feedback be reviewed with? In terms of the rater groups, this would often depend on the nature of the feedback they gave. So, if the feedback from peers was rather critical but the feedback from subordinates was generally very positive, it would be more important to discuss it with the former. However, talking over feedback directly with those giving it might be too difficult for one or both parties in some instances. The individual's boss, though, is in a slightly different position. Whilst making discussion of the feedback received with the line manager mandatory might seem a draconian step in a developmental context, it should be remembered that any significant development activity is likely to involve the boss at some stage, even if is only informing him or her that the focal manager is going off to do a course. Usually, it would require their support and active cooperation for the development to achieve anything. Perhaps ideally, feedback would be discussed initially with a coach who is experienced in helping people use feedback to formulate development plans, and then those plans (and if necessary, the feedback) are discussed with the line manager and any other feedback givers judged to be important. However, it is also possible that either the coach or the focal manager might have to go back to feedback givers to clarify feedback before a personal development plan can be finalized. Where qualitative feedback has been included in the process, less clarification is likely to be needed.

Moving to consideration of the issues raised in looking at feedback characteristics, it seems clear that allowing focal managers to choose their feedback givers is the best approach, as without this there is a danger that the credibility of the source will be reduced and hence decrease the likelihood of a constructive use of the feedback. Though the research suggests that the concern over an individual only nominating people they know they will get good ratings from is not justified, it still leaves possible the option of the individual's line manager or HR to "approve" the suggested list of feedback givers or to, with the consent of the focal manager, add one or two more.

One aspect of feedback that cannot really be controlled is how positive or negative it is. Covering letters to feedback givers can emphasize the need for evidence-based, helpful feedback, but little more. This is an area of concern, as in the conventional performance appraisal setting it has long been recognized that an appraisee's tolerance of critical comments is limited, and that after more than just a couple of areas of weakness being highlighted (especially if they are not balanced with any positive feedback) they may switch off or become too defensive to be open-minded about improvement and development (Fletcher, 2008). This is borne out in the MSMR context by Smither and Walker (2004) who analyzed the impact of upward feedback ratings as well as narrative comments over a one-year period for 176 managers. They found that those who received a small number of unfavorable behaviorally based comments improved more than other managers but that those who received a large number (relative to positive comments) significantly declined in performance. Interestingly, Nowack (2009) links these findings on responses to criticism with recent neuroscience research (Eisenberger, Lieberman, & Williams, 2003), which shows that emotional hurt and rejection – as in poorly designed and delivered feedback interventions – can actually trigger the same neurophysiologic pathways associated with physical pain and suffering. There are stories of focal managers suffering nervous break-downs or attempting self-harm following feedback, but the truth of these is difficult to establish – they may be apocryphal or at least greatly exaggerated. However, just the pos-sibility of adverse emotional reactions to negative feedback is perhaps a reason in itself why someone other than the focal manager should have access to the feedback report and thus be in a position to identify and handle the risks that might arise if a vulnerable or insecure focal manager might receive painful feedback. This raises a question about the possible "vetting" or "filtering" of 360-degree feedback – a few organizations have been known to remove any especially blunt, unhelpful, or potentially hurtful written comments from the feedback report before the focal manager sees them. This kind of partial censorship raises ethical issues, some of which support it and some of which go against it.

When it comes to using feedback for development, setting realistic improvement goals, both in terms of difficulty and quantity, is likely to be very important. Following on from the observation above that after more than a couple of critical comments people tend to switch off, seeking to tackle more than two development needs in one review period might be too much for some managers (though they can cope with additional strength-based development actions). This will also be impacted by the individual's self-efficacy (see below). One of the clearest messages from the research is that in terms of feedback, one size most definitely does *not* fit all. Characteristics of the focal manager have a crucial bearing on how feedback is received and the extent to which it results in developmental action. As we have seen, three interlinked attributes in particular stand out – self efficacy, core self-evaluation, and having a consistent tendency to over-rate oneself. Individuals who have a high generalized level of self-efficacy are more likely to attempt development activities, so it would be helpful for a coach working with focal managers to implement the development implications of feedback to have a measure of their self-efficacy; this could be taken pre- or post-feedback from one of the various short questionnaires avail-able. Indeed, it would be helpful to look beyond just self-efficacy and to have a measure of core self-evaluation (Judge et al., 2003). Both the kind and degree of support given and the number and difficulty of the development goals set might be adjusted in light of the focal manager's scores on these measures. Likewise, if it appears that an individual consistently rates themselves higher than they are rated by others – and especially if this is associated with very high levels of self-esteem – then the approach to using the feedback in development will need to be adjusted. As suggested by Halman and Fletcher (2001), a much tougher and probably more persistent approach to discussing the feedback may be necessary with such people, and closer monitoring of post-feedback development action. On the other hand, under-raters may need a softer, more encouraging approach; this is particularly so where the under-rating seems to stem from some lack of self-efficacy or of self-belief generally. Feedback counselors need to be aware that women in particular seem to be more modest in their self-assessments; obviously this is not true in every case, but it does come through in the literature quite often (e.g., Ostroff, Atwater, & Feinberg, 2004).

Finally, in this domain, a feedback coach would find it helpful to have some other per-sonality questionnaire data in deciding what approach to take in helping a focal manager to arrive at, and implement, a personal development plan. In particular, if the individual scores high on Openness to Experience and on Conscientiousness, they are more likely to be constructive and diligent in their attitude and approach to their own development than if they are low in these attributes. Overall, then, making available measures of core self-evaluation and of the "Big 5" personality dimensions, along with identifying over- and under-rating tendencies should help feedback coaches tailor their approach to suit the focal manager's make-up. Quite apart from that, though, using personality questionnaires in combination with 360-degree feedback is likely to be fruitful in working out development strategies. As Guenole et al. (2011) and others have found, 360-feedback ratings correlate with the focal managers' personality attributes, and an understanding of that relationship should help focal managers and the coaches working with them to understand some of the characteristics that underlie the behaviors reflected in the feedback, and as a result to target development activities accordingly. For instance, if an individual is deeply introverted, there is likely to be limited mileage in targeting behavioral change that would need them to adopt a much more outgoing approach to others – better by far to find situations that suit their make-up and strengths.

With regard to culture, the picture is perhaps more complicated and also rather thin in terms of the amount of research. Nonetheless, the implications from the studies we do have suggest the need for particular care to be taken both in the pre-feedback briefing and in post-feedback developmental follow up where focal managers and feedback givers may well be from different cultural backgrounds. In particular, feedback givers from high-PD and highly collectivist cultures may need support and encouragement to give honest and direct feedback, while focal managers who are from high-PD cultures may need more persuasion than most of the value of (in particular) upward feedback and perhaps also in the merits of modesty and realism in self-assessments. In contrast, focal managers from highly collectivist cultures might benefit from encouragement to be a little less modest and more inclined to take personal credit for what they have achieved where this is appropriate.

Future Research

Growth in the use of 360-degree feedback was swift, and – partly because it lent itself to it – attracted a good deal of research, though perhaps in that sense it has become a little less "fashionable" as a topic because so many issues have already been investigated. But the question of how best to use the feedback to drive development is still one that needs further study. There are some general themes that would be desirable in future research, and two of these are, first, more use of control groups or conditions, and, second, better measures of actual development activity (both in terms of its relevance to the feedback and its effectiveness) undertaken post-feedback by focal managers. However, to move to more specific issues, the following are important to address.

1   It would be helpful to have more research that made planned comparisons of the effects of different coaching approaches to using feedback. There is little doubt that this is one of the weakest features of the research profile in this area. Although writers such as Nowack (2009) have offered models for coaching using 360 feedback that are based on research done to date, such models are inferred from data mostly collected for other purposes rather than being based on studies that sought to directly compare and evaluate the effectiveness of different methods of coaching and of using 360 feedback within them. Much as this is needed, it has to be recognized that carrying out research of this kind is bedeviled with methodological problems. For example, how does one disentangle the possible effects (e.g., through personality or competence) of the individual coach from the method of coaching and feedback use, or indeed of the efficacy of the 360 feedback system itself? How often do we encounter circumstances that allow us to randomly allocate people seeking coaching, or the coaches themselves, to one method or another? The likelihood is that any studies of this kind are likely to be rather limited in scale and involve small samples or possibly be limited to qualitative methods – but they would still be helpful and certainly a lot better than no studies at all!

2   Another area that should prove fruitful is research on the impact of adopting different feedback development strategies according to focal manager personality attributes. Thus, for example, with individuals who display a tendency to over-rate themselves (compared to others) when invited to do self-assessment in the context of 360 feedback, is there more change in subsequent self-view as a result of a direct and "tougher" feedback giving style being adopted with them than when the traditionally more tentative feedback style is used? The relationship between a focal manager's core self-evaluation and responses to feedback more generally is a subject that warrants further study.

3   In performance appraisal, research has generally shown that a balanced amount of positive and negative feedback produces the best results in terms of post-appraisal motivation and attitude. In particular, more than a couple of critical comments seem to reduce motivation. There has been only one study in the 360-feedback context that addresses this (Smither & Walker, 2004 – mentioned above) and that examined the degree of criticism only. It would be useful to have more research on this and in particular on what is the optimal balance between negative and positive comments to achieve the best post-feedback results.

4   As noted earlier, the amount of empirical evidence on cultural differences and their potential impact in giving and receiving 360-degree feedback is rather small – so almost any research on this subject would be welcome! In particular, examining some of the consequences of the kinds of contrast that can occur in PD and/or individualism between feedback givers and focal managers in multicultural workforces, using qualitative methods, might be illuminating in terms of how to avoid or handle the possible problems and misunderstandings that could arise.

Conclusions

Multisource feedback can, we know, achieve positive outcomes in the right circumstances. It continues to be widely applied, though less often in the same way it originally was because when it was very new, organizations were inclined to follow a "sheep-dip" approach, that is, all managers at a certain level would be put through it. This was usually for developmental purposes. Now, it is increasingly used as an input to performance appraisal. In some respects, 360-degree feedback is a victim of its own success – today, many managers have been through it several times and whilst familiarity may not actually breed contempt, it may lead to the process being approached a little less assiduously by both them and their feedback givers. Fortunately, in the developmental context, there is a tendency for it to be applied in a more targeted manner, for individual managers, or for a specific team, or in one section of an organization, which helps keep it "fresh." This targeted use makes much sense, as it can be a powerful diagnostic tool in looking at team functioning as well as for an individual. However, this does often mean it has to be tailored to the specific situation or group, potentially making it a more resource-intensive exercise if the questionnaires devised are to be properly validated. When used for an individual manager, very often it will be a largely qualitative exercise carried out by a coach. Irrespective of these trends, only when we can factor in all the varying influences on eliciting and using 360-degree feedback will we be in a position to predict its outcomes and effectiveness in generating positive behavioral change. Indeed, the more focused application of such feedback places even greater emphasis on understanding the variables that might be relevant to its effectiveness in a particular situation or context.

References

Antonioni, D. (1996). Designing an effective 360-degree appraisal feedback process. *Organizational Dynamics*, 25, 24–38.

Antonioni, D., & Wohr, D. (2001). Improving the quality of multisource rater performance. In D. Bracken, C., Timmreck, & A. Church (Eds.), *Handbook of Multisource Feedback* (pp. 114–129). San Francisco: Jossey-Bass.

Atwater, L., & Brett, J. (2006). Feedback format: Does it influence manager's reactions to feedback? *Journal of Occupational and Organizational Psychology*, 79, 517–532.

Atwater, L., Ostroff, C., Waldman, D., Robie, C., & Johnson, K. M. (2005). Self–other agreement: Comparing its relationship with performance in the US and Europe. *International Journal of Selection and Assessment*, 13, 25–40.

Bailey, C., & Austin, M. (2006). 360 degree feedback and development outcomes: The role of feedback characteristics, self-efficacy, and importance of feedback dimensions to focal managers' current role. *International Journal of Selection and Assessment*, 14, 51–66.

Bailey, C., & Fletcher, C. (2002a). When do other people's opinions matter? The credibility of feedback from co-workers. BPS Occupational Psychology Conference, Blackpool, January.

Bailey, C. & Fletcher, C. (2002b). The impact of multiple source feedback on management development: Findings from a longitudinal study. *Journal of Organizational Behaviour*, 23, 853–867.

Bailey, C., & Fletcher, C. (2008). Performance management and appraisal – An international perspective. In M. M. Harris (Ed.), *The Handbook of Research in International Human Resource Management* (pp. 125–143). Organization Management Series. Mahwah, NJ: Erlbaum.

Bandura, A. (1977). Self-efficacy: Towards a unifying theory of behavioral change. *Psychological Review*, 84, 191–215.

Bastos, M., & Fletcher, C. (1995). Exploring the individual's perception of sources and credibility of feedback in the work environment. *International Journal of Selection and Assessment*, 3, 29–40.

Bernadin, H., Tyler, C., & Villanova, P. (2009). Rating level and accuracy as a function of rater personality. *International Journal of Selection and Assessment*, 17, 300–310.

Bono, J. E., & Colbert, A. E. (2005). Understanding responses to multi-source feedback: The role of core self-evaluations. *Personnel Psychology*, 58, 171–203.

Bracken, D., & Rose, D. (2011). When does 360-degree feedback create behavior change? And how would we know it when it does? *Journal of Business and Psychology*, 26, 183–192.

Brett, J. F., & Atwater, L. E. (2001). 360 degree feedback: Accuracy, reactions and perceptions of usefulness. *Journal of Applied Psychology*, 86, 930–942.

Brutus, S., Derayeh, M., Fletcher, C., Bailey, C., Velazquez, P., Shi, K., Simon, C., & Labath, V. (2006). Multisource feedback systems: A six-country comparative analysis. *International Journal of Human Resource Management*, 17, 1888–1906.

Brutus, S., Fleenor, J., & London, M. (1998). Does 360 degre feedback work in different industries? A between-industry comparison of the reliability and validity of multi-source performance ratings. *Journal of Management Development*, 17, 177–190.

Brutus, S., Petosa, S., & Aucoin, E. (2005). Who will evaluate me? Rater selection in multi-source assessment contexts. *International Journal of Selection and Assessment*, 13, 129–138.

Carrick, P., & Williams, R. (1999). Development centres: A review of assumptions. *Human Resource Management Journal*, 9, 77–92.

Church, A. H. (1997). Managerial self-awareness in high performing individuals in organizations. *Journal of Applied Psychology*, 82, 281–292.

Dai, G., De Meuse, K., & Peterson C. (2010). Impact of multi-source feedback on leadership competency development: A longitudinal field study. *Journal of Managerial Issues*, 22, 197–219.

Eisenberger, N., Lieberman, M., & Williams, K. (2003). Does rejection hurt? An MRI study of social exclusion. *Science*, 302, 290–292.

Facteau, J., & Craig, S. B. (2001). Are performance appraisal ratings from different rater sources comparable? *Journal of Applied Psychology*, 86, 215–227.

Fletcher, C. (1997). "Self-awareness – a neglected attribute in selection and assessment'. *International Journal of Selection and Assessment,* 5, 183–187.

Fletcher, C. (2001). Performance appraisal and performance management: The developing research agenda. *Journal of Occupational and Organizational Psychology,* 74, 473–487.

Fletcher, C. (2008). *Appraisal, Feedback and Development: Making Performance Review Work.* London: Routledge.

Fletcher, C., & Baldry, C. (1999). Multi-source feedback systems: A research perspective. In C. L. Cooper & I. Robertson (Eds.), *International Review of Industrial and Organizational Psychology* (vol. 14, pp. 149–193). New York/Chichester: John Wiley & Sons, Inc.

Fletcher, C., & Baldry, C. (2000). A study of individual differences and self-awareness in the context of multi-source feedback. *Journal of Occupational and Organizational Psychology,* 73, 303–319.

Fletcher, C., Baldry, C., & Cunningham-Snell, N. (1997). The psychometric properties of 360-degree feedback: An empirical study and a cautionary tale. *International Journal of Selection and Assessment,* 5, 183–187.

Fletcher, C., & Perry, E. (2001). Performance appraisal and feedback: A consideration of national culture and a review of contemporary trends. In N. Anderson, D. Ones, H. Sinangil, & C. Viswesvaran (Eds.), *International Handbook of Industrial, Work and Organizational Psychology* (vol. 1, pp. 127–144). Beverly Hills, CA: Sage.

Gentry, W., Yip, J., & Hannum, K. (2010). Self–observer rating discrepancies of managers in Asia: A study of derailment characteristics and behaviours in Southern and Confucian Asia. *International Journal of Selection and Assessment,* 18, 237–250.

Gillespie, T. L. (2005). Internationalizing 360-degree feedback: Are subordinate ratings comparable? *Journal of Business and Psychology,* 19, 361–382.

Greguras, G. J., Robie, C., Schleicher, D. J., & Goff, M. (2003). A field study of the effects of rating purpose on the quality of multisource ratings. *Personnel Psychology,* 56, 1–21.

Guenole, N., Cockerill, T., Chamurro-Premuzic T., & Smillie, L. (2011). Evidence of the validity of 360 dimensions in the presence of rater-source factors. *Consulting Psychology: Practice and Research,* 63, 203–218.

Halman, F., & Fletcher, C. (2000). The impact of development center participation and the role of individual differences in changing self assessments. *Journal of Occupational and Organizational Psychology,* 73, 423–442.

Hoffman, B., Lance, C. E., Bynum, B., & Gentry, W. A. (2010). Rater source effects are alive and well after all. *Personnel Psychology,* 63, 119–151.

Hofstede, G. (1980). *Culture's Consequences: International Differences in Work-Related Values.* Beverly Hills, CA: Sage.

Hofstede, G. (2001). *Culture's Consequences: Comparing Values, Behaviors, Institutions and Organizations Across Nations.* Thousand Oaks, CA: Sage.

Jones, L., & Fletcher, C. (2002). Self-assessment in a selection situation: An evaluation of different measurement approaches. *Journal of Occupational and Organizational Psychology,* 75, 145–161.

Jones, L., & Fletcher, C. (2004). The impact of measurement conditions on the validity of self-assessment in a selection setting. *European Journal of Work and Organizational Psychology,* 13, 101–111.

Judge, T. A., Erez, A., Bono, J., & Thoreson, C. (2003). The core self-evaluations scale: Development of a measure. *Personnel Psychology,* 56, 303–332.

Kluger, A. N., & DeNisi, A. (1996). The effects of feedback interventions on performance: A historical review, a meta-analysis, and a preliminary feedback intervention theory. *Psychological Bulletin,* 119, 254–284.

Kwiatkowski, R. (2006). Inside-out and outside-in: The use of personality and 360 degree data in executive coaching. In H Brunning (Ed.), *Executive Coaching: Systems-Psychodynamic Perspectives* (pp. 153–182). London: Karnac.

London, M., & Smither, J. W. (1995). Can multi-source feedback change self awareness and behavior? Theory-based applications and directions for research. *Personnel Psychology,* 48, 803–839.

Malling, B., Bonderup, T., Mortensen, L., Riingsted, C., & Scherpbier, A. (2009). Effects of multi-source feedback on developmental plans for leaders of postgraduate medical eduction. *Medical Education,* 43, 159–167.

Maurer, T., Mitchell, D., & Barbeite, F. (2002). Predictors of attitudes toward a 360 degree feedback system and involvement in post-feedback management development activity. *Journal of Occupational and Organizational Psychology, 75*, 87–107.

McDowall, A., & Kurtz, R. (2008). Effective integration of 360 degree feedback into the coaching process. *Coaching Psychologist, 4*, 7–19.

Meyer, H. H., Kay, E., & French, J. R. P. (1965). Split roles in performance appraisal. *Harvard Business Review, 43*, 123–129.

Nowack, K. M. (2009). Leveraging multirater feedback to facilitate successful behavioral change. *Consulting Psychology Journal: Practice and Research, 61*(4), 280–297.

Ostroff, C., Atwater, L. E., & Feinberg, B. J. (2004). Understanding self–other agreement: A look at rater and ratee characteristics, context and outcomes. *Personnel Psychology, 57*, 333–376.

Peretz, H., & Fried, Y. (2012). National cultures, performance appraisal practices, and organizational absenteeism and turnover: A study across 21 countries. *Journal of Applied Psychology, 97*, 448–459.

Pfau, B., & Kay, I. (2002). Does 360-degree feedback negatively affect company performance? *HR Magazine, 47*(6), 54–59.

Randall, R., & Sharples, D. (2012). The impact of rater agreeableness and rating context on the evaluation of poor performance. *Journal of Occuptional and Organizational Psychology, 85*, 42–59.

Salam, S., Cox, J., & Sims, H. (1997). In the eye of the beholder: How leadership relates to 360 degree performance ratings. *Group & Organization Management, 22*, 185–209.

Smither, J., Brett, J., & Atwater, L. (2008). What do leaders recall about their multisource feedback? *Journal of Leadership and Organizational Studies, 14*, 202–218.

Smither, J. W., London, M., Flautt, R., Vargas, Y., & Kucine, I. (2003). Can working with an executive coach improve multisource feedback ratings over time? A quasi-experimental field study. *Personnel Psychology, 56*, 23–44.

Smither, J. W., London, M., & Reilly, R. R. (2005). Does performance improve following multi-source feedback? A theoretical model, meta-analysis, and review of empirical findings. *Personnel Psychology, 58*, 33–66.

Smither, J. W., & Walker, A. G. (2004). Are the characteristics of narrative comments related to improvement in multi-rater feedback ratings over time? *Personnel Psychology, 89*, 575–581.

Tyson, S., & Ward, P. (2004). The use of 360 degree feedback technique in the evaluation of management learning. *Management Learning, 35*(2), 205–223.

Varela, O., & Primeaux, S. (2008). Do cross-cultural values affect multisource feedback dynamics? The case of high power distance and collectivism in two Latin American countries. *International Journal of Selection and Assessment, 16*, 134–142.

Violato, C., Lockyer, J., & Fidler, H. (2008). Changes in performance: A 5-year longitudinal study of participants in a multi-source feedback programme. *Medical Education, 42*, 1007–1013.

Walker, A. G., & Smither, J. W. (1999). A five year study of upward feedback: What managers do with their results matters. *Personnel Psychology, 52*, 393–423.

Woo, S., Sims, C., Rupp, D., & Gibbons A. (2008). Development engagement within and following development assessment centers: Considering feedback favourability and self–assessor agreement. *Personnel Psychology, 61*, 727–759.

25

Feedback, Development, and Social Networks

Piet Van den Bossche, Sara Van Waes, and Janine van der Rijt

Introduction

This chapter explores the idea that professional development is for a large part driven by discursive interactions with other persons. Specifically, we will look into feedback as a crucial aspect of these interactions. This interest in the social aspect of professional development correlates with a lot of current research that suggests that a majority of what people learn is learned informally on-the-job from the people with whom they work (Eraut, 2007; Tannenbaum et al., 2010). Given this social nature of learning in the workplace, the ways in which professionals actively form and use their interpersonal relations has become an increasing focus in the literature (Brueller & Carmelli, 2011; van der Rijt et al., 2013; Grant & Ashford, 2008; Hakkarainen et al., 2004). The perspective of social networks is forwarded to grasp the learning that takes place in interpersonal interactions. In this chapter, we provide an overview of research that touches upon the role of these social networks in professional development. In this way we also show the potential of social network methodology to understand the social nature of professional development in general and feedback processes specifically.

First, we will provide a reflection on the different strands of research and theoretical perspectives that have taken this "social turn" in the understanding of professional development. This sets the scene to focus on the value of feedback provided by people in our surroundings. Next, we will describe how a social network perspective can be used to provide a common angle to grasp the role of the relationships that provide feedback. This is followed by a description of different aspects of networks that are identified in research as potentially important in relation to feedback in the workplace. This chapter finishes by identifying paths for future research and theoretical and practical implications.

The Wiley Blackwell Handbook of the Psychology of Training, Development, and Performance Improvement,
First Edition. Edited by Kurt Kraiger, Jonathan Passmore, Sigmar Malvezzi, and Nuno Rebelo dos Santos.
© 2015 John Wiley & Sons Ltd. Published 2020 by John Wiley & Sons Ltd.

Social Turn in Professional Development

The increasing need for highly skilled professionals with up-to-date competences has resulted in a growing interest of organizations for learning and development. Organizations realize that talented employees are their "most valuable asset and the key to organizational success" (van der Rijt et al., 2012, p. 234; Whelan, Collings, & Donnellan, 2010). This has resulted in investment in formalized training programs (Tannenbaum et al., 2010). Nowadays, it is acknowledged that informal learning is at least as – if not more – important as formal learning in organizational settings (Eraut, 2004; Tynjälä, 2008).

Research has increasingly taken a more social perspective on expertise development. Borgatti and Cross (2003), for example, discussed how high performance is not only determined by an individual's know-what (declarative knowledge) and know-how (procedural knowledge), but also by his or her "know-who." These studies have revealed how high-performers in organizations succeed by developing networks that target and extend their abilities (Cross & Thomas, 2008). Palonen and colleagues emphasized that learning from the experiences of others is important for expertise development, which they described as "networked expertise" (Palonen et al., 2004). This "social turn" has given rise to (renewed) interest in and recognition of communities of practice, networking, developmental networks, and so on. They all share that learning is foremost social, collaborative, and to a high extent informal.

A key component of this social and collaborative informal learning in the workplace is feedback (Tannenbaum et al., 2010). Developing professionals are in need of feedback to be able to adjust their behavior and processes (Salas & Rosen, 2010). Exemplary is the research of Sonnentag (2000), which showed that expert performers actively sought more feedback from colleagues than moderate performers in technical jobs. The next section elaborates on the importance of feedback for professional development.

Feedback and Professional Development

Feedback

The value of feedback in supporting learning and motivation to learn has been long-standing and widely accepted (Ashford & Cummings, 1983; Herold & Greller, 1977; Ilgen, Fisher, & Taylor, 1979). Feedback can be defined as information provided by an agent (e.g., teacher, peer, book, parent, self, experience) about aspects of performance or understanding (Hattie & Timperley, 2007). Based on feedback, the recipient can identify the causes of his/her effective or ineffective performance and adjust to achieve higher levels of performance (Salas & Rosen, 2010). London (2003) stressed that this includes a dynamic interaction process between the source of the feedback and the recipient, which offers information about performance.

Despite the established importance of feedback for any learning process, scholars contend that the mechanisms of feedback remain unclear (Anseel, Lievens, & Levy, 2007; Mulder & Ellinger, 2013; Van der Rijt et al., 2012). This call to further our understanding of feedback processes in the workplace is reflected in the available evidence on the relationship between feedback and performance: feedback does not uniformly improve performance nor produce the expected effects in organizational settings (Alvero, Bucklin, & Austin, 2001; Kluger & DeNisi, 1996).

(Informal) feedback and feedback seeking

The belief in feedback and the constant need for highly skilled employees with up-to-date competences has led organizations to invest in formal human resource programs in which feedback is incorporated, such as performance management, training programs, mentoring, coaching, and 360-degree feedback (Higgins & Kram, 2001; van der Rijt et al., 2012; Van Gennip et al., 2010).

On the other hand, together with the insight that the majority of what employees learn is gained informally on the job from their colleagues and peers, more attention has been drawn to informal feedback processes. Moreover, employees are expected to take more responsibility for their own professional development (Grant, Parker, & Collins, 2009; Kim, Hon, & Crant, 2009). An important aspect of this proactive attitude is feedback seeking (van der Rijt et al., 2012). Research showed that employees are not passively waiting for feedback but are proactive in seeking feedback during casual day-to-day interactions (Ashford, Blatt, & Vande Walle, 2003; Crant, 2000; Grant & Ashford, 2008).

The concept of feedback seeking is sometimes used interchangeably with similar concepts of information seeking and help seeking. These concepts all stress the proactive search to gain specific resources. Research on information seeking refers to a proactive search for information, advice, or knowledge (e.g., Borgatti & Cross, 2003; Cross, Borgatti, & Parker, 2001; Cross & Sproull, 2004). Feedback-seeking behavior and help-seeking behavior can be considered as specific types of information-seeking behavior. "Feedback seeking" concerns the proactive search for day-to-day feedback information and can be described as a self-evaluation process (Anseel, Lievens, & Levy, 2007). Feedback information is often more "emotionally charged" (Ashford, Blatt, & Vande Walle, 2003, p. 779) as it concerns information about the self. Help seeking typically is problem-focused, involves intentional action, and requires interpersonal interaction (Cornally & McCarthy, 2011). Conversely, feedback and information seeking do not necessarily involve a specific problem or difficulty, and direct interaction with other people is not required (Bamberger, 2009; Lee, 1997, 2002). Feedback and information can be attained indirectly without interacting with other people, for example, by monitoring, while help seeking needs direct interaction with others.

Dimensions of feedback

Major dimensions identified in feedback studies are helpfulness, sign (positive vs. negative), frequency, and source of the feedback (Becker & Klimosky, 1989; Shute, 2008). In this respect the dimension's source and helpfulness of the feedback are of particular importance.

The *source* of feedback is studied within feedback literature. In this case, an interesting field of research is that of multirater or multisource feedback. It is argued that by involving multiple sources of feedback, the information received is much richer and therefore more informative for behavioral change. The review study of Smither, London, and Reilly (2005) evidenced small but significant effects of receiving feedback from multiple raters on performance improvement. In addition, it is questioned if the source of feedback makes a difference in the reaction to the multirater feedback (i.e., performance improvement, undertaken of developmental activities). In general there are five sources of feedback that can be categorized in three distinct sets. Firstly, there are the other individuals who have been able to observe the recipient's behavior and can evaluate it. Most frequently cited in this category are peers, co-workers, and supervisors. Secondly, there is the task itself and the task environment as a source of feedback. Thirdly, individuals are also able to judge themselves and act as a source of feedback (Herold & Greller, 1977). An interesting study conducted by Maurer, Mitchell, and Barbeite (2002) noted that, one might logically believe that the order of importance of feedback source to those being rated would reflect the traditional hierarchy of power. Ratings from one's supervisors should be more important than those of one's peers. In turn, ratings from one's peers should be more important than those of one's subordinates. (p. 88)

However, the results of their study using multirater feedback for developmental purposes indicated that peer feedback had more effect on the developmental activities undertaken than the supervisor feedback. This line of research on sources of feedback underlines the importance of understanding the feedback network around people.

With regard to *helpfulness*, Kluger and Denisi (1996) proposed the feedback intervention theory (FIT) explaining the effectiveness of feedback or: "how helpful is feedback for the learner?" The theory states that when we notice a gap between feedback and our goal, we strive to reduce the gap. According to DeNisi and Kluger (2000) the effectiveness of feedback and the mechanism of feedback centers around the attention created at the appropriate level. Feedback on the task motivation level (i.e., related to the actual performance), or feedback at the task learning level (i.e., related to the details of performing the task) in combination with the proper information as to how to improve, will provide for the necessary behavioral change and thereby increase performance. This theory makes clear that feedback is not only about providing an evaluation against certain standards. Appreciating the value of feedback requires understanding of the information and advice that is part of the interaction.

These different insights into the broad field of feedback research underline that feedback is crucial for professional development. Hereby, attention has shifted from formal feedback processes to the more informal feedback seeking of employees. With regard to this feedback, the value of multiple sources has been shown and helpfulness is crucial. With respect to the latter, FIT argued that the informational value of these feedback processes is crucial. Thus, feedback should not be seen as a strict evaluative response, but also includes information, advice, and help.

In spite of this generalized belief in the value of feedback and the abundant research that is available on feedback and feedback seeking, our understanding of the processes by which feedback is informally initiated is still incomplete (van der Rijt et al., 2012). In particular, we know little about the relational aspects that facilitate the processes by which feedback is initiated (van der Rijt et al., 2012). This is of importance, as these social interactions have become more prominent in current workplaces.

These insights bring us to our argument that a social network perspective on feedback (seeking) in the workplace can further our understanding of processes of feedback (seeking), given that these are relational by nature and involve multiple sources. In the following section, we will first present the foundations of a social network perspective. Next, we will show how this perspective can further our understanding of feedback (seeking) processes and their influence on professional development.

A Social Network Perspective

In the past couple of decades, research has emphasized the degree to which employees use information obtained from people in their networks to do their work more effectively (Borgatti & Cross, 2003; Cross et al., 2001; Reinholt, Pedersen, & Foss, 2011). Social networks can be defined as "a group of collaborating (and/or competing) entities that are related to each other" (Håkansson, Havila, & Pedersen, 1999). The theory behind social networks focuses on explaining the interpersonal mechanisms and social structures that exist among interacting units such as people within an organization (Wasserman & Faust, 1994; Hatala & Fleming, 2007).

A number of theories have been developed that draw on a social network perspective. The most popular linkage to social network theory is the notion of *social capital* (Adler & Kwon, 2002; Halpern, 2005; Lin, 2001). Coleman (1988, p. 16) argued that "unlike other forms of capital, social capital inheres in the structure of relations between actors and among actors. It is lodged neither in the actors themselves nor in physical implements of production." The central proposition of social capital theory is that networks of relationships constitute a valuable resource (Nahapiet & Ghoshal, 1998). Social networks and their central theoretical foundation describe the transmission of knowledge or useful information through interpersonal ties and social contacts with individuals (Kali & Reyes, 2007). Networks can take on various forms including friendship or advice and cut across formal and informal relationships (Nohria, 1992). This also implies that multiple things can flow through these ties such as information but also resources or affection (Nohria, 1992; Nohria & Eccles, 1992). Developing personal ties (i.e., relations), whether dyadic or multiple, gives individuals the chance to be exposed to different kinds of information and exists as the precondition for knowledge transfer (Dal Fiore, 2007) and learning (Borgatti & Cross, 2003; Reinholt, Pederson, & Foss, 2011).

Social network theory takes shape in a variety of mechanisms that may explain the flow of resources in a network (Carrington, Scott, & Wasserman, 2005; Scott, 2000; Wasserman & Faust, 1994; Moolenaar, 2010). The most notable mechanisms are weak-tie theory (Granovetter, 1973), structural hole theory (Burt, 1992), and social resources theory (e.g., Lin, Ensel, & Vaughn, 1981).

Weak-tie theory focuses on the characteristics of ties between actors, where *tie* stands for the relationship between actors (strength of ties); structural hole theory emphasizes the bridging properties between individual groups or networks; and social resources theory focuses on the characteristics of the contacts within the network versus the nature of the tie or the tie pattern among contacts. A subset of work in the network field has clearly emphasized the importance of networks for individual performance (Borgatti & Cross, 2003). Most of this work has focused on the structural aspects of networks (e.g., Burt, 1992). Recently, increasing attention has been paid to relational aspects. Scholars have started to examine the nature and content of relations, and the behavioral network aspects related to individual behavior and performance (e.g., Cross & Thomas, 2008; Hayton, Carnabuci, & Eisenberger, 2012; van der Rijt et al., 2013).

Social network analysis (SNA) provides a methodology aimed at analyzing participants' interactions to map the relationships between actors in the network, and uncovers the specific dynamics that exist in a group (Hatala & Fleming, 2007). Wasserman and Faust (1994, p. 21), in this respect, note the following: "these methods translate core concepts in social and behavioral theories into formal definitions expressed in relational terms." In this way the social network perspective is providing a methodology (SNA) that is able to present a fine-grained insight into the social environment and its structural, relational, and behavioral aspects. This indicates the potential of this perspective and methodology to enhance our understanding of feedback processes in the workplace.

Structural and Relational Characteristics of the Networks

In this chapter, we pointed out that providing feedback (including help, information, or advice) is an essential ingredient of professional development. We established the emerging consensus that relationships and interactions in the workplace are instrumental for professional development in general and for the provision of feedback in particular. Social network theory provides the tools to investigate professional development through a social lens. Network theory helps us to understand the structural properties and relational characteristics of networks. We will review how structural network properties affect the flow of resources (including feedback) between people. Moreover, we discuss how relational network characteristics influence the process of tie formation: which resources are available from what kind of people.

Structural network characteristics

Social network theory capitalizes on structural aspects of networks. Gaining insight into the structure or underlying patterns of networks enables us to grasp the connections between individuals, and to gain insight into the flow of resources between these individuals, such as information, knowledge, and materials. Social network theory enables us to capture these connections and resources in structural patterns. These structural patterns may enhance or constrain individuals' perceptions, opinions, and behavior. Network theory comprises a variety of mechanisms that enable the measurement of these structural properties.

Based on research on social networks, we will now review mechanisms that affect the decision to seek information from other people in or outside the workplace, and thus influence the extent to which feedback can be sought or received. Structural network boundaries affect the extent to which resources can flow between ties, and which resources can be fed back to individuals. The concepts forwarded (centrality, density, structural holes, and structural balance) are exemplary. They are identified in social network research as explanatory to understand effectiveness in social networks. For that reason, we forward them and discuss their implications for understanding feedback in organizations.

Centrality Centrality as a structural characteristic is frequently studied (Reinholt, Pedersen, & Foss, 2011; Sparrowe, Liden, & Kramer, 2001).Centrality provides an indication of which actors are most central in the network (Freeman, 1979). Employees in central network positions are defined as those that have many ties (Wasserman & Faust, 1994). Being connected to well-connected others means greater centrality. Ample research demonstrates a positive relationship between a central network position and knowledge sharing (e.g., Anderson, 2008; Reinholt, Pedersen, & Foss, 2011). Anderson (2008) points out that every tie in someone's network is a channel through which information may flow to and from that employee. This implies that employees in more central network positions have more relationships to draw on (Reinholt, Pedersen, & Foss, 2011). Degree centrality is probably the best known and straightforward form of centrality. It is measured by calculating "in-degree" and "out-degree." In-degree captures the amount of people who seek an individual out for resources. The more someone is nominated as a valuable resource in the network, the higher the in-degree. Whereas out-degree stands for the number of times an individual reaches out for resources. Applying the idea of centrality in networks to feedback processes implies that insight is given into the number ties (i.e., relationships) one receives or seeks feedback from. Or, in other words, the number of different feedback sources an employee can rely on.

In the past, feedback research that focused on formal feedback environments has studied multirater or multisource feedback. It has been argued that by involving multiple sources of feedback, the information received is much richer and therefore more informative for behavioral change. The review study of Smither, London, and Reilly (2005) evidenced small but significant effects of receiving feedback from multiple raters on performance improvement. These findings suggest that centrality is also in the case of feedback a positive characteristic.

A study by Van den Bossche, Segers, and Jansen (2010) provided evidence for this idea in the context of informal feedback processes. This research questioned the role of feedback generated within the social network in the work environment. It was studied how this relates to creating motivation-to-transfer and fostering transfer after having followed a training. This is of particular importance as the feedback provided in the work environment on the application of newly learned skills in the workplace helps to close the gap between the current performance and the desired goal of full application of what is learned during the training. In the light of centrality as structural network characteristic, an interesting pattern of results was found. The number of ties (or feedback sources) within the social network –higher centrality – has a positive effect. This in contrast to the frequency of feedback; no relation was established with outcomes. In this regard, it is important to note that when the feedback literature refers to the frequency of feedback, it aims at how much and how often feedback is given (Becker & Klimoski, 1989). The social network perspective and methodology that was taken in this research enabled disentanglement of two different aspects: (a) the number of ties, that is the number of people (or relationships) someone receives feedback from, and (b) the frequency, referring to how often one receives feedback from a particular person in his/her network. The results confirmed that this separation between number of ties and frequency is valuable to further insight into the impact of increased feedback. These results suggest that simply giving more feedback is not sufficient. Becker and Klimoski (1989) noted and that simply increasing feedback can even be detrimental for learning (Schmidt, 1991). This study underscores the importance of centrality in feedback networks.

Density Network density or cohesion is related to the size of the network (Blau, 1977). It refers to the concentration of relationships within a network, and is calculated by dividing the possible number of ties by the actual number of ties. This implies that the greater the proportion of ties in the network, the more dense the network. People with denser networks might have more and more diverse access to resources as they have a higher number of connections. Resources can also be moved more quickly in a dense network than in a network with fewer ties (Scott, 2000).

The density of a feedback network can be of consequence for the availability and use of the feedback in that network. As the timeliness and accessibility of feedback are described as important characteristics of effective feedback, it would be interesting to question if the density of a network is facilitating this.

Structural holes Structural holes are holes in social structure that result from absent or weaker connections between individuals or groups in a social structure (Burt, 2002). Generally, the greater the density of a network, the fewer structural holes exist within the network. Structural holes can be "brokered" or bridged" by an individual connected to others that are sparsely connected or disconnected (Burt, 2005). Individuals acting as brokers or occupying bridging roles between people or groups can gain early access to information and control over how resources flow within the network. Ties that span across structural holes facilitate access to resources not readily available.

This would also imply that these "brokers" can provide feedback containing information that is new in the network. When describing the importance of centrality, it was shown that, with regard to feedback processes, having more ties is more effective as these bring different points of view. It is worthwhile questioning if these brokers bring more value into the network than others in the network.

Structural balance   Over time people seek balance in their networks. Structural balance theory poses that networks tend to be "transitive" (Heider, 1958). This means that people are more likely to exchange information, knowledge, or materials with friends of friends (transitive structures) than with friends of enemies or enemies of friends (intransitive structures) (Wasserman & Faust, 1994). Structural balance is said to reduce psychological discomfort arising from cognitive dissonance (Festinger, 1957). It is one of the mechanisms that explains why subgroups or cliques emerge, offering the network some balance or stability over time (Kossinets & Watts, 2006). However, structural balance may also result in network homogeneity and redundant relationships, which can limit access to valuable information, knowledge, or materials (Burt, 1997).

This tendency in networks to look for balance can also be unfavorable in the context of informative feedback. Cognitive dissonance can be an attribute of valuable feedback, so lacking this in the network is not optimal.

Relational network characteristics

As we discussed, mainstream network research capitalizes on structural properties of networks. Recent network research somewhat breaks with this mainstream network research by not only measuring structural properties of networks, but also investigating how networks come to have such structures in the first place. Therefore, scholars increasingly paid attention to relational characteristics of network (Monge & Contractor, 2000; Borgatti & Cross, 2003). Seeking feedback from others is often informed by the seeker's perception of relational characteristics of others. Hence, relational network characteristics give us insight into the process of tie formation (or: how to build networks more effectively). Maintaining a broad conception of feedback, we will review exemplary relational network characteristics that influence the exchange of knowledge and information in networks.

Expertise, value and location   Borgatti and Cross (2003) indicate that network formation is facilitated by the following relational characteristics: (a) awareness of expertise, (b) value of expertise, (c) access to expertise, and (d) the possible cost of information. Seeking resources in the face of a new problem or opportunity is most likely affected by one's perception of the expertise of others. Tie formation based on perception of expertise requires that the individual knows that the other person has certain information, knowledge, or material, and that he or she values these resources. Determining how to gain timely access to this person affects the probability of seeking that person out for information in the future. Finally, Borgatti and Cross suggest that people consider the potential costs involved when seeking information from others. "Cost" implies interpersonal risks, for example, esteem and reputation issues, or obligations incurred. They also demonstrate that physical proximity plays an important part in information exchange (Borgatti & Cross, 2003). Access to resources is facilitated when they are available in the proximal workplace environment. Physical propinquity leads to exchange of resources, which stimulates organizations to enhance access between employees by considering open spaces, face-to-face meetings, or virtual (visual) work.

These relational characteristics can also be used to further understanding of feedback seeking. Being aware of expertise and valuing this expertise are important conditions of being able to find informative feedback and will therefore impact feedback-seeking behavior of professionals. Nadler, Ellis, and Bar (2003) suggested that employees sought more help from individuals whom they perceive as more knowledgeable than themselves. Also van de Wiel et al. (2011) found in their study on the learning of physicians that their primary reason to go to colleagues for advice was their expertise. Of course, one needs to be able to access the sources to gain feedback. Within feedback-seeking literature there is some evidence that accessibility affects the likelihood of asking a particular source for feedback (Vancouver & Morrison, 1995). Moreover, asking for feedback often implies the willingness to be vulnerable and put themselves at risk to another person; all possible costs of looking for feedback. In other words, trust seems crucial (Hofmann, Lei, & Grant, 2009). Eraut's study (2007) also showed that individuals were less reluctant to ask questions and look for input when they had a good trusting relationship with the help provider.

A study of van der Rijt et al. (2013) made use of a social network perspective to investigate some of these characteristics. They examined employees' relationships within their professional network, and their effect on help-seeking behavior. Participants in this study were 133 professionals working for various (multi)national corporations in the fields of management, accounting, finance, and control. An ego-centric survey was administered. This approach pictures the ego network, which consist of the focal node (i.e., ego) and the alters to whom the ego is directly connected (in some instances also the ties between the alters are considered). The studied relational characteristics of their professional network were awareness of expertise, accessibility, and trust. The purpose was to examine the extent to which these characteristics had an influence on the help-seeking behavior within these relations. More specifically, it was studied how these characteristics relate to the likelihood and frequency of help seeking, and to the quality of help that is received. The results of this study indicated that the perceptions of the provider's expertise, accessibility, and trust were positively associated with the likelihood to seek help, the frequency by which help is sought, and the perceived quality of help received.

Homophily Another key guiding principle in network formation is homophily. Homophily refers to the principle that "a contact between similar people occurs at a higher rate than between dissimilar people" (McPherson, Smith-Lovin, & Cook, 2001). People tend to interact with people similar to them (Kossinets & Watts, 2006), for example, people who share demographic similarities or equal work status generally interact (Boud & Middleton, 2003). Homophily influences the information people receive, the attitudes they form, and the interactions they experience (Burt, 2000b; Hinds et al., 2000). For example, people with more diverse networks demonstrate more innovation (Kilduff & Krackhardt, 2008, whereas homophily or similarity between people enhances the decay of their networks (Burt, 2000a).

In their research on feedback-seeking behavior, Van der Rijt, Van den Bossche, and Segers (2013) touched upon the issue of homophily, and in particular on the influence of (equal) work status. The purpose of this study was to investigate whether the position of employees in the organizational hierarchy is important in explaining their feedback-seeking behavior. They adopted a social network perspective by using an ego-centric network survey to investigate employees' feedback-seeking behavior within their professional networks. Data were collected from an online questionnaire returned from 243 employees working in a large multinational organization located in the Netherlands. The results of this study indicated that there is indeed an impact of employees' position in the organizational hierarchy on feedback-seeking behavior. In particular, the findings showed that employees frequently seek feedback from colleagues within the same department. However, managers or leaders seek significantly less feedback from colleagues in the same department and from coaches, compared to feedback seekers in other positions. In addition, the findings indicated that employees particularly value the feedback they received from employees in equal or higher hierarchical positions. Furthermore, the results showed that managers/leaders, coaches, and colleagues in the same department were strong predictors for the value someone attaches to the received feedback of these persons. In this way, this study showed how feedback seeking is impacted by the hierarchical relationships. These results also suggests that the tendencies in network development impact the feedback and information available to employees.

Strength of ties Another important concept in the exchange of resources, is strength of ties. Tie strength is an umbrella term that indicates the closeness or strength of relationships by measuring the frequency, (emotional) intensity, reciprocity, depth duration, or time spent in a relation (Marsden & Campbell, 1984). Strong relationships or ties connect to people that are close, whereas weak ties are looser contacts or acquaintances. Strong ties are instrumental in the diffusion of innovation, the transfer of tacit, sensitive, nonroutine, or complex information, and increased problem solving across boundaries within organizations (Reagans & McEvily, 2003; Uzzi, 1996). Strong social networks are also associated with increased individual and organizational performance (Burt, 1992; Hansen, 1999). In contrast, weak ties are more likely to bridge socially distant regions of a network, and thus more likely to gain access to new resources. Hence, the commonly adopted phrase "the strength of weak ties" (Granovetter, 1973). Weak ties play an important role in the formation of novel ideas and nonredundant information (Hansen, 1999; Levin & Cross, 2004). Clearly, both weak and strong ties bring different kinds of resources into a network. Therefore, a combination of both strong and weak ties in networks is often advised (Tenkasi & Chesmore, 2003).

With regard to feedback, the issue of strength of ties raises some interesting questions. We can question if the general reasoning on informational strength of each kind of tie (strong vs. weak) can be generalized to feedback processes. Given the fact that seeking, giving, and receiving feedback entails trust, the extent to which feedback processes in weak ties will be effective can be questioned (i.e., whether the receiver sees it as valuable feedback). Therefore, research should question if and under which circumstances potential valuable feedback sources available through weak ties are used.

Future Research

The above-presented insights provide arguments for the value of taking a social network perspective on feedback processes. Given this potential, we forward a range of challenges ahead. These challenges concern the methodology, network levels, content of interactions, and practical interventions.

Method

As indicated above, the use of social network methodology in feedback research can be a next step in understanding the complexities of feedback processes and their effectiveness. Instead of aggregating feedback from different sources (i.e., colleagues and supervisors), which is commonly the case when using questionnaires to assess feedback behavior in organizations, this methodology defines the different sources of feedback and enables questions on the influence of tie characteristics on feedback behavior. Findings suggested that applying such a social network methodology is valuable. In the research of van der Rijt et al. (2013) it has been showed through multilevel analyses that more variation is present at the tie level (relationships) than at the ego level (employees). This showed the significance of paying attention to the characteristics of the relationships in employees' networks. Future research on feedback that wants to grasp the relational aspects of feedback (seeking) should consider social network methodologies.

Social network analysis has been shown to be a powerful tool to grasp the current state of the network. However, the methodology only starts to explore how it can measure change in networks. Networks are dynamic and change over time. We are in need of ways to examine networks in order to grasp the dynamics of networks over time (Huisman & Snijders, 2003; Snijders, 2001, 2005, 2011). This would enable research on the relationship between network development and professional development. For example, it would provide the tools to study the impact of interventions aimed at the development of networks for professional development.

Level

In this chapter, we have predominantly used the social network perspective to unravel how relationships (i.e., ties) within individuals' networks function with regard to feedback processes. But, this perspective also enables an understanding of the network level. Both conceptually and methodologically, this network approach can help to provide insight in to the feedback environment of organizations.

Moreover, it can take the idea of "professional development through networks" one step further to the idea of "networked expertise" (Hakkarainen et al., 2004). The latter being more a network characteristic than an individual characteristic. In other words, which relationships do we want to foster in a group in order to leverage its collective expertise (Borgatti & Cross, 2003)? Feedback research from a network perspective has the potential to contribute to these issues greatly. The current literature has stressed feedback processes at the individual level to a large extent. Changing the focus to the network level raises the issue of providing feedback to collectives. Feedback to collectives (e.g., networks) brings into play a range of other processes with regard to perception and processing of feedback, which have received far less attention. For example, a recent review of Gabelica et al. (2012) on feedback to teams showed that, although research is widely available, almost no knowledge is gathered on processes that explain the effect of feedback. Also at this level, a social network perspective may provide a valuable contribution.

If we take it one level higher, the concept of culture can – and maybe should – be taken into account, given the central place of relationships in the network approach. Enabling a relational approach to feedback (seeking), the question arises how culture impacts these relations in a network. Does feedback seeking vary according to culture? Does feedback seeking have a greater importance in more relational cultures compared to less relational or more distant cultures?

Content

In this chapter feedback was conceived as a broad/multidimensional concept encompassing various resources, such as evaluation, information, knowledge, advice. We discussed the structural and relational dimension of networks, and the implications they can have for practice. Hereby, we gain insight into the shape or structure of networks, and in the relational factors that can influence the formation of these network structures. Yet, little research has investigated to what extent network content shapes network structure. A network concept that is highly relevant for this line of thought is "multiplexity." Multiplex relationships involve relationships that are characterized by a multiplicity of purposes, that is, the exchange of different types of resources with one tie/relationship (Lazega &

Pattison, 1999). For example, advice ties can be strengthened if a friendship tie also emerges. The more relationships link an individual to another, the stronger the link (Granovetter, 1973). Further research on the impact of multiplex ties on professional development is necessary, in order to further understand how networks at the workplace are shaped by their content by comparing and contrasting networks that transfer different content.

Another content-related matter that deserves further attention is the quality of inter-actions. Complementary to a structural network approach, we also need to pay attention to the quality of the content that flows through ties of networks in the workplace. Recent studies examine the quality of networks by looking at the nature and depth of ties, adopting a qualitative network approach (Coburn & Russell, 2008; Coburn et al., 2012; Van Waes et al., 2013). Qualitative network data enables us to examine whether interactions between people in the workplace involve, for example, swapping enter-taining stories, exchanging basic information, or collaborating intensively on shared products. They also allow us to investigate the interdependency between people, the depth of their exchanges, and the impact of their interactions on their professional development.

(Practical) interventions

Social network methodology is also forwarded and used as a mapping tool informing interventions. With regard to feedback, you can think of making employees' feedback networks visible. This can visualize the characteristics of these feedback networks, making them available for assessment based on our knowledge of qualities of networks for professional development. However, mapping alone does not necessarily provide a clear path to intervention. More information is needed on how to encourage strong networks when they do not exist or how to sustain them when they do (Coburn, Choi, & Mata, 2010). Preliminary research has shown that mapping informal networks using social network analysis can detect multiple (isolated) networks in organizations, connect ideas, and facilitate value creation (de Laat & Schreurs, 2013). Using a network approach enables organizations to link with existing informal networks, and unlock their potential for organizational learning by giving them a voice and making their results more explicit within the organization (de Laat & Schreurs, 2013; and see Cross et al., 2010, for concrete examples of network mapping as an intervention in organizations).

In this respect, Van den Bossche and Segers (2013) argued (from a social network perspective) that one of the main goals of HRD-interventions, such as training, needs to be to affect the social structure of organizations. The creation of a community may be one of the most significant and lasting consequences of training programs (Grup-pen et al., 2006). This is concurrent with a growing awareness in human resource management as a field. Snell, Shadur, and Wright (2002) stated that it is important to consider that HR strategy and practices transcend the development of knowledge, skills, and behaviors, to also incorporate the development of relationships and exchanges inside and outside the organization. This is not to say that these studies argue that installing a social structure is an end in itself, but that by focusing on developing an appropriate structure, processes such as informal learning and knowledge sharing are facilitated. Hatala and Fleming (2007), for example, advocate the use of social network analysis as a tool to analyze participants' organizational network relationships prior to training to help the facilitator, trainee, and supervisor gain an accurate picture of the transfer climate.

By concentrating on development of networks, these trainings indirectly support professional development and behavioral change. In particular, feedback (seeking) networks need to be considered.

Conclusion

Feedback has been established as a key ingredient in the support of learning and professional development. This has resulted in an ongoing interest both from research and practice. Practice has invested in a range of human resource programs that aim to foster valuable feedback for employees. Research has called for further understanding of feedback processes at the workplace.

This interest is concurrent with changes in the (understanding of) learning in the workplace. It is acknowledged that informal learning is an important driver of competence development. Moreover, the social nature of this informal learning is recognized. This is reflected in the development of our thinking about feedback. Feedback seeking is forwarded as important in current workplaces. Employees are expected to look actively for feedback and not to only wait passively for formal feedback. This stresses the relational nature of feedback.

This relational nature brought us to promote the social network perspective as this perspective provides both theories and instruments to grasp this relational aspect of feedback (seeking). We put forward based on research within the social network literature, a range of structural and relational network characteristics that affect the flow of resources (including feedback) between people in organizations. Some of these characteristics were already incorporated in research of feedback (seeking). The results of the available research subscribe to the potential value of taking a social network perspective on feedback (seeking). Moreover, applying general ideas of social network mechanisms on feedback research triggered interesting questions for future research.

References

Adler, P. S., & Kwon, S.-W. (2002). Social capital: Prospects for a new concept. *Academy of Management Review*, 27(1), 17–40.

Alvero, A. M., Bucklin, B. R., & Austin, J. (2001). An objective review of the effectiveness and essential characteristics of performance feedback in organizational settings (1985–1998). *Journal of Organizational Behavior Management*, 21(1), 3–29.

Anderson, M. H. (2008). Social networks and the cognitive motivation to realize network opportunities: A study of managers' information gathering behaviors. *Journal of Organizational Behavior*, 29, 51–78.

Anseel, F., Lievens, F., & Levy, P. E. (2007). A self-motives perspective on feedback-seeking behavior: Linking organizational behavior and social psychology research. *International Journal of Management Reviews*, 9(3), 211–236.

Ashford, S. J., Blatt, R., & Vande Walle, D. (2003). Reflections on the looking glass: A review of research on feedback-seeking behavior in organizations. *Journal of Management*, 29(6), 773–799. doi:10.1016/s0149-2063_03_00079-5.

Ashford, S. J., & Cummings, L. L (1983). Feedback as an individual resources: Personal strategies of creating information. *Organizational Behavior and Human Performance*, 32(3), 370–398.

Bamberger, P. (2009). Employee help-seeking: Antecedents, consequences and new insights for future research. *Research in Personnel and Human Resources Management*, 28, 49–98.

Becker, T. E., & Klimoski, R. J. (1989). A field study of the relationship between the organizational feedback environment and performance. *Personnel Psychology*, 42, 343–358.

Blau, P. M. (1977). *Inequality and Heterogeneity*. New York: Free Press.

Borgatti, S. P., & Cross, R. (2003). A relational view of information seeking and learning in social networks. *Management Science*, 49(4), 432–445.

Boud, D., & Middleton, H. (2003). Learning from others at work: Communities of practice and informal learning. *Journal of Workplace Learning*, 15(5), 194–202.

Brueller, D., & Carmeli, A. (2011). Linking capacities of high-quality relationships to team learning and performance in service organizations. *Human Resource Management*, 50(4), 455–477. doi:10.1002/hrm.20435.

Burt, R. S. (1992). *Structural Holes: The Social Structure of Competition*. Cambridge, MA: Harvard University Press.

Burt, R. S. (1997). A note on social capital and network content. *Social Networks*, 19(4), 355–373. doi: 10.1016/S0378-8733(97)00003-8.

Burt, R. S. (2000a). Decay functions. *Social Networks*, 22(1), 1–28.

Burt, R. S. (2000b). The network structure of social capital. *Research in Organizational Behavior*, 22(0), 345–423. doi:10.1016/s0191-3085(00)22009-1.

Burt, R. S. (2002). Bridge decay. *Social Networks*, 24(4), 333–363.

Burt, R. S. (2005). *Brokerage and Closure: An Introduction to Social Capital*. Oxford: Oxford University Press, 2005.

Carrington, P. J., Scott, J., & Wasserman, S. (2005). *Models and Methods in Social Network Analysis*. New York: Cambridge University Press.

Coburn, C. E., Choi, L., & Mata, W. (2010). I would go to her because her mind is math: Network formation in the context of mathematics reform. In A. J. Daly (Ed.), *Social Network Theory and Educational Change* (pp. 33–50). Cambridge, MA: Harvard Educational Press.

Coburn, C. E., & Russell, J. L. (2008). District policy and teachers' social networks. *Educational Evaluation and Policy Analysis*, 30(3), 203–235.

Coburn, C., Russell, J. L., Kaufman, J. H., & Stein, M. K. (2012). Supporting sustainability: Teachers' advice networks and ambitious instructional reform. *American Journal of Education*, 119(1), 137–182.

Coleman, J. S. (1988). Social capital in the creation of human capital. *American Journal of Sociology*, 94 (Supplement: Organizations and Institutions: Sociological and Economic Approaches to the Analysis of Social Structure), S95–S120.

Cornally, N., & McCarthy, G. (2011). Help-seeking behavior: A concept analysis. *International Journal of Nursing Practice*, 17, 280–288.

Crant, J. M. (2000). Proactive behavior in organizations. *Journal of Management*, 26(3), 435–462.

Cross, R., Borgatti, S. P., & Parker, A. (2001). Beyond answers: Dimensions of the advice network. *Social Networks*, 23(3), 215–235. doi:10.1016/s0378-8733(01)00041-7.

Cross, R., Parker, A., Prusak, L., & Borgatti, S. P. (2001). Knowing what we know: Supporting knowledge creation and sharing in social networks. *Organizational Dynamics*, 30(2), 100–120.

Cross, R., Singer, J., Colella, S., Thomas, R. J., & Silverstone, Y. (2010). *The Organizational Network Fieldbook: Best Practices, Techniques, and Exercises to Drive Organizational Innovation and Performance*. San Francisco: Jossey-Bass.

Cross, R., & Sproull, L. (2004). More than an answer: Information relationships for actionable knowledge. *Organization Science*, 15(4), 446–462.

Cross, R., & Thomas, R. J. (2008). How top talent uses networks and where rising stars get trapped. *Organizational Dynamics*, 37(2), 165–180.

Dal Fiore, F. (2007). Communities versus networks: The implications on innovation and social change. *American Behavioral Scientist*, 50(7), 857–866.

Daly, A. J. (2010). *Social Network Theory and Educational Change*. Cambridge, MA: Harvard Education Press.

De Laat, M., & Schreurs, B. (2013). Visualizing informal professional development networks: Building a case for learning analytics in the workplace. *American Behavioral Scientist*. doi:10.1177/0002764213479364.

DeNisi, A. S., & Kluger, A. N. (2000). Feedback effectiveness: Can 360-degree appraisals be improved? *Academy of Management Executive*, 14(1), 129–139. doi:10.5465/ame.2000.2909845.

Eraut, M. (2004). Informal learning in the workplace. *Studies in Continuing Education*, 26(2), 247–273. doi:10.1080/158037042000225245.

Eraut, M. (2007). Learning from other people in the workplace. *Oxford Review of Education*, 33(4), 403–422. doi:10.1080/03054980701425706.

Festinger, L. (1957). *A Theory of Cognitive Dissonance*. Stanford, CA: Stanford University Press.

Freeman, L. C. (1979). Centrality in social networks conceptual clarification. *Social Networks*, 1(3), 215–239.

Gabelica, C., Van den Bossche, P., Segers, M., & Gijselaers, W. (2012). Feedback, a powerful lever in teams: A review. *Educational Research Review*, 7(2), 123–144. doi:10.1016/j.edurev.2011. 11.003.

Granovetter, M. (1973). The strength of weak ties. *American Journal of Sociology*, 78(6), 1360–1380.

Grant, A. M., & Ashford, S. J. (2008). The dynamics of proactivity at work. *Research in Organizational Behavior*, 28, 3–34.

Grant, A. M., Parker, S. K., & Collins, C. G. (2009). Getting credit for proactive behavior: Supervisor reactions depend on what you value and how you feel. *Personnel Psychology*, 62, 31–55.

Gruppen, L. D., Simpson, D., Searle, N. S., Irby, D. M., & Mullan, P. B. (2006). Educational fellowships programs: Common themes and overarching issues. *Academic Medicine*, 81, 990–994.

Håkansson, H., Havila, V., & Pedersen, A.-C. (1999). Learning in networks. *Industrial Marketing Management*, 28(5), 443–452. doi: http://dx.doi.org/10.1016/S0019-8501(99)00080-2.

Hakkarainen, K., Palonen, T., Paavola, S., & Lehtinen, E. (2004). *Communities of Networked Expertise. Professional and Educational Perspectives*. Amsterdam: Elsevier.

Halpern, D. (2005). *Social Capital*. Cambridge: Polity Press.

Hansen, M. T. (1999). The search-transfer problem: The role of weak ties in sharing knowledge across organization subunits. *Administrative Science Quarterly*, 44(1), 82–111.

Hatala, J., & Fleming, P. (2007). Making transfer climate visible: Utilizing social network analysis to facilitate transfer of training. *Human Resource Development Review*, 6(1), 33–63.

Hattie, J., & Timperley, H. (2007). The power of feedback. *Review of Educational Research*, 77(7), 81–112.

Hayton, J. C., Carnabuci, G., & Eisenberger, R. (2012). With a little help from my friends: A social embeddedness approach to perceived organizational support. *Journal of Organizational Behavior*, 33, 235–249.

Heider, F. (1958). *The Psychology of Interpersonal Relations*. New York: John Wiley & Sons, Inc.

Herold, D. M., & Greller, M. M. (1977). Feedback: The definition of a construct. *Academy of Management Journal*, 20(1), 142–147. doi:10.2307/255468.

Higgins, M. C., & Kram, K. E. (2001). Reconceptualizing mentoring at work: A developmental network perspective. *Academy of Management Review*, 26(2), 264–288.

Hinds, P. J., Carley, K. M., Krackhardt, D., & Wholey, D. (2000). Choosing work group members: Balancing similarity, competence, and familiarity. *Organizational Behavior and Human Decision Processes*, 81(2), 226–251. doi: http://dx.doi.org/10.1006/obhd.1999.2875.

Hofmann, D. A., Lei, Z., & Grant, A. M. (2009). Seeking help in the shadow of a doubt: The sensemaking processes underlying how nurses decide who to ask for advice. *Journal of Applied Psychology*, 94(5), 1261–1274.

Huisman, M., & Snijders, T. A. B. (2003). Statistical analysis of longitudinal network data with changing composition. *Sociological Methods & Research*, 32(2), 253–287. doi:10.1177/004912 4103256096.

Ilgen, D. R., Fisher, C. D., & Taylor, S. M. (1979). Consequences of individual feedback on behavior in organizations. *Journal of Applied Psychology*, 64(4), 349–371.

Kali, R., & Reyes, J. (2007). The architecture of globalization: A network approach to international economic integration. *Journal of International Business Studies*, 38(4), 595–620.

Kilduff, M., & Krackhardt, D. (2008). *Interpersonal Networks in Organizations: Cognition, Personality, Dynamics, and Culture*. Cambridge: Cambridge University Press.

Kim, T.-Y., Hon, A. H., & Crant, J. M. (2009). Proactive personality, employee creativity, and new-comer outcomes: A longitudinal study. *Journal of Business and Psychology*, 24(1), 93–103.

Kluger, A. N., & DeNisi, A. (1996). The effectiveness of feedback interventions on performance: A historical review, a meta-analysis and a preliminary feedback intervention theory. *Psychological Bulletin*, 119(2), 254–284.

Kossinets, G., & Watts, D. J. (2006). Empirical analysis of an evolving social network. *Science*, 311, 88–90.

Lazega, E., & Pattison, P. E. (1999). Multiplexity, generalized exchange and cooperation in organi-zations: A case study. *Social Networks*, 21(1), 67–90.

Lee, F. (1997). When the going gets tough, do the tough ask for help? Help seeking and power motivations in organizations. *Organizational Behavior and Human Decision Processes*, 72(3), 336–363.

Lee, F. (2002). The social costs of seeking help. *Journal of Applied Behavioral Science*, 38(1), 17–35.

Levin, D. Z., & Cross, R. (2004). The strength of weak ties you can trust: The mediating role of trust in effective knowledge transfer. *Management Science*, 50(11), 1477–1490.

Lin, N. (1999). Building a network theory of social capital. *Connections*, 22(1), 28–51.

Lin, N. (2001). *Social Capital. A Theory of Social Structure and Action*. Cambridge: Cambridge University Press.

Lin, N., Ensel, W. M., & Vaughn, J. C. (1981). Social resources and strength of ties: Structural factors in occupational status attainment. *American Sociological Review*, 46(4), 393–405.

London, M. (2003). Job feedback: Giving, seeking and using feedback for performance improve-ment (2nd ed.). Mahwah, NJ: Erlbaum.

Marsden, P. V., & Campbell, K. E. (1984). Measuring tie strength. *Social Forces*, 63, 482–501.

Maurer, T. J., Mitchell, D. R. D., & Barbeite, F. G. (2002). Predictors of attitudes toward a 360-degree feedback system and involvement in post-feedback management development activity. *Journal of Occupational and Organizational Psychology*, 75, 87–107.

McPherson, M., Smith-Lovin, L., & Cook, J. M. (2001). Birds of a feather: Homophily in social networks. *Annual Review of Sociology*, 27, 415–444.

Monge, P. R., & Contractor, N. S. (2003). *Theories of Communication Networks*. New York: Oxford University Press.

Moolenaar, N. M. (2010). Ties with potential: Nature, antecedents, and consequences of social net-works in school teams. PhD thesis. University of Amsterdam.

Mulder, R. M., & Ellinger, A. D. (2013). Perceptions of quality of feedback in organizations. *European Journal of Training and Development*, 37(1), 4–23.

Nadler, A., Ellis, S., & Bar, I. (2003). To seek or not to seek: The relationship between help seeking and job performance evaluations as moderated by task-relevant expertise. *Journal of Applied Social Psychology*, 33(1), 91–109.

Nahapiet, J., & Ghoshal, S. (1998). Social capital, intellectual capital, and the organiza-tional advantage. *Academy of Management Review*, 23(2), 242–266. doi:10.5465/amr. 1998.533225.

Nohria, N. (1992). Is a network perspective a useful way of studying organizations? In N. Nohria & R. G. Eccles (Eds.), *Network and Organizations: Structure, Form, and Action* (pp. 1–22). Boston, MA: Harvard Business School Press.

Nohria, N., & Eccles, R. G. (1992). *Networks and Organizations: Structure, Form, and Action*. Boston, MA: Harvard Business School Press.

Palonen, T., Hakkarainen, K., Talvitie, J., & Lehtinen, E. (2004). Network ties, cognitive centrality, and team interaction within a telecommunication company. In H. P. A. Boshuizen, R. Bromme, & H. Gruber (Eds.), *Professional Learning: Gaps and Transitions on the Way from Novice to Expert* (pp. 271–294). Dordrecht: Kluwer.

Reagans, R., & McEvily, B. (2003). Network structure and knowledge transfer: The effects of cohe-sion and range. *Administrative Science Quarterly*, 48(2), 240–267. doi:10.2307/3556658.

Reinholt, M., Pedersen, T., & Foss, N. J. (2011). Why a central network position isn't enough: The role of motivation and ability for knowledge sharing in employee networks. *Academy of Management Journal*, 54(6), 1277–1297.

Salas, E., & Rosen, M. A. (2010). Experts at work: Principles for developing expertise in organizations. In S. W. J. Kozlowski & E. Salas (Eds.), *Learning, Training, and Development in Organizations* (pp. 99–134). New York: Routledge.

Schmidt, R. A. (1991). Frequent augmented feedback can degrade learning: Evidence and interpretations. In G. E. Stelmach & J. Requin (Eds.), *Tutorials in Motor Neuroscience* (pp. 59–75). Dordrecht: Kluwer.

Scott, J. (2000). *Social Network Analysis* (2nd ed.). London: Sage.

Shute, V. J. (2008). Focus on formative feedback. *Review of Educational Research*, 78(1), 153–189. doi:10.3102/0034654307313795.

Smither, J. W., London, M., & Reilly, R. R. (2005). Does performance improve following multisource feedback? A theoretical model, meta-analysis, and review of empirical findings. *Personnel Psychology*, 58(1), 33–66.

Snell, S. A., Shadur, M. A., & Wright, P. M. (2002). Human resources strategy: The era of our ways. In M. A. Hitt, R. E. Freeman, & J. S. Harrison (Eds.), *Handbook of Strategic Management* (pp. 627–649). Malden, MA: Blackwell.

Snijders, T. A. B. (2001). The statistical evaluation of social network dynamics. *Sociological Methodology*, 31(1), 361–395. doi:10.1111/0081-1750.00099.

Snijders, T. A. B. (2005). Models for longitudinal network data. In P. J. Carrington, J. Scott, & S. Wasserman (Eds.), *Models and Methods in Social Network Analysis* (pp. 215–247). New York: Cambridge University Press.

Snijders T. A. B. (2011). Network dynamics. In J. Scott & P. J. Carrington (Eds.), *The SAGE Handbook of Social Network Analysis* (pp. 501–513). London: Sage.

Sonnentag, S. (2000). Excellent performance: The role of communication and cooperation processes. *Applied Psychology: An International Review*, 49(3), 483–497.

Sparrowe, R. T., Liden, R. C., & Kramer, M. L. (2001). Social networks and the performance of individuals and groups. *Academy of Management Journal*, 44, 316–325.

Tannenbaum, S. I., Beard, R. L., McNall, L. A., & Salas, E. (2010). Informal learning and development in organizations. In S. W. J. Kozlowski & E. Salas (Eds.), *Learning, Training, and Development in Organizations* (pp. 303–331). New York: Routledge.

Tenkasi, R. V., & Chesmore, M. C. (2003). Social networks and planned organizational change: The impact of strong network ties on effective change implementation and use. *Journal of Applied Behavioral Science*, 39(3), 281–300. doi:10.1177/0021886303258338.

Tynjälä, P. (2008). Perspectives into learning at the workplace. *Educational Research Review*, 3, 130–154.

Uzzi, B. (1996). The sources and consequences of embeddedness for the economic performance of organizations: The network effect. *American Sociological Review*, 61(4), 674–698. doi: 10.2307/2096399.

van de Wiel, M. W. J., Van den Bossche, P., Janssen, S., & Jossberger, H. (2011). Exploring deliberate practice in medicine: How do physicians learn in the workplace? *Advances in Health Sciences Education*, 16(1), 81–95. doi:10.1007/s10459-010-9246-3.

Van den Bossche, P., & Segers, M. (2013). Transfer of training: Adding insight through social network analysis. *Educational Research Review*, 8(1), 37–47. doi:10.1016/j.edurev.2012.08.002.

Van den Bossche, P., Segers, M., & Jansen, N. (2010). Transfer of training: The role of feedback in supportive networks. *International Journal of Training and Development*, 14(2), 81–94.

van der Rijt, J., Van den Bossche, P., & Segers, M. (2013). Understanding informal feedback seeking in the workplace: The impact of the position in the organizational hierarchy. *European Journal of Training and Development*, 1, 72–85. doi:10.1108/03090591311293293.

van der Rijt, J., Van den Bossche, P., van de Wiel, M., De Maeyer, S., Gijselaers, W., & Segers, M. (2013). Asking for help: A relational perspective on help seeking in the workplace. *Vocations and Learning*, 6, 259–279. doi:10.1007/s12186-012-9095-8.

van der Rijt, J., van de Wiel, M., Van den Bossche, P., Segers, M., & Gijselaers, W. (2012). Contextual antecedents of informal feedback processes in the workplace. *Human Resource Development Quarterly*, 23(2), 233–257. doi:10.1002/hrdq.21129.

Van Gennip, N., Gijbels, D., Segers, M., & Tillema, H. (2010). Reactions to 360 feedback: The role of trust and trust-related variables. *International Journal of Human Resources Development and Management*, 10(4), 362–379. doi:10.1504/ijhrdm.2010.036088.

Van Waes, S., Van den Bossche, P., Moolenaar, N., De Maeyer, S., & Van Petegem, P. (2013). The importance of know-who in becoming an expert teacher in higher education. Paper presented at the Annual Meeting of the American Educational Research Association (AERA), San Francisco, CA, April 27–May 1.

Vancouver, J. B., & Morrison, E. W. (1995). Feedback inquiry: The effects of source attributes and individual differences. *Organizational Behavior and Human Decision Processes*, 62, 276–285.

Wasserman, S., & Faust, K. (1994). *Social Network Analysis: Methods and Applications*. New York: Cambridge University Press.

Whelan, E., Collings, D. G., & Donnellan, B. (2010). Managing talent in knowledge-intensive settings. *Journal of Knowledge Management*, 14(3), 486–504.

Index

Page numbers in *italics* refer to illustrations; those in **bold** refer to tables

The Wiley Blackwell Handbook of the Psychology of Training, Development, and Performance Improvement,
First Edition. Edited by Kurt Kraiger, Jonathan Passmore, Sigmar Malvezzi, and Nuno Rebelo dos Santos.
© 2015 John Wiley & Sons Ltd. Published 2020 by John Wiley & Sons Ltd.